George Parainlam
4401 ST. THOMAS AVE
21206
325-5527

GMAT

GRADUATE MANAGEMENT ADMISSION TEST

Complete Preparation for the Newly Revised GMAT

Gino Crocetti
and
David Ellis, M.B.A.

ARCO PUBLISHING, INC.
NEW YORK

Published by Arco Publishing, Inc.
215 Park Avenue South, New York, N.Y. 10003

Library of Congress Cataloging in Publication Data

Crocetti, Gino.
Graduate management admission test, GMAT.

1. Management—Examinations, questions, etc.
2. Management—Study and teaching-(Graduate)
I. Ellis, David, 1956- . II. Title.
HD30.413.C76 1983 650'.076 83-8794
ISBN 0-668-05679-7 (pbk.)

Printed in the United States of America

CONTENTS

Part One: About the GMAT and General Test-Taking Information

Part Two: Review of GMAT Question Types

Part Three: Two Full-Length Practice Examinations

Part Four: GMAT Graduate School List

Part One

About the GMAT and General Test-taking Information

HOW TO USE THIS BOOK

HOW THIS BOOK WILL HELP YOU GET A BETTER GMAT SCORE

The book that you hold in your hand is different from other preparation books in several ways that will help you get a better GMAT score.

First, there is much more instructional material in this book than in other preparation books. The Instructional Overviews for each type of question are substantial reviews of what the question type is all about and how to master it. They are not just filled out with more drill work. They really teach you something.

Second, the answer explanations are not only longer than usual, but they discuss all the answer choices—including the reasons that the wrong choices were attractive. There are no one-sentence explanations. There are, after all, four wrong answers to cope with for every right answer.

Third, this book offers a complete program of preparation including both general test-taking hints and specific hints for each type of question in the Instructional Overviews and in the answer explanations, many of which are longer than the questions they explain.

Fourth, there is a separate Attack Strategy for each question type, including detailed timing recommendations on sections and question types where students have had trouble in the past.

Fifth, the problems in the practice tests are just like the test. There will be no surprises.

Sixth, there is nothing in the book that is not going to be on the test. There are no "extras" that only fill up the book without helping your score. Everything you need is here, while anything you don't is not.

For all these reasons we want to tell you how to get the full value of this book toward getting the best possible GMAT score.

THE IMPORTANCE OF THE GMAT SCORE

You know that the GMAT score is important to your admission to graduate school. It is used both as a cutoff for some programs and as one of the two major criteria in evaluating your application in most other programs. The other criterion is usually your grade point average.

The GMAT score and the two subscores—Verbal and Quantitative—are given different relative weights by different business schools, but they all give great weight to the results of the GMAT. The derivation of these scores is discussed in detail in the next section, "All About the GMAT."

WHY AND HOW PREPARATION IS EFFECTIVE

The GMAT is intended by its makers to test mental and academic skills that they regard as taking a long time to develop. These skills are usually referred to as "the ability to read, understand, and reason," but they are somewhat narrower than that designation might imply. There are three separate ways that preparation can raise your score.

1. UNDERSTANDING THE TEST: Preparation will help you to know what each section of the test is about. Good preparation will also analyze each subtype of question and explain what it is asking. Also included in this area of benefit are such technical matters as knowing whether to guess (yes, on the GMAT), how the timing works, etc.

2. IMPROVING YOUR TEST-TAKING SKILLS: Good test-taking skills improve the efficiency of your other academic and mental skills. There are many different test-taking skills. One of the most difficult to master is knowing

just which other skills should be used for different question types. That skill is fully explained in this book. Other test-taking skills include the order in which parts of the section should be read and the emphasis to be given to each, how to tell the answer choices apart, key words to beware of, what you DON'T have to worry about, and how to avoid various common errors.

3. IMPROVING YOUR "ABILITY TO READ, UNDERSTAND, AND REASON": Or at least the mental and academic skills that go by that name on the GMAT. Reading, reasoning, and problem-solving are skills that you use every day, and which, like all skills, can be improved. One of the most effective ways of improving any skill, and the one used in this book, is clear identification of errors and the appropriate times to use these skills.

Perhaps an analogy to a "physical" skill will help (no skill is purely physical; there is always a major mental element). A tennis player may have a dozen excellent shots but still play poorly because he does not know when to use them to best advantage or because he lacks one shot that he needs.

You may be in a similar position. You have spent years learning a large number of mental and academic skills, but if you don't know which ones to use on which parts of the test, you won't do as well as you should. Similarly, you can probably benefit from brushing up on, or perhaps learning in the first place, some of the skills needed for the GMAT.

We won't pretend that a five-year-old could pick up this book and then get a perfect score on the GMAT. But you are not five years old and you don't need a perfect score, just a better one. A better score is just what you will get if you master the skills presented in this book.

WHAT YOU NEED TO DO

How, then, shall you use this book? We will give you guidance in three areas: how to evaluate your needs and resources, how to set up a workable study plan, and how to study this sort of material effectively. Naturally there is some overlap between these three areas.

The first and most important thing that you need to do is take this book seriously. If you are just going to read a page here and there, casually do some problems without regard to timing, and never read the explanations—well, in that case you are not going to benefit nearly as much as you could. It takes work and commitment—YOUR work and YOUR commitment.

Now, having been stirred to action, here is what you do.

Evaluating your Needs and Resources

The most valuable resource you have in this work is your time. You may have a great deal of time or you may have only a little. You need to set priorities so that you can get the most return for the time invested.

Actually, your needs are not too complicated to evaluate. You should assume that you need to study closely each of the Instructional Overviews, unless you are previously both familiar AND successful with the kinds of questions it treats. If you think you don't need to study one or two of the Instructional Overviews, do the appropriate sections in the first practice test as a check. Unless you get over 85% right, study the Overview. By the way, as a first exercise in logical reasoning, note that the use of 85% as a criterion in this context does not mean you should expect to get 85% of every section right on the test. As is explained in the next chapter, the GMAT scoring doesn't require that criterion. Even if you can get 85% right without help, you could still probably benefit from further study.

In addition to the overviews, every student should read the next two chapters on the nature of the GMAT and general test-taking strategies. You should also read the first part of the chapter on anxiety just to check yourself out, and read all of it if you find that you have even a small overanxiety problem.

That leaves the practice tests. You must take at least one test as a full-dress rehearsal. That is the highest priority after the instructional material. It is good to do all of the practice tests, but if time does not permit, you can do extra sections of the question types that give you difficulty.

As you study and do the practice tests, you will develop a list of your problem areas, which will direct your further studying. The development of this list is described later, in the section on effective studying.

Now consider your time. Do not overestimate how much time you have. If you think you have four hours every day, say instead that you have two hours five days a week. If you actually have the extra time, you can always do more studying, but if you plan on more than you actually have, you will feel bad and your priorities may become distorted. Be conservative.

Even if it is just 45 minutes a day, that is fine. Just make sure that it is actually 45 minutes and not 20 minutes of telephone calls and only 25 minutes of study. Regular study in small amounts is much better than occasional larger periods. The practice tests that you take as complete tests should be done in one sitting.

Take a piece of paper right now and write down all the time you want to dedicate to studying for the GMAT between now and the test date. If you don't know the test date, consult the official GMAT bulletin.

Setting Up a Workable Study Plan

Once you know how much time you have, you are halfway to having a plan that will work. Each week, you should plan exactly on which topics or tests you will work. You cannot plan the entire process at the beginning because you won't know how long things take until you have done some of them. Allow TWICE as much time as your best estimate of the time it really takes. If you actually do finish quicker, you'll feel good and there is no harm done. You will find your margin used up very quickly.

Never plan two things for the same time. For the best results, your study time must be totally dedicated to study. If you can do some extra review of your notes while commuting, so much the better, but make that extra time, not prime time.

In sum then, the keys to setting up a workable plan are dedicated time, conservative estimation, and advance planning in writing. Aside from helping you to remember when you are to study for the GMAT, putting the plan in writing will remind you to reschedule those hours that will inevitably be superseded by some "emergency" or special event.

Effective Studying for the GMAT

In addition to the organizing ideas just mentioned, there are several studying hints that are particularly helpful with this type of material.

1. ALWAYS HAVE A POSITIVE ATTITUDE. Start every session with the thought of how much better off you will be because you will know even more after studying than you did before.

2. STUDY IN SHORT SEGMENTS, with rest breaks in between. Most people should study in 20-minute segments with a five-minute review at the end for a total of 25 minutes of studying. Then completely relax yourself and think of nothing at all for two minutes or so. If you rush right into another topic, even another GMAT topic, your memory of the first topic will not be as good. No one should go more than 40 minutes without stopping, reviewing, and resting. It just isn't efficient. You will learn better in short periods.

3. TAKE MEANINGFUL NOTES. Take notes in a separate notebook and not in the margins of this book. Don't rely only on highlighting. Write complete notes that will mean something to you at a later time.

4. PREVIEW, READ, WRITE, AND REMEMBER. Rapidly preview the chapter you are studying. Then read it carefully, taking good notes. Finally, after you are finished, close the book and try to recall all the major ideas of the chapter. If you have any difficulties, check yourself against your notes. If they are unclear or incomplete, check the book. The very act of trying to remember will engrave the material in your memory far better than merely rereading it once or even twice.

5. DO EACH EXERCISE OR PRACTICE TEST BY THE "TRAC" METHOD. The initials TRAC stand for Timed, Rework, Analyze, and Check for clues:

Timed: First do the exercise or test in the time limit. However, mark the questions carefully to indicate the answer choices you have eliminated and the choices and questions about which you felt unsure.

Rework: Before you check your answers, rework all of the questions about which you were unsure and indicate to yourself whether you came up with the same answer or a different one.

Analyze: Now check the answer key and try to analyze any remaining errors for yourself, armed with the knowledge of the right answer. Do a full analysis.

Check for clues: Now read the answer explanations for all of the questions which gave you trouble the first time through the material—now just the ones of which you are still unsure. Look for the clues in the problem and the answer choices which you missed the first time through. Try to see how you might have worked your way to them, or seen them more easily.

This entire process will usually take from two to four times as long as the time limit for the section.

NOTE: The key to improvement in reviewing the exercises is NOT merely understanding the explanation of why the right answer was correct, but, just as important, you must try to see exactly what clues in the problem lead you to the right explanation and the right answer. After all, on the day of the test that is what you will have to do—find the answers, not just understand someone else's explanations of them.

6. LEARN ATTACK STRATEGIES AND TIMINGS. These are the basic summaries of the application of the material in the Instructional Overviews. Consciously use them whenever you are doing problems, even if you think the problem is easy.

7. VIVID IMAGES ARE EASY TO REMEMBER. Whenever you want to remember something from this book or elsewhere, you will find a vivid image easier to remember. For instance, if you want to remember the TRAC method, you might think of yourself "tracking" across a giant book and savagely cutting away the wrong answers, leaving only correct answers and uncertain questions. Then a new round of conquests without the clock shining overhead as a sun, and fewer problems still can withstand your glorious assault. . . . You get the idea. The stranger the image, the easier it is to remember. Don't worry if it is a little weird—you don't have to tell anyone about it, just use it to help remember something.

8. REST. This has been mentioned, but is worth repeating. Rest for at least two to five minutes at the end of each study session. Don't think of anything, or just imagine yourself at your favorite secluded spot, alone, gazing at the sky.

GOOD LUCK AND GOOD STUDYING!

ALL ABOUT THE GMAT

PURPOSE OF THE GMAT

The Graduate Management Admission Test (GMAT) is a standardized test intended to assist graduate schools of management in making admissions decisions by giving a standard assessment of mental skills considered to be important to the study of management. According to the GMAT Bulletin, the GMAT scores are designed to measure "general verbal and mathematical abilities" that are "associated with success in the first year of study at graduate schools of management." The Graduate Management Admission Council, a consortium of the accredited graduate schools of management, owns the test, which is written and administered for the Council by the Educational Testing Service (ETS).

The purpose of a standard measure is to permit graduate schools of management to base their admissions decisions, at least in part, on an "objective" comparison of all the candidates—no matter what their college or background. There has been some controversy about the degree to which this laudable goal of objectivity has been met, but there is no similar disagreement about the importance that graduate schools of management place on the GMAT scores in making their admissions decisions.

Thus the purpose of the GMAT is to be part of the criteria for admission to the graduate study of management. And your purpose in taking it is to do as well as you can so that you will have the best possible chance of getting into the school of your choice.

FORMAT OF THE NEW GMAT

The GMAT has had several changes in content and format during the past few years, but now seems stabilized as eight 30-minute sections covering five question formats—Reading Comprehension, Analysis of Situations (Business Judgment), Writing Ability (Sentence Correction), Discrete Quantitative, and Data Sufficiency. (A brief description of each question type follows. For more details, see the specific chapters devoted to each.) Your score will be reported as a combined three-digit GMAT score and two-digit Quantitative and Verbal scores. The scoring system is explained in more detail later in this section.

Here is a very brief description of each question type.

READING COMPREHENSION questions are based on a reading passage and ask you to demonstrate your understanding of the passage by answering questions about the structure, meaning, and implications of the passage. This type of question also appears on several other standardized examinations, including the SAT, LSAT, and GRE.

ANALYSIS OF SITUATIONS questions are based on passages describing decision situations and require you to classify items of information according to the way in which they are used in the discussion of the decision.

WRITING ABILITY questions present sentences which may contain errors. You are given four alternatives to the original sentence and, if the original contains an error, you must choose the alternative which corrects the error without making additional errors.

DISCRETE QUANTITATIVE questions are similar to the mathematics questions seen on many examinations. You are presented with a mathematical question and must choose which of five answer choices, (A) through (E), is the correct one.

DATA SUFFICIENCY questions are also mathematical in content. After a question is posed, two propositions are presented and you must decide whether one, the other, both, or not even both of the propositions give sufficient additional information to permit the original question to be answered. You do not have to give an actual answer, but only to say whether an answer could be obtained.

As with most standardized tests, not every section of the test administered to you will actually be used to compute your GMAT score. Your score will be based on the sum of your answers to six of the eight sections. The six significant sections will consist of two Discrete Quantitative sections and one section of each of the other question formats. Your work on the remaining two sections will be your contribution to the research and development of future GMATs. One of the major purposes of the change to equal-time sections was to make it impossible for students to know which sections will count toward their GMAT score and which ones won't. Unfortunately, that purpose has been well served and you will not be able to tell which sections are to be counted in your case and which are not. In particular, you cannot conclude that the first occurrence of a particular question type is the one which will be counted. In one recent test, both the first and last sections of the test were Reading Comprehension sections, and the first section did not count and the last section did.

Furthermore, GMATs can present "operational" and "non-operational" sections (as they are called) in any order whatsoever and in different orders for different students. Thus, the sections in your test booklet could conceivably be in a different order than those in the booklets of other students. The significant sections, however, are most likely to be in the same order for all students during a particular administration. The bottom line is that *you must do all of the sections.*

TYPICAL FORMAT

The six operational sections of the GMAT will have 150 questions that count toward your score. While some format variation will occur, a typical test would be:

Reading Comprehension	25 questions, 3 passages
Analysis of Situations	35 questions, 2 passages
Writing Ability	25 questions
Data Sufficiency	25 questions
Discrete Quantitative (2 sections)	20 questions each section

The format and timing of each question type is discussed in much greater detail in the Instructional Overview for that question type.

SCORING OF THE NEW GMAT

There are several issues related to scoring which are worth discussing briefly: first, how your score is derived from the answers you give to the questions; second, how that score is converted into the three scores reported to you and the business schools; and third, how the different scores are used by schools for admissions purposes.

Unlike many other similar tests, the GMAT discourages guessing by subtracting a small penalty for incorrect answers. As discussed in detail in the next section, General Test-Taking Strategies, this should not discourage you from answering any question for which you can eliminate at least one answer.

The GMAT score is reported for a range of 200–800, with Verbal and Quantitative subscores reported for a range of 0–60. The Verbal score is based on the 85 questions in the Reading Comprehension, Sentence Correction, and Business Judgment sections. The Quantitative score is based on the 65 questions in the two Discrete Quantitative sections and the Data Sufficiency sections. The three-digit GMAT score is based on all 150 questions.

The three-digit GMAT score is computed in the following way. First, the number of correct and incorrect answers is computed. Unanswered questions neither increase nor reduce your score. The "raw score" is then computed by subtracting $\frac{1}{4}$ times the wrong answers from your total of right answers. The raw score is then put into a scoring formula to give a "scaled score" of between 200 and 800, which is then rounded off to the nearest ten, since GMAT scores are only reported in tens (i.e., the next score above 530, for instance, is 540, with nothing in between). Each raw-score point is typically worth 4.5 scaled-score points. While GMAT scores above 700 are rare, a score of 800 can be achieved even if as many as 6–8 percent of the questions are answered incorrectly. In contrast, the Verbal and Quantitative subscores frequently have an actual maximum possible score well under the theoretical maximum score of 60. One recent test, for example, had actual maximum reportable Verbal and Quantitative scores of 52 and 56, respectively.

For tactical purposes, you should remember that every question—easy or hard—is worth the same amount; very good scores can be achieved even when many questions are not answered or are answered incorrectly. In the parlance of the trade, the GMAT has a "long top end." On a typical test, a 99th percentile score is possible even if 16 percent of the questions are answered incorrectly.

We won't go into any further details of the scoring system, since your job on the test is to answer correctly as many questions as possible, no matter how the scoring system works.

All business schools are interested in the three-digit GMAT score, and that score is generally given more weight than the subscores. Some schools, particularly those whose programs are oriented toward quantitative methods, give particular weight to the Quantitative subscore. It is always permissible to ask a school whether it does give special weight to a particular subscore, but you will not always receive an answer. Still, it is worth asking.

REGISTRATION FOR THE GMAT

You can obtain registration materials for the GMAT and associated services from your prebusiness advisor or dean, or by writing to:

Graduate Management Admission Test
Educational Testing Service
Box 966–R
Princeton, NJ 08541

You should register well in advance of the test and should get your materials as soon as possible. The registration booklet also contains detailed administrative information and some sample questions.

SPECIAL ADMINISTRATIONS OF THE GMAT

Special arrangements can be made for the physically and visually handicapped students and those with learning disabilities. Special Monday administrations are also available for those whose religious beliefs forbid their taking the test on a Saturday. The key to making satisfactory arrangements is time. If you want to make any special arrangements for taking the GMAT, communicate immediately with ETS at the address given above.

GENERAL TEST-TAKING STRATEGIES

In the chapter "All About the GMAT," we discussed the intellectual skills needed to do well in each specific section (see also our chapter "How to Recognize and Reduce Test Anxiety" for further hints). Later we will provide attack strategies aimed at each section. At this point, we need to take up the more general problem of working within the limits of a standardized test such as the GMAT. The GMAT is to a very large extent a game—a game with its own rules—and the winners and the losers are selected within that framework. This artificiality produces some surprising anomalies. For example, it is conceivable, though extremely unlikely, that a person could score a perfect GMAT just by guessing, and it is also conceivable that a person could turn in a very low score because he picked not the best but the second-best answer on every problem. The test, you see, has this very large blind spot: The machine reads only correct answers—those little black marks on the answer sheet. No one receives any credit for the "thinking" that went into solving the problem. Unless the mark is there in the appropriate spot, the machine will assume the student simply could not answer the question (no partial credit is given for an "almost" answer).

Four Points to Remember

Since you are aware of the limitations of the GMAT, you can turn those limitations to your own advantage. We make the following four suggestions regarding taking the GMAT: (1) preview sections, (2) be attentive to the time, (3) guess when necessary, and (4) watch carefully how you enter your answers on the answer sheet. Let us develop each one of these in a little more detail.

Previewing sections. When the proctor announces that it is time to begin work on a section (remember, each section is separately timed and you will not be allowed to work ahead in other sections, nor will you be allowed to return to a section once time has been called on that section), take a few seconds to preview the material. This procedure is beneficial in two ways. First, it has a calming effect. Instead of beginning work in a frantic manner, you can take a deep breath and remind yourself of the strategy which you have learned for approaching that particular section. Your eye may fall upon a question stem which looks familiar and this will trigger associations. In other words, you will be in a better state of mind to begin work in a systematic fashion. A second benefit of previewing is that you guard against the unexpected. In this book we have followed faithfully the layout which ETS (Educational Testing Service) has officially announced for the GMAT. ETS is under no legal or moral compunction, however, to abide by every detail of this information. To be sure, ETS is not likely to spring a whole new test or new question type on students (that is inconceivable), but it is not out of the realm of possibility that they could make some last-minute adjustments in the test format. For example, it is just conceivable that ETS could add two Quantitative questions to a section, bringing the total number of questions to 22 or 27. If you make it a practice to preview the section before you begin work, you cannot be caught out by any such adjustments in the test.

Timing. A second very important point, which should be always on your mind, is the critical nature of timing. Remember, the computer which grades your paper has no mechanism for judging the depth of your thought. It gives the same credit for a lucky guess as it gives for a well-thought-out answer, and it gives the same credit for a tentative "I'm not sure about this" answer as it gives for a firm "This has to be it" answer. So your entire effort must be aimed at maximizing the *total* *number of correct answers*—without regard to incorrect answers and without regard to the amount of thought which went into finding the answer.

To make this clear, let us compare the performances of two hypothetical students. One student is a very meticulous thinker. He attacks the Data Sufficiency section in a very careful manner, checking his work. At the end of the thirty minutes, he has answered only eighteen questions, but he has gotten fourteen of those correct—missing only four. His raw score is 13 ($14 - \frac{4}{4}$). Another student works more quickly—not that he is careless; it is just that he knows the importance of the time limit—and attempts to answer all twenty-five of the questions. Some of them he sees immediately, so he does not bother to recheck his work. On others he can eliminate only one answer choice, so he makes his best guess. On still others, he is able to limit his choice to two of the five possibilities, and once he reaches that point he knows it would be a bad investment of his time to keep working toward a certainty which might never materialize. Our second student answered twenty-five questions, but he missed eight questions, giving him a total of seventeen questions answered correctly. His raw score is 15 ($17 - \frac{8}{4}$). At first glance, it might have seemed that our careful student is the better student, and under different circumstances (in the real world) that might have been so. But on the GMAT, our second student is the better performer—by a total of two raw-score points, worth *ten* points on his GMAT score.

This demonstrates the importance of careful attention to the time limit. To guide you in learning how quickly you must work, keep the following points in mind:

1. Do not spend too much time on any one problem. Remember, each question on the test counts the same; the difficult questions are not extra-credit questions. It just does not pay to spend extra time answering a hard question when there may be some easy questions left for you to answer.

2. Do not look for certainty. There will be many times when you have eliminated all but two answers. At that point you will probably want to work some more on the problem, thinking to yourself, "If I give this another minute or so, I will definitely figure it out." *This is a mistake.* If you use that minute in answering another problem (taking your chances with a fifty-fifty guess on the first one), you will be better off in the long run than if you try answering only one problem with certainty.

3. Do not try to be "super" accurate. While it is true that the GMAT places a premium on careful reading and attention to detail, you must still work quickly. Rest assured that there are no cheap tricks, such as words written in invisible ink, that you have to find. Try for comprehension, but learn to do it quickly.

4. Finally, there is obviously some trade-off between accuracy and speed, and the optimal point will vary from individual to individual. The best thing to do in preparing for this test is to work to find that point for yourself—remembering that it is the number of correct answers, not the accuracy rate, which determines the GMAT scores.

Guessing. Whenever you have eliminated at least one answer choice, ANSWER—even if it is a guess. As discussed in the section called "All About the GMAT," there is a penalty for wrong answers—$\frac{1}{4}$ of a point is subtracted from the raw score for each wrong answer. However, this penalty makes it neither advantageous nor disadvantageous to guess, leaving aside the time it takes to guess.

Look at the scoring for 60 questions about which we might not be completely certain. If we guess at random, with no answer choices eliminated, we will get on the average $\frac{1}{5}$, or 12 questions, correct and $\frac{4}{5}$, or 48 questions, wrong. The raw score would be calculated as no. right $- \frac{1}{4}$ no. wrong $= 12 - \frac{1}{4}(48) = 12 - 12 = 0$.

If we can eliminate only one answer choice on each question and guess at random among the remaining four answer choices, we will get $\frac{1}{4}$, or 15, correct and 45 wrong, which will yield a raw score of $15 - \frac{1}{4}(45) = 15 - 11\frac{1}{4} = 3\frac{3}{4}$, which is probably 20 points on the 200 to 800 scaled score.

If we can eliminate only two answer choices on each question and guess at random among the remaining three answer choices, we will get $\frac{1}{3}$, or 20, correct and 40 wrong, which will yield a raw score of $20 - \frac{1}{4}(40) = 20 - 10 = 10$ raw-score points, which would probably be 50 points on the 200 to 800 scaled score.

If we can eliminate three answers and guess at random among the remaining two answer choices, we will get $\frac{1}{2}$, or 30, correct and 30 wrong, which will yield a raw score of $30 - \frac{1}{4}(30) = 22\frac{1}{2}$ raw-score points, which is probably 100 points on the 200 to 800 scaled score.

Thus it is absolutely to your advantage to answer whenever you can eliminate one or more answer choices from consideration. It is not worth guessing when you have no idea about the question.

Answer sheets. Finally, it goes without saying that you must be attentive to the mechanics of the testing process; specifically, you must be careful in your management of your answer sheet. As obvious as this is, some students will make a coding error in completing the answer sheet, e.g., putting the answer intended for question twenty-four in the slot for the answer to question twenty-five. Interestingly enough, this kind of mistake seems to be randomly distributed across the scoring range—that is, the very best students seem just as likely to make this kind of error as their colleagues who did not score as well. In order to avoid making this error, we suggest:

1. Keep a separate record of answers in the test booklet (yes, you may write in the test booklet). You get no credit for marks made in the test booklet (only for those answers coded on the answer sheet), but circling the answer you believe to be correct and placing a question mark by those you intend to come back to will provide you with a separate record of your choices. Should you then discover that you have made an error in coding answers, you can retrieve the information more easily.

2. Code answers in blocks. Rather than coding answers one by one (which requires needless paper shuffling), work a group of problems, say four or five, without coding answers (keeping your independent record in the test booklet). Then, when you find a convenient breaking point, e.g., turning a page, take that opportunity to record those answers. Coding in blocks will minimize the danger of a coding error, and it will also save time. Obviously, it is important to watch the time. Make absolutely certain that the proctor does not call time before you have had the opportunity to record answers. It may be a good idea, as time draws to a close, to record answers one by one. In any event, you should practice this technique at home before attempting to use it on the actual GMAT.

HOW TO RECOGNIZE AND REDUCE TEST ANXIETY

HOW TO USE THIS CHAPTER

This chapter will help you to recognize, minimize, and control test anxiety while you prepare for and take the GMAT.

Many students are tense and anxious about the GMAT. Indeed, you need a certain amount of adrenalin flowing in order to do your best on the exam. However, too much tension can be a serious problem for some students. Overanxious students are often unable to think clearly, read quickly and precisely, or remember accurately during the exam. Needless to say, their scores suffer.

This chapter provides a step-by-step program for discovering and addressing these problems. Even if you do not have a severe overanxiety problem, you will probably benefit from following the guidelines contained in this chapter. We will first discuss the nature and sources of anxiety. Then we will analyze the elements of anxiety and give you some hints on how to reduce these problems during your preparation for the test. This is followed by some specific hints on how to recognize and control tension during the test itself.

WHAT IS ANXIETY AND WHERE DOES IT COME FROM?

One definition of anxiety calls it a state of "uncertainty, agitation or dread, and brooding fear." This pretty well describes the feelings of all too many test-takers. Anxious students may find themselves sweating, trembling, or gripped with muscle tension, racing hearts, and pounding pulses.

One critical fact about anxiety that most students don't know or ignore is that it is not solely a phenomenon of the testing room. The seeds of anxiety are sown long before the test and some of the best weeding-out of anxiety can also be done before the test—as part of your preparation for the GMAT.

CONTROLLING ANXIETY BEFORE THE TEST

Let's take each part of the definition of anxiety and see how you can control and minimize it.

UNCERTAINTY: Standardized tests such as the GMAT ask the test-taker to be definite and precise. While speed is not the major problem on the GMAT, most of the problems have to be done fairly quickly.

The best way to combat uncertainty on the GMAT is to focus your study time on issue recognition, which is one major skill required by graduate students and asked for by the test. Many students study problem explanations simply to see if they can follow along with the explanation. Certainly that is required, but it is just as important to look for the clues in the question or the passage which tell you that a certain approach or issue is important in this particular problem. This book tries to help you to do that in the discussions of the basic problem types and in the answer explanations. For Reading Comprehension problems, for instance, you will learn how to tell implicit-meaning problems from use-of-evidence problems, and in knowing what the problem type is you will know how it should be approached.

But there is another, deeper level of uncertainty with which you must cope. When you first read a problem, there will ALWAYS be a moment of ignorance when you don't know what to do. Sometimes the moment is very short, and other times noticeably long. Many anxious students feel this moment of ignorance and become convinced that they can never do the problem. If they take too long to talk themselves out of this defeatist attitude, they lose valuable time.

Let's do an experiment. What is 2 + 2?

"Four," you said to yourself so rapidly it seemed instantaneous.

What is 19 + 19?

For most people this takes a little longer than 2 + 2. However, you have little doubt that you can do the addition, so you get right to work and in a few seconds you have the answer. The fact that there was a moment of ignorance when you were asked to add 19 + 19 was absolutely no indication that you could not do it. All it meant was that you had to work it out rather than pull it directly from memory like 2 + 2.

GMAT problems are more complicated than 19 + 19, but the same principle applies—JUST BECAUSE THE ANSWER OR APPROACH DOESN'T COME IMMEDIATELY TO MIND HAS PRACTICALLY NOTHING TO DO WITH WHETHER OR NOT YOU CAN GET THE ANSWER.

The antidote to uncertainty has three parts:

1. Carefully studying the instructions and different types of problems so that you can recognize what they require for solution. This should take the form of outlined notes and memorized attack strategies and problem recognition clues.

2. Becoming tolerant of your moment of ignorance.

3. Learning that perfection is not the goal. The GMAT scoring system was explained earlier in this book. It is expected that everyone will miss some questions, and a very respectable score may well be the result of a situation where you are certain of fewer than half the questions. If you do not remember this clearly, reread that section of the chapter describing the GMAT.

AGITATION: This is essentially the physical part of the anxiety syndrome—the muscle tension, trembling hands, sweaty palms or brows, pounding pulse, and shortness of breath. Few students experience all of these symptoms, but the significance of these physical symptoms is that they will let you know that you are overanxious and that it is time to do something about it.

Agitation is rarely severe, even on the day of the test. The most common part of the agitation syndrome is muscle tension, usually in the neck, shoulders, arms, or lower back. Such tensions can tire you out and distract you from the task at hand—scoring your best on the test.

In your study sessions prior to the GMAT the best way to reduce tensions is to always be totally relaxed before and during your study sessions. The simplest and most direct way to relax is to follow these steps:

1. Sit in a comfortable chair (your study chair should be comfortable) in a reasonably undisturbed location.

2. Close your eyes, roll your head and shoulders, and take a deep breath—letting it out slowly.

3. Starting with your toes, tense each muscle in your body slowly and then relax it—along with its tension—in a slow rhythm.

4. Once you have relaxed your body just float there for a minute or two, breathing slowly but deeply.

It is also a good idea to do a relaxation exercise at the end of your study session. If you have had successful experiences with other methods of relaxation, you can certainly use them either in addition to or in place of the ones described here. However, a method which is not focused on relaxation so much as on some other object such as on a mantra, a center, etc., is not as likely to be helpful in this particular context.

Using this technique regularly will help you to apply the following anxiety-reducing technique for your use during the test.

DREAD AND BROODING FEAR: While this is much more extreme than most students will ever feel, fear of the test is usually the result of a lack of confidence, from whatever source. If you have previously had bad experiences with tests, you should remind yourself each time you study for this test that you are better prepared this time.

Another trick that some students play on themselves is to always focus on their difficulties with a problem and their errors. Although it is true that studying your errors can help you to correct them, it is also true that you should always keep in mind the things you are doing right. Many times you can be making life tough for yourself by using the wrong standard to measure your performance. Perfection is not, as was previously mentioned, the proper reference point.

As the song says, "Accentuate the positive."

CONTROLLING ANXIETY DURING THE TEST

Your main job during the test is to answer questions. Sometimes, you may be a little over-anxious. If you are, it can be helpful to recognize the signs of overanxiety and take action to relieve the anxiety during the test so that it doesn't become a problem. There are three signs of overanxiety during the test and three ways of relieving it.

Recognizing Overanxiety

1. As previously noted, the most common sign of anxiety is muscle tension. While you can expect to be a little stiff from sitting in a chair for several hours, you will notice excess tension if it is present.
2. If you find yourself reading and rereading sentences or questions without really grasping what you have read, this is the result of overanxiety and not your inability to read the material on the test.
3. Assuming that you have not been so foolish as to have been up late partying the night before the test, any sleepiness that you might feel is the result of anxiety and not fatigue.

Reducing Overanxiety

If you find that you might be becoming a little overanxious, you can do the following things:

1. Remember that you are well prepared. You know a lot about all the types of problems and you CAN work on them.
2. Reduce the tension by moving your muscles. Stretch, rotate, shake your arms. Be sure to get up and move during the break in the test. Don't worry how it looks, just do it.
3. Do a relaxation exercise. You shouldn't take the time during the test to do a full-dress exercise, but you can do a shorter version which can be very effective.
   —Take a deep breath and hold it for one second.
   —Close your eyes, blank your mind, and let out the breath while you relax your upper body (without falling off your chair).

The whole thing should take only four or five seconds. Don't take any longer. If you keep it short, you can do it as often as you need to, even after every question if you need to. You should practice this exercise before the day of the test.

AN OUNCE OF PREVENTION

When you are at the test you may be near someone who is very nervous. Don't talk about the test. Similarly, you should not talk about the test during the break. Use the break to stretch, drink, go to the bathroom, and relax. If you want to calmly review your guidelines for a section which has not yet appeared, that is fine. Just don't give anyone else an opportunity to make themselves feel good by telling you what they think you have done wrong.

Part Two

Review of GMAT Question Types

GENERAL HINTS FOR THE GMAT MATHEMATICS SECTIONS

There are many specific hints in the Mathematics Review about the shortest and best approaches to specific types of problems that you will see on the GMAT. The answer explanations to the mathematical questions in the five practice GMAT tests also contain many hints. You should read the explanations even if you got the problem right, since there are often alternative solutions which take less time or are more accurate or both.

The following hints focus on some of the most common errors that students make in approaching the mathematics sections of the GMAT. Read them carefully and try to follow them conscientiously throughout your preparation and, of course, on the test itself. Although some are very simple, they can all be very helpful.

Do not compute too much. Most mathematics questions require less computation than most students do. The Educational Testing Service consciously designs the GMAT to have relatively little computation on it. The numbers almost always come out neatly and evenly, with perhaps the occasional square root (which should almost never be computed as a number, but left as a square root). They assume, rightly or wrongly, that you know how to compute with numbers by now, so that is not the point of any of the GMAT mathematics questions.

Estimate on chart questions. You will probably have few chart questions. Research indicates that students who feel uncomfortable with math tend to skip chart questions, or only give them a minimum effort. You should do the chart questions whenever you can because they have no mathematics in them beyond simple arithmetic. Again, do not compute, but estimate.

Focus on what you need to answer the question. This sounds so obvious that you may wonder why we mention it at all. When having trouble with a problem, most people go over and over the given information, hoping for a spark to light the way. Sometimes it does, of course, but often it doesn't—and it becomes a waste of time.

On some problems you will see what is going on right away. But on the ones where you don't, work backward from the real question. For example, if a percentage is asked for, think: "In order to get to a percentage, I need a number and a base. Where are they?"

In some questions the needed information is just lying around waiting to be picked up, but in longer, more difficult questions you will sometimes find that you have to figure out one of the items needed for the final solution of the problem. For example, in the above percentage problem, you might find that the base is given, but you need to find the number of whatever it is by using another percentage and another base.

Illustration: There are 150 boys and 250 girls in a school. If two-thirds of the boys are ten years old or older, what percentage of the total students are boys under ten years old?

SOLUTION: 1. To get the percentage of boys under ten years old, you need:

$$\frac{\text{number of boys under ten years old}}{\text{total student body}} = \%\text{ boys under ten.}$$

2. To find total student body, you add boys and girls: $150 + 250 = 400$.

3. To find the number of boys under ten, you have to link this to the given information, which is in terms of total boys and boys TEN AND OVER, thus: boys under ten = total boys − boys ten and over. But you don't know the number of boys ten and over. You have to figure that out.

4. Number of boys ten and over = % or

proportion of boys ten and over × number total boys, which is $(\frac{2}{3})(150) = 100$.

5. Boys under ten = $150 - 100 = 50$
6. % boys under ten of total school = $\frac{50}{400} = \frac{1}{8} = 12\frac{1}{2}\%$.

Answer: $12\frac{1}{2}$.

An alternative to steps 4 and 5 would be to note that if $\frac{2}{3}$ of the boys are ten and over, $\frac{1}{3}$ are under ten and $(\frac{1}{3})(150) = 50$.

The major virtues of this approach are (a) that it will actually get you the correct answer quickly and (b) that it will prevent you from pulling numbers out of the air—getting the problem wrong even when you know perfectly well how to calculate a percentage.

Don't skip geometry. As with chart questions, research indicates that many students simply give up on geometry problems that they could solve using their years of experience with the real world of shapes and objects. You do need to know a few formulas, but the questions are primarily testing your ability to see the connections between different parts of the problem. Again, some backward thinking might be helpful. If asked the area of a triangle, there is one, and only one, formula—height times base divided by two = area. So, go look for the base and the height.

MATHEMATICS REVIEW FOR THE GMAT

In order to solve a mathematical problem, it is essential to know the mathematical meaning of the words used. There are many expressions having the same meaning in mathematics. These expressions may indicate a relationship between quantities or an operation (addition, subtraction, multiplication, division) to be performed. This chapter will help you to recognize some of the mathematical synonyms commonly found in word problems.

Equality

The following expressions all indicated that two quantities are equal (=):

is equal to
is the same as
the result is
yields
gives

Also, the word "is" is often used to mean "equals," as in "8 *is* 5 more than 3," which translates to "8 = 5 + 3".

Addition

The following expressions all indicate that the numbers A and B are to be added:

A + B	**2 + 3**
the sum of A and B	the sum of 2 and 3
the total of A and B	the total of 2 and 3
A added to B	2 added to 3
A increased by B	2 increased by 3
A more than B	2 more than 3
A greater than B	2 greater than 3

Subtraction

The following expressions all indicate that the number B is to be subtracted from the number A:

A − B	**10 − 3**
A minus B	10 minus 3
A less B	10 less 3
the difference of A and B	the difference of 10 and 3
from A subtract B	from 10 subtract 3
A take away B	10 take away 3
A decreased by B	10 decreased by 3
A diminished by B	10 diminished by 3
B is subtracted from A	3 is subtracted from 10
B less than A	3 less than 10

Multiplication

If the numbers A and B are to be multiplied (A × B), the following expressions may be used.

A × B	**2 × 3**
A multiplied by B	2 multiplied by 3
the product of A and B	the product of 2 and 3

The parts of a multiplication problem are indicated in the example below:

$$\begin{array}{rl} 15 & \text{(multiplicand)} \\ \times\ 10 & \text{(multiplier)} \\ \hline 150 & \text{(product)} \end{array}$$

Other ways of indicating multiplication are:

Parentheses: A × B = (A)(B)
Dots: A × B = A · B
In algebra, letters next to each other: A × B = AB

A **coefficient** is a number that shows how many times to multiply a variable, such as in 3B, where 3 is the coefficient.

Inequalities

When two numbers are not necessarily equal to each other, this idea can be expressed by using the "greater than" symbol (>) or the "less than" symbol (<). The wider part of the wedge is always towards the greater number.

A is greater than B $A > B$	A is less than B $A < B$
A is greater than or equal to B $A \geq B$	A is less than or equal to B $A \leq B$

An **integer** is a whole number, either positive or negative.

A **prime number** is a whole number (integer) that is evenly divisible only by itself and 1. *Examples:* 1,2,3,5,7,9,11,13,17,19, etc.

Division

Division of the numbers A and B (in the order $A \div B$) may be indicated in the following ways. (See also the discussion of fractions.)

A ÷ B	**14 ÷ 2**
A divided by B	14 divided by 2
the quotient of A and B	the quotient of 14 and 2

The parts of a division problem are indicated in the example below:

$$\begin{array}{rrl} & 5\frac{1}{7} & \text{(quotient)} \\ \text{(divisor)} \quad 7 & \overline{)\,36} & \text{(dividend)} \\ & \underline{35} & \\ & 1 & \text{(remainder)} \end{array}$$

Factors and Divisors

The relationship $A \times B = C$, for any whole numbers A, B, and C, may be expressed as:

A × B = C	**2 × 3 = 6**
A and B are factors of C	2 and 3 are factors of 6
A and B are divisors of C	2 and 3 are divisors of 6
C is divisible by A and by B	6 is divisible by 2 and by 3
C is a multiple of A and of B	6 is a multiple of 2 and of 3

Symbols

Common symbols used on the exam are*:

≠	is not equal to
>	is greater than (3 > 2)
<	is less than (2 < 3)
≥	is greater than or equal to
≤	is less than or equal to
: and ::	is to; the ratio to (see also section on ratios)
$\sqrt{\ }$	radical sign—used without a number, it indicates the square root of ($\sqrt{9} = 3$) or with an index above the sign to indicate the root to be taken if the root is not a square root ($\sqrt[3]{8} = 2$) (see also section on powers and roots).
$\|x\|$	absolute value of (in this case x) (see section on basic properties of numbers, item 6).

BASIC PROPERTIES OF NUMBERS

1. A number greater than zero is called a **positive number.**

2. A number smaller than zero is called a **negative number.**

3. When a negative number is added to another number, this is the same as subtracting the equivalent positive number.

   Example: $2 + (-1) = 2 - 1 = 1$

4. When two numbers of the same sign are multiplied together, the result is a positive number.

   Example: $2 \times 2 = 4$

   Example: $(-2)(-3) = +6$

*Geometric symbols are reviewed in the section on geometry.

5. When two numbers of different signs are multipled together, the result is a negative number.

   Example: $(+5)(-10) = -50$

   Example: $(-6)(+8) = -48$

6. The **absolute value** of a number is the equivalent positive value.

   Example: $|+2| = +2$

   Example: $|-3| = +3$

7. An even number is an integer that is divisible evenly by two. Zero would be considered an even number for practical purposes.

8. An odd number is an integer that is not an even number.

9. An even number times any integer will yield an even number.

10. An odd number times an odd number will yield an odd number.

11. Two even numbers or two odd numbers added together will yield an even number.

12. An odd number added to an even number will yield an odd number.

FRACTIONS

Fractions and Mixed Numbers

1. A **fraction** is part of a unit.

   a. A fraction has a **numerator** and a **denominator.**

   Example: In the fraction $\frac{3}{4}$, 3 is the numerator and 4 is the denominator.

   b. In any fraction, the numerator is being divided by the denominator.

   Example: The fraction $\frac{2}{7}$ indicates that 2 is being divided by 7.

   c. In a fraction problem, the whole quantity is 1, which may be expressed by a fraction in which the numerator and denominator are the same number.

   Example: If the problem involves $\frac{1}{8}$ of a quantity, then the whole quantity is $\frac{8}{8}$, or 1.

2. A **mixed number** is an integer together with a fraction such as $2\frac{3}{5}$, $7\frac{3}{8}$, etc. The integer is the integral part, and the fraction is the fractional part.

3. An **improper fraction** is one in which the numerator is equal to or greater than the denominator, such as $\frac{19}{6}$, $\frac{25}{4}$, or $\frac{10}{10}$.

4. To change a mixed number to an improper fraction:

   a. Multiply the denominator of the fraction by the integer.

   b. Add the numerator to this product.

   c. Place this sum over the denominator of the fraction.

   Illustration: Change $3\frac{4}{7}$ to an improper fraction.

   SOLUTION:
   $$7 \times 3 = 21$$
   $$21 + 4 = 25$$
   $$3\frac{4}{7} = \frac{25}{7}$$

   Answer: $\frac{25}{7}$

5. To change an improper fraction to a mixed number:

   a. Divide the numerator by the denominator. The quotient, disregarding the remainder, is the integral part of the mixed number.

   b. Place the remainder, if any, over the denominator. This is the fractional part of the mixed number.

   Illustration: Change $\frac{36}{13}$ to a mixed number.

   SOLUTION:
   $$13\overline{)36}\ \text{quotient } 2$$
   $$\frac{26}{10}\ \text{remainder}$$
   $$\frac{36}{13} = 2\frac{10}{13}$$

   Answer: $2\frac{10}{13}$

6. The numerator and denominator of a fraction may be changed, without affecting the

value of the fraction, by multiplying both by the same number.

Example: The value of the fraction $\frac{2}{5}$ will not be altered if the numerator and the denominator are multiplied by 2, to result in $\frac{4}{10}$.

7. The numerator and the denominator of a fraction may be changed, without affecting the value of the fraction, by dividing both by the same number. This process is called **reducing the fraction.** A fraction that has been reduced as much as possible is said to be in **lowest terms.**

Example: The value of the fraction $\frac{3}{12}$ will not be altered if the numerator and denominator are divided by 3, to result in $\frac{1}{4}$.

Example: If $\frac{6}{30}$ is reduced to lowest terms (by dividing both numerator and denominator by 6), the result is $\frac{1}{5}$.

8. As a final answer to a problem:

   a. Improper fractions should be changed to mixed numbers.

   b. Fractions should be reduced as far as possible.

Addition of Fractions

9. **Fractions cannot be added unless the denominators are all the same.**

   a. If the denominators are the same, add all the numerators and place this sum over the common denominator. In the case of mixed numbers, follow the above rule for the fractions and then add the integers.

Example: The sum of $2\frac{3}{8} + 3\frac{1}{8} + \frac{3}{8} = 5\frac{7}{8}$.

   b. If the denominators are not the same, the fractions, in order to be added, must be converted to ones having the same denominator. The lowest common denominator is often the most convenient common denominator to find, but any common denominator will work. You can cancel out the extra numbers after the addition.

10. The **lowest common denominator** (henceforth called the L.C.D.) is the lowest number that can be divided evenly by all the given denominators. If no two of the given denominators can be divided by the same number, then the L.C.D. is the product of all the denominators.

Example: The L.C.D. of $\frac{1}{2}$, $\frac{1}{3}$, and $\frac{1}{5}$ is $2 \times 3 \times 5 = 30$.

11. To find the L.C.D. when two or more of the given denominators can be divided by the same number:

   a. Write down the denominators, leaving plenty of space between the numbers.

   b. Select the smallest number (other than 1) by which one or more of the denominators can be divided evenly.

   c. Divide the denominators by this number, copying down those that cannot be divided evenly. Place this number to one side.

   d. Repeat this process, placing each divisor to one side until there are no longer any denominators that can be divided evenly by any selected number.

   e. Multiply all the divisors to find the L.C.D.

Illustration: Find the L.C.D. of $\frac{1}{5}$, $\frac{1}{7}$, $\frac{1}{10}$, and $\frac{1}{14}$.

SOLUTION:

2)	5	7	10	14
5)	5	7	5	7
7)	1	7	1	7
	1	1	1	1

$7 \times 5 \times 2 = 70$

Answer: The L.C.D. is 70.

12. To add fractions having different denominators:

   a. Find the L.C.D. of the denominators.

   b. Change each fraction to an equivalent fraction having the L.C.D. as its denominator.

   c. When all of the fractions have the same denominator, they may be added, as in the example following item 9a.

Illustration: Add $\frac{1}{4}$, $\frac{3}{10}$, and $\frac{2}{5}$.

SOLUTION: Find the L.C.D.:

$$\begin{array}{r|rrr} 2 & 4 & 10 & 5 \\ \hline 2 & 2 & 5 & 5 \\ \hline 5 & 1 & 5 & 5 \\ \hline & 1 & 1 & 1 \end{array}$$

L.C.D. = 2 × 2 × 5 = 20

$$\begin{array}{rcr} \frac{1}{4} & = & \frac{5}{20} \\ \frac{3}{10} & = & \frac{6}{20} \\ +\ \frac{2}{5} & = & +\ \frac{8}{20} \\ \hline & & \frac{19}{20} \end{array}$$

Answer: $\frac{19}{20}$

13. To add mixed numbers in which the fractions have different denominators, add the fractions by following the rules in item 12 above, then add the integers.

Illustration: Add $2\frac{5}{7}$, $5\frac{1}{2}$, and 8.

SOLUTION: L.C.D. = 14

$$\begin{array}{rcr} 2\frac{5}{7} & = & 2\frac{10}{14} \\ 5\frac{1}{2} & = & 5\frac{7}{14} \\ +\ 8 & = & +\ 8 \\ \hline & & 15\frac{17}{14} = 16\frac{3}{14} \end{array}$$

Answer: $16\frac{3}{14}$

Subtraction of Fractions

14. a. Unlike addition, which may involve adding more than two numbers at the same time, subtraction involves only two numbers.

    b. In subtraction, as in addition, the denominators must be the same.

15. To subtract fractions:

    a. Find the L.C.D.

    b. Change both fractions so that each has the L.C.D. as the denominator.

    c. Subtract the numerator of the second fraction from the numerator of the first, and place this difference over the L.C.D.

    d. Reduce, if possible.

Illustration: Find the difference of $\frac{5}{8}$ and $\frac{1}{4}$.

SOLUTION: L.C.D. = 8

$$\begin{array}{rcr} \frac{5}{8} & = & \frac{5}{8} \\ -\ \frac{1}{4} & = & -\ \frac{2}{8} \\ \hline & & \frac{3}{8} \end{array}$$

Answer: $\frac{3}{8}$

16. To subtract mixed numbers:

    a. It may be necessary to "borrow," so that the fractional part of the first term is larger than the fractional part of the second term.

    b. Subtract the fractional parts of the mixed numbers and reduce.

    c. Subtract the integers.

Illustration: Subtract $16\frac{4}{5}$ from $29\frac{1}{3}$.

SOLUTION: L.C.D. = 15

$$\begin{array}{rcr} 29\frac{1}{3} & = & 29\frac{5}{15} \\ -\ 16\frac{4}{5} & = & -\ 16\frac{12}{15} \\ \hline \end{array}$$

Note that $\frac{5}{15}$ is less than $\frac{12}{15}$. Borrow 1 from 29, and change to $\frac{15}{15}$.

$$\begin{array}{rcr} 29\frac{5}{15} & = & 28\frac{20}{15} \\ -\ 16\frac{12}{15} & = & -\ 16\frac{12}{15} \\ \hline & & 12\frac{8}{15} \end{array}$$

Answer: $12\frac{8}{15}$

Multiplication of Fractions

17. a. To be multiplied, fractions need not have the same denominators.

    b. A whole number can be thought of as having a denominator of 1: $3 = \frac{3}{1}$.

18. To multiply fractions:

    a. Change the mixed numbers, if any, to improper fractions.

    b. Multiply all the numerators, and place this product over the product of the denominators.

    c. Reduce, if possible.

Illustration: Multiply $\frac{2}{3} \times 2\frac{4}{7} \times \frac{5}{9}$.

SOLUTION:

$$2\frac{4}{7} = \frac{18}{7}$$

$$\frac{2}{3} \times \frac{18}{7} \times \frac{5}{9} = \frac{180}{189} = \frac{20}{21}$$

Answer: $\frac{20}{21}$

19. a. **Cancellation** is a device to facilitate multiplication. To cancel means to divide a numerator and a denominator by the same number in a multiplication problem.

Example: In the problem $\frac{4}{7} \times \frac{5}{6}$, the numerator 4 and the denominator 6 may be divided by 2.

$$\frac{\overset{2}{\cancel{4}}}{7} \times \frac{5}{\underset{3}{\cancel{6}}} = \frac{10}{21}$$

b. With fractions (and percentages), the word "of" is often used to mean "multiply."

Example: $\frac{1}{2}$ of $\frac{1}{2} = \frac{1}{2} \times \frac{1}{2} = \frac{1}{4}$

20. To multiply a whole number by a mixed number:

a. Multiply the whole number by the fractional part of the mixed number.

b. Multiply the whole number by the integral part of the mixed number.

c. Add both products.

Illustration: Multiply $23\frac{3}{4}$ by 95.

SOLUTION:

$$\frac{95}{1} \times \frac{3}{4} = \frac{285}{4} = 71\frac{1}{4}$$
$$95 \times 23 = 2185$$
$$2185 + 71\frac{1}{4} = 2256\frac{1}{4}$$

Answer: $2256\frac{1}{4}$

Division of Fractions

21. The **reciprocal** of a fraction is that fraction inverted.

a. When a fraction is inverted, the numerator becomes the denominator and the denominator becomes the numerator.

Example: The reciprocal of $\frac{3}{8}$ is $\frac{8}{3}$.

Example: The reciprocal of $\frac{1}{3}$ is $\frac{3}{1}$, or simply 3.

b. Since every whole number has the denominator 1 understood, the reciprocal of a whole number is a fraction having 1 as the numerator and the number itself as the denominator.

Example: The reciprocal of 5 (expressed fractionally as $\frac{5}{1}$) is $\frac{1}{5}$.

22. To divide fractions:

a. Change all the mixed numbers, if any, to improper fractions.

b. Invert the second fraction and multiply.

c. Reduce, if possible.

Illustration: Divide $\frac{2}{3}$ by $2\frac{1}{4}$.

SOLUTION:

$$2\frac{1}{4} = \frac{9}{4}$$
$$\frac{2}{3} \div \frac{9}{4} = \frac{2}{3} \times \frac{4}{9} = \frac{8}{27}$$

Answer: $\frac{8}{27}$

23. A **complex fraction** is one that has a fraction as the numerator, or as the denominator, or as both.

Example: $\dfrac{\frac{2}{3}}{5}$ is a complex fraction.

24. To clear (simplify) a complex fraction:

a. Divide the numerator by the denominator.

b. Reduce, if possible.

Illustration: Clear $\dfrac{\frac{3}{7}}{\frac{5}{14}}$.

SOLUTION: $\frac{3}{7} \div \frac{5}{14} = \frac{3}{7} \times \frac{14}{5} = \frac{42}{35} = \frac{6}{5} = 1\frac{1}{5}$

Answer: $1\frac{1}{5}$

Comparing Fractions

25. If two fractions have the same denominator, the one having the larger numerator is the greater fraction.

Example: $\frac{3}{7}$ is greater than $\frac{2}{7}$.

26. If two fractions have the same numerator, the one having the larger denominator is the smaller fraction.

Example: $\frac{5}{12}$ is smaller than $\frac{5}{11}$.

27. To compare two fractions having different numerators and different denominators:

 a. Change the fractions to equivalent fractions having their L.C.D. as their new denominator.

 b. Compare, as in the example following item 25, for the largest denominator.

Illustration: Compare $\frac{4}{7}$ and $\frac{5}{8}$.

SOLUTION: L.C.D. = 7 × 8 = 56

$\frac{4}{7} = \frac{32}{56}$

$\frac{5}{8} = \frac{35}{56}$

Answer: Since $\frac{35}{56}$ is larger than $\frac{32}{56}$, $\frac{5}{8}$ is larger than $\frac{4}{7}$.

Note: Actually, any common denominator will work, not only the L.C.D.

28. To compare two fractions, multiply the denominators of the left fraction by the numerator of the right fraction and write the result above the right fraction. Then multiply the denominator of the right fraction by the numerator of the left fraction and write the result over the left fraction. If the number over the left fraction is larger than the number over the right fraction, the left fraction is larger. If the number over the right fraction is larger, the right fraction is larger. If the numbers over the two fractions are equal, the fractions are equal.

Illustration: Compare $\frac{5}{7}$ and $\frac{3}{4}$.

SOLUTION:

$\overset{20}{\frac{5}{7}} \nwarrow\!\!\nearrow \overset{21}{\frac{3}{4}}$

4 × 5 = 20

3 ×7 = 21

20 < 21

Answer: $\frac{5}{7} < \frac{3}{4}$. This method will only determine which fraction is larger. It cannot be used to tell you the size of the difference.

Fraction Problems

29. Most fraction problems can be arranged in the form: "What fraction of a number is another number?" This form contains three important parts:

- The fractional part
- The number following "of"
- The number following "is"

 a. If the fraction and the "of" number are given; multiply them to find the "is" number.

Illustration: What is $\frac{3}{4}$ of 20?

SOLUTION: Write the question as "$\frac{3}{4}$ of 20 is what number?" Then multiply the fraction $\frac{3}{4}$ by the "of" number, 20:

$$\frac{3}{\cancel{4}_1} \times \overset{5}{\cancel{20}} = 15$$

Answer: 15

 b. If the fractional part and the "is" number are given, divide the "is" number by the fraction to find the "of" number.

Illustration: $\frac{4}{5}$ of what number is 40?

SOLUTION: To find the "of" number, divide 40 by $\frac{4}{5}$:

$$40 \div \frac{4}{5} = \frac{\overset{10}{\cancel{40}}}{1} \times \frac{5}{\cancel{4}_1}$$

$$= 50$$

Answer: 50

 c. To find the fractional part when the other two numbers are known, divide the "is" number by the "of" number.

Illustration: What part of 12 is 9?

SOLUTION: $9 \div 12 = \frac{9}{12}$

$= \frac{3}{4}$

Answer: $\frac{3}{4}$

Practice Problems Involving Fractions

1. Reduce to lowest terms: $\frac{60}{108}$.
 (A) $\frac{1}{48}$
 (B) $\frac{1}{3}$
 (C) $\frac{5}{9}$
 (D) $\frac{10}{18}$
 (E) $\frac{15}{59}$

2. Change $\frac{27}{7}$ to a mixed number.
 (A) $2\frac{1}{7}$
 (B) $3\frac{6}{7}$
 (C) $6\frac{1}{3}$

(D) $7\frac{1}{2}$
(E) $8\frac{1}{7}$

3. Change $4\frac{2}{3}$ to an improper fraction.
(A) $\frac{10}{3}$
(B) $\frac{11}{3}$
(C) $\frac{14}{3}$
(D) $\frac{24}{3}$
(E) $\frac{42}{3}$

4. Find the L.C.D. of $\frac{1}{6}$, $\frac{1}{10}$, $\frac{1}{18}$, and $\frac{1}{21}$.
(A) 160
(B) 330
(C) 630
(D) 890
(E) 1260

5. Add $16\frac{3}{8}$, $4\frac{4}{5}$, $12\frac{3}{4}$, and $23\frac{5}{6}$.
(A) $57\frac{91}{120}$
(B) $57\frac{1}{4}$
(C) 58
(D) 59
(E) $59\frac{91}{120}$

6. Subtract $27\frac{5}{14}$ from $43\frac{1}{6}$.
(A) 15
(B) $15\frac{5}{84}$
(C) $15\frac{8}{21}$
(D) $15\frac{15}{20}$
(E) $15\frac{17}{21}$

7. Multiply $17\frac{5}{8}$ by 128.
(A) 2256
(B) 2305
(C) 2356
(D) 2368
(E) 2394

8. Divide $1\frac{2}{3}$ by $1\frac{1}{9}$.
(A) $\frac{2}{3}$
(B) $1\frac{1}{2}$
(C) $1\frac{23}{27}$
(D) 4
(E) 6

9. What is the value of $12\frac{1}{6} - 2\frac{3}{8} - 7\frac{2}{3} + 19\frac{3}{4}$?
(A) 21
(B) $21\frac{7}{8}$
(C) $21\frac{1}{8}$
(D) 22
(E) $22\frac{7}{8}$

10. Simplify the complex fraction $\frac{\frac{4}{9}}{\frac{2}{5}}$.
(A) $\frac{1}{2}$
(B) $\frac{9}{10}$
(C) $\frac{2}{5}$
(D) 1
(E) $1\frac{1}{9}$

11. Which fraction is largest?
(A) $\frac{9}{16}$
(B) $\frac{7}{10}$
(C) $\frac{5}{8}$
(D) $\frac{4}{5}$
(E) $\frac{1}{2}$

12. One brass rod measures $3\frac{5}{16}$ inches long and another brass rod measures $2\frac{3}{4}$ inches long. Together their length is
(A) $6\frac{9}{16}$ in.
(B) $6\frac{1}{16}$ in.
(C) $5\frac{1}{8}$ in.
(D) $5\frac{1}{16}$ in.
(E) $5\frac{1}{32}$ in.

13. The number of half-pound packages of tea that can be weighed out of a box that holds $10\frac{1}{2}$ lb. of tea is
(A) 5
(B) $10\frac{1}{2}$
(C) 11
(D) $20\frac{1}{2}$
(E) 21

14. If each bag of tokens weighs $5\frac{3}{4}$ pounds, how many pounds do 3 bags weigh?
(A) $7\frac{1}{4}$
(B) $15\frac{3}{4}$
(C) $16\frac{1}{2}$
(D) $17\frac{1}{4}$
(E) $17\frac{1}{2}$

15. During one week, a man traveled $3\frac{1}{2}$, $1\frac{1}{4}$, $1\frac{1}{6}$, and $2\frac{3}{8}$ miles. The next week he traveled $\frac{1}{4}$, $\frac{3}{8}$, $\frac{9}{16}$, $3\frac{1}{16}$, $2\frac{5}{8}$, and $3\frac{3}{16}$ miles. How many more miles did he travel the second week than the first week?
(A) $1\frac{37}{48}$
(B) $1\frac{1}{2}$
(C) $1\frac{3}{4}$
(D) 1
(E) $\frac{47}{48}$

16. A certain type of board is sold only in lengths of multiples of 2 feet. The shortest board sold is 6 feet and the longest is 24 feet. A builder needs a large quantity of this type of board in $5\frac{1}{2}$-foot lengths. For minimum waste the lengths to be ordered should be
(A) 6 ft
(B) 12 ft
(C) 22 ft
(D) 24 ft
(E) 26 ft

17. A man spent $\frac{15}{16}$ of his entire fortune in buying a car for $7500. How much money did he possess?
(A) $6000
(B) $6500
(C) $7000
(D) $8000
(E) $8500

18. The population of a town was 54,000 in the last census. It has increased $\frac{2}{3}$ since then. Its present population is
(A) 18,000
(B) 36,000
(C) 72,000
(D) 90,000
(E) 108,000

19. If $\frac{1}{3}$ of the liquid contents of a can evaporates on the first day and $\frac{3}{4}$ of the remainder evaporates on the second day, the fractional part of the original contents remaining at the close of the second day is
(A) $\frac{5}{12}$
(B) $\frac{7}{12}$
(C) $\frac{1}{6}$
(D) $\frac{1}{2}$
(E) $\frac{4}{7}$

20. A car is run until the gas tank is $\frac{1}{8}$ full. The tank is then filled to capacity by putting in 14 gallons. The capacity of the gas tank of the car is
(A) 14 gal
(B) 15 gal
(C) 16 gal
(D) 17 gal
(E) 18 gal

Fraction Problems—Correct Answers

1. **(C)**	6. **(E)**	11. **(D)**	16. **(C)**
2. **(B)**	7. **(A)**	12. **(B)**	17. **(D)**
3. **(C)**	8. **(B)**	13. **(E)**	18. **(D)**
4. **(C)**	9. **(B)**	14. **(D)**	19. **(C)**
5. **(A)**	10. **(E)**	15. **(A)**	20. **(C)**

Problem Solutions—Fractions

1. Divide the numerator and denominator by 12:

$$\frac{60 \div 12}{108 \div 12} = \frac{5}{9}$$

One alternate method (there are several) is to divide the numerator and denominator by 6 and then by 2:

$$\frac{60 \div 6}{108 \div 6} = \frac{10}{18}$$

$$\frac{10 \div 2}{18 \div 2} = \frac{5}{9}$$

Answer: **(C)** $\frac{5}{9}$

2. Divide the numerator (27) by the denominator (7):

$$\begin{array}{r} 3 \\ 7\overline{)27} \\ \underline{21} \\ 6 \end{array} \text{ remainder}$$

$$\frac{27}{7} = 3\frac{6}{7}$$

Answer: **(B)** $3\frac{6}{7}$

3.

$$4 \times 3 = 12$$
$$12 + 2 = 14$$
$$4\frac{2}{3} = \frac{14}{3}$$

Answer: **(C)** $\frac{14}{3}$

4.

2)	6	10	18	21	(2 is a divisor of 6, 10, and 18)
3)	3	5	9	21	(3 is a divisor of 3, 9, and 21)
3)	1	5	3	7	(3 is a divisor of 3)
5)	1	5	1	7	(5 is a divisor of 5)
7)	1	1	1	7	(7 is a divisor of 7)
	1	1	1	1	

L.C.D. $= 2 \times 3 \times 3 \times 5 \times 7 = 630$

Answer: **(C)** 630

5. L.C.D. = 120

$$\begin{aligned} 16\tfrac{3}{8} &= 16\tfrac{45}{120} \\ 4\tfrac{4}{5} &= 4\tfrac{96}{120} \\ 12\tfrac{3}{4} &= 12\tfrac{90}{120} \\ +\ 23\tfrac{5}{6} &= +\ 23\tfrac{100}{120} \\ & \quad 55\tfrac{331}{120} = 57\tfrac{91}{120} \end{aligned}$$

Answer: **(A)** $57\tfrac{91}{120}$

6. L.C.D. = 42

$$\begin{aligned} 43\tfrac{1}{6} &= 43\tfrac{7}{42} = 42\tfrac{49}{42} \\ -\ 27\tfrac{5}{14} &= -\ 27\tfrac{15}{42} = -\ 27\tfrac{15}{42} \\ & \qquad 15\tfrac{34}{42} = 15\tfrac{17}{21} \end{aligned}$$

Answer: **(E)** $15\tfrac{17}{21}$

7.

$$17\tfrac{5}{8} = \tfrac{141}{8}$$

$$\tfrac{141}{8} \times \tfrac{128}{1} = 2256$$

Answer: **(A)** 2256

8.

$$\begin{aligned} 1\tfrac{2}{3} \div 1\tfrac{1}{9} &= \tfrac{5}{3} \div \tfrac{10}{9} \\ &= \tfrac{5}{3} \times \tfrac{9}{10} \\ &= \tfrac{3}{2} \\ &= 1\tfrac{1}{2} \end{aligned}$$

Answer: **(B)** $1\tfrac{1}{2}$

9. L.C.D. = 24

$$\begin{aligned} 12\tfrac{1}{6} &= 12\tfrac{4}{24} = 11\tfrac{28}{24} \\ -\ 2\tfrac{3}{8} &= -\ 2\tfrac{9}{24} = -\ 2\tfrac{9}{24} \\ 9\tfrac{19}{24} &= 9\tfrac{19}{24} \\ -\ 7\tfrac{2}{3} &= -\ 7\tfrac{16}{24} \\ 2\tfrac{3}{24} &= 2\tfrac{3}{24} \\ +19\tfrac{3}{4} &= +19\tfrac{18}{24} \\ & \quad 21\tfrac{21}{24} \end{aligned}$$

$$21\tfrac{21}{24} = 21\tfrac{7}{8}$$

Answer: **(B)** $21\tfrac{7}{8}$

10. To simplify a complex fraction, divide the numerator by the denominator:

$$\begin{aligned} \tfrac{4}{9} \div \tfrac{2}{5} &= \tfrac{4}{9} \times \tfrac{5}{2} \\ &= \tfrac{10}{9} \\ &= 1\tfrac{1}{9} \end{aligned}$$

Answer: **(E)** $1\tfrac{1}{9}$

11. Write all of the fractions with the same denominator. L.C.D. = 80

$$\begin{aligned} \tfrac{9}{16} &= \tfrac{45}{80} \\ \tfrac{7}{10} &= \tfrac{56}{80} \\ \tfrac{5}{8} &= \tfrac{50}{80} \\ \tfrac{4}{5} &= \tfrac{64}{80} \\ \tfrac{1}{2} &= \tfrac{40}{80} \end{aligned}$$

Answer: **(D)** $\tfrac{4}{5}$

12.

$$\begin{aligned} 3\tfrac{5}{16} &= 3\tfrac{5}{16} \\ +\ 2\tfrac{3}{4} &= +\ 2\tfrac{12}{16} \\ & \quad 5\tfrac{17}{16} \\ &= 6\tfrac{1}{16} \end{aligned}$$

Answer: **(B)** $6\tfrac{1}{16}$ in.

13.

$$\begin{aligned} 10\tfrac{1}{2} \div \tfrac{1}{2} &= \tfrac{21}{2} \div \tfrac{1}{2} \\ &= \tfrac{21}{2} \times \tfrac{2}{1} \\ &= 21 \end{aligned}$$

Answer: **(E)** 21

14.

$$\begin{aligned} 5\tfrac{3}{4} \times 3 &= \tfrac{23}{4} \times \tfrac{3}{1} \\ &= \tfrac{69}{4} \\ &= 17\tfrac{1}{4} \end{aligned}$$

Answer: **(D)** $17\tfrac{1}{4}$

15. First week:
L.C.D. = 24

$$\begin{aligned} 3\tfrac{1}{2} &= 3\tfrac{12}{24} \text{ miles} \\ 1\tfrac{1}{4} &= 1\tfrac{6}{24} \\ 1\tfrac{1}{6} &= 1\tfrac{4}{24} \\ +\ 2\tfrac{3}{8} &= +\ 2\tfrac{9}{24} \\ & \quad 7\tfrac{31}{24} = 8\tfrac{7}{24} \text{ miles} \end{aligned}$$

Second week:
L.C.D. = 16

$$\begin{aligned} \tfrac{1}{4} &= \tfrac{4}{16} \text{ miles} \\ \tfrac{3}{8} &= \tfrac{6}{16} \\ \tfrac{9}{16} &= \tfrac{9}{16} \\ 3\tfrac{1}{16} &= 3\tfrac{1}{16} \\ 2\tfrac{5}{8} &= 2\tfrac{10}{16} \\ +\ 3\tfrac{3}{16} &= +\ 3\tfrac{3}{16} \\ & \quad 8\tfrac{33}{16} = 10\tfrac{1}{16} \text{ miles} \end{aligned}$$

L.C.D. = 48

$$\begin{aligned} 10\tfrac{1}{16} &= 9\tfrac{51}{48} \text{ miles second week} \\ -\ 8\tfrac{7}{24} &= -\ 8\tfrac{14}{48} \text{ miles first week} \\ & \quad 1\tfrac{37}{48} \text{ miles more traveled} \end{aligned}$$

Answer: **(A)** $1\tfrac{37}{48}$

16. Consider each choice:
Each 6-ft board yields one $5\frac{1}{2}$-ft board with $\frac{1}{2}$ ft waste.
Each 12-ft board yields two $5\frac{1}{2}$-ft boards with 1 ft waste ($2 \times 5\frac{1}{2} = 11$; $12 - 11 = 1$ ft waste).
Each 24-ft board yields four $5\frac{1}{2}$-ft boards with 2 ft waste ($4 \times 5\frac{1}{2} = 22$; $24 - 22 = 2$ ft waste).
Each 22 ft board may be divided into four $5\frac{1}{2}$-ft boards with no waste ($4 \times 5\frac{1}{2} = 22$ exactly).

Answer: **(C)** 22 ft

17. $\frac{15}{16}$ of fortune is \$7500.
Therefore, his fortune $= 7500 \div \frac{15}{16}$
$= \frac{\overset{500}{\cancel{7500}}}{1} \times \frac{16}{\underset{1}{\cancel{15}}}$
$= 8000$

Answer: **(D)** \$8000

18. $\frac{2}{3}$ of 54,000 = increase

$$\text{Increase} = \frac{2}{\underset{1}{\cancel{3}}} \times \overset{18{,}000}{\cancel{54{,}000}}$$
$$= 36{,}000$$
$$\text{Present population} = 54{,}000 + 36{,}000$$
$$= 90{,}000$$

Answer: **(D)** 90,000

19. First day: $\frac{1}{3}$ evaporates
$\frac{2}{3}$ remains

Second day: $\frac{3}{4}$ of $\frac{2}{3}$ evaporates
$\frac{1}{4}$ of $\frac{2}{3}$ remains

The amount remaining is

$\frac{1}{\underset{2}{\cancel{4}}} \times \frac{\overset{1}{\cancel{2}}}{3} = \frac{1}{6}$ of original contents

Answer: **(C)** $\frac{1}{6}$

20.
$$\frac{7}{8} \text{ of capacity} = 14 \text{ gal}$$
$$\text{Therefore, capacity} = 14 \div \frac{7}{8}$$
$$= \frac{\overset{2}{\cancel{14}}}{1} \times \frac{8}{\underset{1}{\cancel{7}}}$$
$$= 16 \text{ gal}$$

Answer: **(C)** 16 gal

DECIMALS

1. A **decimal,** which is a number with a decimal point (.), is actually a fraction, the denominator of which is understood to be 10 or some power of 10.

 a. The number of digits, or places, after a decimal point determines which power of 10 the denominator is. If there is one digit, the denominator is understood to be 10; if there are two digits, the denominator is understood to be 100, etc.

Example: $.3 = \frac{3}{10}$, $.57 = \frac{57}{100}$, $.643 = \frac{643}{1000}$

 b. The addition of zeros after a decimal point does not change the value of the decimal. The zeros may be removed without changing the value of the decimal.

Example: .7 = .70 = .700 and, vice versa, .700 = .70 = .7

 c. Since a decimal point is understood to exist after any whole number, the addition of any number of zeros after such a decimal point does not change the value of the number.

Example: 2 = 2.0 = 2.00 = 2.000

Addition of Decimals

2. Decimals are added in the same way that whole numbers are added, with the provision that the decimal points must be kept in a vertical line, one under the other. This determines the place of the decimal point in the answer.

Illustration: Add 2.31, .037, 4, and 5.0017

SOLUTION:
```
   2.3100
    .0370
   4.000
 + 5.0017
  11.3487
```

Answer: 11.3487

Subtraction of Decimals

3. Decimals are subtracted in the same way that whole numbers are subtracted, with the provision that, as in addition, the decimal points must be kept in a vertical line, one under the other. This determines the place of the decimal point in the answer.

Illustration: Subtract 4.0037 from 15.3

SOLUTION:

```
  15.3000
–  4.0037
  -------
  11.2963
```

Answer: 11.2963

Multiplication of Decimals

4. Decimals are multiplied in the same way that whole numbers are multiplied.

   a. The number of decimal places in the product equals the sum of the decimal places in the multiplicand and in the multiplier.

   b. If there are fewer places in the product than this sum, then a sufficient number of zeros must be added in front of the product to equal the number of places required, and a decimal point is written in front of the zeros.

Illustration: Multiply 2.372 by .012

SOLUTION:

```
   2.372   (3 decimal places)
×  .012    (3 decimal places)
 -------
   4744
  2372
 -------
 .028464   (6 decimal places)
```

Answer: .028464

5. A decimal can be multiplied by a power of 10 by moving the decimal point to the *right* as many places as indicated by the power. If multiplied by 10, the decimal point is moved one place to the right; if multiplied by 100, the decimal point is moved two places to the right; etc.

Example: .235 × 10 = 2.35
.235 × 100 = 23.5
.235 × 1000 = 235

Division of Decimals

6. There are four types of division involving decimals:

- When the dividend only is a decimal.
- When the divisor only is a decimal.
- When both are decimals.
- When neither dividend nor divisor is a decimal.

a. When the dividend only is a decimal, the division is the same as that of whole numbers, except that a decimal point must be placed in the quotient exactly above that in the dividend.

Illustration: Divide 12.864 by 32

SOLUTION:

```
        .402
32 ) 12.864
     12 8
     ----
        64
        64
        --
```

Answer: .402

b. When the divisor only is a decimal, the decimal point in the divisor is omitted and as many zeros are placed to the right of the dividend as there were decimal places in the divisor.

Illustration: Divide 211327 by 6.817

SOLUTION:

```
  6.817 ) 211327
  (3 decimal places)

               31000
= 6817 ) 211327000
         20451          (3 zeros added)
         -----
          6817
          6817
          ----
```

Answer: 31000,

c. When both divisor and dividend are decimals, the decimal point in the divisor is omitted and the decimal point in the dividend must be moved to the right as many decimal places as there were in the divisor. If there are not enough places in the dividend, zeros must be added to make up the difference.

Illustration: Divide 2.62 by .131

$$\text{SOLUTION: } .131\overline{)\,2.62} = 131\overline{)\,2620}$$

```
            20
131 ) 2620
      262
```

Answer: 20

d. In instances when neither the divisor nor the dividend is a decimal, a problem may still involve decimals. This occurs in two cases: when the dividend is a smaller number than the divisor; and when it is required to work out a division to a certain number of decimal places. In either case, write in a decimal point after the dividend, add as many zeros as necessary, and place a decimal point in the quotient above that in the dividend.

Illustration: Divide 7 by 50.

```
          .14
SOLUTION: 50 ) 7.00
               5 0
               2 00
               2 00
```

Answer: .14

Illustration: How much is 155 divided by 40, carried out to 3 decimal places?

```
               3.875
SOLUTION: 40 ) 155.000
               120
                35 0
                32 0
                 3 00
                 2 80
                   200
```

Answer: 3.875

7. A decimal can be divided by a power of 10 by moving the decimal to the *left* as many places as indicated by the power. If divided by 10, the decimal point is moved one place to the left; if divided by 100, the decimal point is moved two places to the left; etc. If there are not enough places, add zeros in front of the number to make up the difference and add a decimal point.

Example: .4 divided by 10 = .04
.4 divided by 100 = .004

Rounding Decimals

8. To round a number to a given decimal place:
   a. Locate the given place.
   b. If the digit to the right is less than 5, omit all digits following the given place.
   c. If the digit to the right is 5 or more, raise the given place by 1 and omit all digits following the given place.

   Examples:

   4.27 = 4.3 to the nearest tenth
   .71345 = .713 to the nearest thousandth

9. In problems involving money, answers are usually rounded to the nearest cent.

Conversion of Fractions to Decimals

10. A fraction can be changed to a decimal by dividing the numerator by the denominator and working out the division to as many decimal places as required.

Illustration: Change $\frac{5}{11}$ to a decimal of 2 places.

$$\text{SOLUTION: } \frac{5}{11} = 11\overline{)\,5.00}$$

```
     .45 5/11
11 ) 5.00
     4.44
       60
       55
        5
```

Answer: $.45\frac{5}{11}$

11. To clear fractions containing a decimal in either the numerator or the denominator, or in both, divide the numerator by the denominator.

Illustration: What is the value of $\frac{2.34}{.6}$?

$$\text{SOLUTION: } \frac{2.34}{.6} = .6\overline{)\,2.34} = 6\overline{)\,23.4}$$

```
     3.9
6 ) 23.4
    18
     5 4
     5 4
```

Answer: 3.9

Conversion of Decimals to Fractions

12. Since a decimal point indicates a number having a denominator that is a power of 10, a decimal can be expressed as a fraction, the numerator of which is the number itself and the denominator of which is the power indicated by the number of decimal places in the decimal.

Example: $.3 = \frac{3}{10}$, $.47 = \frac{47}{100}$

13. When the decimal is a mixed number, divide by the power of 10 indicated by its number of decimal places. The fraction does not count as a decimal place.

Illustration: Change $.25\frac{1}{3}$ to a fraction.

SOLUTION: $.25\frac{1}{3} = 25\frac{1}{3} \div 100$
$= \frac{76}{3} \times \frac{1}{100}$
$= \frac{76}{300} = \frac{19}{75}$

Answer: $\frac{19}{75}$

14. When to change decimals to fractions:

a. When dealing with whole numbers, do not change the decimal.

Example: In the problem $12 \times .14$, it is better to keep the decimal:
$$12 \times .14 = 1.68$$

b. When dealing with fractions, change the decimal to a fraction.

Example: In the problem $\frac{3}{5} \times .17$, it is best to change the decimal to a fraction:
$$\frac{3}{5} \times .17 = \frac{3}{5} \times \frac{17}{100} = \frac{51}{500}$$

15. Because decimal equivalents of fractions are often used, it is helpful to be familiar with the most common conversions.

$\frac{1}{2} = .5$	$\frac{1}{3} = .3333$
$\frac{1}{4} = .25$	$\frac{2}{3} = .6667$
$\frac{3}{4} = .75$	$\frac{1}{6} = .1667$
$\frac{1}{5} = .2$	$\frac{1}{7} = .1429$
$\frac{1}{8} = .125$	$\frac{1}{9} = .1111$
$\frac{1}{16} = .0625$	$\frac{1}{12} = .0833$

Note that the left column contains exact values. The values in the right column have been rounded to the nearest ten-thousandth.

Practice Problems Involving Decimals

1. Add 37.03, 11.5627, 3.4005, 3423, and 1.141. ______

2. Subtract 4.64324 from 7. ______

3. Multiply 27.34 by 16.943. ______

4. How much is 19.6 divided by 3.2, carried out to 3 decimal places? ______

5. What is $\frac{5}{11}$ in decimal form (to the nearest hundredth)? ______

6. What is $.64\frac{2}{3}$ in fraction form? ______

7. What is the difference between $\frac{3}{5}$ and $\frac{9}{8}$ expressed decimally? ______

8. A boy saved up \$4.56 the first month, \$3.82 the second month, and \$5.06 the third month. How much did he save altogether?
______

9. The diameter of a certain rod is required to be $1.51 \pm .015$ inches. The rod's diameter must be between ______ and ______.

10. After an employer figures out an employee's salary of \$190.57, he deducts \$3.05 for social security and \$5.68 for pension. What is the amount of the check after these deductions?
______

11. If the outer radius of a metal pipe is 2.84 inches and the inner radius is 1.94 inches, the thickness of the metal is ______.

12. A boy earns \$20.56 on Monday, \$32.90 on Tuesday, \$20.78 on Wednesday. He spends half of all that he earned during the three days. How much has he left? ______

13. The total cost of $3\frac{1}{2}$ pounds of meat at \$1.69 a pound and 20 lemons at \$.60 a dozen will be
______.

14. A reel of cable weighs 1279 lb. If the empty reel weighs 285 lb and the cable weighs 7.1

lb per foot, the number of feet of cable on the reel is ______.

15. 345 fasteners at \$4.15 per hundred will cost ______.

Problem Solutions—Decimals

1. Line up all the decimal points one under the other. Then add:

$$\begin{array}{r} 37.03 \\ 11.5627 \\ 3.4005 \\ 3423.0000 \\ +\quad 1.141 \\ \hline 3476.1342 \end{array}$$

Answer: 3476.1342

2. Add a decimal point and five zeros to the 7. Then subtract:

$$\begin{array}{r} 7.00000 \\ -\ 4.64324 \\ \hline 2.35676 \end{array}$$

Answer: 2.35676

3. Since there are two decimal places in the multiplicand and three decimal places in the multiplier, there will be 2 + 3 = 5 decimal places in the product.

$$\begin{array}{r} 27.34 \\ \times\ 16.943 \\ \hline 8202 \\ 1\ 0936 \\ 24\ 606 \\ 164\ 04 \\ 273\ 4 \\ \hline 463.22162 \end{array}$$

Answer: 463.22162

4. Omit the decimal point in the divisor by moving it one place to the right. Move the decimal point in the dividend one place to the right and add three zeros in order to carry your answer out to three decimal places, as instructed in the problem.

$$\begin{array}{r} 6.125 \\ 3.2.\overline{)\,19.6.000} \\ 19\ 2 \\ \hline 4\ 0 \\ 3\ 2 \\ \hline 80 \\ 64 \\ \hline 160 \\ 160 \\ \hline \end{array}$$

Answer: 6.125

5. To convert a fraction to a decimal, divide the numerator by the denominator:

$$\begin{array}{r} .454 \\ 11\overline{)\,5.000} \\ 4\ 4 \\ \hline 60 \\ 55 \\ \hline 50 \\ 44 \\ \hline 6 \end{array}$$

Answer: .45 to the nearest hundredth

6. To convert a decimal to a fraction, divide by the power of 10 indicated by the number of decimal places. (The fraction does not count as a decimal place.)

$$\begin{aligned} 64\tfrac{2}{3} \div 100 &= \tfrac{194}{3} \div \tfrac{100}{1} \\ &= \tfrac{194}{3} \times \tfrac{1}{100} \\ &= \tfrac{194}{300} \\ &= \tfrac{97}{150} \end{aligned}$$

Answer: $\frac{97}{150}$

7. Convert each fraction to a decimal and subtract to find the difference:

$\frac{9}{8} = 1.125 \qquad \frac{3}{5} = .60$

$$\begin{array}{r} 1.125 \\ -\ \ .60 \\ \hline .525 \end{array}$$

Answer: .525

8. Add the savings for each month:

$$\begin{array}{r} \$4.56 \\ 3.82 \\ +\ \ 5.06 \\ \hline \$13.44 \end{array}$$

Answer: \$13.44

9.

$$\begin{array}{r} 1.51 \\ +\ .015 \\ \hline 1.525 \end{array} \qquad \begin{array}{r} 1.510 \\ -\ .015 \\ \hline 1.495 \end{array}$$

Answer: The rod may have a diameter of from 1.495 inches to 1.525 inches inclusive.

10. Add to find total deductions:

$$\begin{array}{r} \$3.05 \\ +\ 5.68 \\ \hline \$8.73 \end{array}$$

Subtract total deductions from salary to find amount of check:

$$\begin{array}{r} \$190.57 \\ -\ 8.73 \\ \hline \$181.84 \end{array}$$

Answer: $181.84

11. Outer radius minus inner radius equals thickness of metal:

$$\begin{array}{r} 2.84 \\ -\ 1.94 \\ \hline .90 \end{array}$$

Answer: .90 in

12. Add daily earnings to find total earnings:

$$\begin{array}{r} \$20.56 \\ 32.90 \\ +\ 20.78 \\ \hline \$74.24 \end{array}$$

Divide total earnings by 2 to find out what he has left:

$$\begin{array}{r} \$37.12 \\ 2\ \overline{)\ \$74.24} \end{array}$$

Answer: $37.12

13. Find cost of 3½ pounds of meat:

$$\begin{array}{r} \$1.69 \\ \times\ 3.5 \\ \hline 845 \\ 5\ 07 \\ \hline \$5.915 \end{array} = \$5.92 \text{ to the nearest cent}$$

Find cost of 20 lemons:

$.60 ÷ 12 = $.05 (for 1 lemon)
$.05 × 20 = $1.00 (for 20 lemons)

Add cost of meat and cost of lemons:

$$\begin{array}{r} \$5.92 \\ +\ 1.00 \\ \hline \$6.92 \end{array}$$

Answer: $6.92

14. Subtract weight of empty reel from total weight to find weight of cable:

$$\begin{array}{r} 1279 \text{ lb} \\ -\ 285 \text{ lb} \\ \hline 994 \text{ lb} \end{array}$$

Each foot of cable weighs 7.1 lb. Therefore, to find the number of feet of cable on the reel, divide 994 by 7.1:

$$\begin{array}{r} 14\ 0. \\ 7.1.\ \overline{)\ 994.0.} \\ 71 \\ \hline 284 \\ 284 \\ \hline 0\ 0 \end{array}$$

Answer: 140

15. Each fastener costs:

$4.15 ÷ 100 = $.0415

345 fasteners cost:

$$\begin{array}{r} 345 \\ \times\ .0415 \\ \hline 1725 \\ 345 \\ 13\ 80 \\ \hline 14.3175 \end{array}$$

Answer: $14.32

PERCENTS

1. The **percent symbol** (%) means "parts out of a hundred." Thus a percent is really a fraction—25% is 25 parts out of a hundred, or $\frac{25}{100}$, which reduces or simplifies to $\frac{1}{4}$, or one part out of four. Some problems involve expressing a fraction or a decimal as a percent. In other problems it is necessary to express a percent as a fraction or decimal in order to perform the calculations efficiently. When you have a percent (or decimal) which

converts to a common fraction (25% = .25 = $\frac{1}{4}$), it is usually best to do any multiplying or dividing by first converting the percent or decimal to the common fraction, since the numbers are usually smaller and will work better. For adding and subtracting, percentages and decimals are often easier.

2. To change a whole number or a decimal to a percent:

   a. Multiply the number by 100.

   b. Affix a % sign.

Illustration: Change 3 to a percent.

SOLUTION: $3 \times 100 = 300$
$3 = 300\%$

Answer: 300%

Illustration: Change .67 to a percent.

SOLUTION: $.67 \times 100 = 67$
$.67 = 67\%$

Answer: 67%

3. To change a fraction or a mixed number to a percent:

   a. Multiply the fraction or mixed number by 100.

   b. Reduce, if possible.

   c. Affix a % sign.

Illustration: Change $\frac{1}{7}$ to a percent.

SOLUTION: $\frac{1}{7} \times 100 = \frac{100}{7}$
$= 14\frac{2}{7}$
$\frac{1}{7} = 14\frac{2}{7}\%$

Answer: $14\frac{2}{7}\%$

Illustration: Change $4\frac{2}{3}$ to a percent.

SOLUTION: $4\frac{2}{3} \times 100 = \frac{14}{3} \times 100 = \frac{1400}{3}$
$= 466\frac{2}{3}$
$4\frac{2}{3} = 466\frac{2}{3}\%$

Answer: $466\frac{2}{3}\%$

4. To remove a % sign attached to a decimal, divide the decimal by 100. If necessary, the resulting decimal may then be changed to a fraction.

Illustration: Change .5% to a decimal and to a fraction.

SOLUTION: $.5\% = .5 \div 100 = .005$
$.005 = \frac{5}{1000} = \frac{1}{200}$

Answer: $.5\% = .005$
$.5\% = \frac{1}{200}$

5. To remove a % sign attached to a fraction or mixed number, divide the fraction or mixed number by 100, and reduce, if possible. If necessary, the resulting fraction may then be changed to a decimal.

Illustration: Change $\frac{3}{4}\%$ to a fraction and to a decimal.

SOLUTION: $\frac{3}{4}\% = \frac{3}{4} \div 100 = \frac{3}{4} \times \frac{1}{100}$
$= \frac{3}{400}$

$\frac{3}{400} = 400\overline{)3.0000}$ = .0075

Answer: $\frac{3}{4}\% = \frac{3}{400}$
$\frac{3}{4}\% = .0075$

6. To remove a % sign attached to a decimal that includes a fraction, divide the decimal by 100. If necessary, the resulting number may then be changed to a fraction.

Illustration: Change $.5\frac{1}{3}\%$ to a fraction.

SOLUTION: $.5\frac{1}{3}\% = .005\frac{1}{3}$
$= \dfrac{5\frac{1}{3}}{1000}$
$= 5\frac{1}{3} \div 1000$
$= \frac{16}{3} \times \frac{1}{1000}$
$= \frac{16}{3000}$
$= \frac{2}{375}$

Answer: $.5\frac{1}{3}\% = \frac{2}{375}$

7. Some fraction-percent equivalents are used so frequently that it is helpful to be familiar with them.

$\frac{1}{25} = 4\%$	$\frac{1}{5} = 20\%$
$\frac{1}{20} = 5\%$	$\frac{1}{4} = 25\%$
$\frac{1}{12} = 8\frac{1}{3}\%$	$\frac{1}{3} = 33\frac{1}{3}\%$
$\frac{1}{10} = 10\%$	$\frac{1}{2} = 50\%$
$\frac{1}{8} = 12\frac{1}{2}\%$	$\frac{2}{3} = 66\frac{2}{3}\%$
$\frac{1}{6} = 16\frac{2}{3}\%$	$\frac{3}{4} = 75\%$

Solving Percent Problems

8. Most percent problems involve three quantities:

- The rate, R, which is followed by a % sign.
- The base, B, which follows the word "of."
- The amount of percentage, P, which usually follows the word "is."

a. If the rate (R) and the base (B) are known, then the percentage (P) = R × B.

Illustration: Find 15% of 50.

SOLUTION:

$$\begin{aligned} \text{Rate} &= 15\% \\ \text{Base} &= 50 \\ P &= R \times B \\ P &= 15\% \times 50 \\ &= .15 \times 50 \\ &= 7.5 \end{aligned}$$

Answer: 15% of 50 is 7.5.

b. If the rate (R) and the percentage (P) are known, then the base (B) = $\frac{P}{R}$.

Illustration: 7% of what number is 35?

SOLUTION:

$$\begin{aligned} \text{Rate} &= 7\% \\ \text{Percentage} &= 35 \\ B &= \frac{P}{R} \\ B &= \frac{35}{7\%} \\ &= 35 \div .07 \\ &= 500 \end{aligned}$$

Answer: 7% of 500 is 35.

c. If the percentage (P) and the base (B) are known, the rate (R) = $\frac{P}{B}$

Illustration: There are 96 men in a group of 150 people. What percent of the group are men?

SOLUTION:

$$\begin{aligned} \text{Base} &= 150 \\ \text{Percentage (amount)} &= 96 \\ \text{Rate} &= \tfrac{96}{150} \\ &= .64 \\ &= 64\% \end{aligned}$$

Answer: 64% of the group are men.

Illustration: In a tank holding 20 gallons of solution, 1 gallon is alcohol. What is the strength of the solution in percent?

SOLUTION:

$$\begin{aligned} \text{Percentage (amount)} &= 1 \text{ gallon} \\ \text{Base} &= 20 \text{ gallons} \\ \text{Rate} &= \tfrac{1}{20} \\ &= .05 \\ &= 5\% \end{aligned}$$

Answer: The solution is 5% alcohol.

9. In a percent problem, the whole is 100%.

Example: If a problem involves 10% of a quantity, the rest of the quantity is 90%.

Example: If a quantity has been increased by 5%, the new amount is 105% of the original quantity.

Example: If a quantity has been decreased by 15%, the new amount is 85% of the original quantity.

10. Percent change, percent increase, or percent decrease are special types of percent problems in which the difficulty is in making sure to use the right numbers to calculate the percent. The full formula is:

$$\frac{\text{(New Amount)} - \text{(Original Amount)}}{\text{(Original Amount)}} \times 100 = \text{percent change}$$

Where the new amount is less than the original amount, the number on top will be a negative number and the result will be a **percent decrease.** When a percent decrease is asked for, the negative sign is omitted. Where the new amount is greater than the original amount, the percent change is positive and is called a **percent increase.**

The percent of increase or decrease is found by putting the amount of increase or decrease over the original amount and changing this fraction to a percent by multiplying by 100.

Illustration: The number of automobiles sold by the Cadcoln Dealership increased from 300 one year to 400 the following year. What was the percent of increase?

SOLUTION: There was an increase of 100, which must be compared to the original 300.

$$\frac{100}{300} = \frac{1}{3} = 33\tfrac{1}{3}\%$$

Answer: $33\frac{1}{3}\%$

Practice Problems Involving Percents

1. 10% written as a decimal is
(A) 1.0
(B) 0.1
(C) 0.01
(D) 0.010
(E) 0.001

2. What is 5.37% in fraction form?
(A) $\frac{537}{10,000}$
(B) $\frac{537}{1000}$
(C) $5\frac{37}{10,000}$
(D) $5\frac{37}{100}$
(E) $\frac{537}{10}$

3. What percent is $\frac{5}{6}$ of $\frac{3}{4}$?
(A) 60%
(B) 75%
(C) 80%
(D) 90%
(E) 111%

4. What percent is 14 of 24?
(A) $62\frac{1}{4}\%$
(B) $58\frac{1}{3}\%$
(C) $41\frac{2}{3}\%$
(D) $33\frac{3}{5}\%$
(E) 14%

5. 200% of 800 equals
(A) 4
(B) 16
(C) 200
(D) 800
(E) 1600

6. If John must have a mark of 80% to pass a test of 35 items, the number of items he may miss and still pass the test is
(A) 7
(B) 8
(C) 11
(D) 28
(E) 35

7. The regular price of a TV set that sold for \$118.80 at a 20% reduction sale is
(A) \$158.60
(B) \$148.50
(C) \$138.84
(D) \$95.04
(E) \$29.70

8. A circle graph of a budget shows the expenditure of 26.2% for housing, 28.4% for food, 12% for clothing, 12.7% for taxes, and the balance for miscellaneous items. The percent for miscellaneous items is
(A) 79.3
(B) 70.3
(C) 68.5
(D) 29.7
(E) 20.7

9. Two dozen shuttlecocks and four badminton rackets are to be purchased for a playground. The shuttlecocks are priced at \$.35 each and the rackets at \$2.75 each. The playground receives a discount of 30% from these prices. The total cost of this equipment is
(A) \$7.29
(B) \$11.43
(C) \$13.58
(D) \$18.60
(E) \$19.40

10. A piece of wood weighing 10 ounces is found to have a weight of 8 ounces after drying. The moisture content was
(A) 80%
(B) 40%
(C) $33\frac{1}{3}\%$
(D) 25%
(E) 20%

11. A bag contains 800 coins. Of these, 10 percent are dimes, 30 percent are nickels, and the rest are quarters. The amount of money in the bag is
(A) less than \$150
(B) between \$150 and \$300

(C) between \$301 and \$450
(D) between \$450 and \$800
(E) more than \$800

12. Six quarts of a 20% solution of alcohol in water are mixed with 4 quarts of a 60% solution of alcohol in water. The alcoholic strength of the mixture is
(A) 80%
(B) 40%
(C) 36%
(D) $33\frac{1}{3}$%
(E) 10%

13. A man insures 80% of his property and pays a $2\frac{1}{2}$% premium amounting to \$348. What is the total value of his property?
(A) \$19,000
(B) \$18,000
(C) \$18,400
(D) \$17,400
(E) \$13,920

14. A clerk divided his 35-hour work week as follows: $\frac{1}{5}$ of his time was spent in sorting mail; $\frac{1}{2}$ of his time in filing letters; and $\frac{1}{7}$ of his time in reception work. The rest of his time was devoted to messenger work. The percent of time spent on messenger work by the clerk during the week was most nearly
(A) 6%
(B) 10%
(C) 14%
(D) 18%
(E) 20%

15. In a school in which 40% of the enrolled students are boys, 80% of the boys are present on a certain day. If 1152 boys are present, the total school enrollment is
(A) 1440
(B) 2880
(C) 3600
(D) 5400
(E) 5760

16. Mrs. Morris receives a salary raise from \$25,000 to \$27,500. Find the percent of increase.
(A) 9
(B) 10
(C) 90
(D) 15
(E) $12\frac{1}{2}$

17. The population of Stormville has increased from 80,000 to 100,000 in the last 20 years. Find the percent of increase.
(A) 20
(B) 25
(C) 80
(D) 60
(E) 10

18. The value of Super Company Stock dropped from \$25 a share to \$21 a share. Find the percent of decrease.
(A) 4
(B) 8
(C) 12
(D) 16
(E) 20

19. The Rubins bought their home for \$30,000 and sold it for \$60,000. What was the percent of increase?
(A) 100
(B) 50
(C) 200
(D) 300
(E) 150

20. During the pre-holiday rush, Martin's Department Store increased its sales staff from 150 to 200 persons. By what percent must it now decrease its sales staff to return to the usual number of salespersons?
(A) 25
(B) $33\frac{1}{3}$
(C) 20
(D) 40
(E) 75

Percent Problems—Correct Answers

1. **(B)**	6. **(A)**	11. **(A)**	16. **(B)**
2. **(A)**	7. **(B)**	12. **(C)**	17. **(B)**
3. **(D)**	8. **(E)**	13. **(D)**	18. **(D)**
4. **(B)**	9. **(C)**	14. **(D)**	19. **(A)**
5. **(E)**	10. **(E)**	15. **(C)**	20. **(A)**

Problem Solutions—Percents

1. $10\% = .10 = .1$

Answer: **(B)** 0.1

2. $5.37\% = .0537 = \frac{537}{10,000}$

Answer: **(A)** $\frac{537}{10,000}$

3. Base (number followed by "of") = $\frac{5}{6}$
Percentage (number followed by "is") = $\frac{3}{4}$

$$\text{Rate} = \frac{\text{Percentage}}{\text{Base}}$$
$$= \text{Percentage} \div \text{Base}$$
$$\text{Rate} = \frac{3}{4} \div \frac{5}{6}$$
$$= \frac{3}{4} \times \frac{6}{5} \quad (\text{cancelled: } \tfrac{3}{\cancel{4}_2} \times \tfrac{\cancel{6}^3}{5})$$
$$= \frac{9}{10}$$
$$\frac{9}{10} = .9 = 90\%$$

Answer: **(D)** 90%

4. Base (number followed by "of") = 24
Percentage (number followed by "is") = 14

Rate = Percentage ÷ Base
Rate = 14 ÷ 24
= $.58\frac{1}{3}$
= $58\frac{1}{3}\%$

Answer: **(B)** $58\frac{1}{3}\%$

5. 200% of 800 = 2.00 × 800
= 1600

Answer: **(E)** 1600

6. He must answer 80% of 35 correctly. Therefore, he may miss 20% of 35.
20% of 35 = .20 × 35
= 7

Answer: **(A)** 7

7. Since $118.80 represents a 20% reduction, $118.80 = 80% of the regular price.

$$\text{Regular price} = \frac{\$118.80}{80\%}$$
$$= \$118.80 \div .80$$
$$= \$148.50$$

Answer: **(B)** $148.50

8. All the items in a circle graph total 100%. Add the figures given for housing, food, clothing, and taxes:

$$\begin{array}{r} 26.2\% \\ 28.4\% \\ 12\ \ \% \\ +\ 12.7\% \\ \hline 79.3\% \end{array}$$

Subtract this total from 100% to find the percent for miscellaneous items:

$$\begin{array}{r} 100.0\% \\ -\ 79.3\% \\ \hline 20.7\% \end{array}$$

Answer: **(E)** 20.7%

9. Price of shuttlecocks = 24 × $.35 = $ 8.40
Price of rackets = 4 × $2.75 = $11.00
Total price = $19.40

Discount is 30%, and 100% − 30% = 70%

Actual cost = 70% of 19.40
= .70 × 19.40
= 13.58

Answer: **(C)** $13.58

10. Subtract weight of wood after drying from original weight of wood to find amount of moisture in wood:

$$\begin{array}{r} 10 \\ -\ 8 \\ \hline 2 \end{array}$$ ounces of moisture in wood

$$\text{Moisture content} = \frac{2 \text{ ounces}}{10 \text{ ounces}} = .2 = 20\%$$

Answer: **(E)** 20%

11. Find the number of each kind of coin:

10% of 800 = .10 × 800 = 80 dimes
30% of 800 = .30 × 800 = 240 nickels
60% of 800 = .60 × 800 = 480 quarters

Find the value of the coins:

80 dimes =	80 × .10 =	$ 8.00
240 nickels =	240 × .05 =	12.00
480 quarters =	480 × .25 =	120.00
	Total	$140.00

Answer: **(A)** less than $150

12. First solution contains 20% of 6 quarts of alcohol.

$$\text{Alcohol content} = .20 \times 6 = 1.2 \text{ quarts}$$

Second solution contains 60% of 4 quarts of alcohol.

$$\text{Alcohol content} = .60 \times 4 = 2.4 \text{ quarts}$$

Mixture contains: 1.2 + 2.4 = 3.6 quarts alcohol
6 + 4 = 10 quarts liquid

$$\text{Alcoholic strength of mixture} = \frac{3.6}{10} = 36\%$$

Answer: **(C)** 36%

13. $2\frac{1}{2}\%$ of insured value = $348

$$\text{Insured value} = \frac{348}{2\frac{1}{2}\%} = 348 \div .025 = \$13{,}920$$

$13,920 is 80% of total value

$$\text{Total value} = \frac{\$13{,}920}{80\%} = \$13{,}920 \div .80 = \$17{,}400$$

Answer: **(D)** $17,400

14. $\frac{1}{5} \times 35 = 7$ hr sorting mail
$\frac{1}{2} \times 35 = 17\frac{1}{2}$ hr filing
$\frac{1}{7} = 35 = 5$ hr reception
$29\frac{1}{2}$ hr accounted for

$35 - 29\frac{1}{2} = 6\frac{1}{2}$ hr left for messenger work

% spent on messenger work:

$$= \frac{6\frac{1}{2}}{35} = 6\frac{1}{2} \div 35 = \frac{13}{2} \times \frac{1}{35} = \frac{13}{70} = .18\frac{4}{7} = 18\frac{4}{7}\%$$

Answer: **(D)** most nearly 18%

15. 80% of the boys = 1152

$$\text{Number of boys} = \frac{1152}{80\%} = 1152 \div .80 = 1440$$

40% of students = 1440

$$\text{Total number of students} = \frac{1440}{40\%} = 1440 \div .40 = 3600$$

Answer: **(C)** 3600

16. Amount of increase = $2500

$$\text{Percent of increase} = \frac{\text{amount of increase}}{\text{original}}$$

$$\frac{2500}{25{,}000} = \frac{1}{10} = 10\%$$

Answer: **(B)** 10%

17. Amount of increase = 20,000

$$\text{Percent of increase} = \frac{20{,}000}{80{,}000} = \frac{1}{4} = 25\%$$

Answer: **(B)** 25%

18. Amount of decrease = $4

$$\text{Percent of decrease} = \frac{4}{25} = \frac{16}{100} = 16\%$$

Answer: **(D)** 16%

19. Amount of increase $30,000

$$\text{Percent of increase} = \frac{30{,}000}{30{,}000} = 1 = 100\%$$

Answer: **(A)** 100%

20. Amount of decrease = 50

$$\text{Percent of decrease} = \frac{50}{200} = \frac{1}{4} = 25\%$$

Answer: **(A)** 25%

SHORTCUTS IN MULTIPLICATION AND DIVISION

There are several shortcuts for simplifying multiplication and division. Following the description of each shortcut, practice problems are provided.

Dropping Final Zeros

1. a. A zero in a whole number is considered a "final zero" if it appears in the units column or if all columns to its right are filled with zeros. A final zero may be omitted in certain kinds of problems.

   b. In decimal numbers, a zero appearing in the extreme right column may be dropped with no effect on the solution of a problem.

2. In multiplying whole numbers, the final zero(s) may be dropped during computation and simply transferred to the answer.

Examples:

$$\begin{array}{r} 2310 \\ \times \quad 150 \\ \hline 1155 \\ 231 \\ \hline 346500 \end{array} \qquad \begin{array}{r} 129 \\ \times \quad 210 \\ \hline 129 \\ 258 \\ \hline 27090 \end{array}$$

$$\begin{array}{r} 1760 \\ \times \ 205 \\ \hline 880 \\ 352 \\ \hline 360800 \end{array}$$

Practice Problems

Solve the following multiplication problems, dropping the final zeros during computation.

1. $\begin{array}{r} 230 \\ \times \quad 12 \\ \hline \end{array}$

2. $\begin{array}{r} 175 \\ \times \ 130 \\ \hline \end{array}$

3. $\begin{array}{r} 203 \\ \times \quad 14 \\ \hline \end{array}$

4. $\begin{array}{r} 621 \\ \times \ 140 \\ \hline \end{array}$

5. $\begin{array}{r} 430 \\ \times \ 360 \\ \hline \end{array}$

6. $\begin{array}{r} 132 \\ \times \ 310 \\ \hline \end{array}$

7. $\begin{array}{r} 350 \\ \times \quad 24 \\ \hline \end{array}$

8. $\begin{array}{r} 520 \\ \times \ 410 \\ \hline \end{array}$

9. $\begin{array}{r} 634 \\ \times \ 120 \\ \hline \end{array}$

10. $\begin{array}{r} 431 \\ \times \ 230 \\ \hline \end{array}$

Solutions to Practice Problems

1. $\begin{array}{r} 230 \\ \times \quad 12 \\ \hline 46 \\ 23 \\ \hline 2760 \end{array}$

2. $\begin{array}{r} 175 \\ \times \ 130 \\ \hline 525 \\ 175 \\ \hline 22750 \end{array}$

3. $\begin{array}{r} 203 \\ \times \quad 14 \\ \hline 812 \\ 203 \\ \hline 2842 \end{array}$
   (no final zeros)

4. $\begin{array}{r} 621 \\ \times \ 140 \\ \hline 2484 \\ 621 \\ \hline 86940 \end{array}$

5. $\begin{array}{r} 430 \\ \times \ 360 \\ \hline 258 \\ 129 \\ \hline 154800 \end{array}$

6.
$$\begin{array}{r} 132 \\ \times\ 310 \\ \hline 132 \\ 396 \\ \hline 40920 \end{array}$$

7.
$$\begin{array}{r} 350 \\ \times\ 24 \\ \hline 140 \\ 70 \\ \hline 8400 \end{array}$$

8.
$$\begin{array}{r} 520 \\ \times\ 410 \\ \hline 52 \\ 208 \\ \hline 213200 \end{array}$$

9.
$$\begin{array}{r} 634 \\ \times\ 120 \\ \hline 1268 \\ 634 \\ \hline 76080 \end{array}$$

10.
$$\begin{array}{r} 431 \\ \times\ 230 \\ \hline 1293 \\ 862 \\ \hline 99130 \end{array}$$

Multiplying Whole Numbers by Decimals

3. In multiplying a whole number by a decimal number, if there are one or more final zeros in the multiplicand, move the decimal point in the multiplier to the right the same number of places as there are final zeros in the multiplicand. Then cross out the final zero(s) in the multiplicand.

Examples:

$$\begin{array}{r} 27500 \\ \times\ \ .15 \\ \hline \end{array} = \begin{array}{r} 275 \\ \times\ 15 \\ \hline \end{array}$$

$$\begin{array}{r} 1250 \\ \times\ .345 \\ \hline \end{array} \qquad \begin{array}{r} 125 \\ \times\ 3.45 \\ \hline \end{array}$$

Practice Problems

Rewrite the following problems, dropping the final zeros and moving decimal points the appropriate number of spaces. Then compute the answers.

1. $\begin{array}{r} 2400 \\ \times\ .02 \\ \hline \end{array}$

2. $\begin{array}{r} 620 \\ \times\ .04 \\ \hline \end{array}$

3. $\begin{array}{r} 800 \\ \times\ .005 \\ \hline \end{array}$

4. $\begin{array}{r} 600 \\ \times\ .002 \\ \hline \end{array}$

5. $\begin{array}{r} 340 \\ \times\ .08 \\ \hline \end{array}$

6. $\begin{array}{r} 480 \\ \times\ .4 \\ \hline \end{array}$

7. $\begin{array}{r} 400 \\ \times\ .04 \\ \hline \end{array}$

8. $\begin{array}{r} 5300 \\ \times\ .5 \\ \hline \end{array}$

9. $\begin{array}{r} 930 \\ \times\ .3 \\ \hline \end{array}$

10. $\begin{array}{r} 9000 \\ \times\ .001 \\ \hline \end{array}$

Solutions to Practice Problems

The rewritten problems are shown, along with the answers.

1. $\begin{array}{r} 24 \\ \times\ 2 \\ \hline 48 \end{array}$

2. $$\begin{array}{r} 62 \\ \times\ .4 \\ \hline 24.8 \end{array}$$

3. $$\begin{array}{r} 8 \\ \times\ .5 \\ \hline 4.0 \end{array}$$

4. $$\begin{array}{r} 6 \\ \times\ .2 \\ \hline 1.2 \end{array}$$

5. $$\begin{array}{r} 34 \\ \times\ .8 \\ \hline 27.2 \end{array}$$

6. $$\begin{array}{r} 48 \\ \times\ 4 \\ \hline 192 \end{array}$$

7. $$\begin{array}{r} 4 \\ \times\ 4 \\ \hline 16 \end{array}$$

8. $$\begin{array}{r} 530 \\ \times\ 5 \\ \hline 2650 \end{array}$$

9. $$\begin{array}{r} 93 \\ \times\ 3 \\ \hline 279 \end{array}$$

10. $$\begin{array}{r} 9 \\ \times\ 1 \\ \hline 9 \end{array}$$

Dividing by Whole Numbers

4. a. When there are final zeros in the divisor but no final zeros in the dividend, move the decimal point in the dividend to the left as many places as there are final zeros in the divisor, then omit the final zeros.

Example: $2700.\overline{)\,37523.} = 27.\overline{)\,375.23}$

b. When there are fewer final zeros in the divisor than there are in the dividend, drop the same number of final zeros from the dividend as there are final zeros in the divisor.

Example: $250.\overline{)\,45300.} = 24.\overline{)\,4530.}$

c. When there are more final zeros in the divisor than there are in the dividend, move the decimal point in the dividend to the left as many places as there are final zeros in the divisor, then omit the final zeros.

Example: $2300.\overline{)\,690.} = 23.\overline{)\,6.9}$

d. When there are no final zeros in the divisor, no zeros can be dropped in the dividend.

Example: $23.\overline{)\,690.} = 23.\overline{)\,690.}$

Practice Problems

Rewrite the following problems, dropping the final zeros and moving the decimal points the appropriate number of places. Then compute the quotients.

1. $600.\overline{)\,72.}$
2. $310.\overline{)\,6200.}$
3. $7600\overline{)\,1520.}$
4. $46.\overline{)\,920.}$
5. $11.0\overline{)\,220.}$
6. $700.\overline{)\,84.}$
7. $90.\overline{)\,8100.}$
8. $8100.\overline{)\,1620.}$
9. $25.\overline{)\,5250.}$
10. $41.0\overline{)\,820.}$
11. $800.\overline{)\,96.}$
12. $650.\overline{)\,1300.}$
13. $5500.\overline{)\,110.}$
14. $36.\overline{)\,720.}$
15. $87.0\overline{)\,1740.}$

Rewritten Practice Problems

1. $6.\,\overline{)\;.72}$

2. $31.\,\overline{)\;620.}$

3. $76.\,\overline{)\;15.2}$

4. $46.\,\overline{)\;920.}$

5. $11.\,\overline{)\;220.}$

6. $7.\,\overline{)\;.84}$

7. $9.\,\overline{)\;810.}$

8. $81.\,\overline{)\;16.2}$

9. $25.\,\overline{)\;5250.}$

10. $41.\,\overline{)\;820.}$

11. $8.\,\overline{)\;.96}$

12. $65.\,\overline{)\;130.}$

13. $55.\,\overline{)\;1.1}$

14. $36.\,\overline{)\;720.}$

15. $87.\,\overline{)\;1740.}$

Solutions to Practice Problems

1. $$\begin{array}{r} .12 \\ 6.\,\overline{)\;.72} \end{array}$$

2. $$\begin{array}{r} 20 \\ 31.\,\overline{)\;620.} \\ 62 \\ \hline 00 \end{array}$$

3. $$\begin{array}{r} .2 \\ 76.\,\overline{)\;15.2} \\ 15\;2 \\ \hline 0\;0 \end{array}$$

4. $$\begin{array}{r} 20 \\ 46.\,\overline{)\;920.} \\ 92 \\ \hline 00 \end{array}$$

5. $$\begin{array}{r} 20 \\ 11.\,\overline{)\;220.} \\ 22 \\ \hline 00 \end{array}$$

6. $$\begin{array}{r} .12 \\ 7.\,\overline{)\;.84} \end{array}$$

7. $$\begin{array}{r} 90 \\ 9.\,\overline{)\;810.} \\ 81 \\ \hline 00 \end{array}$$

8. $$\begin{array}{r} .2 \\ 81.\,\overline{)\;16.2} \\ 16\;2 \\ \hline 0\;0 \end{array}$$

9. $$\begin{array}{r} 210 \\ 25.\,\overline{)\;5250.} \\ 50 \\ \hline 25 \\ 25 \\ \hline 00 \end{array}$$

10. $$\begin{array}{r} 20 \\ 41.\,\overline{)\;820.} \\ 82 \\ \hline 00 \end{array}$$

11. $$\begin{array}{r} .12 \\ 8.\,\overline{)\;.96} \end{array}$$

12. $$\begin{array}{r} 2 \\ 65.\,\overline{)\;130.} \\ 130 \\ \hline 00 \end{array}$$

13. $$\begin{array}{r} .02 \\ 55.\,\overline{)\;1.10} \\ 1\;10 \\ \hline 00 \end{array}$$

14. $$\begin{array}{r} 20 \\ 36.\,\overline{)\;720.} \\ 72 \\ \hline 00 \end{array}$$

15. $$\begin{array}{r} 20 \\ 87.\,\overline{)\;1740.} \\ 174 \\ \hline 00 \end{array}$$

Division by Multiplication

5. Instead of dividing by a particular number, the same answer is obtained by multiplying by the equivalent multiplier.

6. To find the equivalent multiplier of a given divisor, divide 1 by the divisor.

   Example: The equivalent multiplier of $12\frac{1}{2}$ is $1 \div 12\frac{1}{2}$ or .08. The division problem $100 \div 12\frac{1}{2}$ may be more easily solved as the multiplication problem $100 \times .08$. The answer will be the same. This can be helpful when you are estimating answers.

7. Common divisors and their equivalent multipliers are shown below:

Divisor	*Equivalent Multiplier*
$11\frac{1}{9}$	.09
$12\frac{1}{2}$	.08
$14\frac{2}{7}$	.07
$16\frac{2}{3}$	.06
20	.05
25	.04
$33\frac{1}{3}$	.03
50	.02

8. A divisor may be multiplied or divided by any power of 10, and the only change in its equivalent multiplier will be in the placement of the decimal point, as may be seen in the following table:

Divisor	*Equivalent Multiplier*
.025	40.
.25	4.
2.5	.4
25.	.04
250.	.004
2500.	.0004

Practice Problems

Rewrite and solve each of the following problems by using equivalent multipliers. Drop the final zeros where appropriate.

1. $100 \div 16\frac{2}{3} =$
2. $300 \div 25 =$
3. $300 \div 33\frac{1}{3} =$
4. $250 \div 50 =$
5. $80 \div 12\frac{1}{2} =$
6. $800 \div 14\frac{2}{7} =$
7. $620 \div 20 =$
8. $500 \div 11\frac{1}{9} =$
9. $420 \div 16\frac{2}{3} =$
10. $1200 \div 33\frac{1}{3} =$
11. $955 \div 50 =$
12. $900 \div 33\frac{1}{3} =$
13. $275 \div 12\frac{1}{2} =$
14. $625 \div 25 =$
14. $244 \div 20 =$
16. $350 \div 16\frac{2}{3} =$
17. $400 \div 33\frac{1}{3} =$
18. $375 \div 25 =$
19. $460 \div 20 =$
20. $250 \div 12\frac{1}{2} =$

Solutions to Practice Problems

The rewritten problems and their solutions appear below:

1. $100 \times .06 = 1 \times 6 = 6$
2. $200 \times .04 = 2 \times 4 = 8$
3. $300 \times .03 = 3 \times 3 = 9$

4. 250 × .02 = 25 × .2 = 5

5. 80 × .08 = 8 × .8 = 6.4

6. 800 × .07 = 8 × 7 = 56

7. 620 × .05 = 62 × .5 = 31

8. 500 × .09 = 5 × 9 = 45

9. 420 × .06 = 42 × .6 = 25.2

10. 1200 × .03 = 12 × 3 = 36

11. 955 × .02 = 19.1

12. 900 × .03 = 9 × 3 = 27

13. 275 × .08 = 22

14. 625 × .04 = 25

15. 244 × .05 = 12.2

16. 350 × .06 = 35 × .6 = 21

17. 400 × .03 = 4 × 3 = 12

18. 375 × .04 = 15

19. 460 × .05 = 46 × .5 = 23

20. 250 × .08 = 25 × .8 = 20

Multiplication by Division

9. Just as some division problems are made easier by changing them to equivalent multiplication problems, certain multiplication problems are made easier by changing them to equivalent division problems.

10. Instead of arriving at an answer by multiplying by a particular number, the same answer is obtained by dividing by the equivalent divisor.

11. To find the equivalent divisor of a given multiplier, divide 1 by the multiplier.

12. Common multipliers and their equivalent divisors are shown below:

Multiplier	*Equivalent Divisor*
$11\frac{1}{9}$	.09
$12\frac{1}{2}$	.08
$14\frac{2}{7}$	.07
$16\frac{2}{3}$	.06
20	.05
25	.04
$33\frac{1}{3}$	.03
50	.02

Notice that the multiplier-equivalent divisor pairs are the same as the divisor-equivalent multiplier pairs given earlier.

Practice Problems

Rewrite and solve each of the following problems by using division. Drop the final zeros where appropriate.

1. $77 \times 14\frac{2}{7} =$

2. $81 \times 11\frac{1}{9} =$

3. 475 × 20 =

4. 42 × 50 =

5. $36 \times 33\frac{1}{3} =$

6. $96 \times 12\frac{1}{2} =$

7. $126 \times 16\frac{2}{3} =$

8. 48 × 25 =

9. $33 \times 33\frac{1}{3} =$

10. $84 \times 14\frac{2}{7} =$

11. $99 \times 11\frac{1}{9} =$

12. $126 \times 33\frac{1}{3} =$

13. $168 \times 12\frac{1}{2} =$

14. $654 \times 16\frac{2}{3} =$

15. $154 \times 14\frac{2}{7} =$

16. $5250 \times 50 =$

17. $324 \times 25 =$

18. $625 \times 20 =$

19. $198 \times 11\frac{1}{9} =$

20. $224 \times 14\frac{2}{7} =$

Solutions to Practice Problems

The rewritten problems and their solutions appear below:

1. $.07\overline{)\,77.} = 7\overline{)\,7700.}$ $\quad$ 1100.

2. $.09\overline{)\,81.} = 9\overline{)\,8100.}$ $\quad$ 900.

3. $.05\overline{)\,475.} = 5\overline{)\,47500.}$ $\quad$ 9500.

4. $.02\overline{)\,42.} = 2\overline{)\,4200.}$ $\quad$ 2100.

5. $.03\overline{)\,36.} = 3\overline{)\,3600.}$ $\quad$ 1200.

6. $.08\overline{)\,96.} = 8\overline{)\,9600.}$ $\quad$ 1200.

7. $.06\overline{)\,126.} = 6\overline{)\,12600.}$ $\quad$ 2100.

8. $.04\overline{)\,48.} = 4\overline{)\,4800.}$ $\quad$ 1200.

9. $.03\overline{)\,33.} = 3\overline{)\,3300.}$ $\quad$ 1100.

10. $.07\overline{)\,84.} = 7\overline{)\,8400.}$ $\quad$ 1200.

11. $.09\overline{)\,99.} = 9\overline{)\,9900.}$ $\quad$ 1100.

12. $.03\overline{)\,126.} = 3\overline{)\,12600.}$ $\quad$ 4200.

13. $.08\overline{)\,168.} = 8\overline{)\,16800.}$ $\quad$ 2100.

14. $.06\overline{)\,654.} = 6\overline{)\,65400.}$ $\quad$ 10900.

15. $.07\overline{)\,154.} = 7\overline{)\,15400.}$ $\quad$ 2200.

16. $.02\overline{)\,5250.} = 2\overline{)\,525000.}$ $\quad$ 262500.

17. $.04\overline{)\,324.} = 4\overline{)\,32400.}$ $\quad$ 8100.

18. $.05\overline{)\,625.} = 5\overline{)\,62500.}$ $\quad$ 12500.

19. $.09\overline{)\,198.} = 9\overline{)\,19800.}$ $\quad$ 2200.

20. $.07\overline{)\,224.} = 7\overline{)\,22400.}$ $\quad$ 3200.

AVERAGES

1. a. The term average can technically refer to a variety of mathematical ideas, but on the test it refers to the **arithmetic mean.** It is found by adding the numbers given and then dividing this sum by the number of items being averaged.

Illustration: Find the arithmetic mean of 2, 8, 5, 9, 6, and 12.

SOLUTION: There are 6 numbers.

$$\text{Arithmetic mean} = \frac{2 + 8 + 5 + 9 + 6 + 12}{6} = \frac{42}{6} = 7$$

Answer: The arithmetic mean is 7.

b. If a problem calls for simply the average or the mean, it is referring to the arithmetic mean.

2. If a group of numbers is arranged in order, the middle number is called the **median.** If there is no single middle number (this occurs when there is an even number of items), the median is found by computing the arithmetic mean of the two middle numbers.

   Example: The median of 6, 8, 10, 12, and 14 is 10.

   Example: The median of 6, 8, 10, 12, 14, and 16 is the arithmetic mean of 10 and 12.

$$\frac{10 + 12}{2} = \frac{22}{2} = 11.$$

3. The **mode** of a group of numbers is the number that appears most often.

   Example: The mode of 10, 5, 7, 9, 12, 5, 10, 5 and 9 is 5.

4. When some numbers among terms to be averaged occur more than once, they must be given the appropriate weight. For example, if a student received four grades of 80 and one of 90, his average would not be the average of 80 and 90, but rather the average of 80, 80, 80, 80, and 90.

   To obtain the average of quantities that are weighted:

   a. Set up a table listing the quantities, their respective weights, and their respective values.

   b. Multiply the value of each quantity by its respective weight.

   c. Add up these products.

   d. Add up the weights.

   e. Divide the sum of the products by the sum of the weights.

   Illustration: Assume that the weights for the following subjects are: English 3, History 2, Mathematics 2, Foreign Languages 2, and Art 1. What would be the average of a student whose marks are: English 80, History 85, Algebra 84, Spanish 82, and Art 90?

SOLUTION:

Subject	*Weight*	*Mark*
English	3	80
History	2	85
Algebra	2	84
Spanish	2	82
Art	1	90

English	3 × 80 =	240
History	2 × 85 =	170
Algebra	2 × 84 =	168
Spanish	2 × 82 =	164
Art	1 × 90 =	90
		832

Sum of the weights: $3 + 2 + 2 + 2 + 1 = 10$

$832 \div 10 = 83.2$

Answer: Average = 83.2

Note: On the test, you might go directly to a list of the weighted amounts, here totalling 832, and divide by the number of weights; or you might set up a single equation.

Illustration: Mr. Martin drove for 6 hours at an average rate of 50 miles per hour and for 2 hours at an average rate of 60 miles per hour. Find his average rate for the entire trip.

SOLUTION:

$$\frac{6(50) + 2(60)}{8} = \frac{300 + 120}{8} = \frac{420}{8} = 52\tfrac{1}{2}$$

Answer: $52\frac{1}{2}$

Since he drove many more hours at 50 miles per hour than at 60 miles per hour, his average rate should be closer to 50 than to 60, which it is. In general, average rate can always be found by dividing the total distance covered by the time spent traveling.

Practice Problems Involving Averages

1. The arithmetic mean of 73.8, 92.2, 64.7, 43.8, 56.5, and 46.4 is
   (A) 60.6
   (B) 62.9
   (C) 64.48
   (D) 75.48
   (E) 82.9

2. The median of the numbers 8, 5, 7, 5, 9, 9, 1, 8, 10, 5, and 10 is
(A) 5
(B) 7
(C) 8
(D) 9
(E) 10

3. The mode of the numbers 16, 15, 17, 12, 15, 15, 18, 19, and 18 is
(A) 15
(B) 16
(C) 17
(D) 18
(E) 19

4. A clerk filed 73 forms on Monday, 85 forms on Tuesday, 54 on Wednesday, 92 on Thursday, and 66 on Friday. What was the average number of forms filed per day?
(A) 60
(B) 72
(C) 74
(D) 92
(E) 370

5. The grades received on a test by twenty students were: 100, 55, 75, 80, 65, 65, 85, 90, 80, 45, 40, 50, 85, 85, 85, 80, 80, 70, 65, and 60. The average of these grades is
(A) 70
(B) 72
(C) 77
(D) 80
(E) 100

6. A buyer purchased 75 six-inch rulers costing 15¢ each, 100 one-foot rulers costing 30¢ each, and 50 one-yard rulers costing 72¢ each. What was the average price per ruler?
(A) $26\frac{1}{8}$¢
(B) $34\frac{1}{3}$¢
(C) 39¢
(D) 42¢
(E) $77\frac{1}{4}$¢

7. What is the average of a student who received 90 in English, 84 in Algebra, 75 in French, and 76 in Music, if the subjects have the following weights: English 4, Algebra 3, French 3, and Music 1?
(A) 81
(B) $81\frac{1}{2}$
(C) 82
(D) $82\frac{1}{2}$
(E) 83

Questions 8–11 refer to the following information:

A census shows that on a certain block the number of children in each family is 3, 4, 4, 0, 1, 2, 0, 2, and 2, respectively.

8. Find the average number of children per family.
(A) 4
(B) 3
(C) $3\frac{1}{2}$
(D) 2
(E) $1\frac{1}{2}$

9. Find the median number of children.
(A) 1
(B) 2
(C) 3
(D) 4
(E) 5

10. Find the mode of the number of children.
(A) 0
(B) 1
(C) 2
(D) 3
(E) 4

Averages Problems—Correct Answers

1.	**(B)**	6.	**(B)**
2.	**(C)**	7.	**(E)**
3.	**(A)**	8.	**(D)**
4.	**(C)**	9.	**(B)**
5.	**(B)**	10.	**(C)**

Problem Solutions—Averages

1. Find the sum of the values:

$73.8 + 92.2 + 64.7 + 43.8 + 56.5 + 46.4 = 377.4$

There are 6 values.

$$\text{Arithmetic mean} = \frac{377.4}{6} = 62.9$$

Answer: **(B)** 62.9

2. Arrange the numbers in order:

   1, 5, 5, 5, 7, 8, 8, 9, 9, 10, 10

   The middle number, or median, is 8.

   Answer: **(C)** 8

3. The mode is that number appearing most frequently. The number 15 appears three times.

   Answer: **(A)** 15

4. $$\text{Average} = \frac{73 + 85 + 54 + 92 + 66}{5} = \frac{370}{5} = 74$$

   Answer: **(C)** 74

5. Sum of the grades = 1440.

   $$\frac{1440}{20} = 72$$

   Answer: **(B)** 72

6. $$\begin{array}{rl} 75 \times 15¢ = & 1125¢ \\ 100 \times 30¢ = & 3000¢ \\ 50 \times 72¢ = & 3600¢ \\ \hline 225 \qquad & 7725¢ \end{array}$$

   $$\frac{7725¢}{225} = 34\tfrac{1}{3}¢$$

   Answer: **(B)** $34\frac{1}{3}$¢

7.

Subject	*Grade*	*Weight*
English	90	4
Algebra	84	3
French	75	3
Music	76	1

$(90 \times 4) + (84 \times 3) + (75 \times 3) + (76 \times 1)$
$360 + 252 + 225 + 76 = 913$
Weight $= 4 + 3 + 3 + 1 = 11$
$913 \div 11 = 83$ average

Answer: **(E)** 83

8. $$\text{Average} = \frac{3 + 4 + 4 + 0 + 1 + 2 + 0 + 2 + 2}{9} = \frac{18}{9} = 2$$

   Answer: **(D)** 2

9. Arrange the numbers in order:

   0, 0, 1, 2, 2, 2, 3, 4, 4

   Of the 9 numbers, the fifth (middle) number is 2.

   Answer: **(B)** 2

10. The number appearing most often is 2.

    Answer: **(C)** 2

RATIO AND PROPORTION

Ratio

1. A **ratio** expresses the relationship between two (or more) quantities in terms of numbers. The mark used to indicate ratio is the colon (:) and is read "to."

   Example: The ratio 2:3 is read "2 to 3."

2. A ratio also represents division. Therefore, any ratio of two terms may be written as a fraction, and any fraction may be written as a ratio.

   Example: $3:4 = \frac{3}{4}$
   $\frac{5}{6} = 5:6$

3. To simplify any complicated ratio of two terms containing fractions, decimals, or percents:

   a. Divide the first term by the second.

   b. Write as a fraction in lowest terms.

   c. Write the fraction as a ratio.

   Illustration: Simplify the ratio $\frac{5}{6}:\frac{7}{8}$

   SOLUTION: $\frac{5}{6} \div \frac{7}{8} = \frac{5}{6} \times \frac{8}{7} = \frac{20}{21}$
   $\frac{20}{21} = 20:21$

   Answer: 20:21

4. To solve problems in which the ratio is given:

   a. Add the terms in the ratio.

   b. Divide the total amount that is to be put into a ratio by this sum.

c. Multiply each term in the ratio by this quotient.

Illustration: The sum of $360 is to be divided among three people according to the ratio 3:4:5. How much does each one receive?

SOLUTION: $3 + 4 + 5 = 12$

$$360 \div 12 = 30$$
$$30 \times 3 = 90$$
$$30 \times 4 = 120$$
$$30 \times 5 = 150$$

(all amounts in dollars: \$360 ÷ 12 = \$30; \$30 × 3 = \$90; \$30 × 4 = \$120; \$30 × 5 = \$150)

Answer: The money is divided thus: $90, $120, $150.

Proportion

5. a. A **proportion** indicates the equality of two ratios.

Example: 2:4 = 5:10 is a proportion. This is read "2 is to 4 as 5 is to 10."

b. In a proportion, the two outside terms are called the **extremes,** and the two inside terms are called the **means.**

Example: In the proportion 2:4 = 5:10, 2 and 10 are the extremes, and 4 and 5 are the means.

c. Proportions are often written in fractional form.

Example: The proportion 2:4 = 5:10 may be written $\frac{2}{4} = \frac{5}{10}$.

d. In any proportion, the product of the means equals the product of the extremes. If the proportion is a fractional form, the products may be found by cross-multiplication.

Example: In $\frac{2}{4} = \frac{5}{10}$, $4 \times 5 = 2 \times 10$.

e. The product of the extremes divided by one mean equals the other mean; the product of the means divided by one extreme equals the other extreme.

6. Many problems in which three terms are given and one term is unknown can be solved by using proportions. To solve such problems:

a. Formulate the proportion very carefully according to the facts given. (If any term is misplaced, the solution will be incorrect.) Any symbol may be written in place of the missing term.

b. Determine by inspection whether the means or the extremes are known. Multiply the pair that has both terms given.

c. Divide this product by the third term given to find the unknown term.

Illustration: The scale on a map shows that 2 cm represents 30 miles of actual length. What is the actual length of a road that is represented by 7 cm on the map?

SOLUTION: The map lengths and the actual lengths are in proportion—that is, they have equal ratios. If m stands for the unknown length, the proportion is:

$$\frac{2}{7} = \frac{30}{m}$$

As the proportion is written, m is an extreme and is equal to the product of the means, divided by the other extreme:

$$m = \frac{7 \times 30}{2}$$
$$m = \frac{210}{2}$$
$$m = 105$$

Answer: 7 cm on the map represents 105 miles.

Illustration: If a money bag containing 500 nickels weighs 6 pounds, how much will a money bag containing 1600 nickels weigh?

SOLUTION: The weights of the bags and the number of coins in them are proportional. Suppose w represents the unknown weight. Then

$$\frac{6}{w} = \frac{500}{1600}$$

The unknown is a mean and is equal to the product of the extremes, divided by the other mean:

$$w = \frac{6 \times 1600}{500}$$
$$w = 19.2$$

Answer: A bag containing 1600 nickels weighs 19.2 pounds.

Practice Problems Involving Ratio and Proportion

1. The ratio of 24 to 64 is
(A) 1:64
(B) 1:24
(C) 20:100
(D) 24:100
(E) 3:8

2. The Baltimore Colts won 8 games and lost 3. The ratio of games won to games played is
(A) 11:8
(B) 8:3
(C) 8:11
(D) 3:8
(E) 3:11

3. The ratio of $\frac{1}{4}$ to $\frac{3}{5}$ is
(A) 1 to 3
(B) 3 to 20
(C) 5 to 12
(D) 3 to 4
(E) 5 to 4

4. If there are 16 boys and 12 girls in a class, the ratio of the number of girls to the number of children in the class is
(A) 3 to 4
(B) 3 to 7
(C) 4 to 7
(D) 4 to 3
(E) 7 to 4

5. 259 is to 37 as
(A) 5 is to 1
(B) 63 is to 441
(C) 84 is to 12
(D) 130 is to 19
(E) 25 is to 4

6. 2 dozen cans of dog food at the rate of 3 cans for $1.45 would cost
(A) $10.05
(B) $10.20
(C) $11.20
(D) $11.60
(E) $11.75

7. A snapshot measures $2\frac{1}{2}$ inches by $1\frac{7}{8}$ inches. It is to be enlarged so that the longer dimension will be 4 inches. The length of the enlarged shorter dimension will be
(A) $2\frac{1}{2}$ in
(B) 3 in
(C) $3\frac{3}{8}$ in
(D) 4 in
(E) 5 in

8. Men's white handkerchiefs cost $2.29 for 3. The cost per dozen handkerchiefs is
(A) $27.48
(B) $13.74
(C) $9.16
(D) $6.87
(E) $4.58

9. A certain pole casts a shadow 24 feet long. At the same time another pole 3 feet high casts a shadow 4 feet long. How high is the first pole, given that the heights and shadows are in proportion?
(A) 18 ft
(B) 19 ft
(C) 20 ft
(D) 21 ft
(E) 24 ft

10. The actual length represented by $3\frac{1}{2}$ inches on a drawing having a scale of $\frac{1}{8}$ inch to the foot is
(A) 3.5 ft
(B) 7 ft
(C) 21 ft
(D) 28 ft
(E) 120 ft

11. Aluminum bronze consists of copper and aluminum, usually in the ratio of 10:1 by weight. If an object made of this alloy weighs 77 lb, how many pounds of aluminum does it contain?
(A) 0.7
(B) 7.0
(C) 7.7
(D) 70.7
(E) 77.0

12. It costs 31 cents a square foot to lay vinyl flooring. To lay 180 square feet of flooring, it will cost
(A) \$16.20
(B) \$18.60
(C) \$55.80
(D) \$62.00
(E) \$180.00

13. If a per diem worker earns \$352 in 16 days, the amount that he will earn in 117 days is most nearly
(A) \$3050
(B) \$2575
(C) \$2285
(D) \$2080
(E) \$1170

14. Assuming that on a blueprint $\frac{1}{8}$ inch equals 12 inches of actual length, the actual length in inches of a steel bar represented on the blueprint by a line $3\frac{3}{4}$ inches long is
(A) $3\frac{3}{4}$
(B) 30
(C) 36
(D) 360
(E) 450

15. A, B, and C invested \$9,000, \$7,000 and \$6,000, respectively. Their profits were to be divided according to the ratio of their investment. If B uses his share of the firm's profit of \$825 to pay a personal debt of \$230, how much will he have left?
(A) \$30.50
(B) \$32.50
(C) \$34.50
(D) \$36.50
(E) \$37.50

Ratio and Proportion Problems—Correct Answers

1.	**(E)**	6.	**(D)**	11.	**(B)**
2.	**(C)**	7.	**(B)**	12.	**(C)**
3.	**(C)**	8.	**(C)**	13.	**(B)**
4.	**(B)**	9.	**(A)**	14.	**(D)**
5.	**(C)**	10.	**(D)**	15.	**(B)**

Problem Solutions—Ratio and Proportion

1. The ratio 24 to 64 may be written 24:64 or $\frac{24}{64}$. In fraction form, the ratio can be reduced:

$$\frac{24}{64} = \frac{3}{8} \quad \text{or} \quad 3:8$$

Answer: **(E)** 3:8

2. The number of games played was 3 + 8 = 11. The ratio of games won to games played is 8:11.

Answer: **(C)** 8:11

3. $$\begin{aligned} \tfrac{1}{4}:\tfrac{3}{5} &= \tfrac{1}{4} \div \tfrac{3}{5} \\ &= \tfrac{1}{4} \times \tfrac{5}{3} \\ &= \tfrac{5}{12} \\ &= 5:12 \end{aligned}$$

Answer: **(C)** 5 to 12

4. There are 16 + 12 = 28 children in the class. The ratio of number of girls to number of children is 12:28.

$$\frac{12}{28} = \frac{3}{7}$$

Answer: **(B)** 3 to 7

5. The ratio $\frac{259}{37}$ reduces by 37 to $\frac{7}{1}$. The ratio $\frac{84}{12}$ also reduces to $\frac{7}{1}$. Therefore, $\frac{259}{37} = \frac{84}{12}$ is a proportion.

Answer: **(C)** 84 is to 12

6. The number of cans are proportional to the price. Let p represent the unknown price:

Then $$\frac{3}{24} = \frac{1.45}{p}$$

$$p = \frac{1.45 \times 24}{3}$$

$$p = \frac{34.80}{3}$$

$$= \$11.60$$

Answer: **(D)** \$11.60

7. Let s represent the unknown shorter dimension:

$$\frac{2\frac{1}{2}}{4} = \frac{1\frac{7}{8}}{s}$$

$$s = \frac{4 \times 1\frac{7}{8}}{2\frac{1}{2}}$$

$$= \frac{\overset{1}{\not{4}} \times \frac{15}{\not{8}_2}}{2\frac{1}{2}}$$

$$= \frac{15}{2} \div 2\frac{1}{2}$$

$$= \frac{15}{2} \div \frac{5}{2}$$

$$= \frac{15}{2} \times \frac{2}{5}$$

$$= 3$$

Answer: **(B)** 3 in

8. If p is the cost per dozen (12):

$$\frac{3}{12} = \frac{2.29}{p}$$

$$p = \frac{\overset{4}{\not{12}} \times 2.29}{\underset{1}{\not{3}}}$$

$$= 9.16$$

Answer: **(C)** $9.16

9. If f is the height of the first pole, the proportion is:

$$\frac{f}{24} = \frac{3}{4}$$

$$f = \frac{\overset{6}{\not{24}} \times 3}{\underset{1}{\not{4}}}$$

$$= 18$$

Answer: **(A)** 18 ft

10. If y is the unknown length:

$$\frac{3\frac{1}{2}}{\frac{1}{8}} = \frac{y}{1}$$

$$y = \frac{3\frac{1}{2} \times 1}{\frac{1}{8}}$$

$$= 3\frac{1}{2} \div \frac{1}{8}$$

$$= \frac{7}{2} \times \frac{8}{1}$$

$$= 28$$

Answer: **(D)** 28 ft

11. Since only two parts of a proportion are known (77 is total weight), the problem must be solved by the ratio method. The ratio 10:1 means that if the alloy were separated into equal parts, 10 of those parts would be copper and 1 would be alumninum, for a total of 10 + 1 = 11 parts.

$$77 \div 11 = 7 \text{ lb per part}$$

The alloy has 1 part aluminum.

$$7 \times 1 = 7 \text{ lb aluminum}$$

Answer: **(B)** 7.0

12. The cost (c) is proportional to the number of square feet.

$$\frac{\$.31}{c} = \frac{1}{180}$$

$$c = \frac{\$.31 \times 180}{1}$$

$$= \$55.80$$

Answer: **(C)** $55.80

13. The amount earned is proportional to the number of days worked. If a is the unknown amount:

$$\frac{\$352}{a} = \frac{16}{117}$$

$$a = \frac{\$352 \times 117}{16}$$

$$a = \$2574$$

Answer: **(B)** $2575

14. If n is the unknown length:

$$\frac{\frac{1}{8}}{3\frac{3}{4}} = \frac{12}{n}$$

$$n = \frac{14 \times 3\frac{3}{4}}{\frac{1}{8}}$$

$$= \frac{\overset{3}{\not{12}} \times \frac{15}{\not{4}_1}}{\frac{1}{8}}$$

$$= \frac{45}{\frac{1}{8}}$$

$$= 45 \div \frac{1}{8}$$

$$= 45 \times \frac{8}{1}$$

$$= 360$$

Answer: **(D)** 360

15. The ratio of investment is:

9,000:7,000:6,000 or 9:7:6

9 + 7 + 6 = 22

$825 ÷ 22 = $37.50 each share of profit

7 × $37.50 = $262.50 B's share of profit

$262.50	
− 230.00	
$ 32.50	amount B has left

Answer: **(B)** $32.50

WORK AND TANK PROBLEMS

Work Problems

1. a. In work problems, there are three items involved: the number of people working, the time, and the amount of work done.

   b. The number of people working is directly proportional to the amount of work done; that is, the more people on the job, the more the work that will be done, and vice versa.

   c. The number of people working is inversely proportional to the time; that is, the more people on the job, the less time it will take to finish it, and vice versa.

   d. The time expended on a job is directly proportional to the amount of work done; that is, the more time expended on a job, the more work that is done, and vice versa.

Work at Equal Rates

2. a. When given the time required by a number of people working at equal rates to complete a job, multiply the number of people by their time to find the time required by one person to do the complete job.

   Example: If it takes 4 people working at equal rates 30 days to finish a job, then one person will take 30 × 4 or 120 days.

   b. When given the time required by one person to complete a job, to find the time required by a number of people working at equal rates to complete the same job, divide the time by the number of people.

   Example: If 1 person can do a job in 20 days, it will take 4 people working at equal rates 20 ÷ 4 or 5 days to finish the job.

3. To solve problems involving people who work at equal rates:

   a. Multiply the number of people by their time to find the time required by 1 person.

   b. Divide this time by the number of people required.

   Illustration: Four workers can do a job in 48 days. How long will it take 3 workers to finish the same job?

   SOLUTION: One worker can do the job in 48 × 4 or 192 days.
   3 workers can do the job in 192 ÷ 3 = 64 days.

   Answer: It would take 3 workers 64 days.

4. In some work problems, the rates, though unequal, can be equalized by comparison. To solve such problems:

   a. Determine from the facts given how many equal rates there are.

   b. Multiply the number of equal rates by the time given.

   c. Divide this by the number of equal rates.

   Illustration: Three workers can do a job in 12 days. Two of the workers work twice as fast as the third. How long would it take one of the faster workers to do the job himself?

   SOLUTION: There are two fast workers and one slow worker. Therefore, there are actually five slow workers working at equal rates.

   1 slow worker will take 12 × 5 or 60 days.
   1 fast worker = 2 slow workers; therefore, he will take 60 ÷ 2 or 30 days to complete the job.

   Answer: It will take 1 fast worker 30 days to complete the job.

5. Unit time is expressed in terms of 1 minute, 1 hour, 1 day, etc.

6. The rate at which a person works is the amount of work he can do in **unit time.**

7. If given the time it will take one person to do a job, then the reciprocal of the time is the part done in unit time.

   Example: If a worker can do a job in 6 days, then he can do $\frac{1}{6}$ of the work in 1 day.

8. The reciprocal of the work done in unit time is the time it will take to do the complete job.

   Example: If a worker can do $\frac{3}{7}$ of the work in 1 day, then he can do the whole job in $\frac{7}{3}$ or $2\frac{1}{3}$ days.

9. If given the various times at which each of a number of people can complete a job, to find the time it will take to do the job if all work together:

   a. Invert the time of each to find how much each can do in unit time.

   b. Add these reciprocals to find what part all working together can do in unit time.

   c. Invert this sum to find the time it will take all of them together to do the whole job.

   Illustration: If it takes A 3 days to dig a certain ditch, whereas B can dig it in 6 days, and C in 12, how long would it take all three to do the job?

   SOLUTION: A can do it in 3 days; therefore, he can do $\frac{1}{3}$ in one day. B can do it in 6 days; therefore, he can do $\frac{1}{6}$ in one day. C can do it in 12 days; therefore, he can do $\frac{1}{12}$ in one day.

   $$\frac{1}{3} + \frac{1}{6} + \frac{1}{12} = \frac{7}{12}$$

   A, B, and C can do $\frac{7}{12}$ of the work in one day; therefore, it will take them $\frac{12}{7}$ or $1\frac{5}{7}$ days to complete the job.

   Answer: A, B, and C, working together, can complete the job in $1\frac{5}{7}$ days.

10. If given the total time it requires a number of people working together to complete a job, and the times of all but one are known, to find the missing time:

   a. Invert the given times to find how much each can do in unit time.

   b. Add the reciprocals to find how much is done in unit time by those whose rates are known.

   c. Subtract this sum from the reciprocal of the total time to find the missing rate.

   d. Invert this rate to find the unknown time.

   Illustration: A, B, and C can do a job in 2 days. B can do it in 5 days, and C can do it in 4 days. How long would it take A to do it himself?

   SOLUTION: B can do it in 5 days; therefore, he can do $\frac{1}{5}$ in one day. C can do it in 4 days; therefore, he can do $\frac{1}{4}$ in one day. The part that can be done by B and C together in 1 day is:

   $$\frac{1}{5} + \frac{1}{4} = \frac{9}{20}$$

   The total time is 2 days; therefore, all can do $\frac{1}{2}$ in one day.

   $$\frac{1}{2} - \frac{9}{20} = \frac{1}{20}$$

   A can do $\frac{1}{20}$ in 1 day; therefore, he can do the whole job in 20 days.

   Answer: It would take A 20 days to complete the job himself.

11. In some work problems, certain values are given for the three factors—number of workers, the amount of work done, and the time. It is then usually required to find the changes that occur when one or two of the factors are given different values.

   One of the best methods of solving such problems is by directly making the necessary cancellations, divisions and multiplications.

   In this problem it is easily seen that more workers will be required since more houses are to be built in a shorter time.

   Illustration: If 60 workers can build 4 houses in 12 months, how many workers would be required to build 6 houses in 4 months?

   SOLUTION: To build 6 houses instead of 4 in the same amount of time, we would need $\frac{6}{4}$ of the number of workers.

   $$\frac{6}{4} \times 60 = 90$$

   Since we now have 4 months where previously we needed 12, we must triple the number of workers.

$$90 \times 3 = 270$$

Answer: 270 workers will be needed to build 6 houses in 4 months.

12. In general, a work problem in which the workers work at different rates can be fitted into the following formula for combining their work:

$$\frac{\text{work done by worker A}}{\text{time taken by worker A}} + \frac{\text{work done by worker B}}{\text{time taken by worker B}} = \frac{\text{Total work done}}{\text{Total time taken}}$$

The problem will, directly or indirectly, give you five of the above six items. Plug in the known quantities and calculate the unknown one.

Note: Be sure your units of work and time are consistent throughout the formula.

Illustration: A can do the job in 4 hours. B can do it in 5. How long do they take together?

SOLUTION: $\frac{1\text{ job}}{4\text{ hrs.}} + \frac{1\text{ job}}{5\text{ hrs.}} = \frac{1\text{ job}}{x\text{ hrs.}}$

$$\frac{1}{4} + \frac{1}{5} = \frac{1}{x}$$
$$\frac{5}{20} + \frac{4}{20} = \frac{1}{x}$$
$$\frac{9}{20} = \frac{1}{x}$$
$$\frac{20}{9} = \frac{x}{1}$$
$$2\tfrac{2}{9} = x$$

Answer: A and B together take $2\frac{2}{9}$ hours to do the job.

Tank Problems

13. The solution of tank problems is similar to that of work problems. Completely filling (or emptying) a tank may be thought of as completing a job.

14. a. If given the time it takes a pipe to fill or empty a tank, the reciprocal of the time will represent that part of the tank that is filled or emptied in unit time.

Example: If it takes a pipe 4 minutes to fill a tank, then $\frac{1}{4}$ of the tank is filled in one minute.

b. The amount that a pipe can fill or empty in unit time is its **rate.**

15. If given the part of a tank that a pipe or a combination of pipes can fill or empty in unit time, invert the part to find the total time required to fill or empty the whole tank.

Example: If a pipe can fill $\frac{2}{5}$ of a tank in 1 minute, then it will take $\frac{5}{2}$ or $2\frac{1}{2}$ minutes to fill the entire tank.

16. To solve tank problems in which only one action (filling or emptying) is going on:

a. Invert the time of each pipe to find how much each can do in unit time.

b. Add the reciprocals to find how much all can do in unit time.

c. Invert this sum to find the total time.

Illustration: Pipe A can fill a tank in 3 minutes whereas B can fill it in 4 minutes. How long would it take both pipes, working together, to fill it?

SOLUTION: Pipe A can fill it in 3 minutes; therefore, it can fill $\frac{1}{3}$ of the tank in one minute. Pipe B can fill it in 4 minutes; therefore, it can fill $\frac{1}{4}$ of the tank on one minute.

$$\frac{1}{3} + \frac{1}{4} = \frac{7}{12}$$

Pipe A and Pipe B can fill $\frac{7}{12}$ of the tank in one minute; therefore, they can fill the tank in $\frac{12}{7}$ or $1\frac{5}{7}$ minutes.

Answer: Pipes A and B, working together, can fill the tank in $1\frac{5}{7}$ minutes.

17. In problems in which both filling and emptying actions are occurring:

a. Determine which process has the faster rate.

b. The difference between the filling rate and the emptying rate is the part of the tank that is actually being filled or emptied in unit time. The fraction representing the slower action is subtracted from the fraction representing the faster process.

c. The reciprocal of this difference is the time it will take to fill or empty the tank.

Illustration: A certain tank can be filled by Pipe A in 12 minutes. Pipe B can empty the tank in 18 minutes. If both pipes are open, how long will it take to fill or empty the tank?

SOLUTION: Pipe A fills $\frac{1}{12}$ of the tank in 1 minute.
Pipe B empties $\frac{1}{18}$ of the tank in 1 minute.

$$\frac{1}{12} = \frac{3}{36}$$
$$\frac{1}{18} = \frac{2}{36}$$

Since $\frac{1}{12}$ is greater than $\frac{1}{18}$, the tank will ultimately be filled. In 1 minute, $\frac{3}{36} - \frac{2}{36} = \frac{1}{36}$ of the tank is actually filled. Therefore, the tank will be completely filled in 36 minutes.

Answer: It will take 36 minutes to fill the tank if both pipes are open.

Work and Tank Practice Problems

1. If 314 clerks filed 6594 papers in 10 minutes, what is the number filed per minute by the average clerk?
(A) .2
(B) 1.05
(C) 2.1
(D) 2.5
(E) 21

2. Four men working together can dig a ditch in 42 days. They begin, but one man works only half-days. How long will it take to complete the job?
(A) 38 days
(B) 42 days
(C) 43 days
(D) 44 days
(E) 48 days

3. A clerk is requested to file 800 cards. If he can file cards at the rate of 80 cards an hour, the number of cards remaining to be filed after 7 hours of work is
(A) 140
(B) 240
(C) 260
(D) 560
(E) 800

4. If it takes 4 days for 3 machines to do a certain job, it will take two machines
(A) 6 days
(B) $5\frac{1}{2}$ days
(C) 5 days
(D) $4\frac{1}{2}$ days
(E) 2 days

5. A stenographer has been assigned to place entries on 500 forms. She places entries on 25 forms by the end of half an hour, when she is joined by another stenographer. The second stenographer places entries at the rate of 45 an hour. Assuming that both stenographers continue to work at their respective rates of speed, the total number of hours required to carry out the entire assignment is
(A) 5
(B) $5\frac{1}{2}$
(C) $6\frac{1}{2}$
(D) 7
(E) $7\frac{1}{14}$

6. If in 5 days a clerk can copy 125 pages, 36 lines each, 11 words to the line, how many pages of 30 lines each and 12 words to the line can he copy in 6 days?
(A) 145
(B) 155
(C) 160
(D) 165
(E) 175

7. A and B do a job together in two hours. Working alone A does the job in 5 hours. How long will it take B to do the job alone?
(A) 2 hrs
(B) $2\frac{1}{3}$ hrs
(C) $2\frac{1}{2}$ hrs
(D) 3 hrs
(E) $3\frac{1}{3}$ hrs

8. A stenographer transcribes her notes at the rate of one line typed in ten seconds. At this

rate, how long (in minutes and seconds) will it take her to transcribe notes, which will require seven pages of typing, 25 lines to the page?
(A) 29 min 10 sec
(B) 20 min 30 sec
(C) 17 min 50 sec
(D) 15 min
(E) 9 min 30 sec

9. A group of five clerks have been assigned to insert 24,000 letters into envelopes. The clerks perform this work at the following rates of speed: Clerk A, 1100 letters an hour; Clerk B, 1450 letters an hour; Clerk C, 1200 letters an hour; Clerk D, 1300 letters an hour; Clerk E, 1250 letters an hour. At the end of two hours of work, Clerks C and D are assigned to another task. From the time that Clerks C and D were taken off the assignment, the number of hours required for the remaining clerks to complete this assignment is
(A) less than 2 hr
(B) more than 2 hr, but less than 4 hr
(C) more than 4 hr, but less than 6 hr
(D) more than 6 hr
(E) none of the above

10. If a certain job can be performed by 18 workers in 26 days, the number of workers needed to perform the job in 12 days is
(A) 24
(B) 30
(C) 39
(D) 45
(E) 52

11. A steam shovel excavates 2 cubic yards every 40 seconds. At this rate, the amount excavated in 45 minutes is
(A) 90 cu yd
(B) 135 cu yd
(C) 270 cu yd
(D) 1200 cu yd
(E) 3600 cu yd

12. If a plant making bricks turns out 1250 bricks in 5 days, the number of bricks that can be made in 20 days is
(A) 5000
(B) 6250
(C) 12,500
(D) 25,000
(E) none of the above

13. A tank is $\frac{3}{4}$ full. Fillpipe A can fill the tank in 12 minutes. Drainpipe B can empty it in 8 minutes. If both pipes are open, how long will it take to empty the tank?
(A) 8 min
(B) 12 min
(C) 16 min
(D) 18 min
(E) 24 min

14. A tank that holds 400 gallons of water can be filled by one pipe in 15 minutes and emptied by another in 40 minutes. How long would it take to fill the tank if both pipes are functioning?
(A) 20 min
(B) 21 min
(C) 23 min
(D) 24 min
(E) 28 min

15. An oil burner in a housing development burns 76 gallons of fuel oil per hour. At 9 A.M. on a very cold day the superintendent asks the housing manager to put in an emergency order for more fuel oil. At that time, he reports that he has on hand 266 gallons. At noon, he again comes to the manager, notifying him that no oil has been delivered. The maximum amount of time that he can continue to furnish heat without receiving more oil is
(A) $\frac{1}{2}$ hr
(B) 1 hr
(C) $1\frac{1}{2}$ hr
(D) 2 hr
(E) none of the above

Work and Tank Problems—Correct Answers

1. **(C)**	6. **(D)**	11. **(B)**
2. **(E)**	7. **(E)**	12. **(A)**
3. **(B)**	8. **(A)**	13. **(D)**
4. **(A)**	9. **(B)**	14. **(D)**
5. **(B)**	10. **(C)**	15. **(A)**

Work and Tank Problem Solutions

1. 6594 papers ÷ 314 clerks = 21 papers per clerk in 10 minutes
   21 papers ÷ 10 minutes = 2.1 papers per minute filed by average clerk

   Answer: **(C)** 2.1

2. It would take 1 man 42 × 4 = 168 days to complete the job, working alone.
   If $3\frac{1}{2}$ men are working (one man works halfdays, the other 3 work full days), the job would take 168 ÷ $3\frac{1}{2}$ = 48 days.

   Answer: **(E)** 48 days

3. In 7 hours the clerk files 7 × 80 = 560 cards. Since 800 cards must be filed, there are 800 − 560 = 240 remaining.

   Answer: **(B)** 240

4. It would take 1 machine 3 × 4 = 12 days to do the job. Two machines could do the job in 12 ÷ 2 = 6 days.

   Answer: **(A)** 6 days

5. At the end of the first half-hour, there are 500 − 25 = 475 forms remaining. If the first stenographer completed 25 forms in half an hour, her rate is 25 × 2 = 50 forms per hour. The combined rate of the two stenographers is 50 + 45 = 95 forms per hour. The remaining forms can be completed in 475 ÷ 95 = 5 hours. Adding the first half-hour, the entire job requires $5\frac{1}{2}$.

   Answer: **(B)** $5\frac{1}{2}$

6. 36 lines × 11 words = 396 words on each page
   125 pages × 396 words = 49,500 words in 5 days
   49,500 ÷ 5 = 9900 words in 1 day
   12 words × 30 lines = 360 words on each page
   9900 ÷ 360 = $27\frac{1}{2}$ pages in 1 day
   $27\frac{1}{2}$ × 6 = 165 pages in 6 days.

   Answer: **(D)** 165

7. If A can do the job alone in 5 hours, A can do $\frac{1}{5}$ of the job in 1 hour. Working together, A and B can do the job in 2 hours, therefore in 1 hour they do $\frac{1}{2}$ the job.
   In 1 hour, B alone does

   $$\frac{1}{2} - \frac{1}{5} = \frac{5}{10} - \frac{2}{10} = \frac{3}{10} \text{ of the job.}$$

   It would take B $\frac{10}{3}$ hours = $3\frac{1}{3}$ hours to do the whole job alone.

   Answer: **(E)** $3\frac{1}{3}$ hr

8. She must type 7 × 25 = 175 lines. At the rate of 1 line per 10 seconds, it will take 175 × 10 = 1750 seconds.

   1750 seconds ÷ 60 = $29\frac{1}{6}$ minutes
   = 29 min 10 sec

   Answer: **(A)** 29 min 10 sec

9.

Clerk	*Number of letters per hr*
A	1100
B	1450
C	1200
D	1300
E	+ 1250
Total =	6300

   All 5 clerks working together process a total of 6300 letters per hour. After 2 hours, they have processed 6300 × 2 = 12,600. Of the original 24,000 letters there are

   24,000
   − 12,600
   11,400 letters remaining

   Clerks A, B, and E working together process a total of 3800 letters per hour. It will take them

   11,400 ÷ 3800 = 3 hours

   to process the remaining letters.

   Answer: **(B)** more than 2 hr, but less than 4 hr

10. The job could be performed by 1 worker in 18 × 26 days = 468 days. To perform the job in 12 days would require 468 × 12 = 39 workers.

   Answer: **(C)** 39

11. The shovel excavates 1 cubic yard in 20 seconds.

There are $45 \times 60 = 2700$ seconds in 45 minutes.

In 2700 seconds the shovel can excavate $2700 \div 20 = 135$ cubic yards.

Answer: **(B)** 135 cu yd

12. In 20 days the plant can produce four times as many bricks as in 5 days.

$$1250 \times 4 = 5000 \text{ bricks}$$

Answer: **(A)** 5000

13. Pipe A can fill the tank in 12 min or fill $\frac{1}{12}$ of the tank in 1 min. Pipe B can empty the tank in 8 min or empty $\frac{1}{8}$ of the tank in 1 min. In 1 minute, $\frac{1}{8} - \frac{1}{12}$ of the tank is emptied (since $\frac{1}{8}$ is greater than $\frac{1}{12}$).

$$\frac{1}{8} = \frac{3}{24}$$
$$-\frac{1}{12} = -\frac{2}{24}$$

$\frac{1}{24}$ of the tank is emptied per minute

It would take 24 min to empty whole tank, but it is only $\frac{3}{4}$ full:

$$\frac{3}{\cancel{4}_1} \times \overset{6}{\cancel{24}} = 18 \text{ minutes}$$

Answer: **(D)** 18 min

14. The first pipe can fill $\frac{1}{15}$ of the tank in 1 minute. The second pipe can empty $\frac{1}{40}$ of the tank in 1 minute. With both pipes open, $\frac{1}{15} - \frac{1}{40}$ of the tank will be filled per minute.

$$\frac{1}{15} = \frac{8}{120}$$
$$-\frac{1}{40} = -\frac{3}{120}$$
$$\frac{5}{120} = \frac{1}{24}$$

In 1 minute, $\frac{1}{24}$ of the tank is filled; therefore, it will take 24 mintues for the entire tank to be filled.

Answer: **(D)** 24 min

15. If 76 gallons are used per hour, it will take $266 \div 76 = 3\frac{1}{2}$ hours to use 266 gallons.

From 9 a.m. to noon is 3 hours; therefore, there is only fuel for $\frac{1}{2}$ hour more.

Answer: **(A)** $\frac{1}{2}$ hr

DISTANCE PROBLEMS

1. In distance problems, there are usually three quantities involved: the distance (in miles), the rate (in miles per hour—mph), and the time (in hours).

   a. To find the distance, multiply the rate by the time: distance = rate × time.

   Example: A man traveling 40 miles an hour for 3 hours travels 40×3 or 120 miles.

   b. The rate is the distance traveled in unit time. To find the rate, divide the distance by the time.

   Example: If a car travels 100 miles in 4 hours, the rate is $100 \div 4$ or 25 miles an hour.

   c. To find the time, divide the distance by the rate.

   Example: If a car travels 150 miles at the rate of 30 miles an hour, the time is $150 \div 30$ or 5 hours.

Combined Rates

2. a. When two people or objects are traveling towards each other, the rate at which they are approaching each other is the sum of their respective rates.

   b. When two people or objects are traveling in directly opposite directions, the rate at which they are separating is the sum of their respective rates.

3. To solve problems involving combined rates:

   a. Determine which of the three factors is to be found.

   b. Combine the rates and find the unknown factor.

   Illustration: A and B are walking towards each other over a road 120 miles long. A walks at a rate of 6 miles an hour, and B walks at a rate of 4 miles an hour. How soon will they meet?

SOLUTION: The factor to be found is the time.

Time = distance ÷ rate
Distance = 120 miles
Rate = 6 + 4 = 10 miles an hour
Time = 120 ÷ 10 = 12 hours

Answer: They will meet in 12 hours.

Illustration: Joe and Sam are walking in opposite directions. Joe walks at the rate of 5 miles an hour, and Sam walks at the rate of 7 miles an hour. How far apart will they be at the end of 3 hours?

SOLUTION: The factor to be found is distance.

Distance = time × rate
Time = 3 hours
Rate = 5 + 7 = 12 miles an hour
Distance = 12 × 3 = 36 miles

Answer: They will be 36 miles apart at the end of 3 hours.

4. To find the time it takes a faster person or object to catch up with a slower person or object:

   a. Determine how far ahead the slower person or object is.

   b. Subtract the slower rate from the faster rate to find the distance the faster person or object gains per unit time.

   c. Divide the slower person or object's lead by the difference in rates (b).

Illustration: Two automobiles are traveling along the same road. The first one, which travels at the rate of 30 miles an hour, starts out 6 hours ahead of the second one, which travels at the rate of 50 miles an hour. How long will it take the second one to catch up with the first one?

SOLUTION: The first automobile starts out 6 hours ahead of the second. Its rate is 30 miles an hour. Therefore, it has traveled 6 × 30 or 180 miles by the time the second one starts. The second automobile travels at the rate of 50 miles an hour. Therefore, its gain is 50 − 30 or 20 miles an hour. The second auto has to cover 180 miles. Therefore, it will take 180 ÷ 20 or 9 hours to catch up with the first automobile.

Answer: It will take the faster auto 9 hours to catch up with the slower one.

Average of Two Rates

5. In some problems, two or more rates must be averaged. When the times are the same for two or more different rates, add the rates and divide by the number of rates.

Example: If a man travels for 2 hours at 30 miles an hour, at 40 miles an hour for the next 2 hours, and at 50 miles an hour for the next 2 hours, then his average rate for the 6 hours is (30 + 40 + 50) ÷ 3 = 40 miles an hour.

6. When the times are not the same, but the distances are the same:

   a. Assume the distance to be a convenient length.

   b. Find the time at the first rate.

   c. Find the time at the second rate.

   d. Find the time at the third rate, if any.

   e. Add up all the distances and divide by the total time to find the average rate.

Illustration: A boy travels a certain distance at the rate of 20 miles an hour and returns at the rate of 30 miles an hour. What is his average rate for both trips?

SOLUTION: The distance is the same for both trips. Assume that it is 60 miles. The time for the first trip is 60 ÷ 20 = 3 hours. The time for the second trip is 60 ÷ 30 = 2 hours. The total distance is 120 miles. The total time is 5 hours. Average rate is 120 ÷ 5 = 24 miles an hour.

Answer: The average rate is 24 miles an hour.

7. When the times are not the same and the distances are not the same:

   a. Find the time for the first distance.

b. Find the time for the second distance.

c. Find the time for the third distance, if any.

d. Add up all the distances and divide by the total time to find the average rate.

Illustration: A man travels 100 miles at 20 miles an hour, 60 miles at 30 miles an hour, and 80 miles at 10 miles an hour. What is his average rate for the three trips?

SOLUTION: The time for the first trip is 100 ÷ 20 = 5 hours. The time for the second trip is 60 ÷ 30 = 2 hours. The time for the third trip is 80 ÷ 10 = 8 hours. The total distance is 240 miles. The total time is 15 hours. Average rate is 240 ÷ 15 = 16.

Answer: The average rate for the three trips is 16 miles an hour.

Gasoline Problems

8. Problems involving miles per gallon (mpg) of gasoline are solved in the same way as those involving miles per hour. The word gallon simply replaces the word hour.

9. Miles per gallon = distance in miles ÷ no. of gallons

   Example: If a car can travel 100 miles using 4 gallons of gasoline, then its gasoline consumption is 100 ÷ 4, or 25 mpg.

Practice Problems Involving Distance

1. A ten-car train took 6 minutes to travel between two stations that are 3 miles apart. The average speed of the train was
   (A) 20 mph
   (B) 25 mph
   (C) 30 mph
   (D) 35 mph
   (E) 40 mph

2. A police car is ordered to report to the scene of a crime 5 miles away. If the car travels at an average rate of 40 miles per hour, the time it will take to reach its destination is
   (A) 3 min
   (B) 7.5 min
   (C) 10 min
   (D) 13.5 min
   (E) 15 min

3. If the average speed of a train between two stations is 30 miles per hour and the two stations are $\frac{1}{2}$ mile apart, the time it takes the train to travel from one station to the other is
   (A) 1 min
   (B) 2 min
   (C) 3 min
   (D) 4 min
   (E) 5 min

4. A car completes a 10-mile trip in 20 minutes. If it does one-half the distance at a speed of 20 miles an hour, its speed for the remainder of the distance must be
   (A) 25 mph
   (B) $33\frac{1}{3}$ mph
   (C) 40 mph
   (D) 50 mph
   (E) 60 mph

5. An express train leaves one station at 9:02 and arrives at the next station at 9:08. If the distance traveled is $2\frac{1}{2}$ miles, the average speed of the train (mph) is
   (A) 15 mph
   (B) 20 mph
   (C) 25 mph
   (D) 40 mph
   (E) 50 mph

6. A motorist averaged 60 miles per hour in going a distance of 240 miles. He made the return trip over the same distance in 6 hours. What was his average speed for the entire trip?
   (A) 40 mph
   (B) 48 mph
   (C) 50 mph
   (D) 60 mph
   (E) 64 mph

7. A city has been testing various types of gasoline for economy and efficiency. It has been found that a police radio patrol car can travel 18 miles on a gallon of Brand A

gasoline, costing $1.30 a gallon, and 15 miles on a gallon of Brand B gasoline, costing $1.25 a gallon. For a distance of 900 miles, Brand B will cost
(A) $10 more than Brand A
(B) $10 less than Brand A
(C) $100 more than Brand A
(D) $100 less than Brand A
(E) the same as Brand A

8. A suspect arrested in New Jersey is being turned over by New Jersey authorities to two New York City police officers for a crime committed in New York City. The New York officers receive their prisoner at a point 16 miles from their precinct station house, and travel directly toward their destination at an average speed of 40 miles an hour except for a delay of 10 minutes at one point because of a traffic tie-up. The time it should take the officers to reach their destination is, most nearly,
(A) 16 min
(B) 18 min
(C) 24 min
(D) 30 min
(E) 34 min

9. The Mayflower sailed from Plymouth, England, to Plymouth Rock, a distance of approximately 2800 miles, in 63 days. The average speed was closest to which one of the following?
(A) $\frac{1}{2}$ mph
(B) 1 mph
(C) 2 mph
(D) 3 mph
(E) 4 mph

10. If a vehicle is to complete a 20-mile trip at an average rate of 30 miles per hour, it must complete the trip in
(A) 20 min
(B) 30 min
(C) 40 min
(D) 50 min
(E) 60 min

11. A car began a trip with 12 gallons of gasoline in the tank and ended with $7\frac{1}{2}$ gallons. The car traveled 17.3 miles for each gallon of gasoline. During the trip gasoline was bought for $10.00, at a cost of $1.25 per gallon. The total number of miles traveled during this trip was most nearly
(A) 79
(B) 196
(C) 216
(D) 229
(E) 236

12. A man travels a total of 4.2 miles each day to and from work. The traveling consumes 72 minutes each day. How many hours would he save in 129 working days if he moved to another residence so that he would travel only 1.7 miles each day, assuming he travels at the same rate?
(A) 98.3
(B) 97.0
(C) 95.6
(D) 93.2
(E) 90.3

13. A man can travel a certain distance at the rate of 25 miles an hour by automobile. He walks back the same distance on foot at the rate of 10 miles an hour. What is his average rate for both trips?
(A) $14\frac{2}{7}$ mph
(B) $15\frac{1}{3}$ mph
(C) $17\frac{1}{2}$ mph
(D) $28\frac{4}{7}$ mph
(E) 35 mph

14. Two trains running on the same track travel at the rates of 25 and 30 miles an hour. If the first train starts out an hour earlier, how long will it take the second train to catch up with it?
(A) 2 hr
(B) 3 hr
(C) 4 hr
(D) 5 hr
(E) 6 hr

15. Two ships are 1550 miles apart sailing towards each other. One sails at the rate of 85 miles per day and the other at the rate of 65 miles per day. How far apart will they be at the end of 9 days?
(A) 180 mi
(B) 200 mi
(C) 220 mi

(D) 785 mi
(E) 1350 mi

Distance Problems—Correct Answers

1.	**(C)**	6.	**(B)**	11.	**(C)**
2.	**(B)**	7.	**(A)**	12.	**(E)**
3.	**(A)**	8.	**(E)**	13.	**(A)**
4.	**(E)**	9.	**(C)**	14.	**(D)**
5.	**(C)**	10.	**(C)**	15.	**(B)**

Problem Solutions—Distance

1. 6 min = $\frac{6}{60}$ hr = .1 hr
Speed (rate) = distance ÷ time
Speed = 3 ÷ .1 = 30 mph

Answer: **(C)** 30 mph

2. Time = distance ÷ rate
Time = 5 ÷ 40 = .125 hr
.125 hr = .125 × 60 min
= 7.5 min

Answer: **(B)** 7.5 min

3. Time = distance ÷ rate
Time = $\frac{1}{2}$ mi ÷ 30 mph
= $\frac{1}{60}$ hr
$\frac{1}{60}$ hr = 1 min

Answer: **(A)** 1 min

4. First part of trip = $\frac{1}{2}$ of 10 miles = 5miles
Time for first part = 5 ÷ 20
= $\frac{1}{4}$ hour
= 15 minutes

Second part of trip was 5 miles, completed in 20 − 15 minutes, or 5 minutes.

5 minutes = $\frac{1}{12}$ hour
Rate = 5 mi ÷ $\frac{1}{12}$ hr
= 60 mph

Answer: **(E)** 60 mph

5. Time is 6 minutes, or .1 hour

Speed = distance ÷ time
= $2\frac{1}{2}$ ÷ .1
= 2.5 ÷ .1
= 25 mph

Answer: **(C)** 25 mph

6. Time for first 240 mi = 240 ÷ 60
= 4 hours
Time for return trip = 6 hours
Total time for round trip = 10 hours
Total distance for round trip = 480 mi
Average rate = 480 mi ÷ 10 hr
= 48 mph

Answer: **(B)** 48 mph

7. Brand A requires 900 ÷ 18 = 50 gal
50 gal × \$1.30 per gal = \$65

Brand B requires 900 ÷ 15 = 60 gal
60 gal × \$1.25 per gal = \$75

Answer: **(A)** Brand B will cost \$10 more than Brand A

8. Time = distance ÷ rate
Time = 16 mi ÷ 40 mph
= $\frac{4}{10}$ hrs
= $\frac{4}{10}$ × 60 minutes
= 24 minutes
24 + 10 = 34 minutes

Answer: **(E)** 34 min

9. 63 days = 63 × 24 hours
= 1512 hours
Speed = 2800 mi ÷ 1512 hr
= 1.85 mph

Answer: **(C)** 2 mph

10. Time = 20 mi ÷ 30 mph
= $\frac{2}{3}$ hr
$\frac{2}{3}$ hr = $\frac{2}{3}$ × 60 min = 40 min

Answer: **(C)** 40 min

11. The car used

12 − $7\frac{1}{2}$ = $4\frac{1}{2}$ gal, plus
\$10.00 ÷ \$1.25 = 8 gal,

for a total of $12\frac{1}{2}$ gal, or 12.5 gal.

12.5 gal × 17.3 mpg = 216.25 mi

Answer: **(C)** 216

12. 72 min = $\frac{72}{60}$ hr = 1.2 hr
Rate = 4.2 mi ÷ 1.2 hr = 3.5 mph

At this rate it would take 1.7 mi ÷ 3.5 mph

= .5 hours (approx.) to travel 1.7 miles. The daily savings in time is 1.2 hr − .5 hr = .7 hr.

.7 hr × 129 days = 90.3 hr

Answer: **(E)** 90.3

13. Assume a convenient distance, say, 50 mi.

Time by automobile = 50 mi ÷ 25 mph
= 2 hr
Time walking = 50 mi ÷ 10 mph
= 5 hr
Total time = 7 hours
Total distance = 100 mi
Average rate = 100 mi ÷ 7 hr
= $14\frac{2}{7}$ mph

Answer: **(A)** $14\frac{2}{7}$ mph

14. 30 mi − 25 mi = 5 mi gain per 1 hr

During first hour, the first train travels 25 miles.

25 mi ÷ 5 mph = 5 hr

Answer: **(D)** 5 hr

15. 85 mi × 9 da = 765 mi
65 mi × 9 da = 585 mi
1350

1550 mi − 1350 = 200 miles apart at end of 9 days.

Answer: **(B)** 200 mi

INTEREST

1. **Interest (I)** is the price paid for the use of money. There are three items considered in interest:

   a. The **principal (p),** which is the amount of money-bearing interest.

   b. The **interest rate (r),** expressed in percent on an annual basis.

   c. The **time (t)** during which the principal is used, expressed in terms of a year.

2. The basic formulas used in interest problems are:

   a. $I = prt$

   b. $p = \frac{I}{rt}$

   c. $r = \frac{I}{pt}$

   d. $t = \frac{I}{pr}$

3. a. For most interest problems, the year is considered to have 360 days. Months are considered to have 30 days, unless a particular month is specified.

   b. To use the interest formulas, time must be expressed as part of a year.

   Examples: 5 months = $\frac{5}{12}$ year
   36 days = $\frac{36}{360}$ year, or $\frac{1}{10}$ year
   1 year 3 months = $\frac{15}{12}$ year

   c. In reference to time, the prefix semi- means every half. The prefix bi- means every two.

   Examples: Semiannually means every half-year (every 6 months).
   Biannually means every 2 years.
   Semimonthly means every half-month (every 15 days, unless the month is specified).
   Biweekly means every 2 weeks (every 14 days).

4. There are two types of interest problems:

   a. **Simple interest,** in which the interest is calculated only once over a given period of time.

   b. **Compound interest,** in which interest is recalculated at given time periods based on previously earned interest.

Simple Interest

5. To find the interest when the principal, rate, and time are given:

   a. Change the rate of interest to a fraction.

   b. Express the time as a fractional part of a year.

   c. Multiply all three items.

Illustration: Find the interest on \$400 at $11\frac{1}{4}\%$ for 3 months and 16 days.

SOLUTION: $11\frac{1}{4}\% = \frac{45}{4}\% = \frac{45}{400}$

3 months and 16 days = 106 days (30 days per month)

106 days = $\frac{106}{360}$ of a year = $\frac{53}{180}$ year (360 days per year)

$$400 \times \frac{45}{400} \times \frac{53}{180} = \frac{53}{4}$$

$$= 13.25$$

Answer: Interest = \$13.25

6. To find the principal if the interest, interest rate, and time are given:

   a. Change the interest rate to a fraction.

   b. Express the time as a fractional part of a year.

   c. Multiply the rate by the time.

   d. Divide the interest by this product.

Illustration: What amount of money invested at 6% would receive interest of \$18 over $1\frac{1}{2}$ years?

SOLUTION:

$$6\% = \frac{6}{100}$$

$$1\tfrac{1}{2} \text{ years} = \tfrac{3}{2} \text{ years}$$

$$\frac{6}{100} \times \frac{3}{2} = \frac{9}{100}$$

$$\$18 \div \frac{9}{100} = \$18 \times \frac{100}{9}$$

$$= \$200$$

Answer: Principal = \$200

7. To find the rate if the principal, time, and interest are given:

   a. Change the time to a fractional part of a year.

   b. Multiply the principal by the time.

   c. Divide the interest by this product.

   d. Convert to a percent.

Illustration: At what interest rate should \$300 be invested for 40 days to accrue \$2 in interest?

SOLUTION: 40 days = $\frac{40}{360}$ of a year

$$300 \times \frac{40}{360} = \frac{100}{3}$$

$$\$2 \div \frac{100}{3} = 2 \times \frac{3}{100}$$

$$= \frac{3}{50}$$

$$\frac{3}{50} = 6\%$$

Answer: Interest rate = 6%

8. To find the time (in years) if the principal, interest, and interest rate are given:

   a. Change the interest rate to a fraction (or decimal).

   b. Multiply the principal by the rate.

   c. Divide the interest by this product.

Illustration: Find the length of time for which \$240 must be invested at 5% to accrue \$16 in interest.

SOLUTION:

$$5\% = .05$$

$$240 \times .05 = 12$$

$$16 \div 12 = 1\tfrac{1}{3}$$

Answer: Time = $1\frac{1}{3}$ years

Compound Interest

9. Interest may be computed on a compound basis; that is, the interest at the end of a certain period (half-year, full year, or whatever time stipulated) is added to the principal for the next period. The interest is then computed on the new increased principal, and for the next period the interest is again computed on the new increased principal. Since the principal constantly increases, compound interest yields more than simple interest.

10. To find the compound interest when given the principal, the rate, and time period:

    a. Calculate the interest as for simple interest problems, using the period of compounding for the time.

    b. Add the interest to the principal.

    c. Calculate the interest on the new principal over the period of compounding.

d. Add this interest to form a new principal.

e. Continue the same procedure until all periods required have been accounted for.

f. Subtract the original principal from the final principal to find the compound interest.

Illustration: Find the amount that $200 will become if compounded semiannually at 8% for $1\frac{1}{2}$ years.

SOLUTION: Since it is to be compounded semiannually for $1\frac{1}{2}$ years, the interest will have to be computed 3 times:

Interest for the first period:	$.08 \times \frac{1}{2} \times \$200 = \$8$
First new principal:	$\$200 + \$8 = \$208$
Interest for the second period:	$.08 \times \frac{1}{2} \times \$208 = \$8.32$
Second new principal:	$\$208 + \$8.32 = \$216.32$
Interest for the third period:	$.08 \times \frac{1}{2} \times \$216.32 = \$8.6528$
Final principal:	$\$216.32 + \$8.6528 = \$224.9728$

Answer: $224.97 to the nearest cent

Bank Discounts

11. A **promissory note** is a commitment to pay a certain amount of money on a given date, called the **date of maturity.**

12. When a promissory note is cashed by a bank in advance of its date of maturity, the bank deducts a discount from the principal and pays the rest to the depositor.

13. To find the bank discount:

a. Find the time between the date the note is deposited and its date of maturity, and express this time as a fractional part of a year.

b. Change the rate to a fraction.

c. Multiply the principal by the time and the rate to find the bank discount.

d. If required, subtract the bank discount from the original principal to find the amount the bank will pay the depositor.

Illustration: A $400 note drawn up on August 12, 1980, for 90 days is deposited at the bank on September 17, 1980. The bank charges a $6\frac{1}{2}\%$ discount on notes. How much will the depositor receive?

SOLUTION: From August 12, 1980, to September 17, 1980, is 36 days. This means that the note has 54 days to run.

$$54 \text{ days} = \frac{54}{360} \text{ of a year}$$
$$6\tfrac{1}{2}\% = \tfrac{13}{2}\% = \tfrac{13}{200}$$
$$\$400 \times \frac{13}{200} \times \frac{54}{360} = \frac{39}{10}$$
$$= \$3.90$$
$$\$400 - \$3.90 = \$396.10$$

Answer: The depositor will receive $396.10.

Practice Problems Involving Interest

1. What is the simple interest on $460 for 2 years at $8\frac{1}{2}\%$? ________

2. For borrowing $300 for one month, a man was charged $6.00. The rate of interest was ________.

3. At a simple interest rate of 5% a year, the principal that will give $12.50 interest in 6 months is ________.

4. Find the interest on $480 on $10\frac{1}{2}\%$ for 2 months and 15 days. ________

5. The interest on $300 at 6% for 10 days is ________.

6. The scholarship board of a certain college loaned a student $200 at an annual rate of 6% from September 30 until December 15. To repay the loan and accumulated interest the student must give the college ________.

7. If $300 is invested at simple interest so as to yield a return of $18 in 9 months, the amount of money that must be invested at the same rate of interest so as to yield a return of $120 in 6 months is ________.

8. When the principal is $600, the difference in one year between simple interest at 12% per annum and interest compounded semiannually at 12% per annum is ________.

9. What is the compound interest on $600, compounded quarterly, at 6% for 9 months? ________.

10. A 90-day note for $1200 is signed on May 12. Seventy-five days later the note is deposited at a bank that charges 8% discount on notes. The bank discount is ________.

Problem Solutions—Interest

1. Principal = $460
Rate = $8\frac{1}{2}\%$ = .085
Time = 2 years
Interest = $460 × .085 × 2
= $78.20

Answer: $78.20

2. Principal = $300
Interest = $6
Time = $\frac{1}{12}$ year
$300 × $\frac{1}{12}$ = $25
$6 ÷ $25 = .24 = 24%

Answer: 24%

3. Rate = 5% = .05
Interest = $12.50
Time = $\frac{1}{2}$ year
.05 × $\frac{1}{2}$ = .025
$12.50 ÷ .025 = $500.00

Answer: $500

4. Time:

2 months 15 days = 75 days or $\frac{75}{360}$ of a year

Rate:

$$10\frac{1}{2}\% = \frac{21}{2}\% = \frac{21}{200}$$

Interest:

$$480 \times \frac{21}{200} \times \frac{75}{360} = \frac{21}{2} = 10.50$$

Answer: $10.50

5. Principal = $300
Rate = .06 = $\frac{6}{100}$
Time = $\frac{10}{360} = \frac{1}{36}$

$$\text{Interest} = \$\overset{3}{\cancel{300}} \times \frac{\overset{1}{\cancel{6}}}{\underset{1}{\cancel{100}}} \times \frac{1}{\underset{6}{\cancel{36}}}$$

$$= \frac{3}{6} = \$.50$$

Answer: $.50

6. Principal = $200
Rate = .06 = $\frac{6}{100}$

Time from Sept. 30 until Dec. 15 is 76 days. (31 days in October, 30 days in November, 15 days in December)

76 days = $\frac{76}{360}$ year

$$\text{Interest} = \$\overset{2}{\cancel{200}} \times \frac{\overset{1}{\cancel{6}}}{\underset{1}{\cancel{100}}} \times \frac{76}{\underset{60}{\cancel{360}}}$$

$$= \$\frac{152}{60} = \$2.53$$

$200 + $2.53 = $202.53

Answer: closest to $202.50

7. Principal = $300
Interest = $18
Time = $\frac{9}{12}$ years = $\frac{3}{4}$ year
$300 × $\frac{3}{4}$ = $225
$18 ÷ $225 = .08

Rate is 8%.

To yield $120 at 8% in 6 months,

Interest = $120
Rate = .08
Time = $\frac{1}{2}$ year
.08 × $\frac{1}{2}$ = .04
$120 ÷ .04 = $3000 must be invested

Answer: $3000

8. Simple interest:
Principal = $600
Rate = .12
Time = 1
Interest = $600 × .12 × 1
= $72.00

Compound interest:
Principal = $600
Period of compounding = $\frac{1}{2}$ year
Rate = .12

For the first period,
Interest = $600 × .12 × $\frac{1}{2}$
= $36
New principal = $600 + $36
= $636

For the second period,
Interest = $636 × .12 × $\frac{1}{2}$
= $38.16
New principal = $636 + $38.16
= $674.16

Total interest = \$74.16
Difference = \$74.16 − 72.00
= \$2.16

Answer: \$2.16

9. Principal = \$600
Rate = 6% = $\frac{6}{100}$
Time (period of compounding) = $\frac{3}{12}$ year = $\frac{1}{4}$ year

In 9 months, the interest will be computed 3 times.

For first quarter,
Interest = \$600 × $\frac{6}{100}$ × $\frac{1}{4}$
= \$9

New principal at end of first quarter:
\$600 + \$9 = \$609

For second quarter,
Interest = \$609 × $\frac{6}{100}$ × $\frac{1}{4}$
= \$$\frac{3654}{400}$ = \$9.135, or \$9.14

New principal at end of second quarter:
\$609 + \$9.14 = \$618.14

For third quarter,
Interest = \$618.14 × $\frac{6}{100}$ × $\frac{1}{4}$
= \$$\frac{3708.84}{400}$
= \$9.27

Total interest for the 3 quarters:
\$9 + \$9.14 + \$9.27 = \$27.41

Answer: \$27.41

10. Principal = \$1200
Time = 90 days − 75 days
= 15 days
15 days = $\frac{15}{360}$ year
Rate = 8% = $\frac{8}{100}$
Bank discount = \$$\overset{12}{\cancel{1200}}$ × $\frac{\overset{1}{\cancel{8}}}{\underset{1}{\cancel{100}}}$ × $\frac{15}{\underset{45}{\cancel{360}}}$
= \$$\frac{180}{45}$ = \$4

Answer: \$4.00

TAXATION

1. a. Taxation problems are a form of percentage or fraction problems since the tax rate is often expressed as a percentage (parts per hundred) or as another sort of fraction such as tax per \$100,000, etc.

b. Taxation problems may also be a form of table or chart problem when the rate of taxation is not a single rate, but changes in accordance with something else, such as total to be taxed, time, etc.

2. In taxation, there are usually three items involved: the amount taxable, henceforth called the base, the tax rate, and the tax itself.

3. To find the tax when given the base and the tax rate in percent:

a. Change the tax rate to a decimal.

b. Multiply the base by the tax rate.

Illustration: How much would be realized on \$4000 if taxed 15%?

SOLUTION: 15% = .15
\$4000 × .15 = \$600

Answer: Tax = \$600

4. To find the tax rate in percent form when given the base and the tax:

a. Divide the tax by the base.

b. Convert to a percent.

Illustration: Find the tax rate at which \$5600 would yield \$784.

SOLUTION: \$784 ÷ \$5600 = .14
.14 = 14%

Answer: Tax rate = 14%

5. To find the base when given the tax rate and the tax:

a. Change the tax rate to a decimal.

b. Divide the tax by the tax rate.

Illustration: What amount of money taxed 3% would yield \$75?

SOLUTION: 3% = .03
\$75 ÷ .03 = \$2500

Answer: Base = \$2500

6. When the tax rate is fixed and expressed in terms of money, take into consideration the denomination upon which it is based; that is, whether it is based on every $100, or $1000, etc.

7. To find the tax when given the base and the tax rate in terms of money:

   a. Divide the base by the denomination upon which the tax is based.

   b. Multiply this quotient by the tax rate.

   Illustration: If the tax rate is $3.60 per $1000, find the tax on $470,500.

   SOLUTION:

   $$\$470{,}500 \div \$1000 = 470.5$$
   $$470.5 \times \$3.60 = \$1{,}693.80$$

   Answer: $1,693.80

8. To find the tax rate based on a certain denomination when given the base and the tax derived:

   a. Divide the base by the denomination indicated.

   b. Divide the tax by this quotient.

   Illustration: Find the tax rate per $100 that would be required to raise $350,000 on $2,000,000 of taxable property.

   SOLUTION: $\$2{,}000{,}000 \div \$100 = 20{,}000$
   $\$350{,}000 \div 20{,}000 = \$17.50$

   Answer: Tax rate = $17.50 per $100

9. Since a surtax is an additional tax besides the regular tax, to find the total tax:

   a. Change the regular tax rate to a decimal.

   b. Multiply the base by the regular tax rate.

   c. Change the surtax rate to a decimal.

   d. Multiply the base by the surtax rate.

   e. Add both taxes.

   Illustration: Assuming that the tax rate is $2\frac{1}{3}\%$ on liquors costing up to $3.00, and 3% on those costing from $3.00 to $6.00, and $3\frac{1}{2}\%$ on those from $6.00 to $10.00, what would be the tax on a bottle costing $8.00 if there is a surtax of 5% on all liquors above $5.00?

   SOLUTION: An $8.00 bottle falls within the category of $6.00 to $10.00. The tax rate on such a bottle is

   $$3\tfrac{1}{2}\% = .035$$
   $$\$8.00 \times .035 = \$.28$$
   $$\text{surtax rate} = 5\% = .05$$
   $$\$8.00 \times .05 = \$.40$$
   $$\$.28 + \$.40 = \$.68$$

   Answer: Total tax = $.68

Practice Problems Involving Taxation

1. Mr. Jones' income for a year is $15,000. He pays $2250 for income taxes. The percent of his income that he pays for income taxes is __________.

2. If the tax rate is $3\frac{1}{2}\%$ and the amount to be raised is $64.40, what is the base? ________

3. What is the tax rate per $1000 if a base of $338,500 would yield $616.07? ________

4. A man buys an electric light bulb for 54¢, which includes a 20% tax. What is the cost of the bulb without tax? ________

5. What tax rate on a base of $3650 would raise $164.25? ________

6. A piece of property is assessed at $22,850 and the tax rate is $4.80 per thousand. What is the amount of tax that must be paid on the property? ________

7. $30,000 worth of land is assessed at 120% of its value. If the tax rate is $5.12 per $1000 assessed valuation, the amount of tax to be paid is ________.

8. Of the following real estate tax rates, which is the largest?
   $31.25 per $1000
   $3.45 per $100
   32¢ per $10
   3¢ per $1

9. A certain community needs \$185,090.62 to cover its expenses. If its tax rate is \$1.43 per \$100 of assessed valuation, what must be the assessed value of its property? ________

10. A man's taxable income is \$14,280. The state tax instructions tell him to pay 2% on the first \$3000 of his taxable income, 3% on each of the second and third \$3000, and 4% on the remainder. What is the total amount of income tax that he must pay? ________

Problem Solutions—Taxation

1. Tax = \$2250
Base = \$15,000
Tax rate = Tax ÷ Base
Tax rate = \$2250 ÷ \$15,000 = .15
Tax rate = .15 = 15%

Answer: 15

2. Tax rate = $3\frac{1}{2}$% = .035
Tax = \$64.40
Base = Tax ÷ Tax rate
Base = \$64.40 ÷ .035
= \$1840

Answer: \$1840

3. Base = \$338,500
Tax = \$616.07
Denomination = \$1000
\$338,500 ÷ \$1000 = 338.50
\$616.07 ÷ 338.50 = \$1.82 per \$1000

Answer: \$1.82

4. 54¢ is 120% of the base (cost without tax)

Base = 54 ÷ 120%
= 54 ÷ 1.20
= 45

Answer: 45¢

5. Base = \$3650
Tax = \$164.25
Tax rate = Tax ÷ Base
= \$164.25 ÷ \$3650
= .045
= $4\frac{1}{2}$%

Answer: $4\frac{1}{2}$%

6. Base = \$22,850
Denomination = \$1000
Tax rate = \$4.80 per thousand

$$\frac{\$22{,}850}{\$1000} = 22.85$$

22.85 × \$4.80 = \$109.68

Answer: \$109.68

7. Base = Assessed val. = 120% of \$30,000
= 1.20 × \$30,000
= \$36,000

Denomination = \$1000
Tax rate = \$5.12 per thousand

$$\frac{\$36{,}000}{\$1000} = 36$$

36 × \$5.12 = \$184.32

Answer: \$184.32

8. Express each tax rate as a decimal:

$$\$31.25 \text{ per } \$1000 = \frac{31.25}{1000} = .03125$$

$$\$3.45 \text{ per } \$100 = \frac{3.45}{100} = .0345$$

$$32¢ \text{ per } \$10 = \frac{.32}{10} = .0320$$

$$3¢ \text{ per } \$1 = \frac{.03}{1} = .0300$$

The largest decimal is .0345

Answer: \$3.45 per \$100

9. Tax rate = \$1.43 per \$100

$$= \frac{1.43}{100} = .0143$$

= 1.43%
Tax = \$185,090.62
Base = Tax ÷ rate
= 185,090.62 ÷ .0143
= \$12,943,400

Answer: \$12,943,400

10.

First \$3000:	.02 × \$3000 = \$ 60.00
Second \$3000:	.03 × \$3000 = \$ 90.00
Third \$3000:	.03 × \$3000 = \$ 90.00
Remainder (\$14,280 − \$9000):	.04 × \$5280 = \$211.20
	Total tax = \$451.20

Answer: \$451.20

PROFIT AND LOSS

1. The following terms may be encountered in profit and loss problems:

   a. The **cost price** of an article is the price paid by a person who wishes to sell it again.

   b. There may be an **allowance** or **trade discount** reducing the cost price.

   c. The **list price** or **marked price** is the price at which the article is listed or marked to be sold.

   d. There may be a **discount** or **series of discounts** (usually expressed as a percent) on the list price.

   e. The **selling price** or **sales price** is the price at which the article is finally sold.

   f. If the selling price is greater than the cost price, there has been a **profit.**

   g. If the selling price is lower than the cost price, there has been a **loss.**

   h. If the article is sold at the same price as the cost, there has been no loss or profit.

   i. A percentage profit or loss may be based either on the cost price or on the selling price.

   j. Profit or loss may be stated in terms of dollars and cents, or in terms of percent.

   k. **Overhead** expenses include such items as rent, salaries, etc., and may be added to cost price or to the profit to increase the selling price.

2. The basic formulas used in profit and loss problems are:

   Selling price = cost price + profit
   Selling price = cost price − loss

   Example: If the cost of an article is \$2.50, and the profit is \$1.50, then the selling price is \$2.50 + \$1.50 = \$4.00.

   Example: If the cost of an article is \$3.00, and the loss is \$1.20, then the selling price is \$3.00 − \$1.20 = \$1.80.

3. a. To find the profit in terms of money, subtract the cost price from the selling price, or selling price − cost price = profit.

   Example: If an article costing \$3.00 is sold for \$5.00, the profit is \$5.00 − \$3.00 = \$2.00.

   b. To find the loss in terms of money, subtract the selling price from the cost price, or: cost price − selling price = loss.

   Example: If an article costing \$2.00 is sold for \$1.50, the loss is \$2.00 − \$1.50 = \$.50.

4. To find the selling price if the profit or loss is expressed in percent based on cost price:

   a. Multiply the cost price by the percent of profit or loss to find the profit or loss in terms of money.

   b. Add this product to the cost price if a profit is involved, or subtract for a loss.

   Illustration: Find the selling price of an article costing \$3.00 that was sold at a profit of 15% of the cost price.

   SOLUTION: 15% of \$3.00 = .15 × \$3.00
   = \$.45 profit
   \$3.00 + \$.45 = \$3.45

   Answer: Selling price = \$3.45

   Illustration: If an article costing \$2.00 is sold at a loss of 5% of the cost price, find the selling price.

   SOLUTION: 5% of \$2.00 = .05 × \$2.00
   = \$.10 loss
   \$2.00 − \$.10 = \$1.90

   Answer: Selling price = \$1.90

5. To find the cost price when given the selling price and the percent of profit or loss based on the selling price:

   a. Multiply the selling price by the percent of profit or loss to find the profit or loss in terms of money.

   b. Subtract this product from the selling price if a profit, or add the product to the selling price if a loss.

Illustration: If an article sells for $12.00 and there has been a profit of 10% of the selling price, what is the cost price?

SOLUTION:

10% of $12,00 = .10 × $12.00
= $1.20 profit
$12.00 − $1.20 = $10.80

Answer: Cost price = $10.80

Illustration: What is the cost price of an article selling for $2.00 on which there has been a loss of 6% of the selling price?

SOLUTION: 6% of $2.00 = .06 × $2.00
= $.12 loss
$2.00 + $.12 = $2.12

Answer: Cost price = $2.12

6. To find the percent of profit or percent of loss based on cost price:

 a. Find the profit or loss in terms of money.

 b. Divide the profit or loss by the cost price.

 c. Convert to a percent.

Illustration: Find the percent of profit based on cost price of an article costing $2.50 and selling for $3.00.

SOLUTION: $3.00 − $2.50 = $.50 profit

$$2.50\;\overline{)\,.50} = 250\;\overline{)\,50.00}^{\;.20}$$
.20 = 20%

Answer: Profit = 20%

Illustration: Find the percent of loss based on cost price of an article costing $5.00 and selling for $4.80.

SOLUTION: $5.00 − $4.80 = $.20 loss

$$5.00\;\overline{)\,.20} = 500\;\overline{)\,20.00}^{\;.04}$$
.04 = 4%

Answer: Loss = 4%

7. To find the percent of profit or percent of loss on selling price:

 a. Find the profit or loss in terms of money.

 b. Divide the profit or loss by the selling price.

 c. Convert to a percent.

Illustration: Find the percent of profit based on the selling price of an article costing $2.50 and selling for $3.00.

SOLUTION:

$3.00 − $2.50 = $.50 profit

$$3.00\;\overline{)\,.50} = 300\;\overline{)\,50.00} = .16\tfrac{2}{3}$$
$$= 16\tfrac{2}{3}\%$$

Answer: Profit = $16\frac{2}{3}\%$

Illustration: Find the percent of loss based on the selling price of an article costing $5.00 and selling for $4.80.

SOLUTION:

$5.00 − $4.80 = $.20 loss

$$4.80\;\overline{)\,.20} = 480\;\overline{)\,20.00} = .04\tfrac{1}{6}$$
$$= 4\tfrac{1}{6}\%$$

Answer: Loss = $4\frac{1}{6}\%$

8. To find the cost price when given the selling price and the percent of profit based on the cost price:

 a. Establish a relation between the selling price and the cost price.

 b. Solve to find the cost price.

Illustration: An article is sold for $2.50, which is a 25% profit of the cost price. What is the cost price?

SOLUTION: Since the selling price represents the whole cost price plus 25% of the cost price,

2.50 = 125% of the cost price
2.50 = 1.25 of the cost price
Cost price = 2.50 ÷ 1.25
= 2.00

Answer: Cost price = $2.00

9. To find the selling price when given the profit based on the selling price:

 a. Establish a relation between the selling price and the cost price.

 b. Solve to find the selling price.

Illustration: A merchant buys an article for $27.00 and sells it at a profit of 10% of the selling price. What is the selling price?

SOLUTION: \$27.00 + profit = selling price

Since the profit is 10% of the selling price, the cost price must be 90% of the selling price.

27.00 = 90% of the selling price
= .90 of the selling price
Selling price = 27.00 ÷ .90
= 30.00

Answer: Selling price = \$30.00

Trade Discounts

10. A **trade discount,** usually expressed in percent, indicates the part that is to be deducted from the list price.

11. To find the selling price when given the list price and the trade discount:

a. Multiply the list price by the percent of discount to find the discount in terms of money.

b. Subtract the discount from the list price.

Illustration: The list price of an article is \$20.00. There is a discount of 5%. What is the selling price?

SOLUTION: \$20.00 × 5%
= 20.00 × .05 = \$1.00 discount
\$20.00 − \$1.00=\$19.00

Answer: Selling price = \$19.00

An alternate method of solving the above problem is to consider the list price to be 100%. Then, if the discount is 5%, the selling price is 100% − 5% = 95% of the list price. The selling price is

95% of \$20.00 = .95 × \$20.00
= \$19.00

Series of Discounts

12. There may be more than one discount to be deducted from the list price. These are called a **discount series.**

13. To find the selling price when given the list price and a discount series:

a. Multiply the list price by the first percent of discount.

b. Subtract this product from the list price.

c. Multiply the difference by the second discount.

d. Subtract this product from the difference.

e. Continue the same procedure if there are more discounts.

Illustration: Find the selling price of an article listed at \$10.00 on which there are discounts of 20% and 10%.

SOLUTION:

\$10.00 × 20% = 10.00 × .20 = \$2.00
\$10.00 − \$2.00 = \$8.00
\$8.00 × 10% = 8.00 × .10 = \$.80
\$8.00 − \$.80 = \$7.20

Answer: Selling price = \$7.20

14. Instead of deducting each discount individually, it is often more practical to find the single equivalent discount first and then deduct. It does not matter in which order the discounts are taken.

15. The single equivalent discount may be found by assuming a list price of 100%. Leave all discounts in percent form.

a. Subtract the first discount from 100%, giving the net cost factor (NCF) had there been only one discount.

b. Multiply the NCF by the second discount. Subtract the product from the NCF, giving a second NCF that reflects both discounts.

c. If there is a third discount, multiply the second NCF by it and subtract the product from the second NCF, giving a third NCF that reflects all three discounts.

d. If there are more discounts, repeat the process.

e. Subtract the final NCF from 100% to find the single equivalent discount.

Illustration: Find the single equivalent discount of 20%, 25%, and 10%.

SOLUTION:

	100%	
	− 20%	first discount
	80%	first NCF
−25% of 80% =	20%	
	60%	second NCF
−10% of 60% =	6%	
	54%	third NCF

100% − 54% = 46% single equivalent discount

Answer: 46%

Illustration: An article lists at $750.00. With discounts of 20%, 25%, and 10%, what is the selling price of this article?

SOLUTION: As shown above, the single equivalent discount of 20%, 25%, and 10% is 46%.

46% of $750 = .46 × $750
= $345
$750 − $345 = $405

Answer: Selling price = $405

Practice Problems Involving Profit and Loss

1. Dresses sold at $65.00 each. The dresses cost $50.00 each. The percentage of increase of the selling price over the cost is ______.

2. A dealer bought a ladder for $27.00. What must it be sold for if he wishes to make a profit of 40% on the selling price? ______

3. A typewriter was listed at $120.00 and was bought for $96.00. What was the rate of discount? ______

4. A dealer sells an article at a loss of 50% of the cost. Based on the selling price, the loss is ______.

5. What would be the marked price of an article if the cost was $12.60 and the gain was 10% of the cost price? ______

6. A stationer buys note pads at $.75 per dozen and sells them at 25 cents apiece. The profit based on the cost is ______.

7. An article costing $18 is to be sold at a profit of 10% of the selling price. The selling price will be ______.

8. A calculating maching company offered to sell a city agency 4 calculating machines at a discount of 15% from the list price, and to allow the agency $85 for each of two old machines being traded in. The list price of the new machines is $625 per machine. If the city agency accepts this offer, the amount of money it will have to provide for the purchase of these 4 machines is ______.

9. Pencils are purchased at $9 per gross and sold at 6 for 75 cents. The rate of profit based on the selling price is ______.

10. The single equivalent discount of 20% and 10% is ______.

Problem Solutions—Profit and Loss

1. Selling price − cost = $65 − $50
= $15

$$\frac{\$15}{\$50} = .30 = 30\%$$

Answer: 30%

2. Cost price = 60% of selling price, since the profit is 40% of the selling price, and the whole selling price is 100%.

$27 = 60% of selling price
Selling price = $27 ÷ 60%
= $27 ÷ .6
= $45

Answer: $45

3. The discount was $120 − $96 = $24

$$\text{Rate of discount} = \frac{\$24}{\$120} = .20 = 20\%$$

Answer: 20%

4. Loss = cost − selling price.

Considering the cost to be 100% of itself, if the loss is 50% of the cost, the selling price is also 50% of the cost. (50% = 100% − 50%)

Since the loss and the selling price are therefore the same, the loss is 100% of the selling price.

Answer: 100%

5. Gain (profit) = 10% of \$12.60
= .10 × \$12.60
= \$1.26

Selling price = cost + profit
= \$12.60 + \$1.26
= \$13.86

Answer: \$13.86

6. Each dozen note pads cost \$.75 and are sold for

12 × \$.25 = \$3.00

The profit is \$3.00 − \$.75 = \$2.25

$$\text{Profit based on cost} = \frac{\$2.25}{\$.75} = 3 = 300\%$$

Answer: 300%

7. If profit = 10% of selling price,
then cost = 90% of selling price
\$18 = 90% of selling price
Selling price = \$18 ÷ 90%
= \$18 ÷ .90
= \$20

Answer: \$20.00

8. Discount for each new machine:

15% of \$625 = .15 × \$625
= \$93.75

Each new machine will cost

\$625 − \$93.75 = \$531.25

Four new machines will cost

\$531.25 × 4 = \$2125

But there is an allowance of \$85 each for 2 old machines:

\$85 × 2 = 170

Final cost to city:

\$2125 − \$170 = \$1955

Answer: \$1955

9. 1 gross = 144 units

Selling price for 6 pencils = \$.75

$$\text{Selling price for 1 pencil} = \frac{\$.75}{6}$$

$$\text{Selling price for 1 gross of pencils} = \frac{\$.75}{\cancel{6}_{1}} \times \cancel{144}^{24} = \$18.00$$

Cost for 1 gross of pencils = \$9.00

Profit for 1 gross of pencils = \$18.00 − \$9.00 = \$9.00

$$\frac{\text{profit}}{\text{selling price}} = \frac{\$9.00}{\$18.00} = .5 = 50\%$$

Answer: 50%

10.

	100%
	− 20%
	80%
−10% of 80% =	− 8%
	72%

100% − 72% = 28% single equivalent discount

Answer: 28%

TABLES

1. **Tables** are used to organize information in easily understandable form. The key to understanding tables is to read the title and the margins, or stubs as they are sometimes called. These items, plus the footnotes to the table, if any, will tell you what the numbers in the table mean. The numbers themselves have no meaning without the writing. For example, consider the following arrangement of numbers:

300	500	800
400	600	1000
700	1100	1800

You may think that the bottom row and the right-hand column represent totals since things seem to add up that way. It is possible that this is correct, but unless there is written information to tell you this, you do not know it to be true.

2. You should be particularly alert to the units that are used in a table, which may be

different from the units asked for in the problem. For example, a table may give you information in tons and the problem might ask for pounds.

3. Other than the fact that the information is presented in a table, there is nothing about a table problem that is different from any of the other sorts of problems which have been discussed.

4. As in other arithmetic computational problems, it is usually a good idea to estimate the numbers that you have to use from a table rather than using them in their printed form. Generally the first and second digits are all that is needed.

GRAPHS

1. **Graphs** illustrate comparisons and trends in statistical information. The most commonly used graphs are **bar graphs, line graphs, circle graphs,** and **pictographs.** The fundamental idea about graphs is that they all use some distance or area to represent value. The distance may be length, width, etc., and the value may be dollars, percents, etc. The graphs are always labelled to show what part of the graph means what value. So read the labels, margins, and notes of each graph carefully.

Bar Graphs

2. **Bar graphs** are used to compare various quantities. Each bar may represent a single quantity or may be divided to represent several quantities.

3. Bar graphs may have horizontal or vertical bars.

Illustration (next column):

Municipal Expenditures, Per Capita

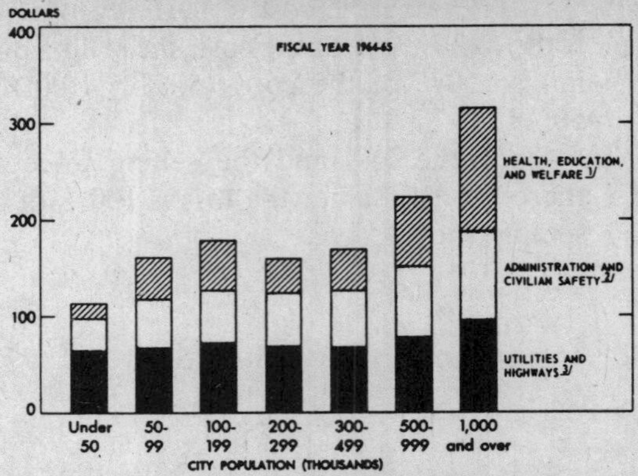

1/PUBLIC WELFARE, EDUCATION, HOSPITALS, HEALTH, LIBRARIES, AND HOUSING AND URBAN RENEWAL
2/POLICE AND FIRE PROTECTION, FINANCIAL ADMINISTRATION, GENERAL CONTROL, GENERAL PUBLIC BUILDINGS, INTEREST ON GENERAL DEBT, AND OTHER.
3/HIGHWAYS, SEWERAGE, SANITATION, PARKS AND RECREATION, AND UTILITIES.
SOURCE: DEPARTMENT OF COMMERCE.

Question 1: What was the approximate municipal expenditure per capita in cities having populations of 200,000 to 299,000?

Answer: The middle bar of the seven shown represents cities having populations from 200,000 to 299,000. This bar reaches about halfway between 100 and 200. Therefore, the per capita expenditure was approximately $150.

Question 2: Which cities spent the most per capita on health, education, and welfare?

Answer: The bar for cities having populations of 1,000,000 and over has a larger striped section than the other bars. Therefore, those cities spent the most.

Question 3: Of the three categories of expenditures, which was least dependent on city size?

Answer: The expenditures for utilities and highways, the darkest part of each bar, varied least as city size increased.

Line Graphs

4. **Line graphs** are used to show trends, often over a period of time.

5. A line graph may include more than one line, with each line representing a different item.

Illustration:

The graph below indicates, at 5 year-intervals, the number of citations issued for various offenses from the year 1960 to the year 1980.

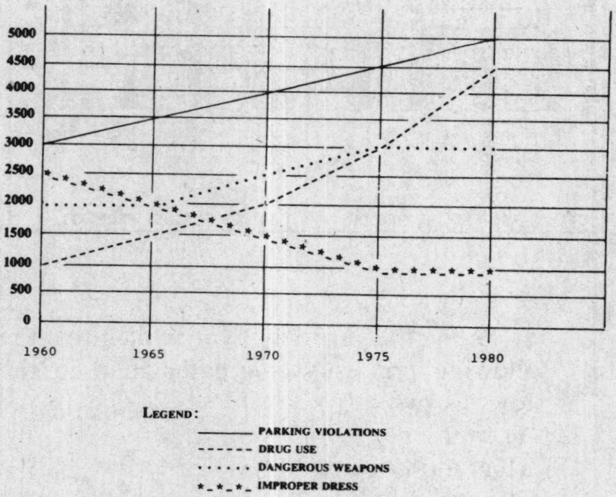

Question 4: Over the 20-year period, which offense shows an average rate of increase of more than 150 citations per year?

Answer: Drug-use citations increased from 1000 in 1960 to 4500 in 1980. The average increase over the 20-year period is $\frac{3500}{20}$ = 175.

Question 5: Over the 20-year period, which offense shows a constant rate of increase or decrease?

Answer: A straight line indicates a constant rate of increase or decrease. Of the four lines, the one representing parking violations is the only straight one.

Question 6: Which offense shows a total increase or decrease of 50% for the full 20-year period?

Answer: Dangerous weapons citations increased from 2000 in 1960 to 3000 in 1980, which is an increase of 50%.

Circle Graphs

6. **Circle graphs** are used to show the relationship of various parts of a quantity to each other and to the whole quantity.

7. Percents are often used in circle graphs. The 360 degrees of the circle represents 100%.

8. Each part of the circle graph is called a **sector.**

Illustration:

The following circle graph shows how the federal budget of $300.4 billion was spent.

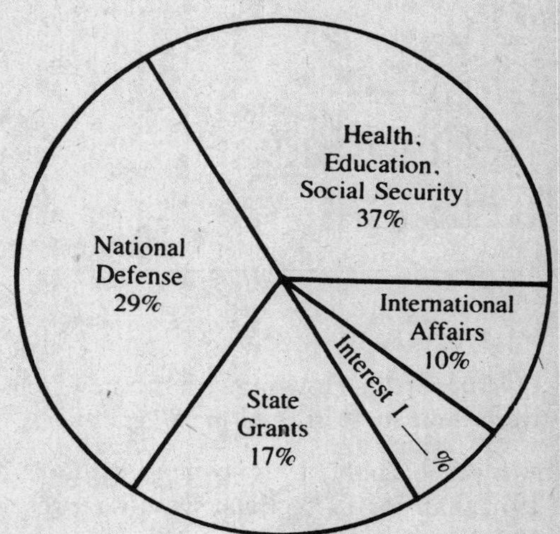

Question 7: What is the value of I?

Answer: There must be a total of 100% in a circle graph. The sum of the other sectors is:

$$17\% + 29\% + 37\% + 10\% = 93\%$$

Therefore, I = 100% − 93% = 7%.

Question 8: How much money was actually spent on national defense?

Answer: 29% × $300.4 billion
= $87.116 billion
= $87,116,000,000

Question 9: How much more money was spent on state grants than on interest?

Answer: 17% − 7% = 10%
10% × $300.4 billion
= $30.04 billion
= $30,040,000,000

Pictographs

9. **Pictographs** allow comparisons of quantities by using symbols. Each symbol represents a given number of a particular item.

Illustration:

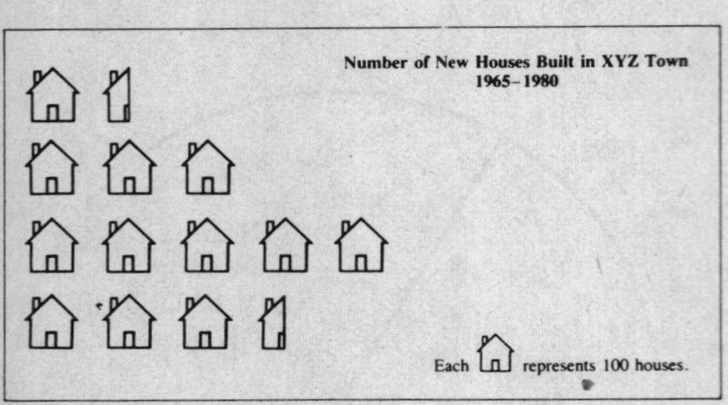

Question 10: How many more new houses were built in 1970 than in 1975?

Answer: There are two more symbols for 1970 than for 1975. Each symbol represents 100 houses. Therefore, 200 more houses were built in 1970.

Question 11: How many new houses were built in 1965?

Answer: There are $3\frac{1}{2}$ symbols shown for 1965; $3\frac{1}{2} \times 100 = 350$ houses.

Question 12: In which year were half as many houses built as in 1975?

Answer: In 1975, 3 × 100 = 300 houses were built. Half of 300, or 150, houses were built in 1980.

Practice Problems Involving Graphs

Questions 1–4 refer to the graph in the next column:

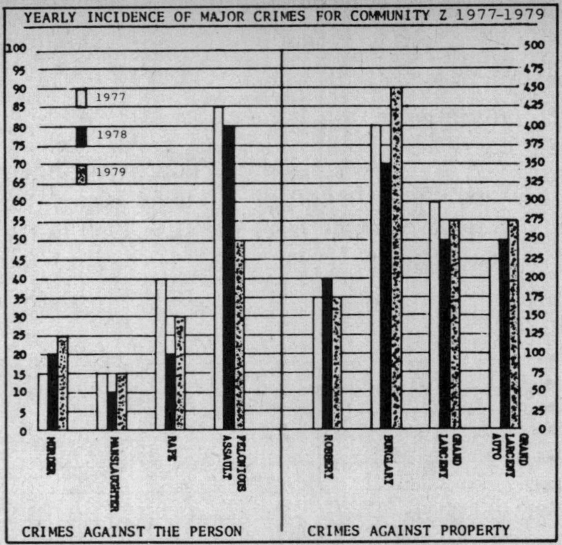

1. In 1979, the incidence of which of the following crimes was greater than in the previous two years?
(A) murder
(B) grand larceny
(C) rape
(D) robbery
(E) manslaughter

2. If the incidence of burglary in 1980 had increased over 1979 by the same number as it had increased in 1979 over 1978, then the average for this crime for the four-year period from 1977 through 1980 would be most nearly
(A) 100
(B) 400
(C) 425
(D) 440
(E) 550

3. The above graph indicates that the *percentage* increase in grand larcency auto from 1978 to 1979 was:
(A) 5%
(B) 10%
(C) 15%
(D) 20%
(E) 25%

4. Which of the following cannot be determined because there is not enough information in the above graph to do so?
   (A) For the three-year period, what percentage of all "Crimes Against the Person" involved murders committed in 1978?
   (B) For the three-year period, what percentage of all "Major Crimes" was committed in the first six months of 1978?
   (C) Which major crimes followed a pattern of continuing yearly increases for the three-year period?
   (D) For 1979, what was the ratio of robbery, burglary, and grand larceny crimes?
   (E) What was the major crime with the greatest annual incidence for the period 1977–1979?

Questions 5–7 refer to the following graph:

In the graph below, the lines labeled "A" and "B" represent the cumulative progress in the work of two file clerks, each of whom was given 500 consecutively numbered applications to file in the proper cabinets over a five-day work week.

5. The day during which the largest number of applications was filed by both clerks was
   (A) Monday
   (B) Tuesday
   (C) Wednesday
   (D) Thursday
   (E) Friday

6. At the end of the second day, the percentage of applications still to be filed was
   (A) 25%
   (B) 30%
   (C) 50%
   (D) 66%
   (E) 75%

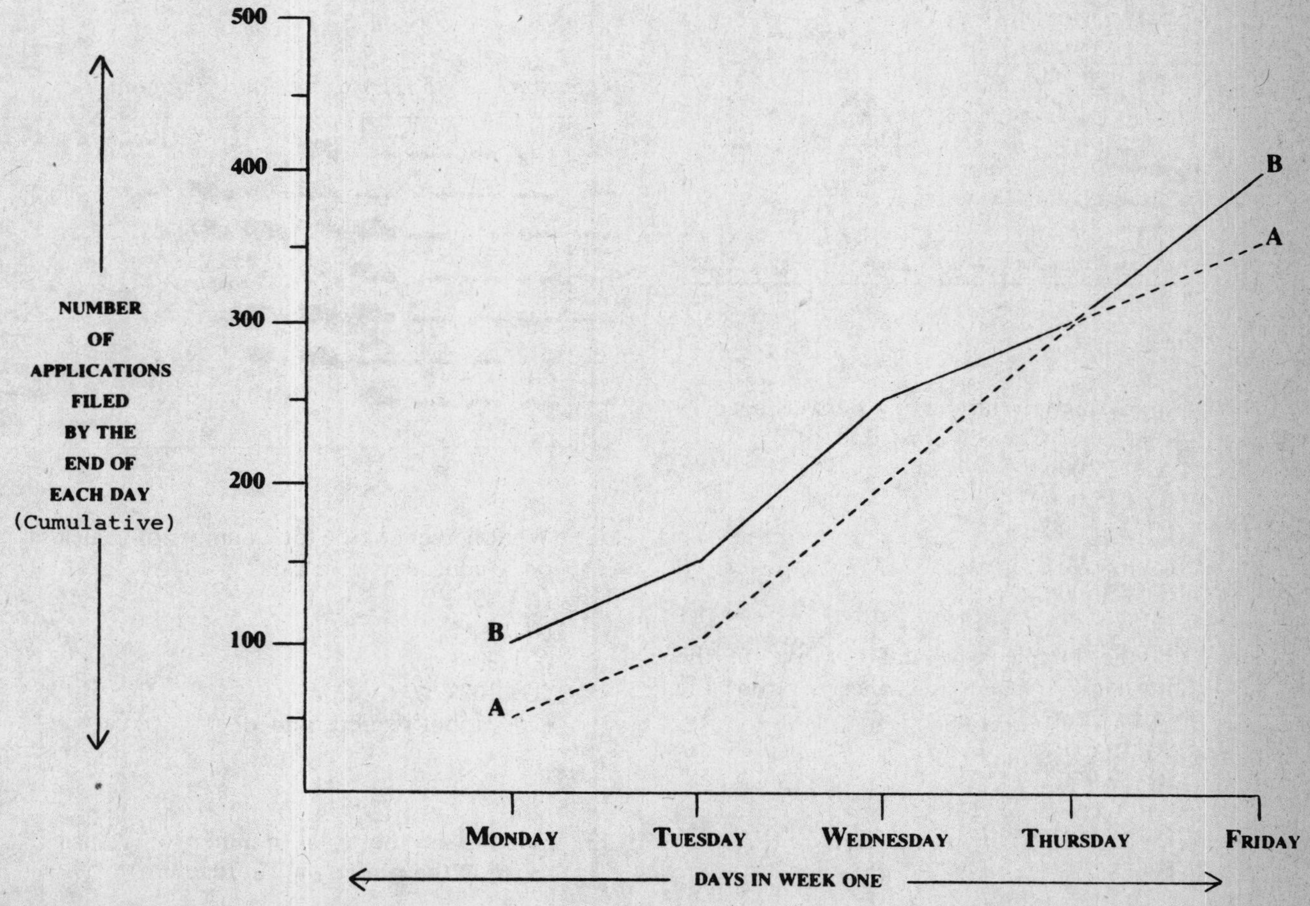

7. Assuming that the production pattern is the same the following week as the week shown in the chart, the day on which Clerk B will finish this assignment will be
   (A) Monday
   (B) Tuesday
   (C) Wednesday
   (D) Thursday
   (E) Friday

Questions 8–11 refer to the following graph:

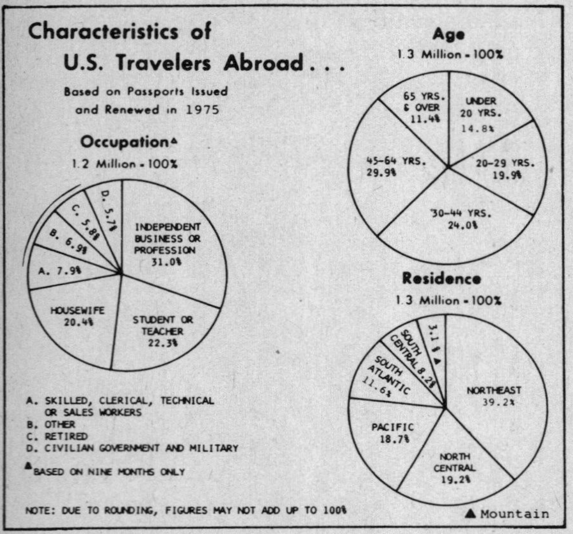

8. Approximately how many persons aged 29 or younger traveled abroad in 1975?
   (A) 175,000
   (B) 245,000
   (C) 350,000
   (D) 415,000
   (E) 450,000

9. Of the people who did *not* live in the Northeast, what percent came from the North Central states?
   (A) 19.2%
   (B) 19.9%
   (C) 26.5%
   (D) 31.6%
   (E) 38.7%

10. The fraction of travelers from the four smallest occupation groups is most nearly equal to the fraction of travelers
    (A) under age 20, and 65 and over, combined
    (B) from the North Central and Mountain states
    (C) between 45 and 64 years of age
    (D) from the Housewife and Other categories
    (E) Northeast and Pacific states

11. If the South Central, Mountain, and Pacific sections were considered as a single classification, how many degrees would its sector include?
    (A) 30°
    (B) 67°
    (C) 108°
    (D) 120°
    (E) 180°

Questions 12–15 refer to the following graph:

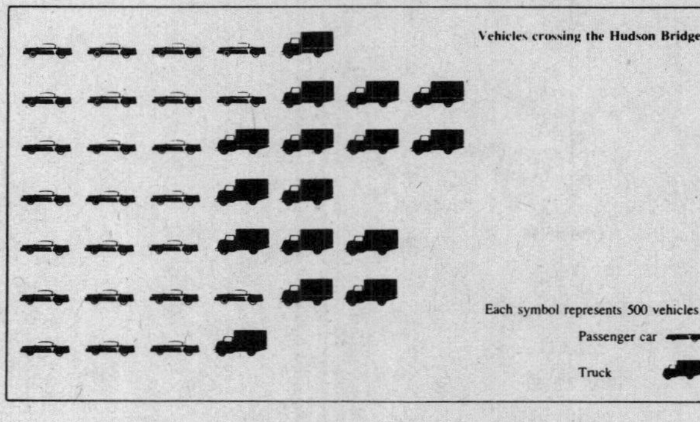

12. What percent of the total number of vehicles on Wednesday were cars?
    (A) 85%
    (B) 60%
    (C) 30%
    (D) 10%
    (E) cannot be determined

13. What was the total number of vehicles crossing the bridge on Tuesday?

(A) 7
(B) 700
(C) 1500
(D) 2000
(E) 3500

14. How many more trucks crossed on Monday than on Saturday?
(A) 200
(B) 1000
(C) 1500
(D) 2000
(E) 3500

15. If trucks paid a toll of $1.00 and cars paid a toll of $.50, how much money was collected in tolls on Friday?
(A) $400
(B) $750
(C) $2000
(D) $2500
(E) $3000

Graphs—Correct Answers

1. **(A)**	6. **(E)**	11. **(C)**
2. **(D)**	7. **(B)**	12. **(B)**
3. **(B)**	8. **(E)**	13. **(E)**
4. **(B)**	9. **(D)**	14. **(B)**
5. **(C)**	10. **(A)**	15. **(C)**

Problem Solutions—Graphs

1. The incidence of murder increased from 15 in 1977 to 20 in 1978 to 25 in 1979.

Answer: **(A)** murder

2. The incidence of burglary in 1977 was 400; in 1978 it was 350; and in 1979 it was 450. The increase from 1978 to 1979 was 100. An increase of 100 from 1979 gives 550 in 1980.
The average of 400, 350, 450, and 550 is

$$\frac{400 + 350 + 450 + 550}{4} = \frac{1750}{4}$$
$$= 437.5$$

Answer: **(D)** 440

3. The incidence of grand larceny auto went from 250 in 1978 to 275 in 1979, an increase of 25.
The percent increase is

$$\frac{25}{250} = .10 = 10\%$$

Answer: **(B)** 10%

4. This graph gives information by year, not month. It is impossible to determine from the graph the percentage of crimes committed during the first six months of any year.

Answer: **(B)**

5. For both A and B, the greatest increase in the cumulative totals occurred from the end of Tuesday until the end of Wednesday. Therefore, the largest number of applications was filed on Wednesday.

Answer: **(C)** Wednesday

6. By the end of Tuesday, A had filed 100 applications and B had filed 150, for a total of 250. This left 750 of the original 1000 applications.

$$\frac{750}{1000} = .75 = 75\%$$

Answer: **(E)** 75%

7. During Week One, Clerk B files 150 applications on Monday, 50 on Tuesday, 100 on Wednesday, 50 on Thursday, and 100 on Friday. If he follows this pattern, he will file 50 on the Monday of Week Two, for a total of 450, and the remaining 50 during Tuesday.

Answer: **(B)** Tuesday

8. 20–29 yrs.: 19.9%
Under 20 yrs.: +14.8%
34.7%

$$34.7\% \times 1.3 \text{ million} = .4511 \text{ million}$$
$$= 451{,}100$$

Answer: **(E)** 450,000

9. 100% − 39.2% = 60.8% did not live in Northeast.

19.2% lived in North Central

$$\frac{19.2}{60.8} = .316 \text{ approximately}$$

Answer: **(D)** 31.6%

10. Four smallest groups of occupation:

$$7.9 + 6.9 + 5.8 + 5.7 = 26.3$$

Age groups under 20 and over 65:

$$14.8 + 11.4 = 26.2$$

Answer: **(A)**

11.

South Central:	8.2%
Mountain:	3.1%
Pacific:	18.7%
	30.0%

$$30\% \times 360° = 108°$$

Answer: **(C)** 108°

12. There are 5 vehicle symbols, of which 3 are cars.

$$\tfrac{3}{5} = 60\%$$

Answer: **(B)** 60%

13. On Tuesday, there were 3 × 500 = 1500 cars and 4 × 500 = 2000 trucks. The total number of vehicles was 3500.

Answer: **(E)** 3500

14. The graph shows 2 more truck symbols on Monday than on Saturday. Each symbol represents 500 trucks, so there were 2 × 500 = 1000 more trucks on Monday.

Answer: **(B)** 1000

15. On Friday there were

$$4 \times 500 = 2000 \text{ cars}$$
$$2 \times 500 = 1000$$

Car tolls:	2000 × $ .50 =	$1000
Truck tolls:	1000 × $1.00 =	+ $1000
Total tolls:		$2000

Answer: **(C)** $2000

POWERS AND ROOTS

1. The numbers that are multiplied to give a product are called the **factors** of the product.

   Example: In 2 × 3 = 6, 2 and 3 are factors.

2. If the factors are the same, an **exponent** may be used to indicate the number of times the factor appears.

   Example: In $3 \times 3 = 3^2$, the number 3 appears as a factor twice, as is indicated by the exponent 2.

3. When a product is written in exponential form, the number the exponent refers to is called the **base.** The product itself is called the **power.**

   Example: In 2^5, the number 2 is the base and 5 is the exponent.
   $2^5 = 2 \times 2 \times 2 \times 2 \times 2 = 32$, so 32 is the power.

4. a. If the exponent used is 2, we say that the base has been **squared,** or raised to the second power.

   Example: 6^2 is read "six squared" or "six to the second power."

   b. If the exponent used is 3, we say that the base has been **cubed,** or raised to the third power.

   Example: 5^3 is read "five cubed" or "five to the third power."

   c. If the exponent is 4, we say that the base has been raised to the fourth power. If the exponent is 5, we say the base has been raised to the fifth power, etc.

   Example: 2^8 is read "two to the eighth power."

5. A number that is the product of a whole number squared is called a **perfect square.**

   Example: 25 is a perfect square because $25 = 5^2$.

6. a. If a number has exactly two equal factors, each factor is called the **square root** of the number.

   Example: 9 = 3 × 3; therefore, 3 is the square root of 9.

   b. The symbol $\sqrt{\ }$ is used to indicate square root.

Example: $\sqrt{9} = 3$ means that the square root of 9 is 3, or $3 \times 3 = 9$.

c. In principle, all numbers have a square root. Although many square roots cannot be calculated exactly, they can be found to whatever degree of accuracy is needed (see item 8). Thus the square root of 10, $\sqrt{10}$, is *by definition* the number that equals 10 when it is squared—$\sqrt{10} \times \sqrt{10} = 10$.

d. If a number has exactly three equal factors, each factor is called a **cube root.** The symbol $\sqrt[3]{}$ is used to indicate a cube root.

Example: $8 = 2 \times 2 \times 2$; thus $2 = \sqrt[3]{8}$

e. In general, the nth root is indicated as $\sqrt[n]{}$

7. The square root of the most common perfect squares may be found by using the following table, or by trial and error; that is, by finding the number that, when squared, yields the given perfect square.

Number	*Perfect Square*	*Number*	*Perfect Square*
1	1	10	100
2	4	11	121
3	9	12	144
4	16	13	169
5	25	14	196
6	36	15	225
7	49	20	400
8	64	25	625
9	81	30	900

Example: To find $\sqrt{81}$, note that 81 is the perfect square of 9, or $9^2 = 81$. Therefore, $\sqrt{81} = 9$.

8. On the GMAT you will only rarely have to find the square root of a number that is not a perfect square. The two most common square roots with which you will have to deal with are $\sqrt{2}$, which equals approximately 1.4, and $\sqrt{3}$, which equals approximately 1.7. Most times you will not have to convert these square roots to their equivalents since the answer choices will be in terms of the square roots, e.g., (A) $4\sqrt{3}$, etc.

The following method is the way to compute square roots of numbers that are not perfect squares. It is very effective, but it is long and you are unlikely to actually need it on the GMAT.

a. Locate the decimal point.

b. Mark off the digits in groups of two in both directions beginning at the decimal point.

c. Mark the decimal point for the answer just above the decimal point of the number whose square root is to be taken.

d. Find the largest perfect square contained in the left-hand group of two.

e. Place its square root in the answer. Subtract the perfect square from the first digit or pair of digits.

f. Bring down the next pair.

g. Double the partial answer.

h. Add a trial digit to the right of the doubled partial answer. Multiply this new number by the trial digit. Place the correct new digit in the answer.

i. Subtract the product.

j. Repeat steaps f–i as often as necessary.

You will notice that you get one digit in the answer for every group of two you marked off in the original number.

Illustration: Find the square root of 138,384.

SOLUTION:

```
                 3
           √13'83'84.
   3² =     9
            4 83

            3  7  2.
           √13'83'84.
   3² =     9
            4 83
7 × 67 =    4 69
              14 84
2 × 742 =     14 84
```

The number must first be marked off in groups of two figures each, beginning at the decimal point, which, in the case of a whole number, is at the right. The number of figures in the root will be the same as the number of groups so obtained.

The largest square less than 13 is 9. $\sqrt{9} = 3$

Place its square root in the answer. Subtract the perfect square from the first digit or pair of digits. Bring down the next pair. To form our trial divisor, annex 0 to this root "3" (making 30) and multiply by 2.

$483 \div 60 = 80$. Multiplying the trial divisor 68 by 8, we obtain 544, which is too large. We then try multiplying 67 by 7. This is correct. Add the trial digit to the right of the doubled partial answer. Place the new digit in the answer. Subtract the product. Bring down the final group. Annex 0 to the new root 37 and multiply by 2 for the trial divisor:

$$2 \times 370 = 740$$
$$1484 \div 740 = 2$$

Place the 2 in the answer.

Answer: The square root of 138,384 is 372.

Illustration: Find the square root of 3 to the nearest hundredth.

SOLUTION:

	1. 7 3 2
	$\sqrt{3.00'00'00}$
$1^2 =$	1
20	2 00
$7 \times 27 =$	1 89
340	11 00
$3 \times 343 =$	10 29
3460	71 00
$2 \times 3462 =$	69 24

Answer: The square root of 3 is 1.73 to the nearest hundredth.

9. When more complex items are raised to powers, the same basic rules apply.

a. To find the power of some multiplied item, find the power of each multiplicand and multiply those powers together.

Example: $(4x)^2 = (4x)(4x) = (4)(4)(x)(x) = (4)^2(x)^2 = 16x^2$

Example: $(2xy)^4 = (2)^4(x)^4(y)^4 = 16x^4y^4$

b. To find the power of some divided item or fraction, find the power of each part of the fraction and then divide in the manner of the original fraction.

Example: $\left(\frac{2}{x}\right)^2 = \left(\frac{2}{x}\right)\left(\frac{2}{x}\right) = \left(\frac{4}{x^2}\right)$

c. To find the result when two powers of the same base are multiplied together, *add* the exponents. You add the exponents because you are adding to the length of the string of the same base all being multiplied together.

Example: $(x^2)(x^3) = (x)(x) \cdot (x)(x)(x) = xxxxx = x^{(2+3)} = x^5$

Example: $2^a \cdot 2^b = 2^{(a+b)}$

d. To find the result when a power is raised to an exponent, *multiply* the exponents. You multiply the exponents together because you are multiplying the length of the string of the same base all being multiplied together.

Example: $(x^2)^3 = (x^2)(x^2)(x^2) = xxxxxx = x^{(2\cdot3)} = x^6$

e. When a power is divided by another power of the same base, the result is found by subtracting the exponent in the denominator (bottom) from the exponent in the numerator (top).

Example: $\frac{x^3}{x^2} = \frac{xxx}{xx} = x^{(3-2)} = x^1 = x$

Note: Any base to the first power, x^1, equals the base.

Example: $\frac{x^9}{x^6} = x^{(9-6)} = x^3$

Example: $\frac{x^2}{x^2} = \frac{xx}{xx} = x^{(2-2)} = x^0 = 1$

Note: Any base to the "zero-th" power, x^0, equals 1.

Example: $\frac{x^3}{x^4} = \frac{xxx}{xxxx} = \frac{1}{x} = x^{(3-4)} = x^{-1}$

f. A **negative exponent** is a reciprocal, as discussed in the earlier section on fractions.

Example: $z^{-3} = \left(\frac{z}{1}\right)^{-3} = \left(\frac{1}{z}\right)^{+3} = \frac{1^3}{z^3} = \frac{1}{z^3}$

Example: $(3p)^{-2} = \frac{1}{(3p)^{+2}} = \frac{1}{9p^2}$

Example: $(r^{-3})^{-6} = \frac{1}{(r^{-3})^{+6}} = \frac{1}{\left(\frac{1}{r^3}\right)^6} = \frac{1}{\frac{1}{r^{18}}}$

$= (1)\left(\frac{r^{18}}{1}\right) = r^{18}$

or $(r^{-3}) = r^{(-3)(-6)} = r^{+18}$

10. Some problems require that different powers be grouped together. Depending on the relationships, they can be grouped by doing the processes explained in #9 in the reverse direction.

Example: $9x^2 = 3^2 \cdot x^2 = (3x)^2$

Example: $\frac{81}{y^2} = \frac{9^2}{y^2} = \left(\frac{9}{y}\right)^2$

Example: $m^{12} = (m^5)(m^7)$ or $(m^{10})(m^2)$ etc.

Example: $z^{24} = (z^6)^4$ or $(z^8)^3$ etc.

11. The conditions under which radicals can be added or subtracted are much the same as the conditions for letters in an algebraic expression. The radicals act as a label, or unit, and must therefore be exactly the same. In adding or subtracting, we add or subtract the coefficients, or rational parts and carry the radical along as a label, which does not change.

Example: $\sqrt{2} + \sqrt{3}$ cannot be added
$\sqrt{2} + \sqrt[3]{2}$ cannot be added
$4\sqrt{2} + 5\sqrt{2} = 9\sqrt{2}$

Often, when radicals to be added or subtracted are not the same, simplification of one or more radicals will make them the same. To simplify a radical, we remove any perfect square factors from underneath the radical sign.

Example: $\sqrt{12} = \sqrt{4}\sqrt{3} = 2\sqrt{3}$
$\sqrt{27} = \sqrt{9}\sqrt{3} = 3\sqrt{3}$

If we wish to add $\sqrt{12} + \sqrt{27}$, we must first simplify each one. Adding the simplified radicals gives a sum of $5\sqrt{3}$.

Example: $\sqrt{125} + \sqrt{20} - \sqrt{500}$

SOLUTION:

$\sqrt{25}\sqrt{5} + \sqrt{4}\sqrt{5} - \sqrt{100}\sqrt{5}$
$5\sqrt{5} + 2\sqrt{5} - 10\sqrt{5}$
$-3\sqrt{5}$

Answer: $-3\sqrt{5}$

12. In multiplication and division we again treat the radicals as we would letters in an algebraic expression. They are factors and must be treated as such.

Example: $(\sqrt{2})(\sqrt{3}) = \sqrt{(2)(3)} = \sqrt{6}$

Example: $4\sqrt{2} \cdot 5\sqrt{3} = 20 \cdot \sqrt{6}$

Example: $(3\sqrt{2})^2 = 3\sqrt{2} \cdot 3\sqrt{2} = 9 \cdot 2 = 18$

Example: $\frac{\sqrt{8}}{\sqrt{2}} = \sqrt{4} = 2$

Example: $\frac{10\sqrt{20}}{\sqrt{4}} = 5\sqrt{5}$

Example: $\sqrt{2}(\sqrt{8} + \sqrt{18}) = \sqrt{16} + \sqrt{36}$
$= 4 + 6 = 10$

13. In simplifying radicals that contain several terms under the radical sign, we must combine terms before taking the square root.

Example: $\sqrt{16 + 9} = \sqrt{25} = 5$

Note: It is not true that $\sqrt{16 + 9} = \sqrt{16} + \sqrt{9}$, which would be 4 + 3, or 7.

Example: $\sqrt{\frac{x^2}{16} - \frac{x^2}{25}} = \sqrt{\frac{25x^2 - 16x^2}{400}}$

$= \sqrt{\frac{9x^2}{400}} = \frac{3x}{20}$

Practice Problems Involving Roots

1. Combine $4\sqrt{27} - 2\sqrt{48} + \sqrt{147}$
(A) $27\sqrt{3}$
(B) $-3\sqrt{3}$
(C) $9\sqrt{3}$

(D) $10\sqrt{3}$
(E) $11\sqrt{3}$

2. Combine $\sqrt{80} + \sqrt{45} - \sqrt{20}$
(A) $9\sqrt{5}$
(B) $5\sqrt{5}$
(C) $-\sqrt{5}$
(D) $3\sqrt{5}$
(E) $-2\sqrt{5}$

3. Combine $6\sqrt{5} + 3\sqrt{2} - 4\sqrt{5} + \sqrt{2}$
(A) 8
(B) $2\sqrt{5} + 3\sqrt{2}$
(C) $2\sqrt{5} + 4\sqrt{2}$
(D) $5\sqrt{7}$
(E) 5

4. Combine $\frac{1}{2}\sqrt{180} + \frac{1}{3}\sqrt{45} - \frac{2}{5}\sqrt{20}$
(A) $3\sqrt{10} + \sqrt{15} + 2\sqrt{2}$
(B) $\frac{16}{5}\sqrt{5}$
(C) $\sqrt{97}$
(D) $\frac{24}{5}\sqrt{5}$
(E) none of these

5. Combine $5\sqrt{mn} - 3\sqrt{mn} - 2\sqrt{mn}$
(A) 0
(B) 1
(C) $\sqrt{mn}$
(D) mn
(E) $-\sqrt{mn}$

6. Multiply and simplify: $2\sqrt{18} \cdot 6\sqrt{2}$
(A) 72
(B) 48
(C) $12\sqrt{6}$
(D) $8\sqrt{6}$
(E) 36

7. Find $(3\sqrt{3})^3$
(A) $27\sqrt{3}$
(B) $81\sqrt{3}$
(C) 81
(D) $9\sqrt{3}$
(E) 243

8. Multiply and simplify: $\frac{1}{2}\sqrt{2}\,(\sqrt{6} + \frac{1}{2}\sqrt{2})$
(A) $\sqrt{3} + \frac{1}{2}$
(B) $\frac{1}{2}\sqrt{3}$
(C) $\sqrt{6} + 1$
(D) $\sqrt{6} + \frac{1}{2}$
(E) $\sqrt{6} + 2$

9. Divide and simplify: $\dfrac{\sqrt{32b^3}}{\sqrt{8b}}$
(A) $2\sqrt{b}$
(B) $\sqrt{2b}$
(C) 2b
(D) $\sqrt{2b^2}$
(E) $b\sqrt{2b}$

10. Divide and simplify: $\dfrac{15\sqrt{96}}{5\sqrt{2}}$
(A) $7\sqrt{3}$
(B) $7\sqrt{12}$
(C) $11\sqrt{3}$
(D) $12\sqrt{3}$
(E) $40\sqrt{3}$

11. Simplify $\sqrt{\dfrac{x^2}{9} + \dfrac{x^2}{16}}$
(A) $\dfrac{25x^2}{144}$
(B) $\dfrac{5x}{12}$
(C) $\dfrac{5x^2}{12}$
(D) $\dfrac{x}{7}$
(E) $\dfrac{7x}{12}$

12. Simplify $\sqrt{36y^2 + 64x^2}$
(A) $6y + 8x$
(B) 10xy
(C) $6y^2 + 8x^2$
(D) $10x^2y^2$
(E) cannot be simplified

13. Simplify $\sqrt{\dfrac{x^2}{64} - \dfrac{x^2}{100}}$
(A) $\dfrac{x}{40}$
(B) $-\dfrac{x}{2}$
(C) $\dfrac{x}{2}$
(D) $\dfrac{3x}{40}$
(E) $\dfrac{3x}{80}$

14. Simplify $\sqrt{\dfrac{y^2}{2} - \dfrac{y^2}{18}}$
(A) $\dfrac{2y}{3}$

(B) $\frac{y\sqrt{5}}{3}$
(C) $\frac{10y}{3}$
(D) $\frac{y\sqrt{3}}{6}$
(E) cannot be simplified

15. $\sqrt{a^2 + b^2}$ is equal to
(A) $a + b$
(B) $a - b$
(C) $\sqrt{a^2} + \sqrt{b^2}$
(D) $(a + b)(a - b)$
(E) none of these

16. Which of the following square roots can be found exactly?
(A) $\sqrt{.4}$
(B) $\sqrt{.9}$
(C) $\sqrt{.09}$
(D) $\sqrt{.02}$
(E) $\sqrt{.025}$

Root Problems—Correct Answers

1.	**(E)**	9.	**(C)**
2.	**(B)**	10.	**(D)**
3.	**(C)**	11.	**(B)**
4.	**(B)**	12.	**(E)**
5.	**(A)**	13.	**(D)**
6.	**(A)**	14.	**(A)**
7.	**(B)**	15.	**(E)**
8.	**(A)**	16.	**(C)**

Problem Solutions—Roots

1. $4\sqrt{27} = 4\sqrt{9}\sqrt{3} = 12\sqrt{3}$
$2\sqrt{48} = 2\sqrt{16}\sqrt{3} = 8\sqrt{3}$
$\sqrt{147} = \sqrt{49}\sqrt{3} = 7\sqrt{3}$
$12\sqrt{3} - 8\sqrt{3} + 7\sqrt{3} = 11\sqrt{3}$

Answer: **(E)** $11\sqrt{3}$

2. $\sqrt{80} = \sqrt{16}\sqrt{5} = 4\sqrt{5}$
$\sqrt{45} = \sqrt{9}\sqrt{5} = 3\sqrt{5}$
$\sqrt{20} = \sqrt{4}\sqrt{5} = 2\sqrt{5}$
$4\sqrt{5} + 3\sqrt{5} - 2\sqrt{5} = 5\sqrt{5}$

Answer: **(B)** $5\sqrt{5}$

3. Only terms with the same radical may be combined.

$6\sqrt{5} - 4\sqrt{5} = 2\sqrt{5}$
$3\sqrt{2} + \sqrt{2} = 4\sqrt{2}$

Therefore we have $2\sqrt{5} + 4\sqrt{2}$

Answer: **(C)** $2\sqrt{5} + 4\sqrt{2}$

4. $\frac{1}{2}\sqrt{180} = \frac{1}{2}\sqrt{36}\sqrt{5} = 3\sqrt{5}$
$\frac{1}{3}\sqrt{45} = \frac{1}{3}\sqrt{9}\sqrt{5} = \sqrt{5}$
$\frac{2}{5}\sqrt{20} = \frac{2}{5}\sqrt{4}\sqrt{5} = \frac{4}{5}\sqrt{5}$
$3\sqrt{5} + \sqrt{5} - \frac{4}{5}\sqrt{5} = 4\sqrt{5} - \frac{4}{5}\sqrt{5} = 3\frac{1}{5}\sqrt{5} = \frac{16}{5}\sqrt{5}$

Answer: **(B)** $\frac{16}{5}\sqrt{5}$

5. $5\sqrt{mn} - 5\sqrt{mn} = 0$

Answer: **(A)** 0

6. $2\sqrt{18} \cdot 6\sqrt{2} = 12\sqrt{36} = 12 \cdot 6 = 72$

Answer: **(A)** 72

7. $3\sqrt{3} \cdot 3\sqrt{3} \cdot 3\sqrt{3} = 27(3\sqrt{3}) = 81\sqrt{3}$

Answer: **(B)** $81\sqrt{3}$

8. Using the distributive law, we have
$\frac{1}{2}\sqrt{12} + \frac{1}{4} \cdot 2 = \frac{1}{2}\sqrt{4}\sqrt{3} + \frac{1}{2} = \sqrt{3} + \frac{1}{2}$

Answer: **(A)** $\sqrt{3} + \frac{1}{2}$

9. Dividing the numbers in the radical sign, we have $\sqrt{4b^2} = 2b$

Answer: **(C)** 2b

10. $3\sqrt{48} = 3\sqrt{16}\sqrt{3} = 12\sqrt{3}$

Answer: **(D)** $12\sqrt{3}$

11. $\sqrt{\frac{16x^2 + 9x^2}{144}} = \sqrt{\frac{25x^2}{144}} = \frac{5x}{12}$

Answer: **(B)** $\frac{5x}{12}$

12. The terms cannot be combined and it is not possible to take the square root of separated terms.

Answer: **(E)** cannot be done

13. $\sqrt{\dfrac{100x^2 - 64x^2}{6400}} = \sqrt{\dfrac{36x^2}{6400}} = \dfrac{6x}{80} = \dfrac{3x}{40}$

Answer: **(D)** $\dfrac{3x}{40}$

14. $\sqrt{\dfrac{18y^2 - 2y^2}{36}} = \sqrt{\dfrac{16y^2}{36}} = \dfrac{4y}{6} = \dfrac{2y}{3}$

Answer: **(A)** $\dfrac{2y}{3}$

15. It is not possible to find the square root of separate terms.

Answer: **(E)** none of these

16. In order to take the square root of a decimal, it must have an even number of decimal places so that its square root will have exactly half as many. In addition to this, the digits must form a perfect square ($\sqrt{.09} = .3$).

Answer: **(C)** $\sqrt{.09}$

ALGEBRAIC FRACTIONS

1. In reducing algebraic fractions, we must divide the numerator and denominator by the same factor, just as we do in arithmetic. We can never cancel terms, as this would be adding or subtracting the same number from the numerator and denominator, which changes the value of the fraction. When we reduce $\frac{6}{8}$ to $\frac{3}{4}$, we are really saying that $\frac{6}{8} = \frac{2 \cdot 3}{2 \cdot 4}$ and then dividing numerator and denominator by 2. We do not say $\frac{6}{8} = \frac{3+3}{3+5}$ and then say $\frac{6}{8} = \frac{3}{5}$. This is faulty reasoning in algebra as well. If we have $\frac{6t}{8t}$, we can divide numerator and denominator by 2t, giving $\frac{3}{4}$ as an answer. However, if we have $\frac{6 + t}{8 + t}$, we can do no more, as there is no factor that divides into the *entire* numerator as well as the *entire* denominator. Cancelling terms is one of the most frequent student errors. Don't get caught! Be careful!

Example: Reduce $\dfrac{3x^2 + 6x}{4x^3 + 8x^2}$ to its lowest terms.

SOLUTION: Factoring the numerator and denominator, we have $\dfrac{3x(x + 2)}{4x^2(x + 2)}$. The factors common to both numerator and denominator are x and (x + 2). Dividing these out, we arrive at $\dfrac{3}{4x}$.

Answer: $\dfrac{3}{4x}$

2. In adding or subtracting fractions, we must work with a common denominator and the same shortcuts we used in arithmetic.

Example: Find the sum of $\frac{1}{a}$ and $\frac{1}{b}$.

SOLUTION: Remember to add the two cross products and put the sum over the denominator product.

Answer: $\dfrac{b + a}{ab}$

Example: Add: $\dfrac{2n}{3} + \dfrac{3n}{2}$

SOLUTION: $\dfrac{4n + 9n}{6} = \dfrac{13n}{6}$

Answer: $\dfrac{13n}{6}$

3. In multiplying or dividing fractions, we may cancel a factor common to any numerator and any denominator. Always remember to invert the fraction following the division sign. Where exponents are involved, they are added in multiplication and subtracted in division.

Example: Find the product of $\dfrac{a^3}{b^2}$ and $\dfrac{b^3}{a^2}$.

SOLUTION: We divide a^2 into the first numerator and second denominator, giving $\dfrac{a}{b^2} \cdot \dfrac{b^2}{1}$. Then we divide b^2 into the first denominator and second numerator, giving $\dfrac{a}{1} \cdot \dfrac{b}{1}$. Finally, we multiply the resulting fractions, giving an answer of ab.

Answer: ab

Example: Divide $\frac{6x^2y}{5}$ by $2x^3$.

SOLUTION: $\frac{6x^2y}{5} \cdot \frac{1}{2x^3}$. Divide the first numerator and second denominator by $2x^2$, giving $\frac{3y}{5} \cdot \frac{1}{x}$. Multiplying the resulting fractions, we get $\frac{3y}{5x}$.

Answer: $\frac{3y}{5x}$

4. Complex algebraic fractions are simplified by the same methods used in arithmetic. Multiply *each term* of the complex fraction by the lowest quantity that will eliminate the fraction within the fraction.

Example: $\dfrac{\frac{1}{a} + \frac{1}{b}}{ab}$

SOLUTION: We must multiply *each term* by ab, giving $\frac{b + a}{a^2b^2}$ Since no reduction beyond this is possible, $\frac{b + a}{a^2b^2}$ is our final answer. Remember *never* to cancel terms unless they apply to the entire numerator or the entire denominator.

Answer: $\frac{b + a}{a^2b^2}$

Practice Problems Involving Algebraic Fractions

1. Find the sum of $\frac{n}{6} + \frac{2n}{5}$.
(A) $\frac{13n}{30}$
(B) 17n
(C) $\frac{3n}{30}$
(D) $\frac{17n}{30}$
(E) $\frac{3n}{11}$

2. Combine into a single fraction: $1 - \frac{x}{y}$
(A) $\frac{1 - x}{y}$
(B) $\frac{y - x}{y}$
(C) $\frac{x - y}{y}$
(D) $\frac{1 - x}{1 - y}$
(E) $\frac{y - x}{xy}$

3. Divide $\frac{x - y}{x + y}$ by $\frac{y - x}{y + x}$.
(A) 1
(B) −1
(C) $\frac{(x-y)^2}{(x+y)^2}$
(D) $-\frac{(x-y)^2}{(x+y)^2}$
(E) 0

4. Simplify: $\dfrac{1 + \frac{1}{x}}{\frac{y}{x}}$
(A) $\frac{x + 1}{y}$
(B) $\frac{x + 1}{x}$
(C) $\frac{x + 1}{xy}$
(D) $\frac{x^2 + 1}{xy}$
(E) $\frac{y + 1}{y}$

5. Find an expression equivalent to $\left(\frac{2x^2}{y}\right)^3$.
(A) $\frac{8x^5}{3y}$
(B) $\frac{6x^6}{y^3}$
(C) $\frac{6x^5}{y^3}$
(D) $\frac{8x^5}{y^3}$
(E) $\frac{8x^6}{y^3}$

6. Simplify: $\dfrac{\frac{1}{x} + \frac{1}{y}}{3}$
(A) $\frac{3x + 3y}{xy}$
(B) $\frac{3xy}{x + y}$
(C) $\frac{xy}{3}$
(D) $\frac{x + y}{3xy}$
(E) $\frac{x + y}{3}$

7. $\frac{1}{a} + \frac{1}{b} = 7$ and $\frac{1}{a} - \frac{1}{b} = 3.$

Find $\frac{1}{a^2} - \frac{1}{b^2}$.

(A) 10
(B) 7
(C) 3
(D) 21
(E) 4

Algebraic Fractions—Correct Answers

1.	**(D)**	5.	**(E)**
2.	**(B)**	6.	**(D)**
3.	**(B)**	7.	**(D)**
4.	**(A)**		

Solutions—Algebraic Fractions

1. $\frac{n}{6} + \frac{2n}{5} = \frac{5n + 12n}{30} = \frac{17n}{30}$

Answer: **(D)** $\frac{17n}{30}$

2. $\frac{1}{1} - \frac{x}{y} = \frac{y - x}{y}$

Answer: **(B)** $\frac{y - x}{y}$

3. $\frac{x - y}{x + y} \cdot \frac{y + x}{y - x}$
Since addition is commutative, we may cancel x + y with y + x, as they are the same quantity. However, subtraction is not commutative, so we may not cancel x − y with y − x, as they are *not* the same quantity. We can change the form of y − x by factoring out a − 1. Thus, $y - x = (-1)(x - y)$. In this form, we can cancel x − y, leaving an answer of $\frac{1}{-1}$, or −1.

Answer: **(B)** −1

4. Multiply every term in the fraction by x, giving $\frac{x + 1}{y}$.

Answer: **(A)** $\frac{x + 1}{y}$

5. $\frac{2x^2}{y} \cdot \frac{2x^2}{y} \cdot \frac{2x^2}{y} = \frac{8x^6}{y^3}$

Answer: **(E)** $\frac{8x^6}{y^3}$

6. Multiply every term of the fraction by xy, giving $\frac{y + x}{3xy}$.

Answer: **(D)** $\frac{y + x}{3xy}$

7. $\frac{1}{a^2} - \frac{1}{b^2}$ is equivalent to $\left(\frac{1}{a} + \frac{1}{b}\right)\left(\frac{1}{a} - \frac{1}{b}\right)$.
We therefore multiply 7 by 3 for an answer of 21.

Answer: **(D)** 21

PROBLEM-SOLVING IN ALGEBRA

1. In solving verbal problems, the most important technique is to read accurately. Be sure you understand clearly what you are asked to find. Then try to evaluate the problem in common-sense terms; use this to eliminate answer choices.

Example: If two people are working together, their combined speed is greater than either one, but not more than twice as fast as the fastest one.

Example: The total number of the correct answers cannot be greater than the total number of answers. Thus if x questions are asked and you are to determine from other information how many correct answers there were, they cannot come to 2x.

2. The next step, when common sense alone is not enough, is to translate the problem into algebra. Keep it as simple as possible.

Example: 24 = what % of 12?

Translation: $24 = x\% \cdot 12$
or $24 = x\frac{1}{100} \cdot 12$
or $24 = \frac{x}{100} \cdot \frac{12}{1}$

Divide both sides by 12.

$2 = \frac{x}{100}$

Multiply both sides by 100.

200 = x IN PERCENT

3. Be alert for the "hidden equation." This is some necessary information so obvious in the stated situation that the question assumes that you know it.

Example: Boys plus girls = total class

Example: Imported wine plus domestic wine = all wine.

Example: The wall and floor, or the shadow and the building, make a right angle (thus permitting use of the Pythagorean Theorem).

4. Always remember that a variable (letter) can have any value whatsoever within the terms of the problem. Keep the possibility of fractional and negative values constantly in mind.

5. **Manipulating Equations.** You can perform any mathematical function you think helpful to one side of the equation, *provided* you do precisely the same thing to the other side of the equation. You can also substitute one side of an equality for the other in another equation.

6. **Manipulating Inequalities.** You can add to or subtract from both sides of an inequality without changing the direction of the inequality.

Example:

$$8 > 5$$
$$8 + 10 > 5 + 10$$
$$18 > 15$$

Example:

$$3x > y + z$$
$$3x + 5 > y + z + 5$$

You can also multiply or divide both sides of the inequality by any POSITIVE number without changing the direction of the inequality.

Example:

$$12 > 4$$
$$3(12) > 3(4)$$
$$36 > 12$$

Example:

$$x > y$$
$$3x > 3y$$

If you multiply or divide an inequality by a NEGATIVE number, you REVERSE the direction of the inequality.

Example:

$$4 > 3$$
$$(-2)(4) < (-2)(3)$$
$$-8 < -6$$

Example:

$$x^2y > z^2x$$
$$-3(x^2y) < -3(z^2x)$$

7. **Solving Equations.** The first step is to determine what quantity or letter you wish to isolate. Solving an equation for x means getting x on one side of the equals sign and everything else on the other.

Example: $5x + 3 = y$

Subtract 3.

$$5x = y - 3$$

Divide by 5.

$$x = \frac{y - 3}{5}$$

Aside from factoring, discussed later in this review, unwrapping an equation is a matter of performing three steps. These rules are stated in terms of *x,* but apply equally to all variables or variable expressions.

Put all x on one side of the equation, if not already there. This can be done by adding, subtracting, dividing or multiplying. Sometimes other quantities come along.

Example:

$$4x + 2 = 29 + bxy$$

Subtract bxy.

$$4x + 2 - bxy = 29$$

(continued below)

Unpeel x by considering the structure of the whole side x is on as a single expression and perform the opposite operation. Addition and subtraction are opposites; multiplication and division are opposites; raising to powers and taking roots are opposites.

Example: $14k + 8 = 22$

Left is addition, so subtract 8.

$$14k = 14$$

Divide by 14.

$$k = 1$$

Continue step b until only terms with x in them are left.

Example: (from above)

$$4x + 2 - bxy = 29$$

Subtract 2.

$$4x - bxy = 29 - 2 = 27$$

If only one x term is left, unravel to just x.

Example: $8x = 24$
Divide by 8.
$x = 3$

Example: $4x^2 = 36$
Divide by 4.
$x^2 = 9$
Take square root. Note $\pm$.
$x = \pm 3$

If more than one term with x in it is left, try to factor. While, in principle, many things are not factorable, on the GMAT most polynomials will be factorable. (Factoring and polynomial multiplication are discussed in the next section of the math review.)

8. If there are two variables in an equation, it may be helpful to put all expressions containing one variable on one side and all the others on the other.

9. Expressing x in terms of y means having an equation with x alone on one side and some expression of y on the other, such as $x = 4y^2 + 3y + 4$.

10. We will review some of the frequently encountered types of algebra problems, although not every problem you may get will fall into one of these categories. However, thoroughly familiarizing yourself with the types of problems that follow will help you to translate and solve all kinds of verbal problems.

A. Coin Problems

In solving coin problems, it is best to change the value of all monies involved to cents before writing an equation. Thus, the number of nickels must be multiplied by 5 to give their value in cents; dimes must be multiplied by 10; quarters by 25; half-dollars by 50; and dollars by 100.

Example: Richard has $3.50 consisting of nickels and dimes. If he has 5 more dimes than nickels, how many dimes does he have?

SOLUTION:

Let $x =$ the number of nickels
$x + 5 =$ the number of dimes
$5x =$ the value of the nickels in cents
$10x + 50 =$ the value of the dimes in cents
$350 =$ the value of the money he has in cents

$$5x + 10x + 50 = 350$$
$$15x = 300$$
$$x = 20$$

Answer: He has 20 nickels and 25 dimes.

In a problem such as this, you can be sure that 20 would be among the multiple-choice answers. You must be sure to read carefully what you are asked to find and then continue until you have found the quantity sought.

B. Consecutive Integer Problems

Consecutive integers are one apart and can be represented by x, x+1, x+2, etc. Consecutive even or odd integers are two apart and can be represented by x, x+2, x+4, etc.

Illustration: Three consecutive odd integers have a sum of 33. Find the average of these integers.

Solution: Represent the integers as x, x+2 and x+4. Write an equation indicating the sum is 33.

$$3x + 6 = 33$$
$$3x = 27$$
$$x = 9$$

The integers are 9, 11, and 13. In the case of evenly spaced numbers such as these, the average is the middle number, 11. Since the sum of the three numbers was given originally, all we really had to do was to divide this sum by 3 to find the average, without ever knowing what the numbers were.

Answer: 11

C. Age Problems

Problems of this type usually involve a comparison of ages at the present time, several years from now, or several years ago. A person's age x years from now is found by adding x to his present age. A person's age x years ago is found by subtracting x from his present age.

Illustration: Michelle was 12 years old y years ago. Represent her age b years from now.

SOLUTION: Her present age is 12 + y. In b years. her age will be 12 + y + b.

Answer: 12 + y + b

D. Interest Problems

The annual amount of interest paid on an investment is found by multiplying the amount of principal invested by the rate (percent) of interest paid.

Principal · Rate = Interest income

Illustration: Mr. Strauss invests $4,000, part at 6% and part at 7%. His income from these investments in one year is $250. Find the amount invested at 7%.

SOLUTION: Represent each investment.
Let x = the amount invested at 7%. Always try to let x represent what you are looking for.
4000 − x = the amount invested at 6%
.07x = the income from the 7% investment
.06(4000 − x) = the income from the 6% investment

$$.07x + .06(4000 - x) = 250$$
$$7x + 6(4000 - x) = 25000$$
$$7x + 24000 - 6x = 25000$$
$$x = 1000$$

Answer: He invested $1,000 at 7%.

E. Mixture

There are two kinds of mixture problems with which you could be familiar. These problems are rare, so this is best regarded as an extra-credit section and not given top priority. The first is sometimes referred to as dry mixture, in which we mix dry ingredients of different values, such as nuts or coffee.

Also solved by the same method are problems such as those dealing with tickets at different prices. In solving this type of problem, it is best to organize the data in a chart of three rows and three columns, labeled as illustrated in the following problem.

Illustration: A dealer wishes to mix 20 pounds of nuts selling for 45 cents per pound with some more expensive nuts selling for 60 cents per pound, to make a mixture that will sell for 50 cents per pound. How many pounds of the more expensive nuts should he use?

SOLUTION:

	No. of lbs.	Price/lb.	= Total Value
Original	20	.45	.45(20)
Added	x	.60	.60(x)
Mixture	20 + x	.50	.50(20+x)

The value of the original nuts plus the value of the added nuts must equal the value of the mixture. Almost all mixture problems require an equation that comes from adding the final column.

$$.45(20) + .60(x) = .50(20 + x)$$
Multiply by 100 to remove decimals.
$$45(20) + 60(x) = 50(20 + x)$$
$$900 + 60x = 1000 + 50x$$
$$10x = 100$$
$$x = 10$$

Answer: He should use 10 lbs. of 60-cent nuts.

In solving the second type, or chemical, mixture problem, we are dealing with percents rather than prices, and amounts instead of value.

Illustration: How much water must be added to 20 gallons of solution that is 30% alcohol to dilute it to a solution that is only 25% alcohol?

SOLUTION:

	No. of gals.	% alcohol	= Amt. alcohol
Original	20	.30	.30(20)
Added	x	0	0
New	20 + x	.25	.25(20 + x)

Note that the percent of alcohol in water is 0. Had we added pure alcohol to strengthen the solution, the percent would have been 100. The equation again comes from the last column. The amount of alcohol added (none in this case) plus the amount we had to start with must equal the amount of alcohol in the new solution.

$$.30(20) = .25(20 + x)$$
$$30(20) = 25(20 + x)$$
$$600 = 500 + 25x$$
$$100 = 25x$$
$$x = 4$$

Answer: 4 gallons.

F. Motion Problems

The fundamental relationship in all motion problems is that Rate · Time = Distance. The problems at the level of this examination usually derive their equation from a relationship concerning distance. Most problems fall into one of three types.

Motion in opposite directions. When two objects start at the same time and move in opposite directions, or when two objects start at points at a given distance apart and move toward each other until they meet, then the distance the second travels will equal the total distance covered.

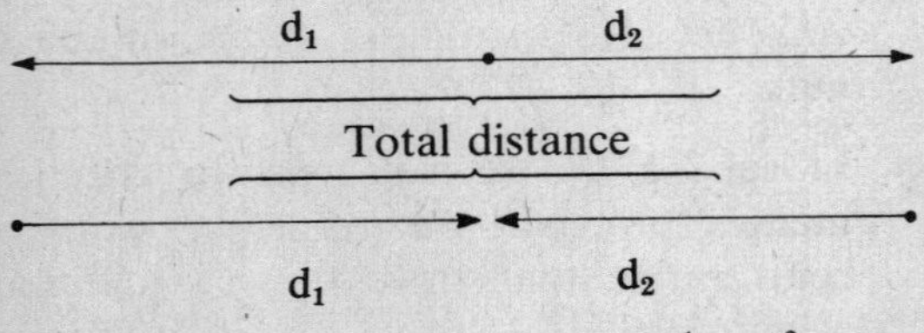

In either of the above cases, $d^1 + d^2$ = Total distance.

Motion in the same direction. This type of problem is sometimes called the "catch-up" problem. Two objects leave the same place at different times and different rates, but one "catches up" to the other. In such a case, the two distances must be equal.

Round trip. In this type of problem, the rate going is usually different from the rate returning. The times are also different. But if we go somewhere and then return to the starting point, the distances must be the same.

To solve any motion problem, it is helpful to organize the data in a box with columns for rate, time, and distance. A separate line should be used for each moving object. Remember that if the rate is given in *miles per hour,* the time must be in *hours* and the distance in *miles.*

Illustration: Two cars leave a restaurant at 1 P.M., with one car traveling east at 60 miles per hour and the other west at 40 miles per hour along a straight highway. At what time will they be 350 miles apart?

SOLUTION:

	Rate	Time	= Distance
Eastbound	60	x	60x
Westbound	40	x	40x

Notice that the time is unknown, since we must discover the number of hours traveled. However, since the cars start at the same time and stop when they are 350 miles apart, their times are the same.

$$60x + 40x = 350$$
$$100x = 350$$
$$x = 3\tfrac{1}{2}$$

Answer: In $3\frac{1}{2}$ hours, it will be 4:30 P.M.

Illustration: Gloria leaves home for school, riding her bicycle at a rate of 12 MPH. Twenty minutes after she leaves, her mother sees Gloria's English paper on her bed and leaves to bring it to her. If her mother drives at 36 MPH, how far must she drive before she reaches Gloria?

SOLUTION:

	Rate	Time	= Distance
Gloria	12	x	12x
Mother	36	$x - \frac{1}{3}$	$36(x - \frac{1}{3})$

Notice that 20 minutes has been changed to $\frac{1}{3}$ of an hour. In this problem the times are not equal, but the distances are.

$$12x = 36(x - \tfrac{1}{3})$$
$$12x = 36x - 12$$
$$12 = 24x$$
$$x = \frac{1}{2}$$

Answer: If Gloria rode for $\frac{1}{2}$ hour at 12 m.p.h., the distance covered was 6 miles.

Illustration: Judy leaves home at 11 A.M. and rides to Mary's house to return her bicycle. She travels at 12 miles per hour and arrives at 11:30 A.M. She turns right around and walks home. How fast does she walk if she returns home at 1 P.M.?

SOLUTION:

	Rate	Time =	Distance
Going	12	$\frac{1}{2}$	6
Return	x	$1\frac{1}{2}$	$\frac{3}{2}x$

The distances are equal.

$$6 = \frac{3}{2}x$$
$$12 = 3x$$
$$x = 4$$

Answer: She walked at 4 m.p.h.

G. Work Problems

In most work problems, a complete job is broken into several parts, each representing a fractional part of the entire job. For each fractional part, which represents the portion completed by one man, one machine, one pipe, etc., the numerator should represent the time actually spent working, while the denominator should represent the total time needed to do the entire job alone. The sum of all the individual fractions should be 1.

Illustration: John can wax his car in 3 hours. Jim can do the same job in 5 hours. How long will it take them if they work together?

SOLUTION: If multiple-choice answers are given, you should realize that the correct answer must be smaller than the quickest worker, for no matter how slow a helper may be, he does part of the job and therefore it will be completed in less time.

$$\frac{\text{Time spent}}{\text{Total time needed to do job alone}} \qquad \overset{\text{John}}{\frac{x}{3}} + \overset{\text{Jim}}{\frac{x}{5}} = 1$$

Multiply by 15 to eliminate fractions.

$$5x + 3x = 15$$
$$8x = 15$$
$$x = 1\tfrac{7}{8} \text{ hours}$$

11. In general, you need as many equations as you have unknowns in order to get a unique numerical solution.

12. The two methods for coping with two or more equations are called **substitution** and **simultaneous.** They overlap. You have used both many times.

Substitution. Whenever one unknown equals something, you can substitute that something for it.

Example: (1) $2x + 3y = 14$ (2) $x = 2y$ } given

Substitute 2y for x in first equation.

$$2(2y) + 3y = 14$$
$$4y + 3y = 14$$

Add up y's; divide by 7.

$$7y = 14$$
$$y = 2$$

Substitute for y in second equation.

$$x = 2(2)$$
$$x = 4$$

Simultaneous. Sometimes adding or subtracting whole equations is shorter.

Example: (1) $5x + 3y = 13$
(2) $2x + 3y = 7$

Subtract (2) from (1).

$$5x + 3y = 13$$
$$-\ [2x + 3y = 7]$$
$$[5x - 2x] + [3y - 3y] = [13 - 7]$$
$$3x = 6$$

Divide by 3.

$$x = 2$$
$$y = 1 \quad \text{by substitution}$$

Practice Problems—Algebra

1. Sue and Nancy wish to buy a gift for a friend. They combine their money and find they have $4.00, consisting of quarters, dimes, and nickels. If they have 35 coins and the number of quarters is half the number of nickels, how many quarters do they have?
   (A) 5
   (B) 10
   (C) 20
   (D) 3
   (E) 6

2. Three times the first of three consecutive odd integers is 3 more than twice the third. Find the third integer.
   (A) 9
   (B) 11
   (C) 13
   (D) 15
   (E) 7

3. Robert is 15 years older than his brother Stan. However, y years ago Robert was twice as old as Stan. If Stan is now b years old and b > y, find the value of b − y.
   (A) 13
   (B) 14
   (C) 15
   (D) 16
   (E) 17

4. How many ounces of pure acid must be added to 20 ounces of a solution that is 5% acid to strengthen it to a solution that is 24% acid?
   (A) $2\frac{1}{2}$
   (B) 5
   (C) 6
   (D) $7\frac{1}{2}$
   (E) 10

5. A dealer mixes a lbs. of nuts worth b cents per pound with c lbs. of nuts worth d cents per pound. At what price should he sell a pound of the mixture if he wishes to make a profit of 10 cents per pound?
   (A) $\frac{ab + cd}{a + c} + 10$
   (B) $\frac{ab + cd}{a + c} + .10$
   (C) $\frac{b + d}{a + c} + 10$
   (D) $\frac{b + d}{a + c} + .10$
   (E) $\frac{b + d + 10}{a + c}$

6. Barbara invests $2,400 in the Security National Bank at 5%. How much additional money must she invest at 8% so that the total annual income will be equal to 6% of her entire investment?
   (A) $2,400
   (B) $3,600
   (C) $1,000
   (D) $3,000
   (D) $1,200

7. Frank left Austin to drive to Boxville at 6:15 P.M. and arrived at 11:45 P.M. If he averaged 30 miles per hour and stopped one hour for dinner, how far is Boxville from Austin?
   (A) 120
   (B) 135
   (C) 180
   (D) 165
   (E) 150

8. A plane traveling 600 miles per hour is 30 miles from Kennedy Airport at 4:58 P.M. At what time will it arrive at the airport?
   (A) 5:00 P.M.
   (B) 5:01 P.M.
   (C) 5:02 P.M.
   (D) 5:20 P.M.
   (E) 5:03 P.M.

9. Mr. Bridges can wash his car in 15 minutes, while his son Dave takes twice as long to do the same job. If they work together, how many minutes will the job take them?
   (A) 5
   (B) $7\frac{1}{2}$
   (C) 10
   (D) $22\frac{1}{2}$
   (E) 30

10. The value of a fraction is $\frac{2}{5}$. If the numerator is decreased by 2 and the denominator increased by 1, the resulting fraction is equivalent to $\frac{1}{4}$. Find the numerator of the original fraction.
(A) 3
(B) 4
(C) 6
(D) 10
(E) 15

Algebra Problem-Solving—Correct Answers

1.	**(B)**	6.	**(E)**
2.	**(D)**	7.	**(B)**
3.	**(C)**	8.	**(B)**
4.	**(B)**	9.	**(C)**
5.	**(A)**	10.	**(C)**

Problem Solutions—Algebra Problem-Solving

1. Let x = number of quarters
2x = number of nickels
35 − 3x = number of dimes
Write all money values in cents.
25(x) + 5(2x) + 10(35 − 3x) = 400
25x + 10x + 350 − 30x = 400
5x = 50
x = 10

Answer: **(B)** 10

2. Let x = first integer
x + 2 = second integer
x + 4 = third integer
3(x) = 3 + 2(x + 4)
3x = 3 + 2x + 8
x = + 11
The third integer is 15.

Answer: **(D)** 15

3. b = Stan's age now
b + 15 = Robert's age now
b − y = Stan's age y years ago
b + 15 − y = Robert's age y years ago
b + 15 − y = 2(b − y)
b + 15 − y = 2b − 2y
15 = b − y

Answer: **(C)** 15

4.

	No. of oz.	% acid	= Amt. acid
Original	20	.05	1
Added	x	1.00	x
Mixture	20 + x	.24	.24(20 + x)

1 + x = .24(20 + x) Multiply by 100 to eliminate decimal.
100 + 100x = 480 + 24x
76x = 380
x = 5

Answer: **(B)** 5

5. The a lbs. of nuts are worth a total of ab cents. The c lbs. of nuts are worth a total of cd cents. The value of the mixture is ab + cd cents. Since there are a + c pounds, each pound is worth $\frac{ab + cd}{a + c}$ cents.

Since the dealer wants to add 10 cents to each pound for profit, and the value of each pound is in cents, we add 10 to the value of each pound.

Answer: **(A)** $\frac{ab + cd}{a + c} + 10$

6. If Barbara invests x additional dollars at 8%, her total investment will amount to 2400 + x dollars.
.05(2400) + .08(x) = .06(2400 + x)
5(2400) + 8(x) = 6(2400 − x)
1200 + 8x = 14400 + 6x
2x = 2400
x = 1200

Answer: **(E)** $1,200

7. Total time elapsed is $5\frac{1}{2}$ hours. However, one hour was used for dinner. Therefore, Frank drove at 30 m.p.h. for $4\frac{1}{2}$ hours, covering 135 miles.

Answer: **(B)** 135

8. Time $= \dfrac{\text{Distance}}{\text{Rate}} = \dfrac{30}{600} = \dfrac{1}{200}$ hour, or 3 minutes.

Answer: **(B)** 5:01 P.M.

9. Dave takes 30 minutes to wash the car alone.

$$\frac{x}{15} + \frac{x}{30} = 1$$
$$2x + x = 30$$
$$3x = 30$$
$$x = 10$$

Answer: **(C)** 10

10. Let $2x$ = original numerator
$5x$ = original denominator

$\dfrac{2x - 2}{5x + 1} = \dfrac{1}{4}$ Cross multiply

$$8x - 8 = 5x + 1$$
$$3x = 9$$
$$x = 3$$

Original numerator is 2(3), or 6.

Answer: **(C)** 6

POLYNOMIAL MULTIPLICATION AND FACTORING

1. A polynomial is any expression with two or more terms, such as $2x + y$ or $3z + 9m^2$.

2. A single term multiplied by another expression must multiply *every* term in the second expression.

Example: $4(x + y + 2z) = 4x + 4y + 8z$

3. The same holds true for division.

Example: $\dfrac{(a + b + 3c)}{3} = \dfrac{a}{3} + \dfrac{b}{3} + \dfrac{3c}{3}$
$= \dfrac{a}{3} + \dfrac{b}{3} + c$

4. The FOIL method should be used when multiplying two binomials together.

Example: $(x + y)(x + y)$

First $(x + y)(x + y) = x^2$

Outer $(x + y)(x + y) = xy$

Inner $(x + y)(x + y) = xy$

Last $(x + y)(x + y) = y^2$

$(x + y)(x + y) = x^2 + 2xy + y2$

5. You should know these three equivalencies by heart for the GMAT.

$(x + y)^2 = (x + y)(x + y) = x^2 + 2xy + y^2$
$(x - y)^2 = (x - y)(x - y) = x^2 - 2xy + y^2$
$(x + y)(x - y) = x^2 - y^2$

Work all three out with the FOIL method. The x or y could stand for a letter, a number, or an expression.

Example: $(m + 3)^2 = m^2 + 2 \cdot 3 \cdot m + 3^2$
$= m^2 + 6m + 9$

Example: $(2k - p)^2 = (2k)^2 - 2 \cdot 2k \cdot p + p^2$
$= 4k^2 - 4kp + p^2$

6. You will not need much factoring on the exam. Most of what you do need was covered in the preceding points—if you just reverse the process of multiplication.

Example: $3x + 6xy = 3x(1 + 2y)$

Example: $2xyz + 4xy = 2xy(z + 2)$

7. One special situation (called a quadratic equation) occurs when an algebraic multiplication equals zero. Since zero can only be achieved in multiplication by multiplying by zero itself, one of the factors must be zero.

Example: $(x + 1)(x + 2) = 0$
Therefore, either $x + 1 = 0, x = -1$
or $x + 2 = 0, x = -2$.

In such a situation you simply have to live with two possible answers. This uncertainty may be important in Quantitative Comparison questions.

8. You may also need to factor to achieve a quadratic format.

Example: $x^2 + 2x + 1 = 0$
$(x + 1)(x + 1) = 0$

Thus, $x + 1 = 0$
$x = -1$ since both factors are the same.

GEOMETRY

Symbols

The most common symbols used in GMAT geometry problems are listed below. The concepts behind the symbols will be explained in this section.

Angles
∠ or ∡ angle (∠ C = angle C or ∡ C = angle C)
∟ right angle (90°)

Lines
⊥ perpendicular, at right angles to
∥ parallel (line B ∥ line C)
$\overline{BD}$ line or line segment BD

Circles
⊙ circle
$\widehat{AC}$ arc AC

Angles

1. a. An **angle** is the figure formed by two lines meeting at a point.

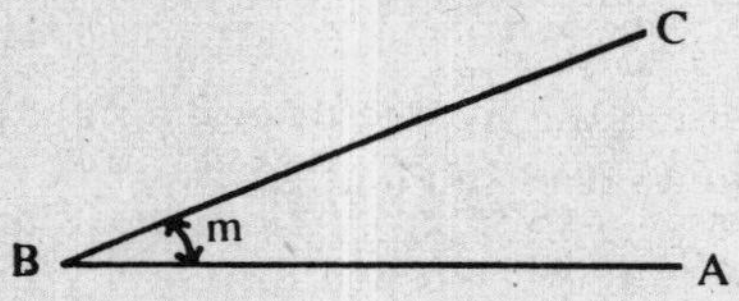

b. The point B is the **vertex** of the angle and the lines BA and BC are the **sides** of the angle.

2. There are three common ways of naming an angle:

a. By a small letter or figure written within the angle, as ∡m.

b. By a capital letter at its vertex, as ∡B.

c. By three capital letters, the middle letter being the vertex letter, as ∠ABC.

3. a. When two straight lines intersect (cut each other), four angles are formed. If these four angles are equal, each angle is a **right angle** and contains 90°. The symbol ∟ is used to indicate a right angle.

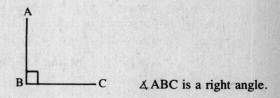

Example:

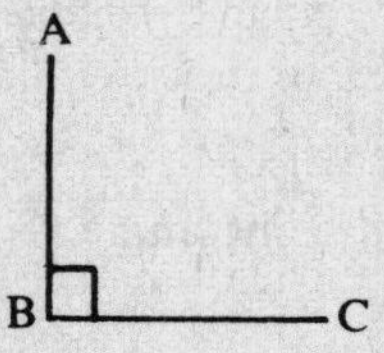

∡ABC is a right angle.

b. An angle less than a right angle is an **acute angle.**

c. If the two sides of an angle extend in opposite directions forming a straight line, the angle is a **straight angle** and contains 180°.

d. An angle greater than a right angle (90°) and less than a straight angle (180°) is an **obtuse angle.**

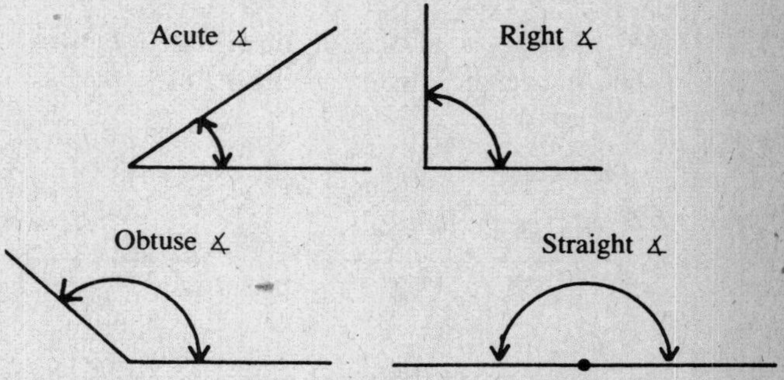

4. a. Two angles are **complementary** if their sum is 90°.

b. To find the complement of an angle, subtract the given number of degrees from 90°.

Example: The complement of 60° is 90° − 60° = 30°.

5. a. Two angles are **supplementary** if their sum is 180°.

b. To find the supplement of an angle, subtract the given number of degrees from 180°.

Example: The supplement of 60° is 180° − 60° = 120°.

Lines

6. a. Two lines are **perpendicular** to each other if they meet to form a right angle. The symbol ⊥ is used to indicate that the lines are perpendicular.

Example: ∠ABC is a right angle. Therefore, AB ⊥ BC.

b. Lines that do not meet no matter how far they are extended are called **parallel lines.** Parallel lines are always the same perpendicular distance from each other. The symbol ‖ is used to indicate that two lines are parallel.

Example: AB ‖ CD

Triangles

7. A **triangle** is a closed, three-sided figure. The figures below are all triangles.

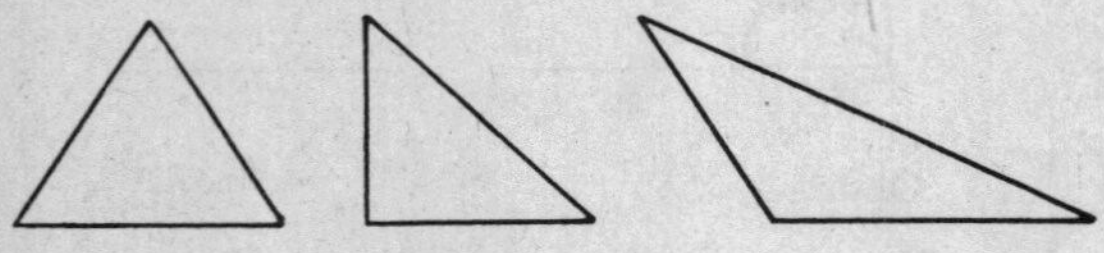

8. a. The sum of the three angles of a triangle is 180°.

b. To find an angle of a triangle when you are given the other two angles, add the given angles and subtract their sum from 180°.

Illustration: Two angles of a triangle are 60° and 40°. Find the third angle.

SOLUTION: 60° + 40° = 100°
180° − 100° = 80°

Answer: The third angle is 80°.

9. a. A triangle that has two equal sides is called an **isosceles triangle.**

b. In an isosceles triangle, the angles opposite the equal sides are also equal.

10. a. A triangle that has all three sides equal is called an **equilateral triangle.**

b. Each angle of an equilateral triangle is 60°.

11. a. A triangle that has a right angle is called a **right triangle.**

b. In a right triangle, the two acute angles are complementary.

c. In a right triangle, the side opposite the right angle is called the **hypotenuse** and is the longest side. The other two sides are called **legs.**

Example: AC is the hypotenuse.
AB and BC are the legs.

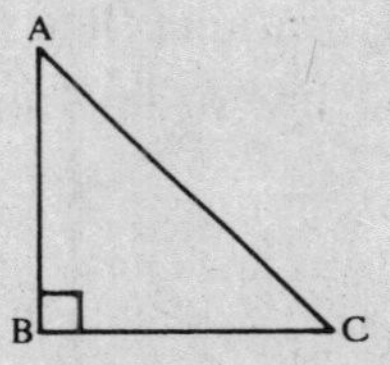

12. The **Pythagorean Theorem** states that in a right triangle the square of the hypotenuse equals the sum of the squares of the legs. In the triangle above, this would be expressed as $\overline{AB}^2 + \overline{BC}^2 = \overline{AC}^2$. The simplest whole number example is $3^2 + 4^2 = 5^2$.

13. a. To find the hypotenuse of a right triangle when given the legs:

a. Square each leg.

b. Add the squares.

c. Extract the square root of this sum.

Illustration: In a right triangle the legs are 6 inches and 8 inches. Find the hypotenuse.

SOLUTION: $6^2 = 36$ $8^2 = 64$
$36 + 64 = 100$
$\sqrt{100} = 10$

Answer: The hypotenuse is 10 inches.

b. To find a leg when given the other leg and the hypotenuse of a right triangle:

a. Square the hypotenuse and the given leg.

b. Subtract the square of the leg from the square of the hypotenuse.

c. Extract the square root of this difference.

Illustration: One leg of a right triangle is 12 feet and the hypotenuse is 20 feet. Find the other leg.

SOLUTION: $12^2 = 144 \qquad 20^2 = 400$

$$400 - 144 = 256$$
$$\sqrt{256} = 16$$

Answer: The other leg is 16 feet.

14. Within a given triangle, the largest side is opposite the largest angle; the smallest side is opposite the smallest angle; and equal sides are opposite equal angles.

Quadrilaterals

15. a. A **quadrilateral** is a closed, four-sided figure in two dimensions. Common quadrilaterals are the **parallelogram, rectangle,** and **square.**

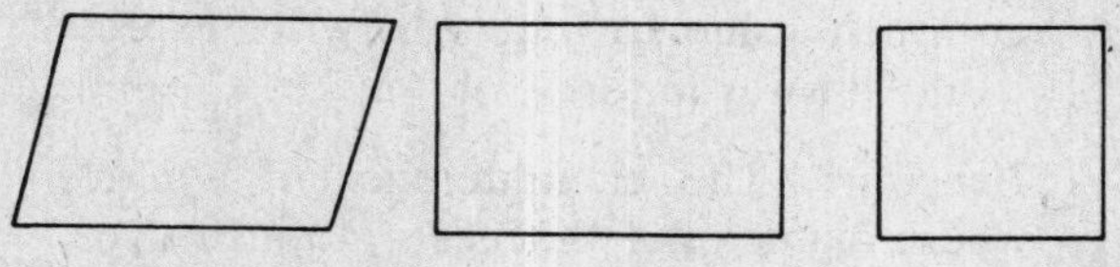

b. The sum of the four angles of a quadrilateral is 360°.

16. a. A **parallelogram** is a quadrilateral in which both pairs of opposite sides are parallel.

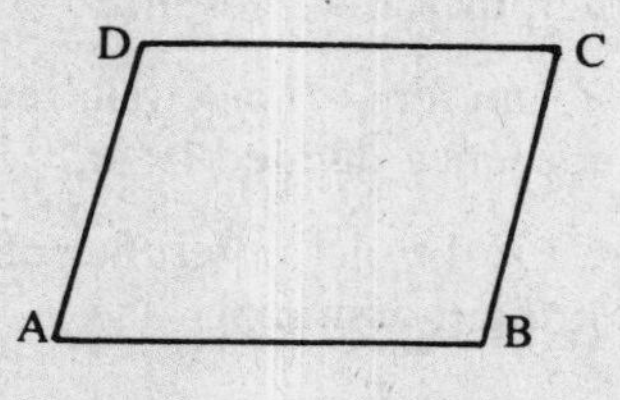

b. Opposite sides of a parallelogram are also equal.

c. Opposite angles of a parallelogram are equal.

17. A **rectangle** has all of the properties of a parallelogram. In addition, all four of its angles are right angles.

18. A **square** is a rectangle having the additional property that all four of its sides are equal.

Circles

19. A **circle** is a closed plane curve, all points of which are equidistant from a point within called the **center.**

20. a. A **complete circle** contains 360°.

b. A **semicircle** contains 180°.

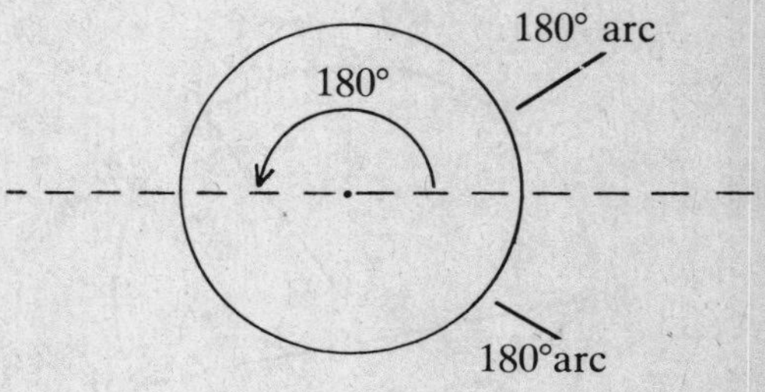

21. a. A **chord** is a line segment connecting any two points on the circle.

b. A **radius** of a circle is a line segment connecting the center with any point on the circle.

c. A **diameter** is a chord passing through the center of the circle.

d. A **secant** is a chord extended in either one or both directions.

e. A **tangent** is a line touching a circle at one and only one point.

f. The **circumference** is the curved line bounding the circle.

g. An **arc** of a circle is any part of the circumference.

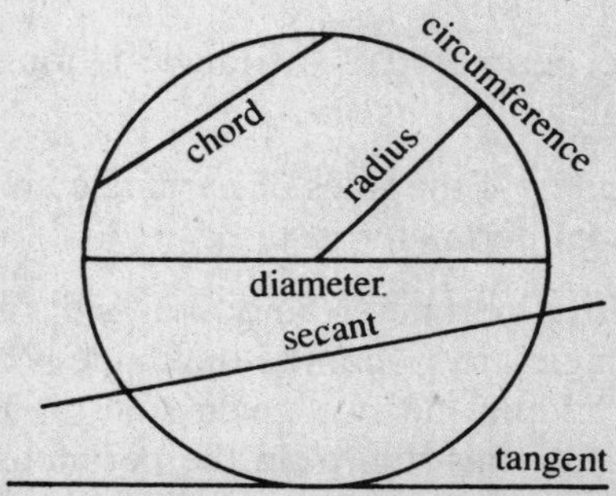

Note: The terms secant and chord are rarely used on the test.

22. a. A **central angle,** as ∠AOB in the figure below, is an angle whose vertex is the center of the circle and whose sides are radii. A central angle is equal to, or has the same number of degrees as, its intercepted arc.

b. An **inscribed angle,** as ∠MNP, is an angle whose vertex is on the circle and whose sides are chords. An inscribed angle has half the number of degrees as its intercepted arc. ∠MNP intercepts arc MP and has half the degrees of arc MP.

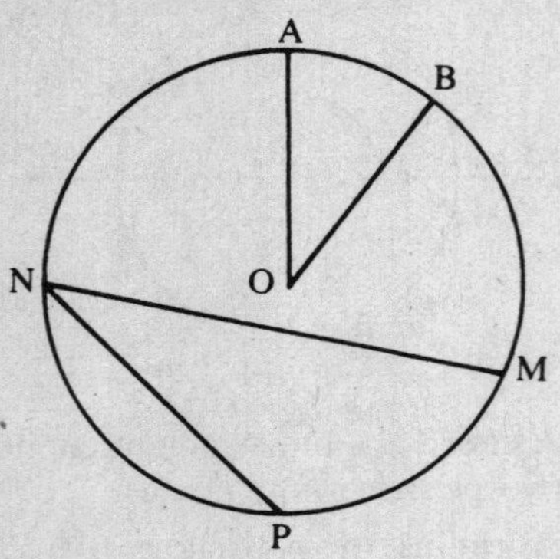

Perimeter

23. The **perimeter** of a two-dimensional figure is the distance around the figure.

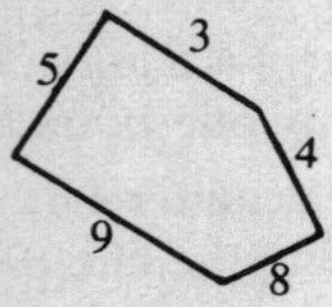

Example: The perimeter of the figure above is 9 + 8 + 4 + 3 + 5 = 29.

24. a. The perimeter of a triangle is found by adding all of its sides.

Example: If the sides of a triangle are 4, 5, and 7, its perimeter is 4 + 5 + 7 = 16.

b. If the perimeter and two sides of a triangle are given, the third side is found by adding the two given sides and subtracting this sum from the perimeter.

Illustration: Two sides of a triangle are 12 and 15, and the perimeter is 37. Find the other side:

SOLUTION: 12 + 15 = 27
37 − 27 = 10

Answer: The third side is 10.

25. The perimeter of a rectangle equals twice the sum of the length and the width. The formula is P = 2(l + w).

Example: The perimeter of a rectangle whose length is 7 feet and width is 3 feet equals 2 × 10 = 20 feet.

26. The perimeter of a square equals one side multiplied by 4. The formula is P = 4s.

Example: The perimeter of a square, one side of which is 5 feet, is 4 × 5 feet = 20 feet.

27. a. The circumference of a circle is equal to the product of the diameter multiplied by π. The formula is $C = \pi d$.

b. The number π (pi) is approximately equal to $\frac{22}{7}$, or 3.14 (3.1416 for greater accuracy). A problem will usually state which value to use; otherwise, express the answer in terms of "pi," π.

Example: The circumference of a circle whose diameter is 4 inches = 4π inches; or, if it is stated that $\pi = \frac{22}{7}$, the circumference is $4 \times \frac{22}{7} = \frac{88}{7} = 12\frac{4}{7}$ inches.

c. Since the diameter is twice the radius, the circumference equals twice the radius multiplied by π. The formula is $C = 2\pi r$.

Example: If the radius of a circle is 3 inches, then the circumference = 6π inches.

d. The diameter of a circle equals the circumference divided by π.

Example: If the circumference of a circle is 11 inches, then, assuming

$$\pi = \frac{22}{7},$$

$$\text{diameter} = 11 \div \frac{22}{7} \text{ inches}$$

$$= \overset{1}{\cancel{11}} \times \frac{7}{\underset{2}{\cancel{22}}} \text{ incheses}$$

$$= \frac{7}{2} \text{ inches, or } 3\frac{1}{2} \text{ inches}$$

Area

28. a. In a figure of two dimensions, the total space within the figure is called the **area.**

b. Area is expressed in square denominations, such as square inches, square centimeters, and square miles.

c. In computing area, all dimensions must be expressed in the same denomination.

29. The area of a square is equal to the square of the length of any side. The formula is $A = s^2$.

Example: The area of a square, one side of which is 6 inches, is $6 \times 6 = 36$ square inches.

30. a. The area of a rectangle equals the product of the length multiplied by the width. The length is any side; the width is the side next to the length. The formula is $A = l \times w$.

Example: If the length of a rectangle is 6 feet and its width 4 feet, then the area is $6 \times 4 = 24$ square feet.

b. If given the area of a rectangle and one dimension, divide the area by the given dimension to find the other dimension.

Example: If the area of a rectangle is 48 square feet and one dimension is 4 feet, then the other dimension is $48 \div 4 = 12$ feet.

31. a. The altitude, or height, of a parallelogram is a line drawn from a vertex perpendicular to the opposite side, or base.

Example: DE is the height.
AB is the base.

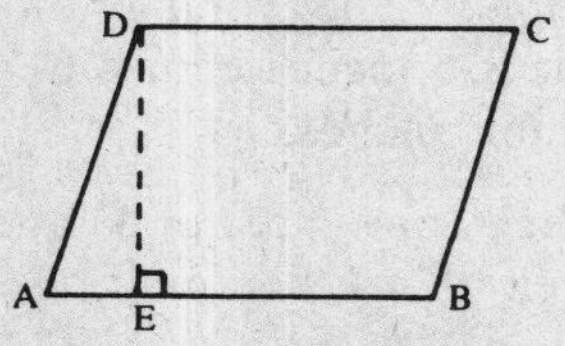

b. The area of a parallelogram is equal to the product of its base and its height: $A = b \times h$.

Example: If the base of a parallelogram is 10 centimeters and its height is 5 centimeters, its area is $5 \times 10 = 50$ square centimeters.

c. If given one of these dimensions and the area, divide the area by the given dimension to find the base or the height of a parallelogram.

Example: If the area of a parallelogram is 40 square inches and its height is 8 inches, its base is $40 \div 8 = 5$ inches.

32. a. The altitude, or height, of a triangle is a line drawn from a vertex perpendicular to the opposite side, called the base. Each triangle has three sets of altitudes and bases.

b. The area of a triangle is equal to one-half the product of the base and the height: $A = \frac{1}{2}b \times h$.

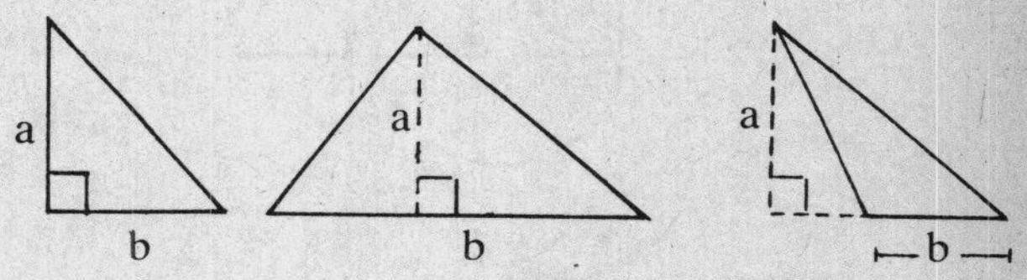

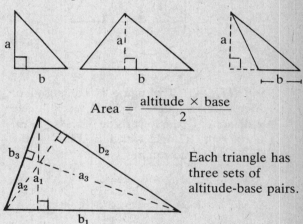

$$\text{Area} = \frac{\text{altitude} \times \text{base}}{2}$$

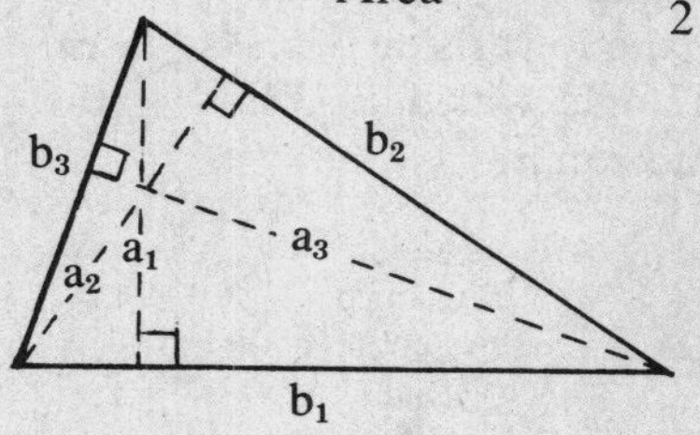

Each triangle has three sets of altitude-base pairs.

Example: The area of a triangle having a height of 5 inches and a base of 4 inches is $\frac{1}{2} \times 5 \times 4 = \frac{1}{2} \times 20 = 10$ square inches.

c. In a right triangle, one leg may be considered the height and the other leg the base. Therefore, the area of a right triangle is equal to one-half the product of the legs.

Example: The legs of a right triangle are 3 and 4. Its area is $\frac{1}{2} \times 3 \times 4 = 6$ square units.

33. a. The area of a circle is equal to the radius squared, multiplied by π: $A = \pi r^2$.

Example: If the radius of a circle is 6 inches, then the area $= 36\pi$ square inches.

b. To find the radius of a circle given the area, divide the area by π and find the square root of the quotient.

Example: To find the radius of a circle of area 100π:

$$\frac{100\pi}{\pi} = 100$$
$$\sqrt{100} = 10 = \text{radius.}$$

34. Some figures are composed of several geometric shapes. To find the area of such a figure it is necessary to find the area of each of its parts.

Illustration: Find the area of the figure below:

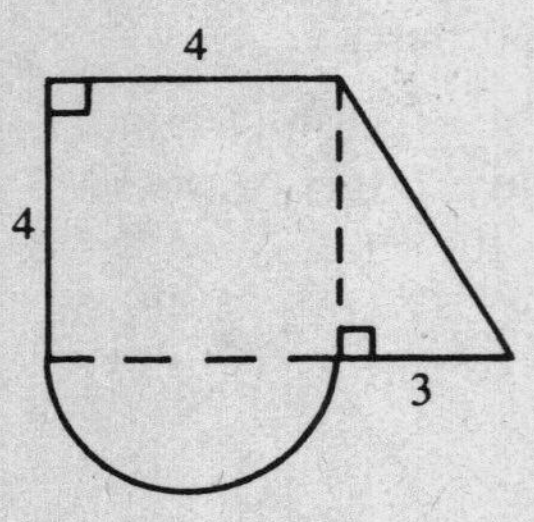

SOLUTION: The figure is composed of three parts: a square of side 4, a semi-circle of diameter 4 (the lower side of the square), and a right triangle with legs 3 and 4 (the right side of the square).

$$\text{Area of square} = 4^2 = 16$$
$$\text{Area of triangle} = \tfrac{1}{2} \times 3 \times 4 = 6$$
$$\text{Area of semicircle is } \tfrac{1}{2} \text{ area of circle} = \tfrac{1}{2}\pi r^2$$
$$\text{Radius} = \tfrac{1}{2} \times 4 = 2$$
$$\text{Area} = \tfrac{1}{2}\pi r^2$$
$$= \tfrac{1}{2} \times \pi \times 2^2$$
$$= 2\pi$$

Answer: Total area $= 16 + 6 + 2\pi = 22 + 2\pi$.

Three-Dimensional Figures

35. a. In a three-dimensional figure, the total space contained within the figure is called the **volume;** it is expressed in **cubic denominations.**

b. The total outside surface is called the **surface area;** it is expressed in **square denominations.**

c. In computing volume and surface area, all dimensions must be expressed in the same denomination.

36. a. A **rectangular solid** is a figure of three dimensions having six rectangular faces meeting each other at right angles. The three dimensions are length, width and height.

The figure below is a rectangular solid; "l" is the length, "w" is the width, and "h" is the height.

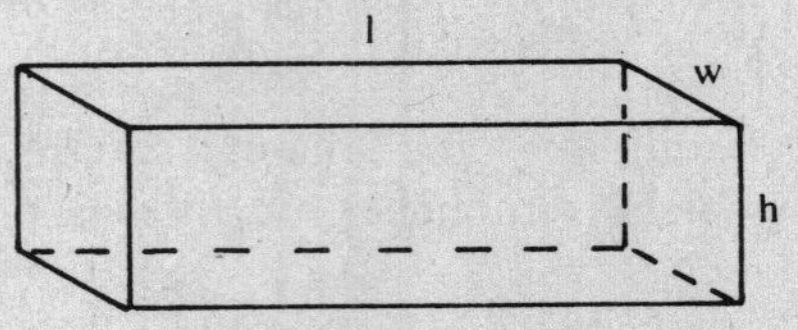

b. The volume of a rectangular solid is the product of the length, width, and height; $V = l \times w \times h$.

Example: The volume of a rectangular solid whose length is 6 feet, width 3 feet, and height 4 feet is $6 \times 3 \times 4 = 72$ cubic feet.

37. a. A **cube** is a rectangular solid whose edges are equal. The figure below is a cube; the length, width, and height are all equal to "e."

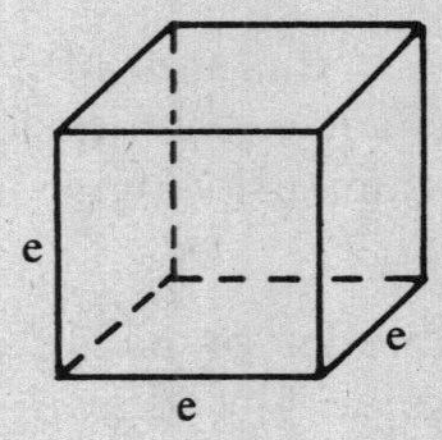

b. The volume of a cube is equal to the edge cubed: $V = e^3$.

Example: The volume of a cube whose height is 6 inches equals $6^3 = 6 \times 6 \times 6 =$ 216 cubic inches.

c. The surface area of a cube is equal to the area of any side multiplied by 6.

Example: The surface area of a cube whose length is 5 inches $= 5^2 \times 6 = 25 \times 6 =$ 150 square inches.

38. The volume of a **circular cylinder** is equal to the product of π, the radius squared, and the height.

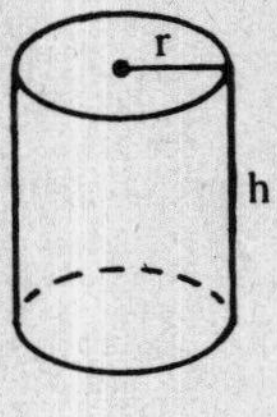

$V = \pi r^2 h$

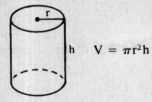

Example: A circular cylinder has a radius of 7 inches and a height of $\frac{1}{2}$ inch. Using $\pi = \frac{22}{7}$, its volume is

$$\frac{22}{7} \times 7 \times 7 \times \frac{1}{2} = 77 \text{ cubic inches}$$

39. The volume of a **sphere** is equal to $\frac{4}{3}$ the product of π and the radius cubed.

$V = \frac{4}{3}\pi r^3$

Example: If the radius of a sphere is 3 cm, its volume in terms of π is

$$\frac{4}{3} \times \pi \times 3 \text{ cm} \times 3 \text{ cm} \times 3 \text{ cm} = 36\pi \text{ cm}^3$$

Practice Problems Involving Geometry

1. If the perimeter of a rectangle is 68 yards and the width is 48 feet, the length is
(A) 10 yd
(B) 18 yd
(C) 20 ft
(D) 46 ft
(E) 56 ft

2. The total length of fencing needed to enclose a rectangular area 46 feet by 34 feet is
(A) 26 yd 1 ft
(B) $26\frac{2}{3}$ yd
(C) 48 yds
(D) 52 yd 2 ft
(E) $53\frac{1}{3}$ yd

3. An umbrella 50″ long can lie on the bottom of a trunk whose length and width are, respectively,
(A) 26″, 30″
(B) 39″, 36″
(C) 31″, 31″
(D) 40″, 21″
(E) 40″, 30″

4. A road runs 1200 ft from A to B, and then makes a right angle going to C, a distance of 500 ft. A new road is being built directly from A to C. How much shorter will the new road be?
(A) 400 ft
(B) 609 ft
(C) 850 ft
(D) 1000 ft
(E) 1300 ft

5. A certain triangle has sides that are, respectively, 6 inches, 8 inches, and 10 inches long. A rectangle equal in area to that of the triangle has a width of 3 inches. The perimeter of the rectangle, expressed in inches, is
(A) 11
(B) 16
(C) 22
(D) 24
(E) 30

6. A ladder 65 feet long is leaning against the wall. Its lower end is 25 feet away from the wall. How much further away will it be if the upper end is moved down 8 feet?
(A) 60 ft
(B) 52 ft
(C) 14 ft
(D) 10 ft
(E) 8 ft

7. A rectangular bin 4 feet long, 3 feet wide, and 2 feet high is solidly packed with bricks whose dimensions are 8 inchs, 4 inches, and 2 inches. The number of bricks in the bin is
(A) 54
(B) 320
(C) 648
(D) 848
(E) none of these

8. If the cost of digging a trench is \$2.12 a cubic yard, what would be the cost of digging a trench 2 yards by 5 yards by 4 yards?
(A) \$21.20
(B) \$40.00

(C) $64.00
(D) $84.80
(E) $104.80

9. A piece of wire is shaped to enclose a square, whose area is 121 square inches. It is then reshaped to enclose a rectangle whose length is 13 inches. The area of the rectangle, in square inches, is
(A) 64
(B) 96
(C) 117
(D) 144
(E) 234

10. The area of a 2-foot-wide walk around a garden that is 30 feet long and 20 feet wide is
(A) 104 sq ft
(B) 216 sq ft
(C) 680 sq ft
(D) 704 sq ft
(E) 1416 sq ft

11. The area of a circle is 49π. Find its circumference, in terms of π.
(A) 14π
(B) 28π
(C) 49π
(D) 98π
(E) 147π

12. In two hours, the minute hand of a clock rotates through an angle of
(A) 90°
(B) 180°
(C) 360°
(D) 720°
(E) 1080°

13. A box is 12 inches in width, 16 inches in length, and 6 inches in height. How many square inches of paper would be required to cover it on all sides?
(A) 192
(B) 360
(C) 720
(D) 900
(E) 1440

14. If the volume of a cube is 64 cubic inches, the sum of its edges is
(A) 48 in
(B) 32 in
(C) 24 in
(D) 16 in
(E) 12 in

Geometry Problems—Correct Answers

1. **(B)**	6. **(C)**	11. **(A)**
2. **(E)**	7. **(C)**	12. **(D)**
3. **(E)**	8. **(D)**	13. **(C)**
4. **(A)**	9. **(C)**	14. **(A)**
5. **(C)**	10. **(B)**	

Problem Solutions—Geometry

1.

Perimeter = 68 yards
Each width = 48 feet = 16 yards
Both widths = 16 yd + 16 yd = 32 yd
Perimeter = sum of all sides
Remaining two sides must total 68 − 32 = 36 yards.
Since the remaining two sides are equal, they are each 36 ÷ 2 = 18 yards.

Answer: **(B)** 18 yd

2. Perimeter $= 2(46 + 34)$ feet
$= 2 \times 80$ feet
$= 160$ feet
160 feet $= 160 \div 3$ yards $= 53\frac{1}{3}$ yards

Answer: **(E)** $53\frac{1}{3}$ yd

3. The umbrella would be the hypotenuse of a right triangle whose legs are the dimensions of the trunk.

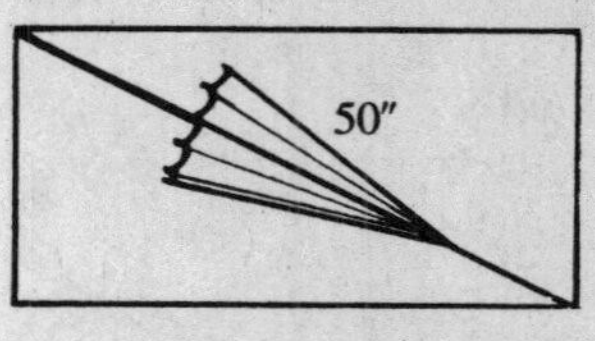

The Pythagorean Theorem states that in a right triangle, the square of the hypotenuse equals the sum of the squares of the legs. Therefore, the sum of the dimensions of the trunk squared must at least equal the length of the umbrella squared, which is 50^2 or 2500.

The only set of dimensions filling this condition is **(E):**

$$40^2 = 30^2 = 1600 + 900$$
$$= 2500$$

Answer: **(E)** 40″, 30″

4. The new road is the hypotenuse of a right triangle, whose legs are the old road.

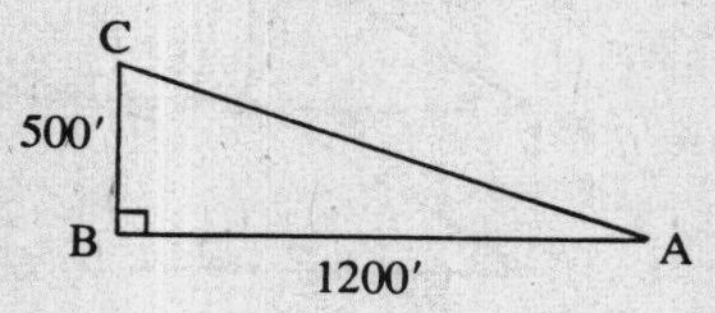

$$AC^2 = AB^2 + BC^2$$
$$AC = \sqrt{500^2 + 1200^2}$$
$$= \sqrt{250{,}000 + 1{,}440{,}000}$$
$$= \sqrt{1{,}690{,}000}$$
$$= 1300 \text{ feet}$$
$$\text{Old road} = 1200 + 500 \text{ feet}$$
$$= 1700 \text{ feet}$$
$$\text{New road} = 1300 \text{ feet}$$
$$\text{Difference} = 400 \text{ feet}$$

Answer: **(A)** 400 ft

5. Since $6^2 + 8^2 = 10^2$ $(36 + 64 = 100)$, the triangle is a right triangle. The area of the triangle is $\frac{1}{2} \times 6 \times 8 = 24$ square inches. Therefore, the area of the rectangle is 24 square inches.

If the width of the rectangle is 3 inches, the length is $24 \div 3 = 8$ inches. Then the perimeter of the rectangle is $2(3 + 8) = 2 \times 11 = 22$ inches.

Answer: **(C)** 22

6. The ladder forms a right triangle with the wall and the ground.

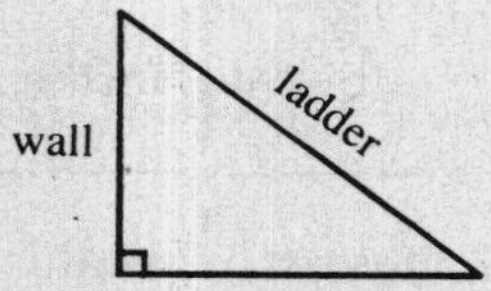

First, find the height that the ladder reaches when the lower end of the ladder is 25 feet from the wall:

$$65^2 = 4225$$
$$25^2 = 625$$
$$65^2 - 25^2 = 3600$$
$$\sqrt{3600} = 60$$

The ladder reaches 60 feet up the wall when its lower end is 25 feet from the wall.

If the upper end is moved down 8 feet, the ladder will reach a height of $60 - 8 = 52$ feet.

The new triangle formed has a hypotenuse of 65 feet and one leg of 52 feet. Find the other leg:

$$65^2 = 4225$$
$$52^2 = 2704$$
$$65^2 - 52^2 = 1521$$
$$\sqrt{1521} = 39$$

The lower end of the ladder is now 39 feet from the wall. This is $39 - 25 = 14$ feet further than it was before.

Answer: **(C)** 14 ft

7. Convert the dimensions of the bin to inches:

$$4 \text{ feet} = 48 \text{ inches}$$
$$3 \text{ feet} = 36 \text{ inches}$$
$$2 \text{ feet} = 24 \text{ inches}$$
$$\text{Volume of bin} = 48 \times 36 \times 24 \text{ cubic inches}$$
$$= 41{,}472 \text{ cubic inches}$$
$$\text{Volume of each brick} = 8 \times 4 \times 2 \text{ cubic inches}$$
$$= 64 \text{ cubic inches}$$
$$41{,}472 \div 64 = 648 \text{ bricks}$$

Answer: **(C)** 648

8. The trench contains

$$2 \text{ yd} \times 5 \text{ yd} \times 4 \text{ yd} = 40 \text{ cubic yards}$$
$$40 \times \$2.12 = \$84.80$$

Answer: **(D)** $84.80

9. Find the dimensions of the square: If the area of the square is 121 square inches, each side is $\sqrt{121} = 11$ inches, and the perimeter is $4 \times 11 = 44$ inches.

Next, find the dimensions of the rectangle: The perimeter of the rectangle is the same as the perimeter of the square, since the same length of wire is used to enclose either figure. Therefore, the perimeter of the rectangle is 44 inches. If the two lengths are each 13 inches, their total is 26 inches, and 44 − 26 inches, or 18 inches, remain for the two widths. Each width is equal to 18 ÷ 2 = 9 inches.

The area of a rectangle with length 13 in and width 9 in is 13 × 9 = 117 sq in.

Answer: **(C)** 117

10.

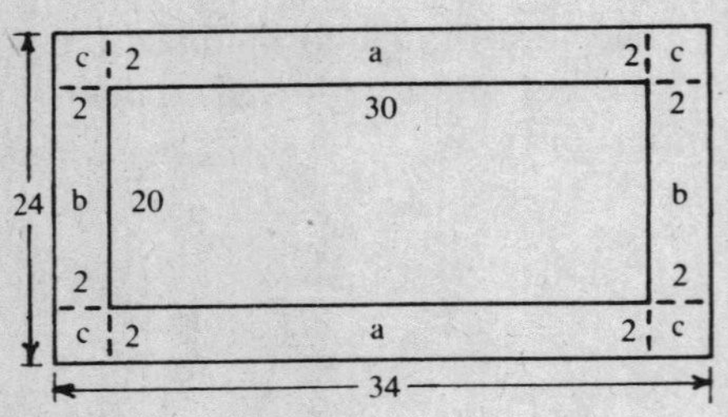

The walk consists of:

a. 2 rectangles of length 30 feet and width 2 feet.

Area of each rectangle = 2 × 30 = 60 sq ft
Area of both rectangles: = 120 sq ft

b. 2 rectangles of length 20 feet and width 2 feet.

Area of each = 2 × 20 = 40 sq ft
Area of both = 80 sq ft

c. 4 squares, each having sides measuring 2 feet.

Area of each square = 2^2 = 4 sq ft
Area of 4 squares = 16 sq ft

Total area of walk = 120 + 80 + 16
= 216 sq ft

Alternate solution:

Area of walk = Area of large rectangle − area of small rectangle
= 34×24−30×20
= 816 − 600
= 216 sq ft

Answer: **(B)** 216 sq ft

11. If the area of a circle is 49π, its radius is $\sqrt{49}$ = 7. Then, the circumference is equal to 2 × 7 × π = 14π.

Answer: **(A)** 14π

12. In one hour, the minute hand rotates through 360°. In two hours, it rotates through 2 × 360° = 720°.

Answer: **(D)** 720°

13. Find the area of each surface:

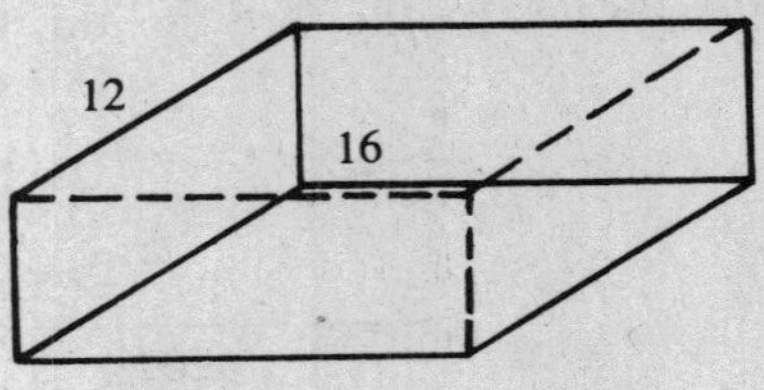

Area of top =	12 × 16 =	192 sq in
Area of bottom =	12 × 16 =	192 sq in
Area of front =	6 × 16 =	96 sq in
Area of back =	6 × 16 =	96 sq in
Area of right side =	6 × 12 =	72 sq in
Area of left side =	6 × 12 =	+ 72 sq in
Total surface area =		720 sq in

Answer: **(C)** 720

14. For a cube, V = e^3. If the volume is 64 cubic inches, each edge is $\sqrt[3]{64}$ = 4 inches.

A cube has 12 edges. If each edge is 4 inches, the sum of the edges is 4 × 12 = 48 inches.

Answer: **(A)** 48 in

COORDINATE GEOMETRY

Perhaps the easiest way to understand the coordinate axis system is as an analog to the points of the compass. If we take a plot of land, we can divide it into quadrants:

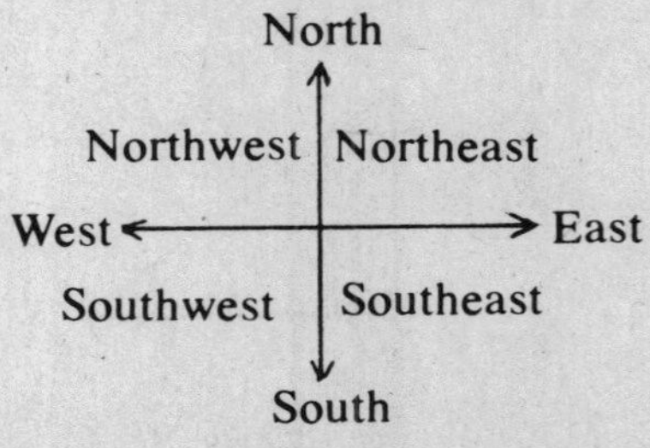

Now, if we add measuring units along each of the directional axes, we can actually describe any location on this piece of land by two numbers. For example, point P is located at 4 units East and 5 units North. Point Q is located at 4 units West and 5 units North. Point R is located at 5 units West and 2 units South. And Point T is located at 3 units East and 4 units South.

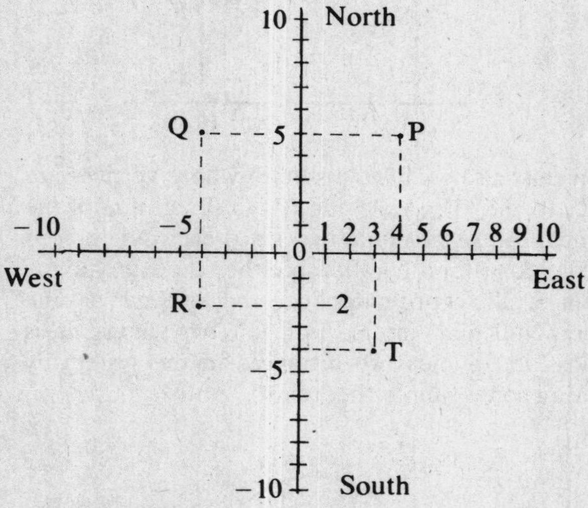

The coordinate system used in coordinate geometry differs from our map of a plot of land in two respects. First, it uses x and y axes divided into negative and positive regions.

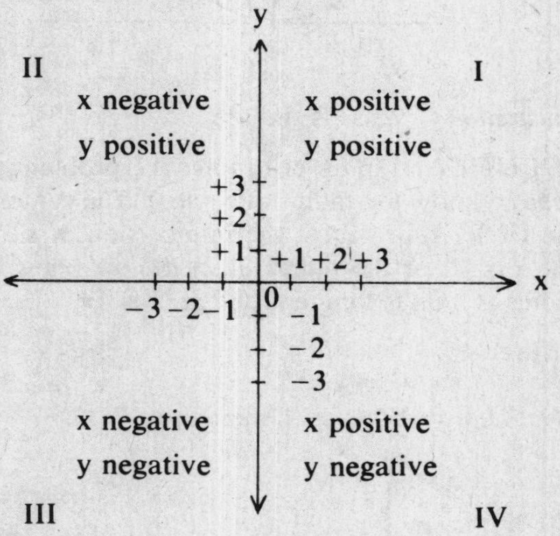

It is easy to see that Quadrant I corresponds to our Northeast quarter, and in it the measurements on both the x and y axes are positive. Quadrant II corresponds to our Northwest quarter, and in it the measurements on the x axis are negative and the measurements on the y axis are positive. Quadrant III corresponds to the Southwest quarter, and in it both the x axis measurements and the y axis measurements are negative. Finally, Quadrant IV corresponds to our Southeast quarter, and there the x values are positive while the y values are negative.

Second, mathematicians adopt a convention called **ordered pairs** to eliminate the necessity of specifying each time whether one is referring to the x axis or the y axis. An ordered pair of coordinates has the general form (a, b). The first element always refers to the x value (distance left or right of the *origin*, or intersection, of the axes) while the second element gives the y value (distance up or down from the origin).

To make this a bit more concrete, let us *plot* some examples of ordered pairs, that is, find their locations in the system: Let us start with the point (3, 2). We begin by moving to the positive 3 value on the x axis. Then from there we move up two units on the y axis.

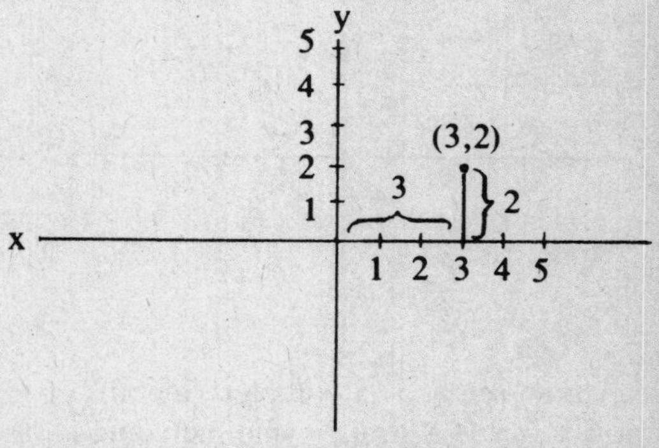

An alternative way of speaking about this is to say that the point (3, 2) is located at the intersection of a line drawn through the x value 3 parallel to the y axis and a line drawn through the y value 2 parallel to the x axis:

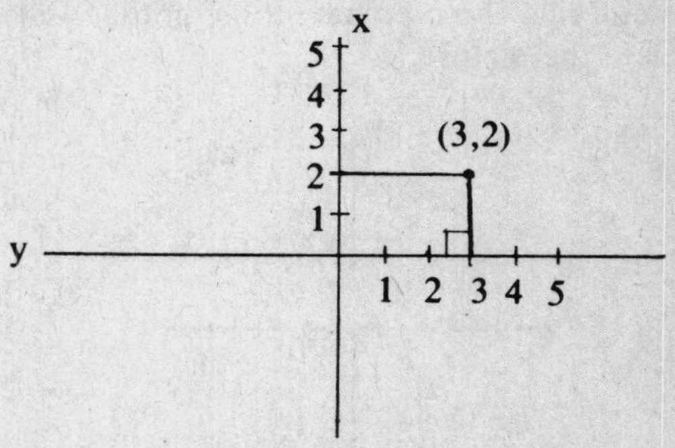

Both methods locate the same point. Let us now use the ordered pairs (−3, 2), (−2, −3) and (3, −2):

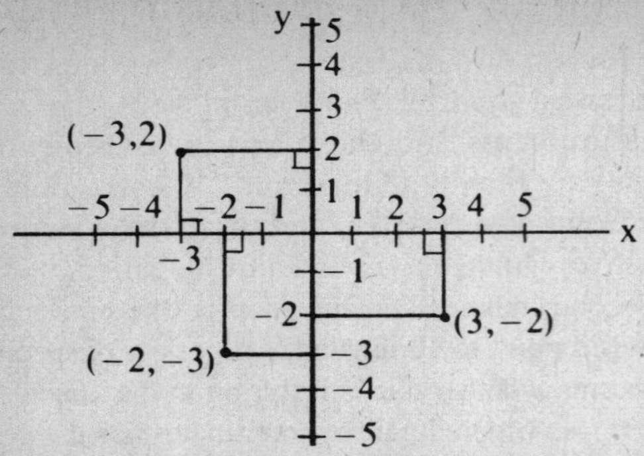

One important use of the coordinate axis system is that it can be used to draw a picture of an equation. For example, we know that the equation x = y has an infinite number of solutions:

x	1	2	3	5	0	−3	−5	etc.
y	1	2	3	5	0	−3	−5	

We can plot these pairs of x and y on the axis system:

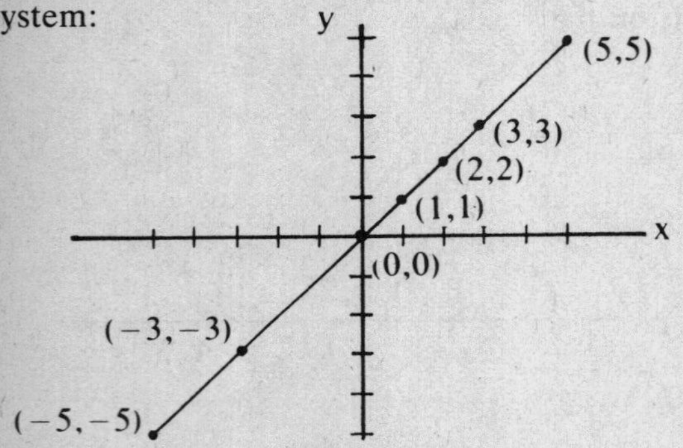

We can now see that a complete picture of the equation x = y is a straight line including all the real numbers such that x is equal to y.

Similarly, we might graph the equation x = 2y

x	−4	−2	−1	0	1	2	4
y	−8	−4	−2	0	2	4	8

After entering these points on the graph, we can complete the picture:

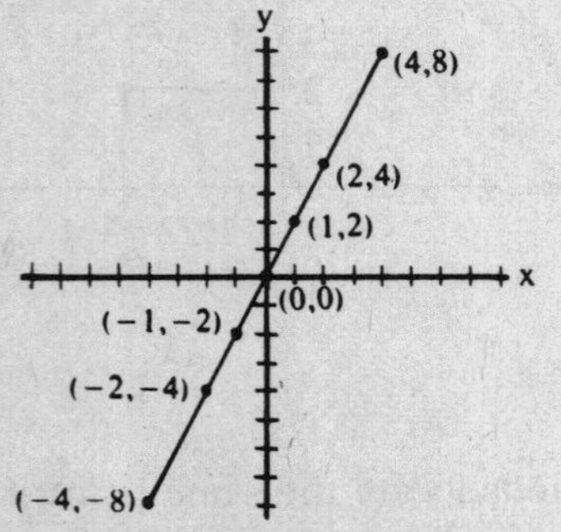

It too is a straight line, but it rises at a more rapid rate than does x = y.

A final use one might have for the coordinate system on the GMAT is in graphing geometric figures:

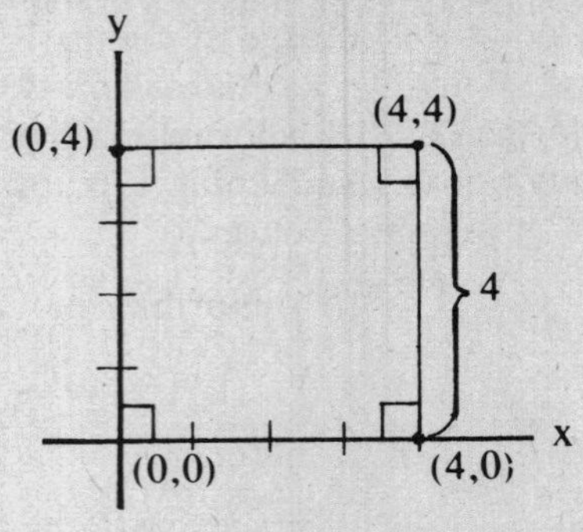

In this case we have a square whose vertices are (0, 0), (4, 0), (4, 4) and (0, 4). Each side of the square must be equal to 4 since each side is four units long (and parallel to either the x or y axis). Since all coordinates can be viewed as the perpendicular intersection of two lines, it is possible to measure distances in the system by using some simple theorems.

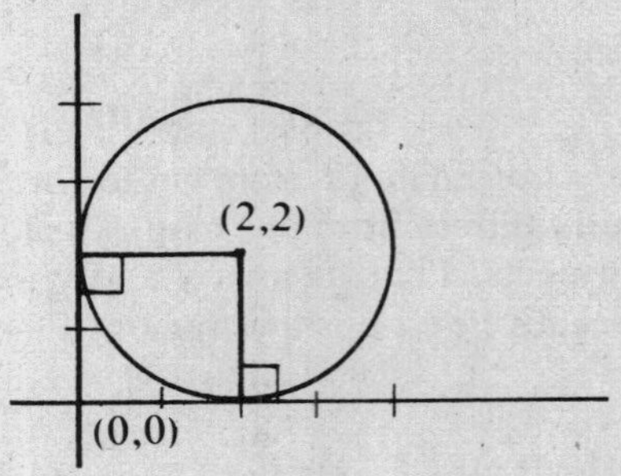

Illustration: What is the area of circle 0?

SOLUTION: In order to solve this problem, we need to know the radius of circle 0. The center of the circle is located at the intersection of x = 2 and y = 2, or the point (2, 2). So we know the radius is 2 units long and the area is 4π.

Answer: 4π

Illustration: What is the length of PQ?

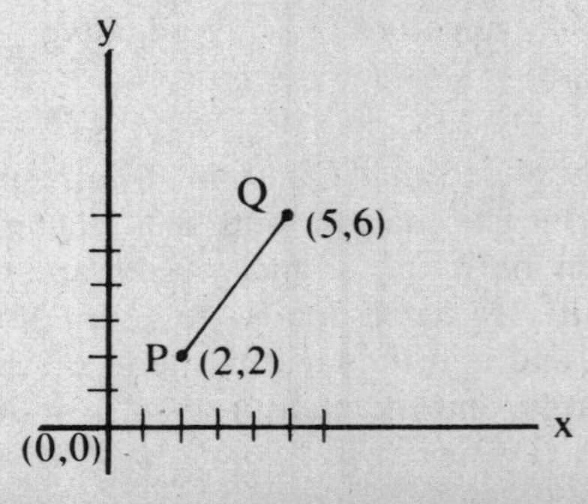

SOLUTION: We can find the length of PQ by constructing a triangle:

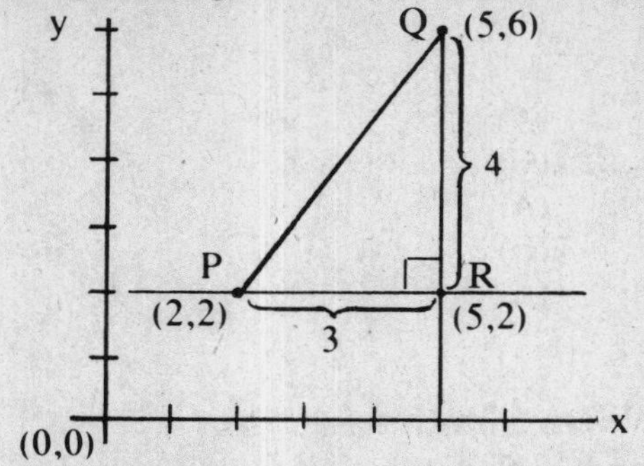

Now, we see that PR runs from (5, 6) to (5, 2) and so it must be 4 units long. We see that QR runs from (2, 2) to (5, 2) so it is 3 units long. We then use the Pythogorean Theorem to determine that PQ, which is the hypotenuse of our triangle, is 5 units long.

Answer: 5 units

It is actually possible to generalize on this example. Let us take any two points on the graph (for simplicity's sake we will confine the discussion to the First Quadrant, but the method is generally applicable, that is, will work in all quadrants and even with lines covering two or more quadrants) P and Q. Now let us assign the value (x_1,y_1) to P and (x_2,y_2) to Q.

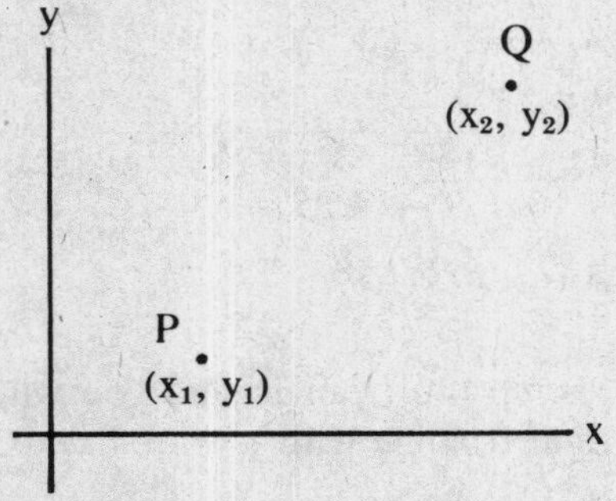

Then, following our method above, we construct a triangle so that we can use the Pythagorean Theorem:

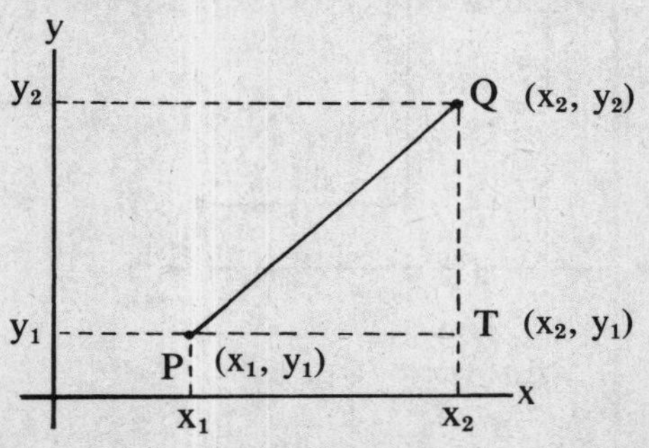

Point T now has the coordinates (x_2,y_1). Side PT will be $x_2 - x_1$ units long (the y coordinate does not change, so the length is only the distance moved on the x axis), and QT will be $y_2 - y_1$ (again, the distance is purely vertical, moving up from y_1 to y_2, with no change in the x value). Using the Pythagorean Theorem:

$$PQ^2 = PT^2 + QT^2$$
$$PQ^2 = (x_2 - x_1)^2 + (y_2 - y_1)^2$$
$$PQ = \sqrt{(x_2 - x_1)^2 + (y_2 - y_1)^2}$$

And we have just derived what is called the **Distance Formula.** We can find the length of any straight line segment drawn in a coordinate axis system (that is, the distance between two points in the system) using this formula.

Illustration: What is the distance between P and Q?

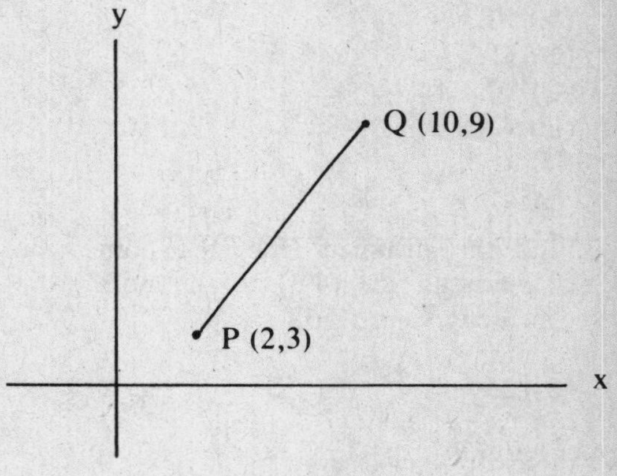

SOLUTION: Point P has the coordinates (2,3) and Q the coordinates (10,9). Using the formula:

$$PQ^2 = \sqrt{(10 - 2)^2 + (9 - 3)^2}$$
$$PQ = \sqrt{8^2 + 6^2}$$
$$PQ = \sqrt{64 + 36}$$
$$PQ = \sqrt{100}$$
$$PQ = 10$$

Answer: 10

For those students who find the Distance Formula a bit too technical, be reassured that the Pythagorean Theorem (which is more familiar) will work just as well on the GMAT. In fact, as a general rule, any time one is asked to calculate a distance which does not move parallel to one of the axes, the proper attack is to use the Pythagorean Theorem.

Practice Problems Involving Coordinate Geometry

1. AB is the diameter of a circle whose center is O. If the coordinates of A are (2,6) and the coordinates of B are (6,2), find the coordinates of O.
   (A) (4,4)
   (B) (4,−4)
   (C) (2,−2)
   (D) (0,0)
   (E) (2,2)

2. AB is the diameter of a circle whose center is O. If the coordinates of O are (2,1) and the coordinates of B are (4,6) find the coordinates of A.
   (A) $(3,3\frac{1}{2})$
   (B) $(1,2\frac{1}{2})$
   (C) (0,−4)
   (D) $(2\frac{1}{2},1)$
   (E) $(-1,-2\frac{1}{2})$

3. Find the distance from the point whose coordinates are (4,3) to the point whose coordinates are (8,6).
   (A) 5
   (B) 25
   (C) $\sqrt{7}$
   (D) $\sqrt{67}$
   (E) 15

4. The vertices of a triangle are (2,1), (2,5), and (5,1). The area of the triangle is
   (A) 12
   (B) 10
   (C) 8
   (D) 6
   (E) 5

5. The area of a circle whose center is at (0,0) is 16π. The circle passes through each of the following points *except*
   (A) (4,4)
   (B) (0,4)
   (C) (4,0)
   (D) (−4,0)
   (E) (0,−4)

Coordinate Geometry Problems—Correct Answers

1. **(A)**
2. **(C)**
3. **(A)**
4. **(D)**
5. **(A)**

Problem Solutions—Coordinate Geometry

1. Find the midpoint of AB by averaging the x coordinates and averaging the y coordinates.

   $$\left(\frac{6+2}{2}, \frac{2+6}{2}\right) = (4, 4)$$

   Answer: **(A)** (4,4)

2. O is the midpoint of AB.

   $$\frac{x+4}{2} = 2 \qquad x + 4 = 4 \qquad x = O$$

   $$\frac{y+6}{2} = 1 \qquad y + 6 = 2 \qquad y = -4$$

   A is the point (0,−4)

   Answer: **(C)** (0,−4)

3. $d = \sqrt{(8-4)^2 + (6-3)^2} = \sqrt{4^2 + 3^2} = \sqrt{16 + 9} = \sqrt{25} = 5$

   Answer: **(A)** 5

4. Sketch the triangle and you will see it is a right triangle with legs of 4 and 3.

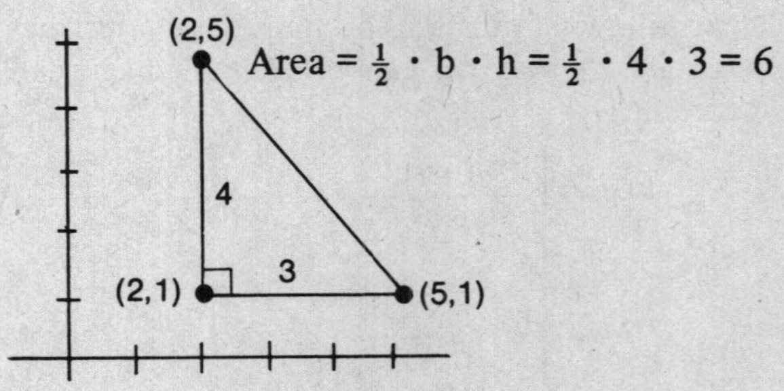

   Answer: **(D)** 6

5. Area of a circle = πr^2

$\pi r^2 = 16\pi \qquad r = 4$

Points B, C, D, and E are all 4 units from the origin. Point A is not.

Answer: **(A)** (4, 4)

SETS

In the past few years a new type of problem—called set problems—has been introduced in the Discrete Quantitative Math sections of the GMAT. These problems give you information about the relationships between different groupings and combinations of persons or objects and ask for the number or percentage in one of the combinations or groupings. The information given in the problem is often in the form of totals for two or more groupings and the approach is to break the situation into separate groupings. This means that your diagram or analysis must always be in terms of the smallest groupings. If the members of a class of students are referred to by sex and by major, then the smallest groupings are males with a certain major, females with that major, etc.

Set problems can also be classified in terms of what is being counted. Usually it is the number of persons or objects that is being discussed, as shown in the following two examples. The third example shows a problem in which the number of memberships, entries, etc., is being counted.

Example: In the ABC Coat Company 85% of the employees are non-managerial and three-quarters are women. If two-thirds of the managers are men, what proportion of the men are non-managers?

(A) 10%
(B) 15%
(C) $33\frac{1}{3}$%
(D) 60%
(E) 75%

SOLUTION: Since there are two ways in which the total work force is divided—sex and managerial status—and the information is given in percentages and proportions, a table can be constructed and filled in, in percentages of the total work force.

	Men	Women	Total
Manager			**15**
Non-Manager			85
Total	**25**	75	100

The numbers in bold type can be calculated by subtraction from 100%. Then we can use the information that two-thirds of the managers are men, which is 10% of the total ($\frac{2}{3} \times 15\% = 10\%$). From this, the entire table can be constructed by subtraction from the known totals:

	Men	Women	Total
Manager	10	5	15
Non-Manager	15	70	85
Total	25	75	100

Answer: $\frac{15}{25}$ = 60% of the men are non-managers, choice (D).

Such a problem could be solved by making a system of equations, but it is much quicker and simpler to do it with a chart.

Another type of problem which is also classified as a set problem is one in which there are two categories and a group of people or objects that are in one or the other of the categories or in both. The key to approaching such a problem is to consider there to be three categories: the first alone, the second alone, and both together.

Example: Thirty-five members of the Sigma fraternity are taking German or French classes. If 25 fraternity members are taking German and eighteen members are taking French, how many are taking both French and German?

(A) 6
(B) 8
(C) 10
(D) 12
(E) 14

SOLUTION: Labeling our three types of fraternity members as F for those taking only French, G for those taking only German, and FG for those taking both classes, we can establish the following equations: F + FG = 18, G + FG = 25, and F + FG + G = 35.

By comparing these three equations we can see that: F must be 10 (difference between second and third equations), G must be 17 (difference between first and third equations), and FG must be 8 (by plugging the values of F and G into the third equation).

Answer: **(B)** 8

This same solution can be achieved by using a diagram, such as two overlapping circles, to indicate the relationships.

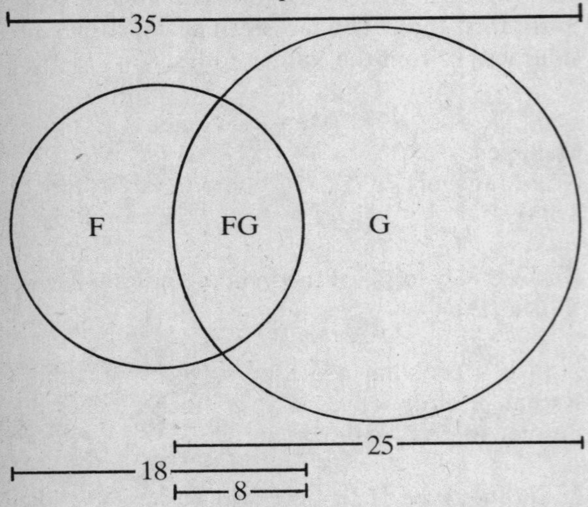

When a problem gives information about the number of memberships, etc., there will be multiple memberships. The solution can be most easily found by counting the number of memberships, etc.

Example: Of 30 adults, 12 belong to club A, 15 belong to club B and 19 belong to club C. If 7 belong to all three clubs and exactly 6 belong to two clubs, how many belong to none of the clubs?
(A) 0
(B) 2
(C) 4
(D) 6
(E) 8

SOLUTION: Adding up the number of memberships in the three clubs gives a total of 12 + 15 + 19 = 46 memberships to be accounted for by the 30 adults. The seven adults with triple memberships account for 21 memberships among them and the six with two memberships account for another 12. Thus 33 memberships are accounted for and only adults with one or no memberships remain. The 46 − 33 = 13 remaining memberships must be 13 people with one membership apiece. Thus

7 adults × 3 memberships =	21 memberships
6 adults × 2 memberships =	12 memberships
13 adults × 1 membership =	13 memberships
4 adults × 0 memberships =	0 memberships
30 adults	46 memberships

Answer: **(C)** 4

Practice Problems Involving Sets

1. Nineteen diners at Joe's Pizzeria are eating only pizza and 26 diners are eating only calzone. If a total of 55 different people are eating either calzone or pizza or both, how many diners are eating both calzone and pizza?
(A) 10
(B) 12
(C) 14
(D) 16
(E) 18

2. Twenty percent of the animals at the Westside Dog and Cat Shelter are male cats. If there are twice as many male dogs as male cats and three times as many dogs as cats at the shelter, what percentage of the cats in the shelter are female?
(A) 5%
(B) 15%
(C) 20%
(D) 30%
(E) 50%

3. A troop of 20 scouts earned a total of 14 merit badges in first aid, 13 merit badges in woodcraft, and 12 merit badges in knot tying. If 10 scouts had earned three merit badges and 5 scouts had earned only one merit badge each, what percentage of the troop had earned no merit badges?
(A) 0%
(B) 5%
(C) 10%
(D) 15%
(E) 25%

Set Problems—Correct Answers

1. (A) 2. (C) 3. (D)

Problem Solutions—Sets

1. There are three categories: calzone only, pizza only, and both. Pizza only plus calzone only comes to 19 + 26 = 45, so 55 − 45 = 10 are eating both. The problem states that the 55 total of diners does not include any other possibility.

   Answer: **(A)**

2. Setting up the table with only the male cats:

	Dogs	Cats	Total
Male		20	
Female			
Total			100

Then, noting the fact that the number of male dogs is twice that of male cats (2 × 20 = 40), and that dogs plus cats must come to 100%, there must be 75% dogs in order for there to be three times as many dogs as cats. (You would know that dogs and cats are the total population both from the title of the shelter and from the fact that those are the only animals mentioned.)

This yields the following table:

	Dogs	Cats	Total
Male	40	20	
Female			
Total	75	25	100

Filling in the remaining boxes by addition and subtraction:

	Dogs	Cats	Total
Male	40	20	60
Female	35	5	40
Total	75	25	100

Thus there are 5% female cats and 25% total cats out of the total animal population, and one-fifth or 20% of the cats are females.

Answer: **(C)**

3. The total number of merit badges earned is 14 + 13 + 12 = 39. The ten scouts with three badges each account for 30 of the badges and the five with one badge each account for another five. This leaves only 4 badges to be earned by those with exactly two badges each, which is two scouts with two badges each. Thus 3 scouts had no badges and $\frac{3}{20}$ = 15% of the scouts had no badges.

10 scouts × 3 badges =	30 badges
2 scouts × 2 badges =	4 badges
5 scouts × 1 badge =	5 badges
3 scouts × 0 badges =	0 badges
20 scouts	39 badges

Answer: **(D)**

DATA SUFFICIENCY INSTRUCTIONAL OVERVIEW

INTRODUCTION

The substance of the Data Sufficiency (DS) section is, of course, very much the same as the Discrete Quantitative (DQ) sections of the test. The scope and relative frequencies of the problem types vary somewhat, but the differences in math content are of little or no use in preparing for this section. The fundamental difference between the DS section and the regular math format sections is precisely the format and the different requirements of that format as well as the different opportunities that the DS format presents for shortcuts and errors.

Since the format difference is of overriding importance, the first step in attacking this section is to develop a comprehensive understanding of both the format and the implications of the format. It is not enough merely to have a knowledge of the stated differences between the five answer choices. Such formal understanding is only the starting point.

Only one counting section of the GMAT will be composed of Data Sufficiency questions. The Data Sufficiency section of the test will have 25 questions and a 30-minute time limit. These questions will be roughly in order of increasing difficulty, but most students have a reasonable chance of getting any question correct; thus, no matter how weak you may feel your math skills are, it is not wise to write off questions without giving them at least a reading. In practice, many students find that once the format is mastered, DS questions actually are easier to do than regular-format (DQ) mathematics questions. The fact that 25 DS questions are given in the same time limit as 20 DQ questions shows that the test makers feel that there is less work to be done on each DS question than on each regular-format math question, whatever the relative difficulties may be in other regards.

THE PARTS OF A DS PROBLEM

If m and n are positive numbers, is m greater than n?

(1) The sum of i, j and k is m.
(2) The average of i, j and k is n.

Every DS problem can be considered to have four parts: the original, or given, information; the question; and the two statements.

Original Information

The given, or original, information is the information given at the beginning of the question, including the diagram (when one is present), which is to be used in considering both of the statements. In one quarter to one half of the problems, there will be no given information separate from the question. In some problems the given information is stated as a conditional, such as "If $p > q > 1$, what is the ratio of p to q?" Usually the given information is in the form of definite statements about the situation, such as "In a certain store, the price of a coat is discounted by 50%. . . ."

When a diagram is part of the given information, it will conform to the rest of the given information but might not conform to one or both of the statements. However, that is unusual. In most cases, the diagram can be used without much limitation.

The Question

The questions that are asked in DS problems divide into two types according to the type of answer they require. One type of question asks

Answer Choice	Is (1) sufficient by itself?	Is (2) sufficient by itself?	Are (1) and (2) together sufficient?
A	Yes	No	Not applicable
B	No	Yes	Not applicable
C	No	No	Yes
D	Yes	Yes	Not applicable
E	No	No	No

for a specific number as an answer. For example, "What is the area of the rectangle ABCD?" or "How many workers will be needed to do the job in three days?" Whenever a specific number is asked for, a definite answer can be considered to be achieved only when there is one, and only one, number that fits the information.

The second type of question requires "yes" or "no" as an answer. Usually one-third of the questions will ask yes/no questions; the remainder will ask for specific numbers.

The Two Statements

The two statements can contain any sort of information that is appropriate to the problem and could even have diagrams associated with them, though that is rare. Each statement will give a particular fact or describe a relationship, or even two facts or relationships on occasion.

The chart above shows another way of presenting the relationship between the sufficiency of the statements and the answer choices. The chart shows that only answer choices C and E raise the issue of using both of the statements together. If either or both of the statements is sufficient by itself to answer the question posed (choices A, B and D), you do not even consider how the two statements work together. Only when you have decided that neither of the statements is adequate by itself (C and E) do you try to evaluate the results of using both statements together.

The chart also shows how you can eliminate answer choices based on your decision about one of the statements if the other one is giving you trouble. If statement (1) is not sufficient by itself, (A) and (D) are eliminated. If statement (1) by itself is sufficient, then choices (B), (C) and (E) are eliminated. Thus, determining the sufficiency of one of the statements will eliminate at least two of the answer choices and lead you to make an educated guess even if you have no idea how to evaluate the other statement.

There is no necessity for you to evaluate statement (1) first. Most of the time you might as well, but where (2) is clearly simpler or easier, or you are having trouble with (1), it is wise to evaluate (2) first.

THE DS INSTRUCTIONS AND ANSWER FORMAT

DIRECTIONS: Each question below is followed by two numbered facts. You are to determine whether the data given in the statements is sufficient for answering the question. Use the data given, plus your knowledge of math and everyday facts, to choose between the five possible answers.

(A) if statement 1 alone is sufficient to answer the question, but statement 2 alone is not sufficient.
(B) if statement 2 alone is sufficient to answer the question, but statement 1 alone is not sufficient.
(C) if both statements together are needed to answer the question, but neither statement alone is sufficient.
(D) if either statement alone is sufficient to answer the question asked.
(E) if not enough facts are given to answer the question.

The essential nature of the DS problem is clear from the instructions. A question is posed, with or without original information, and two additional pieces of evidence are presented. Your task is to identify the degree to which the question posed can be answered by either of the statements independently or by the combination of the two statements.

The first element of these instructions deserving of special attention is the word alone, which appears in the definition of answer choices (A), (B), (C) and (D). The order of attack on the problem is very strict: you *must* consider each statement alone before combining them in any way. This is contrary to your normal, reasonable practice of quickly using all available information when trying to solve a problem. To some extent, this section tests your ability to keep different pieces of information separate and to use only what is appropriate at each step of the problem solution. Since you now know that this mental discipline is precisely what is being tested, you can carefully observe your own thinking as you do these problems to make sure that you do not fall into the trap of using the wrong information at the wrong time.

If you find yourself answering (C) (both statements together are sufficient) when the correct answer is either (A) or (B), it is possible that you are not keeping the information in the two statements separate, and think you are using both when one statement was enough. On the other hand, if you find yourself answering (A) or (B) when the correct answer is (C), you may be using the information from one answer while you are considering the sufficiency of the other.

FURTHER NOTES ON THE ANSWER CATEGORIES AND FORMAT

When the correct answer to a DS question is (D)—each of the statements is enough by itself to answer the question posed—the answers given by the two statements must be compatible. That is, if statement (1) answers the question "What is the value of x?" by showing that x is equal to 5, then if statement (2) gives an answer to the question, it will also be $x = 5$. This is only common sense. They would not set up a situation and give you two different answers. In the case of yes/no questions such as "Is x greater than 0?", a (D) situation will give two statements that answer the question the same way, but they might not be exactly the same numerically. Thus, statement (1) might show that $x = 5$, which gives a yes answer to the question while statement (2) might show that x is greater than 4, which will also give a yes answer to the question and is compatible with $x = 5$.

The way in which this piece of structural information is best used is to help you get a handle on a problem in which the two statements are very different, either in form or difficulty. If one of the statements has proved to be sufficient, this will cast some light on the ways in which the second statement might work. For example:

Does $(a - b)^2 - (a + b)^2 = 24$?
(1) $ab = -6$
(2) $a = 3$ and $b = -2$

It is clear at a glance that (2) is sufficient, since if you know the values of a and b, you will definitely know the value of any equation constructed out of a and b. The real issue is whether (1) is sufficient. There are several possible approaches. One good approach would be to quickly check the values in (2) and see that the expression in the question does equal 24. The next step might be to see a relationship between the -6 found in statement (1) and the 24 found in the question. The relationship is -4, so you know you are looking for a -4. Another approach would be to simply multiply out the quantities that are indicated as squares in the original question. Generally it is good practice to change the forms of algebraic expressions if they are not helpful in their original form. When factors are given and that is not helpful, multiply the factors out. If it is already multiplied out and that is not helpful, then find the factors. In this case, when the two squares are multiplied out you will get $(a^2 - 2ab + b^2) - (a^2 + 2ab + b^2)$. The a^2 and b^2 will cancel out and you are left with $-4ab$. Thus, knowing the value of ab is enough to evaluate the entire expression, and the answer to the problem is (D). This is a good example of the value of having memorized the forms of $(a + b)^2$ and $(a - b)^2$. There is a very good chance that you will need them on the test.

Another hint that can be helpful in a difficult problem is that yes/no questions such as the one above ("Does . . . equal 24?") are almost always answered with a "yes," *if they are answerable at all.* There is no clue that a yes/no question is more likely to be answerable—not an (E)—than any other form of question, nor is there any clue that either or both of the statements is more likely to provide sufficient information. The clue is only that when the statements are sufficient to answer a yes/no question, they almost always answer it "yes." You will almost surely not see more than two yes/no questions per section that are answered "no," and often there are none.

COMMON SITUATIONS IN DS QUESTIONS

The Missing Base

The amount of money, or other measurable quantity, that is represented by a certain percentage cannot be computed unless the base for that percentage is also known.

Which of the two companies, TopFlight, or HiFlyer, has earned the greatest amount of profit in 1981?
(1) TopFlight has earned a profit equal to 10% of its total revenues for 1981.
(2) HiFlyer has earned a profit equal to 5% of its total revenues for 1981.

The amount of 1981 profits cannot be computed. The key word in the question is "amount." TopFlight might have had total sales of $10,000, and HiFlyer total sales of $10,000,000, or the other way around. When the base is given, the amount can be computed. You will often see statements that are insufficient for this reason.

Alternate:
(1) TopFlight earned a 1981 profit 25% greater than its 1980 profit of 10% based on total sales of $876,000.

This would be sufficient. You do not need to compute the actual profit; indeed, it would be a serious error to waste time doing so. However, the 1981 profit is given as a percent of the 1980 profit. If 1980 is computable, so is 1981. 1980 is given as a percent of a stated amount of sales; thus 1980 is computable.

Equivalencies

Some problems will ask you to equate two quantities, both of which are unknown at the start.

In a certain city, two types of snowplows are used, tractor-driven and truck-mounted. The tractor-driven plows clear the roads more slowly than do the truck-mounted plows. How many truck-mounted plows working an 8-hour shift would be needed to clear the same number of miles of streets as 12 tractor-driven plows working 8 hours each?
(1) The tractor-driven plows can clear 2 miles of street per hour.
(2) It takes a tractor-driven plow 50% longer to clear a given street than it takes a truck-mounted plow to clear the same street.

In this problem, you must be careful to seek only what is actually asked. You are asked "how many are equivalent," not "how many," but you are given the equivalent amount of work for the tractor-driven plows. Thus a stated ratio or equivalence between the two types of plows will enable you to find the answer you seek. You do not actually need to know how many miles of street were plowed, but only how many of one type of plow would substitute for a given number of the other. Thus (2) is sufficient by itself and (1) is not needed, which gives an answer of (B).

The Limitations of the Product

In algebra problems, you will sometimes be given information in one or both of the statements about the value of the product of the two variables in the problem. All you know from the result of multiplying two variables together is exactly that—the result of multiplying the two variables together. And a little bit about their signs. If you know that ab = 8, you do not know anything about a in particular. The equation could be rewritten in the form $b = \frac{8}{a}$. The variable a could be any number at all. All that is required is to adjust b to fit. If a times b equals a positive number, then you know that both a and b have the same sign, either positive or negative, and if a times b equals a negative number, then you know that one is positive and one is negative, but you do not know which is which. Of course, if a times b equals zero, you know that one, or both of them, is zero, though again you do not know which one.

This limitation is particularly useful to keep in mind when the question asks something about the specific variables a and b, such as "Is a greater than b?" or does one of them equal a particular number.

A variation in the presentation of information about a product is the presentation of information in the form $\frac{3}{a} = \frac{b}{9}$ or the like. When this particular equation is cross-multiplied, it will take the form ab = 27. It is unusual for a statement to have as complicated a form as $(a + b)^2 - (a - b)^2 = 24$. If such a statement does appear, you can conclude that it can be reduced to a much simpler final result; in this case 4ab = 24.

Number of Variables

In word problems of all sorts (see the discussion of word problems in the Math Review) there will be some number of variables. In a percent problem, the basic relationship is $\frac{\text{number}}{\text{base}}$ = percent. In order to solve for one of these variables, you must have information about the other two. This same idea holds true for any word problem. If you are asked what percent x is of y, you will need either an equation that can show a ratio between those two variables or you will need to link them through some other process. If the average of x, y and z is equal to p, then you can link the sum to p because you have been given the number of items, which is also part of the average equation $\frac{\text{sum}}{\text{of items}}$ = average. Listings of items are often a sneaky way of giving you the total number of items in an average problem. You don't care what the number is, but only that you do have the number available.

Another aspect of the idea of the number of variables comes up when a system of equations is to be used in order to find the value of one of the variables. If there are two variables, p and q, then two equations linking p and q (without any squares or p times q) will be enough to give the value of p and of q because the entire system of equations can be solved. In such situations, however, it is a good idea to look for some shortcut that would make one of the statements sufficient. This is particularly likely to occur when the question is a yes/no question.

If x and y are positive numbers, is x greater than y?
(1) 3x + 2 = y
(2) 5x = y

The kicker here is that both x and y are positive numbers. While this information is not as powerful as an entire equation, it does, in this case, permit answering the question using only statement (2). Note that if x and y were not limited to being positive numbers, (2) would not be sufficient to answer the question since both could be negative numbers, such as x = −1 and y = −5. If the statement about both x and y being positive numbers were not present, then both (1) and (2) would be needed to answer the question. (1) is not sufficient by itself because of the +2.

Integer Questions

Sometimes the question will ask whether a particular variable is an integer or, more often, whether a variable divided by a particular small integer is an integer. In either case, the usual issue is whether some number of variable is evenly divisible by some small integer. For example, if $\frac{x}{333,666}$ is an integer, this means that x is also divisible by 3 since 333,666 is factorable into 111,222 times 3. You can tell, in a pinch, whether any number has a factor of 3 (that is, whether it is divisible by 3) by adding up the digits and seeing if the sum of the digits is divisible by 3. The number 123,456 is divisible by three because the sum of the digits (1 + 2 + 3 + 4 + 5 + 6 = 21) is divisible by three. Of course, all even numbers are divisible by two, and all numbers ending in 5 or 0 are divisible by 5. Knowing that $\frac{x}{512}$ is an integer tells you that x is divisible by 2, but leaves open the question of whether it is divisible by 3 since the sum of the digits in 512 is not divisible by 3 (5 + 1 + 2 = 8).

Regular Geometric Figures

The regular geometric figures that you will see on the exam are the square, the circle, the equilateral triangle, the cube, the sphere and occasionally the hexagon. These figures are called regular because they have the maximum symmetry possible for that type of figure. The practical effect of this symmetry is that if you know almost anything about these figures, you know everything. In a cube, for example, knowing the area of one side will give you the length of the side of the cube ($A = s^2$), and the side of the cube will give you the volume, the length of the diagonals of the sides, and the diagonal of the whole cube. Similarly, knowing the surface area of a sphere will enable you to compute the radius and the volume, etc.

If you are asked to find any specific number having to do with any one of these figures, it will be sufficient to have a specific value for any defined segment of that figure. Or, similarly, if you are asked about some triangle inside of a cube and you are given the side of the cube, this will be sufficient.

Extending Parallel Lines

In most figures that have parallel lines, it is helpful to extend the lines in the figure to show the full intersections with parallel lines. For example:

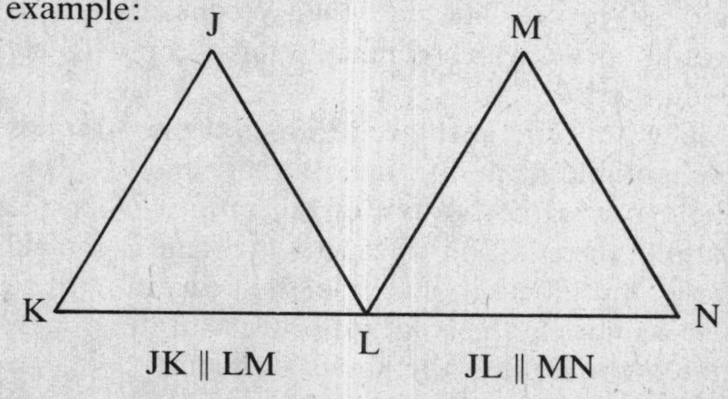

This is much clearer when the lines are extended.

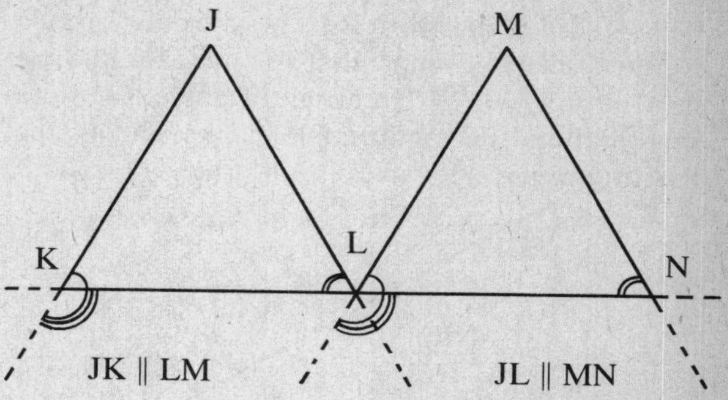

This permits the corresponding angles to be more easily seen and used. If the question asks whether a pair of lines are parallel, extending the lines may be helpful as well.

Key Numbers

There are some numbers which, when they appear, are often clues to the type of situation being presented. These are based on the right-angle triangles formed when the angles are 45–45–90 or 30–60–90. These triangles are discussed in detail in the Math Review. If there is a geometry problem and $\sqrt{2}$ appears, you should check to see if there might be a 45–45–90 right triangle in the diagram. If $\sqrt{3}$ appears, there might be a 30–60–90 right triangle. These numbers sometimes appear in problems without the triangles, but the triangles seldom appear without the numbers.

Plus Does Not Equal Minus

A simple error that many students make is to suppose that when they know the value of the sum of two variables, they know the value of the difference of the same two variables, or *vice versa*. This is not true. If $x + y = 8$, there are many possible x and y pairs which can add up to 8, e.g., 3 + 5 = 8, 4 + 4 = 8. Thus, you do not know $x - y$.

Area of a Triangle

As stated in the Math Review, the only formula for the area of a triangle that you need for this test is Area $= \frac{\text{height} \times \text{base}}{2}$. In a right triangle, the sides surrounding the right angle can serve as the height and base:

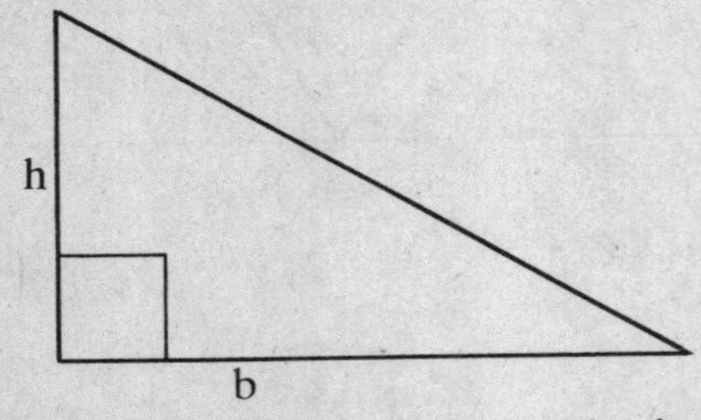

To give the area, this is true of only those two sides. You must be certain that these are, in fact, the sides you are dealing with before you can be certain that the area can be computed. If all that is stated is "Triangle ABC is a right triangle with sides 3 and 4," you do not know that the sides referred to are the legs of the triangle, and not its hypotenuse.

Triangle Errors

The mere fact that two of the sides of a triangle equal 3 and 4, or 3 and 5, or 4 and 5, does not make the triangle a right triangle. If the three sides are 3, 4 and 5, then it is a right triangle because it obeys the Pythagorean theorem as described in the Math Review. Similarly, the fact that the hypotenuse of a right triangle is 5 is not sufficient to determine that it is a 3–4–5 right triangle. There are many solutions to the Pythagorean equation $a^2 + b^2 = 25$; 3–4–5 is simply the only *integer* solution.

Exponent Errors

If the given information, or the question, presents a complicated exponent situation, you will be best advised to simplify it before evaluating the sufficiency of the statements. For example:

If $xy \neq 0$, what is the value of $\frac{x^7\sqrt{y^8}}{(y^2)^2x^4}$?

(1) $x = 3$
(2) $y = 4$

The structure of this problem points out that the concern of this question is precisely whether or not the values of both x and y are needed in order to evaluate the question. The given expression can be simplified as follows:

$$\frac{x^7\sqrt{y^8}}{(y^2)^2x^4} = \frac{x^7y^4}{y^4x^4} = x^3$$

which means that only the value of x is needed, and the answer is (A).

Ratios Don't Add

Sometimes you will be given a ratio or rate or percentage for one time or place or company and then asked for the analogous ratio, rate or percentage for the next year or another place or company. If the information given in the statements allows you to recompute the top and bottom of the ratio, then you can find the new ratio. Also, if a ratio between the old ratio and the new ratio is given in the statements, then you can find the new ratio. However, the test will sometimes give you an absolute number to add to the top and bottom of the ratio and this is not always sufficient:

The ratio of dogs to cats in the New City Animal Home on Tuesday is $\frac{2}{3}$. What is the ratio of dogs to cats on Wednesday if no cats or dogs were taken from the Home on either Tuesday or Wednesday?
(1) 20 dogs were brought to the Home on Wednesday.
(2) 20 cats were brought to the Home on Wednesday.

In this case, you cannot find the new ratio. If there were 2 dogs and 3 cats on Tuesday, then Wednesday's ratio is $\frac{22}{23}$. If there were 200 dogs and 300 cats on Tuesday, then Wednesday's ratio would be $\frac{220}{320}$, which is not the same as previously computed.

The only circumstance in which the new ratio is computable from information that simply adds to the top and the bottom of the ratio is when the ratio of the additions is exactly the same as the old ratio. In that case, of course, the new ratio will be the same as the old ratio. Substitute a new statement (2) into the above problem:

Alternate: (2) 30 cats were brought to the home on Wednesday.

Now the ratio of the added cats and dogs on Wednesday is $\frac{20}{30} = \frac{2}{3}$, which is the same as Tuesday's ratio, so Wednesday's ratio will also be $\frac{2}{3}$. To take the two examples used above, $\frac{2+20}{3+30} = \frac{22}{33} = \frac{2}{3}$, and $\frac{200+20}{300+30} = \frac{220}{330} = \frac{2}{3}$.

Statements Are Not Impossible

Sometimes there will be a statement that gives a relationship which appears at first glance to be impossible, or at least highly unlikely. Since the statements are to be taken as givens, at least for the purposes of seeing whether they will give you enough information to answer the question, you should never just throw up your hands and say that the statement is impossible. The statements will never contradict the given information. If the statement says that $a - b = b - a$, then this fact, by its very unlikelihood, has restricted the possible values of a and b. In fact, $a - b$ can equal $b - a$ only if $a = b$ and $a - b = b - a = 0$. This information would probably be enough to answer the question.

ATTACK STRATEGY

The attack strategy for Data Sufficiency questions is straightforward.

- Read the given information and the question.
- Simplify the given information or the question, if needed.
- Add the information from one of the statements and see if the question can be answered.
- Add the information from the other statement (having put aside the first statement) and see if that is sufficient to answer the question.
- Only if neither statement alone was sufficient to answer the question, consider whether both together are sufficient.

All the relationships that apply to regular math format questions (DQ) also can appear in Data Sufficiency questions.

A LAST WORD

The most common reason for time pressure on Data Sufficiency problems is for students to do too much computing and figuring. In principle, almost none of the Data Sufficiency questions need to be specifically computed or answered in order for you to determine whether you have enough information. In practice, you will need to compute or answer some of the questions to be confident that an answer is indeed obtainable. These should be as few as possible.

READING COMPREHENSION INSTRUCTIONAL OVERVIEW

INTRODUCTION

"Reading comprehension?" you snort. "I know how to read." And you do. But somehow you still make errors on reading comprehension problems.

While reading is a skill that you have practiced nearly all your life, it is one that you—like almost everyone else—could probably improve greatly. We don't mean just speed, or even primarily speed, but COMPREHENSION—getting the meaning, the whole meaning, and nothing but the meaning. Having made that global statement, let us focus on the much narrower and simpler task of improving your score on the Reading Comprehension questions on the GMAT.

We will approach this task by first describing how the Reading Comprehension question appears in the GMAT; second, by identifying different kinds of reading tasks and approaches that you will need on the test; third, by analyzing the types of questions you will be asked and the answer choices among which you will be choosing; and, fourth, by developing an attack strategy.

STRUCTURE AND TIMING OF READING COMPREHENSION QUESTIONS

The Reading Comprehension section of the GMAT will have three reading passages. Each of the passages will have eight or nine questions. The passages will usually be from 450 to 550 words long, with the total number of words in the questions and answer choices for each passage coming to somewhat more than the passage itself. The section will contain a total of 25 questions to be done in 30 minutes.

The passages will usually be writings that are, or could be, from textbooks, journal articles, academic essays, and the like. While they will not often be intrinsically interesting to you personally, they are fairly well written, with definite structure and considerable implicit meaning. Later we will discuss this further. The topics presented will range widely and will usually include passages from the humanities and social sciences, with some fairly technical-sounding passages from such fields as economics, psychology, and occasionally even the physical sciences. The topics are not really important since in principle you can always answer all of the questions even if you have no knowledge of the field other than what the passage says.

You will often, correctly, be told: THE RC SECTION IS NOT A TEST OF KNOWLEDGE, BUT ONLY OF READING SKILLS. While this is basically true, it is also true that you are expected to use two general areas of knowledge—language and common sense. The linguistic knowledge required is not knowledge of esoteric vocabulary, but the ability to read closely and know the precise relationships expressed by common words. Common sense knowledge is merely what any reasonably alert college graduate could be expected to know. For example:

Cows are the source of beef, cows are deliberately raised by humans for food and not simply harvested like fish. China is a country, theology has to do with God, etc.

TIMING FOR READING COMPREHENSION PASSAGES

Many students are very worried that their reading speed is inadequate for the test. They often base this feeling on the experience of having wanted more time than was available for the reading sections of this or other tests. READING SPEED IS NOT THE KEY TO THE GMAT.

You will only have to read about 115 words per minute, perhaps less, for the whole section, including passages, questions, and answer choices. This is well within the capacities of virtually any college graduate. Of course there is one other little matter—you have to think about the questions and answer them.

Although one of the passages will have nine questions and there is some variation in the total number of words among the passages, it is generally best to allocate your time equally among the three passages—that is, ten minutes for each passage. The first passage is usually slightly easier than the others, but it is often the one with nine questions. If you finish the first passage in less than ten minutes, you can always go on to the next passage. You should be rather careful that you do not let yourself run over the ten minutes for each of the first and second passages or you will not have adequate time to do any good work on the third passage. It is better to leave one or two of the harder questions unresolved on the first two passages than to sacrifice a good understanding of all eight or nine questions on the last passage. For most students, the ten minutes available for each passage should be devoted to that one passage including reviewing or reattacking of questions that may have to be done. To try to come back to the first passage, for example, after completing the third passage is not usually efficient, since the passage will no longer be fresh in your mind and you will need to reread the passage and the questions. The ten minutes per passage is best divided as shown in the chart below. The timing is approximately the same for both eight-question and nine-question passages.

Previewing Questions	45 seconds
Reading Passage	4 minutes
Answering Questions	5 minutes 15 seconds
Total	10 minutes

This works out to approximately five seconds per question for the previewing, 25–30 seconds per question for reading the passage, and 35–40 seconds per question for answering the questions.

The most important thing for you to remember about this timing recommendation is that it is not rigid. It is certain that you will not follow it exactly for most passages, so don't worry. The second most important thing is that you spend more time answering the questions than reading the passage. While this will not always be possible with a longer or more obscure passage, it's the goal you should strive for. The questions and answers between them will usually have even more words to read than the passage, words that are not all connected together. In addition, you will have to think about the answer choices to the questions since many are rather similar, as we will discuss later. While it is true that you have to think about the passage while you read it, there is still more work to be done with the questions than with the passage. Furthermore, your natural impulse is to feel that if you could memorize the passage all your troubles would be over and the questions would answer themselves. Nothing could be further from the truth. Practically none of the RC questions will merely ask you to parrot back what was in the passage. At the least, you will need to use different words and often you will need to work from underlying structures and implicit ideas, again as we will discuss later. All of this means that your goal is to read the passage carefully but briskly once, thinking all the while, and then to work the problems briskly but carefully.

The previewing of the question stem that is recommended is a very quick reading of just the part of the question which asks the question, not the answer choices or roman numeral propositions, if any. There are three purposes to this preview. First, it can alert you to most of the questions that concern details or have references to specific parts of the passage ("line 20" or "first paragraph," etc.); this foreknowledge can save you time and improve accuracy, though it only applies to a few questions. Second, it can give you some idea of the topic and approach of the passage so that you can more easily follow it; this can be particularly helpful when the passage has a broad range, or a beginning that is quite different from its body. Third, by giving you some clues and structure for your reading of the passage, this preview can combat both fatigue and boredom. As interested as you are in your score, you may find the passages less than thrilling. If you can persuade yourself that it is a detective game—which it is, of sorts—you might keep up your interest and do better.

Most students find previewing the questions very helpful and reassuring. Try this technique on the practice tests in this book. If you personally find that you are not comfortable with it and you can do well without previewing the questions, then don't do it.

Another issue that affects timing is the question of referring back to the passage while considering a particular question. Naturally, it is quickest to answer a question without referring back to the passage. You should make as much progress as possible in eliminating answer choices and choosing the correct answer before you let yourself refer back to the passage. You should be able to answer most questions without having to refer to the passage—provided you have done a reasonably good job in reading the passage in the first place. On some questions, you will need to refer back to the passage to distinguish between a few answer choices or to get a handle on a particular idea or phrase.

When you do need to refer back to the passage it is very important to do so efficiently. You certainly do not have time to re-read the entire passage for each question. Before you go back to the passage, try to be clear in you mind just which part or parts of the passage are relevant. This can be deduced from the overall structure of the passage and your understanding of where the idea you are checking fits into that structure. For instance, a passage may trace the chronological development of theories of electricity. If the question asks about Galvani's ideas, you may remember that Galvani was fairly early on and thus go to the earlier parts of the passage. A few seconds (two or three) spent in fixing the position of the idea you are checking in the structure of the passage will not only save time in the review, but also improve your ability to understand the material you are reviewing.

If you have no idea where or how the idea in the question relates to the passage, leave the question to the end of the time allotted for that passage and do the rereading only if you do have time after answering the other questions.

DIFFERENT KINDS OF READING AND HOW TO DO THEM

Four aspects of reading will concern us here:

1. literal versus implicit meaning
2. precision versus imprecision
3. active versus passive reading
4. "test reading" versus "real-world" reading

These are not entirely separate ideas, nor will you find them strange. You have been reading successfully for many years and all we will try to do in this section is help you to improve by making you conscious of and emphasizing the reading skills most used on the GMAT.

We will use the following short passage as the basis of our discussions of both the different kinds of reading and the different kinds of questions on the GMAT. Whenever a question is asked about the passage, try to answer it before you read the explanation.

> One dependable characteristic of the cattle cycle is the biologic time lag in the production process.
>
> Heifers are not bred for their first calf until they are 14 to 18 months old. Then the gestation period is 9 months. The calf, in turn, won't reach mature slaughter weight for another 17 to 19 months, depending on the individual calf's rate of gain and the feeding program.
>
> Consequently, it takes up to 4 years from the time a cattle producer's heifer is born until her offspring reaches slaughter weight. If this offspring is retained to expand the herd rather than sent to slaughter, it could be about 5½ years from the time the first calf is retained in the herd until an offspring reaches slaughter.
>
> Because of the time lag, beef production continues to increase well beyond the time price signals change. This happened in the 1974–76 period. Beef production kept increasing despite the large financial losses to cattle producers.

Literal Versus Implicit Meaning

Literal meaning is the meaning of the passage that is explicitly stated. For instance:

1. What is the period of gestation in cattle?

The answer is found by looking up the period in the second paragraph of the passage (or by memory) and noting that it is 9 months.

2. What happened to beef production and prices during 1974–76?

In the last paragraph it is stated that the production kept increasing despite lower prices and large losses.

Although it is hard to do anything with a passage if you do not even see its literal meaning, most of the questions and most of the information in a passage—even one as simple and descriptive as this one—is carried in the implicit meanings. There are many kinds of implicit meanings, but they are all essentially the same idea. The connections between the different parts of the passage and the fact that the specific literal ideas are presented in particular orders and with particular emphases and relationships conveys additional meaning. There is, of course, no absolute dividing line between explicit and implicit. Some ideas can be understood in several ways.

3. What is a heifer?

A heifer is a young cow. This could be known by prior knowledge (not much of that on the GMAT, though) or you could see that it is implied from the statement in the passage that heifers are the cattle which give birth, hence female by our common knowledge of mammalian reproduction, and are young since it is the earliest they can be bred. The latter is a little less sure than the former.

4. What is the cattle cycle referred to in the first sentence?

Here we begin to get into what the answer is not. The cattle cycle is not the generations of cattle or the process of getting one cow from another. That would be the biologic cycle perhaps. We know this because if something (the biologic cycle) is a characteristic of something else (the cattle cycle), then the characteristic is not likely to be the whole thing.

What, then, is the cattle cycle? The last paragraph tells us that there is a price movement as well, and that the price movement and the biologic movement have been out of synchrony. This leads to the idea that the cattle cycle is some sort of cycle involving the prices, the production or number of cattle, and the biologic cycle of cattle. Since it is referred to as a cycle, it presumably goes up and down. Therefore, we might see a further question of this sort.

5. What probably happened to beef prices and cattle supplies after 1976?

Since the cycle had been on a down price and up cattle supplies part of the cycle through 1976, one would expect a reduction in herd size and an increase in prices after 1976. This would be followed by a natural desire for the cattle producers to increase their herds to take advantage of the higher prices (deduced from the cyclic nature of things, reinforced by common sense applied to basic business). This would gradually lead to a general increase in cattle supplies and an eventual decrease in prices, thus completing the cycle.

6. How long does a cattle cycle probably take?

This is not a question that can be answered with great confidence. One would actually have to work with the answer choices to some extent as will be described in the section on questions. However, we CAN imply from the passage that the cycle must involve at least 6 years or more since it will take at least that long for the herds to have increased through two generations. An answer choice of less than 5 years would be too short to allow really major changes in cattle supplies and one longer than 15 years (maybe 10) would not be good since it would not recognize the building up of oversupply. The upper limit is much less certain than the lower.

We will leave this topic now, though it will be carried forward further in the discussion of the kinds of questions which you will be asked, and the proper approaches to them. Many examples of this sort of reading are explained in the answer explanations for the practice test RC questions.

Precision in Reading

Many of the implications which you will be called upon to see in the passages on the test will be strong or weak or even possible because of the precise wording of the passage. It is very important, however, to remember that precision is not the same as subtlety. An example of precision is the difference between *can* and *will* in these two sentences:

> Inflation can be controlled.
> Inflation will be controlled.

These sentences have very different meanings. The first states that it is possible to control inflation, while the second states that not only can it be controlled, but also that this happy outcome will occur. The difference is not subtle in any way, even though it turns on a single word.

In the passage about cattle, the first sentence used the word cycle, and we were able to learn a lot from the fact that the cattle situation was a cycle. If the sentence had only referred to a problem or an industry we would have known much less about what was happening.

There are too many possible sentences for us to hope to classify them all for you, nor is that needed. There is one fundamental idea which you need to apply: EVERYTHING COUNTS.

In order to fully understand this injunction that everything counts, let us remember just what the test-writers are interested in and with what sorts of passages you will be dealing. The test-writers want to see how well you can get the fullest understanding—comprehension—from a passage. To permit a good test of that skill, they will usually give you passages that—unlike much writing—are highly structured and fairly well written. We must immediately point out that interest, vitality, and style are not within the scope of the writing we are now describing, though some passages have those qualities. What we are referring to is the fact that the authors of the passages have thought about the structure of their sentences and paragraphs and about their choice of words rather carefully. We may assume that whatever words or structures are in the passages are intended to convey every bit of meaning that can reasonably be wrung from them.

Thus, if the word cycle is used, you must conclude that it was precisely a cycle that was meant and not merely an event, period, or circumstance.

How, you may be wondering, can the reader possibly catch all of this precision in less than 39 readings of the passage? The answer to this reasonable question is contained in the third aspect of reading we will treat in this section.

Active Versus Passive Reading

Every piece of reading is done differently. If you are reading a book in bed at night in order to relax and go to sleep, you will probably read more slowly and without as much attention to detail than if you were studying the same book in order to write a major analytic paper on it. But no matter how fast or with how much concentration you are reading, you are always thinking about what you are reading as you are reading it.

When you are watching television or looking up at the clouds after a summer picnic, you may be doing practically nothing but passively receiving visual stimuli.

When you read, however, your understanding depends on how much thinking you are doing while you are reading. Indeed, even pure memorization of a passage will be improved if you have done some good thinking about it while you were reading.

Active reading, then, is reading accompanied by sustained, intense thought about the passage being read: not a conscious counterpoint to the passage, but just feeling the gears whirring underneath, where most thought occurs.

As we have mentioned, it is the structure and implicit meanings of the passage that will be the major subjects of the questions on the test. Therefore, you will want to be constantly trying to "dig the bones" of the passage. Here are some of the questions you should be considering as you read:

—How is this idea connected to previous ones in the passage?
—What is likely to follow (from) this idea?
—What is the author's purpose in making this particular statement at this particular place in the passage?
—What does this prove, exemplify, demonstrate, etc.?
—Is this a continuation of some previous idea or the introduction of a new line of thought?

Connections, connections—that is always your concern. Always working while you are reading is your method of finding them in the time available. You do this all the time; all that you need to do on the GMAT is do this a little bit more.

"Test Reading" Versus "Real-world" Reading

When you are reading an article in the real world you will be trying to link what the article is telling you to everything else that you know. This is the most powerful sort of reading that you can do. In practice, of course, you don't quite manage to make a complete cross-referencing to everything you know about every topic, but you probably pretty well cross-reference to a lot of what you know about the specific topic of the passage and related topics.

On the test you don't do the same thing. The GMAT is not a test of your previous knowledge of the topic of the passage, nor of any particular previous knowledge at all except language and reading skills. All the test is concerned with is the INTERNAL linkages within the passage. This makes your job much easier. All you have to do is correlate all of the parts of the passage with each other and understand whatever can be implied from that. While there are hard and easy questions, you will find after a while that the difficulty of the questions is largely a matter of the range of answer choices and not so much a matter of the passage's difficulty. Focusing on the internal linkages within the passage actually reduces the work a great deal.

ANSWERING THE DIFFERENT TYPES OF RC QUESTIONS

We will analyze RC questions in two ways: formal structure and linkage to the passage. In the latter we will analyze the different types of question stems and what they are asking of you. Then we will discuss the fundamental rules for answering RC questions prior to developing an attack strategy in the next section.

Formal Structure

The directions ask you to select the best answer choice out of the five available. This means just what it says. The correct answer choice will be better than any of the others. It may be all but perfect and surrounded by other good choices, or it may be fairly poor and surrounded by totally unacceptable choices. While all of the correct answer choices have merit, there are wrong answer choices which also have merit and some correct ones whose main claim is the poverty of their competition. For this reason you always read all of the answer choices.

The question stem for the RC question, as for most Verbal questions, sets up a criterion by which to judge the answer choices. Any answer choice may relate to the criterion in three basic ways: definitely meets the criterion, definitely fails the criterion, or it is not known how it relates to the criterion. Therefore, when the question asks which answer choice is, for example, true, the incorrect answer choices may be either false or indeterminate. In addition, two or more of the answer choices may have some measure of truth and you have to choose the one which is most strongly deducible.

When the question states that all of the answers are, for example, agreeable to the author EXCEPT . . . , then the incorrect answers are agreeable, though the agreeableness of some may be more strongly supported than that of others, and the correct answer choice may be either known to be disagreeable or something whose agreeableness is not determinable.

For Roman-numeral-format questions, you can make good progress even if you only know one or two of the propositions. Use the ones you know to eliminate answer choices.

The strength and scope of the questions and the answer choices is very important.

Linkage to the Passage

Each and every question that you face on the test has the unstated introductory clause "In light of what the passage says or implies. . . ." Some questions actually say "according to the passage," or "according to the author," etc. But you will always have that in your mind whether it is said or not.

While it is possible to consider every question to be asking for you to make some sort of inference, we shall first sort out some other, slightly more restricted sorts of questions before addressing the general topic of inference questions as the residual category of questions. We will discuss the following kinds of questions:

—Specific details (0–2)
—Purpose (1–3)
—Tone (1–3)
—Identity of author or other person (0–2)
—Use of evidence (2–5)
—Main idea, including title (4–7)
—Logical reasoning or method of argument (1–3)
—Inference, implication, author agree, trend, or stated or implied (5–8)

The numbers in parentheses following each question type are a very approximate indication of the typical range of frequency for that question type in a single Reading Comprehension Section. The types are not utterly distinct, and some variants, combinations, or just plain oddball questions are perfectly possible, but there won't be many.

Specific details questions. There may be a few questions which essentially ask you to report something which is specifically stated in the passage. These would be questions such as questions 1, 2, or 3 previously discussed. If you see this sort of question, be very careful in checking the answer choices for qualifiers and limiters that may be the difference between one choice and another. Also, more than one quality or descriptor may go with a particular idea and the correct answer choice may be somewhat more comprehensive than the incorrect ones.

Purpose of the passage or author. If the passage is just a description of something, then the purpose will be to describe whatever the passage describes. The purpose can also be explanatory of some aspect of the passage which is implicit. In the illustrative passage about the cattle cycle, for example, you might have the following:

7. What is the author's purpose in writing the passage?
   (A) To describe the problems of ranchers.
   (B) To justify the cattle cycle.
   (C) To explain how the cattle cycle can lead to apparently irrational actions by cattle producers.

(A) has the merit of saying that some problem is being explained, which is true of the passage. It is not, however, especially the problem of ranchers, but of cattle producers. This is a matter of precision reading.

(B) has the merit of referring to the cattle cycle, which is certainly a major part of the passage. However, justify means to show why something is good, usually in spite of appearances to the contrary. The cycle just is, and the author isn't in favor of it.

(C) is the best answer since it amounts to saying that the purpose of the passage is to justify the cattle producers' actions as being not irrational in the least because of the lag time. Justify might be too strong anyway, so the use of explain in (C) is better.

Thus, a purpose must match the passage as precisely and completely as possible. Generally, it will reflect the bulk of the passage similar to the way a main idea problem does as discussed in the "Tone of the Passage" section below.

The only exception would be a passage which makes a specific proposal for some change. In that case, the purpose of the passage was to make the proposal.

Tone of the passage. As in any other question, the answer chosen must have a basis—preferably a strong one—in the passage. This passage might be described as factual, objective, explanatory, and so on. It would be too strong to call it apologetic or alarmed or worried. Some tone questions have single-word answer choices; others have longer choices. The longer the choices, the more accurately they can reflect the texture of the passage—factual but concerned.

Identity of author or other person. Usually this is a matter of time and job description. Typically the inferences are a bit on the thin side, and frequently fall far short of perfection. In the illustrative passage, the perfect description might be "an agricultural economist writing in the late 1970's." The time could not be before 1977, and the job must be something to do with economics or agriculture. An answer choice such as "Congressional aide" is tempting, but there is nothing "Congressional" about the passage. There is no basis.

Use of evidence. This question type asks you to identify the role of some piece of evidence or sub-argument in the overall scheme of things. Occasionally, the role of a piece of evidence in the development of a sub-argument or a quoted argument may be sought. The basic type would be of this sort:

8. What does the author demonstrate by referring to "large financial losses" in the last paragraph?
   (A) foolishness of cattle producers
   (B) financial weakness of cattle producers
   (C) poor prospects of small cattle producers
   (D) inevitability of the biologic time lag
   (E) futility of trying to plan anything in cattle production

As discussed for question 7, the author does not feel that the cattle producers are especially foolish, but is explaining the difficulties they face; hence (A) is inadequate. (B) has a superficial appeal since large losses surely cannot strengthen the financial strength of the cattle producers, but that is not related to the flow of the actual passage, which is concerned with explaining the interactions of the cattle and biologic cycles. (C) fails on precision reading grounds since nothing is said in the passage about small producers as such. The prospects of all cattle producers are tainted by the seeming unavoidability of the cattle cycle, but "small" is unfounded.

(D) is the best answer because the author's purpose in mentioning the losses (and low prices) is to show just how inevitable the biologic lag is. Even when they lose money, they still have to increase the production of beef (slaughter) since they started growing the animals years previously. This highlights the need ALWAYS to consider your answer in light of the actual passage.

(E) is appealing because it captures the feeling of inevitability just referred to in (D). However, the word anything is far too strong since the passage is only describing a part of the cattle production process.

Main idea including title. In the previous two problems we had different statements of the main idea of the passage. It is important in the longer passages that you will see on the test that you make certain that the main idea answer choice that you choose covers as much of the passage as possible. No significant part should be left out if it can be avoided. Typically, several of the answer choices in this type of problem are quite good, and you have to examine the differences between the various answer choices closely in order to choose the correct one. Any outright error would eliminate an answer choice, but scope and fit are usually the final issues you must consider. Always be aware of how well the answer choices reflect the range of ideas, generality, causality, or other connecting ideas and strength of the passage.

A title question is treated the same way except that the potential titles are usually shorter than the answer choices in a main idea question, which means that the fit to the passage will be somewhat rougher.

Logical reasoning or method of argument. Occasionally there will be a question that asks you what the premises of the author are in the passage. This type of question stem might ask you to identify assumptions—ideas in which the author must also believe, and propositions with which the author would probably agree. You are to select an answer choice that is implied by the passage to be in the mind of the author in order for him to have written the passage the way he did. For example, if a passage states that the invention of atomic weapons forever changed the nature of foreign affairs, you may conclude the author believed that the nature of war technology has an impact on the conduct of foreign affairs. The basic idea is that if the author of a passage uses evidence to prove a conclusion, he must believe that the evidence applies to that conclusion, that it was used in the correct way, and that it does prove what he claims it proves. If the author is analyzing the reasoning of someone else, the strength and effectiveness of the arguments analyzed are not assumed.

Inference, implication, etc. This large class of questions is unified not so much by the varied question stems as by the method of attack. Questions 4, 5, and 6 are all examples of this question type. Let us take one more example:

9. All of the following may be inferred from the passage EXCEPT
   (A) Weight is a more important determinant of a calf's readiness for slaughter than age.
   (B) Successful cattle producers usually

have either considerable ready capital or substantial lines of credit.

(C) The cattle cycle is a dependable phenomenon and will continue indefinitely.

(D) It would be an improvement over current practice if market prices coordinated with beef supplies.

(E) The 1974–76 period was not an unusual one for cattle producers.

(A) can be inferred from the second paragraph. This is practically stated since the only reference to "slaughterability" is in terms of weight. (B) is much more implicit and derives from some of the same considerations as (E). The passage makes it clear that the cattle cycle is a cycle—a repetitive event. The biologic lag is dependable and it was the biologic lag which led to the mismatch between prices and supplies, and thus the losses. Therefore, cyclical losses (presumably offset by gains at other times) are typical of cattle producing, hence (E). If cyclical losses are typical, then any successful cattle producer must have some way of surviving these losses, hence (B).

(C) and (D) are both candidates for not being inferable, but by definition of the problem, one will turn out to be inferable and the other won't. (C) has two ideas in it about the cattle cycle. One is that the cycle AS A WHOLE is dependable and the other is that it will continue indefinitely. The first is only very weakly supported. The fact that it is a cycle is all that we needed for (E) and (B). (C) adds the modifier dependable. The only thing which is known to be dependable is the biologic lag (cycle), which, while important to the cattle cycle, is not necessarily the whole thing. Furthermore, we must see what the author means by dependable in the passage. When he refers to the biologic lag, he means that it is both necessary and of fairly well-defined duration. While the cattle cycle appears to be occurring, neither its necessity nor the regularity of its timing are known to be.

(D), on the other hand, has a somewhat weaker claim, which is thus easier to infer. (D) holds that the current situation, where the market prices and beef supplies are not in synchrony, is not as good as one where they would be in synchrony. This is supported by the last paragraph's reference to price signaling change in beef production (thus, one should follow the other) and, to a lesser extent, by the author's basically sympathetic view of the cattle producers' problems.

On a test, many of these ideas will not come to you neatly sorted out in reference to each answer choice, but will derive from a close examination of each choice and its differences from the other answer choices.

ATTACK STRATEGY FOR READING COMPREHENSION

The final section of the Instructional Overview will review a number of tips, tricks, and traps for RC questions. Here we will summarize our discussion in the form of an attack strategy for this type of question.

1. **Do each passage separately.** Do not jump back and forth for each passage.
2. **Preview the question stems only.** Become alert to specific references and idea of passage.
3. **Read passage actively, briskly, precisely.** See linkages, structural clues, and flow. Checkmark specific references known from preview.
4. **Read question and all answer choices.** Read precisely and actively. Watch for key words. Identify question type.
5. **Choose answer choice by elimination and contrast.** Focus on differences between answers to eliminate. Resolve close calls by strength of inference and closeness to main idea of passage.
6. **Refer back to passage only when necessary or for specific-detail questions.**
7. **Do not get hung up on one question.**

Tips, Tricks, and Traps

This section is a listing of hints that may help to improve your speed or accuracy on RC passages.

1. **Topic sentences.** Most paragraphs will have a topic sentence giving the idea of the paragraph. This sentence is usually the first or last sentence.

2. Structural clues in passage. The following items are all clues to the structure of a paragraph or passage and should be noted by you as you read. In each case ask yourself how this structural clue advances the ideas of the passage.

—Comparison (finding similarities, what is basis)
—Contrast (finding differences, what is basis)
—Causes (exactly what causes what, and how)
—Sequences (order and basis of order)
—Processes (steps and underlying idea, what next)
—Metaphors or images (how do they work, what in the image represents what in the world, what does it prove, where does it lead)
—Quotations and examples (what does it prove, why is it at this point in the passage)
—Numbers and dates (don't memorize, do they connect to anything else, do they limit the other ideas)
—Generality and specificity (is this a universal situation, limited, limited to what, how)
—Modifiers (why is it this kind of thing, what is the significance of the modifier, what else also is this way)
—Where is the evidence/conclusion (if one is given look for the other, either can be first)
—Definitions (do you understand it and how it works in the development of the passage's ideas)
—Buzzwords, jargon, technical terms (what you need to know about them is in the passage, but the definition might be implicit—note if it isn't defined)

3. Flow of the argument. It is usually important to notice when the argument is definitely continuing in the same vein or when it is making a change. The change may only be within a sentence or it may be a basic change in the flow of the entire passage. Many words and phrases indicate these ideas, but here are a few examples:

—Flow continuers: *and, also, in addition to, moreover, thus, since, because, then,* etc.
—Flow changers: *instead, on the other hand, unless, despite, although, but,* etc.

4. Key words. The following words are the kinds of words which are likely to be important in interpreting questions, answers, and passages. This list is only exemplary, not exhaustive: *always, never, ever, possible, definite, impossible, exactly, precisely, necessar(y)(ily), primar(y)(ily), most, least, unless, without, entire, all, no, part(ial)(ly),* etc.

5. Reading speed and speed reading. It is better to read faster with the same or increased comprehension. It is true that many persons do not read as fast as they could, even maintaining the same comprehension. Many people report increased comprehension as well as speed with a speed reading course. Leaving aside the question of the comprehension tests having been given by the speed reading schools, this is reasonable since the essence of speed reading is better concentration and mental and physical discipline. Both of those should increase speed and also comprehension.

However, the key limit on the GMAT is comprehension, not speed. Just as the increased concentration resulting from speed study often yields increased comprehension, the increased concentration resulting from comprehension study almost always results in increased speed. If you have only a few weeks to study for the GMAT, you should concentrate on improving your comprehension through practicing precise and active reading. If you make sure that you don't let yourself slack off on the speed, you will probably find that your speed has increased along with your comprehension.

One of the key fallacies that many people believe about reading is that a good reader just sails through the material at top speed and understands it. This may be true for fairly easy material. However, it is often the poor reader who will finish a particular passage most quickly, but with very little understanding. A good reader will slow down his reading speed to suit the difficulty of the particular sentence, or part of a sentence, and then speed up when the going is easier. The key difference between a good reader and a poor reader in terms of speed and comprehension is that a good reader will be constantly checking himself while he is reading to make sure that he is understanding at least the basic flow of ideas and will take the time *during* the reading process to get it right the first time. A poor reader, in a time pressure situation such as the GMAT, will frequently feel that he does not have the time to get it really right and thus goes so fast that he does not understand very much at all. In other words, doing the job correctly the first time is more efficient than trying to do it quickly and then fixing it up later.

Do not worry if you find yourself subvocalizing some of the more difficult parts of the passage (you don't need to subvocalize the whole thing). This is just a way of concentrating on the material, and can even be helpful.

On the other hand, you do not need to pore over every word for ten minutes. Every passage consists of a series of thoughs and your only job is to interpret the sentences one by one to see this structure.

6. Eyes. Physically, we can all read a thousand words a minute unless there is something wrong with our eyes. Mentally, that is usually not so practical. The point is that if you feel eyestrain or have a lot of trouble physically reading, you should go to an ophthalmologist or optometrist and have your eyes checked. It probably is the tension of studying, but if you do need glasses or some other treatment, get it at once.

7. Practice makes better, but only if it is practice of the right things. For everything that you read from now to the test, especially the practice tests in this book, analyze them carefully and check any errors you might make to see which clue(s) you missed—so you won't miss them next time.

WRITING ABILITY INSTRUCTIONAL OVERVIEW

The current format of the Writing Ability section of the GMAT consists of 25 questions of a type called Sentence Correction that you must complete in 30 minutes. As on most of the other sections of the GMAT, the questions increase in their level of difficulty as they progress from question one to question twenty-five.

QUESTION FORMAT

Each question consists of a sentence of which either all or part is underlined. Answer choice (A) always repeats the underlined portion exactly, and answer choices (B) through (E) are alternative ways of expressing the idea contained in the underlined portion. With respect to the rules of grammar and usage in Standard Written English, brevity of expression, and the appropriate use of words and idiomatic expressions within the sentence (these criteria will be discussed below, with examples), you must choose the best alternative from among the answer choices, without changing the meaning of the original underlined portion. Spelling, capitalization and punctuation are not directly tested; only rarely are they even indirectly tested (and then only as they relate to grammar, usage, etc.). Also not tested is your knowledge of the terminology that is used to classify the various structural components of sentences (e.g., predicate nominative, dangling participle, gerundive, etc.). Rather, the Writing Ability section of the GMAT is a functional test of your ability to recognize incorrect expressions and errors of structure in sentences and your ability to choose the best ways of correcting those errors and incorrect expressions.

ANSWERING THE QUESTION

While reading the original sentence, pay careful attention to the meaning and structure of all the elements (words, phrases and clauses) of the sentences, both in the underlined and nonunderlined portions of the sentence. Remember that for purposes of evaluating correct grammatical and structural agreement among different parts of the sentence, the nonunderlined portion of the sentence is correct by definition. Also remember that the meaning of the idea expressed in the underlined portion of the sentence must be preserved in the answer choice that you select as the correct one. The underlined portion, if it contains an error, is usually not completely incorrect, but only partially so. Only one word or just a few words in the underlined portion may need to be changed, deleted, added or rearranged in order to correct any errors in the sentence. It is also true, however, that more than one error may appear in the underlined portion: in that event, all errors need to be corrected. Do not select an answer choice as correct until you have examined all of the answer choices, since there may be an answer choice among the later alternatives that is better than one you have provisionally selected. Determining the best answer on this section of the test should always be a process of eliminating the incorrect answer choices from consideration and constantly narrowing the field of answer choices down to the correct one. Even if you are not able to select one answer choice as being correct to the exclusion of the other four, it is in your best interests, for purposes of maximizing your score, to take a guess if you can make any eliminations of answer choices; the more eliminations of incorrect answer choices, the better. Random guessing is not a wise tactic on the GMAT, since a percentage of the number of your incorrect answers is subtracted from the number of your correct answers to yield your raw score (which is then converted to the scaled score that business schools receive when you apply).

As you read the underlined portion of the sentence, try to pick out both errors and correct expressions. Whichever answer choices fail to correct the errors and, conversely, whichever answer choices change correct expressions into incorrect ones, cannot be correct and therefore should be eliminated. For example, the preposition among should be used with an object that refers to more than two things, and the preposition between should be used with an object that refers to exactly two things. If the underlined portion of a sentence uses among or between, it will be either correct or incorrect, depending on the number of things to which its object refers. If several of the answer choices use among and several use between in the same construction as the underlined portion, whichever choices use the preposition incorrectly should be eliminated, regardless of the correctness or incorrectness of the rest of the answer choice.

The following example will further illustrate this tactic.

<u>Between you and I, there can be no other swimmer in the country faster than he.</u>

(A) Between you and I, there can be no other swimmer in the country faster than he.
(B) Between you and me, there can be no swimmer in the country faster than he.
(C) Among you and me, there can be no swimmer in the country as fast as he.
(D) There can be no other swimmer in the country faster than him, between you and me.
(E) Among you and I, in the country there can be no other swimmer as fast as he.

In this example, the object of the preposition "Between" in the original sentence, is "you and I," which is exactly two people. So "Between," not "Among" [in answer choices (C) and (E)], must be correct. (C) and (E) should be eliminated on that basis alone, without reading the remainder of (C) and (E). Likewise, the pronoun "I" in the original sentence is incorrect, since a preposition ("Between") must take an object, not a subject ("I" is a subject, and "me" is an object). So choice (A) should be eliminated, as well as choice (E) (which was already eliminated because of "Among"). Either (B) or (D) must therefore be the answer at this point. Even if you cannot choose between (B) and (D), you should guess one or the other. In choice (D), the word "him" should be "he," because the expression "faster than he (or him)" is an example of an ellipsis (the omission of a word or words from a sentence). The complete expression would be "faster than he is fast." Since "faster than him is fast" incorrectly uses an object ("him") instead of a subject ("he"), choice (D) is incorrect and choice (B) is correct. An ellipsis in a sentence, by the way, is perfectly acceptable in Standard Written English (if used properly, of course). The general point is that, whenever possible, specific errors within answer choices should be isolated and should cause you to eliminate those choices in which the errors appear. Another comment on the above example is that choices (C) and (E), in addition to using among incorrectly, also change the meaning of the original sentence by stating that no swimmer (or no *other* swimmer) in the country is *as fast as* he, which is different from stating that no swimmer (or no *other* swimmer) is *faster than* he. Furthermore, it is logically impossible to say that no swimmer in the country is as fast as he, since *he* is certainly as fast as he himself.

BASIC STRATEGY

Since the questions tend, as a general rule, to become more difficult as you progress toward the end of the section, it is a good idea to try to work quickly at the outset, when the questions are relatively easy. The rule of questions increasing in difficulty has its exceptions, of course, so you shouldn't be surprised to find one or two difficult questions toward the beginning of the section and one or two easy questions toward the end. Another point to keep in mind is that certain questions will be easy for you and more difficult for someone else, and vice versa, regardless of where in the section they appear. Therefore, you should not feel compelled to answer the questions in the order in which they appear. Rather, you should be prepared to omit temporarily (or perhaps permanently) a particular question from consideration and go on to the next question if it seems too difficult for you after giving it and the answer choices one or two careful readings. If you're drawing a blank on a particular question, don't feel compelled to keep working on it until you figure out the correct answer. Rather, go on to the next question. Similarly, if you come to a question whose underlined portion is particularly long compared to some other questions that follow, it is a good idea to skip (again, temporarily or permanently) that question in the interest of saving time. All the questions count the same. It is not the case that the longer or more difficult questions give you more points than the shorter or easier questions. The idea is to do as many questions correctly as quickly as possible.

Before skipping a question, you may want to eliminate some answer choices, so that if you come back to that question, you will have fewer answer choices to choose among. Also, if you skip a question, you should make sure that you also skip that question on your answer sheet, so that the answers that you mark on your answer sheet correspond to the correct questions. Work as quickly as possible (but carefully) the first time you go through the section. If you have time left at the end of the section, go back to work on the questions you omitted, or use the remaining time to check the accuracy of your work if you have put an answer on your answer sheet for all of the questions in the section. Sometimes when you reconsider a question that you have previously read carefully (and perhaps have eliminated some answer choices), the correct answer will "click" in your mind, even though it was not apparent to you the first time. (Perhaps a later question jogged your memory of the linguistic principle or rule involved, or perhaps you were thinking about the question on a "subconscious" level.)

If you find, as a result of doing the timed sample sections of Writing Ability questions in this book, that you are having difficulty finishing the sections in the allotted time, then omit only those questions (the first time through) in which you cannot eliminate any answer choices. On the others (when you do not feel sure of one answer choice to the exclusion of the other four, but can eliminate one or more answer choices), it is in your best interest to take a guess.

WHAT IS TESTED

The terms grammar and usage refer to the form and structure of sentences and sentence parts, as distinct from the meaning of the words and phrases of a sentence. The general rules of grammar and usage that are tested on the GMAT are the following (these will be discussed more fully in a series of examples that follows):

1. Subjects of clauses must agree in number with their verbs.
2. Pronouns must agree in number with their antecedents.
3. Cases of pronouns must be used correctly.
4. Pronouns must refer unambiguously to their antecedents.
5. Verb forms, including tenses, voices, moods and participles, must be used correctly.
6. Adjectives and adverbs, including degrees of comparison, must be used correctly.
7. Grammatically equivalent elements of sentences must be parallel with each other.
8. Dangling and misplaced modifiers must be avoided.
9. Comparisons must be made between like classes of things.
10. Sentence fragments and run-on sentences must be avoided.
11. Coordinate and subordinate clauses must be properly used, introduced and joined together.

The term brevity of expression refers to the avoidance of unnecessarily long sentence parts and of redundant words and phrases.

The appropriate use of words and idiomatic expressions within sentences is known as proper diction. The use of a word in a sentence will be considered poor diction if the meaning of the word, according to its standard dictionary definition, does not fit the meaning of the rest of the sentence.

In the remainder of this section, we will discuss proper diction, brevity of expression and the various rules of sentence construction by the use of examples.

Example 1

If one begins to smoke at an early age, <u>it is likely that he will go on smoking further.</u>

(A) it is likely that he will go on smoking further.

(B) he will probably keep smoking more and more.
(C) it is hard to stop him from smoking more.
(D) he is likely to continue smoking.
(E) he will have a tendency to continue smoking.

Example 1 illustrates a lack of brevity of expression in the original underlined portion, which is the same as answer choice (A)—do not make the mistake of reading choice (A), since you've already read the original. In shortening a wordy expression such as the above (and, in fact, any time you select an answer choice that changes the original wording), you need to make sure that the meaning of the original is preserved. Choice (C) changes the meaning of the original and therefore should be eliminated. Choice (E) changes the meaning slightly but is a possibility. Choices (A) and (B) are quite wordy in comparison with the correct answer, choice (D). Choice (D) expresses the meaning of the original clearly and concisely. None of the answer choices in this question contains any grammatical mistakes, which is rare. Also, you should not blindly choose the shortest answer choice.

Example 2

After being in school for sixteen years, <u>Jack couldn't wait to get out to get a job.</u>
(A) Jack couldn't wait to get out to get a job.
(B) there was great desire in Jack to get out and get a job.
(C) Jack was eager to get a job.
(D) Jack wanted out and a job badly.
(E) Jack arranged to look for a job.

Example 2 also illustrates a lack of brevity of expression, as well as poor diction in answer choice (D). Choice (C) expresses the idea of the underlined portion clearly and concisely. In choice (D) "out" used without "to get" is poor diction. Choice (E) changes the meaning of the original by using "arranged to look" (the reader of the sentence does not know what steps, if any, Jack has taken in pursuit of a job). Both choices (A) and (B) are wordy.

Example 3

The prisoner was expedited from California to Florida.
(A) <u>The prisoner was expedited from California to Florida.</u>
(B) From California to Florida, the prisoner was expedited.
(C) The prisoner from California was extradited to Florida.
(D) The prisoner was extradited from California to Florida.
(E) From California, the prisoner was expedited to Florida.

In this example, "expedited" (meaning "speeded up, hastened or accomplished promptly") is used incorrectly; therefore, answer choices (A), (B), and (E) should be eliminated. The proper word to use in this context is extradited (meaning "surrendered by one state or authority to another"), which appears in choices (C) and (D). The meaning of the original is changed in (C): "The prisoner from California" seems to mean that the prisoner is a person from the state of California, not necessarily that the state of California is extraditing him. The error in choice (C) is an example of a misplaced modifier (in this instance, the prepositional phrase "from California") (see Rule 8). Choices (B) and (E) also contain misplaced modifiers—"From California to Florida" in choice (B); "From California" in choice (E). Therefore, (D) is the best choice.

The above examples have primarily been illustrations of poor diction and a lack of brevity of expression. The remaining examples will primarily be illustrations of the grammatical rules enumerated above. These next examples will primarily illustrate Rule 1.

Example 4

<u>The phenomena of public education is another example of the workings of democracy.</u>
(A) The phenomena of public education is another example of the workings of democracy.
(B) The phenomena of public education is yet another example of democracy at work.
(C) The phenomenon of public education is another example of how the workings of democracy work.
(D) The phenomenon of public education is another example of democracy at work.
(E) Public education, a phenomena, is another working example of democracy.

In this example there is a lack of agreement in number between the subject ("phenomena") and the verb ("is") because "phenomena" is plural ("phenomenon" is singular). The same error eliminates choices (B) and (E) ("*a* phenomena" is incorrect). Choice (C) is redundant ("the workings of democracy work"). Choice (D) is correct. The general rule is that a singular subject requires a singular verb, and a plural subject requires a plural verb.

Example 5

Everyone on both sides except the pitcher and me was injured in that game.

(A) except the pitcher and me was
(B) except the pitcher and me were
(C) except the pitcher and I was
(D) accept the pitcher and I were
(E) accept the pitcher and me was

The underlined portion contains no errors. The "was" is correctly used since "Everyone" is always considered to be singular. Everyone is an indefinite pronoun, of which there are three types. The pronouns of the first type are always singular: everyone, each, either, neither, someone, somebody, nobody, anyone, anybody, everybody, one and no one. Those of the second type are always plural: both, few, many and several. Those of the third type may be singular or plural, depending on whether the noun to which they refer is singular or plural: some, more, most and all ("some of the cake (singular) is . . ."; "some of the boys (plural) are . . ."). In choice (C), "I" should be "me" because it is the object of "except" (Rule 3). Choices (D) and (E) are both incorrect because "accept" is a verb, not a preposition (an error of diction).

Example 6

His dog, along with his cat and goldfish, prevent him from taking long trips.

(A) along with his cat and goldfish, prevent
(B) as well as his cat and goldfish, prevents
(C) in addition to his cat and goldfish, are preventing
(D) together with his cat and goldfish, were preventing
(E) accompanied by his cat and goldfish, prevent

The subject of the sentence is "dog," which is singular; therefore, a singular verb is required. Only choice (B) has a singular verb ("prevents"). The general rule is that the joining of a singular subject with another noun or pronoun, or with several nouns or pronouns, singular or plural, by along with, together with, with, as well as, in addition to, accompanied by, or any similar word or phrase except *and,* does not make the singular subject into a plural one (only and will do so). Choice (D) also changes the meaning of the original by making the tense of the verb past instead of present.

Example 7

Neither the councilmen nor the mayor take responsibility for the passage of the controversial bill.

(A) Neither the councilmen nor the mayor take
(B) Neither the councilmen or the mayor takes
(C) Neither the councilmen take nor the mayor takes
(D) Neither the mayor nor the councilmen takes
(E) Neither the councilmen nor the mayor takes

Choice (E) is correct. The general rule is that when two distinct words or phrases are joined by the correlatives either . . . or, neither . . . nor, or not only . . . but also, the number (singular or plural) of the word or phrase nearer to the verb determines the number of the verb. Choices (A) and (D) are wrong for that reason ("mayor take" and "councilmen takes"). Choice (B) is wrong because "Neither" is incorrectly correlated with "or" (rather than "nor"). Choice (C) is wrong because of the insertion of "take"; the neither . . . nor correlation must be *directly* between two nouns or pronouns.

Example 8

Faulty construction of storage vessels and that the water supply was inadequately supervised is the cause of the present shortage.

(A) vessels and that the water supply was inadequately supervised is the cause
(B) vessels and that the water supply was inadequately supervised are the causes
(C) vessels, together with an inadequately supervised water supply, are the causes

(D) vessels and an inadequately supervised water supply are the causes
(E) vessels, as well as that the water supply was inadequately supervised, are the causes

This example illustrates both subject-verb agreement and lack of parallelism (Rule 7). Choices (A) (B) and (E) lack parallelism between "construction" and "that the water supply. . . ." Choices (C) and (D) correct this error (joining "construction" with "supply," two nouns), but (C) has a singular subject ("construction") and plural verb ("are"). (Compare Example 6: "together with" does not make the subject of a sentence plural.) Note also that "vessels," as the object of the preposition "of," has no effect on the number of "construction." On the GMAT Writing Ability section, it is quite important to *isolate the subject of the sentence* in order to ascertain whether the subject agrees in number with the verb in all of the clauses of a sentence.

The next two examples illustrate Rule 2.

Example 9

The preacher said that everyone will burn in eternal damnation for their sins.
(A) that everyone will burn in eternal damnation for their sins.
(B) that everyone for his sins in eternal damnation will burn.
(C) that everyone will burn in eternal damnation for his sins.
(D) about everyone that they will burn in eternal damnation for their sins.
(E) that all of us should burn in eternal damnation for their sins.

Everyone is always singular. Therefore, any pronoun that refers back to "everyone" must also be singular. Choices (A) and (D) use their (plural) instead of his (singular) to refer to everyone and are therefore wrong. Choice (B) uses his correctly but has its prepositional phrase modifiers placed in an unusual fashion. Choice (E) uses their correctly to refer to "all of *us*" (plural "all" because of "us," which is plural), but changes the meaning of the sentence to "should burn" instead of "will burn." Choice (C) is correct.

Example 10

Of the two leaders, neither Trotsky nor Lenin was most brilliant, but each worked in their sphere for the party.
(A) was most brilliant, but each worked in their sphere
(B) was most brilliant, but each worked in their own sphere
(C) was most brilliant, but each worked in his sphere
(D) was more brilliant, but each in their own sphere worked
(E) was more brilliant, but each worked in his sphere

Each is always singular. Therefore, any pronoun which refers back to each must also be singular. Choices (A), (B), and (D) use "their" (plural) instead of "his" (singular) to refer to "each" and are therefore wrong. After the commas in choices (C) and (E), the wording is the same and is correct. In choice (C) "most" is incorrect because only two people are mentioned in the sentence: a comparison between two people or things uses the comparative degree, more (*adjective*) or (*adjective*)er, not the superlative degree most (*adjective*) or (*adjective*)est (see Rule 6). Both (D) and (E) use the proper comparative form, but (A), (B) and (C) do not. Therefore choice (E) is the correct answer.

The next three examples illustrate Rule 3, as well as several errors of diction.

Example 11

Every conservative candidate except Smith and she was defeated in the primary election.
(A) except Smith and she
(B) except Smith and her
(C) excepting Smith and she
(D) but not she and Smith
(E) outside of her and Smith

Since except is a preposition, it must take an object (her), not a subject (she). Therefore, choices (A) and (C) are wrong. Choice (C) is also wrong because "excepting" is poor diction as used in this context, as a substitute for "except." In choice E, "outside of" is also poor diction; either except or other than should be used instead. In choice D, "but not she and Smith" is an awkward construction, and even if it were used, it should be set off from the rest of the sentence by commas.

Example 12

If I were he, I would lay that manuscript on the sofa, and keep it away from the kitchen table.

(A) If I were he, I would lay that manuscript
(B) If I were him, I would lay that manuscript
(C) If I were he I would lie that manuscript
(D) If I was he, I would lay that manuscript
(E) If I was he, I would lie that manuscript

The various answer choices in this example contain three places where an error may occur: "was" or "were"; "he" or "him"; and "lay" or "lie." The correct choices from the three pairs of alternatives are "were" because the first clause is known as a condition contrary to fact (the "I" is *not* "he") and therefore requires the subjunctive mood of the verb ("I were" rather than the normal, or indicative, mood, "I was") (see Rule 5); "he" because whenever a form of the verb to be is used (in this case, "were"), the pronouns on both sides of the verb must be subjects (the "I" is a subject, and the "he" is a predicate nominative) (see Rule 3); and "lay," which means "to put or place," not "lie," which means "to recline" (an error of diction). Therefore, the correct answer is (A).

Example 13

The contest judges were told to give the prize to whomever drew the best picture.

(A) to give the prize to whomever drew the best picture.
(B) to give the prize to whoever drew the best picture.
(C) to give to whomever drew the best picture the prize.
(D) to give to whoever drew the best picture the prize.
(E) to give the prize to whomever it was who drew the best picture.

In this sentence the preposition to (the second "to" of the sentence) has as its object the rest of the sentence, not merely the word whomever. The part of the sentence after the second "to" is a clause (a group of words containing a subject and a verb) which has "whomever" as its subject ("drew" is its verb, and "picture is the object of "drew"). But whomever is an object; the correct word is whoever. That eliminates choices (A), (C) and (E). Choice (D) is awkwardly phrased because "the prize" does not immediately follow "give." Therefore, choice (B) is correct. As a comparison, a sentence that would use whomever correctly (as the object of the verb liked) would be the following: ". . . to give the prize to whomever the audience liked best."

The next two examples illustrate Rule 4.

Example 14

The coal strike reduced Indiana's energy reserves, which caused unemployment among the workers.

(A) which caused unemployment among the workers.
(B) which caused the workers to unemployed.
(C) a circumstance which resulted in unemployment.
(D) a fact that created unemployed workers.
(E) which led many workers to be unemployed.

In this sentence, "which" has no other word in the sentence to which it can logically refer: neither the "reserves" nor the "strike" "caused unemployment," but rather the fact that the energy reserves were reduced "caused unemployment." Therefore, choices (A), (B) and (E) are incorrect. Either "a circumstance" or "a fact" is correct. Since the reduction of energy reserves did not *create workers* (unemployed or otherwise), choice (C) is correct. The "circumstance" resulted in employment (and unemployment *of workers* is understood; the context implies that it is workers, and not some other group, who are unemployed). The general rule is that a pronoun in a sentence must unambiguously refer to some other noun or pronoun in the sentence. Otherwise, as here, another word ("circumstance") must be supplied. The next example will further illustrate Rule 4.

Example 15

In this article they imply that everybody who dislike this philosophy must still accept its principal tenet themselves.

(A) In this article they imply that everybody who dislike this philosophy must still accept its principal tenet themselves.
(B) The author of this article implies that everybody who dislikes this philosophy must still except its principal tenet themselves.
(C) The author of this article implies that everybody who dislikes this philosophy must still accept its principal tenet himself.
(D) The author in this article implies that everybody who dislike this philosophy must himself still except its principle tenet.
(E) The author implies that everybody who dislike this philosophy must themselves still accept its principle tenet.

In this sentence, "they" has no reference, unambiguous or otherwise. Therefore, an appropriate change must be made, as in choices (B), (C), (D) or (E) ("The author"). Choices (A), (D) and (E) contain a second error, namely, "dislike" instead of "dislikes," because "who," which refers to "everybody," must be singular because "everybody" is singular (see Rule 2 and Example 5). Choices (B) and (D) contain diction errors (the use of "except" instead of "accept"), so those choices are incorrect. Choices (D) and (E) contain a second diction error, the use of "principle" instead of "principal." Choices (A), (B) and (E) incorrectly use the plural "themselves" instead of the singular "himself," as in choices (C) and (D), to refer to "everybody." Choices (D) and (E) misplace "himself" (or "themselves"); it should appear at the end of the sentence in order to achieve a natural-sounding word order (see Rule 8, concerning misplaced modifiers).

The next three examples illustrate Rule 5.

Example 16

When I opened the hood and saw smoke pouring from the engine, I realized that I forgot to add oil.

(A) I realized that I forgot to add oil.
(B) I had realized that I forgot to add oil.
(C) I had realized that I had forgotten to add oil.
(D) I realized that I would forget to add oil.
(E) I realized that I had forgotten to add oil.

Verb tenses must be in proper sequence. When two or more events have taken place, are taking place, or will take place at the same time, their tenses must be the same. If two events have taken place in the past but one event occurred prior to the other, the later of the two events must be in the past tense, and the earlier of the two must be in the past perfect tense (had plus the past tense of the verb). In this sentence, the "opening," the "seeing" and the "realizing" all took place in the past at the same time and therefore should all be in the (simple) past tense. So choices (B) and (C) (with "had realized," which is the past perfect tense) are wrong. The "forgetting" also took place in the past but prior to the other three events and therefore should be in the past perfect tense ("had forgotten"). So choices (A), (B) and (D) are wrong. Only choice (E) contains the proper sequence of tenses.

Example 17

If they would have paid attention, they would not have had to be told again.

(A) would have paid attention
(B) would pay attention
(C) had paid attention
(D) paid attention
(E) were to pay attention

This sentence provides another example of the proper sequence of tenses, in a slightly different format. If the two events had actually occurred (neither event did occur), the "paying attention" would have occurred prior to the "having to be told again." Therefore, the earlier event must be in the past perfect tense ("had paid"). Only choice (C) has the correct form of the verb. The if clause is known as a condition contrary to fact (in fact, they did not pay attention).

Example 18

She is not and does not intend to run for political office.

(A) She is not and does not intend to run

(B) She is not running and does not intend to
(C) She is not and will not intend to run
(D) She is not running and does not intend to run
(E) She has not and does not intend to run

This sentence contains an example of an ellipsis (the omission of a word or words from a sentence) in the omission of some form of "run" after the first "not." In a construction like this one, the verb may properly be omitted only if it is in the same form as another appearance of the same verb. Since "running" is the omitted form and "run" is the form that appears later in the sentence, "running" must appear after the first "not." Choice (B) corrects that error but omits "run" at the end of the underlined portion; therefore, choice (B) is wrong. Choices (C) and (E) also do not correct the error of the original; furthermore, the meaning of the original is changed by the changing of tenses. Only choice (D) is correct.

The next three examples illustrate Rule 6.

Example 19

He disapproves of you insisting that the rope of pearls were misplaced on purpose.

(A) He disapproves of you insisting that the rope of pearls were misplaced on purpose.
(B) He disapproves of you insisting that the rope of pearls were purposely misplaced.
(C) He disapproves of your insisting that the rope of pearls was purposely misplaced.
(D) He disapproves of you insisting that she misplaced the rope of pearls purposely.
(E) How could you insist she misplaced the rope of pearls on purpose.

In this sentence the object of the preposition "of" is "insisting," not "you." Therefore, your, not you, must be used since that word is acting as a modifier of "insisting" (which is a gerund—that is, a form of a verb, ending in -ing, which acts as a noun). Choices (B) and (D) contain the same error. Additionally, choices (A) and (B) contain an error of agreement between the subject of a clause ("rope") and its verb ("were misplaced"). The fact that the "rope" is "of pearls" (plural) does not make the subject grammatically plural (see Rule 1). Choices (D) and (E) also change the meaning of the original (the reader does not know who misplaced the pearls). Either "on purpose," choices (A) and (E), or "purposely," choices (B), (C) and (D), may be used interchangeably without affecting the grammar or meaning of the sentence. Only choice (C) contains no errors.

Example 20

The car runs quieter when I add a more heavy transmission fluid.

(A) The car runs quieter when I add a more heavy transmission fluid.
(B) The car runs more quietly when I add a heavier transmission fluid.
(C) The car runs quieter when I add a more heavier transmission fluid.
(D) The car runs more quietly when I add a more heavy transmission fluid.
(E) The car runs quieter when I add a heavier transmission fluid.

The only glaring grammatical error in this sentence is the use of "quieter" (the adjective form of quiet) instead of "more quietly." "Quieter" (or "more quietly") modifies "run" (a verb) and therefore should be in its adverb form (adverbs modify verbs, adjectives or other adverbs) rather than its adjective form (adjectives modify nouns and pronouns). The other error in the original is the use of "more heavy" instead of "heavier." As a matter of word choice, it is preferable to use an *-er* ending for a comparative adjective when one is readily available and in common use; such a word choice is more idiomatic (but not "idiomaticer"). Choices (C) and (E) do not correct the "quieter" error; additionally, in choice (C), "more heavier" is incorrect because it joins two comparative forms in one construction. Choice (D) does not correct the "more heavy" error. Therefore, choice (B) is correct.

Example 21

John maintained that his scholastic record was better or at least as good as hers.

(A) John maintained that his scholastic record was better or at least as good as hers.
(B) John maintained that his scholastic record at its least was as good as hers.

(C) John maintained that his scholastic record was as good or better than hers.
(D) John maintained that his scholastic record was better or at least as good as her scholastic record.
(E) John maintained that his scholastic record was better than or at least as good as hers.

When two items are being compared and one is stated to be better than the others, the than in the comparison is essential. Likewise, when one item is stated to be as good as another, the second as is essential. Therefore, the correct construction in the sentence above should be ". . . better *than* or at least as good *as* hers" or ". . . at least as good *as* or better *than* hers" (either order is acceptable). Choices (A) and (D) omit "than," and choice (C) omits the second "as." Choice (B) changes the meaning of the sentence slightly and therefore is incorrect. In choice (D), it is unnecessary to replace "hers" (at the end of the sentence) with "her scholastic record." Only choice (E) contains no errors.

The next four examples illustrate Rule 7.

Example 22

The stranger was affable, with good manners and has a keen wit.
(A) with good manners and has a keen wit.
(B) with good manners and a keen wit.
(C) well-mannered and keen-witted.
(D) good manners as well as keen-witted.
(E) and has good manners as well as a keen wit.

This sentence contains two illustrations of a lack of parallelism among grammatically equivalent elements of the sentence. "Affable," an adjective, is used to describe the "stranger." Therefore, the other two descriptions of the "stranger" must agree in form (that is, must be parallel) with "affable." "With good manners" is a prepositional phrase and "has a keen wit" is the predicate portion of a clause; both must be changed into their adjective forms. Only choice (C) makes that correction.

Example 23

To run for an important political office, to manage a large organization and practicing law effectively all require organizational and problem-solving skills.
(A) To run for an important political office, to manage a large organization and practicing law effectively
(B) To run for an important political office and to manage a large organization, practicing law effectively
(C) Running for an important political office, managing a large organization and to practice law effectively
(D) To run and manage political offices and large organizations and practicing law effectively
(E) Running for an important office, managing a large organzation and practicing law effectively

This sentence, like the previous example, is a very straightforward example of a lack of parallelism in the subject matter of the sentence: two infinitives ("to run" and "to manage") are used along with a gerund ("practicing"; a gerund is a form of a verb that ends in -ing and functions as a noun). Either all three terms must be infinitives *or* all three terms must be gerunds. Only choice (E) uniformly uses one construction or the other.

Example 24

Edward not only resists learning to correlate new facts but also remembering old lessons.
(A) Edward not only resists learning to correlate new facts but also remembering old lessons.
(B) Edward not only resists learning to correlate new facts but also to remember old lessons.
(C) Edward resists not only learning to correlate new facts but also remembering old lessons.
(D) Edward resists not only learning to correlate new facts but also to remember old lessons.
(E) Edward resists learning to correlate new facts and remembering old lessons.

The terms not only and but also (just like neither and nor and either and or) must introduce grammatically equivalent, and therefore parallel, sentence elements. In this sentence, "not only" introduces "resists" and "but also" introduces "remembering." "Resists" is the verb of the sentence, and "remembering," along with "learning," is an object of "resists." One way to correct this error would be "Edward not only resists learning . . . but also *resists* remembering. . . ." But the use of "resists" twice is unnecessarily wordy. A better way to correct the error is choice (C), the correct answer. Choice (B) compounds the error of the original underlined portion by using "to remember" instead of "remembering," so that the new term is not parallel with "learning." Choice (D) corrects the original error, but makes the same mistake as choice B. Choice (E) slightly changes the meaning of the original sentence by eliminating the comparative emphasis between "learning" and "remembering."

Example 25

A speaker's physical impact—including gestures, facial expression and body carriage—is as important as listening to his message.

(A) A speaker's physical impact—including gestures, facial expression and body carriage—is
(B) A speaker's physical impact—gestures, facial expression and body carriage—are
(C) The examination of a speaker's physical impact—including gestures, facial expression and body carriage—is
(D) Examining a speaker's physical impact—gestures, facial expression and body carriage—are
(E) Examining a speaker's physical impact—including gestures, facial expression and body carriage—is

This question is relatively difficult. The sentence as it stands makes a comparison between "impact" and "listening," which are neither grammatically nor conceptually parallel (see Rule 9 and Example 27). Since "listening" is not underlined, the subject of the sentence, "impact," must be changed so as to be parallel with "listening." "Examination" comes close, but "Examining" is even closer to being parallel with "listening." Thus the correct answer is either (D) or (E). Since the subject of the sentence is singular—"impact" in (A) and (B), "examination" in (C), and "Examining" in choices (D) and (E)—the verb must be singular ("is" instead of "are") even though the subject *seems* to be plural ("gestures, facial expression and body carriage" does not make the subject plural). Thus choices (B) and (D) are incorrect. Furthermore, (B) and (D) are wrong because they eliminate "including" before "gestures" and therefore imply that "gestures, facial expression and body carriage" are the *only* characteristics of a "speaker's physical impact," whereas "including" implies that there may be other characteristics. Therefore, choices (B) and (D) slightly change the meaning of the original underlined portion. Thus, only choice (E) is correct.

The next two examples illustrate Rule 8.

Example 26

By leading trump the contract was defeated resoundingly by the defenders.

(A) By leading trump the contract was defeated resoundingly by the defenders.
(B) By leading trump the defenders defeated the contract resoundingly.
(C) The defenders resounded the defeat of the contract by leading trump.
(D) The contract, by leading trump, was defeated resoundingly by the defenders.
(E) Resoundingly, the contract was defeated by the defenders by leading trump.

An introductory modifier of a noun or pronoun, in this case the prepositional phrase "By leading trump," must modify the subject of the main clause, in this case "the contract." But clearly the "contract" did not lead trump; rather, the "defenders" led trump and "defeated the contract resoundingly." Therefore, the subject of the main clause must be "defenders," if "By leading trump" is to remain as the introductory modifier. The error here is known as a dangling, or misplaced, modifier because it does not *logically* modify the noun or pronoun that it *grammatically* modifies. Choice (B) corrects the error and is the correct answer. Choice (C) changes the meaning of the original by stating that "The defenders resounded the defeat . . ." (D) and (E) still imply, grammatically, that the contract led trump. An additional point concerning the construction of these answer choices is that, as a matter of writing style (but not as a matter of grammar or usage), the active voice ("the defenders defeated the contract") is preferable to the passive voice ("the contract was defeated by the defenders").

Example 27

In addition to those specified for professions, the corporations maintained endowments in purely academic fields, especially in the physical sciences.

(A) the corporations maintained endowments in purely academic fields, especially in the physical sciences.
(B) the corporations had maintained purely academic endowments like those of the physical sciences.
(C) in purely academic fields, endowments, especially in the physical sciences, were maintained by the corporations.
(D) endowments were maintained in purely academic fields, especially in the physical sciences, by the corporations.
(E) purely academic endowments, especially for those fields like the physical sciences, were maintained by the corporations.

Grammatically, this sentence states that "the corporations" are "In addition to those specified for professions," whereas it is the "endowments" that are "In addition to those specified for professions." One way to classify this error is to say that the nonunderlined portion of the sentence is a dangling, or misplaced, modifier because it grammatically modifies "the corporations" but logically should modify the "endowments." Another way to classify the error is to say that the reference of the pronoun "those" is ambiguous (see Rule 4) because "those" grammatically refers to "corporations" (the general rule is that a pronoun should refer, whenever possible, to the noun or other pronoun closest to it in the sentence) but logically should refer to "endowments." In either case, the subject of the main clause must be "endowments" rather than "corporations." (C), (D) and (E) all use "endowments" as the subject of the main clause. In choice (C) the prepositional-phrase modifiers "in purely academic fields" and "especially in the physical sciences" are misplaced so that the sentence is awkwardly constructed, causing the reader to slow down when he reads it in order to put the pieces (of the sentence) back together. Choice (D) corrects the awkwardness and misplacement of modifiers of choice (C) and is therefore the correct answer. Choice (E) is more brief in its use of "purely academic endowments" rather than "endowments in purely academic fields" (making the sentence more concise and therefore better, probably without changing the meaning), but changes the meaning of the next expression by using "especially for those fields like the physical sciences": the endowments were maintained "especially in the physical sciences," not "especially for those fields *like* the physical sciences."

The next example illustrates Rule 9.

Example 28

Your courage is as great as any other man in defending your country.

(A) as great as any other man
(B) so great as any other man
(C) great like any other man
(D) as great as that of any other man
(E) as that of any man

A comparison is being made in this sentence between "Your courage" and "any other man." But "courage" and "man" are not like classes of things. Since "courage" is not underlined, "man" must be altered to make the comparison logical. Only (D) corrects the error, by comparing "courage" to "that of any other man," that is to the courage of "any other man." The correct construction could be either choice (D) or "as great as the courage of any other man" or "as great as any other man's courage" or "as great as any other man's" (where "courage" after "man's" would be understood).

The next example illustrates Rule 3 and Rule 10.

Example 29

The lovestruck boy was sad because the girl who he loved and who had left him for another.

(A) the girl who he loved and who had left him for another
(B) the girl whom he loved and whom had left him for another
(C) the girl whom he loved and who had left him for

(D) the girl whom he loved had left him for another
(E) the girl who he loved had left him for another

The underlined portion of this sentence is a fragment (not a sentence fragment but a clause fragment) because it contains a subject ("girl") but no verb to act as a predicate for the subject (the two clauses that begin with "who" act as modifiers of "girl"). Removing "and who" after "loved" will correct this error, as in choices (D) and (E); "had left" then becomes the verb that acts as the predicate for "girl." Another error in the original underlined portion is the first "who," which is in the form of a subject but which should be in the form of an object ("whom") since it acts as the object of "loved" ("he" is the subject of "loved"). The second "who" is correct since it is the subject of "had left" ("him" is the object). Therefore, choice (D) is correct.

The next example illustrates Rules 10 and 11.

Example 30

Initially Bob was the group's spokesman, afterwards it occurred to them that Jane was more articulate and more diplomatic.
(A) afterwards it occurred to them that
(B) that wasn't the best thing to do since
(C) but they came to realize that
(D) they concluded, however, that
(E) then they decided that

This sentence is an example of a run-on sentence, that is, a sentence which contains two independent clauses that are not properly joined together. The portion of this sentence before the comma is an independent clause (which means a clause that can act as a sentence all by itself), and the portion of the sentence after the comma is also an independent clause. A comma by itself is not sufficient to separate two independent clauses; rather, a coordinating conjunction like and, but, yet, for, or, or nor must be used between the comma and the second independent clause. Only choice (C) provides such a conjunction at the beginning of the second clause. Since "they came to realize" has virtually the same meaning as "it occurred to them," choice (C) is the correct answer. The main consideration here is that choices (A), (B), (D) and (E) are run-on sentences.

The next three examples illustrate Rule 11.

Example 31

The Beatles were to be honored on account they bolstered the sagging British economy.
(A) on account they bolstered the sagging British economy
(B) being that they bolstered the sagging British economy
(C) when they bolstered the sagging British economy
(D) the reason being on account of their bolstering the sagging British economy
(E) since they bolstered the sagging British economy

The underlined portion of this sentence is a subordinate (or dependent) clause, that is, one that cannot stand by itself as a complete sentence but which must be joined to an independent or other dependent clause by a subordinate conjunction. Both (C) and (E) introduce the clause by a subordinate conjunction ("when" and "since"). Since the relationship between the two clauses of the sentence is one of cause and effect, since is a better word than when. On account, if used at all, should be in the form on account of; furthermore, since of is a preposition, it must take an object, for example "their bolstering of the sagging British economy." Being that is poor diction (because it is not acceptable in Standard Written English, that is, it is a slang expression, as is being as) if used as a substitute for "since" or "because." Choice (D) is redundant ("the reason being" and "on account of" say the same thing).

Example 32

Because he agrees with you does not signify that his reasons are the same as yours.
(A) Because he agrees with you
(B) If he agrees with you
(C) When he agrees with you
(D) Because you and he agree
(E) That he agrees with you

The underlined portion of the sentence acts as the subject of the sentence, that is, the underlined portion "does not signify . . ." The correct answer is choice (E) because "That" is short for "The fact that," and "fact" is the true subject of the sentence. The omission of "The fact" from choice (E) is another example of an ellipsis (the omission of a word or words from a sentence). None of the other choices can act as the subject of the sentence.

Example 33

The scholar's reluctance over committing himself as to judging the authenticity of the manuscript may be caused as a result of his uncertainty of its recent history.

(A) over committing himself as to judging the authenticity of the manuscript may be caused as a result of
(B) to judge the authenticity of the manuscript may be caused as a result of
(C) to judge the authenticity of the manuscript may be a result of
(D) over committing himself as to judgment of the authenticity of the manuscript may be caused by
(E) over committing himself as to judging of the authenticity of the manuscript may be a result of

The underlined portion of this sentence uses too many words to express two ideas and also uses poor diction. "Over committing himself as to judging" should be either "to commit himself to judge" ("reluctance over committing" uses poor diction; "reluctance" in this context should be followed by an infinitive) or merely "to judge," which is even better. "Caused as a result of" is redundant: his "reluctance" either "is caused by his uncertainty" or "is a result of his uncertainty," not both. Therefore, the correct answer is (C).

Keep in mind that although there are other linguistic rules of sentence construction, the GMAT concentrates on the rules discussed above. Controversial topics and rules of grammar are avoided (for example, the rule that it is preferable to avoid splitting an infinitive by placing a word or phrase between the "to" and the verb).

BASIC ENGLISH REVIEW

PUNCTUATION RULES

1. Apostrophe (')

The apostrophe is used

1. *to indicate possession*
   Bob's hat; Burns' poems; Jones's houses;

NOTE: Use *apostrophe only* (without the s) for certain words that end in s:

a. When *s* or *z* sound comes before the final *s*
   Moses' journey
   Cassius' plan

b. after a plural noun
   girls' shoes
   horses' reins

Where to place the Apostrophe
EXAMPLE:
These (ladie's, ladies') blouses are on sale.

The apostrophe means *belonging to everything to the* left *of the apostrophe.*

ladie's means *belonging to ladie* (no such word)
ladies' means *belonging to ladies* (correct)

EXAMPLE:
These (childrens', children's) coats are size 8.

One cannot say *belonging to childrens* (childrens'); therefore, children's (belonging to children) is correct.

ALSO NOTE:

a. When two or more names comprise one firm, possession is indicated in the last name.

Lansdale, Jackson and Roosevelt's law firm.
Sacks and Company's sale.

b. In a compound noun, separated by hyphens, the apostrophe belongs in the last syllable—*father-in-law's.*

Note that the *plurals* of compound nouns are formed by adding the s (no apostrophe, of course) to the *first* syllable: I have three *brothers-in-law.*

The apostrophe has two other uses besides indicating possession:

2. *for plurals of letters and figures*
   three d's; five 6's

3. *to show that a letter has been left out*
   let's (for let us)

NOTE A: ours, yours, his, hers, its, theirs, and whose—all are possessive but have no apostrophe.

NOTE B: The apostrophe is omitted occasionally in titles: Teachers College: Actors Equity Association.

2. Colon (:)

The colon is used

1. *after such expressions as "the following," "as follows," and their equivalents*
   The sciences studied in high schools are as follows: biology, chemistry, and physics.

2. *after the salutation in a business letter*
   Gentlemen:
   Dear Mr. Jones:

NOTE: A comma (see below) is used after the salutation in a friendly letter:

Dear Ted,

The semicolon is *never* used in a salutation.

3. Comma (,)

In general, the comma is used in writing just as you use a pause in speaking. Here are the specific situations in which commas are used:

1. *direct address*
   Mr. Adams, has the report come in yet?

2. *apposition*
   Sam, our buyer, gave us some good advice.

3. *parenthetical expressions*
   We could not, however, get him to agree.

4. *letter*
   Sincerely,
   Truly yours,

5. *dates, addresses*
   November 11, 1918
   Cleveland, Ohio

6. *series*
   We had soup, salad, ice cream, and milk for lunch.

NOTE: Comma before the *and* in a series is not necessary.

7. *phrase or clause at beginning of sentence (if the phrase or clause is long)*
   As I left the room to go to school, my mother called me.

8. *separating clauses of long sentence*
   We asked for Mr. Smith, but he had already left for home.

9. *clearness*
   After planting, the farmer had his supper.

10. *direct quotation*
    Mr. Arnold blurted out, "This is a fine mess!"

11. *modifier expressions that do not restrict the meaning of the thought which is modified*
    Air travel, which may or may not be safe, is an essential part of our way of life.

NOTE: Travel that is on the ground is safer than air travel. (NO COMMAS)

4. Dash (—)

The dash is about twice as long as the hyphen. The dash is used

1. *to break up a thought*
   There are five—remember I said five—good reasons to refuse their demands.

2. *instead of parentheses*
   A beautiful horse—Black Beauty is its name—is the hero of the book.

5. Exclamation Mark (!)

The exclamation mark is used after an expression of *strong feeling:*

Ouch! I hurt my thumb.

6. Hyphen (-)

The hyphen divides a word:

mother-in-law

NOTE: When written out, numbers from twenty-one through ninety-nine are hyphenated.

7. Parentheses ( )

1. Parentheses set off that part of the sentence that is not absolutely necessary to the completeness of the sentence:

   I was about to remark (this may be repetition) that we must arrive there early.

2. Parentheses are also used to enclose figures, letters, signs and dates in a sentence:

   Shakespeare (1564–1616) was a great dramatist.

   The four forms of discourse are a) narration b) description c) exposition d) argument.

8. Period (.)

The period is used

1. *after a complete thought unit*
   The section manager will return shortly.

2. *after an abbreviation*
   Los Angeles, Calif.

9. Question Mark (?)

The question mark is used after a *request for information:*

When do you leave for lunch?

10. Quotation Marks (" ")

Quotation marks are used

1. *to enclose what a person says directly*
   "No one could tell," she said, "that it would occur."
   He exclaimed, "This is the end!"
   "Don't leave yet," the boss told her.

2. *to enclose a title*
   I have just finished reading "Arrowsmith."

11. Semicolon (;)

The semicolon is not used much. It is to be avoided where a comma or a period will suffice.

Following, however, are the common uses of the semicolon:

1. *to avoid confusion with numbers*
   Add the following: $1.25; $7.50; and $12.89.

2. *before explanatory words or abbreviations—namely, e.g.,* etc.
   We are able to supply you with two different gauges of nylon stockings; namely, 45 and 51.

NOTE: *The semicolon goes before the expression "namely." A comma follows the expression.*

3. *to separate short statements of contrast*
   War is destructive; peace is constructive.

CAPITALIZATION RULES

1. *the first word of a sentence*
   With cooperation, a depression can be avoided.

2. *all proper names*
   America, Sante Fe Chief, General Motors, Abraham Lincoln.

3. *days of the week and months*
   The check was mailed on *Thursday.*

NOTE: The seasons are not capitalized.
Example: In Florida, *winter* is mild.

4. *the word* dear *when it is the first word in the salutation of a letter*
   Dear Mr. Jones:
   but
   My *dear* Mr. Jones:

5. *the first word of the complimentary close of a letter*
   Truly yours,
   Very *truly* yours,

6. *the first and all other important words in a title*
   The *Art* of *Salesmanship*

7. *a word used as part of a proper name*
   William *Street* (but—That *street* is narrow.)
   Morningside *Terrace* (but—We have a *terrace* apartment.)

8. *titles, when they refer to a particular official or family member*
   The report was read by *Secretary* Marshall.
   (but—Miss Shaw, our *secretary,* is ill.)
   Let's visit *Uncle* Harry.
   (but—I have three *uncles.*)

9. *points of a compass, when they refer to particular regions of a country*
   We're going *South* next week. (but—New York is *south* of *Albany.*)

NOTE: Write: the Far West, the Pacific Coast, the Middle East, etc.

10. *the first word of a direct quotation*
    It was Alexander Pope who wrote, "*A* little learning is a dangerous thing."

NOTE: When a direct quotation sentence is broken, the *first* word of the *second half* of the sentence is not capitalized.

"Don't phone," Lily told me, "*because* they're not in yet."

THE RULES OF GRAMMAR

Parts of Speech

A **NOUN** is the name of a person, place, thing, or idea:

teacher   city   desk   democracy

PRONOUNS substitute for nouns:

he   they   ours   those

An **ADJECTIVE** describes a noun:

warm   quick   tall   blue

A **VERB** expresses action or state of being:

yell   interpret   feel   are

An **ADVERB** modifies a verb, an adjective, or another adverb:

fast   slowly   friendly   well

CONJUNCTIONS join words, sentences, and phrases:

and   but   or

A **PREPOSITION** shows position in time or space:

in   during   after   behind

Nouns

There are different kinds of nouns.

Common nouns are general:

house   girl   street   city

Proper nouns are specific:

White House   Jane   Main Street   New York

Collective nouns name groups:

team   crowd   organization   Congress

Nouns have *cases:*

Nominative—the subject, noun of address, or predicate noun

Objective—the direct object, indirect object, or object of the preposition

Possessive—the form that shows possession

Pronouns

Antecedent of the pronoun—the noun to which a pronoun refers. A pronoun must agree with its antecedent in gender, person, and number.

There are several kinds of pronouns. (Pronouns also have cases.)

Demonstrative pronoun: this, that, these, those

Indefinite pronoun: all, any, nobody

Interrogative pronoun: who, which, what

Personal pronoun:

		NOMINATIVE CASE	OBJECTIVE CASE	POSSESSIVE CASE
SINGULAR	1st person	I	me	my, mine
	2nd person	you	you	your, yours
	3rd person	he, she, it	him, her, it	his, her, hers
PLURAL	1st person	we	us	our, ours
	2nd person	you	you	your, yours
	3rd person	they	them	their, theirs

Adjectives

Adjectives answer the questions "Which one?", "What kind?", and "How many?"

There are three uses of adjectives:

A **noun modifier** is usually placed directly before the noun it describes: He is a *tall* man.

A **predicate adjective** follows an inactive verb and modifies the subject: He is *happy*. I feel *terrible*.

An **article** or **noun marker** are other names for these adjectives: the, a, an

Adverbs

Adverbs answer the questions "Why?", "How?", "Where?", "When?", and "To what degree?"

Adverbs should not be used to modify nouns.

CORRECT ENGLISH USAGE

accede—means *to agree with.*
concede—means *to yield,* but not necessarily in agreement.
exceed—means *to be more than.*

We shall *accede* to your request for more evidence.
To avoid delay, we shall *concede* that more evidence is necessary.
Federal expenditures now *exceed* federal income.

access—means *availability*
excess—means *too much.*

The lawyer was given *access* to the grand jury records.
The expenditures this month are far in *excess* of income.

accept—means *to take when offered.*
except—means *excluding.* (preposition)
except—means *to leave out.* (verb)

The draft board will *accept* all seniors as volunteers before graduation.
All eighteen-year-olds *except* seniors will be called.
The draft board will *except* all seniors until after graduation.

adapt—means *to adjust or change.*
adopt—means *to take as one's own.*
adept—means *skillful.*

Children can *adapt* to changing conditions very easily.
The war orphan was *adopted* by the general and his wife.
Proper instruction makes children *adept* in various games.
NOTE: adapt *to,* adopt *by,* adept *in* or *at.*

adapted to—implies *original or natural suitability.*

The gills of the fish are *adapted to* underwater breathing.

adapted for—implies *created suitability.*

Atomic energy is constantly being *adapted for* new uses.

adapted from—implies *changed to be made suitable.*

Many of Richard Wagner's opera librettos were *adapted from* old Norse sagas.

addition—means *the act or process of adding.*
edition—means *a printing of a publication.*
In *addition* to a dictionary, he always used a thesaurus.
The first *edition* of Shakespeare's plays appeared in 1623.

advantage—means *a superior position.*
benefit—means *a favor conferred* or *earned* (as a profit).
He had an *advantage* in experience over his opponent.
The rules were changed for his *benefit.*
NOTE: to *take* advantage *of,* to *have* an advantage *over.*

adverse—(pronounced AD-verse) means *unfavorable.*
averse—(pronounced a-VERSE) means *disliking.*
He took the *adverse* decision in poor taste.
Many students are *averse* to criticism by their classmates.

advise—means *to give advice. Advise* is losing favor as a synonym for *notify.*
Acceptable: The teacher will *advise* the student in habits of study.
Unacceptable: We are *advising* you of a delivery under separate cover. (SAY: *notifying*)

affect—means *to influence.* (verb)
effect—means *an influence* (noun)
effect—means *to bring about.* (verb)
Your education must *affect* your future.
The *effect* of the last war is still being felt.
A diploma *effected* a tremendous change in his attitude.
NOTE: *Affect* also has a meaning of *pretend.* She had an *affected* manner.

after—is unnecessary with the *past* participle.
SAY: *After* checking the timetable, I left for the station.
DON'T SAY: *After having checked* (omit *after*) the timetable, I left for the station.

ain't—is an *unacceptable* contraction for *am not, are not,* or *is not.*

aisle—is *a passageway* between seats.
isle—is *a small island.* (Both words rhyme with *pile.*)

all ready—means *everybody* or *everything ready.*
already—means *previously.*
They were *all ready* to write when the teacher arrived.
They had *already* begun writing when the teacher arrived.

alright—is *unacceptable.*
all right—is *acceptable.*

all-round—means *versatile* or *general.*
all around—means *all over a given area.*
Rafer Johnson, decathlon champion, is an *all-round* athlete.
The police were lined up for miles *all around.*

all together—means *everybody* or *everything together.*
altogether—means *completely.*
The boys and girls sang *all together.*
This was *altogether* strange for a person of his type.

all ways—means *in every possible way.*
always—means *at all times.*
He was in *all ways* acceptable to the voters.
His reputation had *always* been spotless.

allude—means *to make a reference to.*
elude—means *to escape from.*
Only incidentally does Coleridge *allude* to Shakespeare's puns.
It is almost impossible for one to *elude* tax collectors.

allusion—means *a reference.*
illusion—means *a deception of the eye or mind.*
The student made *allusions* to his teacher's habits.
Illusions of the mind, unlike those of the eye, cannot be corrected with glasses.

alongside of—means *side by side with.*
Bill stood *alongside of* Henry.
alongside—means *parallel to the side.*
Park the car *alongside* the curb.

alot—is *unacceptable.* It should always be written as two words: *a lot.*

among—is used with *more than two persons or things.*
NOTE: *Amongst* should be avoided.
between—is used with *two persons or things.*
The inheritance was equally divided *among* the four children.
The business, however, was divided *between* the oldest and the youngest one.

amount—applies to quantities *that cannot be counted one by one.*
number—applies to quantities *that can be counted one by one.*
A large *amount* of grain was delivered to the storehouse.
A large *number* of bags of grain was delivered.

annual—means *yearly.*
biannual—means *twice a year.* (*Semiannual* means the same.)
biennial—means *once in two years* or *every two years.*

anywheres—is *unacceptable.*
anywhere—is *acceptable.*
SAY we can't find it *anywhere.*
ALSO SAY *nowhere* (NOT nowheres), *somewhere* (NOT somewheres)

aren't I—is colloquial. Its use is to be discouraged.
SAY: *AM I not* entitled to an explanation?
(preferred to *Aren't I . . .*)

as—(used as a conjunction) is followed by a verb
like—(used as a preposition) is NOT followed by a verb.
Do *as* I do, not *as* I say.
Try not to behave *like* a child.
Unacceptable: He acts *like* I do.

as far as—expresses *distance.*
so far as—indicates *a limitation.*
We hiked *as far as* the next guest house.
So far as we know, the barn was adequate for a night's stay.

as good as—should be used *for comparisons only.*
This motel is *as good as* the next one.
NOTE: *As good as* does NOT mean *practically.*
Unacceptable: They *as good as* promised us a place in the hall.
Acceptable: They *practically* promised us a place in the hall.

as if—is correctly used in the expression, "He talked *as if* his jaw hurt him."
Unacceptable: "He talked *like* his jaw hurt him."

ascared—no such word. It is *unacceptable* for *scared.*
The child was *scared* of ghosts. (NOT *ascared*).

ascent—is *the act of rising.*
assent—means *approval.*
The *ascent* to the top of the mountain was perilous.
Congress gave its *assent* to the President's emergency directive.

assay—means *to try* or *experiment.*
essay—means *to make an intellectual effort.*
We shall *assay* the ascent of the mountain tomorrow.
The candidate's views were expressed in a well-written *essay.*

attend to—means *to take care of.*
tend to—means *to be inclined to.*
One of the clerks will *attend to* mail in my absence.
Lazy people *tend* to gain weight.

back—should NOT be used with such words as *refer* and *return* since the prefix *re* means *back.*
Unacceptable: Refer *back* to the text, if you have difficulty recalling the facts.

backward Both are *acceptable* and may be
backwards used interchangeably as an adverb.
We tried to run *backward.* (or *backwards*)
Backward as an adjective means *slow in learning.* (DON'T say *backwards* in this case)
A *backward* pupil should be given every encouragement.

berth—is *a resting place.*
birth—means *the beginning of life.*
The new liner was given a wide *berth* in the harbor.
He was a fortunate man from *birth.*

beside—means *close to.*
besides—refers *to something that has been added.*
He lived *beside* the stream.
He found wild flowers and weeds *besides.*

better—means *recovering.*
well—means *completely recovered.*
He is *better* now than he was a week ago.
In a few more weeks, he will be *well.*

both—means *two considered together.*
each—means *one of two or more.*
Both of the applicants qualified for the position.
Each applicant was given a generous reference.
NOTE: Avoid using such expressions as the following:
Both girls had a new typewriter. (Use *each girl* instead.)
Both girls tried to outdo the other. (Use *each girl* instead.)
They are *both* alike (Omit *both*).

breath—means *an intake of air.*
breathe—means *to draw air in and give it out.*
breadth—means *width.*
Before you dive in, take a very deep *breath.*
It is difficult to *breathe* under water.
In a square, the *breadth* should be equal to the length.

bring—means *to carry toward the person who is speaking.*
take—means *to carry away from the speaker.*
Bring the books here.
Take your raincoat with you when you go out.

broke—is the past tense of *break.*
broke—is *unacceptable* for *without money.*
He *broke* his arm.
"Go for broke" is a slang expression widely used in gambling circles.

bunch—refers to *things.*
group—refers to *persons* or *things.*
This looks like a delicious *bunch* of bananas.
What a well-behaved *group* of children!
NOTE: The colloquial use of bunch applied to *persons* is to be discouraged.
A *bunch* of the boys were whooping it up. (*Number* is preferable.)

certainly—(and *surely*) is an *adverb.*
sure—is an *adjective.*
He was *certainly* learning fast.
Unacceptable: He *sure* was learning fast.

cite—means *to quote.*
sight—means *seeing.*
site—means *a place for a building.*
He was fond of *citing* from the Scriptures.
The *sight* of the wreck was appalling.
The Board of Education is seeking a *site* for the new school.

coarse—means *vulgar* or *harsh.*
course—means a *path* or a *study.*
He was shunned because of his *coarse* behavior.
The ship took its usual *course.*
Which *course* in English are you taking?

come to be—should NOT be replaced with the expression *become to be,* since *become* means *come to be.*
True freedom will *come to be* when all tyrants have been overthrown.

comic—means *intentionally funny.*
comical—means *unintentionally funny.*
A clown is a *comic* figure.
The peculiar hat she wore gave her a *comical* appearance.

conscience—means *sense of right.*
conscientious—means *faithful.*
conscious—means *aware of one's self.*
Man's *conscience* prevents him from becoming completely selfish.
We all depend on him because he is *conscientious.*
The injured man was completely *conscious.*

considerable—is properly used *only as an adjective,* NOT as a noun.

cease—means *to end.*
seize—means *to take hold of.*
Will you please *cease* making those sounds?
Seize him by the collar as he comes around the corner.

cent—means *a coin.*
scent—means *an odor.*
sent—is the past tense of *send.*
The one-*cent* postal card is a thing of the past.
The *scent* of roses is pleasing.
We were *sent* to the rear of the balcony.

calendar—is *a system of time.*
calender—is *a smoothing and glazing machine.*
colander—is *a kind of sieve.*
In this part of the world, most people prefer the twelve-month *calendar.*
In ceramic work, the potting wheel and the *calender* are indispensable.
Garden-picked vegetables should be washed in a *colander* before cooking.

can—means *physically able.*
may—implies *permission.*
I *can* lift this chair over my head.
You *may* leave after you finish your work.

cannot help—must be followed by an *-ing* form.
We cannot help *feeling* (NOT *feel*) distressed about this.
NOTE: *cannot help but* is *unacceptable.*

can't hardly—is a *double negative.* It is *unacceptable.*
SAY: The child *can hardly* walk in those shoes.

capital—is *the city.*
capitol—is *the building*
Paris is the *capital* of France.
The Capitol in Washington is occupied by the Congress. (The Washington *Capitol* is capitalized.)
NOTE: *Capital* also means wealth.

compare to—means *to liken to something which has a different form.*
compare with—means *to compare persons or things with each other when they are of the same kind.*
contrast with—means *to show the difference between two things.*
A minister is sometimes *compared to* a shepherd.
Shakespeare's plays are often *compared with* those of Marlowe.
The writer *contrasted* the sensitivity of the dancer *with* the grossness of the pugilist.

complement—means *a completing part.*
compliment—is *an expression of admiration.*
His wit was a *complement* to her beauty.
He *complimented* her attractive hairstyle.

consul—means *a government representative.*
council—means *an assembly that meets for deliberation.*
counsel—means *advice.*
Americans abroad should keep in touch with their *consuls.*
The City *Council* enacts local laws and regulations.
The defendant heeded the *counsel* of his friends.

convenient to—should be followed by a *person.*
convenient for—should be followed by a *purpose.*
Will these plans be *convenient to* you?
You must agree that they are *convenient for* the occasion.

copy—is *an imitation of an original work.* (not necessarily an exact imitation)
facsimile—is *an exact imitation of an original work.*
The counterfeiters made a crude *copy* of the hundred-dollar bill.
The official government engraver, however, prepared a *facsimile* of the bill.

could of—is *unacceptable.* (*Should of* is also *unacceptable.*)
could have—is *acceptable.* (*Should have* is *acceptable.*)
Acceptable: You *could have* done better with more care.
Unacceptable: I *could of* won.
ALSO AVOID: *must of, would of.*

decent—means *suitable.*
descent—means *going down.*
dissent—means *disagreement.*
The *decent* thing to do is to admit your fault.
The *descent* into the cave was treacherous.
Two of the nine justices filed a *dissenting* opinion.

deduction—means *reasoning from the general (laws or principles) to the particular (facts).*
induction—means *reasoning from the particular (facts) to the general (laws or principles).*
All men are mortal. Since John is a man, he is mortal. (*deduction*)
There are 10,000 oranges in this truckload. I have examined 100 from various parts of the load and find them all of the same quality. I conclude that the 10,000 oranges are of this quality. (*induction*)

delusion—means *a wrong idea* that will probably influence action.
illusion—means *a wrong idea* that will probably *not* influence action.
People were under the *delusion* that the earth was flat.
It is just an *illusion* that the earth is flat.

desert—(pronounced DEZZ-ert) means *an arid area.*
desert—(pronounced di-ZERT) means *to abandon;* also *a reward or punishment.*
dessert—(pronounced di-ZERT) means *the final course of a meal.*
The Sahara is the world's most famous *desert.*
A husband must not *desert* his wife.
Execution was a just *desert* for his crime.
We had plum pudding for *dessert.*

different from—is *acceptable.*
different than—is *unacceptable.*
Acceptable: Jack is *different from* his brother.
Unacceptable: Florida climate is *different than* New York climate.

doubt that—is *acceptable.*
doubt whether—is *unacceptable.*
Acceptable: I *doubt that* you will pass this term.
Unacceptable: We *doubt whether* you will succeed.

dual—means *relating to two.*
duel—means *a contest between two persons.*
Dr. Jekyll had a *dual* personality.
Alexander Hamilton was fatally injured in a *duel* with Aaron Burr.

due to—is *unacceptable* at the beginning of a sentence. Use *because of, on account of,* or some similar expression instead.
Unacceptable: Due to the rain, the game was postponed.
Acceptable: Because of the rain, the game was postponed.
Acceptable: the postponement was *due to* the rain.

each other—refers to *two persons.*
one another—refers to *more than two persons.*
The two girls have known *each other* for many years.
Several of the girls have known *one another* for many years.

either . . . or—is used when referring to choices.
neither . . . nor—is the *negative* form.
Either you *or* I will win the election.
Neither Bill *nor* Henry is expected to have a chance.

eliminate—means *to get rid of.*
illuminate—means *to supply with light.*
Let us try to *eliminate* the unnecessary steps.
Several lamps were needed to *illuminate* the corridor.

emerge—means *to rise out of.*
immerge—means *to sink into. (also* **immerse**)
The swimmer *emerged* from the pool.
The laundress *immerged* the dress in the tub of water.

emigrate—means *to leave one's country for another.*
immigrate—means *to enter another country.*
The Norwegians *emigrated* to America in the mid-1860's.
Many of the Norwegian *immigrants* settled in the Middle West

everyone—is written as one word when it is a *pronoun.*

every one—(two words) is used when each individual is stressed.

Everyone present voted for the proposal.

Every one of the voters accepted the proposal.

NOTE: *Everybody* is written as one word.

everywheres—is *unacceptable.*
everywhere—is *acceptable.*

We searched *everywhere* for the missing book.

NOTE: *Everyplace* (one word) is likewise *unacceptable.*

feel bad—means *to feel ill.*
feel badly—means *to have a poor sense of touch.*

I *feel bad* about the accident I saw.

The numbness in his limbs caused him to *feel badly.*

feel good—means *to be happy.*
feel well—means *to be in good health.*

I *feel* very *good* about my recent promotion.

Spring weather always made him *feel well.*

flout—means *to insult.*
flaunt—means *to make a display of.*

He *flouted* the authority of the principal.

Hester Prynne *flaunted* her scarlet "A."

formally—means *in a formal way.*
formerly—means *at an earlier time.*

The letter of reference was *formally* written.

He was *formerly* a delegate to the convention.

former—means *the first of two.*
latter—means *the second of two.*

The *former* half of the book was in prose.

The *latter* half of the book was in poetry.

forth—means *forward.*
fourth—*comes after third.*

They went *forth* like warriors of old.

The *Fourth* of July is our Independence Day.

NOTE: spelling of *forty* (40) and *fourteen* (14).

get—is a verb that strictly means *to obtain.*

Please *get* my bag.

There are many slang forms of GET that should be avoided:

AVOID: Do you *get* me? (SAY: Do you *understand* me?)

AVOID: You can't *get* away with it. (SAY: You won't *avoid* punishment if you do it.)

AVOID: *Get* wise to yourself. (SAY: *Use* common sense.)

AVOID: We didn't *get* to go. (SAY: We didn't *manage* to go.)

got—means *obtained.*

He *got* the tickets yesterday.

AVOID: You've *got* to do it. (SAY: You *have* to do it.)

AVOID: We *have got* no sympathy for them. (SAY: We *have* no sympathy for them.)

AVOID: They have *got* a great deal of property. (SAY: They *have* a great deal of property.)

hanged—is used in reference to a *person.*
hung—is used in reference to a *thing.*

The prisoner was *hanged* at dawn.

The picture was *hung* above the fireplace.

however—means *nevertheless.*
how ever—means *in what possible way.*

We are certain, *however,* that you will like this class.

We are certain that, *how ever* you decide to study, you will succeed.

if—introduces a *condition.*
whether—introduces a *choice.*

I shall go to Europe *if* I win the prize.

He asked me *whether* I intended to go to Europe. (not *if*)

if it was—implies that *something might have been true in the past.*
if it were—implies *doubt,* or indicates *something that is contrary to fact.*

If your book was there last night, it is there now.

If it were summer now, we would all go swimming.

in—usually refers to *a state of being.* (no motion)
into—is used for *motion from one place to another.*

The records are *in* that drawer.
I put the records *into* that drawer.
NOTE: "We were walking in the room" is correct even though there is motion. The motion is *not* from one place to another.

irregardless—is *unacceptable.*
regardless—is *acceptable.*
Unacceptable: Irregardless of the weather, I am going to the game.
Acceptable: Regardless of his ability, he is not likely to win.

its—means *belonging to it.*
it's—means *it is.*
The house lost *its* roof.
It's an exposed house, now.

kind of / **sort of** are *unacceptable* for *rather.*
SAY: We are *rather disappointed in you.*

last—refers to *the final member in a series.*
latest—refers to *the most recent in time.*
latter—refers to *the second of two.*
This is the *last* bulletin. There won't be any other bulletins.
This is the *latest* bulletin. There will be other bulletins.
Of the two most recent bulletins, the *latter* is more encouraging.

lay—means *to place.*
lie—means *to recline.*
Note the forms of each verb:

TENSE	LIE (RECLINE)
Present	The child *is lying* down.
Past	The child *lay* down.
Pres. perf.	The child *has lain* down.

TENSE	LAY (PLACE)
Present	The chicken *is laying* an egg.
Past	The chicken *laid* an egg.
Pres. Perf.	The chicken *has laid* an egg.

lightening—is the present participle of *to lighten.*
lightning—means *the flashes of light accompanied by thunder.*
Leaving the extra food behind resulted in *lightening* the pack.
Summer thunderstorms produce startling *lightning* bolts.

many—refers to *a number.*
much—refers to *a quantity in bulk.*
How *many* inches of rain fell last night?
I don't know; but I would say *much* rain fell last night.

may—is used in the *present tense.*
might—is used in the *past tense.*
We are hoping that he *may* come today.
He *might* have done it if you had encouraged him.

it's I—is always *acceptable.*
it's me—is *acceptable* only in colloquial speech or writing.

It's him / This is her / It was them } always *unacceptable*

It's he / This is she / It was they } always *acceptable*

noplace—as a solid word, is *unacceptable* for *no place* or *nowhere.*
Acceptable: You now have *nowhere* to go.

number—is singular *when the total is intended.*
The *number* (of pages in the book) is 500.
number—is plural *when the individual units are referred* to.
A *number of pages* (in the book) were printed in italic type.

of any—(and *of anyone*) is *unacceptable* for *of all.*
SAY: His was the highest mark *of all.*
(NOT *of any* or *of anyone*)

off of—is *unacceptable.*
SAY: He took the book *off* the table.

out loud—is *unacceptable* for *aloud.*
SAY: He read *aloud* to his family every evening.

outdoor—(and *out-of-door*) is an adjective.
outdoors—is an adverb.
We spent most of the summer at an *outdoor* music camp.
Most of the time we played string quartets *outdoors.*
NOTE: *Out-of-doors* is *acceptable* in either case.

people—comprise *a united* or *collective group of individuals.*
persons—are *individuals that are separate and unrelated.*
Only five *persons* remained in the theater after the first act.
The *people* of New York City have enthusiastically accepted "Shakespeare-in-the-Park" productions.

persecute—means *to make life miserable for someone.* (Persecution is illegal.)
prosecute—means *to conduct a criminal investigation.* (Prosecution is legal.)
Some racial groups insist upon *persecuting* other groups.
The District Attorney is *prosecuting* the racketeers.

precede—means *to come before.*
proceed—means *to go ahead.* (*Procedure* is the noun.)
supersede—means *to replace.*
What were the circumstances that *preceded* the attack?
We can then *proceed* with our plan for resisting a second attack.
It is then possible that Plan B will *supersede* Plan A.

principal—means *chief* or *main* (as an adjective); *a leader* (as a noun).
principle—means *a fundamental truth* or *belief.*
His *principal* supporters came from among the peasants.
The *principal* of the school asked for cooperation from the staff.
Humility was the guiding *principle* of Buddha's life.
NOTE: *Principal* may also mean *a sum placed at interest.*
Part of his monthly payment was applied as interest on the *principal.*

sit—means *take a seat.* (intransitive verb)
set—means *place.* (transitive verb)
Note the forms of each verb:

TENSE	SIT (TAKE A SEAT)
Present	He *sits* on a chair.
Past	he *sat* on the chair.
Pres. Perf.	He *has sat* on the chair.

TENSE	SET (PLACE)
Present	He *sets* the lamp on the table
Past	He *set* the lamp on the table.
Pres. Perf.	He *has set* the lamp on the table.

some time—means *a portion of time.*
sometime—means *at an indefinite time in the future.*
sometimes—means *occasionally.*
I'll need *some time* to make a decision.
Let us meet *sometime* after twelve noon.
Sometimes it is better to hesitate before signing a contract.

somewheres—is *unacceptable.*
somewhere—is *acceptable.*

stationary—means *standing still.*
stationery—means *writing materials.*
In ancient times people thought the earth was *stationary.*
We bought writing paper at the *stationery* store.

stayed—means *remained.*
stood—means *remained upright* or *erect.*
The army *stayed* in the trenches for five days.
The soldiers *stood* at attention for one hour.

sure—for *surely* is *unacceptable.*
SAY: You *surely* (NOT *sure*) are not going to write that!

take in—is *unacceptable* in the sense of *deceive* or *attend.*
SAY: We were *deceived* (NOT *taken in*) by his oily manner.
We should like to *attend* (NOT *take in*) a few plays during our vacation.

their—means *belonging to them.*
there—means *in that place.*
they're—means *they are.*
We took *their* books home with us.
You will find your books over *there* on the desk.
They're going to the ballpark with us.

theirselves—is *unacceptable* for *themselves.*
SAY: Most children of school age are able to care for *themselves* in many ways.

these kind—is *unacceptable.*
this kind—is *acceptable.*
I am fond of *this kind* of apples.
NOTE: *These kinds* would be also *acceptable.*

through—meaning *finished* or *completed* is *unacceptable.*
SAY: We'll finish (NOT *be through with*) the work by five o'clock.

try to—is *acceptable.*
try and—is *unacceptable.*
Try to come (NOT *try and* come).
NOTE: *plan on going* is *unacceptable. plan to go* is *acceptable.*

two—is the *numeral* 2.
to—means *in the direction of.*
too—means *more than* or *also.*
There are *two* sides to every story.
Three *twos* (or 2's) equal six.
We shall go *to* school.
We shall go, *too.*
The weather is *too* hot for school.

was
were If something is contrary to fact (not a fact), use *were* in every instance.
I wish I *were* in Bermuda.
Unacceptable: If he *was* sensible, he wouldn't act like that.
(SAY: If he *were* . . .)

ways—is *unacceptable* for *way.*
SAY: We climbed a little *way* (NOT *ways*) up the hill.

went and took—(*went and stole,* etc.) is *unacceptable.*
SAY: They *stole* (NOT *went and stole*) our tools.

when—(and *where*) should NOT be used to introduce a definition of a noun.
SAY: A tornado *is a* twisting, high wind on land (NOT *is when a twisting, high wind is on land*).
A pool *is a place for swimming.* (NOT *is where people swim*)

whereabouts—is *unacceptable* for *where.*
SAY: *Where* (NOT *whereabouts*) do you live?
NOTE: *Whereabouts* as a noun meaning a place is *acceptable.*
Do you know his *whereabouts?*

whether—should NOT be preceded by *of* or *as to.*
SAY: The President will consider the question *whether* (NOT *of whether*) it is better to ask for or demand higher taxes now.
He inquired *whether* (NOT *as to whether*) we were going or not.

which—is used *incorrectly* in the following expressions:
He asked me to stay, *which I did.* (CORRECT: He asked me to stay and I did.)
It has been a severe winter, *which* is unfortunate. (CORRECT: Unfortunately, it has been a severe winter.)
You did not write; besides *which* you have not telephoned. (CORRECT: Omit *which*)

while—is *unacceptable* for *and* or *though.*
SAY: The library is situated on the south side; (OMIT *while*) the laboratory is on the north side.
Though (NOT while) I disagree with you, I shall not interfere with your right to express your opinion.
Though (NOT *while*) I am in my office every day, you do not attempt to see me.

who
whom The following is a method (without going into grammar rules) for determining when to use WHO or WHOM.
"Tell me (*Who, Whom*) you think should represent our company?"
STEP ONE: Change the who—whom part of the sentence to its natural order.
"You think (*who, whom*) should represent our company?"
STEP TWO: Substitute HE for WHO, HIM for WHOM.
"You think (he, him) should represent our company?"
You would say *he* in this case.
THEREFORE: "Tell me WHO you think should represent the company?" is correct.

who is
who am Note these constructions:

It is I who *am* the most experienced.
It is he who *is* . . .
It is he or I who *am* . . .
It is I or he who *is* . . .
It is he and I who *are* . . .

whose—means *of whom.*

who's—mean *who is.*
Whose is this notebook?
Who's in the next office?

would have—is *unacceptable* for *had.*
SAY: I wish you *had* (NOT *would have*) called earlier.

you all—is *unacceptable* for *you* (plural).
SAY: We welcome *you,* the delegates from Ethiopia.
You are all welcome, delegates of Ethiopia.

TWENTY PRINCIPLES OF GRAMMAR

1. The subject of a verb is in the nominative case even if the verb is understood and not expressed.
2. The word *who* is in the nominative case. *Whom* is in the objective case.
3. The word *whoever* is in the nominative case. *Whomever* is in the objective case.
4. Nouns or pronouns connected by a form of the verb *to be* should always be in the nominative case.
5. The object of a preposition or of a transitive verb should use a pronoun in the objective case.
6. It is unacceptable to use the possessive case in relation to inanimate objects.
7. A pronoun agrees with its antecedent in person, number, gender, and case.
8. A noun or pronoun linked with a gerund should be in the possessive case.
9. *Each, every, everyone, everybody, anybody, either, neither, no one, nobody,* and similar words are singular and require the use of singular verbs and pronouns.
10. When modifying the words *kind* and *sort,* the words *this* and *that* always remain in the singular.
11. The word *don't* is not used with third person singular pronouns or nouns.
12. A verb agrees in number with its subject. A verb should not be made to agree with a noun that is part of a phrase following the subject.
13. The number of the verb is not affected by the addition to the subject of words introduced by *with, together with, no less than, as well as,* etc.
14. Singular subjects joined by the words *nor* and *or* take a singular verb.
15. A subject consisting of two or more nouns joined by the word *and* takes a plural verb.
16. A verb should agree in number with the subject, not with the predicate noun.
17. In *there is* and *there are,* the verb should agree in number with the noun that follows it.
18. An adjective should not be used to modify a verb.
19. Statements equally true in the past and in the present are usually expressed in the present tense.
20. The word *were* is used to express a condition contrary to fact, or a wish.

ANALYSIS OF SITUATIONS (PRACTICAL BUSINESS JUDGMENT) INSTRUCTIONAL OVERVIEW

For many years the GMAT has had a Practical Business Judgment section in it. This type of question also appeared on the LSAT for some years. The name of the section was changed to Analysis of Situations in 1982 and that name is used in this book (Analysis of Situations will be abbreviated AS).

FORMAT OF SECTION

The AS section on the GMAT will consist of two passages, each of which are 900 to 1500 words in length. A total of 35–40 questions will be associated with the two passages, generally divided roughly in half between the passages. Each question is a partial sentence that conveys an idea that must be classified in accordance with the section's instructions.

The AS section is based on a predetermined answer schema and much of our work in this Instructional Overview will be to understand what this schema really means. This is a difficult task because the instructions given by the Educational Testing Service use words that have many connotations and meanings other than the ones that they are used to convey in the instructions. Furthermore, there is a certain amount of indirection in the ways that the instructions are phrased that makes it difficult for most students to clearly see what the issues are.

TIMING

This section also presents most students with some time pressure, since there are 35 or more questions to answer in 30 minutes. Focusing your attention on one passage, you should allow 15 minutes for each passage. Of those 15 minutes, no more than nine minutes should be spent reading the passage. This is an outside limit since it leaves you only six minutes to answer approximately 18 questions. Even though these questions are relatively short and there is a consistent answer schema, spending nine minutes reading the passage leaves you only 20 seconds to answer each question. This is enough time if you work quickly and efficiently, but it does not leave much room for error. Ideally, the passage should be read in six minutes, which is still a rate of less than 200 words per minute for most passages. If the reading takes only six minutes, this leaves you 30 seconds for answering each question, which, while not overlong, is definitely adequate for a well-schooled student.

If you finish with a passage and its questions in less than 15 minutes, it is usually best to do whatever reviewing you can within the 15 minutes. It is most efficient to recheck your work on a particular passage while that passage is still fresh in your mind. If you finish only one or two minutes ahead of schedule, you should probably move right to the second passage—unless there is a particular question that you want to rethink. Unfortunately, most students do not have this problem. While you cannot afford to run over the 15 minutes on the first passage, since the second tends to be a trifle longer and certainly no easier, you should not fail to read and work any of the AS problems. This means that you *must* read quickly and you *must* be disciplined in quickly answering the problems as you come to them. Your overall score will be better if you answer all of the AS questions quickly than if you agonize over two-thirds of them and then have to make blind guesses at the remaining third.

BASIC IDEA OF THE SECTION

The basic idea of the AS section is to present you with a decision situation, usually in a business context, and the discussion of that decision and its options, and to require you to classify the various ideas presented in the passage in terms of the predetermined answer schema. The authors of this section refer to it as a precision reading test, and the precision reading is as much in the questions as it is in the passage, probably more so. As in Reading Comprehension, the goal is not to memorize the passage. That takes too long and ignores the fact that a good deal of work must be done with the questions, short as they are. Perhaps the most important part of reading the passage is determining exactly what the decision is in the most precise way possible. This is not necessarily hard, just important. We will discuss the proper ways of reading AS passages later in this Overview.

WHY YOU MUST UNDERSTAND DECISION SITUATIONS

You probably are aching to get right at the answer categories that the GMAT uses in this section. Indeed, many readers have probably already read them in the GMAT *Bulletin*. However, it will be better if we first discuss the nature of a decision situation and the types of ideas which naturally are used in such a situation before we make a detailed analysis of the instructions for the section and the five answer choices. The reason for this delay is simply that the wording of the instructions is, as mentioned above, less than perfectly clear. By studying the nature of decision situations before referring to the test's instructions, you will be better able to focus on those aspects of the instructions that are truly helpful.

After analyzing decision situations, we will present an extended analysis of the five answer categories, followed by a detailed attack strategy and some rules for making productive guesses when you are stuck.

WHAT IS A DECISION SITUATION?

A decision situation is one in which some person (or persons) needs to make a decision about some particular topic. On the GMAT, all of the decision situations that you will actually have to analyze concern a decision among a group of defined options. In real life, of course, trying to identify the options in a situation is often the most difficult part of the decision. On the GMAT you will rarely be concerned with that aspect of the decision.

Let us take a simple decision situation with which all college students are familiar: choosing a schedule. To make the situation even simpler, we will state that you have only one open spot on your schedule and you have determined that you must choose among the following three courses: Math #101, French and Tibetan Studies. Now we have the decision clearly defined, but we still cannot make the decision without more information. We need to know what the goals and/or purposes of the student are. We need to know what the differences are among the options. We need to know something about the general situation in which the decision-maker finds himself.

For instance:

What could be the goals or purposes for taking a particular course?

Fulfilling academic requirements; taking a course with a certain teacher; academic interest; other students taking the course; likely grade achievable in the course. There are other possible goals or purposes in taking a course in college, but these will do for now.

The next step in arriving at a decision is trying to see how good a match there is between the available courses (options) and the goals or purposes that the student is hoping to fulfill by this decision. How do we know whether a particular option meets a goal, or—more realistically—how do we know the extent to which the various options meet particular goals? In order to know how well the options meet the goals, we must know what the goals are and also what the options consist of.

Let us look at our scheduling problem. Our goal is to meet academic requirements. Do we know yet whether Math 101 will meet academic requirements? Of course not. We need new and different information—information about the state of the world outside the options that will help us to see how well the options meet the goals. In this example, let us suppose that the academic requirements of the school are that each student must take at least three math courses. This helps, but we would also like to know which courses the student has taken in earlier semesters (if any). If we know that three math courses are required and the student has taken only two, then we are able to say that there is a distinct plus for the Math 101 option: it will help to meet the math requirement. Thus we needed more information than merely what the options were and what our desires, purposes or goals were before we could make a judgment about the options in respect to that goal.

We have thus identified three basic types of information that we might use in a decision situation: (1) goals or purposes, (2) what the option is and (3) the relevant parts of the world that connect goals to the options and allow us to measure them.

Consider the following student's situation:

George is a senior at State College. He is majoring in Philosophy and is interested in taking as wide a variety of courses as he can and still meet the college's graduation requirements. He must take three additional philosophy courses in order to complete the requirements for a major in Philosophy and he only has enough money to take four courses in all.

George works three days a week and is active in the Philosophy Society, which meets every week, so his schedule is crowded. In addition to the three philosophy courses, the only courses he is eligible to take and which also fit into this schedule are Math 200, French 300 and Tibetan Studies 400. The Math 200 and French 300 classes meet early enough on Tuesday afternoon for George to make the Philosophy Society meeting. However, the Math 200 class meets on the downtown campus and George would have to take a cab if he wished to be absolutely sure of making the meeting on time. Since he is an officer of the Society and presides at the debates which the Society stages, he feels he should be on time for the meetings. The Tibetan Studies course meets on Thursday.

George has already taken three mathematics courses, so the math course is not as different from his other courses as is the Tibetan Studies course. The math course is, however, about a different branch of mathematics than he has previously studied. George has also taken two French courses from the same instructor and is afraid that this French course will be just more of the same.

George is also concerned about his grade-point average. It is just a fraction of a point below the 3.75 average needed for graduation with honors. While he knows that a fraction of a point won't make any difference to his prospects of getting into graduate school, his parents will be very pleased if he manages to graduate with honors. He would like it himself. Professor Strong, who teaches the Tibetan Studies course, is well known on campus as a very tough grader. George intends to do the work and knows he will do good work, but the margin for error will be less with Professor Strong than with the professors of the other two courses.

A related advantage of the math course is that his good friend Shelly is going to be taking it. She is an excellent math student and if they study together, he is sure of getting an A in the course.

What is the decision being discussed in this passage?

Which course to take as a fourth course. Note that the issue of the rest of George's curriculum is irrelevant, since that has already been decided and George has progressed to the current decision of choosing a fourth course.

Who is the decisionmaker?

George.

What are the options?

Math 200, French 300 and Tibetan Studies 400. We are unconcerned about why the other courses have been thrown out of consideration, because George doesn't say; it's moot.

What are the goals?

Making the Philosophy Society's meetings on time; taking an unusual or different course;

taking a course (or professor) in which a good grade can be achieved; taking a course that a friend is taking. The academic requirements for majoring in Philosophy are *not* a goal in this particular decision. These requirements and the goal of meeting them have been satisfied by the three courses that are already selected. The current decision does not in any way further the satisfaction of the goal of meeting academic requirements.

What is the nature of the options? (That is, what are the differences between the options which are relevant to the goals or purposes of the current decision?)

In answering this question, we need to develop a method of organizing and connecting our ideas so that we can understand their relationships to the decision more clearly. This passage has discussed the various options, characteristic by characteristic. First the timing problem was discussed for all the options, then the diversity issue, and lastly the grading issue. In some passages the discussion is organized by option; that is, all the aspects of one option are discussed in one place and then all the aspects of the next option, etc. Occasionally, a passage will have both structures by discussing some characteristics across all the options and also having some discussion option by option.

If we think of a decision discussion as being primarily concerned with the extent to which the various options meet the various goals and purposes of the decision, then it is logical to organize the consideration of the nature of the options by goals and purposes. The general discussion of the issue of diversity, for instance, constitutes one line of consideration that is directly tied to a clearly defined goal. Similarly for the discussions concerning timing and grading. These three general ideas are the ones that directly connect to the goals. We can therefore call them "direct."

But what does it mean to say that the math course is on another campus and thus George must take a cab in order to be sure of arriving on time for the Philosophy Society meetings? Does this automatically disqualify the option? Clearly it is not the best conceivable arrangement, but this is not the best of all possible worlds. It is often the case that the best that can be done in practice is not the best in theory. The influence of the issue of timing on the decision can only be based on the consideration of the total discussion of all the options in regard to timing. Knowing how one option works is not enough. Knowledge is needed about how *all* the options work in regard to the goal of making the Philosophy Society meetings. So it is as well for the other lines of reasoning—diversity and grading. The nature of all of the options in these regards is necessary in order to have real impact on the decision.

We thus distinguish between complete or total consideration of an idea relating to meeting a goal and an incomplete or partial consideration of the same idea. "The potential grade achievable in the math class" is only part of the grading discussion. "The grades achievable in the different classes under consideration" demands a complete discussion of the issue of meeting the goal of achieving good grades.

What ideas are useful in evaluating, but not part of, the options?

The schedule of the Philosophy Society; the location of the Philosophy Society meeting; George's previous courses; George's previous grades. These are all ideas which help to set the stage for the consideration of how well the options meet the goals. They are yardsticks of a sort which can be applied to all the options and which aid in the understanding of the significance of that option.

What ideas in the passage do not help to make the decision?

The effect of the grade achieved in each course under consideration on George's chances of admission to graduate school; the fact that George is majoring in Philosophy. The impact on any possible admission to graduate school is not helpful because the passage says that the kinds of grade changes that are being considered could not make any difference to George's chances of admission. You must simply accept this because the passage says so. It is just the same as in reading, where you must accept the passage in order to answer the questions.

The fact that George is majoring in philosophy would and did affect the choice of the first three courses, but has no impact on the last course. It could have, if the passage had been different. But don't go making things tough for yourself; only concern yourself with the issues which are raised in the passage.

ANALYSIS OF THE INSTRUCTIONS

Now the instructions can be analyzed in a reasonable manner. You are to choose:

(A) if the item is a MAJOR OBJECTIVE in making the decision; that is, one of the outcomes or results sought by the decision-maker.
(B) if the item is a MAJOR FACTOR in making the decision; that is, a consideration, explicitly mentioned in the passage, that is basic in determining the decision.
(C) if the item is a MINOR FACTOR in making the decision; that is, a secondary consideration that affects the criteria tangentially, relating to a Major Factor rather than to an Objective.
(D) if the item is a MAJOR ASSUMPTION in making the decision; that is, a supposition or projection made by the decisionmaker before weighing the variables.
(E) if the item is an UNIMPORTANT ISSUE in making the decision; that is, a factor that is insignificant or not immediately relevant to the situation.

These instructions are quite explicit, even if they are not entirely clear. One aspect of the instructions that must be explained is the use of the word major. Between choices B and C, the difference is between a major factor and a minor factor, however defined, so that the use of major seems to have some sort of justification. For (A) "Major Objective," and (D), "Major Assumption," there is seemingly little justification for the word major. There are many (A)s and (D)s for each passage, so the use of major does not mean that there is one, most important objective or assumption that is to be identified. Nor is it made clear what "minor" objectives and assumptions would be and what would be the proper way to classify them.

The only resolution to this problem is to consider the word major to imply that the item being described has a direct relationship to the decision. Thus a "major" objective is any goal, purpose or objective that is directly achievable by the making of the decision at hand. "Directly achievable" does not mean that the goal in question is going to be totally achieved, but rather that the decision will directly help to achieve it, at least in part.

Similarly, the differences between a major factor and a minor factor will be how directly they impact on the decision. What the instructions do not state, but what examination of past tests shows clearly, is that the major and minor factors, (B) and (C), are all aspects of the option or things that give the option the characteristics that it does have. (B) is the complete discussion of an issue we identified in the previous discussion as having a direct impact on the decision, while (C) is the other idea in the passage that either expresses what the option is or explains why the option has the characteristics it does. When characteristics of the option are referred to here, they can be any characteristic at all EXCEPT the evaluation of the significance of the other characteristics. In other words, the location of the math class is an idea that *causes the existence of* another characteristic of the math-class option, namely, that it will require a cab ride to be on time for the Philosophy Society meetings. Thus, the location of the math class is not the complete discussion of the issue of timing but only a sub-part of that issue, for the math-class option. Thus the location of the math class would be a minor factor (C), and the "ability of each option to permit timely attendance of the Philosophy Society meetings" would be the complete discussion of that issue and thus bears directly on the decision and is the "major" factor (B).

The major assumption (D) is particularly poorly named and you are well advised to banish the word assumption from your mind and think of these ideas only as (D). In common usage, the word assumption implies that something is not certain. However, in the AS section, this is not the distinction between ideas classified as (D) and those classified as other choices. While it is true that (D) tends to look to the future, terms of contracts that have already been signed are also (D). Furthermore, (B) and (C) generally are also future-looking since they concern the characteristics of options that have not yet been adopted.

In our analysis of the course-selection decision facing George, we identified three major uses of ideas. The goals and objectives are clearly (A). The characteristics of the options (and the causes thereof) are (B) and (C). The third category, the table- or stage-setter, corresponds to (D). The instructions speak of "presuppositions or projections," and the ideas that the decisionmaker has about the world and about his own values are presuppositions, however firm or weak their basis in reality.

In the instructions, (E), or the "Unimportant Issue," corresponds to the ideas in the passage which are not used, or are not usable, in making the decision.

It is interesting to note that there are several important aspects of the decision which are not classifiable under the answer schema put forward by the test. First of all, the options are not classifiable—their characteristics, however, are. Thus you will not see a partial sentence question that simply names an option. Also, the decisionmaker is not a classifiable idea, nor is a bald statement of the decision. All of these are important ideas to keep in mind when you are answering the questions, but they are not going to be questions themselves.

IDENTIFYING UNIMPORTANT ISSUES (E)

(E) is presented out of order because the identification of the irrelevancies is logically the first step in the solution of AS questions. There are two major types of (E) choices: irrelevancies and dismissals.

Irrelevancies are ideas that do not and cannot contribute to the discussion of the decision as defined in the particular passage. It is not that one could not imagine a passage in which these ideas are relevant, but rather that they do not help, given the structure in the actual passage before you. The easiest way to determine that something is an irrelevancy is to turn it into its negative and see whether that would make any difference to the outcome of the decision, as far as you can tell.

Dismissals are ideas that are unimportant to the making of the decision because the decisionmaker has stated that they are unimportant, negligible, of no conern, have no impact on the decision, etc. In the passage involving George, the effect of the courses and the grades in the courses on his admission to graduate school is stated to be negligible. Even though you might think it ought to be important, it isn't; you must always follow what the passage says.

It is important for the student to remember at all times that (E)s are not merely ideas that are less important than other ideas; (E)s are ideas that have absolutely no importance at all, given any reasonable interpretation of the situation. Therefore, the situations in which a dismissal can occur are very definite. There must be no doubt that the idea has been totally dismissed from consideration. Sometimes there is a group discussing the decision. A president of a corporation might call in several advisors, or a group of people might be engaged in a joint venture. The usual rule is to consider any comment that is made to, or in the presence of, the decisionmaker as having been accepted by the decisionmaker unless he or she objects. For example, a junior advertising consultant might propose that the product be promoted by association with hockey stars and the decisionmaker might object that the hockey association connotes violence and would not appeal to the right market. In that case, the concept of using the hockey stars is dead and anything associated with it is dead (except perhaps the fact that it is dead and the violence association that killed it). A simpler example would be a marketing decision in which one advisor suggests that the fact that one of the options under consideration can get to the stores more quickly than the others is an advantage. If it is then stated that they do not care about the date the item is marketed, but only about the success of the marketing plan, then the speed with which a proposal will get the product to the market is an (E). It has been dismissed.

In past exams, there have sometimes been (E) choices that were ideas that were simply not mentioned in the passage. More recent exams have not had (E)s of this sort, but have instead had fragments, classified as (D)s, that were only very weakly and indirectly referred to in the passage. This sort of (D) is discussed in the section on (D)s. As far as (E) goes, the best approach with an idea that you do not recognize as having been in the passage is to consider whether it could have been an implied (D), as described later, and to mark it as an (E) only if it would not make any difference anyway.

IDENTIFYING MAJOR OBJECTIVES (A)

There are several key clues that will help you to identify an (A) on the exam. (Throughout the remainder of this Instructional Overview, the answer choices will be referred to almost exclusively by their letters to encourage you to think of them that way rather than by their names.)

Action noun. If the first noun in the partial sentence is an action noun (usually the noun form of an action verb: taking, paying, making, sending, saving, overcoming, expanding, acquisition, controlling), then you should consider that the partial sentence might be an (A).

The grammatical construction of an (A) can be either the action noun related to some object, such as "Increasing the profitability of the corporation," or it can refer directly to the state of affairs to be accomplished, such as "Higher profits for the corporation." All of the following are partial sentences that would be classified as (A)s, based on the previous course-choice passage, but which are phrased differently:

1. Making the Philosophy Society's meetings on time
   On-time attendance of Philosophy Society meetings
   Scheduling classes so that they do not conflict with the meetings of the Philosophy Society
2. Taking an unusual or different course
   Enrollment in a course different from previous courses
   Maximizing the variety of courses taken in college
3. Taking a course in which a good grade can be achieved
   High grades in the course chosen
   Achievement of high grades (in the course chosen)

Positive phrasing. Another characteristic of (A) is that it will always be phrased positively. If an animal is caught in a trap and can only escape by chewing off its leg, the goal is not "chew off leg" but "escape from trap."

Achieved at least in part. Remember that (A)s will likely be things that can only be partly achieved in the decision situation. If a goal is to increase market share, the decision being discussed may only have the potential to increase market share a small amount, but this will still be a goal of that decision as long as there is the real possibility of an actual increase in market share as a result of the decision.

The test—use the whole of the partial sentence. Ask yourself the following question, substituting the exact wording of the partial sentence for the blank space: By making this decision properly, does the decisionmaker hope to, at least to some noticeable degree, achieve the goal of (having the) ________? If the answer is yes, then the fragment is an (A). A slight awkwardness of expression is okay, but if it sounds truly bizarre, then it is probably not an (A).

Need not be explicitly stated in the passage. The last point to keep in mind about (A)s is that they are not always explicitly stated in the passage. Sometimes an (A) can be introduced implicitly by the decisionmaker's discussion of an advantage of some difference between the options. For instance, if the passage says that option 1 has the advantage of permitting the new product to be introduced more quickly, the goal of "Quick introduction of the new product" has been implicitly stated. While most of the (A)s will be explicitly stated in some way (though the wording of the partial sentence may be quite different from the passage), some (A)s are introduced by the sort of value judgment just mentioned.

DISTINGUISHING (B)s AND (C)s FROM (D)s—MAJOR ASSUMPTIONS

At this point in the discussion of partial sentences, two of the choices have been dealt with. The remaining three choices can be naturally separated into two groups: the (B)s and (C)s, which are both related to the options by being characteristics of the options for causes thereof), and (D)s, which are other relevant aspects of the world. It is usually more fruitful and efficient to first ask whether the partial sentence is a (B) or (C), since the odds are 2 to 1 in favor of this. Also, the majority of (B)s and

(C)s are straightforward statements of some characteristic of one or all of the options, which makes the task easier.

The process by which you distinguish the (B)s and (C)s from the (D)s is as follows:

Characteristic of an option. If the partial sentence gives a characteristic of an option, or of all of the options, then it is a (B) or (C). This is a simple enough idea, but a few refinements are occasionally needed. In the "George" passage, a partial sentence could have been, "The ability of each option to permit on-time attendance of George at the Philosophy Society meetings." Even though one of the options might not permit the on-time attendance of George at the Philosophy Society meetings, the idea is still present. Another, even sharper example would be the partial sentence "Difficulty in convincing each of the companies to agree to the proposed sales plan" in a passage where one or more of the companies did not seem to be difficult to convince at all. It is still a complete discussion of the point involved.

Another refinement is needed to adjust to the different ways that the partial sentences may refer to the options, even on the same exam. For instance, several partial sentences referring to a passage may refer to "(each of) the businesses under consideration"; and then there will be a partial sentence that refers to "each of the businesses." This is still the same idea. However, if a passage has stated the decisionmaker's belief that only small stores will be receptive to a particular product whose promotion is the subject of the decision, then a partial sentence that refers to "the unwillingness of large stores to stock the product" is neither a B nor C because it is not referring to an option, but rather to a guideline that the decisionmaker has established, which is a (D)-type of idea.

Another example might be helpful here. If the passage concerns a decision on how best to increase the profits of a company, one of the goals might be a preference for the original owners of the company to maintain operating control of the company. One of the options might be to seek financing from a large corporation, but the decisionmaker has the guideline that such corporations are only willing to give such financing when they have operational control of the company, in order to protect their investment. This does not mean that the option of getting such financing does not exist, only that it does not meet one of the goals. A partial sentence in such a situation might be, "The unwillingness of large corporations to give financial assistance without also assuming operational control." This is *not* a (C) or (B). It does not refer to a particular option, which was to have a particular large corporation finance the company. This partial sentence refers instead to the decisionmaker's guideline or presupposition about the nature of the world to the effect that large corporations have certain characteristics. This is not the specific application of the idea to the specific corporation. The partial sentence "The unwillingness of the ABC Corporation to finance the company without its assuming operational control of the company" *is* a (C) or a (B)—actually it would almost surely be a (C), as is discussed below—because it is a characteristic of one of the specific options considered in the passage.

Causing the existence of a characteristic of an option. While most (B)s and (C)s are relatively straightforward statements of some characteristic of one or more options, there are some (C)s that are a little more indirect. Consider a situation in which three locations are being considered for the relocation of a business. If one of the goals of the decision is to retain as many of the current customers as possible, then there will be a (B) about the capability of the various locations being considered to retain the patronage of current customers. This characteristic of the degree to which each of the options can retain the current customers could be influenced by many other ideas. One possibility could be that the transportation available between the current location and the various options is too poor to permit the current customers to travel to the new location. In that case there might be a partial sentence which reads "Poor transportation between current neighborhood and location X." This would be a (C) that causes the existence of the factor of customer retention at location X. To be sure, it can also be seen as a characteristic of the new location, which is an option and thus it is also a characteristic of an option. Many students find, however, that it is helpful to have this additional string to their bow.

Not mentioning or referring to an option by name. If a partial sentence does not refer to the whole group of options, to any one of the options, or to an option by name, it is almost surely not a (B) or (C). In the context of having already sorted out the (A)s and (E)s, this makes it a (D). However, as noted above, some (D)s do have references that seem to refer to options to some extent, but which actually refer to some general rule or guideline about the world.

DISTINGUISHING MAJOR FACTORS (B) FROM MINOR FACTORS (C)

Along with the task of differentiating (D) from (B) and (C), the task of distinguishing (B) from (C) is a major source of difficulty on this section for most students. The basic conceptual difference between (B) and (C) is that a (B) is the complete discussion of a logically distinct issue and thus directly impacts on the decision, while a (C) is only a partial discussion of such an issue and thus must join with other ideas in order to directly impact on the decision. Another way of stating the same idea is to view (B) as the overall ability of the various options to satisfy some goal and (C) as either the ability of a single option to satisfy the goal or an aspect of the option that influences its ability to satisfy the goal. The only problem with the formulation in terms of goals is that many goals are only stated in an implicit manner through the discussion of the characteristics of the options.

For example, a passage describing a company's decision discussion about the various products that could be manufactured in a newly acquired building might say: "The team of advisers considered the reports it had commissioned on the crucial issues of machinery availability, personnel requirements, compatibility with existing products and cash flow requirements for each of the products being considered." Such a sentence almost certainly means that each of these crucial issues is to be considered as a (B)—a logical separate line of consideration. However, no goal has been explicitly mentioned. Furthermore, by simply stating that such and such is a crucial issue, the passage has not necessarily fully described the goal that is sought. "Machinery availability" fairly clearly implies the goal of "choosing a product to produce for which the needed manufacturing machinery is available." "Personnel requirements" does not so easily imply the goal in relation to personnel for the new product. The best that can be done is to say that the goal would be something like "choosing an option the personnel requirements of which can be met." This is a goal of sorts, and it is enough to support "personnel requirements of the various options under consideration" as a (B).

Partial sentences that refer to one option. Virtually every partial sentence that gives a characteristic of only one option, especially when there are more than two options, is going to be a (C). While it is theoretically possible to have a (B) that refers only to one option, it is extremely rare. In a situation where the options are extremely different from each other, it might occur that one characteristic of one of the options simply has no counterpart in the other option(s) and thus may fully describe the issue. If one of the options were illegal (something that the test writers do not in fact do), then the illegality of that option would be a sufficient description of the issue and a partial sentence such as "Illegality of bribing union officials to get work completed" might be a (B). With that extraordinarily rare exception, any partial sentence that refers to only one option by name or clear reference—and is not an (E)—is a (C).

Partial sentences that refer to all the options or to each option. The large majority, but not all, of the partial sentences that refer to all of the options, either as options or by some general term will be (B)s. The references will use such locutions as "the packages under consideration," "the various locations being studied," "the piano factories under consideration," or simply "the product lines," "the houses/stores/sites/factories/etc." As mentioned before, the (B)s are a complete discussion of the idea and thus usually refer to all of the options in one way or another. However, there are occasional partial sentences which refer to all of the options but which are still only partial discussions of some line of consideration. One example of such a "general" (C) would be in a passage which considered the potential sales at each of three locations for a new clothing store. The passage could analyze the potential sales by different kinds of clothing, projecting higher or lower sales for suits, dresses and haberdashery at the three locations. The goal is to have the highest possible total sales; thus the (B) is "total sales at each of the three locations under consideration." The partial sentence "dress sales at each of the three locations under consideration" is a (C), since dress sales are only part of the story about sales. Similarly, "total sales achievable at location X" would also be a (C) because it, too, is an incomplete discussion of the issue of total sales at all the various locations.

In summary, a partial sentence that refers to all or most of the options should first be evaluated in terms of its completeness. Ask yourself whether there are any other aspects of this issue which the partial sentence does not include. If there are, then it is a (C). If the partial sentence describes the entire issue, then it is a (B).

IDENTIFYING MAJOR ASSUMPTIONS—(D)

If a partial sentence is not an (A), (B), (C) or (E), then it is a (D). In practice, the attack strategy that is given below adopts an elimination method in which the (D)s are a sort of residual category. The major reason for this approach is that it works best. The theoretical reason for this approach is that (D)s are the most diffuse of the categories into which you are classifying the partial sentences. "D-ness" is diffuse because it has several distinct parts. The function of being a (D) is actually several different functions that are lumped together in the test instructions. They do have the common thread of being some idea about the world—as distinct from the options—which is useful in discussing the decision and is not a goal.

(D) as the significance of differences between options. The most common function of the (D) idea is that it is an idea which permits or requires the decisionmaker to attach a significance to the differences between the options. (C)s and (B)s describe what the options *are,* their characteristics and the specific things that cause the characteristics to exist. The facts that Option 1 is seven years old and has scaly green wings while Option 2 is 23 years old and has golden feathers on its legs are (C)s and (B)s; they tell you what the option consists of. The fact that there is a great demand for green scaly winged things in the world of commerce allows the decisionmaker to see that the significance of the differences between these two options is that one is more desirable in the world of commerce than the other. The fact of what is desirable, either to the decisionmaker or in the world at large, is a (D) idea.

Terms of relevant contracts or schedules are almost always (D)s, since they provide a framework for judging the value or utility of the options in meeting the goals.

(D) as the existence of a goal or of a useful fact. Another function that (D)s serve in the decision discussion is to support the existence of an (A) or of some other useful fact. For instance, a particular decisionmaker may have the goal of delaying payments on a particular invoice. There might be the partial sentence "Need to delay paying the invoices." This partial sentence is a (D) because it is the idea of the existence of this goal. The decisionmaker does not wish to promote the existence of the goal in any way; he simply wishes to accomplish it. This sort of fragment is not too common.

More common is the simple existence of some fact that is useful in making the decision. If there is some fact that has eliminated a particular option from consideration before it is even discussed, this could be a (D)—for example, if a trucking company has received a contract to transport milk, but their own milk truck has a broken transmission so that it cannot be available when the delivery is needed. Normally, the company would use its own truck, but the option of using the truck is now not available. This might lead to the partial sentence "Infeasibility of repairing the company's own milk tanker in time to make the deliveries." This does not relate to an option under consideration, but it does relate to the decision in that this fact has totally ruled out a particular reasonable option from the decision discussion. You will see no more than one or two of this sort of (D) on a given test, or you may not see any at all.

(D) as a necessary but not explicitly stated idea. The instructions furnished by the Educational Testing Service refer to the fact that (B)s need to be explicitly stated in the passage. Since none of the other instructions make this claim, it is reasonable to suppose that the other ideas do not have to be explicitly stated. In practice, however, the (C)s are always ideas that are stated in the passage, though the phrasing may be somewhat different. (A)s and (D)s are both sometimes not stated in the passage, but are ideas that can be inferred directly from the passage. In the case of implicit (D)s, they are ideas that meet two criteria: they are ideas that would be Ds if they were stated in the passage, and they are ideas that you can be certain that any reasonable decisionmaker would have had to have had in his mind in order to conduct the decision discussion that you have just read.

For instance, if a manufacturer and marketer of gourmet foods is considering buying one of three companies that make fancy almond dishes so that this line can be greatly expanded over the next decade, then the manufacturer must have in his mind the idea that there will be "sufficient almond crops over the next ten years to permit the expansion in production." If the manufacturer did not believe that there would be enough crops, then it would be unreasonable for him to have had the decision discussion about which of the almond companies to buy. This fragment would be a (D) even if the passage contained absolutely no statement about the future of almond crops.

ATTACK STRATEGY

The attack strategy is essentially a summation of the ideas that have just been discussed about the different answer choices combined with the idea of eliminating answer choices. This strategy should be used consciously in answering *every* single Analysis of Situations question. If you do this conscientiously during your practice, you will be able to do it very quickly during the test. However, if you short-circuit the attack strategy during your practice, you will stand a higher chance of misapplying it during the actual exam.

Step One

Read the passage looking for *the* decision and *the* options and *the* differences between the options.

Step Two

After reading the passage, spend 20 seconds reviewing in your mind the answers to these questions:

Who is the decisionmaker?
What, precisely, is the decision to be made?
What are the options, at least generally?
What are some of the basic distinctions to be made between these options?

Step Three

For each and every question, apply the following series of questions to determine which answer to choose:

Question one: Is it an (E)? Does this idea help the decisionmaker to make the decision in any way? If this idea were totally reversed, would that affect the choice between the options?

If the answer to either of these question is *no,* then mark answer (E).

If the answer to these questions is *yes,* then go to question 2.

Question two: Is it an (A)? Substitute the *exact* partial sentence into the following sentence: "By making this decision properly, does the decisionmaker hope to, at least to some noticeable degree, achieve the goal of (having the) ________?"

If the answer is *yes,* mark the partial sentence as an (A).

If the answer is *no,* go to question 3.

Question three: Is it a (B)/(C) or is it a (D)? Is the idea in the partial sentence a characteristic or the cause of a characteristic of one or more options?

If the answer is *yes,* go to question 4.

If the answer is *no,* go to question 5.

Question four: Is it a (B) or is it a (C)? Is the idea in the partial sentence the complete discussion of that line of consideration in the decision discussion?

If the answer is *yes,* mark answer (B). (*Note:* It must be an idea explicitly mentioned in the passage, though it can be in different words.)

If the answer is *no,* mark answer (C). (*Note:* It must be an idea that is subsumed under some other characteristic of the options discussed in the passage, but that larger idea need not be in the list of actual questions on the test.)

Question five: Confirming that it is a (D). Does this idea help the decisionmaker to appreciate the significance of the differences between the options? If this idea is not explicitly stated in the passage, is it an idea that the decisionmaker must have had in his mind in order to have the decision discussion that the passage recounts?

If the answer to either of these questions is *no,* then you should reconsider whether the partial sentence might actually be some sort of (C) or some other classification of idea.

If the answer to these questions is *yes,* then mark answer (D).

FINAL NOTES

Most passages will not come to a specific conclusion that either chooses one of the options or eliminates some of them after discussion. (See the discussion of (D)s for the case of elimination of an option prior to discussion.) If the passage does come to some decision, this does not mean that the discussion was any different, nor does it mean that everything about the non-chosen options is an (E). You are classifying the ideas used in the discussion, not the final decision.

Sometimes the decision discussion is the product of a group discussion. In that case, all discussants are to be considered decisionmakers.

When there are only two options—retire or continue working, sign or reject the contract—there is a greater likelihood of having (B)s that refer directly to only one of the options.

You will answer *all* of the partial-sentence questions because you can always have a reasonable idea as to whether it is an (A) or an (E), and thus you can always eliminate at least one answer choice.

The partial-sentence questions are not in order of difficulty, so you should work through the questions, dividing your time fairly evenly. You should read and consider every partial sentence because you have a good chance of getting any particular question right.

Each passage will contain many more ideas than are asked obout in the particular set of questions that are based on the passage. Thus the set of partial sentences that you are called upon to classify will not be a complete representation of the passage. (C)s may appear in the question set without the corresponding (B)s or (A)s being in the set, etc. However, if you do notice that two partial sentences have a relationship along the lines discussed in this Instructional Overview, you should check (time permitting) that you have been consistent in your answers.

GLOSSARY OF SELECTED BUSINESS TERMS

Directions: You should briefly review these business terms. Some of them might appear in the course of the discussion of a business decision in an Analysis of Situations Passage.

ABATEMENT. A deduction or allowance, as, a discount given for prompt payment.

ACCOUNT. A detailed statement of items affecting property or claims, listed respectively as Debits or Credits, and showing excess of Debits or Credits in form of a balance. Sufficient explanatory material should be given to set forth the complete history of the account. There need not be both Debits and Credits, nor more than one of either of these. If Debits and Credits, or both are made frequently, the account is active. Items held in suspense awaiting future classification or allocation may be charged or credited to an adjustment account. When desirable to keep a separate accounting for specific shipments of goods, it is known as an Adventure Account. If more than one party is interested in such shipment, it is a joint venture account.

Asset Accounts record value owned.

Book Accounts are kept in books, and show in formal manner the details regarding transactions between parties. To be of legal effect the entries must be original, not transferred or posted.

Capital Accounts show the amounts invested in an enterprise either net, as in case of the Capital Accounts of proprietors, partners, and stockholders shown on the liability side of Balance Sheets; or gross, as in case of the Asset Accounts which show both owned and borrowed Capital invested.

Cash Accounts set forth receipts and disbursements of cash as well as balance on hand at beginning and end of period.

Clearing Accounts are employed to collect items preliminary to their allocation to a more detailed classification of the accounts, or preliminary to the determination of the accounts to which such items properly belong.

Contingent Accounts are those which list liabilities or assets dependent for their validity upon some event which may or may not occur.

Contra Accounts are those which offset each other.

Controlling Accounts are those which summarize and afford an independent check upon detailed accounts of a given class which are usually kept in a subordinate ledger. The controlling accounts are kept in the General Ledger. The balance of the controlling account equals the aggregate of the balances of the detailed accounts when all postings affecting these accounts are completed.

Current Accounts are open or running accounts not balanced or stated.

Deficiency Accounts supplement statements of affairs of an insolvent enterprise, showing what items comprise the deficiency of assets subject to lien for payment of unsecured creditors.

Depreciation Accounts are expense accounts which are charged periodically with the amounts credited to the respective Depreciation Reserve Accounts.

Depreciation Reserve Accounts are credited periodically with the amounts charged to contra depreciation expense accounts. Depreciation Reserve Accounts are valuation accounts because they supplement or evaluate the asset accounts for the ultimate replacement of which they are intended.

Discount Accounts are accounts which are either charged with discounts allowed to customers or credited with discounts secured from creditors; or accounts which are charged with amounts paid to have Notes Discounted; or accounts which are carried unamortized differences between par of Bonds sold and the amounts realized at time of sale, such amounts realized being less than the par of the Bonds.

Dividend Accounts are credited with amounts declared payable as dividends by boards of directors. These accounts are charged for amounts disbursed in payment, the charge being made either at time checks are sent out and for full amount of dividend, or for the amounts of the individual checks as they are returned for payment.

Impersonal Accounts record expenses and revenues, assets and liabilities, but do not make reference to persons in their titles.

Income Accounts show sources and amounts of operating revenues, expenses incurred for operations, sources and amounts of nonoperating revenues, fixed charges, net income and disposition thereof.

Investment Accounts record property owned but not used for operating purposes.

Liability Accounts record value owed.

Merchandise Accounts are charged with cost of buying goods and crediting with sales, thus exhibiting Gross Profit when opening and closing inventories are taken into consideration.

Nominal Accounts are those which, during the accounting period, record changes which affect proprietorship favorably or unfavorably.

Open Accounts are those not balanced or closed.

Personal Accounts are those with individuals, usually customers and creditors.

Profit and Loss Account is an account into which all earnings and expenses are closed.

Real Accounts record Assets and Liabilities.

Revenue Accounts are equivalent to nominal accounts, showing income and expense.

Sales Accounts are rendered by agents to principals in explanation of consigned goods sold.

Sinking Fund Accounts record periodic installments paid into sinking funds and interest accretions added thereto.

Surplus Accounts record accretions to capital from profits.

ACCOUNTING. The science of accounts, their construction, classification and interpretation.

ACCRUE. Accumulation of wealth or liabilities based on passage of time.

ACCRUED EXPENSE. A liability representing expense that has accrued but is not yet due and payable. It is in reality postpaid expense, and therefore the opposite of prepaid expense, which is an asset.

ACCRUED INCOME. Income that has accrued but is not yet due. It is in reality postpaid income, and therefore the opposite of prepaid income, which is a liability.

AGENT. One possessing authority to act for another to a more or less limited extent.

ALLOCATION. Determination of the proper distribution of a given sum among a series of accounts.

AMORTIZATION. Extinction of a debt by systematic application of installments to a sinking fund, or reduction of premiums or discount incurred on sale or purchase of bonds by application of the effective interest rate.

ANNUITY. A sum of money payable periodically in installments.

APPRECIATION. Increase in value of assets.

ASSET. Wealth owned. Assets may be classified in various ways. From the point of view of ease of liquidation they are Quick or Fixed in varying degrees.

AUDIT. Verification of the accuracy books by examination of supporting vouchers, making tests of postings and computations and determining whether all entries are made according to correct accounting principles, and making sure that there are no omissions.

BALANCE. The excess of the sum of the items on one side of an account over the sum of the items on the other side.

BALANCE SHEET. A schedule of Assets and Liabilities so classified and arranged as to enable an intelligent study to be made of the important financial ratios existing between different classes of assets, between different classes of liabilities and between assets and liabilities; also to enable one to observe the origin of the equity existing in the assets and to determine to whom it belongs.

BOND. A bond is a written promise under seal to pay a certain sum of money at a specified time. Bonds bear interest at a fixed rate, usually payable semiannually. Bonds may be sold either above or below par, in which case the coupon rate of interest differs from the effective rate when the bonds are sold below par and higher when bonds are sold above par.

BURDEN. Elements of production cost which, not being directly allocable to output, must be distributed on a more or less arbitrary basis.

CAPITAL. In accounting, capital is excess of assets over liabilities of a given enterprise.

Fixed Capital consists of wealth in form of land, buildings, machinery, furniture and fixtures, etc.

Floating Capital is capital which can be readily converted into cash.

Nominal Capital is the authorized capital stock of a corporation.

Paid-Up Capital is the amount of capital stock issued and fully paid.

Working Capital is the excess of current assets over current liabilities.

CASH. All forms of exchange media which by custom are received in settlement of debts.

CHARGES. Items debited in accounts.

CHECK OR CHEQUE. See Draft.

COLLATERAL SECURITY. Personal property transferred by the owner to another to secure the carrying out of an obligation.

CONSIGNEE. An agent who receives shipments of goods from his principal to be sold on commission basis, title to goods remaining in the principal or consignor.

CONSIGNMENT. A shipment of goods to another and held by him for account of the principal or consignor.

CONSIGNOR. One who ships goods to an agent or factor who holds them for account of the principal or consignor.

CONSOLIDATION. Unification or affiliation of enterprises engaged in competitive or supplementary undertakings.

CONTINGENT. That which depends upon some happening or occurrence; doubtful, conditional.

CORPORATION. An artificial person created by law to carry out a certain purpose or purposes.

COST. Cost is the outlay, usually measured in terms of money, necessary to buy or to produce a commodity. The two elements of Cost are Prime Cost and Overhead or Burden. Prime Cost is the outlay on direct labor and raw materials necessary to produce a commodity. Burden includes all elements of Cost other than direct labor and raw materials.

COST ACCOUNTING. Determination, by means of applying accounting principles, of the elements of Cost entering into the production of a commodity or service.

CREDITOR. One who gives credit in business matters; one to whom money is due.

DEBT. An obligation to pay money or that which one owes to another.

DEBTOR. One who owes money.

DEFERRED ASSET OR CHARGE. See Prepaid Expense.

DEFERRED CREDIT & INCOME OR LIABILITY. See Prepaid Income.

DEFICIENCY. Insufficiency of assets to discharge debts or other obligations.

DEPRECIATION. Decline in value of assets resulting from one or more of the following:

1. Wear and tear
2. Tenure of holding
3. Permanency or steadiness of industry
4. Exhaustion of raw materials
5. Obsolescence
6. Accidents
7. Fluctuations in trade
8. Inadequacy

DISBURSEMENTS. Cash payments.

DISCOUNT. Deduction from a listed or named figure, usually computed on a percentage basis.

DIVIDEND. Division of profits among stockholders on a pro rata basis.

DRAFT. A draft or bill of exchange is defined by Uniform Negotiable Instrument Law as, "an unconditional order in writing addressed by one person to another, signed by the person giving it, requiring the person to whom it is addressed to pay on demand or at a fixed or determinable future time a certain sum in money to order or to bearer."

DRAWEE. The person against whom a draft is drawn and who becomes primarily liable upon acceptance.

DRAWER. The maker of a draft or bill of exchange.

ENTRY. Written description of a business transaction or adjustment made in books of accounts.

ESTATE. A right of ownership in property.

FIXED ASSETS. Those assets which are not readily convertible into cash and in the usual routine of business are not so converted.

FRANCHISE. A privilege or liberty given by the Government to certain individuals.

GOOD WILL. Present right to receive expected future superprofits, superprofits being the amount by which future profits are expected to exceed all economic expenditure incident to its production.

IMPREST SYSTEM. Plan used to account for petty cash disbursements whereby the cashier is at intervals reimbursed for the amount disbursed by him through a check drawn to Cash and charged to the accounts against which such disbursements were made.

INCOME. A flow of benefits from wealth over a period of time.

INTEREST. Expense or income resulting from use of wealth over a period of time.

INVENTORY. An itemized list of goods giving amounts and prices.

INVOICE. A statement issued by a seller of goods to the purchaser giving details regarding quantities, prices and terms of payment.

JOURNAL. The book of original entry in double entry bookkeeping.

Cash Journal is a combination cash book and journal, containing columns for both cash and non-cash transactions.

Purchases Journal records purchases made and the names of persons credited therefor.

Sales Journal records sales and the names of persons charged therefor.

LEDGER. A ledger is the book in which transactions are classified according to function. When subordinate ledgers are used, the General Ledger becomes a digest of details kept in subordinate ledgers, as well as the record of all usual ledger accounts.

Accounts Receivable Ledger contains a record of all transactions affecting trade debtors.

Accounts Payable Ledger contains a record of all transactions affecting trade creditors.

LIABILITY. A debt.

Capital Liabilities are those which are incurred in the acquisition of permanent assets, and which are usually in form of bonded indebtedness having a maturity date removed more than a year.

Contingent Liabilities are those which may or may not become definite obligations, depending upon some event.

Current Liabilities are those which will fall due within a period of a year.

Deferred Liabilities are income received but not yet due; see Prepaid Income.

Fixed Liabilities are those in form of bonds or long term notes.

NOTES PAYABLE. The sum of all notes and acceptances upon which a concern is primarily liable as maker, endorser or acceptor.

NOTES RECEIVABLE. The sum of all notes and acceptances upon which others are liable to the holding concern.

NOTES RECEIVABLE DISCOUNTED. Contingent Liability for all notes receivable discounted at bank but not yet liquidated by the makers.

OVERDRAFT. A debit balance in a deposit account which should normally have a credit balance.

POSTING. Transferring items from journals to ledgers, and making the necessary cross-references in folio columns.

PREMIUM ON BONDS. Amount above par at which bonds are bought or sold.

PREPAID EXPENSE. An asset representing expenditures for services not yet rendered. Also known as Deferred Charge or Deferred Asset.

PREPAID INCOME. Income received for services not yet rendered. It is therefore a liability. Also known as Deferred Credit or Deferred Liability.

PROFIT. Increase in net worth resulting from business operations.

PROPRIETORSHIP. Equity in assets over and above liability.

QUICK ASSETS. Assets that can ordinarily be readily converted into cash without involving heavy loss.

RESERVE. A segregation of surplus, or a retention of revenues equivalent to losses in asset values. In the former case it is a reserve of surplus, in the latter case, a valuation reserve.

RESERVE FUND. An amount set aside in form of cash or investments for general or special purposes.

REVENUE. Income from all sources.

SINKING FUND. An amount set aside in form of cash or investments for the purpose of liquidating some liability.

STATEMENT. To set forth in systematic form all data with reference to some phase of a business undertaking. To present essential details, subordinate schedules are frequently appended. A statement of Assets and Liabilities.

Balance Sheets set forth the status of a business as of a given date.

Consolidated Balance Sheets set forth the status of affiliated businesses as of a given time.

Consolidated Income Statements set forth the results of operations of affiliated enterprises over a period.

Income Statements set forth the result of operations over a period.

Statement of Affairs set forth the status of an insolvent business as of a given time, the arrangement being such as to show both book value of assets, what they are expected to realize, and gross liabilities, and how they are expected to rank.

STOCK. Share issued by a corporation, evidenced by formal certificates representing ownership therein. The total amount of such shares is known as the Capital Stock of the corporation.

Common Stock is that upon which dividends are paid only after dividend requirements on preferred stock and interest requirements on bonds are met.

Donated Stock is stock of a corporation which has been given back to be sold at a discount, usually to afford working capital in cases where the stock was originally issued in payment for fixed assets.

Guaranteed Stock is that which is guaranteed as to principal or interest or both by some other corporation or corporations.

Inactive Stock is that which is seldom traded on the exchange.

Preferred Stock is that which has prior rights over common stock either as to dividends or assets or both. Various provisions are found relative to the voting power, as for example, the preferred stock may be given control of the corporation if dividends thereon remain unpaid for two consecutive years. In case of cumulative preferred stock, unpaid dividends become a lien upon profits of following years.

Treasury Stock is that which has been returned to the treasury of the issuing corporation.

Unissued Stock is the excess of Authorized over Issued Stock.

STOCK BONUSES. Gifts of stock offered to furnish incentive to investors to buy some other security of the issuing company.

STOCK RIGHTS. Privileges extended to stockholders to subscribe to new stock at a price below the market value of outstanding stock.

STOCK SUBSCRIPTIONS. Agreements to purchase the stock of a corporation. They become effective only when ratified by the corporation, unless accepted by a trustee in behalf of the corporation.

SURPLUS. In case of corporations having only par value stock, surplus ordinarily measures excess of net worth or proprietorship over par value of stock outstanding.

Capital Surplus is that derived from extraordinary sources, as sale of stock at premium or sale of fixed assets at a profit.

Surplus from Operations is that derived from undertakings from the carrying out of which the business was established.

TRIAL BALANCE. A list of balances of all General Ledger accounts made to determine the correctness of postings from books of original entry as well as the correctness of the work of determining these balances.

TURNOVER. Rapidity of replacement of capital invested in inventories, accounts receivable, etc.

VOUCHER. Any document which serves as proof of a transaction.

VOUCHER SYSTEM. A scheme of accounting under which distribution of all expenditures is made on vouchers preliminary to their entry in the voucher register.

WORK IN PROCESS. Materials in process of manufacture, partly finished goods including all material, labor and overhead costs incurred on those goods up to the time of taking inventory.

Part Three

Two Full-Length Practice Examinations

ANSWER SHEET—PRACTICE EXAMINATION 1

SECTION I

1 Ⓐ Ⓑ Ⓒ Ⓓ Ⓔ	6 Ⓐ Ⓑ Ⓒ Ⓓ Ⓔ	11 Ⓐ Ⓑ Ⓒ Ⓓ Ⓔ	16 Ⓐ Ⓑ Ⓒ Ⓓ Ⓔ	21 Ⓐ Ⓑ Ⓒ Ⓓ Ⓔ
2 Ⓐ Ⓑ Ⓒ Ⓓ Ⓔ	7 Ⓐ Ⓑ Ⓒ Ⓓ Ⓔ	12 Ⓐ Ⓑ Ⓒ Ⓓ Ⓔ	17 Ⓐ Ⓑ Ⓒ Ⓓ Ⓔ	22 Ⓐ Ⓑ Ⓒ Ⓓ Ⓔ
3 Ⓐ Ⓑ Ⓒ Ⓓ Ⓔ	8 Ⓐ Ⓑ Ⓒ Ⓓ Ⓔ	13 Ⓐ Ⓑ Ⓒ Ⓓ Ⓔ	18 Ⓐ Ⓑ Ⓒ Ⓓ Ⓔ	23 Ⓐ Ⓑ Ⓒ Ⓓ Ⓔ
4 Ⓐ Ⓑ Ⓒ Ⓓ Ⓔ	9 Ⓐ Ⓑ Ⓒ Ⓓ Ⓔ	14 Ⓐ Ⓑ Ⓒ Ⓓ Ⓔ	19 Ⓐ Ⓑ Ⓒ Ⓓ Ⓔ	24 Ⓐ Ⓑ Ⓒ Ⓓ Ⓔ
5 Ⓐ Ⓑ Ⓒ Ⓓ Ⓔ	10 Ⓐ Ⓑ Ⓒ Ⓓ Ⓔ	15 Ⓐ Ⓑ Ⓒ Ⓓ Ⓔ	20 Ⓐ Ⓑ Ⓒ Ⓓ Ⓔ	25 Ⓐ Ⓑ Ⓒ Ⓓ Ⓔ

SECTION II

1 Ⓐ Ⓑ Ⓒ Ⓓ Ⓔ	5 Ⓐ Ⓑ Ⓒ Ⓓ Ⓔ	9 Ⓐ Ⓑ Ⓒ Ⓓ Ⓔ	13 Ⓐ Ⓑ Ⓒ Ⓓ Ⓔ	17 Ⓐ Ⓑ Ⓒ Ⓓ Ⓔ
2 Ⓐ Ⓑ Ⓒ Ⓓ Ⓔ	6 Ⓐ Ⓑ Ⓒ Ⓓ Ⓔ	10 Ⓐ Ⓑ Ⓒ Ⓓ Ⓔ	14 Ⓐ Ⓑ Ⓒ Ⓓ Ⓔ	18 Ⓐ Ⓑ Ⓒ Ⓓ Ⓔ
3 Ⓐ Ⓑ Ⓒ Ⓓ Ⓔ	7 Ⓐ Ⓑ Ⓒ Ⓓ Ⓔ	11 Ⓐ Ⓑ Ⓒ Ⓓ Ⓔ	15 Ⓐ Ⓑ Ⓒ Ⓓ Ⓔ	19 Ⓐ Ⓑ Ⓒ Ⓓ Ⓔ
4 Ⓐ Ⓑ Ⓒ Ⓓ Ⓔ	8 Ⓐ Ⓑ Ⓒ Ⓓ Ⓔ	12 Ⓐ Ⓑ Ⓒ Ⓓ Ⓔ	16 Ⓐ Ⓑ Ⓒ Ⓓ Ⓔ	20 Ⓐ Ⓑ Ⓒ Ⓓ Ⓔ

SECTION III

1 Ⓐ Ⓑ Ⓒ Ⓓ Ⓔ	8 Ⓐ Ⓑ Ⓒ Ⓓ Ⓔ	15 Ⓐ Ⓑ Ⓒ Ⓓ Ⓔ	22 Ⓐ Ⓑ Ⓒ Ⓓ Ⓔ	29 Ⓐ Ⓑ Ⓒ Ⓓ Ⓔ
2 Ⓐ Ⓑ Ⓒ Ⓓ Ⓔ	9 Ⓐ Ⓑ Ⓒ Ⓓ Ⓔ	16 Ⓐ Ⓑ Ⓒ Ⓓ Ⓔ	23 Ⓐ Ⓑ Ⓒ Ⓓ Ⓔ	30 Ⓐ Ⓑ Ⓒ Ⓓ Ⓔ
3 Ⓐ Ⓑ Ⓒ Ⓓ Ⓔ	10 Ⓐ Ⓑ Ⓒ Ⓓ Ⓔ	17 Ⓐ Ⓑ Ⓒ Ⓓ Ⓔ	24 Ⓐ Ⓑ Ⓒ Ⓓ Ⓔ	31 Ⓐ Ⓑ Ⓒ Ⓓ Ⓔ
4 Ⓐ Ⓑ Ⓒ Ⓓ Ⓔ	11 Ⓐ Ⓑ Ⓒ Ⓓ Ⓔ	18 Ⓐ Ⓑ Ⓒ Ⓓ Ⓔ	25 Ⓐ Ⓑ Ⓒ Ⓓ Ⓔ	32 Ⓐ Ⓑ Ⓒ Ⓓ Ⓔ
5 Ⓐ Ⓑ Ⓒ Ⓓ Ⓔ	12 Ⓐ Ⓑ Ⓒ Ⓓ Ⓔ	19 Ⓐ Ⓑ Ⓒ Ⓓ Ⓔ	26 Ⓐ Ⓑ Ⓒ Ⓓ Ⓔ	33 Ⓐ Ⓑ Ⓒ Ⓓ Ⓔ
6 Ⓐ Ⓑ Ⓒ Ⓓ Ⓔ	13 Ⓐ Ⓑ Ⓒ Ⓓ Ⓔ	20 Ⓐ Ⓑ Ⓒ Ⓓ Ⓔ	27 Ⓐ Ⓑ Ⓒ Ⓓ Ⓔ	34 Ⓐ Ⓑ Ⓒ Ⓓ Ⓔ
7 Ⓐ Ⓑ Ⓒ Ⓓ Ⓔ	14 Ⓐ Ⓑ Ⓒ Ⓓ Ⓔ	21 Ⓐ Ⓑ Ⓒ Ⓓ Ⓔ	28 Ⓐ Ⓑ Ⓒ Ⓓ Ⓔ	35 Ⓐ Ⓑ Ⓒ Ⓓ Ⓔ

SECTION IV

1 Ⓐ Ⓑ Ⓒ Ⓓ Ⓔ	6 Ⓐ Ⓑ Ⓒ Ⓓ Ⓔ	11 Ⓐ Ⓑ Ⓒ Ⓓ Ⓔ	16 Ⓐ Ⓑ Ⓒ Ⓓ Ⓔ	21 Ⓐ Ⓑ Ⓒ Ⓓ Ⓔ
2 Ⓐ Ⓑ Ⓒ Ⓓ Ⓔ	7 Ⓐ Ⓑ Ⓒ Ⓓ Ⓔ	12 Ⓐ Ⓑ Ⓒ Ⓓ Ⓔ	17 Ⓐ Ⓑ Ⓒ Ⓓ Ⓔ	22 Ⓐ Ⓑ Ⓒ Ⓓ Ⓔ
3 Ⓐ Ⓑ Ⓒ Ⓓ Ⓔ	8 Ⓐ Ⓑ Ⓒ Ⓓ Ⓔ	13 Ⓐ Ⓑ Ⓒ Ⓓ Ⓔ	18 Ⓐ Ⓑ Ⓒ Ⓓ Ⓔ	23 Ⓐ Ⓑ Ⓒ Ⓓ Ⓔ
4 Ⓐ Ⓑ Ⓒ Ⓓ Ⓔ	9 Ⓐ Ⓑ Ⓒ Ⓓ Ⓔ	14 Ⓐ Ⓑ Ⓒ Ⓓ Ⓔ	19 Ⓐ Ⓑ Ⓒ Ⓓ Ⓔ	24 Ⓐ Ⓑ Ⓒ Ⓓ Ⓔ
5 Ⓐ Ⓑ Ⓒ Ⓓ Ⓔ	10 Ⓐ Ⓑ Ⓒ Ⓓ Ⓔ	15 Ⓐ Ⓑ Ⓒ Ⓓ Ⓔ	20 Ⓐ Ⓑ Ⓒ Ⓓ Ⓔ	25 Ⓐ Ⓑ Ⓒ Ⓓ Ⓔ

SECTION V

1 Ⓐ Ⓑ Ⓒ Ⓓ Ⓔ	6 Ⓐ Ⓑ Ⓒ Ⓓ Ⓔ	11 Ⓐ Ⓑ Ⓒ Ⓓ Ⓔ	16 Ⓐ Ⓑ Ⓒ Ⓓ Ⓔ	21 Ⓐ Ⓑ Ⓒ Ⓓ Ⓔ
2 Ⓐ Ⓑ Ⓒ Ⓓ Ⓔ	7 Ⓐ Ⓑ Ⓒ Ⓓ Ⓔ	12 Ⓐ Ⓑ Ⓒ Ⓓ Ⓔ	17 Ⓐ Ⓑ Ⓒ Ⓓ Ⓔ	22 Ⓐ Ⓑ Ⓒ Ⓓ Ⓔ
3 Ⓐ Ⓑ Ⓒ Ⓓ Ⓔ	8 Ⓐ Ⓑ Ⓒ Ⓓ Ⓔ	13 Ⓐ Ⓑ Ⓒ Ⓓ Ⓔ	18 Ⓐ Ⓑ Ⓒ Ⓓ Ⓔ	23 Ⓐ Ⓑ Ⓒ Ⓓ Ⓔ
4 Ⓐ Ⓑ Ⓒ Ⓓ Ⓔ	9 Ⓐ Ⓑ Ⓒ Ⓓ Ⓔ	14 Ⓐ Ⓑ Ⓒ Ⓓ Ⓔ	19 Ⓐ Ⓑ Ⓒ Ⓓ Ⓔ	24 Ⓐ Ⓑ Ⓒ Ⓓ Ⓔ
5 Ⓐ Ⓑ Ⓒ Ⓓ Ⓔ	10 Ⓐ Ⓑ Ⓒ Ⓓ Ⓔ	15 Ⓐ Ⓑ Ⓒ Ⓓ Ⓔ	20 Ⓐ Ⓑ Ⓒ Ⓓ Ⓔ	25 Ⓐ Ⓑ Ⓒ Ⓓ Ⓔ

SECTION VI

1 Ⓐ Ⓑ Ⓒ Ⓓ Ⓔ	5 Ⓐ Ⓑ Ⓒ Ⓓ Ⓔ	9 Ⓐ Ⓑ Ⓒ Ⓓ Ⓔ	13 Ⓐ Ⓑ Ⓒ Ⓓ Ⓔ	17 Ⓐ Ⓑ Ⓒ Ⓓ Ⓔ
2 Ⓐ Ⓑ Ⓒ Ⓓ Ⓔ	6 Ⓐ Ⓑ Ⓒ Ⓓ Ⓔ	10 Ⓐ Ⓑ Ⓒ Ⓓ Ⓔ	14 Ⓐ Ⓑ Ⓒ Ⓓ Ⓔ	18 Ⓐ Ⓑ Ⓒ Ⓓ Ⓔ
3 Ⓐ Ⓑ Ⓒ Ⓓ Ⓔ	7 Ⓐ Ⓑ Ⓒ Ⓓ Ⓔ	11 Ⓐ Ⓑ Ⓒ Ⓓ Ⓔ	15 Ⓐ Ⓑ Ⓒ Ⓓ Ⓔ	19 Ⓐ Ⓑ Ⓒ Ⓓ Ⓔ
4 Ⓐ Ⓑ Ⓒ Ⓓ Ⓔ	8 Ⓐ Ⓑ Ⓒ Ⓓ Ⓔ	12 Ⓐ Ⓑ Ⓒ Ⓓ Ⓔ	16 Ⓐ Ⓑ Ⓒ Ⓓ Ⓔ	20 Ⓐ Ⓑ Ⓒ Ⓓ Ⓔ

SECTION VII

1 Ⓐ Ⓑ Ⓒ Ⓓ Ⓔ	6 Ⓐ Ⓑ Ⓒ Ⓓ Ⓔ	11 Ⓐ Ⓑ Ⓒ Ⓓ Ⓔ	16 Ⓐ Ⓑ Ⓒ Ⓓ Ⓔ	21 Ⓐ Ⓑ Ⓒ Ⓓ Ⓔ
2 Ⓐ Ⓑ Ⓒ Ⓓ Ⓔ	7 Ⓐ Ⓑ Ⓒ Ⓓ Ⓔ	12 Ⓐ Ⓑ Ⓒ Ⓓ Ⓔ	17 Ⓐ Ⓑ Ⓒ Ⓓ Ⓔ	22 Ⓐ Ⓑ Ⓒ Ⓓ Ⓔ
3 Ⓐ Ⓑ Ⓒ Ⓓ Ⓔ	8 Ⓐ Ⓑ Ⓒ Ⓓ Ⓔ	13 Ⓐ Ⓑ Ⓒ Ⓓ Ⓔ	18 Ⓐ Ⓑ Ⓒ Ⓓ Ⓔ	23 Ⓐ Ⓑ Ⓒ Ⓓ Ⓔ
4 Ⓐ Ⓑ Ⓒ Ⓓ Ⓔ	9 Ⓐ Ⓑ Ⓒ Ⓓ Ⓔ	14 Ⓐ Ⓑ Ⓒ Ⓓ Ⓔ	19 Ⓐ Ⓑ Ⓒ Ⓓ Ⓔ	24 Ⓐ Ⓑ Ⓒ Ⓓ Ⓔ
5 Ⓐ Ⓑ Ⓒ Ⓓ Ⓔ	10 Ⓐ Ⓑ Ⓒ Ⓓ Ⓔ	15 Ⓐ Ⓑ Ⓒ Ⓓ Ⓔ	20 Ⓐ Ⓑ Ⓒ Ⓓ Ⓔ	25 Ⓐ Ⓑ Ⓒ Ⓓ Ⓔ

SECTION VIII

1 Ⓐ Ⓑ Ⓒ Ⓓ Ⓔ	5 Ⓐ Ⓑ Ⓒ Ⓓ Ⓔ	9 Ⓐ Ⓑ Ⓒ Ⓓ Ⓔ	13 Ⓐ Ⓑ Ⓒ Ⓓ Ⓔ	17 Ⓐ Ⓑ Ⓒ Ⓓ Ⓔ
2 Ⓐ Ⓑ Ⓒ Ⓓ Ⓔ	6 Ⓐ Ⓑ Ⓒ Ⓓ Ⓔ	10 Ⓐ Ⓑ Ⓒ Ⓓ Ⓔ	14 Ⓐ Ⓑ Ⓒ Ⓓ Ⓔ	18 Ⓐ Ⓑ Ⓒ Ⓓ Ⓔ
3 Ⓐ Ⓑ Ⓒ Ⓓ Ⓔ	7 Ⓐ Ⓑ Ⓒ Ⓓ Ⓔ	11 Ⓐ Ⓑ Ⓒ Ⓓ Ⓔ	15 Ⓐ Ⓑ Ⓒ Ⓓ Ⓔ	19 Ⓐ Ⓑ Ⓒ Ⓓ Ⓔ
4 Ⓐ Ⓑ Ⓒ Ⓓ Ⓔ	8 Ⓐ Ⓑ Ⓒ Ⓓ Ⓔ	12 Ⓐ Ⓑ Ⓒ Ⓓ Ⓔ	16 Ⓐ Ⓑ Ⓒ Ⓓ Ⓔ	20 Ⓐ Ⓑ Ⓒ Ⓓ Ⓔ

PRACTICE EXAMINATION 1

SECTION I

Time—30 Minutes
25 Questions

Directions: Below each of the following passages, you will find questions or incomplete statements about the passage. Each statement or question is followed by lettered words or expressions. Select the word or expression that most satisfactorily completes each statement or answers each question in accordance with the meaning of the passage. After you choose the best answer, blacken the corresponding space on the answer sheet.

There is a confused notion in the minds of many persons, that the gathering of the property of the poor into the hands of the rich does no ultimate harm, since in whosesoever hands it may be, it must be spent at last, and thus, they think, return to the poor again. This fallacy has been again and again exposed; for granting the plea true, the same apology may, of course, be made for blackmail, or any other form of robbery. It might be (though practically it never is) as advantageous for the nation that the robber should have the spending of the money he extorts, as that the person robbed should have spent it. But this is no excuse for the theft. If I were to put a turnpike on the road where it passes my own gate, and endeavor to exact a shilling from every passenger, the public would soon do away with my gate, without listening to any pleas on my part that I should spend their shillings, as that they themselves should. But if, instead of outfacing them with a turnpike, I can only persuade them to come in and buy stones, or old iron, or any other useless thing, out of my ground, I may rob them to the same extent, and be moreover, thanked as a public benefactor and promoter of commercial prosperity. And this main question for the poor of England—for the poor of all countries—is wholly omitted in every treatise on the subject of wealth. Even by the laborers themselves, the operation of capital is regarded only in its effect on their immediate interests, never in the far more terrific power of its appointment of the kind and the object of labor. It matters little, ultimately, how much a laborer is paid for making anything; but it matters fearfully what the thing is, which he is compelled to make. If his labor is so ordered as to produce food, fresh air, and fresh water, no matter that his wages are low;—the food and the fresh air and water will be at last there, and he will at last get them. But if he is paid to destroy food and fresh air, or to produce iron bars instead of them,—the food and air will finally *not* be there, and he will *not* get them, to his great and final inconvenience. So that, conclusively, in political as in household economy, the great question is, not so much what money you have in your pocket, as what you will buy with it and do with it.

1. We may infer that the author probably lived in the
   (A) 1960's in the United States
   (B) early days of British industrialization
   (C) 18th-century France
   (D) Golden Age of Greece
   (E) England of King Arthur

2. It can be inferred that the author probably favors
   (A) capitalism
   (B) totalitarianism
   (C) socialism
   (D) anarchism
   (E) theocracy

3. According to the passage, the individual should be particularly concerned with
   (A) how much wealth he can accumulate
   (B) the acquisition of land property rather than money
   (C) charging the customer a fair price

(D) the quality of goods which he purchases with his funds
(E) working as hard as possible

4. The passage implies that
   (A) "A stitch in time saves nine."
   (B) "It is better later than never."
   (C) "He who steals my purse steals trash."
   (D) "None but the brave deserve the fair"
   (E) "All's well that ends well."

5. It can be inferred that in regard to the accumulation of wealth the author
   (A) equates the rich with the thief
   (B) indicates that there are few honest businessmen
   (C) condones some dishonesty in business dealings
   (D) believes destruction of property is good because it creates consumer demand
   (E) says that the robber is a benefactor

6. What is the "main question for the poor" referred to by the author in the passages?
   (A) the use to which the laborer can put his money
   (B) the methods by which capital may be accumulated
   (C) the results of their work and their lack of authority to determine to what ends their work shall be put
   (D) whether full measure of recompense shall be accorded to the laboring person for the investment of his time in worthy work
   (E) the extent to which a man can call his life his own

7. According to the views expressed in the passage, people should be happiest doing which of the following?
   (A) mining ore for the manufacture of weapons
   (B) cleaning sewage ponds at a treatment plant
   (C) waiting tables for a rich man
   (D) helping a poor man do his job
   (E) studying economic theory

8. The author of the above passage would probably react to an energy shortage by
   (A) blaming the rich for the problem
   (B) urging that energy be used more efficiently and effectively
   (C) supporting the search for more oil, coal, and other energy-producing mineral deposits
   (D) denying that there is really any shortage at all
   (E) fomenting revolution by the poor

Davis, California, like many other American cities, has been threatened by unchecked growth, swarming automobiles, and deeply rising energy costs. But unlike towns and cities which leave energy policy to the federal government or energy corporations, the citizens of Davis have acted on their own.

After lengthy debate, Davis' City Council moved to curb growth. It turned against the automobile and embraced the bicycle as a means of transport. It sponsored an inquiry into energy uses and endorsed a series of measures aimed at reducing energy consumption by as much as one half. It cut back the use of petroleum-derived pesticides on the thousands of trees and shrubs that shade the city's streets, adopting instead a policy of biological control for insects. The city's own cars and trucks have been transformed into a fleet of compact vehicles. When a Davis employee has to get around town, he borrows a bike from the city rack. Davis even passed a law formally and solemnly sanctioning the clothesline.

The citizens of Davis have been involved in progressive city planning and energy conservation since 1968, when they persuaded the City Council to facilitate bicycle transportation by developing a system of bikeways. The city's general plan for development, drawn up in 1972, was based on questionnaires distributed to residents. When a survey of residents showed that automobiles represented 50% of energy consumption and space heating and cooling accounted for 25%, transportation and building construction became important focal points in the Davis plan.

Armed with survey information revealing that a building's east-west orientation on a lot, as well as its insulation, window area, roof and wall colors, overhang shading, and other factors greatly influenced space heating and cooling needs, the City Council drew up a building construction code which greatly reduces the cost of winter heating and eliminates the need for air conditioning even on Davis' hottest (114°+) days. To demonstrate to local builders and developers methods for complying with the new code, Davis built two model solar homes, a single-family dwelling which takes advantage of natural southern exposure sunlight and a duplex adaptable to difficult siting situations where direct sunlight is blocked. Many of Davis' measures simply facilitate natural solar heating or sun-shading. Where most communities require that fences be built close to houses, Davis realized that that practice meant blocking winter sunlight. New fences in Davis must be placed closer to the street, giving residents the benefit of natural solar heat in winter. Reducing required street widths provided more shade and saved asphalt to boot.

Davis' other energy-conserving moves run the gamut—from a city ordinance encouraging cottage industry (to cut down on commuting and the need for new office building construction) to planting evergreens on city streets to reduce leaf pickup in the fall, from a ban on non-solar swimming pool heaters to a recycling center that supports itself selling $3,000 worth of recyclables a month.

9. It can be inferred from the passage that Davis' City Council felt that
   (A) bicycles are healthful because they promote physical fitness
   (B) control of automobile traffic is an essential part of energy management
   (C) Davis citizens are always ready to do the most modern, up-to-date thing
   (D) clotheslines are an important part of energy management for everyone
   (E) survey results should always determine legislative actions

10. Why did Davis build two model solar homes instead of just one?
   (A) to show what they could do when they put their minds to it
   (B) to show that even the hottest days could be mastered without air conditioning
   (C) to demonstrate that even multiple dwellings in difficult locations could be solar powered
   (D) to indicate that other cities were inadequate to the job
   (E) to prove that winter sunlight could be used for heating

11. The purpose of this article is probably to
   (A) congratulate Davis on their fine work
   (B) help Davis to spread their message
   (C) chide the federal government for not doing enough to help cities like Davis
   (D) poke fun at Davis' "clothesline law"
   (E) hold up Davis as an example to other cities

12. It appears that Davis is
   (A) a "good old American town"
   (B) committed to social justice
   (C) a medium- to small-sized city
   (D) governed by a Council-Manager form of municipal government
   (E) blessed by a strong radical element in the population

13. The passage supports the conclusion that
   (A) Davis does not have much industry
   (B) Davis cannot go any further than it already has toward being energy efficient
   (C) Davis' example will work for any city
   (D) the days of the automobile are numbered
   (E) planning can solve all our problems

14. If, after continuing its programs, Davis did another energy survey in 1992 and found that its total energy use had gone up from 1972, all of the following could help to explain this finding, EXCEPT
   (A) population growth might have been substantial because Davis became such a nice place to live
   (B) builders were unable to comply with the stringent and complex building code
   (C) new facilities were constructed that used considerable energy even with advanced design

(D) as the population got older they could no longer use bicycles as much and had to use cars more
(E) the 1972 energy survey seriously underestimated the energy used at that time

15. Which of the following factors did the Davis City Council consider to be factors that significantly affected the energy efficiency of a building's design?

I. the number of people living in a residence
II. the location of the building on its plot
III. the size of the windows installed in the house

(A) I only
(B) II only
(C) I and III only
(D) II and III only
(E) I, II, and III

16. According to the passage, the official policy of the city of Davis, as embodied in their new building code, is that air conditioning
(A) can only be eliminated in residential buildings
(B) is not needed when buildings are designed to be energy efficient
(C) is a complete waste of electricity and should be forbidden in all buildings
(D) constitutes an unnecessary luxury that energy-conscious citizens can learn to live without
(E) is less essential in residential buildings than in public buildings because of the type of work being done in public buildings

It has always been difficult for the philosopher or scientist to fit time into his view of the universe. Prior to Einsteinian physics, there was no truly adequate formulation of the relationship of time to the other forces in the universe, even though some empirical equations included time quantities. However, even the Einsteinian formulation is not perhaps totally adequate to the job of fitting time into the proper relationship with the other dimensions, as they are called, of space. The primary problem arises in relation to things which might be going faster than the speed of light, or have other strange properties.

Examination of the Lorentz-Fitzgerald formulas yields the interesting speculation that if something did actually exceed the speed of light it would have its mass expressed as an imaginary number and would seem to be going backwards in time. The barrier to exceeding the speed of light is the apparent need to have an infinite quantity of mass moved at exactly the speed of light. If this situation could be leaped over in a large quantum jump—which seems highly unlikely for masses that are large in normal circumstances—then the other side may be achieveable.

The idea of going backwards in time is derived from the existence of a time vector that is negative, although just what this might mean to our senses in the unlikely circumstance of our experiencing this state cannot be conjectured.

There have been, in fact, some observations of particle chambers which have led some scientists to speculate that a particle called the tachyon may exist with the trans-light properties we have just discussed.

The difficulties of imagining and coping with these potential implications of our mathematical models points out the importance of studying alternative methods of notation for advanced physics. Professor Zuckerkandl, in his book *Sound and Symbol,* hypothesizes that it might be better to express the relationships found in quantum mechanics through the use of a notation derived from musical notations. To oversimplify greatly, he argues that music has always given time a special relationship to other factors or parameters or dimensions. Therefore, it might be a more useful language in which to express the relationships in physics, where time again has a special role to play and cannot be treated as just another dimension.

The point of this, or any other alternative to the current methods of describing basic physical processes, is that time does not appear—either by common experience or sophisticated scientific understanding—to be the same sort of dimension or parameter as physical dimensions, and is deserving of completely special treatment, in a system of notation designed to accomplish that goal.

One approach would be to consider time to be a field effect governed by the application of energy to mass—that is to say, by the interaction of different forms of energy, if you wish to keep in mind the equivalence of mass and energy. The movement of any normal sort of mass is bound to produce a field effect that we call positive time. An imaginary mass would produce a negative time field effect. This is not at variance with Einstein's theories, since the "faster" a given mass moves the more energy was applied to it and the greater would be the field effect. The time effects predicted by Einstein and confirmed by experience are, it seems, consonant with this concept.

17. The "sound" Professor Zuckerkandl's book title probably refers to
    (A) the music of the spheres
    (B) music in the abstract
    (C) musical notation
    (D) the seemingly musical sounds produced by tachyons
    (E) quantum mechanics

18. The passage supports the inference that
    (A) Einstein's theory of relativity is wrong
    (B) the Lorentz-Fitzgerald formulas contradict Einstein's theories
    (C) time travel is clearly possible
    (D) tachyons do not have the same sort of mass as any other particles
    (E) it is impossible to travel at precisely the speed of light

19. The tone of the passage is
    (A) critical but hopeful
    (B) hopeful but suspicious
    (C) suspicious but speculative
    (D) speculative but hopeful
    (E) impossible to characterize

20. The central idea of the passage can be best described as being which of the following?
    (A) Anomalies in theoretical physics notation permit intriguing hypotheses and indicate the need for refined notation of the time dimension.
    (B) New observations require the development of new theories and new methods of describing the new theories.
    (C) Einsteinian physics can be much improved on in its treatment of tachyons.
    (D) Zuckerkandl's theories of tachyon formation are preferable to Einstein's.
    (E) Time requires a more imaginatiave approach than tachyons.

21. According to the author, it is too soon to
    (A) call Beethoven a physicist
    (B) adopt proposals such as Zuckerkandl's
    (C) plan for time travel
    (D) study particle chambers for tachyon traces
    (E) attempt to improve current notation

22. It can be inferred that the author sees Zuckerkandl as believing that mathematics is a
    (A) necessary evil
    (B) language
    (C) musical notation
    (D) great hindrance to full understanding of physics
    (E) difficult field of study

23. In the first sentence, the author refers to "philosopher" as well as to "scientist" because
    (A) this is part of a larger work
    (B) philosophers study all things
    (C) physicists get Doctor of Philosophy degrees
    (D) the study of the methods of any field is a philosophical question
    (E) the nature of time is a basic question in philosophy as well as physics

24. When the passage says the "particle called the tachyon may exist," the reader may infer that
    (A) scientists often speak in riddles
    (B) the tachyon was named before it existed
    (C) tachyons are imaginary in existence as well as mass
    (D) the tachyon was probably named when its existence was predicted by theory but its existence was not yet known
    (E) many scientific ideas may not exist in fact

25. Which of the following formulations of the function of physics in human thought is closest to that of the author of the above passage?
    (A) Physics explains the movement of objects.
    (B) Physics describes the basis of interactions between different material objects.
    (C) Physics attempts to provide an explanation of the relationships between energy and matter and time and motion.
    (D) Physics tries to link subatomic particles with larger objects.
    (E) Physics provides the fundamental description of all aspects of the universe as they appear to human beings.

STOP

END OF SECTION. IF YOU HAVE ANY TIME LEFT, GO OVER YOUR WORK IN THIS SECTION ONLY. DO NOT WORK IN ANY OTHER SECTION OF THE TEST.

SECTION II

Time—30 Minutes
20 Questions

Directions: For each of the following questions, select the best of the answer choices and blacken the corresponding space on your answer sheet.
Numbers: All numbers used are real numbers.
Figures: The diagrams and figures that accompany these questions are for the purpose of providing information useful in answering the questions. Unless it is stated that a specific figure is not drawn to scale, the diagrams and figures are drawn as accurately as possible. All figures are in a plane unless otherwise indicated.

1. If w, x, y, and z are real numbers, each of the following equals $w(x + y + z)$ EXCEPT
(A) $wx + wy + wz$
(B) $(x + y + z)w$
(C) $wx + w(y + z)$
(D) $3w + x + y + z$
(E) $w(x + y) + wz$

2. A carpenter needs four boards, each 2 feet 10 inches long. If wood is sold only by the foot, what is the minimum length, in feet, of wood he must buy?
(A) 9
(B) 10
(C) 11
(D) 12
(E) 13

3. If $x = +4$, then $(x - 7)(x + 2) =$
(A) -66
(B) -18
(C) 0
(D) 3
(E) 17

4. If $2x + y = 7$ and $x - y = 2$, then $x + y =$
(A) 6
(B) 4
(C) $\frac{3}{2}$
(D) 0
(E) -5

5. A girl rode her bicycle from home to school, a distance of 15 miles, at an average speed of 15 miles per hour. She returned home from school by walking at an average speed of 5 miles per hour. What was her average speed for the round trip if she took the same route in both directions?
(A) 7.5 miles per hour
(B) 10 miles per hour
(C) 12.5 miles per hour
(D) 13 miles per hour
(E) 25 miles per hour

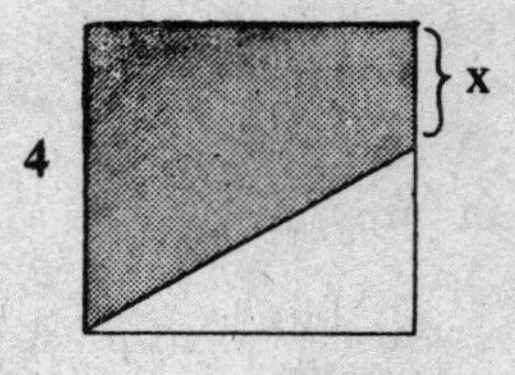

6. In the square above with side 4, the ratio $\frac{\text{area of shaded region}}{\text{area of unshaded region}} =$
(A) $\frac{2 + x}{4}$
(B) $\frac{4 - x}{8}$
(C) 2
(D) $\frac{4 + x}{4 - x}$
(E) $2x$

7. Ned is two years older than Mike, who is twice as old as Linda. If the ages of the three total 27 years, how old is Mike?
(A) 5 years
(B) 8 years
(C) 9 years
(D) 10 years
(E) 12 years

8. A taxicab charges \$1.00 for the first one-fifth mile of a trip and 20¢ for each following one-fifth mile or part thereof. If a trip is $2\frac{1}{2}$ miles long, what will be the fare?
(A) \$2.60
(B) \$3.10
(C) \$3.20
(D) \$3.40
(E) \$3.60

9. What is the side of a square if its area is $36x^2$?
(A) 9
(B) 9x
(C) $6x^2$
(D) 6
(E) 6x

10. If Susan has $5 more than Tom, and if Tom has $2 more than Ed, which of the following exchanges will ensure that each of the three has an equal amount of money?
(A) Susan must give Ed $3 and Tom $1.
(B) Tom must give Susan $4 and Susan must give Ed $5.
(C) Ed must give Susan $1 and Susan must give Tom $1.
(D) Susan must give Ed $4 and Tom must give Ed $5.
(E) Either Susan or Ed must give Tom $7.

11. A perfect number is one which is equal to the sum of all its positive factors that are less than the number itself. Which of the following is a perfect number?
(A) 1
(B) 4
(C) 6
(D) 8
(E) 10

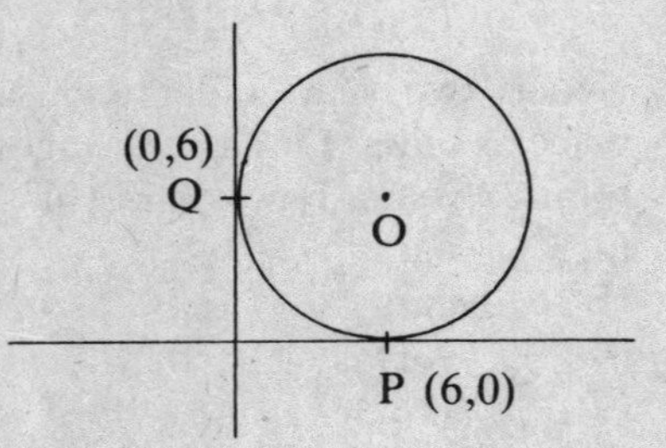

12. In the figure above, the coordinates of points P and Q are (6,0) and (0,6), respectively, What is the area of the circle O?
(A) 36π
(B) 12π
(C) 9π
(D) 6π
(E) 3π

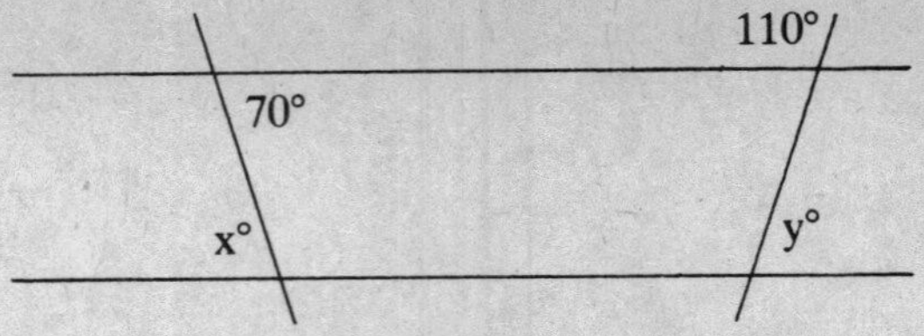

13. In the figure above, x + y =
(A) 50
(B) 140
(C) 180
(D) 220
(E) 240

14. A cylinder has a radius of 2 ft and a height of 5 ft. If it is already 40% filled with a liquid, how many more cubic feet of liquid must be added to completely fill it?
(A) 6π
(B) 8π
(C) 10π
(D) 12π
(E) 16π

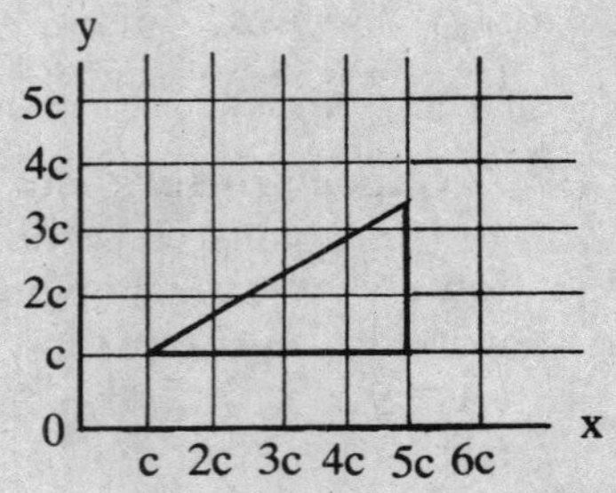

15. If the area of the above triangle is 54, then c =
(A) 3
(B) 6
(C) 10
(D) 12
(E) Cannot be determined from the information given.

16. A carpenter is building a frame for a large wall painting. The painting is in the shape of a rectangle. If the sides of the rectangle are in the ratio of 3:2 and the shorter side has a length of 15 inches, how much framing material does the carpenter need to frame the painting?
(A) 12 inches
(B) $22\frac{1}{2}$ inches
(C) $37\frac{1}{2}$ inches

(D) 50 inches
(E) 75 inches

17. In 1972, country X had a population of P and M cases of meningitis, for a per capita rate of meningitis of $\frac{M}{P}$. If, over the next ten years, the number of cases of meningitis decreased by 50% and the population of country X increased by 50%, what is the percentage change in the per capita rate of meningitis over the ten-year period?
(A) $33\frac{1}{3}$% increase
(B) no change
(C) $33\frac{1}{3}$% decrease
(D) 50% decrease
(E) $66\frac{2}{3}$% decrease

18. In the Excel Manufacturing Company, 46 percent of the employees are men. If 60 percent of the employees are unionized and 70 percent of these are men, what percent of the non-unionized workers are women?
(A) 90%
(B) 87.5%
(C) 66.7%
(D) 50%
(E) 36%

19. A slot machine in a Las Vegas casino has an average profit of $600 for each 8-hour shift for the five days Sunday through Thursday, inclusive. If the average per-shift profit on Friday and Saturday is 25% greater than on the other days of the week and the slot machine is in operation every hour of every day, what is the total weekly profit that the casino makes from the slot machine?
(A) $4,500
(B) $9,000
(C) $13,500
(D) $15,500
(E) $27,000

20. An apartment dweller pays $125 per quarter for theft insurance. The policy will cover the loss of cash and valuables during the course of a year in excess of $350 by reimbursing him 75% of the value of the loss above $350. During the course of a certain year, the apartment dweller suffers the theft of $1250 in cash—but no other losses—by theft. What is the difference between the combined amount he pays in theft insurance and his unreimbursed losses for that year, and the amount that he would have lost if he had not had any insurance?
(A) $125
(B) $175
(C) $225
(D) $350
(E) $675

STOP

END OF SECTION. IF YOU HAVE ANY TIME LEFT, GO OVER YOUR WORK IN THIS SECTION ONLY. DO NOT WORK IN ANY OTHER SECTION OF THE TEST.

SECTION III

Time—30 Minutes
35 Questions

Directions: This section consists of reading selections which detail business situations. After each selection you will be asked to classify certain of the facts presented in the passage on the basis of their importance.

As of 1970, Wingfleet, Inc., was the fourth-largest aircraft manufacturer in the world. That year, the company's sales revenues were slightly under two billion dollars. Wingfleet, an old company in terms of aviation history, started production in 1921, struggled through the Depression, and entered World War II a medium-size company. Thousands of fighters and bombers rolled out of Wingfleet factories. It gained a worldwide reputation for well-designed and well-constructed military aircraft and continued to grow until the late 1960s. By 1970 it employed over 100,000 people in many plants throughout the U.S. The suppliers of Wingfleet employed another 75,000 workers. In short, Wingfleet was a solid supporter of the nation's economy.

John Franco, chairman of the Board of Directors of Wingfleet, carefully studied a lengthy proposal by an executive committee, consisting of three board members and three vice-presidents, recommending that the company bid on a new military-transport plane, the 2L-1000. This would be the largest and one of the fastest transport planes in the world. It would take at least six years to design, test, and bring into full production the 115 planes to be built for the government. The project would provide jobs for 25,000 Wingfleet workers, plus 20,000 jobs for Wingfleet suppliers.

Nearly 90 percent of Wingfleet's business was with the U.S. government. Therefore the aircraft manufacturer's sales revenue was dependent on the federal budget. During times of national emergency (such as the cold war, the Vietnam and Korean conflicts), Wingfleet did very well. But then Congress had cut defense expenditures, and these cuts greatly reduced Wingfleet earnings. In 1966, for example, Wingfleet had shown a profit of 51 million dollars. But in 1969, the company lost 33 million.

Thus it seemed advantageous for Wingfleet to enter the commercial aircraft field to diversify its sources of revenue, and, paradoxically, this was one of the reasons why the executive committee recommended going all out to get the 2L-1000 contract. The huge transport, with slight alteration in design, would make an excellent commercial passenger plane, the committee claimed.

In this connection, a preliminary survey of major airlines showed that nine domestic and foreign airlines had indicated their willingness to order a total of 201 of these commercial planes. Furthermore, should Wingfleet get the government contract, these airlines would order the planes and place immediate and substantial down payments.

Wingfleet had a tentative, but exclusive, contract with Ponzol Company, one of Europe's leading engine manufacturers, to design and produce the plane's engines. This contract depended, of course, on whether Wingfleet decided to bid on the military contract and got it. The fact that Ponzol engines would power the 2L-1000 would probably make the Pentagon regard the Wingfleet bid favorably.

John Franco pondered the possible problems that might arise should Wingfleet take on this enormous project. In order to get the contract against vigorous competition, Wingfleet had to make the lowest bid. The costs were estimated at 1.7 billion dollars if everything went perfectly. Therefore, the executive committee suggested a bid of 2 billion dollars. But John Franco was aware, after 33 years with the company, that it is rare when actual development costs did not exceed estimates. He realized that two or three major structural problems would quickly eat up the estimated gross profit.

On the other hand, he figured if costs exceeded the bid, it might not be disastrous. It was possible to renegotiate a government contract when cost overruns occurred. Wingfleet had done this many times. In fact, cost overruns averaged 50 percent over accepted bids, and these had usually been made up by the government. However, John Franco wondered if Congress in its current limited spending mood would approve an appropriation to make up the difference.

Franco was also uneasy about the Ponzol Company. He had no doubt about the quality of Ponzol engines, but the foreign firm was nationalized. Its profits had been almost nonexistent for the past few years, and governments, he had discovered, were far less patient with losses than were capitalist shareholders. Suppose the European government that owned Ponzol decided to liquidate the engine company in the middle of the 2L-1000 contract? He shuddered at the thought.

Even though the airlines would put down substantial payments for the 201 civilian planes, this money would not solve Wingfleet's poor cash position. The company would have to depend on 25 banks to advance half a billion dollars for the 2L-1000 project, and this would add substantially to Wingfleet's overall debt.

Finally, Wingfleet had previously tried to enter the commercial airplane field three times without success. The failures could not be blamed on inefficiency or lack of knowledge of the market, because careful surveys preceded each attempt. Yet each time Wingfleet had guessed incorrectly. Could this happen again?

Despite his many misgivings, John Franco decided to recommend to the full Board of Directors that Wingfleet make a 2-billion-dollar bid for the 2L-1000 contract.

Directions: Based on your analysis of the previous passage, classify each of the following items in one of five categories. Mark:

(A) if the item is a *Major Objective* in making the decision; that is, one of the outcomes of results sought by the decision-maker.
(B) if the item is a *Major Factor* in making the decision; that is, a consideration, explicitly mentioned in the passage, that is basic in determining the decision.
(C) if the item is a *Minor Factor* in making the decision; that is, a secondary consideration that affects the criteria tangentially, relating to a Major Factor rather than to an Objective.
(D) if the item is a *Major Assumption* in making the decision; that is, a supposition or projection made by the decision-maker before weighing the variables.
(E) if the item is an *Unimportant Issue* in making the decision; that is, a factor that is insignificant or not immediately relevant to the situation.

1. Entrance into the commercial aircraft market.
2. Possibility that the 2L-1000 will cost more than projected.
3. Length of time needed to produce the 2L-1000.
4. The capacity of the 2L-1000 to be modified to a commercial plane.
5. The possible liquidation of Ponzol by its owners.
6. Proportion of Wingfleet's business with the United States government.
7. Down payments by airlines to Wingfleet for new planes.
8. The willingness of airlines to order 201 planes.
9. Diversification of Wingfleet's sales.
10. Congress's anti-military spending mood.
11. The increase in the size of Wingfleet from 1921 to the start of World War II.
12. Composition of the executive committee reporting to Franco.
13. Prospect of Ponzol engines for 2L-1000s causing a favorable Pentagon attitude toward Wingfleet bid.
14. Quality of Ponzol engines.
15. Improving Wingfleet's earnings position.
16. Preserving Wingfleet's reputation as a leading manufacturer of military aircraft.
17. Franco's work experience before joining Wingfleet.

Mike Herd had been a mortician's assistant all his working life—twelve years—and hated his job. His dream was to own a business and to earn at least $28,000 a year at it. This figure amounted to exactly twice his current salary. Then, in May 1982, he saw the following advertisement in a neighborhood newspaper:

> BUSINESS OPPORTUNITY. Established dry-cleaning business for sale: $35,000 firm. Last year's net profits: $30,000. Contact Jerrold Myers, 777-7711.

Mike was electrified. His grandfather had recently died and left him $22,000. Mike's savings amounted to $9,000. With a $4,000 bank loan or with a reduction in the asking price on the part of Myers, he could finally realize his dream and say goodbye to life as an employee.

Mike contacted Myers and inspected the cleaning establishment the next day, learning all he could about the soundness of the business from an examination of Myers' account books for the last few years. After a week of negotiating and reflecting, Mike bought Bus Stop Dry Cleaners for $33,500. He quit his job, and was trained on the job by Myers for two weeks. Finally, at the start of June 1982, he was on his own.

Six months passed. Myers had told him that summer would be the slow season, but profits had totaled only $1,500 for the three summer months. Now at the beginning of December 1982, Mike began to wonder whether Myers had somehow misled him. Mike's uncle, who was an accountant, showed him how a detailed analysis of Myers' books, which Mike had retained, showed actual net earnings of $9,500 for 1981 and $8,300 for 1980. Accounting tricks had been used to yield a bogus figure of $30,000 for the 1981 profits.

Mike's dream burst, and he became gloomy and funereal for several days. Finally, he succumbed to the urgings of his uncle, who felt responsible in a way for this catastrophe, as he had been unwilling to contribute his accounting expertise when Mike first had informed him of his project. At his uncle's insistence, Mike began to consider three possible courses of action.

First, he could sue Myers, who, according to Mike's uncle, was certainly guilty of fraud. When two local lawyers were telephoned for their opinions, both stated informally that Mike had a good case. Second, Mike could look on the brighter side of things, which was that he now possessed his own business, and try to build up his profits until they actually did reach or exceed his cherished $28,000 figure. Mike and his uncle thought that Myers could be persuaded to refund a portion of the sale price when confronted with the facts and threatened with a suit. Third, Mike could obtain some sort of refund from Myers and then sell the store to a third party, thereby recovering the bulk of his investment.

In favor of the first suggestion, the suit, was Mike's moral position that his duty was now to prevent Myers from profiting, insofar as possible, from his misdeeds. A successful suit would accomplish this, Mike believed. Of course, Mike also wished, for his own sake, to recover as much as possible of his inheritance and his life savings, not to mention the rest of the purchase price, which he had borrowed from First Bank for State Development. Again, suing Myers appeared the surest and most direct way of bringing this about.

Arguing against the idea of bringing a court action was, first, the consideration that court costs and legal fees would require cash outlays that were simply beyond Mike's current means. Second, it would probably be several years before Mike would have his money back if he sued. Third, Mike foresaw a lengthy, drawn-out legal battle, and felt reluctant to devote so much of his time to courtroom appearances. It was important to him to spend his time pursuing his dream: self-employment and a $28,000 income. Finally, Mike was the nervous sort and always tried to avoid tension at all costs. The legal proceedings would be anxiety-provoking, to say the least.

Mike's uncle thought the second option—keeping the business—was the one to choose. He thought Mike could get half the purchase price back from Myers, and that he would be able to earn $20,000 from the store in 1984. With that and the $8,000, Mike, a black belt in judo, could probably make by teaching this sport on weekends, he would meet his goal of earning $28,000 per year. He would recover his investment within a few years. Mike would probably be able to get Myers to refund half the purchase price, according to his uncle, because Myers knew he would lose in court. If Mike chose this path, he would not be making any more cash outlays. They both knew that Mike would undergo considerable tension for an indefinite period if he left his business and went out seeking employment, and such emotional upset was to be avoided if at all possible. If he kept the business, Mike would be spending his time pursuing his dream and not looking for a job or languishing in a courtroom, if he kept the store.

Mike's uncle let his nephew know the reasons for his expectation that Mike could bring revenues up from $9,500 to $20,000 by the end of 1984. The only competing dry cleaner in the neighborhood had just gone out of business and had sold his store to a stationer. This meant Mike would now be serving the clients of both establishments. Further, since there were no laundromats in the vicinity and few residents had their own washer and dryer, Mike could do well by offering to launder garments by the pound, his uncle suggested. This would require no additional cash outlay, since the contractors with whom Mike worked performed laundry as well as dry-cleaning services. Finally, by offering reduced rates to senior citizens, Mike could pull in business from the residents of the three adult homes in the surrounding area.

Mike agreed with his uncle that the case for holding onto the store was strong. Nonetheless, he observed, there were disadvantages to such a course of action. In particular, he would probably be allowing Myers to make some amount of profit from his fraudulent activities.

As a third and final option, Mike could sell the business, once he had obtained a refund of some sort from Myers. Advantages here were, first, that the only additional cash outlay would consist of advertising or brokerage fees; and, second, that whatever of his initial investment he would be getting back would be his in a matter of months, not years. Disadvantages were numerous: Myers would be profiting illicitly; Mike would probably not recover the full amount of his investment, since he intended to be quite frank with prospective buyers as to the earnings of the business in the past. He might have to spend a lot of time job-hunting, instead of pursuing his dream. Finally, there would be a period during which Mike would experience tension from two sources at the same time: the uncertainty of his being able to locate a serious buyer for the business, and the anxiety of job-seeking.

Directions: Based on your analysis of the previous passage, classify each of the following items in one of five categories. Mark:

(A) if the item is a *Major Objective* in making the decision; that is, one of the outcomes or results sought by the decision-maker.

(B) if the item is a *Major Factor* in making the decision; that is, a consideration, explicitly mentioned in the passage, that is basic in determining the decision.

(C) if the item is a *Minor Factor* in making the decision; that is, a secondary consideration that affects the criteria tangentially, relating to a Major Factor rather than to an Objective.

(D) if the item is a *Major Assumption* in making the decision; that is, a supposition or projection made by the decision-maker before weighing the variables.

(E) if the item is an *Unimportant Issue* in making the decision; that is, a factor that is insignificant or not immediately relevant to the situation.

18. Degree of anxiety Mike would experience if a given course of action were chosen.

19. Number of businesses on the same block as Bus Stop Dry Cleaners.

20. Recovering a large part of the initial investment in Bus Stop Dry Cleaners.

21. Continuing to be self-employed.

22. Mike's uncle's unwillingness to help his nephew when Mike originally decided to buy Bus Stop.

23. Likelihood that Myers can be persuaded to make a rebate in some amount to Mike.

24. Preventing Myers from profiting from his wrongdoing.

25. Monthly income of the new stationer on Mike's block.

26. Expense of legal fees and court costs if Mike sues Myers for misrepresentation and return of the purchase price of the business.

27. Number of years Mike worked as a mortician's assistant prior to buying the cleaning store.

28. Mike's expertise in judo.

29. Earning $28,000 a year.

30. Myers' belief that he would lose a suit initiated by Mike.

31. The recent closing of the only competing business in Mike's vicinity.

32. Mike's desire to utilize his time pursuing his dream.

33. Extent to which a given alternative allowed Mike to prevent Myers from profiting from his misdeeds.

34. Proportion of his initial investment that Mike could recover under each of the alternatives.

35. Minimizing current cash outlays.

STOP

END OF SECTION. IF YOU HAVE ANY TIME LEFT, GO OVER YOUR WORK IN THIS SECTION ONLY. DO NOT WORK IN ANY OTHER SECTION OF THE TEST.

SECTION IV

Time—30 Minutes
25 Questions

Directions: Each question below is followed by two numbered facts. You are to determine whether the data given in the statements is sufficient for answering the question. Use the data given, plus your knowledge of math and everyday facts, to choose between the five possible answers.

(A) if statement 1 alone is sufficient to answer the question, but statement 2 alone is not sufficient
(B) if statement 2 alone is sufficient to answer the question, but statement 1 alone is not sufficient
(C) if both statements together are needed to answer the question, but neither statement alone is sufficient
(D) if either statement by itself is sufficient to answer the question asked
(E) if not enough facts are given to answer the question

1. What is the value of x?
   (1) $x^2 + x = 2$
   (2) $x^2 + 2x - 3 = 0$

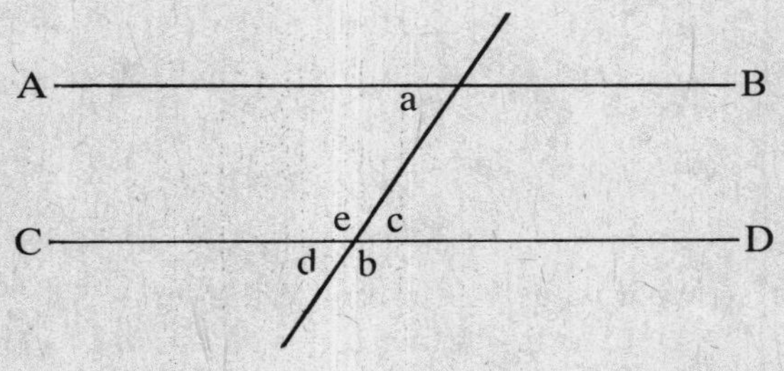

2. Is AB parallel to CD?
   (1) Angle a + angle b = 180°
   (2) Angle a + angle c + angle d + angle e = 360°

3. A, B, and C are three consecutive even integers (not necessarily in order). Which has the greatest value?
   (1) A + B = C
   (2) C is a positive number.

4. How many hours does it take Bill to do a certain job?
   (1) Working together, Bill and Jim can complete it in eight hours.
   (2) Jim can do the job in twelve hours.

5. If x and y are non-negative, is (x + y) greater than xy?
   (1) x = y
   (2) x + y is greater than $x^2 + y^2$

6. How heavy is one brick?
   (1) Two bricks weigh as much as three 6-lb. weights.
   (2) Three bricks weigh as much as one brick plus 18 lbs.

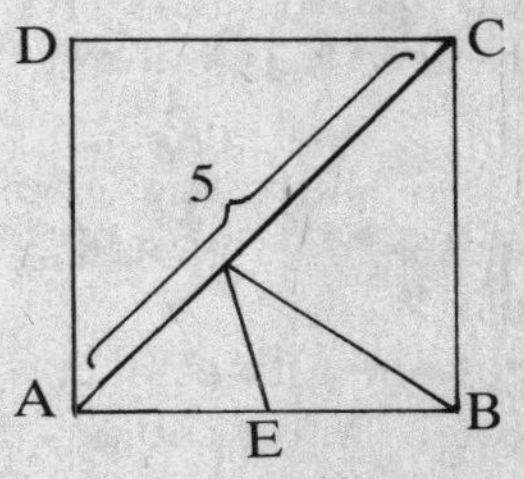

7. In the diagram, find the length of AB.
   (1) ABCD is a rectangle.
   (2) AC − AE = AB + BE

8. A man has eight 3-lb weights, ten 5-lb weights, and seven 10-lb weights. He places eight of these weights on a scale. How many 5-lb weights are used?
   (1) The scale registers 47 lbs.
   (2) The number of 10-lb weights used is one less than the number of 3-lb weights used.

9. What is the value of p?
   (1) p=4q
   (2) q=4p

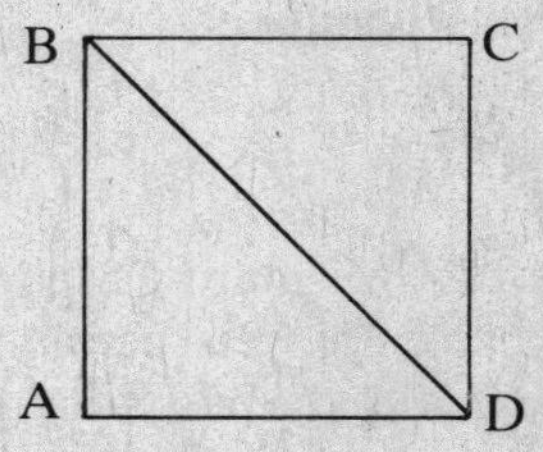

10. Is ABCD a square?
    (1) AB is parallel to CD.
    (2) BCD is an equilateral triangle.

11. A marathon runner running along a prescribed route passes through neighborhoods J, K, L and M, not necessarily in that order. How long does he take to run from J to M?
    (1) The runner averages 8 miles per hour on the route from J to M.
    (2) M is 4 miles from K and 12 miles from L, but J is 15 miles from K.

12. Mary has qualified to become a police officer. Has Albert qualified to become a police officer?
    (1) If Albert qualifies to become a police officer, then Mary will qualify to be come a police officer.
    (2) If Albert does not qualify to become a police officer, then Mary will not qualify to become a police officer.

13. A package of 40 cookies is divided among three children, W, X and Y. How many cookies did X get?
    (1) W got one-fifth as many cookies as Y.
    (2) W got 16 fewer cookies than Y.

14. Is $\frac{x}{5}$ an integer?
    (1) $\frac{x}{12{,}345}$ is an integer.
    (2) $\frac{x}{336}$ is an integer.

15. What is the volume of cube X?
    (1) The diagonal of one of the faces of X is $\sqrt{6}$.
    (2) The diagonal of the cube from the upper rear left corner to the lower front right corner is 3.

16. What is the value of $p^8 - q^8$?
    (1) $p^7 + q^7 = 127$
    (2) $p - q = 0$

17. Is x a negative number?
    (1) $4x + 24 > 0$
    (2) $4x - 24 < 0$

18. In 1980 the Maximo Corporation spent $12,000 on employee pension payments. How much did the corporation spend on employee pension payments in 1981?
    (1) In 1981 the number of employees on the Maximo Corporation pension plan decreased by 15% compared to 1980.
    (2) In 1981 the average cost of employee pension payments per employee increased by 30% over the cost of such payments in 1980.

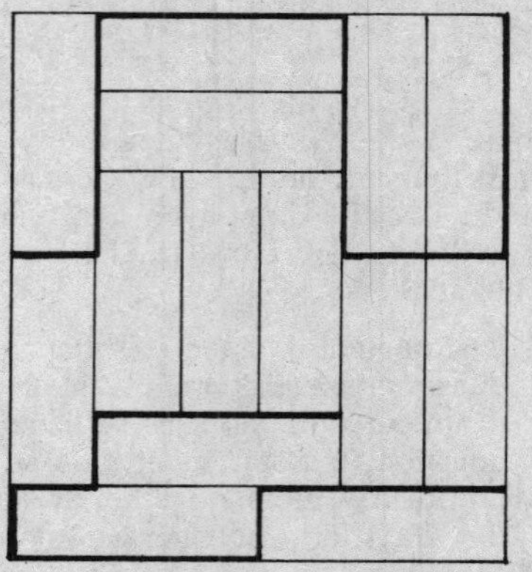

19. In the figure above, a rectangle is divided into smaller rectangles of the same shape and size. What is the area of the large rectangle?
    (1) The length of the darkened path at the top of the diagram is 45.
    (2) The length of the darkened path at the bottom of the diagram is 39.

20. Does $(x + y)^2 + (x - y)^2$ equal 130?
    (1) $x^2 + y^2 = 65$
    (2) $x = 7$ and $y = 7$.

21. What is the 999th term of the series S?
    (1) The first 4 four terms of S are $(1 + 1)^2$, $(2 + 1)^2$, $(3 + 1)^2$, and $(4 + 1)^2$.
    (2) For every x, the xth term of S is $(x + 1)^2$.

22. If x and y are integers, is x less than y?
    (1) The cube of x is less than the cube of y.
    (2) The square of x is less than the square of y.

23. When one piece of fruit is taken at random from a fruit bowl, what is the chance that it is an apple?
    (1) There are twice as many apples as oranges in the fruit bowl.
    (2) A third of the fruit in the fruit bowl are oranges.

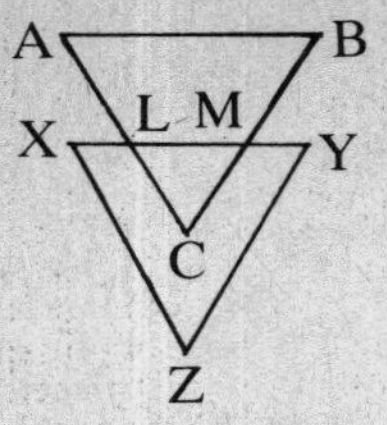

24. Triangles ABC and XYZ are equilateral triangles. Are lines AB and XY parallel?
(1) ∠ BAL = ∠ CLM
(2) Triangle CLM is an equilateral triangle.

25. How many chocolate bars 2 inches wide and 4 inches long can be packed into carton Q?
(1) The inside dimensions of carton Q are 8 inches by 8 inches by 12 inches.
(2) The width of carton Q is equal to the height and $\frac{3}{4}$ of the length.

STOP

END OF SECTION. IF YOU HAVE ANY TIME LEFT, GO OVER YOUR WORK IN THIS SECTION ONLY. DO NOT WORK IN ANY OTHER SECTION OF THE TEST.

SECTION V

Time—30 Minutes
25 Questions

Directions: Below each of the following passages, you will find questions or incomplete statements about the passage. Each statement or question is followed by lettered words or expressions. Select the word or expression that most satisfactorily completes each statement or answers each question in accordance with the meaning of the passage. After you have chosen the best answer, blacken the corresponding space on the answer sheet.

Suppose you go into a fruiterer's shop, wanting an apple—you take up one, and on biting it you find it is sour; you look at it, and see that it is hard and green. You take up another one, and that, too, is hard, green, and sour. The shopman offers you a third; but, before biting it, you examine it, and find that it is hard and green, and you immediately say that you will not have it, as it must be sour, like those that you have already tried.

Nothing can be more simple than that, you think; but if you will take the trouble to analyze and trace out into its logical elements what has been done by the mind, you will be greatly surprised. In the first place you have performed the operation of induction. You find that, in two experiences, hardness and greenness in apples went together with sourness. It was so in the first case, and it was confirmed by the second. True, it is a very small basis, but it is still enough from which to make an induction; you generalize the facts, and you expect to find sourness in apples where you get hardness and greeness. You found upon that a general law, that all hard and green apples are sour; and that, so far as it goes, is a perfect induction. Well, having got your natural law in this way, when you are offered another apple which you find is hard and green, you say, "All hard and green apples are sour; this apple is hard and green; therefore, this apple is sour." That train of reasoning is what logicians call a syllogism, and has all its various parts and terms—its major premises, its minor premises, and its conclusion. And, by the help of further reasoning, which, if drawn out, would have to be exhibited in two or three other syllogisms, you arrive at your final determination. "I will not have that apple." So that, you see, you have, in the first place, established a law by induction, and upon that you have founded a deduction, and reasoned out the special particular case.

Well now, suppose, having got your conclusion of the law, that at some time afterwards, you are discussing the qualities of apple with a friend; you will say to him, "It is a very curious thing, but I find that all hard and green apples are sour!" Your friend says to you, "But how do you know that?" You at once reply, "Oh, because I have tried them over and over again, and have always found them to be so." Well, if we were talking science instead of common sense, we should call than an experimental verification. And, if still opposed, you go further, and say, "I have heard from the people in Somersetshire and Devonshire, where a large number of apples are grown, and in London, where many apples are sold and eaten, that they have observed the same thing. It is also found to be the case in Normandy, and in North America. In short, I find it to be the universal experience of mankind wherever attention has been directed to the subject." Whereupon, your friend, unless he is a very unreasonable man, agrees with you, and is convinced that you are quite right in the conclusion you have drawn. He believes, although perhaps he does not know he believes it, that the more extensive verifications have been made, and results of the same kind arrived at—that the more varied the conditions under which the same results are attained, the more certain is the ultimate conclusion, and he disputes the question no further. He sees that the experiment has been tried under all sorts of conditions, as to time, place, and people, with the same result; and he says with you, therefore, that the law you have laid down must be a good one, and he must believe it.

1. The writer is probably
   (A) French
   (B) English
   (C) American
   (D) Italian
   (E) none of the above

2. "All giraffes are beautiful and graceful.
Twiga is a giraffe.
Twiga is beautiful and graceful."

According to the passage, the above reasoning is a(n)
(A) empirical verification
(B) induction from cases
(C) syllogism
(D) experimental conclusion
(E) developmental sequence

3. Apples are used
(A) in order to convince the reader that fruit has no intellect
(B) to illustrate the subject of the passage
(C) to give color to the story
(D) to show how foolish logic is
(E) to compare various types of persons

4. The author has the approach of a(n)
(A) scientist
(B) artist
(C) novelist
(D) economist
(E) businessman

5. The term "natural law," as it appears in the text, refers to
(A) common sense
(B) the "honor system"
(C) the result of an induction
(D) the order of nature
(E) a scientific discovery

6. Which of the following would be the best title for the passage?
(A) Discovering the Natural Laws of Apples
(B) The Uses of Induction
(C) Syllogistic Reasoning in Common Circumstances
(D) Experimental Verification As an Adjunct to Reasoning
(E) The Logic of Everyday Reasoning

7. If you find a hard and green apple that is not sour, you should
(A) try more apples to see if the natural law has changed
(B) eat the rest of the apple at once
(C) reject the law stating that hard and green apples are usually sour
(D) conduct further investigations and make adjustments to the law of apples as necessary
(E) all of the above

8. According to the above passage, the significance of "extensive verification" of a general law is that

I. general laws are difficult to disprove
II. the more extensively a law is tested, the truer it is
III. if a law holds up in a variety of situations, then it is more likely based on some general characteristic of the world

(A) I only
(B) II only
(C) III only
(D) II and III only
(E) I, II, and III

The Planning Commission asserts that the needed reduction in acute care hospital beds can best be accomplished by closing the smaller hospitals, mainly voluntary and proprietary. This strategy follows from the argument that closing entire institutions saves more money than closing the equivalent number of beds scattered throughout the health system.

The issue is not that simple. Larger hospitals generally are designed to provide more complex care. Routine care at large hospitals costs more than the same care given at smaller hospitals. Therefore, closure of all the small hospitals would commit the city to paying considerably more for inpatient care delivered at acute care hospitals than would be the case with a mixture of large and small institutions. Since reimbursement rates at the large hospitals are now based on total costs, paying the large institutions a lower rate for routine care would simply raise the rates for complex care by a comparable amount. Such a reimbursement rate adjustment might make the charges for each individual case more accurately reflect the actual costs, but there would be no reduction in total costs.

There is some evidence that giant hospitals are not the most efficient. Service organizations—and medical care remains largely a service industry—frequently find that savings of scale have an upper limit. Similarly, the quality of routine care in the very largest hospitals appears to be less than optimum. Also, the concentration of all hospital beds in a few locations may affect the access to care.

Thus, simply closing the smaller hospitals will not necessarily save money or improve the quality of care.

Since the fact remains that there are too many acute care hospital beds in the city, the problem is to devise a proper strategy for selecting and urging the closure of the excess beds, however many it may turn out to be.

The closing of whole buildings within large medical centers has many of the cost advantages of closing the whole of smaller institutions, because the fixed costs can also be reduced in such cases. Unfortunately, many of the separate buildings at medical centers are special use facilities, the relocation of which is extremely costly. Still, a search should be made for such opportunities.

The current lack of adequate ambulatory care facilities raises another possibility. Some floors or other large compact areas of hospitals could be transferred from inpatient to ambulatory uses. Reimbursement of ambulatory services is chaotic, but the problem is being addressed. The overhead associated with the entire hospital should not be charged even *pro rata* to the ambulatory facilities. Even if it were, the total cost would probably be less than that of building a new facility. Many other issues would also need study, especially the potential over-centralization of ambulatory services.

The Planning Commission language seems to imply that one reason for closing smaller hospitals is that they are "mainly voluntary and proprietary," thus preserving the public hospital system by making the rest of the hospital system absorb the needed cuts. It is important to preserve the public hospital system for many reasons, but the issue should be faced directly and not hidden behind arguments about hospital size—if indeed that was the meaning.

9. The best title for the passage would be
   (A) Maintaining Adequate Hospital Facilities
   (B) Defending the Public Hospitals
   (C) Methods of Selecting Hospital Beds to be Closed
   (D) Protecting the Proprietary and Voluntary Hospitals
   (E) Economic Efficiency in Hospital Bed Closings

10. The Planning Commission is accused by the author of being
    (A) unfair
    (B) racist
    (C) foolish
    (D) shortsighted
    (E) ignorant

11. On the subject of the number of hospital beds, the author
    (A) is in complete agreement with the Planning Commission
    (B) wishes to see large numbers of beds closed
    (C) wishes to forestall the closing of any more hospital beds
    (D) is unsure of the number of excess beds there really are
    (E) wishes to avoid exchanging quantity for quality

12. All of the following are reasons the author opposes the Planning Commission's Recommendation EXCEPT
    (A) service industries have an upper limit for savings of scale
    (B) single buildings of large centers may be closable instead of smaller hospitals
    (C) public hospitals have a unique contribution to make and should not be closed
    (D) the smaller hospitals recommended for closure provide services more cheaply than do larger hospitals
    (E) hospitals are service organizations

13. With which of the following would the author probably NOT agree?
    (A) Large medical centers provide better and more complex care than do smaller hospitals.
    (B) Reimbursement rates do not necessarily reflect the actual costs of providing medical care to a given patient.
    (C) Patients needing only routine medical care can often be distinguished from those requiring complex care prior to hospitalization.

(D) Too much centralization of ambulatory care is possible.
(E) Access to medical care is an important issue.

14. The author's purpose in discussing ambulatory care is to
(A) discuss alternatives to closing hospital beds
(B) present a method of reducing the fiscal disadvantages of closing only parts of larger hospitals
(C) show another opportunity for saving money
(D) help preserve the public hospital system
(E) attack the inefficient use of space in larger hospitals

15. With which of the following is the author LEAST likely to agree?
(A) a proposal to save costs in a prison system by building only very large prison complexes
(B) a plan to stop the closing of any beds whatsoever in the city until the costs of various alternatives can be fully considered
(C) an order by the Planning Commission mandating that no public hospitals be closed
(D) a proposal by an architecture firm that new hospital buildings have centralized record systems
(E) a mayoral commission being formed to study the plight of the elderly

16. How does the author feel that his suggestions for closing inpatient beds could impact on the ambulatory care system?
(A) Ambulatory care costs will probably be reduced.
(B) A reduction of hospital beds will increase the demand for ambulatory services.
(C) Smaller hospitals will have to cut back ambulatory services to stay fiscally viable.
(D) The Planning Commission would order the opening of new ambulatory services.
(E) The use as ambulatory facilities of the space made available in large hospitals by bed closings might result in having too many ambulatory services based in large hospitals.

Just as the non-manager is dependent on his boss for motiviational opportunities, so is the manager dependent on his boss for conditions of motivation which have meaning at his level. Since the motivation of an employee at any level is strongly related to the supervisory style of his immediate boss, sound motivation patterns must begin at the top. Being closer to the policymaking level, the manager has more opportunity to understand and relate his work to company goals. However, high position alone does not guarantee motivation or self-actualization.

Motivation for the manager, as well as the non-manager, is usually both a consequence and a symptom of effective job performance. Job success is dependent on cyclical conditions created by interpersonal competence, meaningful goals, and helpful systems. After sustained conditioning in the developmental cycle, an individual has amazing capacity and incentive to remain in it. Moreover, if forced into the reductive cycle, unless he has pathological needs to remain there, organizational conditions must be remarkably and consistently bad to suppress his return to the developmental cycle.

Sustained confinement of a large percentage of the work force in the reductive cycle is symptomatic of organizational illness. It is usually a culmination of a chain of events beginning with top management, and is reversible only by changes at the top. Consequences of reductive conditions such as militant unionism and other forms of reactive behavior usually provoke management into defensive and manipulative behavior which only reinforces the reductive cycle. The vicarious pleasure sought by the rank and file through seeing the management giant felled by their union is a poor substitute for the self-actualization of being a whole person doing a meaningful job, but in the absence of motivational opportunities, it is an understandable compromise.

The seeds of concerted reactive behavior are often brought to the job from broadly shared frustrations arising from social injustice, economic deprivation, and moral decadence either to sprout in a reductive climate or become infertile in a developmental climate. Hence, the unionization of a work group is usually precipitated by management failure to provide opportunities for employees to achieve personal goals through the achievement of organization goals. Organizations survive these failures only because most other companies are equally handicapped by the same failures.

Management failures in supervision do not, of course, stem from intentional malice. They may result, in part, from a lingering tradition of "scientific management" which fractionated tasks and "protected" employees from the need to think, and perpetrated management systems based on automaton conformity. But more often such failures stem from the manager's insensitivity to the needs and perceptions of others, particularly from his inability to see himself as others see him.

Insensitivity or the inability to empathize is manifested not only as interpersonal incompetence, but also as the failure to provide meaningful goals, the misuse of management systems, or a combination of both. Style of supervision, then, is largely an expression of the personality characteristics and mental health of the manager, and his potential for inducing developmental or reductive cyclical reactions.

17. A reductive cycle is one in which
    (A) an employer attempts to reduce costs
    (B) the work force is gradually reduced in number
    (C) costs decrease as a firm gains experience
    (D) a union, step by step, takes over control of a business
    (E) there is less productive effort on the part of employees

18. Upon whom do managers and other employees ultimately depend for their motivation?
    (A) their spouses
    (B) their chief executive officers
    (C) their union
    (D) their fellow workers
    (E) themselves

19. The passage indicates that the unionization of a work group is most commonly brought about by management's failure to provide
    (A) opportunities for the workers to realize individual objectives by way of group objectives
    (B) opportunities for the workers to achieve a feeling of self-identification
    (C) more pleasant working surroundings, including modern conveniences available both at their work and during rest-periods and lunch-periods
    (D) greater fringe benefits, including more holidays and health insurance
    (E) opportunities for socialization during working hours as well as after work

20. If a substantial number of the employees remain in the reductive cycle, one may assume that
    (A) the organization is enjoying increased business
    (B) the personnel department has been functioning effectively
    (C) the boss is not giving sufficient attention to the business
    (D) the organization is failing to provide adequate motivation for its employees
    (E) they belong to unions

21. Which of the following is likely to result initially from reductive conditions in an organization?

    I. militant unionism
    II. pension plans
    III. higher wages

    (A) I only
    (B) II only
    (C) I and II only
    (D) I and III only
    (E) I, II, and III

22. Employees will get together to seek an improvement of conditions because of dissatisfactions stemming from

    I. social injustice
    II. economic deprivation
    III. moral decadence

    (A) I only
    (B) II only
    (C) I and II only
    (D) I and III only
    (E) I, II, and III

23. According to the author, management failures in supervision are mainly attributable to the supervisor or manager's
    (A) currying favor with the boss
    (B) being soft-hearted
    (C) ignorance
    (D) lack of feeling
    (E) inability to gain respect

24. Based on the passage, it can be inferred that the author views the top management of most businesses as basically
    (A) handicapped
    (B) scientific
    (C) ineffective
    (D) reactionary
    (E) unconcerned

25. It can be inferred from the passage that the author believes that a company whose management uses "scientific management" practices will probably
    (A) be unable to achieve a reductive cycle in labor-management relations
    (B) achieve developmental cycles in all areas of production
    (C) lack sufficient managerial skill to create a self-actualizing workplace
    (D) build an effective management system based on the division of labor
    (E) prevent the breakdown of labor-management relations

STOP

END OF SECTION. IF YOU HAVE ANY TIME LEFT, GO OVER YOUR WORK IN THIS SECTION ONLY. DO NOT WORK IN ANY OTHER SECTION OF THE TEST.

SECTION VI

Time—30 Minutes
20 Questions

Directions: For each of the following questions, select the best of the answer choices and blacken the corresponding space on your answer sheet.
Numbers: All numbers used are real numbers.
Figures: The diagrams and figures that accompany these questions are for the purpose of providing information useful in answering the questions. Unless it is stated that a specific figure is not drawn to scale, the diagrams and figures are drawn as accurately as possible. All figures are in a plane unless otherwise indicated.

1. If $x + 6 = 3$, then $x + 3 =$
(A) -9
(B) -3
(C) 0
(D) 3
(E) 9

2. A person is standing on a staircase. He walks down 4 steps, up 3 steps, down 6 steps, up 2 steps, up 9 steps, and down 2 steps. Where is he standing in relation to the step on which he started?
(A) 2 steps above
(B) 1 step above
(C) the same place
(D) 1 step below
(E) 4 steps above

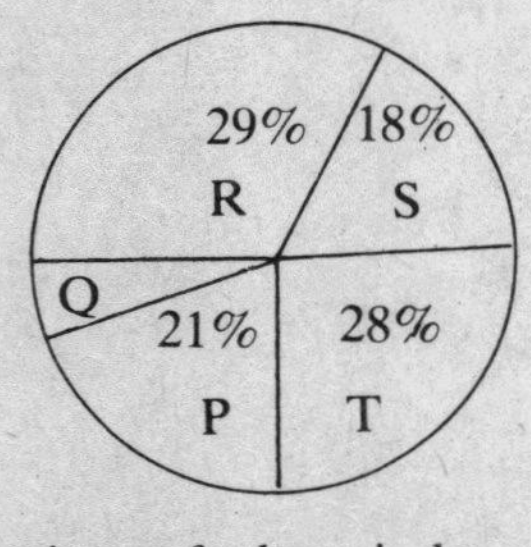

3. What portion of the circle graph above belongs to sector Q?
(A) 4%
(B) 5%
(C) 6%
(D) 75%
(E) 96%

4. A professor begins his class at 1:21 P.M. and ends it at 3:36 P.M. the same afternoon. How many minutes long was the class?
(A) 457
(B) 215
(C) 150
(D) 135
(E) 75

5. A sales representative will receive a 15% commission on a sale of $2800. If she has already received an advance of $150 on that commission, how much more is she due on the commission?
(A) $120
(B) $270
(C) $320
(D) $420
(E) $570

6. If a circle has an area of $9\pi x^2$ units, what is its radius?
(A) 3
(B) $3x$
(C) $3\pi x$
(D) $9x$
(E) $81x^4$

7. Hans is taller than Gertrude, but he is shorter than Wilhem. If Hans, Gertrude, and Wilhelm are heights x, y, and z, respectively, which of the following accurately expresses the relationships of their heights?
(A) $x > y > z$
(B) $x < y < z$
(C) $y > x > z$
(D) $z < x < y$
(E) $z > x > y$

8. For which of the following figures can the perimeter of the figure be determined if the area is known?

I. a trapezoid
II. a square

III. an equilateral triangle
IV. a parallelogram

(A) I only
(B) II only
(C) III only
(D) I and III only
(E) I, II, III, and IV

9. A child withdraws from his piggy bank 10% of the original sum in the bank. If he must add 90¢ to bring the amount in the bank back up to the original sum, what was the original sum in the bank?
(A) $1.00
(B) $1.90
(C) $8.10
(D) $9.00
(E) $9.90

10. If cylinder P has a height twice that of cylinder Q and a radius half that of cylinder Q, what is the ratio between the volume of cylinder P and the volume of cylinder Q?
(A) 1:8
(B) 1:4
(C) 1:2
(D) 1
(E) 2:1

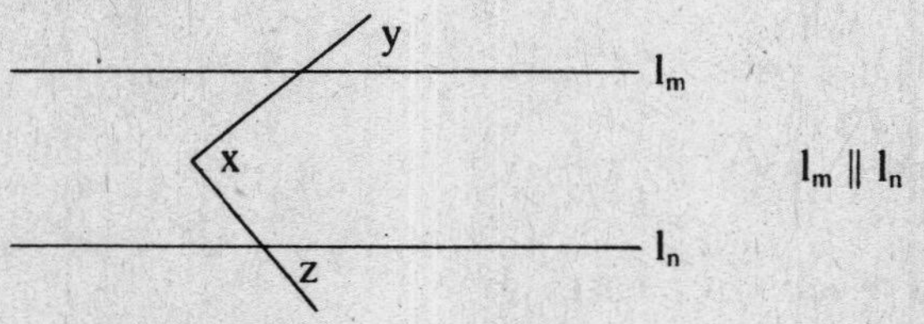

11. In the figure above, which of the following is true?
(A) $y + z = x$
(B) $y = 90°$
(C) $x + y + z = 180$
(D) $y = x + z$
(E) $z = x + y$

12. If the width of a rectangle is increased by 25% while the length remains constant, the resulting area is what percent of the original area?
(A) 25%
(B) 75%
(C) 125%
(D) 225%
(E) Cannot be determined from the information given.

13. The average of four consecutive odd positive integers is always
(A) an odd number
(B) divisible by 4
(C) the sum of two prime numbers
(D) a multiple of 3
(E) an even number

14. A snapshot measures $2\frac{1}{2}$ inches by $1\frac{7}{8}$ inches. It is to be enlarged so that the longer dimension will be 4 inches. The length of the enlarged shorter dimension will be
(A) $2\frac{1}{2}$ inches
(B) 3 inches
(C) $3\frac{3}{8}$ inches
(D) $2\frac{5}{8}$ inches
(E) none of these

15. From a piece of tin in the shape of a square 6 inches on a side, the largest possible circle is cut out. Of the following, the ratio of the area of the circle to the area of the original square is closest in value to
(A) $\frac{3}{4}$
(B) $\frac{2}{3}$
(C) $\frac{3}{5}$
(D) $\frac{1}{2}$
(E) $\frac{1}{4}$

16. In the Peterson Company, the ratio of upper-management to middle-management personnel is 4:3. If 75% of upper management has experience on the production line, what is the greatest proportion of the total of upper- and middle-management personnel who could have experience on the production line?
(A) $\frac{5}{7}$
(B) $\frac{3}{4}$
(C) $\frac{6}{7}$
(D) $\frac{7}{6}$
(E) $\frac{7}{4}$

17. The function # is defined for any positive whole number N as being the product $\#N = (N - 1)(N - 2)(N - 3)$. What is the sum of #1, #2, #3, and #4?
(A) −10
(B) 6
(C) 12
(D) 60
(E) 256

18. A basketball club meets on a certain night with 12 members in attendance. The club members form two 6-member teams to play against each other. If five players on each team must be on the basketball court for a game to be played, how many different groups of players could be playing during the course of the game?
(A) 6
(B) 18
(C) 24
(D) 36
(E) 144

19. Two crystal spheres of diameter $\frac{x}{2}$ are being packed in a cubic box with a side of x. If the crystal spheres are in the box and the rest of the box is completely filled with packing powder, approximately what proportion of the box is filled with packing powder? (The volume of a sphere of radius r is $\frac{4}{3}\pi r^3$.)
(A) $1\frac{1}{16}$
(B) $\frac{1}{8}$
(C) $\frac{1}{2}$
(D) $\frac{3}{4}$
(E) $\frac{7}{8}$

20. All of the coffee mixtures sold in a certain store contain either Colombian, Jamaican, or Brazilian coffee or some combination of these. Of all the mixtures, 33 contain Colombian coffee, 43 contain Jamaican coffee, and 42 contain Brazilian coffee. Of these, 16 contain at least Colombian and Jamaican coffees, 18 contain at least Jamaican and Brazilian coffees, 8 contain at least Brazilian and Colombian coffees, and 5 contain all three. How many different coffee mixtures are sold in the store?
(A) 71
(B) 81
(C) 109
(D) 118
(E) 165

STOP

END OF SECTION. IF YOU HAVE ANY TIME LEFT, GO OVER YOUR WORK IN THIS SECTION ONLY. DO NOT WORK IN ANY OTHER SECTION OF THE TEST.

SECTION VII

Time—30 Minutes
25 Questions

Directions: In each problem below, either part or all of the sentence is underlined. The sentence is followed by five ways of writing the underlined part. Answer choice A repeats the original; the other answer choices vary. If you think that the original phrasing is the best, choose A. If you think one of the other answer choices is the best, select that choice.

This section tests the ability to recognize correct and effective expression. Follow the requirements of standard written English: grammar, choice of words, and sentence construction. Choose the answer which results in the clearest, most exact sentence, but do not change the meaning of the original sentence.

1. During the summer of 1981, when it looked like parts of New York and New Jersey were going to run short of water, many businesses and homes were affected by the stringent restrictions on the use of water.
   (A) it looked like parts of New York and New Jersey were going to run
   (B) it looked as if parts of New York and New Jersey would have run
   (C) it appeared that parts of New York and New Jersey would run
   (D) appearances were that parts of New York and New Jersey would run
   (E) it was the appearance that parts of New York and New Jersey would be running

2. The books of W.E.B. DuBois before World War I constituted as fundamental a challenge to the accepted ideas of race relations that, two generations later, will be true of the writings of the radical writers of the 1960's.
   (A) that, two generations later, will be true of
   (B) that, two generations later, would be true of
   (C) as, two generations later, would be true of
   (D) as, two generations later, would
   (E) just in the way that, two generations later, did

3. For the reason that gasoline was relatively cheap and twenty-five cents per gallon in the 1960's, the average American came to view unfettered, inexpensive driving as a right rather than a lucky privilege.
   (A) For the reason that gasoline was relatively cheap and
   (B) Because gasoline was relatively cheap and
   (C) Due to the fact that gasoline was a relatively inexpensive
   (D) In that gasoline was a relatively inexpensive
   (E) Because gasoline was a relatively cheap

4. The political masters of the health care system have not listened to professional health planners because it has not been profitable for them to do that thing.
   (A) has not been profitable for them to do that thing.
   (B) has not been profitable for them to do so.
   (C) has been unprofitable for them to do that thing.
   (D) has been unprofitable for them to do so.
   (E) doing so had not been profitable for them.

5. Because of the efforts of Amory Lovins and other advocates of the "soft" path of solar energy, the economics of nuclear power are being more closely examined now than ever before.
   (A) being more closely examined now than ever before.
   (B) being attacked more vigorously than ever before.
   (C) open to closer examination than they ever were before.
   (D) more closely examined than before.
   (E) more examined than they ever were before now.

6. Most bacterial populations grown in controlled conditions will quickly expand to the limit of the food supply, produce toxic waste products that inhibit further growth, and reached an equilibrium state within a relatively short time.
   (A) produce toxic waste products that inhibit further growth, and reached an equilibrium state within a relatively short time.
   (B) will have produced toxic waste products that inhibit further growth and also will reach an equilibrium state within a relatively short time.
   (C) will then produce a toxic waste product that inhibits further growth and thus reached an equilibrium state in a very short time.
   (D) produce toxic waste products that inhibit further growth and reach equilibrium.
   (E) produce toxic waste products that inhibit further growth, and reach an equilibrium state in a fairly prompt way.

7. A little-known danger of potent hallucinogens such as lysergic acid diethylamide-25 is that not only is the user immediately disoriented, but also he will experience significant ego suppression for a period of three weeks as well.
   (A) but also he will experience significant ego suppression for a period of three weeks as well.
   (B) but also he will experience significant ego suppression for a period of three weeks.
   (C) but also there will be a three-week period of ego suppression as well.
   (D) but the ego is suppressed for a period of three weeks as well.
   (E) but the user's ego is suppressed for a period of three weeks in addition.

8. Many people mistakenly believe that the body's nutritional requirements remain the same irregardless of the quantity and form of other nutrients ingested, physical activity and emotional state.
   (A) irregardless of the quantity and form of other nutrients ingested, physical activity and emotional state.
   (B) irregardless of the other nutrients, physical activity and emotional state.
   (C) regardless of the quantity of nutrients or physical exercise or emotional excitation.
   (D) regardless of the quantity or form of nutrients or physical exercise and emotional statement.
   (E) regardless of the quantity or form of other nutrients ingested, physical activity or emotional state.

9. Measuring the brainwaves of human beings while they are engaged in different types of thought hopefully will enable neuropsychologists to better understand the relationship between the structures of the brain and thinking.
   (A) hopefully will enable
   (B) hopefully might enable
   (C) will, it is hoped, enable
   (D) would hopefully enable
   (E) will, it is to be hoped by all, enable

10. It appears from a study of the detailed grammar of the Hopi Indians that their system of assigning tenses is very different from that of English or other European languages.
    (A) It appears from a study of the detailed grammar of the Hopi Indians that their system
    (B) It seems that study of the Hopi Indians indicates that their system
    (C) A detailed study of the grammar of the Hopi Indian language indicates that its system
    (D) Detailed study of Hopi Indians reveals that their system
    (E) The Hopi Indians have a system

11. While everyone continues to hope for their survival, it is unlikely that the astronauts could have made it back to the shelter before the power plant exploded.
    (A) could have made it back to the shelter before the power plant exploded.
    (B) were making it back to the shelter before the power plant exploded.
    (C) were able to make it back to the shelter before the power plant explodes.

(D) have been able to make it back to the shelter before the power plant will explode.
(E) could have made it to the shelter before the power plant explosion would have destroyed them.

12. By the time peace and happiness will have come to the planet, many lives will be wasted.
(A) will have come to the planet, many lives will be wasted.
(B) come to the planet, many lives will have been wasted.
(C) will have come to the planet, many lives will have been wasted.
(D) shall have come to the planet, many lives shall be wasted.
(E) would have come to the planet, many lives would have been wasted.

13. It could be argued that the most significant virtue of a popular democracy is not the right to participate in the selection of leaders, but rather that it affirms our importance in the scheme of things.
(A) but rather that it affirms
(B) but rather its affirmation of
(C) but rather it's affirmation in terms of
(D) but instead of that, its affirming that
(E) affirming rather

14. Long popular among the connoisseurs of Indian music, Ravi Shankar first impressed Western listeners with his phenomenal technical virtuosity, but they soon came to appreciate his music as an artful expression of an older culture's musical insights.
(A) but they soon came to appreciate his music as an artful
(B) but it soon occurred that they appreciated his artful music as an
(C) but soon this was surpassed by an appreciation of it as an artful
(D) which was soon surpassed by an even deeper appreciation of it as an artful
(E) soon surpassed by an artful appreciation of an

15. Primarily accomplished through the use of the electron microscope, researchers have recently vastly increased their knowledge of the process of cell division.
(A) Primarily accomplished through the use of the electron microscope,
(B) Through the competent use of advanced electron microscopy,
(C) Primarily through the use of electron microscopy,
(D) In a large sense through the use of the electron microscope,
(E) In the main, particularly through the use of electron microscopes,

16. Though garlic is often associated with Italian cuisine, it is actually the use of oregano which most distinguishes the Italians from the French.
(A) which most distinguishes the Italians from the French.
(B) which primarily distinguishes Italians from Frenchmen.
(C) which generally serves to distinguish an Italian sauce from a French one.
(D) which is the major distinction between the two great cuisines.
(E) which most distinguishes Italian cookery from French.

17. While controversy rages over whether the sign language taught to some great apes is truly human-like speech, there is no similar dispute that our powers of communication are greater by far than that of any other animal.
(A) are greater by far than that of any other animal.
(B) are far greater than that of any other animal.
(C) are greater by far than any other animal.
(D) are far greater than those of any other animal.
(E) have been far greater than those of other animals.

18. Despite the money that has been invested by industry in the attempt to persuade Americans that highly processed foods are the best foods, the populace stubbornly clings to the belief that such foods are neither particularly healthy or tasty.

(A) are neither particularly healthy or tasty.
(B) are neither particularly healthful nor tasty.
(C) are not particularly healthy or tasty.
(D) are not particularly healthful or tasteful.
(E) are not very healthy nor tasty.

19. While it is certainly true that almost all literate citizens could be taught to improve their ability to read and reason, it must first be demonstrated that such an undertaking would increase the general welfare.
(A) While it is certainly true that almost all literate citizens could be taught to improve their ability to read and reason, it must first be demonstrated that such an undertaking would increase the general welfare.
(B) While it is certainly true that almost all literate citizens could improve their reading and reasoning skills, such a vast undertaking requires a clear demonstration of benefit before being undertaken.
(C) Before undertaking to improve the reading and reasoning of almost all citizens, it is necessary to show that the project will work.
(D) Before the project of improving almost all citizens' reading and reasoning skills is undertaken, that the outcome will be increased happiness must be demonstrated.
(E) Prior to the improvement of citizens' reading and reasoning skills, it must be shown that they will be happier with the improved skills than they are now.

20. The closing of small, inexpensive hospitals while large expensive hospitals remain open seems a luxury that we can no longer afford in order to maintain them.
(A) seems a luxury that we can no longer afford in order to maintain them.
(B) seems to emphasize luxury over economy, which we can no longer afford.
(C) seems to be a waste of valuable resources.
(D) seems a luxury we can no longer afford.
(E) seems too luxurious to be any longer affordable.

21. The ancient question of the exact difference between plants and animals, which was so complicated with the discovery of microscopic members of both groups, was somewhat sidestepped with the establishment of a third phylum, the Protista, reserved just for them.
(A) reserved just for them.
(B) consisting only of them.
(C) inhabited only by them.
(D) which includes all microscopic life.
(E) which would have included all microscopic plants and animals.

22. The Lake Manyara Park in Tanzania affords the visitor with unequalled opportunities to photograph lions playing in trees without the aid of telephoto lenses.
(A) The Lake Manyara Park in Tanzania affords the visitor with unequalled opportunities to photograph lions playing in trees without the aid of telephoto lenses.
(B) The Lake Manyara Park in Tanzania permits the visitor unequalled opportunities to photograph lions playing in trees without the aid of telephoto lenses.
(C) The Lake Manyara Park in Tanzania gives the visitor the unequalled opportunity to photograph lions playing in trees without telephoto lenses.
(D) The visitor to the Lake Manyara Park in Tanzania has the unequalled opportunity to photograph lions playing in trees without the aid of telephoto lenses.
(E) Even without the aid of telephoto lenses, the visitor to Tanzania's Lake Manyara Park has an unequalled opportunity to photograph lions playing in trees.

23. One school of thought maintains that a person's susceptibility to hypnosis is able to

be measured by their performance on the "eye roll" test.

(A) is able to be measured by their
(B) can be measured by their
(C) can be measured by his
(D) is measurable by their
(E) is possibly measurable by his

24. Many observers of the demonstration were appalled at the violence with which it was broken up, grieved by the large number of injuries to both demonstrators and militia, and promising that this sort of horror would never be repeated.

(A) grieved by the large number of injuries to both demonstrators and militia, and promising that this sort of horror would never be repeated.
(B) aggrieved by the large number of injuries to both demonstrators and militia, and promised that this sort of horror would never be repeated.
(C) grieved by the large number of injuries to both demonstrators and militia and determined that this sort of horror would never be repeated.
(D) saddened by the large number of injuries to both sides and promised that this horror would never be repeated.
(E) grieving about the large number of injuries to both demonstrators and militia and promising that this sort of horror would never be repeated.

25. In order to survive, prisoners may have to adapt to the harsh conditions of jail, but to do so may be to lose much that is human and admirable in their original personalities.

(A) In order to survive, prisoners may have to adapt to the harsh conditions of jail, but to do so may be to lose much that is human and admirable in their original personalities.
(B) To survive, prisoners may have to jettison much that is human and admirable in the original personality.
(C) In order to survive, prisoners must adapt to the harsh conditions of jail, thus losing much that is human and admirable of their original personalities.
(D) Survival in jail may require the prisoner to discard much that was human and admirable from their original personality.
(E) Survival in a harsh prison environment often requires the discarding of much that is human and admirable in the prisoner's original personalities.

STOP

END OF SECTION. IF YOU HAVE ANY TIME LEFT, GO OVER YOUR WORK IN THIS SECTION ONLY. DO NOT WORK IN ANY OTHER SECTION OF THE TEST.

SECTION VIII

Time—30 Minutes
20 Questions

Directions: For each of the following questions, select the best of the answer choices and blacken the corresponding space on your answer sheet.
Numbers: All numbers used are real numbers.
Figures: The diagrams and figures that accompany these questions are for the purpose of providing information useful in answering the questions. Unless it is stated that a specific figure is not drawn to scale, the diagrams and figures are drawn as accurately as possible. All figures are in a plane unless otherwise indicated.

1. What is 40% of $\frac{10}{7}$?
(A) $\frac{2}{7}$
(B) $\frac{4}{7}$
(C) $\frac{10}{28}$
(D) $\frac{1}{28}$
(E) $\frac{28}{10}$

2. A prime number is one with 2 divisors and which is divisble only by itself and 1. Which of the following are prime numbers?

I. 17
II. 27
III. 51
IV. 59

(A) I only
(B) I and II only
(C) I, III, and IV only
(D) I and IV only
(E) III and IV only

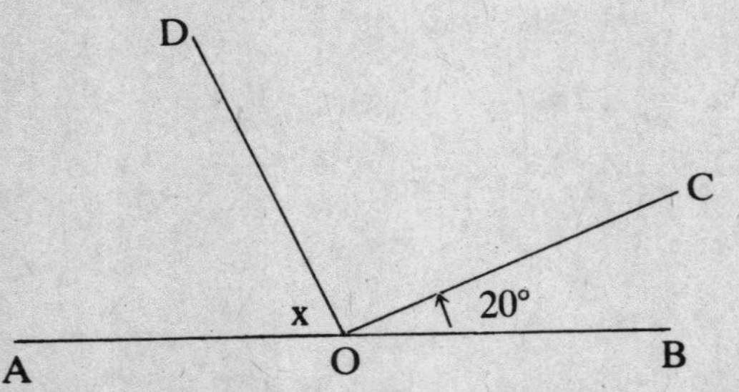

3. As shown in the above diagram, AB is a straight line and angle BOC = 20°. If the number of degrees in angle DOC is 6 more than the number of degrees in angle x, find the number of degrees in angle x.
(A) 77
(B) 75
(C) 78
(D) $22\frac{6}{7}$
(E) 87

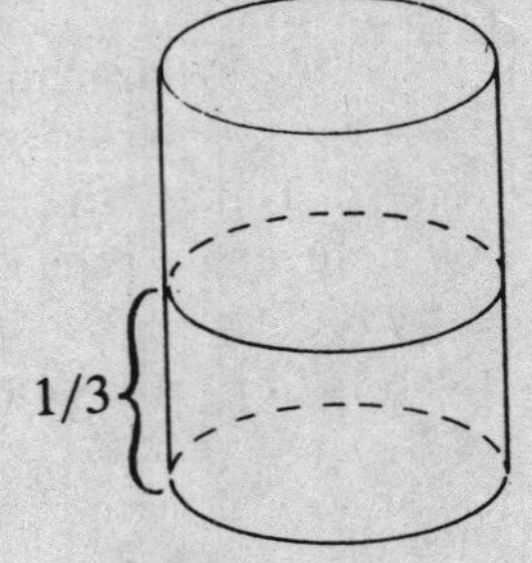

4. As shown in the figure, a cylindrical oil tank is $\frac{1}{3}$ full. If 3 more gallons are added, the tank will be half full. What is the capacity, in gallons, of the tank?
(A) 15
(B) 16
(C) 17
(D) 18
(E) 19

5. A boy receives grades of 91, 88, 86, and 78 in four of his major subjects. What must he receive in his fifth major subject in order to average 85?
(A) 86
(B) 85
(C) 84
(D) 83
(E) 82

6. If a steel bar is 0.39 feet long, its length in *inches* is
(A) less than 4
(B) between 4 and $4\frac{1}{2}$
(C) between $4\frac{1}{2}$ and 5
(D) between 5 and 6
(E) more than 6

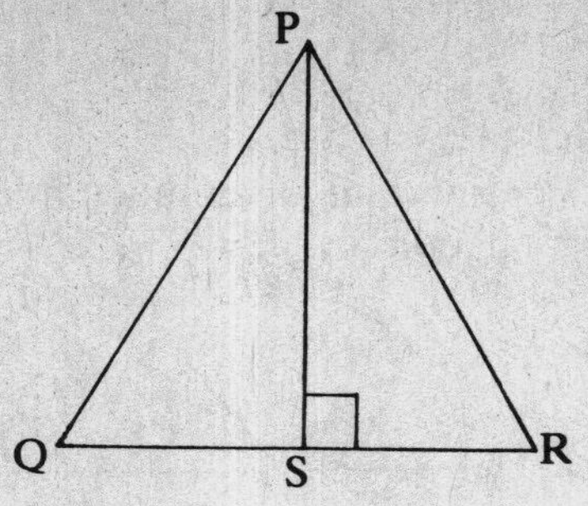

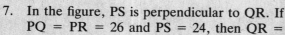

7. In the figure, PS is perpendicular to QR. If PQ = PR = 26 and PS = 24, then QR =
   (A) 14
   (B) 16
   (C) 18
   (D) 20
   (E) 22

8. If x = 0, for what value of y is the following equation valid? $5x^3 + 7x^2 - (4y + 13)x - 7y + 15 = 0$
   (A) $-2\frac{1}{7}$
   (B) 0
   (C) $+2\frac{1}{7}$
   (D) $\frac{15}{11}$
   (E) $3\frac{1}{7}$

9. A man buys some shirts and some ties. The shirts cost $7 each and the ties cost $3 each. If the man spends exactly $81 and buys the maximum number of shirts possible under these conditions, what is the ratio of shirts to ties?
   (A) 5:3
   (B) 4:3
   (C) 5:2
   (D) 4:1
   (E) 3:2

10. If a man walks $\frac{2}{5}$ mile in 5 minutes, what is his average rate of walking in miles per hour?
    (A) 4
    (B) $4\frac{1}{2}$
    (C) $4\frac{4}{5}$
    (D) $5\frac{1}{5}$
    (E) $5\frac{3}{4}$

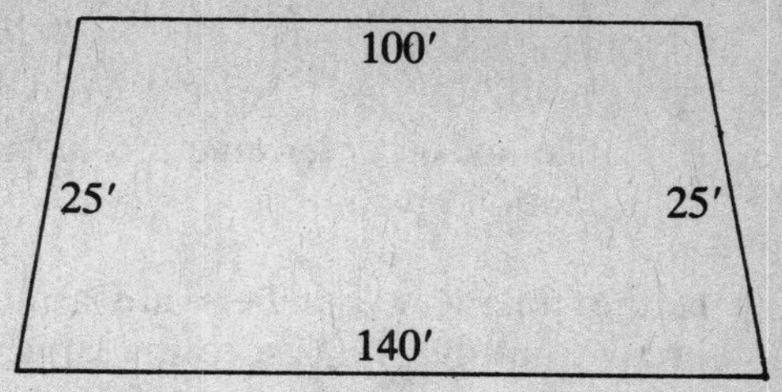

11. One end of a dam has the shape of a trapezoid with the dimensions indicated. What is the dam's area in square feet?
    (A) 1000
    (B) 1200
    (C) 1500
    (D) 1800
    (E) Cannot be determined from the information given.

12. If $1 + \frac{1}{t} = \frac{t+1}{t}$, what does t equal?
    (A) +2 only
    (B) +2 or − 2 only
    (C) +2 or −1 only
    (D) −2 or +1 only
    (E) t is any number except 0

13. Point A is 3 inches from line b as shown in the diagram. In the plane that contains point A and line b, what is the total number of points which are 6 inches from A and also 1 inch from b?
    (A) 0
    (B) 1
    (C) 2
    (D) 3
    (E) 4

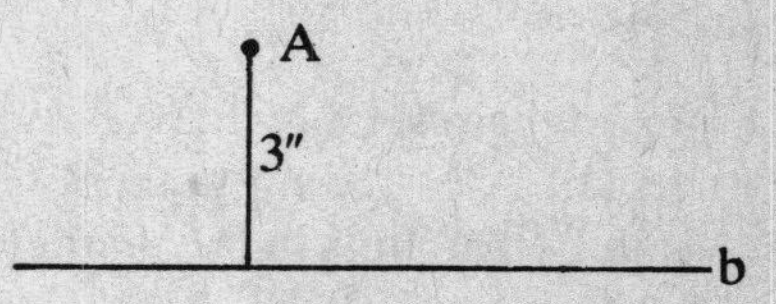

14. If R and S are different integers, both divisible by 5, then which of the following is *not necessarily* true?
    (A) R − S is divisible by 5
    (B) RS is divisible by 25
    (C) R + S is divisible by 5
    (D) $R^2 + S^2$ is divisible by 5
    (E) R + S is divisible by 10

15. If a triangle of base 7 is equal in area to a circle of radius 7, what is the altitude of the triangle?
    (A) 8π
    (B) 10π

(C) 12π
(D) 14π
(E) Cannot be determined from the information given.

16. If the following numbers are arranged in order from the smallest to the largest, what will be their correct order?

I. $\frac{9}{13}$
II. $\frac{13}{9}$
III. 70%
IV. $\frac{1}{.70}$

(A) II, I, III, IV
(B) III, II, I, IV
(C) III, IV, I, II
(D) II, IV, III, I
(E) I, III, IV, II

17. The coordinates of the vertices of quadrilateral PQRS are P(0, 0), Q(9, 0), R(10, 3) and S(1, 3), respectively. The area of PQRS is
(A) $9\sqrt{10}$
(B) $\frac{9}{2}\sqrt{10}$
(C) $\frac{27}{2}$
(D) 27
(E) not determinable from the information given

18. In the circle shown, AB is a diameter. If secant AP = 8 and tangent CP = 4, find the number of units in the diameter of the circle.
(A) 6
(B) $6\frac{1}{2}$
(C) 8
(D) $3\sqrt{2}$
(E) Cannot be determined from the information given.

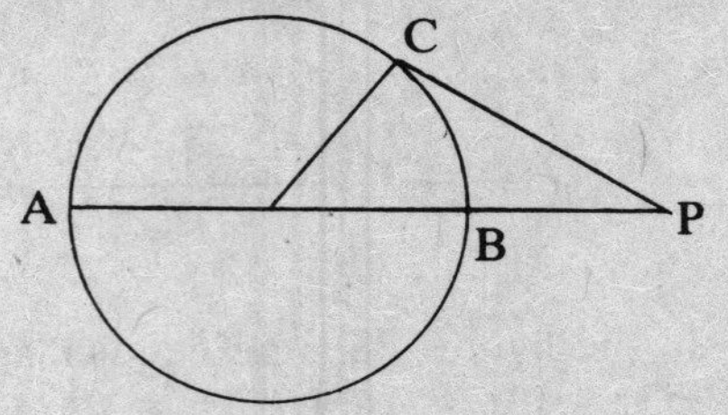

19. A certain type of siding for a house costs $10.50 per square yard. What does it cost for the siding for a wall 4 yards wide and 60 feet long?
(A) $800
(B) $840
(C) $2520
(D) $3240
(E) $5040

20. A circle whose radius is 7 has its center at the origin. Which of the following points are outside the circle?

I. (4, 4)
II. (5, 5)
III. (4, 5)
IV. (4, 6)

(A) I and II only
(B) II and III only
(C) II, III, and IV only
(D) II and IV only
(E) III and IV only

STOP

END OF SECTION. IF YOU HAVE ANY TIME LEFT, GO OVER YOUR WORK IN THIS SECTION ONLY. DO NOT WORK IN ANY OTHER SECTION OF THE TEST.

ANSWER KEY—PRACTICE EXAMINATION I

SECTION I

1. B
2. C
3. D
4. E
5. A
6. C
7. B
8. B
9. B
10. C
11. E
12. C
13. A
14. B
15. D
16. B
17. B
18. E
19. D
20. A
21. C
22. B
23. E
24. D
25. C

SECTION II

1. D
2. D
3. B
4. B
5. A
6. D
7. D
8. D
9. E
10. A
11. C
12. A
13. B
14. D
15. A
16. E
17. E
18. A
19. C
20. B

SECTION III

1. A
2. B
3. E
4. C
5. C
6. B
7. C
8. D
9. A
10. C
11. E
12. E
13. C
14. C
15. A
16. E
17. E
18. B
19. E
20. A
21. A
22. E
23. D
24. A
25. E
26. C
27. E
28. C
29. A
30. D
31. C
32. A
33. B
34. B
35. B

SECTION IV

1. C
2. A
3. C
4. C
5. B
6. D
7. B
8. A
9. C
10. B
11. E
12. B
13. C
14. A
15. D
16. B
17. E
18. C
19. D
20. D
21. B
22. A
23. C
24. D
25. E

SECTION V

1. B
2. C
3. B
4. A
5. C
6. E
7. D
8. C
9. E
10. D
11. D
12. C
13. A
14. B
15. A
16. E
17. E
18. B
19. A
20. D
21. A
22. E
23. D
24. C
25. C

SECTION VI

1. C
2. A
3. A
4. D
5. B
6. B
7. E
8. D
9. D
10. C
11. A
12. C
13. E
14. B
15. A
16. C
17. B
18. D
19. E
20. B

SECTION VII

1. C
2. D
3. E
4. B
5. A
6. D
7. B
8. E
9. C
10. C
11. A
12. B
13. B
14. A
15. C
16. E
17. D
18. B
19. A
20. D
21. D
22. E
23. C
24. C
25. A

SECTION VIII

1. B
2. D
3. A
4. D
5. E
6. C
7. D
8. C
9. E
10. C
11. D
12. E
13. E
14. E
15. D
16. E
17. D
18. A
19. B
20. D

EXPLANATORY ANSWERS

Section I

1. **(B)** The passage makes only one geographic reference, and that is to England, with the use of "this is the question" for England. Thus, (A), (C), and (D) are out. Since the author is doing a fairly modern analysis of the problems of distributing wealth, it is not likely that he lived in King Arthur's time. Hence, (B) rather than (E).

2. **(C)** (B), (D), and (E) are eliminated on the simple grounds that there is nothing in the passage on which to base them. The preference for (C) over (A) is not great but can be arrived at by considering that the author is advocating paying less attention to the wages and the money part of the economy and more towards its ultimate ends. The denial of the virtue of money and the implication that the rich are robbers (by analogy) also tend away from capitalism at least, if not toward socialism.

3. **(D)** (D) is included in the concluding sentence of the passage. (A) and (E) are specifically disputed in the passage, since it is the entire process that matters and not merely the pay rate or effort. (C) is not disputed, but is not emphasized either, while (B) is simply absent.

4. **(E)** The passage emphasizes that it is the ends of the productive process that are critical, thus giving some support to (E). (C) has some appeal since money as such is not too important to the author, but its uses are important. (A), (B), and (D) derive any attractiveness they may have solely from the relative obscurity of (E).

5. **(A)** While the author stops short of outright accusation of the rich as robbers, they are treated in much the same manner in the passage, which creates the analogy desired.
   (E) is untrue. The author says that one might as well say the robber is a benefactor, or at least does no harm, but this is a way of disputing a statement, not agreeing with it.
   (D) fails since the passage is generally opposed to waste, while (B) and (C) are incorrect because only dishonesty is mentioned in relation to business.

6. **(C)** The choice is between (A) and (C). (B) is of no interest to the author, while (D) is only acceptable for the last three words. (E) is relevant but far too general.
   (A) refers to the last sentence and (C) refers to the sentences immediately after the posing of the great question. The distinction here is that (A) describes the great question for ALL members of society, while (C) describes the plight of the poor specifically.

7. **(B)** (B) is preferable because it is something that helps to provide the necessities of life—clean air and water, etc. (D) fails since it does not specify the job. (A) is not strong since weapons are generally destructive, though this is not impossible. (C) is less attractive than (B) since it has no stated positive value. The dislike of the rich would also enter into it. (E) is attractive since it is clear that this is something of which the author has done a great deal. It is clearly the second-best choice, but it is not as good as (B) since there is no clear message in the passage as to the value of studying theory. If (E) specifically were the arousal of the laborer to his best interests, that might be even better than (B) since it would mean all would do good work and not just the one.

8. **(B)** (A) is attractive since the author certainly is not in favor of the rich or most of their works. However, his main point—the

"main question for the poor"—is the use to which the resources of society are to be put. He will definitely see that it is waste and poor use of resources which lead to such problems as an energy shortage, since he has claimed that there will be enough of the good things if only everyone would work at the right things in the right way.

While (C) has the advantages of being a very simple and direct response to an energy shortage, we are looking for something in the passage to link to our answer, and there is really nothing to support the idea that the author wishes to see more mineral exploitation. On the contrary, he denigrates such activities.

(D) has no basis in the passage, but might appear to have the connection that the author does believe that there are enough resources to go around. Thus it might be mistakenly inferred that he would deny the shortage altogether. This is mistaken because the author says in the passage that all sorts of shortages and a despoiling of the environment are perfectly possible—even likely—if nothing is changed.

(E), like (A), is something the author might well like to do on general principles, but there is no immediate link to the question, especially not in preference to (B).

9. **(B)** The council acted on the basis of a study that showed that automobiles were the major users of energy in the city. Further, the encouragement of bicycles and other automobile-use-reducing measures indicated that (B) is correct. (A), while perhaps true and an ancillary benefit of the bikeways, is not mentioned in the passage. (D) is false since the strong terms important and everyone are unsupported by the passage's almost humorous reference to this action of the council. (E) is similarly too strong because of "always." (C) has some superficial merit, but the passage does not really say that the measures undertaken by Davis are all modern or up-to-date. Some might well be viewed as old-fashioned, though excellent for saving energy. The standard applied to the actions was whether they save energy, not whether they are fashionable.

10. **(C)** The purpose of the demonstration homes was to show the local contractors that the new regulations could be met with ease. (B) and (E), thus, have some appeal, but the question asks why two instead of just one, which (C) addresses. (A) has a little merit in that it is certainly true that a demonstration project shows what you can do, but that was not why two houses instead of one were built. (D) has no basis.

11. **(E)** Here we must look to the reasons for writing an article about Davis. The first paragraph provides the best support for (E), though both (A) and (B) have some appeal. (C) is not an implication of the passage and (D) is trivial. (B) fails since the passage does not state that Davis wishes or needs to "spread" its message, since its actions were intended to be suited to its own particular circumstances. (A) is part of (E) and if (E) stands up, as it does, then it is preferable to (A) since it covers more of the passage.

12. **(C)** The fact that Davis has thousands of trees and a fleet of cars indicates that it is not a tiny town, yet the utility of bikeways for general transportation even by city employees indicates that Davis is not too large either. The limitation of the model homes to single- and two-family dwellings also indicates less than major urban concentration, as does the recycling center's sales volume.

(A) is a meaningless term not defined in the passage. (B) has to do with social issues not dealt with in the passage at all. The citizens of Davis could be all kinds of horrible things, and still be concerned enough to save energy. (D) has the tempting half-truth that it is known that the city has a council, but nothing is said of a manager, mayor, or whatever else there might be. The lack of reference to a mayor is some small argument against it, but not for a manager. (E) is unsupported by the passage in any way.

13. **(A)** The analysis of energy-use patterns in Davis does not even mention industry, and thus supports (A). (B) has some merit, but is stated in terms—"any further"—too strong to be supported. If (C) means that the same

actions will work in any city, this is clearly false, since Davis' actions are based on a close analysis of its own situation. The passage does support the idea that other cities should do something about their energy use, but it is perhaps too strong to say "any" city. (E) is good and bad in the same ways as (C). Yes, planning helps, but not necessarily to solve all problems. Also, the passage only speaks to energy management, not to crime, etc. (D) has no support. Even in Davis, the automobile was only restricted, not eliminated, and nothing in the passage would support that conclusion.

14. **(B)** (B) is known to be false since the feasibility of meeting the new code was demonstrated by the two model houses. The answer choice does not address the question of whether the builders will meet the code, only that they can.

(A) will mean more energy even if each person uses less. (C) clearly means more energy and (E) explains the discrepancy very easily. (D) shows that more cars were used, but has the weakness that we are unsure of the breakdown between cars and bicycles before the energy survey. However, the passage noted that the town had been involved in building bikeways in 1968, four years before the 1972 survey. This means that reduced bicycle use will reflect on the 1972 results.

15. **(D)** Proposition I is not an element considered by the Davis City Council. While it is true that they did build a model house that was a multiple dwelling, this refers to the number of units, or apartments, in the building and not to the number of individuals living in a house. I is logical in terms of the overall heat balance of a house, but the Council is designing a building code, not a code that limits the number of people in a house. The reference to the population growth affecting energy use is to total energy use by the city. II is specifically referred to in the phrase "east-west orientation." III is also referred to directly in terms of window area.

16. **(B)** The passage states that air conditioning can be eliminated when the building is properly designed. Although the two model buildings are both residential, there is nothing in the passage to indicate that *only* residential buildings are at issue. (E) and (A) both suffer on this count. (C) fails because it implies that all buildings should stop using air conditioning, no matter what their design. The passage does not deny the need for cool areas within the buildings, but simply argues that this goal can be achieved without the use of air conditioning. (D) is good in its insistence that air conditioning can be eliminated, but it is wrong in saying that it is a luxury. (D) implies that you simply turn off the air conditioning, while the passage holds that you can get the same effect in a different way.

17. **(B)** (A) and (D) are simply not related to the passage at all.

(B), (C), and (E) have some merit. (E) has the merit of being a topic in the book, but it is not clear that sound is a good reference to quantum mechanics. While quantum mechanics is mentioned by the book as a thing to be symbolized, the book also has to discuss the symbolization of music, and that seems to be much more related to sound than quantum mechanics.

Both (B) and (C) have the merit of referring to the music, but with a title that refers to "sound" AND "symbol," it seems likely that the sound part refers to music and the symbol part to the notational system, rather than the other way around.

18. **(E)** (A) becomes unlikely when the first paragraph calls Einsteinian physics a "truly adequate" system, even though it may not be totally correct. Other keys to not choosing this otherwise appealing answer choice are the reference to the Theory of Relativity, which is not specifically mentioned at all, and the last paragraph's reiteration of the correctness of Einstein.

(B) is referred to in the passage as a specification of the strangeness of Einsteinian physics, and thus is part of them rather than contradictory to them. (C) fails because of the several cautionary statements such as the "unlikely" event of our ever experiencing a reversed time flow.

(D) refers to the imaginary mass of tachyons, but the passage says only that the tachyon "may" exist, not that it does.

(E) has the flag word precisely, which tells you that the answer choice is not referring to going faster than light, but to attaining exactly the speed of light. The need to move an infinite quantity of mass to go exactly the speed of light is referred to as a barrier, and is intuitively unlikely.

19. **(D)** Speculative is certainly a fair characterization of the passage. (D) is preferable to (C) because the passage is hopeful that some of these speculative things may come to pass, rather than suspicious of anything. (E) is an unlikely choice for any question of this sort.

20. **(A)** As is usual with this sort of question, there are several good answers among which to choose. (D) is clearly wrong because Zuckerkandl is not stated to have any theories of tachyon formation. (E) similarly fails for lack of reference to the passage. Its only appeal is its obscurity.

(A), (B), and (C) require closer inspection. (C) seems to find that Einsteinian physics cannot treat tachyons; but actually it is predicted by the formulas associated with Einsteinian physics that such strange things as reverse time flow might occur, so (C) is out. The primary difference between (A) and (B) is the question of whether it is the notation and theories on the one hand or the observations on the other which indicates the need for improved notation. (B), while a good abstract statement of the progress of science, does not "cover the waterfront" on this passage. The only observations cited in the passage support the theoretical speculations rather than disprove the theories. Hence, (A).

21. **(C)** It is certainly not too soon for (D), since that has happened. It seems likely that the time for (A) will never arrive, but it is not discussed in the passage. The author is clearly not satisfied with the current notational system, and thus (E) is definitely in order. While (B) has merit because the author does not endorse Zuckerkandl's ideas, (C) has more merit since (C) is definitely stated to be far from accomplishment, if indeed it is possible at all.

22. **(B)** In the author's admitted oversimplification of Zuckerkandl, he says that music might be a better language for physics. Better than what? Better than math, which is, thus, also seen as a language. (D) fails because of the word great, though even without that disqualifier it would be inferior to (B).

23. **(E)** Without attempting to probe the nature of philosophy, which is certainly not an issue on a test question, (E) best links the topic of the passage to philosophy. (A), (B), and (C) are flack and (D) should not seem very good. Perhaps the nature of any field is a philosophical question, but the methods must usually be just technical matters within the field.

24. **(D)** By citing the particular part of the passage, the question requires you to see what follows from that particular phraseology. The cited phrase has the interesting aspect that something is named by scientists which is not definitely in existence. The rest of the passage certainly spoke of the tachyon as being a theoretical object, so (D)'s statement about the timing of the naming of the tachyon is certainly a good bet. It is still not certainly known—in the passage's terms—but it does have a name. It is theoretically described and it therefore seems likely that no one would have named the object without some reason, though it was not yet actually discovered.

(A) is flack and should be dismissed quickly. Such an answer choice is rarely correct unless it reflects a specific statement in the passage.

(C) may well be true, in a witty but somewhat paradoxical statement. However, even if it turns out there is no such thing as a tachyon, that is not what can be inferred from the cited passage.

Both (E) and (B) have some appeal. (B)'s dissolves on close inspection. The difference between (B) and (D) is that the issue of whether the particle was named before it was known to exist or before it actually existed in the world. While it is possible that it is named and will only later come into existence, there is nothing in the passage about creating tachyons. Thus (D) is preferable to (B). (E) is a meritorious statement in that it is certainly true and we do know that it is true (definitely true that the ideas *may* not exist) but we have no information to support the qualifier many; so (E) fails.

25. **(C)** (C) is the best answer, although there is some merit to some of the other answers as well. (A) is incomplete when compared to (C) since (A) only refers to objects, while the passage is clearly concerned with more than objects since time cannot be called an object in the physical sense. (B) suffers from a similar deficit. Although the passage does refer to the equivalence of mass and energy, this is used in the passage to justify referring to the situation of the universe as the interaction between different energies, not different masses, much less material objects. (D) is not entirely unreasonable, but it is lacking any reference to motion and time, which are found in the passage. (E) is clearly the second-best answer. There are two differences between (C) and (E). First of all, (C) refers to four specific aspects of the universe, which are all in the passage, while (E) refers to all aspects of the universe. That might be all right, but when (E) adds the qualification "as they appear to human beings," this is much too broad and would include a lot of emotions, psychology, and whatnot, which the passage clearly does not mean to include within the purview of physics.

Section II

1. **(D)** By multiplying out the given expression, we learn $w(x + y + z) = wx + wy + wz$, which shows that (A) is an equivalent expression. Second, given that it does not matter in multiplication in which order the elements are listed (i.e., $2 \times 3 = 3 \times 2 = 6$), we can see that (B) is also an equivalent expression. From $wx + wy + wz$, we can factor the w's out of the first two terms: $w(x + y) + wz$, which shows that (E) is an equivalent expression. Finally, we could also factor the w's from the last two terms: $wx + w(y + z)$, which shows that (C) is an equivalent expression. (D) is not, however, equivalent: $w + w + w + x + y + z$. The 3 would make you suspicious of (D).

2. **(D)** The problem requires you to find the amount of wood that is needed and then find the number of whole feet that will give you the wood that is needed. In this particular problem there is no question about trying to fit different lengths together, as there might be if, for instance, the wood were only available in 5-foot sections. To find the total wood needed, you must multiply 2 feet, 10 inches by four. Two feet times 4 is 8 feet. Ten inches times 4 is 40 inches, which is between 3 feet (36 inches) and 4 feet (48 inches). There is no way to get 40 inches of wood out of 3 feet. You should round up, so that there is enough wood and the answer is thus 8 feet plus 4 feet = 12 feet.

3. **(B)** The most direct solution to this problem is to substitute the value +4 for x: $(+4-7)(+4+2) = (-3)(6) = -18$. Substitute before multiplying to keep it simple.

4. **(B)** Here we need to solve the simultaneous equations. Though there are different methods, one way to find the values of x and y is first to redefine y in terms of x. Since $x - y = 2$, $x = 2 + y$. We can now use $2 + y$ as the equivalent of x and substitute $2 + y$ for x in the other equation:

$$\begin{aligned} 2(2 + y) + y &= 7 \\ 4 + 2y + y &= 7 \\ 3y &= 3 \\ y &= 1 \end{aligned}$$

Once we have a value of y, we substitute that value into either of the equations. Since the second is a bit simpler, we may prefer to use it: $x - 1 = 2$, so $x = 30$. Now we can determine that $x + y$ is $3 + 1$, or 4.

Another approach would be to add the two equations together so that the y terms will cancel themselves out:

$$\begin{array}{rl} 2x + y &= 7 \\ +(\;x - y &= 2) \\ \hline 3x \quad &= 9, \text{ thus } x = 3. \end{array}$$

Find y by substituting 3 for x in either equation.

5. **(A)** Average speed requires total distance divided by total time. Therefore it is incorrect to average the two speeds together, for, after all, the girl moved at the slower rate for three times as long as she moved at the faster rate, so they cannot be weighted equally. The correct way to solve the problem is to reason that the girl covered the 15 miles by bicycle in 1 hour. She covered the 15 miles by walking in 3 hours. Therefore, she traveled a total of 30 miles in a total of 4 hours. 30 miles/4 hours = 7.5 miles per hour.

6. **(D)** While we know by inspection that the shaded area is larger—the diagonal of a rectangle divides the rectangle in half—the answer choices tell us more is needed, though (C) is eliminated. We begin by noting that the area which is left unshaded is a triangle with a 90° angle. This means that we have an altitude and a base at our disposal. Then we note that the shaded area is the area of the square minus the area of the triangle. So we are in a position to compute the area of the square, the triangle, and the shaded part of the figure. In the first place, the base of the triangle—which is the unshaded area of the figure—is equal to the side of the square, 4. The altitude of that triangle is four units long less the unknown distance x, or 4 − x. So the area of the triangle, $\frac{1}{2}ab$, is $\frac{1}{2}(4 - x)(4)$. The area of the square is 4 × 4, or 16, so the shaded area is 16 minus the triangle, which we have just determined is $\frac{1}{2}(4 - x)(4)$. Let us first pursue the area of the triangle:

$$\tfrac{1}{2}(4 - x)(4) = (4 - x)(2) = 8 - 2x$$

Substituting in the shaded portion:

$$16 - (8 - 2x) = 8 + 2x$$

Now we complete the ratio. 8 + 2x goes on the top, since that is the shaded area, and 8 − 2x goes on the bottom, since that is the unshaded area:

$\dfrac{8 + 2x}{8 - 2x}$. And we reduce by 2 to yield $\dfrac{4 + x}{4 - x}$.

7. **(D)** Since Linda is the youngest and the other ages are derived from hers, let us assign the value x for Linda's age. In that case Mike will be 2x years old, since he is twice as old as Linda. Finally, Ned will be 2x + 2 since he is two years older than Mike. Our three ages are: Linda, x; Mike, 2x; and Ned, 2x + 2. We know that these three ages total 27. Hence, x + 2x + 2x + 2 = 27. And now we solve for x:

$$\begin{aligned} 5x + 2 &= 27 \\ 5x &= 25 \\ x &= 5 \end{aligned}$$

So Linda is 5 years old. Then, if Linda is 5, Mike must be 10 years old.

If Mike is used as a basis, $M = y$, $L = \frac{y}{2}$, $N = y + 2$. Thus, $y + \frac{y}{2} + (y + 2) = 27$; $2\frac{1}{2}y = 25$, $y = 10$.

8. **(D)** Since our rates are by fifths of a mile, let us begin the solution by figuring out how many fifths of a mile (or parts thereof) there are in this trip. In $2\frac{2}{5}$ miles there are 12 fifths. Then we add another fifth for the additional bit of distance between $2\frac{2}{5}$ and $2\frac{1}{2}$ miles. So the whole trip can be broken down into 13 segments of one-fifth (or part of one-fifth) of a mile. For the first, the charge is $1.00. That leaves 12 more segments, the charge for each of which is 20¢, giving a total charge for those 12 segments of $2.40. Now, the total charge for the trip is $1.00 for the first one-fifth of a mile and $2.40 for the remaining segments, or $3.40.

9. **(E)** We know that the formula for the area of a square is s^2 = area. So $s^2 = 36x^2$, and, taking the square root of both sides, we learn $s = 6x$. (Note: there is no question here of a negative solution, since geometrical distances are always positive.)

10. **(A)** Since we do not know how much money Ed has, we must assign that amount the value of x. We now establish that Tom has x + $2 since he has $2 more than Ed; and we know that Susan has (x + $2) + $5, which is x + $7, since she has $5 more than Tom. We want to divide this money equally. The natural thing to do, then, is to add up all

the money and divide it by 3. The total held by all three individuals is: x + (x + 2) + (x + 2 + 5) = 3x + 9. Dividing that by 3, we want everyone to have x + 3. Ed has x, so he needs to receive 3. Tom as x + 2, so he needs to receive 1. Susan has x + 7, so she needs to rid herself of 4. Susan gets rid of this 4 by giving 1 to Tom and 3 to Ed, giving us answer choice (A).

Some shortcutting is possible by considering that Susan has the most money, and then Tom and then Ed. Therefore, any answer which has Ed give up money cannot result in equal shares, eliminating (C) and (E). Furthermore, since Susan has the most, she must give up the most. In (D) Tom gives more than Susan, so this is eliminated. In (B), Susan gives out more than Tom, but she also receives from Tom, so her net giving out is only $1, compared to Tom's $4, so this is also wrong, which leaves (A).

11. **(C)** Do not let the term perfect number throw you. Accept the definition of any such oddball term and apply it to the problem. Since the factors of 6 less than 6 itself are 1, 2, and 3, 6 is the perfect number (1 + 2 + 3 = 6). 1 is not a perfect number since there are no factors of 1 less than itself. 4 is not a perfect number since the factors of 4 less than 4 are 1 and 2 and 1 + 2 ≠ 4. Nor is 8 a perfect number since the factors of 8 which are less than 8 itself are 1, 2, and 4, and those total 7, not 8. Finally, 10 is not a perfect number since the key factors here are 1, 2, and 5, which total 8, not 10.

12. **(A)** By connecting Q and O or P and O, it can be seen that the radius of circle O is 6 units. (Remember, when a circle is named after a point, that point is the center of the circle.) The formula for the area of a circle is πr^2, so the area of circle O is: $\pi(6)^2 = 36\pi$.

13. **(B)** We are given information about angles in the top of the figure and asked about angles in the bottom. The task, then, is to connect these items. We do not know that the horizontal lines are parallel, nor can we prove it. We do, however, have a quadrilateral figure and several straight lines to work with. Considering the figure with a, b, and c as the three angles of the quadrilateral other than the 70°, we see:

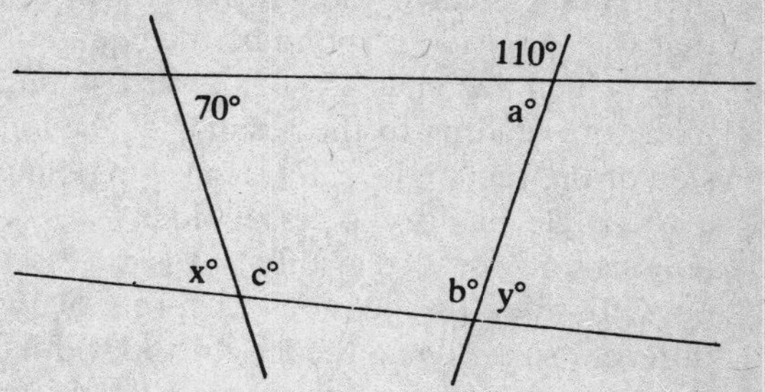

Angle A is on a straight line with 110° and thus equals 70°. We are looking only for x + y, so we need not have each individually. Working our way down through the quadrilateral, we see that the total degrees in the quadrilateral, as for all such figures, is 360°. Thus, b + c + 70° + 70° = 360° and b + c = 220°. Now, at last, we are on the right line. Again using the fact that a straight line totals 180°, we see:

$$\begin{aligned} x + c &= 180 \\ \underline{y + b} &= 180 \\ x + y + b + c &= 360 \end{aligned}$$

Since we know b + c = 220, we can solve by substituting to get x + y + 220 = 360; thus x + y = 140.

14. **(D)** We begin by computing the capacity of the cylinder, which is πr^2 times height. Since the radius is 2 and the height is 5, the capacity of this cylinder is $\pi(2)^2 \times 5 = 20\pi$ cu. ft. It is already 40% full, which means that 60% of the capacity is left. 60% of 20π cu. ft. = 12π cu. ft., and that is the answer we seek.

15. **(A)** We are seeking c, but the given information is about the area of the triangle, while c is a distance. However, the formula for the area of triangles connects distance to area, so we should compute the area in terms of c. We know that we have a right angle in the lower right-hand corner of the figure. So this gives us an altitude and a base. The altitude is 3c units long and the base is 4c units long. So, the area is $\frac{1}{2}ab$ or $\frac{1}{2}(3c)(4c) = \frac{1}{2}(12c^2) = 6c^2$. And this is equal to 54. $6c^2 = 54$; so $c^2 = 9$ and c = 3.

16. **(E)** Since the shorter side of the rectangle is 15 inches, the statement that the sides of the rectangle have the ratio of 3:2 means that the long side is found by the equation $\frac{3}{2} = \frac{x}{15}$, which becomes $45 = 2x$ by cross-multiplication, leading to the result that the long side of the rectangle is $22\frac{1}{2}$ inches long. Since a rectangle has two pairs of sides (the two lengths and the two widths), it is necessary only to refer to the sides in terms of two different sizes. Once the length and width of the rectangle have been calculated, the length of framing needed will be found by computing the perimeter of the rectangle by $2(22\frac{1}{2}) + 2(15) = \text{perimeter} = 45 + 30 = 75$ inches. Answer choice (C) is the result of adding only one set of sides. Choice (D) is reached through the error of considering the side of 15 to be the longer side.

17. **(E)** Since the number of cases is the numerator of the fraction that represents the per capita rate of meningitis and the population is the denominator, both a decrease in the number of cases and an increase in the population will tend to lower the rate. Since we have both, and both changes are substantial, we may expect a substantial decrease in the rate. Thus (A) and (B) may be eliminated on logical grounds. The new rate is found by computing $\frac{50\%\ M}{150\%\ P} = \frac{1M}{3P}$, which is $\frac{1}{3}$ of the original rate of $\frac{M}{P}$. If the new rate is one-third of the old rate, then the percentage change is a decrease of $1 - \frac{1}{3} = \frac{2}{3}$, or $66\frac{2}{3}\%$.

18. **(A)** Since we have a set of non-overlapping groupings, we can construct a table showing the sex and union status of the workers. Putting in the original information and the fact that 70% of 60% is 42%, we get:

	Men	Women	Total
Unionized	42%		60%
Non-unionized			
Total	46%		100%

Filling in the table by subtraction and addition:

	Men	Women	Total
Unionized	42%	18%	60%
Non-unionized	4%	36%	40%
Total	46%	54%	100%

Thus the percentage of the non-unionized workers that are women can be determined by the computation $\frac{36\%}{40\%} = \frac{36}{40} = \frac{9}{10} = 90\%$.

19. **(C)** The total profit is the sum of the profit for the five-day period and the profit for the two-day period Friday and Saturday. You must also remember that there are 24 hours in a day, and thus the profit per 8-hour shift must be multiplied by 3 in order to get the daily profit. For the five-day period, the profit is \$600 (per shift) × 3 (shifts per day) × 5 (days) = \$9000. The profit per shift for the other days is 25% greater and is thus \$600 + $\frac{1}{4}$ (\$600) = \$600 + \$150 = \$750. The total profit for the two-day period is calculated as \$750 (per shift) × 3 (shifts per day) × 2 (days) = \$4500. The total profit for the week is \$9000 + \$4500 = \$13,500.

20. **(B)** When a question is as convoluted as this one, the issue must assuredly be the unraveling of just what is being asked for. Thinking backwards is a good approach. We are asked for the difference between two numbers: (cost of insurance + unreimbursed losses) − (loss if no insurance) = answer. The cost of the insurance is \$125 per quarter, which means that the annual cost is 4 × \$125 = \$500. That is the first number in our equation. The unreimbursed losses consist of two items. First, there is the deductible, that is, the amount of loss that must be sustained before any reimbursement is made. Here, the first \$350 of loss is not reimbursed, so that is one part of the unreimbursed loss. In addition, even when reimbursement is made, it is only made for 75%, or $\frac{3}{4}$ of the value of the loss above \$350. The total loss was \$1250, \$900 above the \$350 deductible. Three-quarters of \$900 is \$675, but that is the portion of the \$900 that *is* reimbursed; so $\frac{1}{4}$ × \$900 = \$225 is the portion that is *not* reimbursed. Thus the total non-reimbursed amount is \$350 + 225 = \$575, which is the second figure we needed for our computation. The third figure is the total amount of the loss, since without insurance it would all have been a loss; this is \$1250. We thus can compute (\$500 + \$575) − \$1250 = −\$175. But the negative sign is irrelevant because the differ-

ence is all that is asked, not whether one is greater than the other.

Section III

1. **(A)** It is stated that Wingfleet wishes to enter the commercial aircraft field, which is a major reason to try to secure the 2L-1000 contract.

2. **(B)** This is an aspect of the option of bidding the project and constitutes a separate line of discussion.

3. **(E)** The length of time it will take to produce the 2L-1000 does not seem to concern anyone.

4. **(C)** The possibility that the 2L-1000 can be converted to a commercial plane is a major factor contributing to a major objective of Wingfleet diversifying its market (#6).

5. **(C)** The possible liquidation of Ponzol by a foreign government is a factor relating to the exclusive contract held by Wingfleet.

6. **(B)** This proportion would be reduced in the long term by bidding the project since more civilian than military sales are projected. Thus this is an aspect of the option of bidding which contributes to the goal of diversification (#9).

7. **(C)** The down payments are a contributing factor to the issue of Wingfleet's cash flow, thus a minor factor.

8. **(D)** This idea is used to show the significance of the difference between the options of bidding and not bidding, in terms of the achievement of the goal of diversification.

9. **(A)** Diversification is a major objective since Wingfleet has had to depend on the single market of government contracts.

10. **(C)** This idea causes the existence of the possibility that cost overruns will not be recoverable and thus causes the existence of the option of bidding leading a great loss.

11. **(E)** This has nothing to do with the decision facing Franco.

12. **(E)** The committee was merely the instrument through which Franco obtained his information. Who provided it to him has nothing to do with his decision-making process.

13. **(C)** Even though the passage says this is something that is only probably true, it impacts on the decision through the major factor of the bid's acceptability to the government.

14. **(C)** The quality of the engines causes the existence of the factor of their being acceptable to the government (#13). This is an aspect of the option of making the contemplated bid.

15. **(A)** While this is never stated outright, it is implied in the initial discussion. For instance, it is conveyed in the sentence, "*Thus* it seemed advantageous for Wingfleet to enter the commercial aircraft field. . . ."

16. **(E)** This is never even implied as a goal of *this* decision.

17. **(E)** This has no bearing on his current dilemma, which is whether or not to bid on the 2L-1000 contract.

18. **(B)** Minimizing anxiety is a concern for Mike in all the decisions he made. This factor is emphasized in the discussions of all the options.

19. **(E)** This is never stated or implied to be a factor Mike considered in arriving at a decision. The issue discussed was the number of other cleaners and laundromats, not all other businesses. Also, the area was the neighborhood, not the block.

20. **(A)** While there is no one portion of this passage where Mike's major objectives are enumerated, certain goals are stated each time an option is presented. Among these goals is regaining as much of Mike's investment as possible.

21. **(A)** this is stated many times as a goal.

22. **(E)** Remember that (E) means that the statement has no bearing on the decision to be made. It may be related in some way to the situation, but is not currently relevant.

23. **(D)** Options two and three are based on this assumption.

24. **(A)** This is stated, in the discussion of each possible choice, as a major goal.

25. **(E)** Mike does not plan to buy the stationer out. There is no other way this factor will influence Mike's decision, based on the passage. Note that you are not asked whether it is possible to think up a way the stationer's income might influence *your* decision in such a case. These questions are based on the situation as presented, and no hint appears of any role for this factor in Mike's planning.

26. **(C)** Avoiding additional cash outlays is a major objective. The extent to which current costs can be minimized is a major factor. Legal costs only apply to one of the three courses of action, so this is a minor factor. In general, any genuine concern that has to do with a single option is a minor factor.

27. **(E)** This has nothing at all to do with the decision facing our hero. Did you find yourself thinking the following: Because he had been at a job he disliked for so long, Mike would at all costs want to avoid returning to the job market. This would predispose him against opting for the suit or the sale. Therefore we have a minor factor, (C).

    If this was your reasoning, you show ingenuity, but you'll have to rein yourself in and stick to the text if you want to do well on this question type.

28. **(C)** This skill is what would enable him to supplement his income by teaching on weekends. Part of the argument for keeping the store is that Mike would manage, through various means, to put together $28,000 a year. What is of interest in this item is that a minor factor can be "several layers deep" in the sense that it sometimes relates to its major factor only by backing up another minor factor, which, in its turn, supports the major factor.

29. **(A)** If you did not recognize this as a major goal, you were just not paying attention to your reading. Wake up!

30. **(D)** In arguing that Mike should keep the business, the uncle argues that Myers knows he will be the loser in such a confrontation. Mike accepts this.

31. **(C)** This argues in favor of keeping the store. This directly affects the major factor of each option's ability to achieve the goal of Mike's achieving a $28,000 income. The closing of the competition means that the option of keeping the business has a different income projection.

32. **(A)** This is stated throughout as a chief consideration for Mike.

33. **(B)** As each possible avenue is explored, the desire to deal with Myers as he deserves guides Mike's steps.

34. **(B)** While Mike is altruistic, he is no fool. His desire to recover his initial investment surfaces each time he ponders a possible move.

35. **(B)** When a concern turns up each time a possible move is presented, it is normally a major factor. This is the case here.

Section IV

1. **(C)** From equation (1), x may be either 1 or −2. From equation (2), x may be 1 or −3. Thus, if both are true, $x = 1$.

2. **(A)** Angle b = angle e, $a + e = 180°$, which means AB is parallel to CD. Equation (2) shows us only that $a = b$, which makes the two lines parallel only where $a = b = 90°$.

3. **(C)** There are three possible combinations fulfilling (1): $-2 + (-4) = (-6)$; $-2 + 2 = 0$; and $2 + 4 = 6$. Of these, only the last satisfies property (2).

4. **(C)** Jim does $\frac{1}{12}$ of the job in 1 hour. Together, Jim and Bill do $\frac{1}{8}$ of the job in 1 hour. Bill alone, therefore, does $\frac{1}{8} - \frac{1}{12}$ of the job in 1 hour $= \frac{1}{24}$. Accordingly, it will take Bill 24 hours to do the entire job by himself.

5. **(B)** (1) does not work by itself since $x = y = 0$ and $x = y = 1$ give different answers. (2) means that either x or y are both fractions between 0 and 1, since that is the only way squaring can reduce the result. Adding a fraction $(x + y)$ increases the result, but multiplying by a fraction (xy) decreases it. Thus $x + y > xy$ under (2). Checking for zero gives a compatible result.

6. **(D)** Since there is only one unknown, the weight of a brick, you only need a single equation to give you sufficient information. Each of the propositions (1) and (2) give an equation, so each is sufficient. You should not bother to calculate the actual weight of the brick, though it is 9 pounds.

7. **(B)** It is tempting to leap to an answer saying that both propositions are needed, but although (1) is clearly not sufficient by itself because it leaves open the issue of the relative proportions of the sides of the rectangle, (2) must be evaluated separately. As it happens, (2) is sufficient. Taking equation (2) and adding AE to both sides, we have: $AC = AB + BE + AE$. Since $BE + AE = AB$, $AC = 2AB$, so $AB = 2\frac{1}{2}$.

8. **(A)** For the last digit of the total weight to be a 7, there must be either four 3's or nine 3's, or more. Nine or more are impossible, so there must be four 3's. This leaves four weights chosen from the 5's and 10's to make up 35 lbs. The only possible way to do this is by using three 10's and one 5.

9. **(C)** On one level, this is an easy problem. There are two unknowns in the situation, p and q. There are two different equations without any squares or exponents, so there is enough information using both equations. If you try to actually solve the problem, which is not really necessary, you may have some difficulty since it appears insoluble at first. Since we are interested in p, substitute from equation (2) into (1), getting $p = 4(4p)$; $p = 16p$, which seems impossible. However, there is one value of p that will work, and that is zero. Thus p is determined by the two equations.

10. **(B)** This is one of the rare problems in which you are asked a "yes/no" question, and the answer is "no." (1) is nice, but not enough by itself. (2) makes it impossible for ABCD to be a square since the diagonal of a square is not equal to its sides. Some suspicion that this might be a "no" question is raised by the fact that equilateral triangles have nothing to do with squares.

11. **(E)** In order to know how long a moving object takes, you need to know the distance traveled and the rate of speed. Neither is given in the original information. The rate is given in (1), but that is not enough by itself; nor is (2). The question then comes down to whether (2) actually gives the distance between J and M. Note that the order of the neighborhoods along the marathon route is not necessarily in alphabetic order. (2) is not sufficient because the order of the neighborhoods could be either with K between J and M, or with J between K and M. Thus the distance is not specified and the answer is (E).

12. **(B)** Both of the given propositions establish a definite relationship between the officerships of Albert and Mary. Since the original information gives us the actual officership status of Mary (she is qualified), the temptation is to say that both propositions are sufficient. (1), however, is not sufficient by itself. It leaves open the question of what happens if Albert does not qualify, because Mary may still qualify even if Albert doesn't. (2) is sufficient because it tells us that if Albert did not qualify, then it is certain that Mary did not qualify. Since

Mary did qualify, we must know that Albert must also have qualified.

13. **(C)** There are three unknowns—the number of cookies received by W, X, and Y. We have one equation in the original information—that the sum of the three is 40—and we get one more equation in each of the propositions, making three equations for three unknowns, which is enough. You do not need to actually solve the equations.

14. **(A)** The issue is whether 5 is an integral factor of x. According to (1), x can be divided by 12,345 and yield an integer. Since 12,345 ends in 5, it has a factor of five, and thus x must have a factor of five in order to have 12,345 divide evenly into it. (2) is not enough because 336 does not have a factor of five in it, so that we cannot say for certain that x/5 is an integer; although it is still possible [suppose x = (12345)(336)].

15. **(D)** A cube is a highly structured figure. All the edges must, by definition, be equal to each other and all the opposite faces parallel, and all the other symmetries of a cube maintained no matter what size the cube may be. Therefore, in principle, if you know any well-defined line in the cube—any edge or any diagonal of a side, or the diagonal of the whole cube—you can compute the lengths of any other line, the area of the sides, or the volume of the cube. Thus, in principle, both statement (1) and statement (2) are sufficient to permit the computation of the volume of the cube. On the actual test, you would leave it there, answer (D), and go on to the next problem. For instructional purposes only, we include a brief description of the way in which each statement could be used.

Statement (1): Each face of a cube is a square. Since the diagonal of a square forms a 45–45–90 right triangle with two of the sides, the length of the diagonal can be computed as $\sqrt{2}$ times the length of a side using the Pythagorean Theorem, or from your knowledge of right triangles. Once an edge of the cube is known, the volume of the cube can be computed as the third power (or cube) of the edge.

Statement (2): The diagonal of the cube forms a right triangle with the diagonal of a face and one of the edges, as shown below. By the same process described in the explanation of statement (1), the length of a diagonal is $\sqrt{2}$ times the length of an edge. Thus the Pythagorean Theorem equation for the triangle which includes the diagonal of the whole cube is $d^2 = (\sqrt{2}\,s)^2(s)^2$, and thus the diagonal = $\sqrt{3}$ times the length of the side. Therefore, knowing the length of the diagonal permits calculation of the length of an edge and of the volume of the cube.

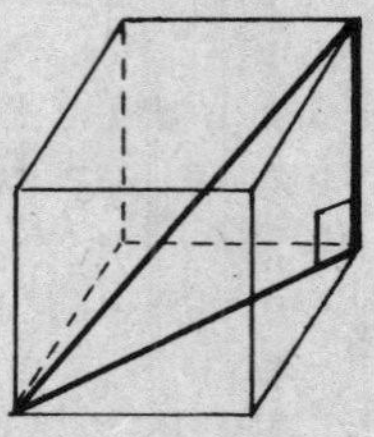

16. **(B)** Since the p and q terms are to the eighth power, simply having two equations for two unknowns is not sufficient. Usually, it is a good idea to try and factor polynomials if they are not easy to deal with in their original form. In this case, we can factor $p^8 - q^8$ into the difference between squares since the square of something to the fourth power is the same base to the eighth power. Thus:

$p^8 - q^8 = (p^4 - q^4)(p^4 + q^4)$. This in turn factors to

$$= (p^2 - q^2)(p^2 + q^2)(p^4 + q^4),$$

which factors to

$$= (p - q)(p + q)(p^2 + q^2)(p^4 + q^4)$$

This gives us something that we can use since (p − q) is stated in proposition (2) and is equal to zero. If p − q is equal to zero, then anything multiplied by zero is equal to zero and the whole thing is equal to zero.

A shorter method would be to note that (2) transforms into p = q, which means that $p^8 = q^8$, which means that $p^8 - q^8 = 0$. The factoring approach might be needed if the propositions referred to $p^2 + q^2 = 0$ or to some other intermediate factor.

17. **(E)** Manipulating (1) to get x alone, we get:

$4x + 24 > 0$
$4x > -24$ (subtract +24 from both sides)
$x > -6$ (divide both sides by +4)

Manipulating (2), we get:

$4x - 24 < 0$
$4x < +24$ (add +24 to both sides)
$x < +6$ (divide both sides by +4)

Each statement allows for the possibility that x may be either positive or negative, and the question cannot be answered.

18. **(C)** In order to know the dollar amount that the corporation spent on pension payments, it is necessary to know the number of employees and the average payment per employee. The alternative of adding up all the individual payments is impractical on the test and, in any case, the propositions point you toward the idea of averages. The given information is the amount in 1980. Since we need the amount in 1981, this could be gotten either by a direct comparison, or linkage, between the two years or by using 1980 information to reconstruct 1981.

(1) and (2) address part of the needed information and thus are not enough by themselves. They do not link the 1980 total to the 1981 total. If 1980 is viewed as the product of two numbers: 1980 total payments = (1980 no. of employees)(1980 average payment). Then we can link 1980 to 1981 by making the adjustments called for in (1) and (2): 1981 total payments = (85%)(1980 no. of employees) (130%)(1980 average payment).

Rearrange the items: 1981 total payments = (85%)(130%) (1980 no. of employees) (1980 average payment); but the last two are equal to the 1980 total payments, or $12,000. Thus 1981 total payments = (85%)(130%) ($12,000) = $13,260.

You should not calculate this answer. It is worked out only to show you that you have enough information with the two propositions.

19. **(D)** In order to find the area of the large rectangle, you need to find its length and width. The only measures of those dimensions that the problem gives you are the small rectangles. Since the only information that is given is that all of the small rectangles are the same shape and size, the first place to look for additional understanding is to the ways that the small rectangles build up into the large rectangle. In addition, the fact that both of the statements concern paths made up of pieces of small rectangles should also focus your attention on the small rectangles. Since the small rectangles are rectangles, their length and width are the key dimensions. Since all of the small rectangles are the same shape and size, the fact that three widths equal one length gives you the proportions of the small rectangles. This is shown in the following details from the diagram:

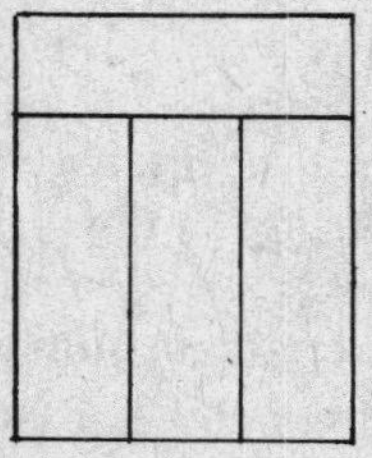

Once you know that three widths of a small rectangle is equal to one length, the information given in the propositions becomes very useful. The upper path referred to in proposition (1) is composed of four lengths and three widths, which is equal to 15 widths (or 5 lengths). Since the proposition gives the value of this path as 45, you can calculate that one width is equal to 45 divided by 15 or 3. Knowing the value of a width of the small rectangle allows you to calculate the value of the length of the small rectangle and thus its area and the area of the large rectangle. You could also directly calculate the length and width of the large rectangle 21 (7 small rectangle widths) and 18 (6 small rectangle widths), respectively. Similarly, the lower path is equivalent to 13 small rectangle widths and knowing its length as 39 permits the area of the large rectangle to be calculated.

20. **(D)** As usual with polynomials, when they are not helpful in one form, change them to the other form. Here they are in factors, but the expanded form will be most useful.

$$(x^2 + y^2) + (x^2 - y^2) = x^2 + 2xy + y^2 + x^2 - 2xy + y^2 = 2x^2 + 2y^2 = 2(x^2 + y^2)$$

(2) is certainly sufficient by itself; the only issue is whether (1) is also sufficient. As the simplification of the equation shows, (1) is sufficient because it gives the value needed to compute $2(x^2 + y^2)$.

21. **(B)** (2) is sufficient because it gives a rule for calculating any term of the series. (1) looks good, but does not actually tell us that the series continues in the same manner beyond the terms listed; thus it is not sufficient.

22. **(A)** (1) is sufficient because the cube of a number retains the same sign as the original number or base, e.g., $(-2)^3 = -8$; $(+2)^3 = +8$. However, the square of a number is always positive, and thus x and y might be negative without changing the relationship between their squares. If $x = -2$ and $y = +3$, (2) is true; but (2) is also true if $x = +2$ and $y = -3$.

23. **(C)** In order to know the chances of taking an apple, it is necessary to know the fraction of apples in the fruit bowl. It is not necessary to know the fractions of all of the fruits in the fruit bowl. (1) only tells the relationship between oranges and apples, but there may be other fruits. (2) only tells the fraction of oranges. Together they permit the calculation that one-sixth of the fruits in the fruit bowl are apples.

24. **(D)** In order to prove that two lines are parallel, you will usually need to either know that there are equal corresponding angles, or that the two lines are opposite sides of a rectangle or square. Since there are no rectangles or squares in this diagram, you should concentrate on the corresponding angles approach. Statement (1) gives the information that two angles are equal. If these are corresponding angles, that will immediately be enough to show that the two lines AB and XY are parallel. Extending some of the lines to make the intersections clearer we see that the angles cited are, in fact, corresponding angles of the intersection of line CA with the two lines we are interested in:

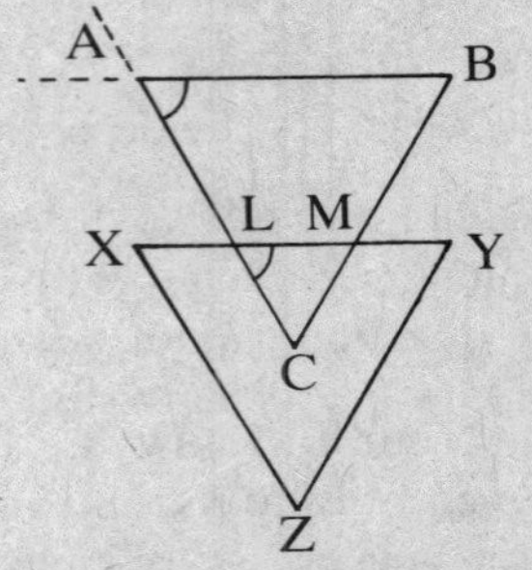

Statement (2) tells you that the smaller, interior triangle is an equilateral triangle. This connects to the facts given in the original question that the larger triangles are also equilateral triangles. Since you are interested in finding out whether the corresponding angles are equal, you should consider what you know about angles of equilateral triangles. Of course, the angles of equilateral triangles are all equal to 60 degrees. Thus, $\angle BAL = 60°$ and $\angle CLM = 60°$, which are the same corresponding angles discussed for statement (1). Angles ABM and CML would also be equal to 60 degrees and form a pair of corresponding angles.

25. **(E)** To know the number of chocolate bars that can be packed into the carton, you need to know at least the three dimensions of the chocolate bars and the three dimensions of the carton. Only two dimensions of the chocolate bar are given in the initial information and the third dimension is never supplied, hence (E). The two propositions do give the three dimensions of the carton, but that is not enough.

Section V

1. **(B)** The references to the shires and London are detailed and imply a closeness to hand. (A), France, is only mentioned with one reference, and thus is not as good as

(B). America, (C), is only supported by a reference to North America, which is insufficiently detailed to override the English references. (D) is nowhere mentioned.

2. **(C)** The only trick here is to remember that the third line of a syllogism does not always have the word thus or its equivalent. The other methods are all in the passage, but not for this sort of reasoning. (See also the instructional materials for the Logical Reasoning questions).

3. **(B)** While it is true that the use of apples gives the story a pedestrian flavor, this is merely to exemplify the author's view that there is real reasoning even in very ordinary events. The apples are the subject of an analogy between the situation with them and all everyday reasoning, which is likened and explained through that example. (C) has a little merit, but (B) is far better since it goes with the basic ideas of the passage. (D) is attractive, but it is false since the author shows how common logic is, not how foolish. (A) and (E) are merely flack.

4. **(A)** While the answer choice of "philosopher" would be better yet, the scientist's reference to experimental method and logic make (A) the best available choice. All the others may use logic and experiment, of course, but the topic here is science—in the sense of its root, meaning "knowing"—not art, fiction, economics, or business, nor the distinguishing methods of those fields.

5. **(C)** The passage notes that you establish a natural law as the result of the induction in just those words—hence, (C). (D) and (E) are other meanings of the term natural law, but not the ones used in this particular passage. (A) and (B) have little connection to the passage.

6. **(E)** All the answer choices reflect part of the passage, but (E) covers the largest portion of the passage, and thus is best. Each of the others can be subsumed under it since (A) is the example used, and (B), (C), and (D) are the methods of everyday reasoning brought out through the use of the example of apples.

7. **(D)** The law of apples is a construct based, as noted in the passage, on experimental verification of an induction. If further verification should show that the law is not perfect, then it must be modified, as (D) suggests. (C) is particularly attractive, but the word usually makes it fail, since it is still the case that hard and green apples are usually sour. If (C) had said always, it would have been hard to refute.

(A) is subsumed under (D) and is incorrect in supposing that the nature of apples has changed, when it is only that our original understanding of them proved to be inadequate. (B), while attractive in the real world, where tasty apples are all too rare, has little to do with standardized tests. Since (A), (B), and (C) are faulty, (E) does not apply.

8. **(C)** Extensive verification is brought up in the last part of the passage as something that makes an argument or proposed general law more attractive. Proposition I is just flack. There is nothing in the passage that says whether general laws are harder or easier to prove or disprove than any other kind of law. Proposition III is precisely what the passage does say. This is why the friend will find it persuasive for you to show him that the law has been tested in a variety of situations. Proposition II is a bit of precision reading that turns on the word tested. Tested means that something is put to some sort of test; it does not mean that the something passed the test. The reason that II is attractive is that a law or proposal that was not passing its tests would soon be dropped and no longer subjected to tests. Thus, there is a potential for erroneously leaping from the fact that something was widely tested to the conclusion that it passed most of its tests. This is, however, based on an idea not present in the passage.

9. **(E)** (D) is of no interest to the author. (A), (B), and (C) are topics mentioned in the passage, but only as serving the general analysis of the Planning Commission's proposal. Thus, (E) is more descriptive of the actual passage.

10. **(D)** The author's argument essentially states that the commission may be right as far as it goes, but it "is not that simple." This implies that the commission has been shortsighted. It is true that because of the shortsightedness the author views the plan as foolish, and perhaps somewhat ignorant, but these derive from the shortsightedness, and the tone is respectful rather than condemnatory. (A) and (B) have no basis.

11. **(D)** (A) is attractive, but the word complete kills it. The author is clearly unsure of the number of beds that should be closed and sees that as a future issue. (B) and (C) fail for the same reason. (E) sounds good, but is not really mentioned.

12. **(C)** All of the statements are agreeable to the author, but (C) is specifically stated by the passage not to be properly addressed in the context of the commission's proposal. Because of (A) and (E), large hospitals may not be more efficient. (B) and (D) are both reasons why small hospitals should not be closed.

13. **(A)** (A) is only half agreeable. The author states the larger centers provide more complex care, and if the larger hospitals do not provide the most efficient care—as the author claims they don't—then it is certainly probable that they do not definitely provide better care than smaller hospitals—care of the sort that can be received at both kinds of facilities.

    (B) is inferable from the statement that only overall costs are used to set rates. (C) is inferable from the author's support of the existence of institutions that can only provide that sort of care while also supporting quality. (D) is stated to be a possible problem. (E) is inferable from the concern shown for greater or lesser access in the third and fifth paragraphs.

14. **(B)** The author knows that he cannot simply say to the commission that they shouldn't close the smaller hospitals. He must present evidence that it is not the best approach to the agreed-upon goal of saving money and closing unneeded beds—hence, (B). (A) is false since closing beds is agreed to by the author. (C) is true, but not as precise as (B); also, the word another is troublesome since it is actually an alternative that is proposed. (D) is not currently at issue. (E) is appealing, but the inefficiencies of larger hospitals are not stated to be in the use of space.

15. **(A)** Prisons are, in a manner of speaking, service organizations (like hospitals), and thus very large ones may not be more efficient, according to the author; thus, (A). (B) is probably just what the author wants, since he is unsure of the number of beds that should be closed anyway. (C) is stated to be agreeable to the author in the last paragraph. (D) and (E) are indeterminable. There is no basis for agreement or disagreement given in the passage.

16. **(E)** The concern about possible *over*-centralization of ambulatory services is raised in the context of the proposal to close portions of the larger hospitals. This juxtaposition of the two means that the author believes that closing parts of the larger hospitals might have the poor result of turning over so much space in those locations to ambulatory care that a disproportionate part of the ambulatory care system would reside at the larger hospitals rather than the entirety of smaller hospitals. His use of the prefix over- indicates disapproval.

    The only references to the costs of ambulatory care are to its chaos and to some needs to keep it down. This implies a concern by the author that ambulatory care costs might increase, not that they might be decreased. Hence, (A) fails.

    (B) and (C) refer to connections that are not in the passage. The author refers to increasing the facilities for ambulatory services, but not to increasing the demand, which he seems to think is there already. If you answered (C), you are answering from current events and not from the passage.

    (D) has the appeal of being something that the author would probably like to have happen, but it is not implicit in the passage that the Planning Commission has the power to bring it about, and he certainly does not ask it. Rather, the force of the argument about the use of the space left by the closed portions of larger medical centers is that this space would certainly not go to waste.

17. **(E)** A reductive cycle is a negative aspect of the psychology of the individual worker, hence, (E). (A), (B), and (C) play on the everyday meaning of *reduce.* (D) may result from a long-term reductive cycle, but is not the cycle itself, which can be changed before (D) occurs.

18. **(B)** The passage says "sound motivation patterns begin at the top." The top is (B).

19. **(A)** This passage traces unionization to failures in the psychological setting of the job. (B), (C), and (D) are more commonly the sorts of things thought of as leading to unionization, but not here. (B) refers to nothing in the passage, but appears to refer to "self-actualization," the lack of which is associated in the passage with unionization. (A) describes the elements of "self-actualization" which must be missing for unionization to occur.

20. **(D)** The passage indicates that motivation is the key. (D) is the cause of a continued reductive cycle. (A) and (B) pretend that a reductive cycle is good, and are thus eliminated. (E) is something that may result from the continued situation, but is here stated in the present rather than future tense, so it fails. (C) is true, but (D) is the specification of just which way the boss is failing.

21. **(A)** Note that the question stem speaks of initial results only. There is some temptation to seek an answer that says that none of the listed propositions is an initial result of reductive conditions since the unionism results from continued reductive conditions and the other two, presumably, result from unionism, though that latter is weak in this passage. However, since that is not an available choice, we choose I only, (A), since that clearly precedes the others.

22. **(E)** All three of these conditions are mentioned in the fourth paragraph. The fact that these are not the only roots of collective action is irrelevant to answering the question.

23. **(D)** The root of the manager's failure is stated to be lack of sensitivity to the needs, etc., of the employees under him. (D) best describes this lack of empathy. (C) may be a cause of the lack of empathy and (E) a possible result, but they are not mentioned specifically in the passage, and thus have a conditional connection to the question at best. (A) and (B) are not the cause of failures or anything else in the passage.

24. **(C)** The author states in the passage that most businesses fail to establish good conditions and that they survive only because of the generally low level of effective management. The management is not scientific (B) because that is seen as only one minor possibility, and it is not in quotes here. Nor are they reactionary (D) since that is not the same as reactive, for which a case could be made. Similarly, unconcerned (E) is not correct since the lack of effectiveness is not necessarily the result of a lack of concern, but erroneous policies to achieve the desired goals. (A) has some merit in that the author states that the primary problem is the insensitivity and lack of perception of the managers. However, in choosing (C) over (A), the balance is swung by considering the major thrust of the passage, which is to explain that the top management of most companies is not doing a good job. Handicapped is a very sweeping term, while ineffective is more within the scope of the entire passage.

25. **(C)** "Scientific management" practices are referred to in the passage as being one possible cause of management failures. Thus, they are viewed negatively by the author of the passage. (A) is incorrect because it holds that this negative characteristic will not achieve the negative goal of a reductive cycle, while the passage states, as just noted, that these practices are one possible cause of a reductive cycle. (B) fails because it refers to a positive achievement. (C) is correct, although at first it seems to confuse two ideas that are somewhat sepa-

rate in the passage. The passage holds that the practice of "scientific management" is bad and ineffective. Those that follow this path lack proper managerial skills. The particular aspect of managerial skill with which the entire passage is most concerned is the provision of a self-actualizing workplace; thus (C) is correct. (D) is correct in noting that "scientific management" divides the labor to be done, but the passage holds that this does not result in an effective management system. (E) is incorrect since the practices will lead to, rather than prevent, the breakdown of labor-management relations.

Section VI

1. **(C)** Since $x + 6 = 3$, $x = -3$. Then, substituting -3 for x in the second expression, $x + 3$ is $-3 + 3 = 0$.

2. **(A)** Probably the easiest way to solve this problem is just to count the steps on your fingers, but the same process can be expressed mathematically. Let those steps he walks down be assigned negative values, and those steps he walks up be positive. We then have: $-4 + 3 - 6 + 2 + 9 - 2 = +2$. So the person comes to rest two steps above where he started.

3. **(A)** In a circle graph such as this, the sectors must total 100%. The sectors P, R, S, and T account for 21%, 29%, 18%, and 28%, respectively, for a total of 96%. So Q must be 4%.

4. **(D)** This is a problem which is most easily solved directly. From 1:21 to 2:21 is 60 minutes. From 2:21 to 3:21 is 60 minutes. So far we have a total of 120 minutes. Then, from 3:21 to 3:36 is 15 minutes, for a total of 135 minutes.

5. **(B)** First, we must compute the total commission that will be owed: 15% of \$3200 = \$420. Then we must take into account the fact that the sales representative has already received \$150 of that sum. So she is now owed: \$420 − \$150 = \$270.

6. **(B)** The area of a circle is pi times radius squared, or $A = \pi r^2$. Here the area is $9\pi x^2$. So we write: $9\pi x^2 = \pi r^2$. Notice that the π terms cancel out, leaving: $9x^2 = r^2$. Taking the square root of both sides of the equation: $\sqrt{9x^2} = \sqrt{r^2}$, so $r = 3x$.

7. **(E)** Since this problem deals with the heights of the individuals, a quite natural starting point would be to draw a diagram:

Hans is taller than Gertrude: H
G

Hans is shorter than Wilhelm: W (z)
H (x)
G (y)

Given the picture, it is easily determined that W is taller than H, who is taller than G; so z is greater than x is greater than y, or $x > x > y$.

8. **(D)** First, we can show that the area of the square and the area of the equilateral triangle are determinable from their respective perimeters. The square is more easily handled. Since the perimeter of the square is 4 times the length of one side, given the perimeter of the square it is possible to determine the side of the square. Then, once the side of the square is known, the area can be computed as side times side. The equilateral triangle is a bit trickier:

$P = 3x$ $\quad A = \frac{1}{2}\left(\frac{\sqrt{3}x}{2}\right)\left(\frac{x}{2}\right)$

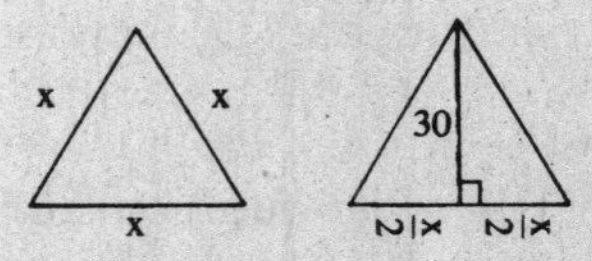

Given the perimeter, it is possible to determine the length of each leg of the triangle (leg = P/3, since each leg is equal). Now, since we know that an equilateral triangle has angles of 60°, and that a perpendicular in this triangle drawn to the opposite base bisects the angle, we can set up a 90° − 30° = 60° triangle. It will be possible to compute the length of each leg of such a triangle, given the length of the hypotenuse. Therefore, we can determine the altitude, and we know the base; so, given the perimeter, we can compute the area. Then, the easiest way to demonstrate that it is not possible to compute the area of a trapezoid or of a parallelogram on the basis of perimeter alone is to draw some pictures:

PARALLELOGRAM:

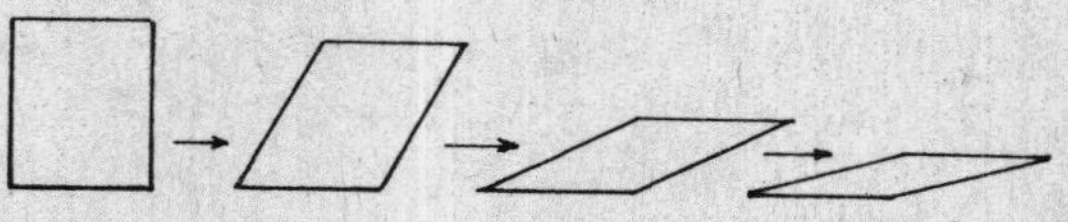

TRAPEZOID:

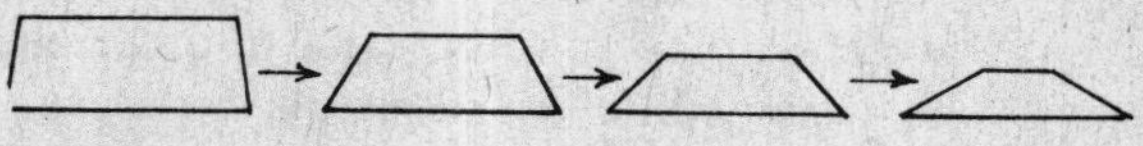

To prove this algebraically would require too much detailed work, but the student should be able to see intuitively that the area of the figures from left to right decreases, and that when the angles eventually become sharp enough, the area will be nearly zero.

9. **(D)** In simple English, the 90¢ the child must replace to bring the amount back up to its original amount is 10% of the original amount. Expressed in notation, that is:

$$90¢ = .10 \text{ of } x$$
$$\$9.00 = x$$

10. **(C)** Let us begin by assigning letters to the height and radius of each cylinder. Since most people find it easier to deal with whole numbers instead of fractions, let us say that cylinder Q has a radius of 2r, so that cylinder P can have a radius of r. Then, we assign cylinder Q a height of h so that P can have a height of 2h. Now, the formula for the volume of a cylinder is $r^2 \times h$. So P and Q have volumes:

$$\text{Volume } P = (r)^2 \times 2h \qquad \text{Volume } Q = (2r)^2 \times h$$
$$P = 2r^2h \qquad Q = 4r^2h$$

Thus, the ratio of P:Q is $\frac{2r^2h}{4r^2h} = 2/4 = 1/2$.

Another way of solving the problem is to use the knowledge that the area of a circle goes up with the square of the radius. This means that if P and Q had equal heights, the volume of Q would be *four* times that of P, since the radius of Q is *twice* that of P. On the other hand, if their radii were equal, P would have a volume of only twice that of Q—the height of P is twice that of Q and the volume increases directly with height. Therefore, the ratio must be two to four, or 1:2.

11. **(A)** We begin by extending the lines to give this picture:

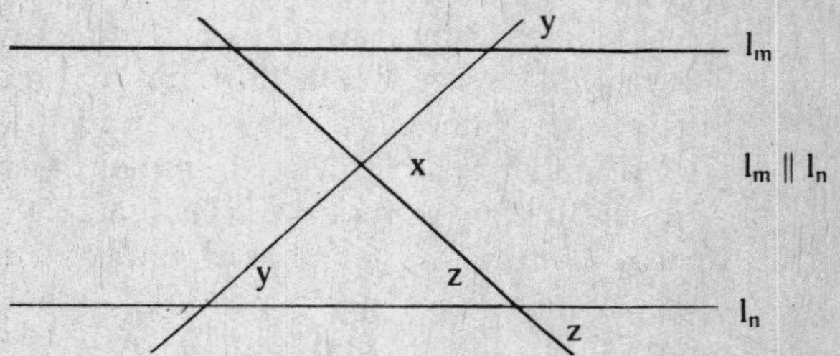

Then we add another angle y (lines l_m and l_n are parallel, so alternate interior angles are equal—for the Liberal Arts majors: all the thin angles are equal) and another z (vertical angles are equal). We know that $x + w = 180°$, and we know that $y + z + w = 180°$. So, $x + w = y + z + w$, and $x = y + z$.

12. **(C)** Let us begin by drawing the rectangle:

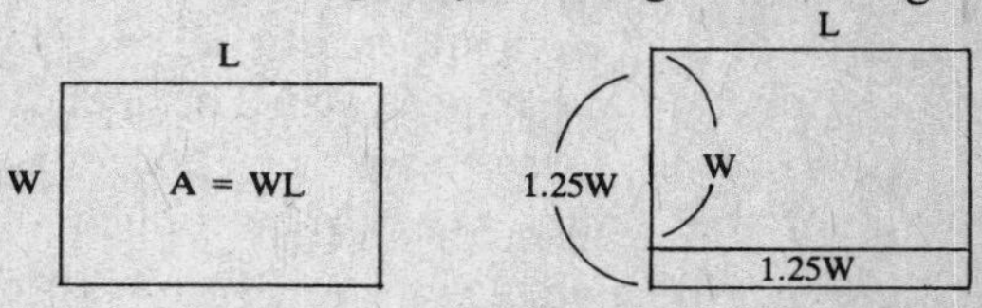

A = 1.25W × L = 1.25WL

The original area is WL. The width of the new rectangle is W + .25%W, or 1.25W. So the new area is 1.25WL. It then follows that the new area is

$\frac{1.25WL}{WL}$, or 125% of the old area.

13. **(E)** Let us take any four consecutive odd positive integers, a,b,c, and d. Between b and c there will be an even integer; let us call that x. The average of the four odd integers will be the even integer between b and c. Therefore the average will always be an even number.

14. **(B)** The proportion to be solved is 2½:4 = 1⅞:x, where x is the length of the shorter dimension of the enlargement. Solving, we get x = 3.

15. **(A)** The area of the circle is π times the square of the radius, or 9π. The area of the square is 36. Thus, the ratio is $\frac{9\pi}{36}$, or $\frac{\pi}{4}$. Approximating π as slightly more than 3, the answer is slightly more than ¾.

16. **(C)** First of all, (D) and (E) are impossible on logical grounds since they are greater than 1, and the proportion of something that has a characteristic cannot be greater than 1. That would be like saying "Five out of three doctors recommend. . . ." We need the total of upper and middle management with production line experience. The ratio 4:3 tells us that the total number of middle- and upper-management personnel in the company can be divided into 7 equal parts, with 4 of them in upper management and 3 in middle management. Of the 4 parts in upper management, 75%, or $\frac{3}{4}$, have experience on the production line. Three-quarters of 4 parts amounts to 3 parts ($\frac{3}{7}$ of the total). You are not told how many of the middle-management personnel have production line experience, but the key word greatest tells you that you should consider *all* of the middle-management personnel as having production line experience. This means that there are 3 parts from the upper-management personnel who have production line experience and that there are 3 more parts from the middle-management personnel that are assumed to have production line experience, for a total of 6 parts out of 7, or $\frac{6}{7}$.

17. **(B)** This sort of problem can seem much more difficult than it actually is. The first step is to understand the instructions for doing the "#" game. For the number N = 1, #1 = (1 − 1)(1 − 2)(1 − 3). The key thing to notice is that the first term in this series of terms being multiplied together (1 − 1) is zero. When you multiply by zero, the result is zero no matter what the other numbers are. Not only should this immediately make you realize that you do not need to compute #1, but it should also alert you to the same sort of possibility in at least some of the other # functions with which you are working. In fact, #2 and #3 also come to zero because they also contain terms which equal zeros (2 − 2 and 3 − 3). Thus, only #4 needs to be evaluated (#4 = (4 − 1)(4 − 2)(4 − 3) = 3 × 2 × 1 = 6).

18. **(D)** The question asks us to determine how many different quintets can be made from each 6-man team, and then how many combinations can there be between the two teams. Taking each team by itself, finding how many quintets can be formed from a given six players is the same as determining how many different single players can be on the sidelines. That is, the same decision that sends a given five players into the game also selects a single player to stay out of the game. Taking the six players one at a time gives six different possibilities; thus there are six different quintets that can be formed out of six players. If there are six different possibilities for each team, the combined possibilities are 6 × 6 = 36.

19. **(E)** The volume of the powder will be determined by subtracting the volume of the two spheres from the volume of the box. The first thing that you must notice is that the quantity $\frac{x}{2}$, which is given to you to show the size of the spheres, is the *diameter*. Thus $\frac{x}{4}$ is the radius of the spheres. Before calculating the answer, it is probably a good idea to try to visualize the situation.

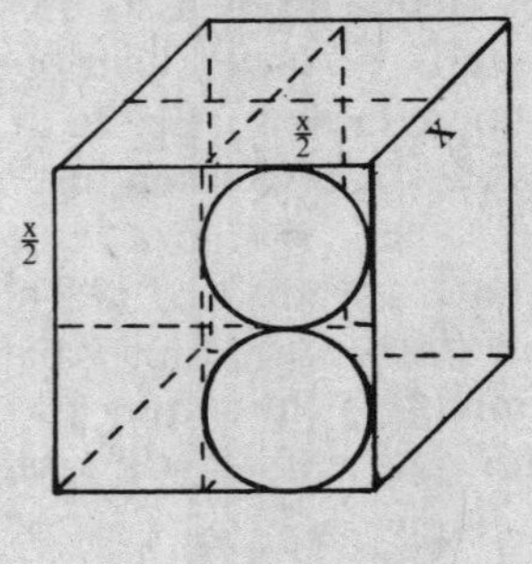

There would be room for 8 spheres in the box if they were placed so that they touched each other. Thus we know that if we divided the box into 8 smaller cubes of side $\frac{x}{2}$, two of them would have spheres in them and the other six would only have packing powder. Having six cubes with only packing powder in them would mean that $\frac{3}{4}$ of the box is completely filled with packing powder, in addition to the powder that is in the two cubes containing the spheres. Thus (E) is the only possible answer.

By calculation, the volume of one sphere is $V = (\frac{4}{3})\pi(\frac{x}{4})^3 = \frac{4\pi x^3}{(3)(64)} = \frac{\pi x^3}{48}$. The volume of a cube of side x is x^3, so the volume of the powder will be $x^3 - 2(\frac{\pi x^3}{48}) = x^3(1 - \frac{\pi}{24})$. If we estimate that π is approximately equal to 3, then we can say that the fraction $\frac{\pi}{24}$ is approximately equal to $\frac{1}{8}$ and the powder makes up approximately $\frac{7}{8}$ of the total volume of the box. You will not often, if ever, need to know the actual value of π; and if you do need to know, it will be sufficient to know that it is slightly more than 3.

20. **(B)** As with all set problems, the key is to break the situation down into non-overlapping groups. There are three basic coffees (B,J, and C) and these three categories can combine in 7 possible ways: B only, C only, J only, B + J only, B + C only, J + C only, and B + J + C. Therefore, your work must start with the information that is given to you in the form of a single category. The only single non-overlapping category that is given is the B + J + C group, of which there are 5 mixtures. The key words at least, when used to describe the information given about combinations of two coffees, tell you that these numbers describe the number of coffee mixtures containing the two coffees only plus the number of coffee mixtures containing all three coffees. Thus the given information that 16 mixtures contain at least Colombian and Jamaican coffees leads to the conclusion that 16 − 5 = 11 mixtures contain Colombian and Jamaican coffees only; 18 − 5 = 13 mixtures contain Jamaican and Brazilian coffees only; and 8 − 5 = 3 mixtures contain Brazilian and Colombian coffees only.

Perhaps the clearest way of seeing how to do the remaining subtractions is to draw three overlapping circles, which show all the possible combinations. The final breakdown looks like this:

Colombian = 33 Jamaican = 43

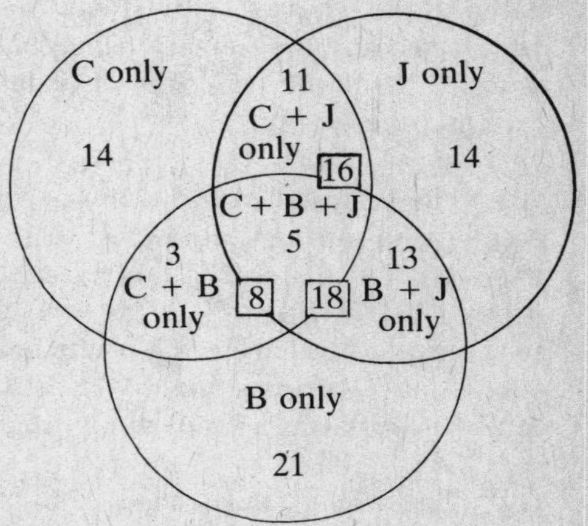

Brazilian = 42

Once the four middle groupings are tied down, then the number of mixtures with only Colombian coffee can be determined by subtraction 33 − 3 − 5 − 11 = 14; Jamaican only is 43 − 11 − 5 − 13 = 14; and Brazilian only is 42 − 3 − 5 − 13 = 21. Adding the seven categories together gives a total of 81.

Another method of approaching this problem is to consider the total number of inclusions of a coffee into a mixture. There are 43 + 42 + 33 = 118 total inclusions. Fifteen of these are from the five mixtures that include all three coffees. The given information states that there are 16 + 18 + 8 = 42 multiple mentions (at least 2 coffees). Since the multiple mentions can only be two or three coffees, we can see that 15 of the 42 multiple mentions are from the three-coffee blends (counted three times, as shown in the diagram), which leaves 27 double mentions. The number of single mentions can be determined by subtraction: 118 − 3(5) − 2(27) = 49. The total number of mixtures is thus 49 + 5 + 27 = 81. This method is a little more abstract and the first method is therefore preferable for most students.

Section VII

1. **(C)** A future possibility of this sort is not expressed by "like." "Looked like" should not be used to mean "appeared." (B) errs in saying "would have" since it is a simple future idea not requiring that construction. (C) correctly uses "appeared" and "would" without the "have." (D) is not so much wrong as an unnecessary change in the sentence structure. (E) similarly is unnecessary and too wordy.

2. **(D)** The first part of the sentence sets up a comparison through the use of "as . . . as," and the original and (B) and (E) fail to carry it out. The "be true of" part of the sentence in (C) is not needed since it is implied in the "as . . . as" construction by the fact that DuBois' work was a fundamental challenge.

3. **(E)** The original fails because the "for the reason" construction is poor, and also the "cheap and" fails to make it clear that the price was cheap, which the sentence intends. (B) fails to correct the "and" and (C) and (D) fail to improve the "for the reason that."

4. **(B)** (A) fails because "that thing" refers to a diffuse idea in the sentence better expressed by (B), (C) and (D) allege that it was *un*profitable, while only a lack of profit was stated. (E) has an unneeded change of tense.

5. **(A)** The original is correct. (B) introduces the new idea of attack, which is not in the original. (C) and (D) lose the idea of "now." (E) trades the idea of the closeness of the examination for one of quantity, which changes the meaning.

6. **(D)** The three verbs in parallel are: "will expand," "(will) produce" and "(will) reached." This shows the original error. Also, the adverb quickly will carry forward to all three verbs. (B) fails for introducing a "have" for "produced." (C) fails to correct the "reached" and adds a gratuitous "then." (E)'s addition of "fairly prompt way" is an error, for level of usage. (D) corrects the "reached" and drops the unneeded time of equilibrium, and the redundant "state."

7. **(B)** "Not only" requires "but also;" hence (D) and (E) fail. "Not only" already includes the idea of an additional item, so the "as well" of the original and (C) are wrong.

8. **(E)** Irregardless is not an English word, eliminating the original and (B). (C) and (D) carelessly drop the term ingested, which changes the meaning. (E) also correctly uses "or" as a connector since the intended meaning of the sentence is to refer to these ideas severally and not as a single group.

9. **(C)** Hopefully is not acceptable in standard written English. The correct phrase is "it is hoped" as in (C). (E)'s phrase denies the fact of the hope expressed by the original sentence.

10. **(C)** There is a lack of coordination between the underlined part's reference to the system of the Hopis and the other part's reference to the system of certain languages. (C) corrects that error. In addition, it seems more likely that it is a detailed study that is at issue than a detailed grammar studied at some unknown depth.

11. **(A)** The original is correct. (B) changes the meaning to a discussion of what they were doing rather than one of their possible success. (C) and (D) change the time of the explosion for no good reason. (E) erroneously has both a "would" and a "could." One of these is sufficient to give the idea of uncertainty.

12. **(B)** The future perfect should be used to refer to an event between the present and some future reference point. In the original it refers to the future reference point, thus (A) is wrong. In (C) and (D) it is used for both the future reference point (time peace . . . comes) and the intermediate point (lives . . . wasted). This is wrong. The use of shall is without meaning here. (E) uses "would have," which introduces an uncertainty not present in the original. (B) does everything correctly.

13. **(B)** Parallelism is the issue here. The parallel creating elements are "not . . . but rather" and the parts after those two must be similar in construction. After the "not" we have a noun, and that is what we should have after "but rather" as well. (E) drops the "but," and (C) and (D) add unneeded words.

14. **(A)** The original is correct. (C), (D), and (E) add the idea of "surpassing," which is not in the original and merely speaks of first and second. (B) is not wrong, but is wordy without cause.

15. **(C)** The element of the sentence following the introductory descriptor or modifier must apply to the first noun after the comma. The researchers were not "primarily accomplished" through the use of electron microscopes, so (A) is out. Though (B)'s idea of competence is not unacceptable, (B) drops the idea of the primacy of the electron microscope in the work, which is wrong. (D) and (E) use locutions that are either meaningless or wordy. (C) keeps everything in order.

16. **(E)** The first part of the sentence speaks of the cuisine, so we do not want to shift suddenly to the peoples themselves as the original does. (B) fails for the same reason. (C) limits itself to sauces, which is unfounded. (D) fails to mention the French cuisine, which is in error. Thus (E), where the word cookery can be carried forward in the reader's mind to yield French cookery being compared to Italian cookery.

17. **(D)** The original errs in its use of "that," which is singular, while "powers," for which it stands, is plural. This eliminates (A) and (B). (C) fails because it is comparing our powers of communication with other animals, rather than with the powers of communication of the other animals. (E) is inferior to (D) because it changes the tense to "have been" without cause. (D)'s change to "far greater," while not strictly necessary, does leave the meaning intact and even improves the sentence.

18. **(B)** "Healthy" refers to the state of health of some organism. "Healthful" is the proper way to describe something that promotes health. "Tasty" refers to the quality of having a good taste when eaten. "Tasteful" refers to being in accord with good aesthetic taste, or having such taste. In addition, the original erred in having "neither . . . or," when "neither . . . nor" is required. Only (D) conveys the intended meaning of the original.

19. **(A)** The original, while not a wonderful sentence, is not wrong. (B) omits the standard of judging benefit (general welfare). (C) leaves aside all consideration of benefit and focuses only on the feasibility of the project. (D) is perhaps second best, though a little convoluted. However, it omits the certainty that the project could be accomplished. (E) incorrectly refers to the happiness of the individuals, while the original referred to the general welfare, which might not be the same thing at all.

20. **(D)** The first part of the sentence, after "in," is surplus. (D) correctly dispenses with that part and preserves the rest.

21. **(D)** The "them" is unclear, eliminating (A), (B), and (C). (D)'s use of the present tense is acceptable since the classification presumably still does what it was set up to do. (E)'s use of the "would" construction isnot acceptable since there is no doubt about what is included.

22. **(E)** The original sentence has the lions playing with lenses while in the trees. This is clearly unacceptable. Only (E) corrects the situation to make it clear that the visitor is the one concerned with telephoto lenses, not the lions.

23. **(C)** We are concerned with the capacity for something to be done, which is expressed best by "can," eliminating (A), (D), and (E). Also, the original refers to "a person," which is singular even with the apostrophe and "s" of the possessive case appended. Thus "his" is needed rather than "their," making (C) preferable to (B).

24. **(C)** The original sentence sets up a parallel structure of "were appalled," "(were) grieved," and "(were) promised." (B)'s use of "aggrieved" is wrong since they were not injured. "Saddened," used in (D), is essentially the same meaning as "grieved," though somewhat weaker. (D) and (E) fail to correct the error with "promise," which leaves (C).

25. **(A)** The original sentence is correct. (B) fails primarily because of its reference to "the" personality rather than "his." The use of "jettison" is not so major a problem. (C) introduces the idea of "must," which is quite different from the "may" of the original and not required by the meaning of the sentence. (D) speaks of "the prisoner" (singular) and "their" (plural) "personality" (singular). (E) fails for similar reasons, since it refers to "prisoner's" (singular) "personalities" (plural), implying multiple personalities for the prisoner, which the original certainly does not support.

Section VIII

1. **(B)** $40\% = \frac{2}{5}$
$\frac{2}{5} - \frac{10}{7} = \frac{4}{7}$

2. **(D)** 27 and 51 are each divisible by 3. 17 and 59 are prime numbers. Hence, I and IV only.

3. **(A)** Angle DOC = 6 + x
$$\begin{aligned} \text{Angle AOC} = (6 + x) + x &= 180 - 20 \\ 6 + 2x &= 160 \\ 2x &= 154 \\ x &= 77 \end{aligned}$$

4. **(D)** Let C = the capacity in gallons. Then $\frac{1}{3}C + 3 = \frac{1}{2}C$. Multiplying through by 6, we obtain $2C + 18 = 3C$, or $C = 18$.

5. **(E)** $$\frac{91 + 88 + 86 + 78 + x}{5} = 85$$
$$\begin{aligned} 343 + x &= 425 \\ x &= 82 \end{aligned}$$

6. **(C)** 12 × .39 = 4.68 inches; that is, between $4\frac{1}{2}$ and 5.

7. **(D)**

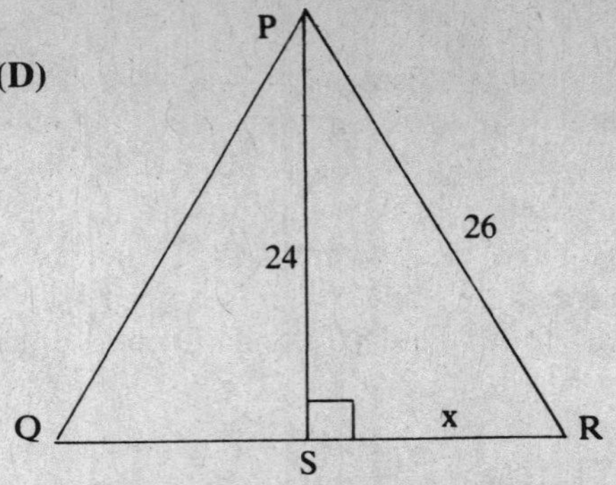

In the figure above, PS ⊥ QR. Then, in right triangle PSR:

$$\begin{aligned} x^2 + 24^2 &= 26^2 \\ x^2 &= 26^2 - 24^2 \\ &= (26 + 24)(26 - 24) \\ x^2 &= 50 \cdot 2 = 100 \\ x &= 10 \end{aligned}$$

Thus, QR = 20.

8. **(C)** All terms involving x are 0. Hence, the equation reduces to:

$$\begin{aligned} 0 - 7y + 15 &= 0 \\ \text{or } 7y &= 15 \\ y &= 2\tfrac{1}{7} \end{aligned}$$

9. **(E)** Let s = number of shirts and t = number of ties, where s and t are integers:

$$\begin{aligned} \text{Then } 7s + 3t &= 81 \\ 7s &= 81 - 3t \\ s &= \frac{81 - 3t}{7} \end{aligned}$$

Since s is an integer, t must have an integral value such that 81 − 3t is divisible by 7. Trial shows that t = 6 is the smallest such number, making $s = \frac{81 - 18}{7} = \frac{63}{7} = 9$. Hence, s:t = 9:6 = 3:2

10. **(C)** $\text{Rate} = \frac{\text{distance}}{\text{time}} = \frac{\frac{2}{5}\text{ mile}}{\frac{5}{60}\text{ hour}} = \frac{\frac{2}{5}}{\frac{1}{12}}$

$\text{rate} = \frac{2}{5} \cdot \frac{12}{1} = \frac{24}{5} = 4\frac{4}{5}$ miles per hour.

11. **(D)** Draw the altitudes indicated. A rectangle and two right triangles are produced. From the figure, the base of each triangle is 20 feet. By the Pythagorean Theorem, the altitude is 15 feet. Hence, the area:

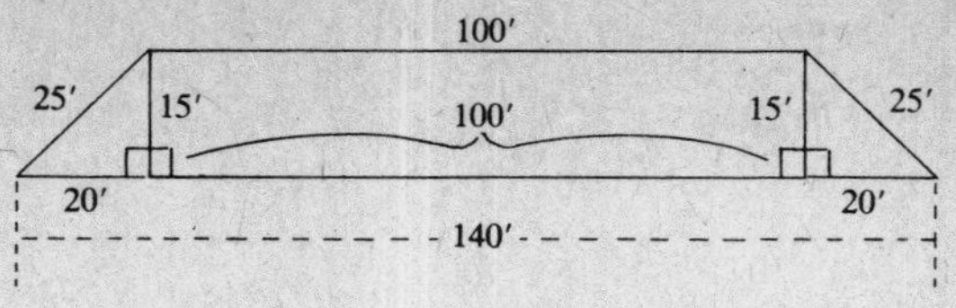

$K = \frac{1}{2} \cdot 15(100 + 140)$
$= \frac{1}{2} \cdot 15 \cdot 240$
$= 15 \cdot 120$
$= 1800$ square feet

12. **(E)** If $1 + \frac{1}{t} = \frac{t+1}{1}$, then the right-hand fraction can also be reduced to $1 = \frac{1}{t}$, and we have an identity, which is true for all values of t except 0.

13. **(E)** All points 6 inches from A are on a circle of radius 6 with center at A. All points 1 inch from b are on 2 straight lines parallel to b and 1 inch from it on each side. These two parallel lines intersect the circle in 4 points.

14. **(E)** Let R = 5P and S = 5Q where P and Q are integers. Then R − S = 5P − 5Q = 5(P − Q) is divisible by 5. RS = 5P · 5Q = 25PG is divisible by 25. R + S = 5P + 5Q = 5(P + Q) is divisible by 5. $R^2 + S^2 = 25P^2 + 25Q^2 = 25(P^2 + Q^2)$ is divisible by 5. R + S = 5P + 5Q = 5(P + Q), which is not necessarily divisible by 10.

15. **(D)** $\frac{1}{2} \cdot 7 \cdot h = \pi \cdot 7^2$. Dividing both sides by 7, we get $\frac{1}{2}h = 7\pi$, or $h = 14\pi$.

16. **(E)**

$\frac{9}{13} = .69$
)9.00
78
120
117

$\frac{13}{9} = 1.44$
)13.00
9
40
36
40
36

70% = .7

$\frac{1}{.70} = \frac{1}{7}$
10

$= \frac{10}{7}$ $\;1.42$
)10.00
7
30
28
20

Correct order is $\frac{9}{13}$, 70%, $\frac{1}{.70}$, $\frac{13}{9}$—or I, III, IV, II.

17. **(D)**

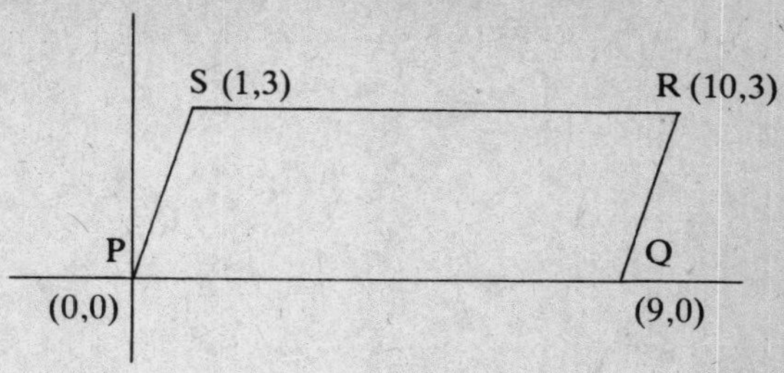

Since PQ and RS are parallel and equal, the figure is a parallelogram of base = 9 and height = 3. Hence, area = 9 · 3 = 27.

18. **(A)**

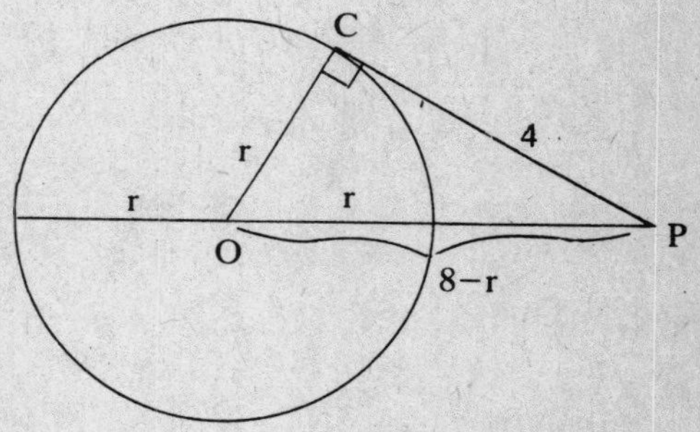

From the figure, in right △PCO:

$$PO^2 = r^2 + 4^2$$
$$(8 - r)^2 = r^2 + 16$$
$$64 - 16r + r^2 = r^2 + 16$$
$$48 = 16r$$
$$r = 3$$

Hence, diameter = 6.

19. **(B)** Area of wall = $4 \cdot \frac{60}{3} = 4 \cdot 20 = 80$ sq. yd. Cost = 80 × \$10.50 = \$840.00.

20. **(D)** Using the distance formula, derived from the Pythagorean Theorem, that the distance from (a,b) to (c,d) is $\sqrt{(a-c)^2 + (b-d)^2}$:
Distance of (4,4) from origin =
$\sqrt{16 + 16} = \sqrt{32} < 7$
Distance from (5,5) from origin =

$\sqrt{25 + 25} = \sqrt{50} > 7$
Distance of (4,5) from origin =
$\sqrt{16 + 25} = \sqrt{41} < 7$

Distance of (4,6) from origin =
$\sqrt{16 + 36} = \sqrt{52} > 7$
Hence, only II and IV are outside circle.

ANSWER SHEET—PRACTICE EXAMINATION 2

SECTION I

1 Ⓐ Ⓑ Ⓒ Ⓓ Ⓔ	6 Ⓐ Ⓑ Ⓒ Ⓓ Ⓔ	11 Ⓐ Ⓑ Ⓒ Ⓓ Ⓔ	16 Ⓐ Ⓑ Ⓒ Ⓓ Ⓔ	21 Ⓐ Ⓑ Ⓒ Ⓓ Ⓔ
2 Ⓐ Ⓑ Ⓒ Ⓓ Ⓔ	7 Ⓐ Ⓑ Ⓒ Ⓓ Ⓔ	12 Ⓐ Ⓑ Ⓒ Ⓓ Ⓔ	17 Ⓐ Ⓑ Ⓒ Ⓓ Ⓔ	22 Ⓐ Ⓑ Ⓒ Ⓓ Ⓔ
3 Ⓐ Ⓑ Ⓒ Ⓓ Ⓔ	8 Ⓐ Ⓑ Ⓒ Ⓓ Ⓔ	13 Ⓐ Ⓑ Ⓒ Ⓓ Ⓔ	18 Ⓐ Ⓑ Ⓒ Ⓓ Ⓔ	23 Ⓐ Ⓑ Ⓒ Ⓓ Ⓔ
4 Ⓐ Ⓑ Ⓒ Ⓓ Ⓔ	9 Ⓐ Ⓑ Ⓒ Ⓓ Ⓔ	14 Ⓐ Ⓑ Ⓒ Ⓓ Ⓔ	19 Ⓐ Ⓑ Ⓒ Ⓓ Ⓔ	24 Ⓐ Ⓑ Ⓒ Ⓓ Ⓔ
5 Ⓐ Ⓑ Ⓒ Ⓓ Ⓔ	10 Ⓐ Ⓑ Ⓒ Ⓓ Ⓔ	15 Ⓐ Ⓑ Ⓒ Ⓓ Ⓔ	20 Ⓐ Ⓑ Ⓒ Ⓓ Ⓔ	25 Ⓐ Ⓑ Ⓒ Ⓓ Ⓔ

SECTION II

1 Ⓐ Ⓑ Ⓒ Ⓓ Ⓔ	5 Ⓐ Ⓑ Ⓒ Ⓓ Ⓔ	9 Ⓐ Ⓑ Ⓒ Ⓓ Ⓔ	13 Ⓐ Ⓑ Ⓒ Ⓓ Ⓔ	17 Ⓐ Ⓑ Ⓒ Ⓓ Ⓔ
2 Ⓐ Ⓑ Ⓒ Ⓓ Ⓔ	6 Ⓐ Ⓑ Ⓒ Ⓓ Ⓔ	10 Ⓐ Ⓑ Ⓒ Ⓓ Ⓔ	14 Ⓐ Ⓑ Ⓒ Ⓓ Ⓔ	18 Ⓐ Ⓑ Ⓒ Ⓓ Ⓔ
3 Ⓐ Ⓑ Ⓒ Ⓓ Ⓔ	7 Ⓐ Ⓑ Ⓒ Ⓓ Ⓔ	11 Ⓐ Ⓑ Ⓒ Ⓓ Ⓔ	15 Ⓐ Ⓑ Ⓒ Ⓓ Ⓔ	19 Ⓐ Ⓑ Ⓒ Ⓓ Ⓔ
4 Ⓐ Ⓑ Ⓒ Ⓓ Ⓔ	8 Ⓐ Ⓑ Ⓒ Ⓓ Ⓔ	12 Ⓐ Ⓑ Ⓒ Ⓓ Ⓔ	16 Ⓐ Ⓑ Ⓒ Ⓓ Ⓔ	20 Ⓐ Ⓑ Ⓒ Ⓓ Ⓔ

SECTION III

1 Ⓐ Ⓑ Ⓒ Ⓓ Ⓔ	6 Ⓐ Ⓑ Ⓒ Ⓓ Ⓔ	11 Ⓐ Ⓑ Ⓒ Ⓓ Ⓔ	16 Ⓐ Ⓑ Ⓒ Ⓓ Ⓔ	21 Ⓐ Ⓑ Ⓒ Ⓓ Ⓔ
2 Ⓐ Ⓑ Ⓒ Ⓓ Ⓔ	7 Ⓐ Ⓑ Ⓒ Ⓓ Ⓔ	12 Ⓐ Ⓑ Ⓒ Ⓓ Ⓔ	17 Ⓐ Ⓑ Ⓒ Ⓓ Ⓔ	22 Ⓐ Ⓑ Ⓒ Ⓓ Ⓔ
3 Ⓐ Ⓑ Ⓒ Ⓓ Ⓔ	8 Ⓐ Ⓑ Ⓒ Ⓓ Ⓔ	13 Ⓐ Ⓑ Ⓒ Ⓓ Ⓔ	18 Ⓐ Ⓑ Ⓒ Ⓓ Ⓔ	23 Ⓐ Ⓑ Ⓒ Ⓓ Ⓔ
4 Ⓐ Ⓑ Ⓒ Ⓓ Ⓔ	9 Ⓐ Ⓑ Ⓒ Ⓓ Ⓔ	14 Ⓐ Ⓑ Ⓒ Ⓓ Ⓔ	19 Ⓐ Ⓑ Ⓒ Ⓓ Ⓔ	24 Ⓐ Ⓑ Ⓒ Ⓓ Ⓔ
5 Ⓐ Ⓑ Ⓒ Ⓓ Ⓔ	10 Ⓐ Ⓑ Ⓒ Ⓓ Ⓔ	15 Ⓐ Ⓑ Ⓒ Ⓓ Ⓔ	20 Ⓐ Ⓑ Ⓒ Ⓓ Ⓔ	25 Ⓐ Ⓑ Ⓒ Ⓓ Ⓔ

SECTION IV

1 Ⓐ Ⓑ Ⓒ Ⓓ Ⓔ	6 Ⓐ Ⓑ Ⓒ Ⓓ Ⓔ	11 Ⓐ Ⓑ Ⓒ Ⓓ Ⓔ	16 Ⓐ Ⓑ Ⓒ Ⓓ Ⓔ	21 Ⓐ Ⓑ Ⓒ Ⓓ Ⓔ
2 Ⓐ Ⓑ Ⓒ Ⓓ Ⓔ	7 Ⓐ Ⓑ Ⓒ Ⓓ Ⓔ	12 Ⓐ Ⓑ Ⓒ Ⓓ Ⓔ	17 Ⓐ Ⓑ Ⓒ Ⓓ Ⓔ	22 Ⓐ Ⓑ Ⓒ Ⓓ Ⓔ
3 Ⓐ Ⓑ Ⓒ Ⓓ Ⓔ	8 Ⓐ Ⓑ Ⓒ Ⓓ Ⓔ	13 Ⓐ Ⓑ Ⓒ Ⓓ Ⓔ	18 Ⓐ Ⓑ Ⓒ Ⓓ Ⓔ	23 Ⓐ Ⓑ Ⓒ Ⓓ Ⓔ
4 Ⓐ Ⓑ Ⓒ Ⓓ Ⓔ	9 Ⓐ Ⓑ Ⓒ Ⓓ Ⓔ	14 Ⓐ Ⓑ Ⓒ Ⓓ Ⓔ	19 Ⓐ Ⓑ Ⓒ Ⓓ Ⓔ	24 Ⓐ Ⓑ Ⓒ Ⓓ Ⓔ
5 Ⓐ Ⓑ Ⓒ Ⓓ Ⓔ	10 Ⓐ Ⓑ Ⓒ Ⓓ Ⓔ	15 Ⓐ Ⓑ Ⓒ Ⓓ Ⓔ	20 Ⓐ Ⓑ Ⓒ Ⓓ Ⓔ	25 Ⓐ Ⓑ Ⓒ Ⓓ Ⓔ

SECTION V

1 Ⓐ Ⓑ Ⓒ Ⓓ Ⓔ	5 Ⓐ Ⓑ Ⓒ Ⓓ Ⓔ	9 Ⓐ Ⓑ Ⓒ Ⓓ Ⓔ	13 Ⓐ Ⓑ Ⓒ Ⓓ Ⓔ	17 Ⓐ Ⓑ Ⓒ Ⓓ Ⓔ
2 Ⓐ Ⓑ Ⓒ Ⓓ Ⓔ	6 Ⓐ Ⓑ Ⓒ Ⓓ Ⓔ	10 Ⓐ Ⓑ Ⓒ Ⓓ Ⓔ	14 Ⓐ Ⓑ Ⓒ Ⓓ Ⓔ	18 Ⓐ Ⓑ Ⓒ Ⓓ Ⓔ
3 Ⓐ Ⓑ Ⓒ Ⓓ Ⓔ	7 Ⓐ Ⓑ Ⓒ Ⓓ Ⓔ	11 Ⓐ Ⓑ Ⓒ Ⓓ Ⓔ	15 Ⓐ Ⓑ Ⓒ Ⓓ Ⓔ	19 Ⓐ Ⓑ Ⓒ Ⓓ Ⓔ
4 Ⓐ Ⓑ Ⓒ Ⓓ Ⓔ	8 Ⓐ Ⓑ Ⓒ Ⓓ Ⓔ	12 Ⓐ Ⓑ Ⓒ Ⓓ Ⓔ	16 Ⓐ Ⓑ Ⓒ Ⓓ Ⓔ	20 Ⓐ Ⓑ Ⓒ Ⓓ Ⓔ

SECTION VI

1 Ⓐ Ⓑ Ⓒ Ⓓ Ⓔ	8 Ⓐ Ⓑ Ⓒ Ⓓ Ⓔ	15 Ⓐ Ⓑ Ⓒ Ⓓ Ⓔ	22 Ⓐ Ⓑ Ⓒ Ⓓ Ⓔ	29 Ⓐ Ⓑ Ⓒ Ⓓ Ⓔ
2 Ⓐ Ⓑ Ⓒ Ⓓ Ⓔ	9 Ⓐ Ⓑ Ⓒ Ⓓ Ⓔ	16 Ⓐ Ⓑ Ⓒ Ⓓ Ⓔ	23 Ⓐ Ⓑ Ⓒ Ⓓ Ⓔ	30 Ⓐ Ⓑ Ⓒ Ⓓ Ⓔ
3 Ⓐ Ⓑ Ⓒ Ⓓ Ⓔ	10 Ⓐ Ⓑ Ⓒ Ⓓ Ⓔ	17 Ⓐ Ⓑ Ⓒ Ⓓ Ⓔ	24 Ⓐ Ⓑ Ⓒ Ⓓ Ⓔ	31 Ⓐ Ⓑ Ⓒ Ⓓ Ⓔ
4 Ⓐ Ⓑ Ⓒ Ⓓ Ⓔ	11 Ⓐ Ⓑ Ⓒ Ⓓ Ⓔ	18 Ⓐ Ⓑ Ⓒ Ⓓ Ⓔ	25 Ⓐ Ⓑ Ⓒ Ⓓ Ⓔ	32 Ⓐ Ⓑ Ⓒ Ⓓ Ⓔ
5 Ⓐ Ⓑ Ⓒ Ⓓ Ⓔ	12 Ⓐ Ⓑ Ⓒ Ⓓ Ⓔ	19 Ⓐ Ⓑ Ⓒ Ⓓ Ⓔ	26 Ⓐ Ⓑ Ⓒ Ⓓ Ⓔ	33 Ⓐ Ⓑ Ⓒ Ⓓ Ⓔ
6 Ⓐ Ⓑ Ⓒ Ⓓ Ⓔ	13 Ⓐ Ⓑ Ⓒ Ⓓ Ⓔ	20 Ⓐ Ⓑ Ⓒ Ⓓ Ⓔ	27 Ⓐ Ⓑ Ⓒ Ⓓ Ⓔ	34 Ⓐ Ⓑ Ⓒ Ⓓ Ⓔ
7 Ⓐ Ⓑ Ⓒ Ⓓ Ⓔ	14 Ⓐ Ⓑ Ⓒ Ⓓ Ⓔ	21 Ⓐ Ⓑ Ⓒ Ⓓ Ⓔ	28 Ⓐ Ⓑ Ⓒ Ⓓ Ⓔ	35 Ⓐ Ⓑ Ⓒ Ⓓ Ⓔ

SECTION VII

1 Ⓐ Ⓑ Ⓒ Ⓓ Ⓔ	5 Ⓐ Ⓑ Ⓒ Ⓓ Ⓔ	9 Ⓐ Ⓑ Ⓒ Ⓓ Ⓔ	13 Ⓐ Ⓑ Ⓒ Ⓓ Ⓔ	17 Ⓐ Ⓑ Ⓒ Ⓓ Ⓔ
2 Ⓐ Ⓑ Ⓒ Ⓓ Ⓔ	6 Ⓐ Ⓑ Ⓒ Ⓓ Ⓔ	10 Ⓐ Ⓑ Ⓒ Ⓓ Ⓔ	14 Ⓐ Ⓑ Ⓒ Ⓓ Ⓔ	18 Ⓐ Ⓑ Ⓒ Ⓓ Ⓔ
3 Ⓐ Ⓑ Ⓒ Ⓓ Ⓔ	7 Ⓐ Ⓑ Ⓒ Ⓓ Ⓔ	11 Ⓐ Ⓑ Ⓒ Ⓓ Ⓔ	15 Ⓐ Ⓑ Ⓒ Ⓓ Ⓔ	19 Ⓐ Ⓑ Ⓒ Ⓓ Ⓔ
4 Ⓐ Ⓑ Ⓒ Ⓓ Ⓔ	8 Ⓐ Ⓑ Ⓒ Ⓓ Ⓔ	12 Ⓐ Ⓑ Ⓒ Ⓓ Ⓔ	16 Ⓐ Ⓑ Ⓒ Ⓓ Ⓔ	20 Ⓐ Ⓑ Ⓒ Ⓓ Ⓔ

SECTION VIII

1 Ⓐ Ⓑ Ⓒ Ⓓ Ⓔ	6 Ⓐ Ⓑ Ⓒ Ⓓ Ⓔ	11 Ⓐ Ⓑ Ⓒ Ⓓ Ⓔ	16 Ⓐ Ⓑ Ⓒ Ⓓ Ⓔ	21 Ⓐ Ⓑ Ⓒ Ⓓ Ⓔ
2 Ⓐ Ⓑ Ⓒ Ⓓ Ⓔ	7 Ⓐ Ⓑ Ⓒ Ⓓ Ⓔ	12 Ⓐ Ⓑ Ⓒ Ⓓ Ⓔ	17 Ⓐ Ⓑ Ⓒ Ⓓ Ⓔ	22 Ⓐ Ⓑ Ⓒ Ⓓ Ⓔ
3 Ⓐ Ⓑ Ⓒ Ⓓ Ⓔ	8 Ⓐ Ⓑ Ⓒ Ⓓ Ⓔ	13 Ⓐ Ⓑ Ⓒ Ⓓ Ⓔ	18 Ⓐ Ⓑ Ⓒ Ⓓ Ⓔ	23 Ⓐ Ⓑ Ⓒ Ⓓ Ⓔ
4 Ⓐ Ⓑ Ⓒ Ⓓ Ⓔ	9 Ⓐ Ⓑ Ⓒ Ⓓ Ⓔ	14 Ⓐ Ⓑ Ⓒ Ⓓ Ⓔ	19 Ⓐ Ⓑ Ⓒ Ⓓ Ⓔ	24 Ⓐ Ⓑ Ⓒ Ⓓ Ⓔ
5 Ⓐ Ⓑ Ⓒ Ⓓ Ⓔ	10 Ⓐ Ⓑ Ⓒ Ⓓ Ⓔ	15 Ⓐ Ⓑ Ⓒ Ⓓ Ⓔ	20 Ⓐ Ⓑ Ⓒ Ⓓ Ⓔ	25 Ⓐ Ⓑ Ⓒ Ⓓ Ⓔ

PRATICE EXAMINATION 2

SECTION I

Time—30 Minutes
25 Questions

Directions: Below each of the following passages, you will find questions or incomplete statements about the passage. Each statement or question is followed by lettered words or expressions. Select the word or expression that most satisfactorily completes each statement or answers each question in accordance with the meaning of the passage. After you have chosen the best answer, blacken the corresponding space on the answer sheet.

When the television is good, nothing—not the theatre, not the magazines, or newspapers—nothing is better. But when television is bad, nothing is worse. I invite you to sit down in front of your television set when your station goes on the air and stay there without a book, magazine, newspaper, or anything else to distract you and keep your eyes glued to that set until the station signs off. I can assure you that you will observe a vast wasteland. You will see a procession of game shows, violence, audience-participation shows, formula comedies about totally unbelievable families, blood and thunder, mayhem, more violence, sadism, murder, Western badmen, Western goodmen, private eyes, gangsters, still more violence, and cartoons. And, endlessly, commercials that scream and cajole and offend. And most of all, boredom. True, you will see a few things you will enjoy. But they will be very, very few. And if you think I exaggerate, try it.

Is there no room on television to teach, to inform, to uplift, to stretch, to enlarge the capacities of our children? Is there no room for programs to deepen the children's understanding of children in other lands? Is there no room for a children's news show explaining something about the world for them at their level of understanding? Is there no room for reading the great literature of the past, teaching them the great traditions of freedom? There are some fine children's shows, but they are drowned out in the massive doses of cartoons, violence, and more violence. Must these be your trademarks? Search your conscience and see whether you cannot offer more to your young beneficiaries whose future you guard so many hours each and every day.

There are many people in this great country, and you must serve all of us. You will get no argument from me if you say that, given a choice between a Western and a symphony, more people will watch the Western. I like Westerns and private eyes, too—but a steady diet for the whole country is obviously not in the public interest. We all know that people would more often prefer to be entertained than stimulated or informed. But your obligations are not satisfied if you look only to popularity as a test of what to broadcast. You are not only in show business; you are free to communicate ideas as well as to give relaxation. You must provide a wider range of choices, more diversity, more alternatives. It is not enough to cater to the nation's whims—you must also serve the nation's needs. The people own the air. They own it as much in prime evening time as they do at six o'clock in the morning. For every hour that the people give you—you owe them something. I intend to see that your debt is paid with service.

—excerpt from speech by Newton H. Minow, chairman of the Federal Communications Commission, before the National Association of Broadcasters.

1. The wasteland referred to by the author describes
   (A) western badlands
   (B) average television programs
   (C) morning television shows
   (D) television shows with desert locales
   (E) children's programs generally

2. The author's attitude toward television can best be described as
   (A) sullenness at defeat
   (B) reconciliation with the broadcasters
   (C) righteous indignation
   (D) determination to prevail
   (E) hopelessness over the size of the problem

3. The author is primarily concerned to tell broadcasters that
   (A) the listener, not the broadcaster, should make the decisions about which programs are aired
   (B) all children's shows are worthless
   (C) mystery programs should be banned
   (D) they had better mend their ways
   (E) televised instruction should become a substitute for classroom lessons

4. Concerning programs for children, it may be inferred that Minow believes that such programs should
   (A) include no cartoons at all
   (B) include ones which provide culture
   (C) be presented only during the morning hours
   (D) be presented without commercial interruption
   (E) not deal with the Old West

5. The statement that "the people own the air" implies that
   (A) citizens have the right to insist on worthwhile television programs
   (B) television should be socialized
   (C) the government may build above present structures
   (D) since air is worthless, the people own nothing
   (E) the broadcasters have no right to commercialize on television

6. It can be inferred from the passage in regard to television programming that the author believes
   (A) the broadcasters are trying to do the right thing but are failing
   (B) foreign countries are going to pattern their programs after ours
   (C) there is a great deal that is worthwhile in present programs
   (D) the listeners do not necessarily know what is good for them
   (E) six o'clock in the morning is too early for a television show

7. Which of the following would NOT be inferable from the passage?
   (A) The needs of minorities must be met by television.
   (B) Minow would probably favor more television stations being established, if they were responsible stations.
   (C) Violence is not a good ingredient for children's shows.
   (D) Children's television is uniformly terrible.
   (E) Minow believes that better shows are possible.

8. Minow believes that his tastes are
   (A) better than most people's
   (B) better than those of the television industry
   (C) the same as most people's
   (D) better than the average child's
   (E) less demanding of television than of other art forms

Every profession or trade, every art, and every science has its technical vocabulary, the function of which is partly to designate things or processes which have no names in ordinary English, and partly to secure greater exactness in nomenclature. Such special dialects, or jargons, are necessary in technical discussion of any kind. Being universally understood by the devotees of the particular science or art, they have the precision of a mathematical formula. Besides, they save time, for it is much more economical to name a process than to describe it. Thousands of these technical terms are very properly included in every large dictionary, yet, as a whole, they are rather on the outskirts of the English language than actually within its borders.

Different occupations, however, differ widely in the character of their special vocabularies. In trades and handicrafts and other vocations, such as farming and fishing, that have occupied great numbers of men from remote times, the technical vocabulary is very old. It consists largely of native words, or of borrowed words that have worked themselves into the very fiber of our language. Hence, though highly technical in many particulars, these vocabularies are more familiar in sound, and more generally understood, than most other technicalities. The special dialects of law, medicine, divinity, and philosophy have also, in their older strata, become pretty familiar to cultivated persons, and have contributed much to the popular vocabulary. Yet, every vocation still possesses a large body of technical terms that remain essentially foreign, even to educated speech. And the proportion has been much increased in the last fifty years, particularly in the various departments of natural and political science and in the mechanic arts. Here new terms are coined with the greatest freedom, and abandoned with indifference when they have served their turn. Most of the new coinages are confined to special discussions and seldom get into general literature or conversation. Yet, no profession is nowadays, as all professions once were, a closed guild. The lawyer, the physician, the man of science, and the cleric associates freely with his fellow creatures, and does not meet them in a merely professional way. Furthermore, what is called popular science makes everybody acquainted with modern views and recent discoveries. Any important experiment, though made in a remote or provincial laboratory, is at once reported in the newspapers, and everybody is soon talking about it—as in the case of the Roentgen rays and wireless telegraphy. Thus, our common speech is always taking up new technical terms and making them commonplace.

9. Which of the following words is least likely to have started its life as jargon?
   (A) sun
   (B) calf
   (C) plow
   (D) loom
   (E) hammer

10. The author's main purpose in the passage is to
   (A) describe a phenomenon
   (B) argue a belief
   (C) propose a solution
   (D) stimulate action
   (E) be entertaining

11. When the author refers to professions as no longer being "closed guilds," he means that
   (A) it is much easier to become a professional today than it was in the past
   (B) there is more social intercourse between professionals and others
   (C) popular science has told their secrets to the world
   (D) anyone can now understand anything in a profession
   (E) apprenticeships are no longer required

12. If the author of the passage wished to study a new field, he would probably
   (A) call in a dictionary expert
   (B) become easily discouraged
   (C) look to the histories of the words in the new field
   (D) pay careful attention to the new field's technical vocabulary
   (E) learn how to coin new jargon in the field

13. The writer of this article was probably a(n)
   (A) linguist
   (B) attorney
   (C) scientist
   (D) politician
   (E) physician

14. The author of the passage probably lived in
   (A) 1904 in India
   (B) 1914 in the United States
   (C) 1944 in Russia
   (D) 1964 in England
   (E) 1974 in France

15. It seems that the passage implies
   (A) the English language is always becoming larger and larger
   (B) the words of the English language are always changing
   (C) one can never be sure of what a word means without consulting an expert
   (D) technical terms in most non-scientific fields have little chance of becoming part of the main body of the language in these scientific days
   (E) such old-time farming words as harrow and farrow are not really technical terms at all

16. Which of the following is (are) NOT advantages of jargon?

    I. Jargon permits experts to make short explanations of technical matters to other experts.
    II. Jargon saves money.
    III. Jargon is mathematical.
    IV. Jargon is more precise than ordinary language for describing special topics.

    (A) I only
    (B) II and III only
    (C) I and IV only
    (D) I, III, and IV only
    (E) I, II, III, and IV

Whenever two or more unusual traits or situations are found in the same place, it is tempting to look for more than a coincidental relationship between them. The high Himalayas and the Tibetan plateau certainly have extraordinary physical characteristics, and the cultures which are found there are also unusual, though not unique. However, there is no intention of adopting Montesquieu's view of climate and soil as cultural determinants. The ecology of a region merely poses some of the problems faced by the inhabitants of the region, and while the problems facing a culture are important to its development, they do not determine it.

The appearance of the Himalayas during the late Tertiary Period and the accompanying further raising of the previously established ranges had a marked effect on the climate of the region. Primarily, of course, it blocked the Indian monsoon from reaching Central Asia at all. Secondarily, air and moisture from other directions were also reduced.

Prior to the raising of the Himalayas, the land now forming the Tibetan uplands had a dry continental climate with vegetation and animal life similar to that of much of the rest of the region on the same parallel, but somewhat different than that of the areas farther north, which were already drier. With the coming of the Himalayas and the relatively sudden drying out of the region, there was a severe thinning out of the animal and plant populations. The ensuing incomplete Pleistocene glaciation had a further thinning effect, but significantly did not wipe out life in the area. Thus, after the end of the glaciation there were only a few varieties of life extant from the original continental species. Isolated by the Kunlun range from the Tarim basin and Turfan depression species which had already adapted to the dry steppe climate, and would otherwise have been expected to flourish in Tibet, the remaining native fauna and flora multiplied. Armand describes the Tibetan fauna as not having great variety, but being "striking" in the abundance of the particular species that are present. The plant life is similarly limited in variety, with some observers finding no more than seventy varieties of plants in even the relatively fertile Eastern Tibetan valleys, with fewer than ten food crops. Tibetan "tea" is a major staple, perhaps replacing the unavailable vegetables.

The difficulties of living in an environment at once dry and cold, and populated with species more usually found in more hospitable climes, are great. These difficulties may well have influenced the unusual polyandrous societies typical of the region. Lattimore sees the maintenance of multiple-husband households as being preserved from earlier forms by the harsh conditions of the Tibetan uplands, which permitted no experimentation and "froze" the cultures which came there. Kawakita, on the other hand, sees the polyandry as a way of easily permitting the best householder to become the head husband regardless of age. His detailed studies of the Bhotea village of Tsumje do seem to support this idea of polyandry as a method of talent mobility in a situation where even the best talent is barely enough for survival.

In sum, though arguments can be made that a pre-existing polyandrous system was strengthened and preserved (insofar as it has been) by the rigors of the land, it would certainly be an overstatement to lay causative factors of any stronger nature to the ecological influences in this case.

17. What are the "unusual situations and traits" referred to in the first sentence?

    I. patterns of animal and plant growth
    II. food and food preparation patterns of the upland Tibetans
    III. social and familial organization of typical Tibetan society

    (A) I only
    (B) II only
    (C) III only

(D) I and III only
(E) I, II, and III

18. What was the significance of the fact that the Pleistocene glaciation did not wipe out life entirely in the area?
(A) Without life, man could not flourish either.
(B) The drying out was too sudden for most plants to adapt to the climate.
(C) If the region had been devoid of life, some of the other species from nearby arid areas might possibly have taken over the area.
(D) The variety of Tibetan life was decreased.
(E) none of the above

19. Which of the following most likely best describes Tibetan "tea"?
(A) a pale brown, clear, broth-like drink
(B) a dark brown tea drink, carefully strained
(C) a nutritious mixture of tea leaves and rancid yak butter
(D) a high caffeine drink
(E) a green-tinted drink similar to Chinese basket-fried green tea

20. The purpose of the passage is to
(A) describe Tibetan fauna and flora
(B) describe the social organization of typical Tibetan villages
(C) analyze the causes of Tibet's unusual animal and plant populations
(D) analyze the possible causal links between Tibetan ecology and society
(E) probe the mysteries of the sudden appearance of the Himalayas

21. The author's knowledge of Tibet is probably
(A) based on firsthand experience
(B) the result of lifelong study
(C) derived only from books
(D) derived from Chinese sources
(E) limited to geological history

22. In which ways are the ideas of Lattimore and Kawakita totally opposed?
(A) Lattimore forbids change and Kawakita requires it.
(B) Kawakita opposes change and Lattimore favors it.
(C) Lattimore sees polyandry as primitive and Kawakita views it as modern.
(D) Lattimore criticizes polyandry as inefficient, but Kawakita finds it highly efficient.
(E) Their ideas are not totally opposed on any point.

23. According to the passage, which of the following would probably be the most agreeable to Montesquieu?
(A) All regions have different soils and, thus, different cultures.
(B) Some regions with similar climates will have similar cultures.
(C) Cultures in the same area, sharing soil and climate, will be essentially identical.
(D) European cultures are liberated to some degree from determinism.
(E) The plants of a country, by being the food of its people, cause the people to have similar views to one another.

24. The species of fauna and flora remaining in Tibet after the Pleistocene glaciation can properly be called continental because they
(A) are originally found in continental climates
(B) are the only life forms in Tibet, which is as big as a continent
(C) have been found in other parts of the Asian continent
(D) are found in a land mass that used to be a separate continent
(E) cannot be found on islands

25. According to the passage, the spread of animal and plant species from one area to another is
(A) least common when the species involved are those adapted to cold and dry steppe climates
(B) unlikely to be affected by the actions of human beings
(C) correlated with the densities of other non-competing species in the originating area
(D) strongly affected by the geological features of the area
(E) independent of the weather conditions in the originating area

STOP

END OF SECTION. IF YOU HAVE ANY TIME LEFT, GO OVER YOUR WORK IN THIS SECTION ONLY. DO NOT WORK IN ANY OTHER SECTION OF THE TEST.

SECTION II

Time—30 Minutes
20 Questions

Directions: For each of the following questions, select the best of the answer choices and blacken the corresponding space on your answer sheet.
Numbers: All numbers used are real numbers.
Figures: The diagrams and figures that accompany these questions are for the purpose of providing information useful in answering the question. Unless it is stated that a specific figure is not drawn to scale, the diagrams and figures are drawn as accurately as possible. All figures are in a plane unless otherwise indicated.

1. From the time 6:15 P.M. to the time 7:45 P.M. of the same day, the minute hand of a standard clock describes an arc of
(A) 30°
(B) 90°
(C) 180°
(D) 540°
(E) 910°

2. Which of the following fractions is the LEAST?
(A) $\frac{7}{8}$
(B) $\frac{7}{12}$
(C) $\frac{8}{9}$
(D) $\frac{1}{2}$
(E) $\frac{6}{17}$

3. The length of each side of a square is $\frac{3x}{4} + 1$. What is the perimeter of the square?
(A) $x + 1$
(B) $3x + 1$
(C) $3x + 4$
(D) $\frac{9}{16}x^2 + \frac{3}{2}x + 1$
(E) It cannot be determined from the information given.

4. A truck departed from Newton at 11:53 A.M. and arrived in Far City, 240 miles away, at 4:41 P.M. on the same day. What was the approximate average speed of the truck on this trip?
(A) $\frac{5640}{5}$ MPH
(B) $\frac{16}{1200}$ MPH
(C) 50 MPH
(D) $\frac{240}{288}$ MPH
(E) $\frac{1494}{240}$ MPH

5. If m, n, o and p are real numbers, each of the following expressions equals m(nop) EXCEPT
(A) (op)(mn)
(B) ponm
(C) p(onm)
(D) (mp)(no)
(E) (mn)(mo)(mp)

ABCD is a square

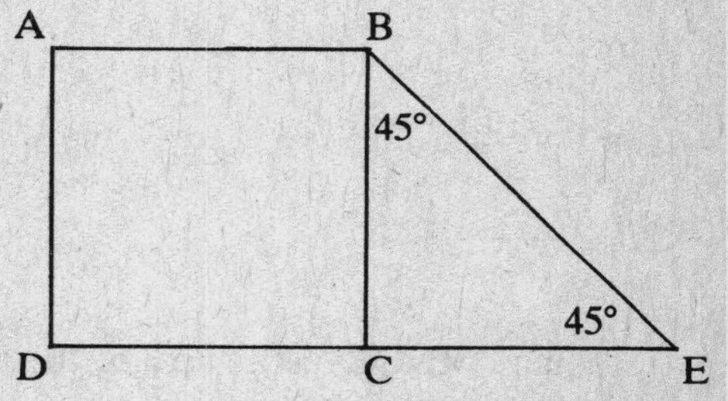

6. If the area of the triangle BCE is 8, what is the area of the square ABCD?
(A) 16
(B) 82
(C) 8
(D) 4
(E) 22

7. The diagonal of the floor of a rectangular closet is $7\frac{1}{2}$ feet. The shorter side of the closet is $4\frac{1}{2}$ feet. What is the area of the closet in square feet?
(A) 37
(B) 27
(C) $\frac{54}{4}$
(D) $\frac{21}{4}$
(E) 5

8. If the ratio of women to men in a meeting is 4 to 1, what percent of the persons in the meeting are men?
(A) 20%
(B) 25%

(C) $33\frac{1}{3}\%$
(D) 80%
(E) 100%

9. Which of the following fractions expressed in the form $\frac{P}{Q}$ is most nearly approximated by the decimal .PQ, where P is the tenths' digit and Q is the hundredths' digit?
(A) $\frac{1}{8}$
(B) $\frac{2}{9}$
(C) $\frac{3}{4}$
(D) $\frac{4}{5}$
(E) $\frac{8}{9}$

10. If b books can be purchased for d dollars, how many books can be purchased for m dollars?
(A) $\frac{bm}{d}$
(B) bdm
(C) $\frac{d}{bm}$
(D) $\frac{b + m}{d}$
(E) $\frac{b - m}{d}$

11. If a square MNOP has an area of 16, then its perimeter is
(A) 4
(B) 8
(C) 16
(D) 32
(E) 64

12. John has more money than Mary but less than Bill. If the amounts held by John, Mary and Bill are x, y, and z, respectively, which of the following is true?
(A) $z < x < y$
(B) $x < z < y$
(C) $y < x < z$
(D) $y < z < x$
(E) $x < y < z$

13. If $x = 3$ and $(x - y)^2 = 4$, then y could be
(A) −5
(B) −1
(C) 0
(D) 5
(E) 9

14. 10% of 360 is how much more than 5% of 360?
(A) 5
(B) 9
(C) 18
(D) 36
(E) 48

15. If $x^2 + 3x + 10 = 1 + x^2$, then $x^2 =$
(A) 0
(B) 1
(C) 4
(D) 7
(E) 9

16. Which of the following must be true?

I. Any of two lines which are parallel to a third line are also parallel to each other.
II. Any two planes which are parallel to a third plane are parallel to each other.
III. Any two lines which are parallel to the same plane are parallel to each other.

(A) I only
(B) II only
(C) I and II only
(D) II and III only
(E) I, II, and III

17. An item costs 90% of its original price. If 90¢ is added to the discount price, the cost of the item will be equal to its original price. What is the original price of the item?
(A) \$.09
(B) \$.90
(C) \$9.00
(D) \$9.90
(E) \$9.99

18. In the figure below, the coordinates of the vertices A and B are (2,0) and (0,2), respectively. What is the area of the square ABCD?
(A) 2
(B) 4
(C) $4\sqrt{2}$
(D) 8
(E) $8\sqrt{2}$

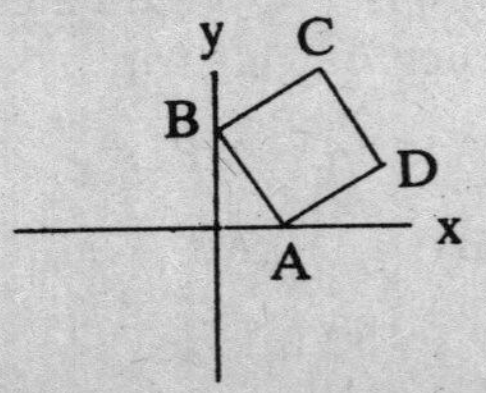

19. If mx + ny = 12my, and my ≠ 0, then $\frac{x}{y} + \frac{n}{m} =$
    (A) 12
    (B) 12 mn
    (C) 12 m + 12y
    (D) 0
    (E) mx + ny

20. In circle 0 shown to the right, MN > NO. All of the following must be true EXCEPT
    (A) MN < 2 MO
    (B) x > y
    (C) z = y
    (D) x = y + z
    (E) x > 60°

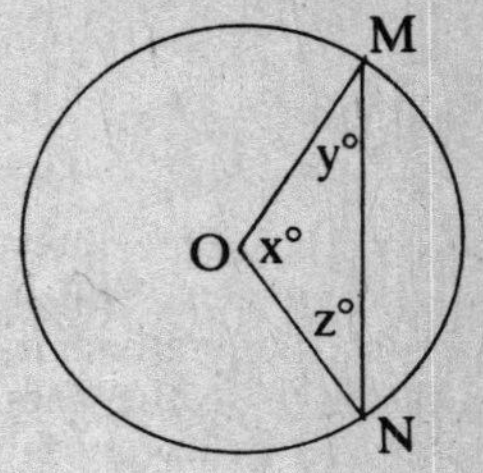

STOP

END OF SECTION. IF YOU HAVE ANY TIME LEFT, GO OVER YOUR WORK IN THIS SECTION ONLY. DO NOT WORK IN ANY OTHER SECTION OF THE TEST.

SECTION III

Time—30 Minutes
25 Questions

Directions: Each question below is followed by two numbered facts. You are to determine whether the data given in the statements is sufficient for answering the question. Use the data given, plus your knowledge of math and everyday facts, to choose between the five possible answers.

(A) if statement 1 alone is sufficient to answer the question, but statement 2 alone is not sufficient
(B) if statement 2 alone is sufficient to answer the question, but statement 1 alone is not sufficient
(C) if both statements together are needed to answer the question, but niether statement alone is sufficient
(D) if either statement by itself is sufficient to answer the question asked
(E) if not enough facts are given to answer the question

1. If the area of a rectangle is 20, what is its perimeter?
   (1) The length of the rectangle is 5.
   (2) The width of the rectangle is 1 unit less than its length.

2. Is the average of ten integers greater than 10?
   (1) Half of the integers are greater than 10.
   (2) Half of the integers are less than 10.

3. Is $A > B$?
   (1) $AX > BX$
   (2) $X < 0$

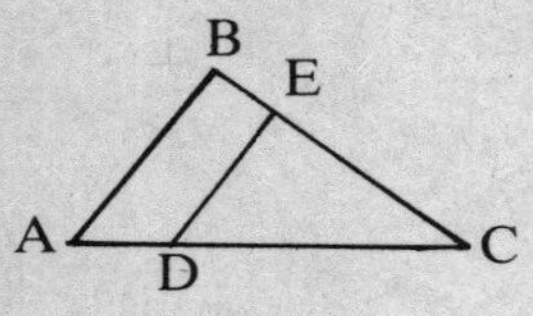

4. Is AB parallel to DE?
   (1) $DC = EC$
   (2) $\angle EDC = \angle BAC$

5. What is the length of the diagonal of a certain rectangle?
   (1) The area of the rectangle is 16.
   (2) The perimeter of the rectangle is 16.

6. If Tim weighs X, where X is a whole number, what is Tim's weight?
   (1) If Tim gains 6 pounds, he will weigh less than 186 pounds.
   (2) If Tim gains 8 pounds, he will weigh more than 186 pounds.

7. Is the integer T divisible by 15?
   (1) The sum of the digits of T equals 15.
   (2) The units digit of T is a 3.

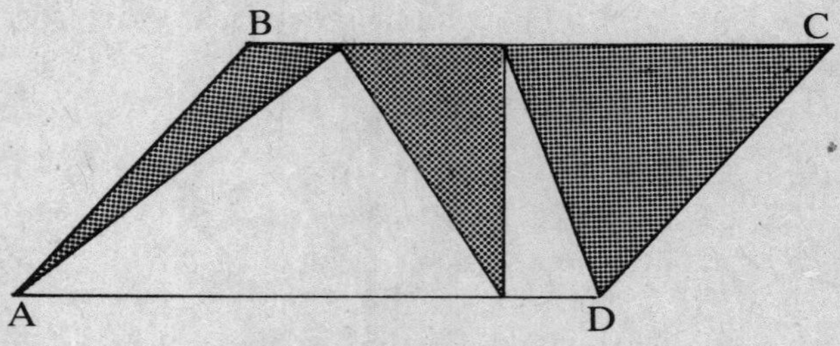

8. What is the area of the shaded region above?
   (1) ABCD is a parallelogram.
   (2) The area of ABCD is 46.

9. What is the length of the diagonal of a cube?
   (1) The sides of the cube have length 1.
   (2) The diagonals of the faces of the cube have length $\sqrt{2}$.

10. How long did a round trip take?
    (1) The outward journey took 1 hour longer than the return journey.
    (2) The return journey was 75 miles.

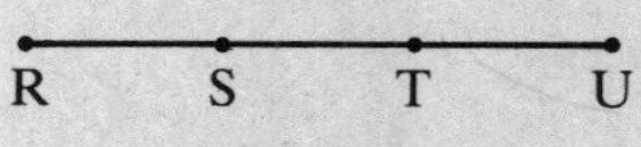

11. Points R, S, T and U are on line RU as shown. Which is larger, TU or ST?
    (1) RU is 15 units long.
    (2) Points S and T trisect line segment RU.

12. John, Peter and Paul together have ten marbles. If each has at least one marble, how many marbles does each boy have?
    (1) John has 5 more than Paul.
    (2) Peter has half as many as John.

13. Is A + B > B?
    (1) $B > 0$
    (2) $A < 0$

14. Is x positive?
    (1) $x^2 - 1 = 0$
    (2) $x^3 + 1 = 0$

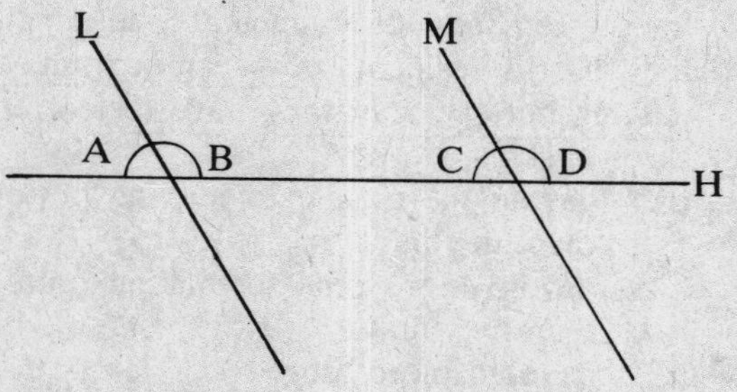

15. L, M and H are straight lines with L ∥ M. Is ∠B equal to 90°?
    (1) ∠A = 55°
    (2) ∠D > 90°

16. A rectangle is 40 inches long. What is its area?
    (1) Its perimeter is 140 inches.
    (2) The length of the diagonal is 50 inches.

17. What are the values of A and B?
    (1) $2A - 3B = 17$
    (2) $6B - 4A = -34$

18. There are 150 bushels to unload from a truck. Joe and Tom, working together take $\frac{1}{2}$ hour to unload the truck. How long should it take Tom working by himself to unload the truck?
    (1) Joe unloads twice as many bushels as Tom.
    (2) Joe would take 45 minutes by himself to unload it.

19. Is A > B?
    (1) A is positive.
    (2) $(A + B)^2$ is positive.

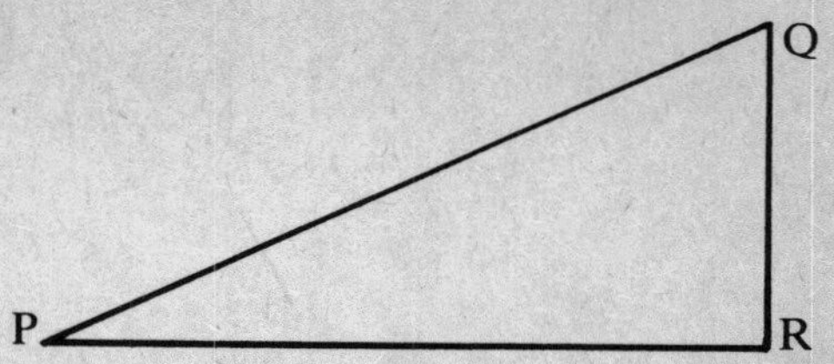

20. Is triangle PQR a right triangle?
    (1) ∠P < ∠Q
    (2) ∠P + ∠Q = ∠R

21. Is K greater than L?
    (1) K is greater than 2L.
    (2) The difference K − L is positive.

22. A piece of wood 7 feet long is cut into three pieces. What is the length of each of the pieces?
    (1) The length of the longest piece is equal to the sum of the lengths of the other two pieces.
    (2) The length of the shortest piece is 6 inches.

23. Is A greater than B?
    (1) $A + B > 2A$
    (2) $A^2 > B^2$

24. N is an integer. Is N divisible by 12?
    (1) N is divisible by 6.
    (2) N is divisible by 2.

25. Is X a whole number?
    (1) 2X is even.
    (2) 3X is odd.

STOP

END OF SECTION. IF YOU HAVE ANY TIME LEFT, GO OVER YOUR WORK IN THIS SECTION ONLY. DO NOT WORK IN ANY OTHER SECTION OF THE TEST.

SECTION IV

Time—30 Minutes
25 Questions

Directions: In each problem below, either part or all of the sentence is underlined. The sentence is followed by five ways of writing the underlined part. Answer choice (A) repeats the original; the other answer choices vary. If you think that the original phrasing is the best, choose (A). If you think one of the other answer choices is the best, select that choice.

This section tests the ability to recognize correct and effective expression. Follow the requirements of Standard Written English: grammar, choice of words, and sentence construction. Choose the answer which results in the clearest, most exact sentence, but do not change the meaning of the original sentence.

1. If they would have found the receipt by mid-April, they would have paid less tax.
   (A) If they would have found the receipt by mid-April, they would have paid less tax.
   (B) If they would have found the receipt by mid-April, they had paid less tax.
   (C) If they had found the receipt by mid-April, they would have paid fewer tax.
   (D) If they had found the receipt by mid-April, they would have paid less tax.
   (E) If they find the receipt by mid-April, they will pay less tax.

2. The libraries with the Corinthian columns that contain almost a million volumes opened last evening.
   (A) The libraries with the Corinthian columns that contain almost a million volumes
   (B) The libraries with the Corinthian columns that contained almost a million volumes
   (C) The libraries with the Corinthian columns that contains almost a million volumes
   (D) The libraries with the Corinthian columns and which contain almost a million volumes
   (E) The libraries which contain almost a million volumes with the Corinthian columns

3. The Russian scientists who have been studying the remnants of an ancient Siberian city feel that its residents devote more time to making pottery than they have to learning survival skills.
   (A) devote more time to making pottery than they have to
   (B) devote more time to making pottery than they do to
   (C) devoted more time to making pottery than they did to
   (D) devote more time to the making of their pottery than to
   (E) devoted more time to making pottery than they do to

4. The leader of the Neanderthal tribe rarely hunted for food, and because of it was never acknowledged as a great hunter.
   (A) The leader of the Neanderthal tribe rarely hunted for food, and because of it
   (B) Because the leader of the Neanderthal tribe rarely hunted for food, he
   (C) In that he rarely hunted for food, the leader of the Neanderthal tribe was
   (D) Rarely hunting for food was the reason that the leader of the Neanderthal tribe
   (E) Hunts were rare, and because of this the leader of the Neanderthal tribe

5. The physicians explained that had the patient known the warning signs of cancer, he would have come in earlier for a check-up.
   (A) had the patient known the warning signs of cancer, he would have come in earlier
   (B) if the patient had known the warning signs of cancer, he would have come in earlier
   (C) if the patient knew the warning signs of cancer, he would have come in earlier

(D) had the patient known the warning signs of cancer, he would come in earlier
(E) if the patient would have known the warning signs of cancer, he would have come in earlier

6. The general's hopes for success in battle were dashed as a result of the willingness of the native population to cooperate with the enemy.
(A) as a result of the willingness of the native population to cooperate with the enemy.
(B) because the native population was willing to cooperate with the enemy.
(C) insofar as the native population was willing to cooperate with the enemy.
(D) because the native population would have a willingness to cooperate with enemy.
(E) by the native population's apparent willingness to cooperate with the enemy.

7. The marines who landed on the beaches of Iwo Jima effected the rescue of several prisoners of war whose assault took the enemy by surprise.
(A) The marines who landed on the beaches at Iwo Jima effected the rescue of several prisoners of war whose assault took the enemy by surprise.
(B) The marines effected the rescue of several prisoners of war who had landed on the beaches at Iwo Jima and whose assult had taken the enemy by surprise.
(C) The marines who landed on the beaches at Iwo Jima effected the rescue of several prisoners of war whose assault had taken the enemy by surprise.
(D) The marines who landed on the beaches at Iwo Jima affected the rescue of several prisoners of war whose assault had taken the enemy by surprise.
(E) The marines who landed on the beaches at Iwo Jima, and whose assault took the enemy by surprise, effected the rescue of several prisoners of war.

8. Unafraid of neither lightning nor thunder during a storm, Mr. Jones enjoyed walking in the park during heavy downpours.
(A) Unafraid of neither lightning nor thunder
(B) Afraid of both lightning and thunder
(C) Unafraid of neither lightning or thunder
(D) Unafraid of either lightning or thunder
(E) Afraid of either lightning or thunder

9. Should we be told that our recommendations pertinent to the kind of use made of our vehicles have been accepted, we will gladly cooperate with the ultimate plan.
(A) Should we be told that our recommendations pertinent to the kind of use made of our vehicles have been accepted, we will
(B) If we are told that recommendations about use of our vehicles has been accepted, we will
(C) Should we be told that our recommendations for the use of our vehicles have been accepted, we will
(D) Our being told of the acceptance of our recommendations pertinent to use made of our vehicles should cause us to
(E) Our being told of all recommendations about the use of our vehicles being accepted will cause us to

10. Authors of the seventeenth century used alliteration to both refine their writing and increase a listener's pleasure.
(A) Authors of the seventeenth century used alliteration to both refine their writing and increase
(B) Authors of the seventeenth century utilized alliteration both to refine their writing and to increase
(C) Seventeenth-century authors utilized alliteration both to refine their writing and to increase
(D) Seventeenth-century authors used alliteration both to refine their writing and to increase
(E) Seventeenth-century authors used alliteration to refine their writing, and also to increase

11. Married women raising young children do not respond to social stresses as poorly as unmarried women do.
(A) as poorly as unmarried women do.
(B) as much as unmarried women do
(C) as poorly as unmarried women.
(D) as much as unmarried women have.
(E) as well as unmarried women.

12. Your incessant meddling in my affairs, your obnoxious ridiculing of my suggestions and sudden departure prevented our conference from yielding significant results.
(A) and sudden departure prevented
(B) and your suddenness of departure prevented
(C) and your sudden departing prevented
(D) and your sudden departing caused the prevention of
(E) plus your sudden departure prevented

13. Breeding and education establishes the rules of behavior for any person, as does occupation and income.
(A) establishes the rules of behavior for any person, as does
(B) establish the rules of behavior for any person, as does
(C) establish the rules of behavior for any person, and so does
(D) establish the rules of behavior for any person, as do
(E) establishes the rules of behavior for any person, and so does

14. If science can find a cure for cancer, if the nuclear arms race can be stopped, and if people can work together to resolve mutual differences are the topics around which the seminar has been planned.
(A) If science can find a cure for cancer, if the nuclear arms race can be stopped, and if people can work together to resolve mutual differences are
(B) Whether science can find a cure for cancer, whether the nuclear arms race can be stopped, and whether people can work together to resolve mutual differences are
(C) If science can find a cure for cancer, if the nuclear arms race can be stopped, and if people can work together to resolve mutual differences is
(D) Whether science can find a cure for cancer, whether the nuclear arms race can be stopped, and whether people can work together toward the resolution of mutual differences
(E) That science can find a cure for cancer, that the nuclear arms race can be stopped, and that people can work together to resolve mutual differences is

15. In the Renaissance, painters were so impressed with Da Vinci that they ignored their own training and designated as a masterpiece anything he painted.
(A) were so impressed with Da Vinci that they ignored
(B) were impressed with Da Vinci to such an extent that they were to ignore
(C) were so impressed with Da Vinci as to ignore
(D) were so impressed with Da Vinci that they had to ignore
(E) were as impressed with Da Vinci as to ignore

16. Most members of the trade union rejected the mayor's demand that they return to work.
(A) that they return to work.
(B) that the members return to work.
(C) for them to return to work.
(D) that they would return to work.
(E) that they ought to return to work.

17. The players were often punished by the referee's lack of alertness who penalized all those who were involved in fighting, regardless of who had instigated it.
(A) The players were often punished by the referee's lack of alertness who penalized
(B) The referee's lack of alertness often caused him to penalize
(C) The players were punished by the lack of alertness of the referee who penalized often
(D) Lacking alertness, the referee's choice was to penalize often
(E) His lack of alertness to brutality often caused the referee to penalize

18. The New York City Police Department was not only responsible for the maintenance of order in the metropolitan area but also for rebuilding the bonds among the various ethnic groups.
   (A) not only responsible for the maintenance of order in the metropolitan area but also for rebuilding the bonds
   (B) responsible not only for maintaining order in the metropolitan area but also for rebuilding the bonds
   (C) responsible not only for the maintenance of order in the metropolitan area and also for rebuilding
   (D) responsible not only for the maintenance of order in the metropolitan area and also for the rebuilding of bonds
   (E) not only responsible for maintaining order in the metropolitan area but also for rebuilding the bonds

19. In comparison with the literature created by the ancient Greeks, today's Greeks have written nothing worth describing.
   (A) In comparison with the literature created by the ancient Greeks, today's Greeks have written nothing worth describing.
   (B) In comparison with the literature created by the ancient Greeks, the literature of today's Greeks are containing nothing worth describing.
   (C) Compared to that of the ancient Greeks, today's Greeks have written nothing worth describing.
   (D) Compared to that of the ancient Greeks, the literature of today's Greeks is not worth describing.
   (E) Compared to the ancient Greek's literature, today's Greeks have written nothing worth describing.

20. Steve, along with his oldest brothers, are going to make a large real estate investment.
   (A) Steve, along with his oldest brothers, are
   (B) Steve, along with his oldest brothers, is
   (C) Steve, in addition to his oldest brothers, are
   (D) Steve, as well as his oldest brothers, are
   (E) Steve and his oldest brothers is

21. During the war, when it looked as if the German army was going to cross into France, English mercenaries joined the French to resist the assault.
   (A) it looked as if the German army was going to cross
   (B) it looked like the German army was going to cross
   (C) it looked like the German army would have crossed
   (D) appearances were that the German army would be crossing
   (E) it appeared that the German army would cross

22. In stating the argument that President Reagan does not care about the plight of the poor, a prominent Democrat inferred that Republicans have never been concerned about them.
   (A) a prominent Democrat inferred that Republicans have never been concerned about them.
   (B) a prominent Democrat inferred that Republicans have never been concerned about the poor.
   (C) a prominent Democrat implied that Republicans have never been concerned about them.
   (D) a prominent Democrat inferred that Republicans have never been concerned about it.
   (E) a prominent Democrat implied that Republicans have never been concerned about it.

23. Although both are rich and famous, Bill and his twin brother differ considerably in temperament; the ambition and sincerity of both are also different.
   (A) Although both are rich and famous, Bill and his twin brother differ considerably in temperament; the ambition and sincerity of both are also different.
   (B) Although both are rich and famous, Bill and his twin brother differ in temperament, ambition, and in how sincere they are.

(C) Although both are rich and famous, the temperament of Bill differs from that of his twin brother; the ambition and sincerity of both are also different.
(D) Although both are rich and famous, Bill and his twin brother differ in temperament, ambition, and sincerity.
(E) Although both rich and famous, the temperament, ambition and sincerity of Bill are different from those of his twin brother.

24. To insist on an oath of allegiance to the government is violating a worker's basic constitutional rights.
(A) To insist on an oath of allegiance to the government is violating a
(B) To insist on an oath of allegiance to the government is to violate a
(C) Insisting on an oath of allegiance to the government is to violate a
(D) Insisting on an oath of allegiance to the government amounts to a violation of a
(E) To insist on an oath to demonstrate loyalty to the government is violating a

25. Excessive exposure to microwave radiation in rats not only damages hearing but also decreases visual acuity as well, thereby reducing the survival potential of the affected organisms.
(A) but also decreases visual acuity as well, thereby reducing
(B) but also decreases visual acuity, thereby reducing
(C) but also decreases visual acuity as well, which reduces
(D) but decreases visual acuity, thereby reducing
(E) but decreases visual acuity, which reduces

STOP

END OF SECTION. IF YOU HAVE ANY TIME LEFT, GO OVER YOUR WORK IN THIS SECTION ONLY. DO NOT WORK IN ANY OTHER SECTION OF THE TEST.

Section V

Time: 30 Minutes
20 Questions

Directions: For each of the following questions, select the best of the answer choices and blacken the corresponding space on your answer sheet.
Numbers: All numbers used are real numbers.
Figures: The diagrams and figures that accompany these questions are for the purpose of providing information useful in answering the questions. Unless it is stated that a specific figure is not drawn to scale, the diagrams and figures are drawn as accurately as possible. All figures are in a plane unless otherwise indicated.

1. If x = 3 and y = 2, then 2x + 3y =
   (A) 5
   (B) 10
   (C) 12
   (D) 14
   (E) 15

2. If the profit on an item is $4 and the sum of the cost and the profit is $20, what is cost of the item.
   (A) $24
   (B) $20
   (C) $16
   (D) $12
   (E) Cannot be determined from the information given.

3. In 1950, the number of students enrolled at a college was 500. In 1970, the number of students enrolled at the college was $2\frac{1}{2}$ times as great as that in 1950. What was the number of students enrolled at the college in 1970?
   (A) 1250
   (B) 1000
   (C) 1750
   (D) 500
   (E) 250

4. If n is an integer between 0 and 100, then any of the following could be 3n + 3 EXCEPT
   (A) 300
   (B) 297
   (C) 208
   (D) 63
   (E) 6

5. A figure that can be folded over along a straight line so that the result is two equal halves which are then lying on top of one another with no overlap is said to have a line of symmetry. Which of the following figures has only one line of symmetry?
   (A) square
   (B) circle
   (C) equilateral triangle
   (D) isosceles triangle
   (E) rectangle

6. A laborer is paid $8 per hour for an 8-hour day and $1\frac{1}{2}$ times that rate for each hour in excess of 8 hours in a single day. If the laborer received $80 for a single day's work, how long did he work on that day?
   (A) 6 hr. 40 min.
   (B) 9 hr. 20 min.
   (C) 9 hr. 30 min.
   (D) 9 hr. 40 min.
   (E) 10 hr.

7. The vertex of the square MNOP is located at the center of circle O. If arc NP is 4π units long, then the perimeter of the square MNOP is

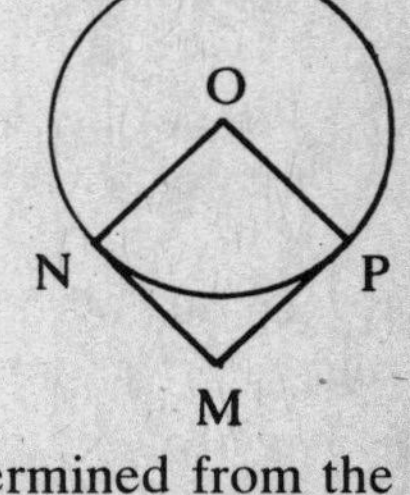

   (A) 32
   (B) 32π
   (C) 64
   (D) 64π
   (E) cannot be determined from the information given

8. How many minutes will it take to completely fill a water tank with a capacity of 3750 cubic feet if the water is being pumped into the tank at the rate of 800 cubic feet per minute and is being drained out of the tank at the rate of 300 cubic feet per minute?
   (A) 3 min. 36 sec.
   (B) 6 minutes
   (C) 7 min. 30 sec.
   (D) 8 minutes
   (E) 1875 minutes

9. Paul is standing 180 yards due north of point P. Franny is standing 240 yards due west of point P. What is the shortest distance between Franny and Paul?
(A) 60 yards
(B) 300 yards
(C) 420 yards
(D) 900 yards
(E) 9000 yards

10. If a rectangle has an area of $81x^2$ and a length of $27x$, then what is its width?
(A) $3x$
(B) $9x$
(C) $3x^2$
(D) $9x^2$
(E) $2128x^3$

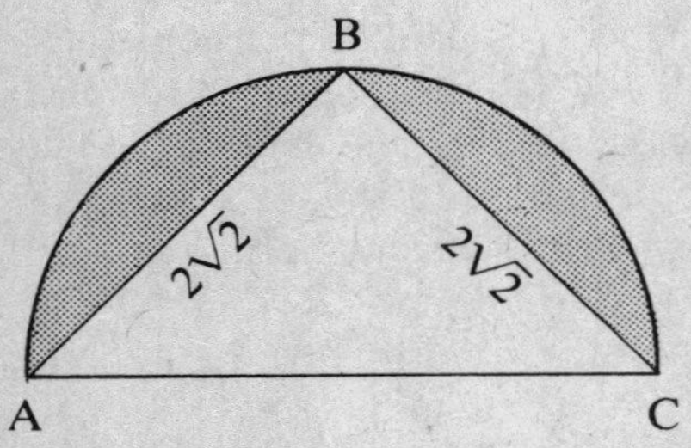

11. Triangle ABC is inscribed in a semicircle. What is the area of the shaded region above?
(A) $32\pi - 4$
(B) $64\pi - 8$
(C) $128\pi - 4$
(D) $256\pi - 4$
(E) Cannot be determined from the information given.

12. The * of any number is defined as the result obtained by adding the square of the number to twice the number. What number is the * of 12?
(A) 12
(B) 168
(C) 1728
(D) 1752
(E) 2024

13. A motorist travels 120 miles to his destination at an average speed of 60 miles per hour and returns to his starting point at an average speed of 40 miles per hour. His average speed for the entire trip is
(A) 53 miles per hour
(B) 50 miles per hour
(C) 48 miles per hour
(D) 45 miles per hour
(E) 52 miles per hour

14. In the figure, AB = BC and angles BAD and BCD are right angles. Which one of the following conclusions may be drawn?

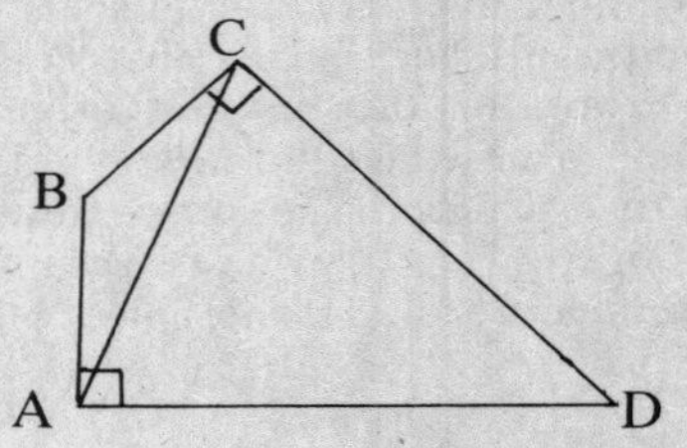

(A) angle BCA = angle CAD
(B) angle B is greater than angle D
(C) AC = CD
(D) AD = CD
(E) BC is shorter than CD

15. A merchant sells a radio for $80, thereby making a profit of 25% of the cost. What is the ratio of cost to selling price?
(A) $\frac{4}{5}$
(B) $\frac{3}{4}$
(C) $\frac{5}{6}$
(D) $\frac{2}{3}$
(E) $\frac{3}{5}$

16. How many degrees are between the hands of a clock at 3:40?
(A) 150°
(B) 140°
(C) 130°
(D) 125°
(E) 120°

17. Two fences in a field meet at an angle of 120°. A cow is tethered at their intersection with a 15-foot rope, as shown in the figure. Over how many square feet may the cow graze?
(A) 50π
(B) 75π
(C) 80π
(D) 85π
(E) 90π

18. If $\frac{17}{10}y = 0.51$, then y =
    (A) 3
    (B) 1.3
    (C) 1.2
    (D) .3
    (E) .03

19. A junior class of 50 girls and 70 boys sponsored a dance. If 40% of the girls and 50% of the boys attended the dance, approximately what percent attended?
    (A) 40
    (B) 42
    (C) 44
    (D) 46
    (E) 48

20. In the same amount of time a new production assembly robot can assemble 8 times as many transmissions as an old assembly line. If the new robot can assemble x transmissions per hour, how many transmissions can the new robot and the old assembly line produce together in five days of round-the-clock production?
    (A) $\frac{45x}{8}$
    (B) 15x
    (C) $\frac{135x}{8}$
    (D) 135x
    (E) 1080x

STOP

END OF SECTION. IF YOU HAVE ANY TIME LEFT GO OVER YOUR WORK IN THIS SECTION ONLY. DO NOT WORK IN ANY OTHER SECTION OF THE TEST.

Section VI

Time—30 Minutes
35 Questions

Directions: This section consists of reading selections which detail business situations. After each selection, you will be asked to classify certain of the facts presented in the passage on the basis of their importance.

Barbara Kellin operates a one-woman typing service from her apartment on the Upper West Side of New York City. She does an active commerce with scores of the writers, graduate students, and miscellaneous professionals who inhabit her neighborhood. In January 1980, Barbara signed a contract with a consortium of social scientists who are professional grantsmen and grantswomen—that is, they make a good living through a succession of government and private foundation research awards. Barbara agreed to give up her other clients for the duration of the contract (one year) and to devote her work time exclusively to the never-ending typing requirements of the consortium. In exchange for this sacrifice, Barbara was guaranteed $500 weekly and was paid double her normal rate of $2.25 per page of typescript. The one difficulty facing Barbara was that, as part of her contract, she had been constrained to agree to finish a massive 15,000-page series of reports within a year of the contract date, that is, by January 31, 1981, at the latest. Should she fail to fulfill this provision of the agreement, she was subject to considerable financial penalties.

To comply with the agreement, Barbara calculated that she had to spend half of each work day on the report. In addition, it was imperative that she obtain an Electroextraordinaire typewriter, with which she could type at the rate of 150 words per minute. By January 15, 1980, Barbara had located, through word of mouth, local classified advertisement, and a series of telephone calls to dealers, five Electroextraordinaire machines for sale in the city: three second-hand and two new models. Awed by the astronomical cost of the typewriters—this would be the biggest investment of her life, so far—and by the urgency and importance of the decision, she called her three best friends to her apartment for a brainstorming session, the result of which would be a decision as to which machine to purchase.

Barbara: "In order for me to comply with the provisions of the contract I have signed, I need to have an Electroextraordinaire in good working order here in my apartment by January 31, about two weeks from today. Should I fail to finish the work for which I must have this typewriter, I'll have to pay a really heavy penalty. What I hope you can help me do is to select from these five the particular machine that is both the most economical and the most reliable. My schedule is so tight that any breakdowns in the machine would jeopardize it. By the way, I have assurances from several banks that I can obtain any loan money necessary to pay for my machine quite easily."

Susan Webb: "Well, old girl, I think you should consider one of the used machines you've located. Runyan's, down the street, has a used model, you mentioned, which they're willing to repair at their own expense. We should keep in mind, though, that they just may not be able to get the parts they need to put it in working order by January 31."

Bob Sankins: "Hey, Remp Corporation downtown has a used model for sale, too, as Barbara told us earlier. Why not try it?"

Will Marsh: "Well, the price on that one sure is right. But it's so old I have my doubts it would hold up as long as Barbara needs it to. Let's face it, buying Remp's machine would be taking a major risk. Probably she shouldn't do that. The third used machine Barbara mentioned is only five months old and should be good without major repairs at least through next January 31."

Barbara: "Yes, but—would you believe it?—that one is missing a single part which the owner, Mr. Graves, told me frankly he may not receive until mid-February. Ordering Graves' typewriter seems like a real gamble."

Susan: "Let's get back to Remp's typewriter. It *is* available now. Barbara could buy it, then use the Graves machine as soon as it's ready. I know that what I'm suggesting is expensive, but at least Barb would be reasonably sure of having a machine that's in good repair for the life of her contract. Also, she could sell the Remp model at the end of the project."

Barbara: "There must be a cheaper way to go. If

your plan were the one I followed, I'd be paying for two machines and have to pay transportation costs for both. You may not realize how expensive transporting the typewriter, or typewriters, is going to be. How about the two new models? They're both available right now, you know."

Will: "You sure would save on repair costs with a new model. There would be no reliability problem, and I understand that the very newest machines are slightly faster than the used models we're considering."

Bob: "The machine that Typo Corporation has for sale is the less expensive of the two new ones, and transportation costs are quite reasonable with Typo. But the other model, sold by Fastype, has been specially programmed so that its automatic correction features save about 20% in time over the Typo machine."

Barbara: "I have to decide about this tonight. Let's draw up a chart, and I'll make up my mind on the basis of the information it features."

ELECTROEXTRAORDINARE MODEL PROS AND CONS

	Sale Price	Repairs	Transportation	Availability
Runyan's model	$3000	$0	$300	?
Remp's model	$2000	?	$300	Immediate
Graves' model	$4000	?	$200	?
Typo's model	$7500	$0	$100	Immediate
Fastype's model	$10,200	$0	$340	Immediate

Directions: Based on your analysis of the previous passage, classify each of the following items in one of five categories. Mark:

(A) if the item is a *Major Objective* in making the decision; that is, one of the outcomes or results sought by the decision-maker.

(B) if the item is a *Major Factor* in making the decision; that is, a consideration, explicitly mentioned in the passage, that is basic in determining the decision.

(C) if the item is a *Minor Factor* in making the decision; that is, a secondary consideration that affects the criteria tangentially, relating to a Major Factor rather than to an Objective.

(D) if the item is a *Major Assumption* in making the decision; that is, a supposition or projection made by the decision-maker before weighing the variables.

(E) if the item is an *Unimportant Issue* in making the decision; that is, a factor that is insignificant or not immediately relevant to the situation.

1. Age of the typewriters under consideration.

2. Overall cost of the model to be purchased.

3. Special programming that is available on the Fastype model.

4. Availability of credit to purchase a typewriter.

5. Higher repair costs for used typewriters under consideration.

6. Possibility of obtaining each typewriter in time for Barbara to meet her contractual obligations.

7. Acquisition of a reliable Electroextraordinaire.

8. Uncertainty of Runyan's typewriter being in working order by January 31.

9. Preservation of Barbara's reputation with her normal, non-consortium clientele.

10. Necessity of obtaining Electroextraordinaire in order to complete contracted job satisfactorily.

11. Availability, by January 31, of a typewriter being considered.

12. Choosing the most economical Electroextraordinare.

13. Provisions of Barbara's contract with the consortium providing for late penalties.

14. Reliability of the typewriters under consideration.

15. Attractiveness of a typewriter considered for purchase.

16. Insuring that a suitable Electroextraordinaire is available by January 31.

17. Number of years Barbara has known Will.

18. Transportation cost of the Graves model.

Wells Company is a large publisher of school textbooks. It has a 15% share of the United States market, as well as a successful operation exporting to other English-speaking countries. Last year its net earnings were $21 million. Until now Wells has been able to maintain a satisfactory growth rate by adding texts on new subjects to their line. At present, however, all school subject areas seem to be adequately represented in the Wells catalogue, and the Wells Board of Directors has approved the purchase of a number of smaller, but prosperous and established, businesses in an effort to preserve Wells' current rate of profit increase and to lessen its dependence on a single product.

Board member Marvin Courtney proposed that one of Wells' new acquisitions be a company publishing romance novels. However, he urged that a well-established company with significant readership should be chosen, since Wells had no familiarity with this new market. Courtney argued that the sales of any such enterprise could be increased if Wells' staff editors and illustrators reworked already accepted romance manuscripts, turning out artistically and stylistically polished products. The board fully endorsed Courtney's program.

Two weeks later, the board met to decide which of three publishing firms suggested for purchase should be acquired. Wells' researchers had studied one company purveying expensive editions, another producing moderately priced paperbacks, and a third marketing inexpensive comic-book-format romances. The board intended to greatly expand whichever company it bought, and to use the new acquisition as a springboard from which to take over, during the next decade, a signficant portion of the romance-novel market.

In considering which business to buy, the board focused on purchase price, prospects for expansion, publisher-name recognition, competition, potential markets, already existing distribution capacity, management efficiency, and employee relations. The board members agreed that a cordial and cooperative attitude on the part of the present owners would be necessary in order to assure a smooth transition. While printing costs would normally be considered in comparing the three operations, Wells had decided to use its own printers to manufacture the romance novels; accordingly, such costs were not taken into account in evaluating the three companies.

First considered was Gilt Edge Productions, which sold leather-bound editions of classic romances to bookstores and, by mail, to individuals. Gilt Edge had a rather large following of well-heeled customers, faced no significant competition, and consistently ranked at the top of the list in name-recognition surveys. Last year, Gilt Edge earned $4 million in profits before taxes on sales of $21 million.

While management efficiency was good, Gilt Edge's authors and leather craftspeople were dissatisfied with their pay and working conditions; it was common knowledge in the industry that Gilt Edge had a "morale problem." In order to enter the romance-novel market on a really large scale, as planned, Wells would need to initiate a $5 million expansion effort right away, to be followed up in the future with additional outlays. Another negative point was that the board was afraid that marketing moderately priced and even inexpensive novels under the Gilt Edge name, a necessary move given their expansion program, would alienate present Gilt Edge customers without drawing in sufficient new readers to replace them. Purchase price of this firm would probably be about $15 million.

Larger than Gilt Edge was Enchanted Heart, Inc., the second company evaluated and a publisher of medium-priced paperback romances. Because of a highly efficient sales program both in the United States and overseas, Enchanted Heart had attained a net profit of $44 million last year, on sales of $108 million. Management was expert at keeping production flowing and at constantly increasing distribution. If Wells bought this firm, only $2 million would be needed for expansion. A few of Enchanted Heart's staff members were so skilled that Wells could use them to write school texts when they were not working on romance novels.

But Enchanted Heart did have some drawbacks. It faced a good deal of competition, and for some reason it always scored low on name-recognition surveys. Although they spent rather lavishly on advertising, management could not seem to improve name-recognition. Finally, there was a labor-relations problem involving the company's sales force.

The last of the three companies under consideration was small but successful. Lovepages, Inc., had $6 million in net profits on $9 million in sales last year. Ranking high in name-recognition surveys, Lovepages produced small comic books with romantic themes. Management had evolved work routines that allowed each artist's talents to be used optimally, and production was streamlined for volume output. Lovepages' distribution system was respected throughout the field. Competition did exist, in the form of Tender Heart, Inc., but it was clear that Lovepages enjoyed the upper hand. There was ample room for expansion. The firm would probably sell for $10 million.

The board voted to make tentative offers to all three of the companies, and to reconvene when responses were available in order to reach a final decision.

Directions: Based on your analysis of the previous passage, classify each of the following items in one of five categories. Mark:

(A) if the item is a *Major Objective* in making the decision; that is, one of the outcomes or results sought by the decision-maker.
(B) if the item is a *Major Factor* in making the decision; that is, a consideration, explicitly mentioned in the passage, that is basic in determining the decision.
(C) if the item is a *Minor Factor* in making the decision; that is, a secondary consideration that affects the criteria tangentially, relating to a Major Factor rather that to an Objective.
(D) if the item is a *Major Assumption* in making the decision; that is, a supposition or projection made by the decision-maker before weighing the variables.
(E) if the item is an *Unimportant Issue* in making the decision; that is, a factor that is insignificant or not immediately relevant to the situation.

19. Maintaining Wells' present profit rate.

20. Labor relations at a publishing firm considered for acquisition by Wells.

21. Quality of the artwork in Wells' school texts.

22. Efficiency of the management of a publishing company under consideration.

23. Wells' $21 million net earnings last year.

24. Gilt Edge's widely recognized name.

25. Current printing costs at a firm under consideration.

26. Competition faced by a firm under consideration.

27. A continuing supply of publishable romance manuscripts for Wells to publish.

28. Continuing demand for romance novels during the next ten years.

29. Publisher-name recognition of the firms being evaluated.

30. Acquisition of a romance-novel publishing company that can be expanded to suit Wells' needs.

31. Expanding into the kind of operations through which Wells can derive profits.

32. Willingness of the ownership of each company considered to sell to Wells.

33. Wells' present advertising budget.

34. Accuracy of the information presented to the board by the researchers.

35. Cooperative attitude of present owners of a firm to be acquired.

STOP

END OF SECTION. IF YOU HAVE ANY TIME LEFT, GO OVER YOUR WORK IN THIS SECTION ONLY. DO NOT WORK IN ANY OTHER SECTION OF THE TEST.

SECTION VII

Time—30 Minutes
20 Questions

Directions: For each of the following questions, select the best of the answer choices and blacken the corresponding space on your answer sheet.
Numbers: All numbers used are real numbers.
Figures: The diagrams and figures that accompany these questions are for the purpose of providing information useful in answering the questions. Unless it is stated that a specific figure is not drawn to scale, the diagrams and figures are drawn as accurately as possible. All figures are in a plane unless otherwise indicated.

1. Into how many line segments, each 2 inches long, can a line segment one and one-half yards long be divided?
   (A) 9
   (b) 18
   (C) 27
   (D) 36
   (E) 48

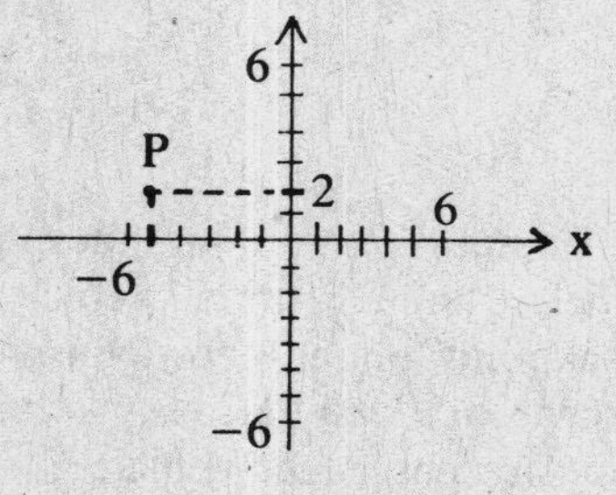

2. In the figure above, the coordinates of point P are
   (A) (−5, −2)
   (B) (−5, 2)
   (C) (−2, 5)
   (D) (2, −5)
   (E) (5, 2)

3. If circle O has a radius of 4, and if P and Q are points on circle O, then the maximum length of arc which could separate P and Q is
   (A) 8π
   (B) 4π
   (C) 4
   (D) 2π
   (E) 2

4. All of the following are prime numbers EXCEPT
   (A) 13
   (B) 17
   (C) 41
   (D) 79
   (E) 91

5. A girl at point X walks 1 mile east, then 2 miles north, then 1 mile east, then 1 mile north, then 1 mile east, then 1 mile north to arrive at point Y. From point Y, what is the shortest distance to point X?
   (A) 7 miles
   (B) 6 miles
   (C) 5 miles
   (D) 2.5 miles
   (E) 1 mile

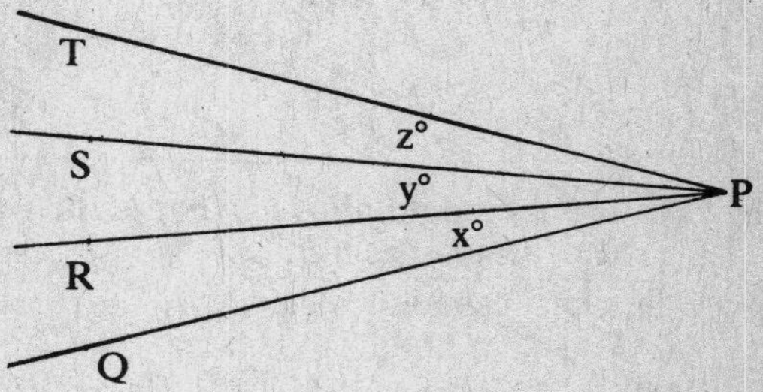

6. In the figure above, the measure ot ∠QPS is equal to the measure of ∠TPR. Which of the following must be true?
   (A) x = y
   (B) y = z
   (C) x = z
   (D) x = y = z
   (E) none of the above

7. Newtown is due north of Oscarville. Highway L runs 31° south of east from Newtown and Highway M runs 44° north of east from Oscarville. If L and M are straight, what is the measure of the acute angle they form at their intersection?
   (A) 105°
   (B) 89°
   (C) 75°

(D) 59°
(E) 46°

8. If a sum of money is divided equally among n children, each child will receive \$60. If another child is added to the group, then when the sum is divided equally among all the children, each child will receive a \$50 share. What is the sum of money?
(A) \$3000
(B) \$300
(C) \$110
(D) \$10
(E) Cannot be determined from the information given.

9. If an item which ordinarily costs \$90 is discounted by 25%, what is the new selling price?
(A) \$22.50
(B) \$25.00
(C) \$45.00
(D) \$67.50
(E) \$112.50

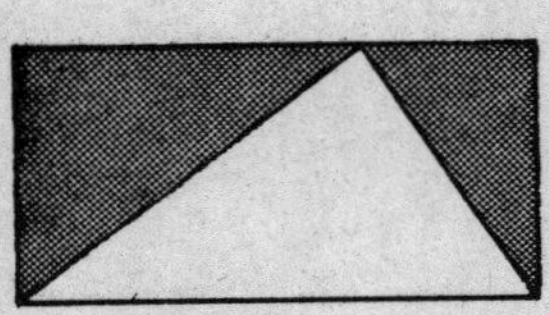

10. In the rectangle above, what is the ratio of $\frac{\text{area of shaded region}}{\text{area of unshaded region}}$?
(A) $\frac{1}{4}$
(B) $\frac{1}{2}$
(C) 1
(D) $\frac{2}{1}$
(E) Cannot be determined from the information given.

11. Earl can stuff advertising circulars into envelopes at the rate of 45 envelopes per minute and Ellen requires a minute and a half to stuff the same number of envelopes. Working together, how long will it take Earl and Ellen to stuff 300 envelopes?
(A) 15 minutes
(B) 4 minutes
(C) 3 minutes 30 seconds
(D) 3 minutes 20 seconds
(E) 2 minutes

DISTRIBUTION	NUMBER IN POPULATION
Having X Having Y	25
Having X Lacking Y	10
Lacking X Having Y	25
Lacking X Lacking Y	40

12. The table above gives the distribution of two genetic characteristics, X and Y, in a population of 100 subjects. What is the ratio of $\frac{\text{number of subjects having X}}{\text{number of subjects having Y}}$?
(A) $\frac{7}{5}$
(B) 1
(C) $\frac{5}{7}$
(D) $\frac{7}{10}$
(E) $\frac{1}{4}$

13. If the ratio of the number of passenger vehicles to all other vehicles passing a checkpoint on a highway is 4 to 1, what percent of the vehicles passing the checkpoint are passenger vehicles?
(A) 20%
(B) 25%
(C) 75%
(D) 80%
(E) 400%

14. If the price of an item is increased by 10% and then decreased by 10%, the net effect on the price of the item is
(A) an increase of 99%
(B) an increase of 1%
(C) no change
(D) a decrease of 1%
(E) a decrease of 11%

15. Lines l_m and l_n lie in the plane x and intersect one another on the perpendicular at point P. Which of the following statements must be true?

    I. A line which lies in plane x and intersects line l_m on the perpendicular at a point other than P does not intersect l_n.
    II. Line segment MN, which does not intersect l_m, does not intersect l_n.
    III. If line l_o lies in plane y and intersects l_m and point P, plane y is perpendicular to plane x.

    (A) I only
    (B) II only
    (C) I and II only
    (D) I and III only
    (E) I, II, and III

16. A student conducts an experiment in biology lab and discovers that the ratio of the number of insects in a given population having characteristic X to the number of insects in the population not having characteristic X is 5:3, and that $\frac{3}{8}$ of the insects having characteristic X are male insects. What proportion of the total insect population are male insects having the characteristic X?
    (A) 1
    (B) $\frac{5}{8}$
    (C) $\frac{6}{13}$
    (D) $\frac{15}{64}$
    (E) $\frac{1}{5}$

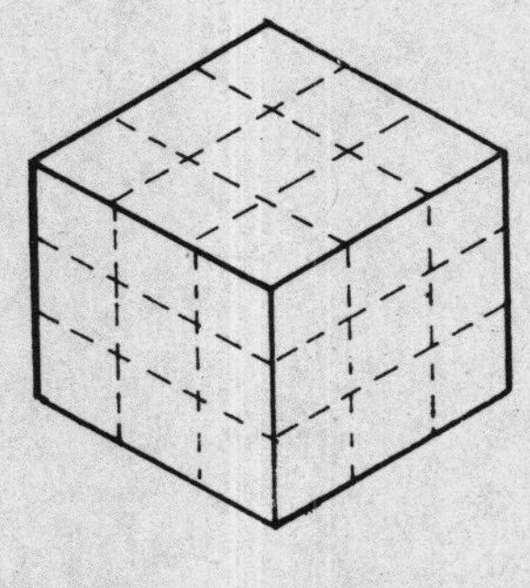

17. The figure above represents a wooden block 3 inches on an edge, all of whose faces are painted black. If the block is cut up along the dotted lines, 27 blocks result, each 1 cubic inch in volume. Of these, how many will have no painted faces?
    (A) 1
    (B) 3
    (C) 4
    (D) 5
    (E) 7

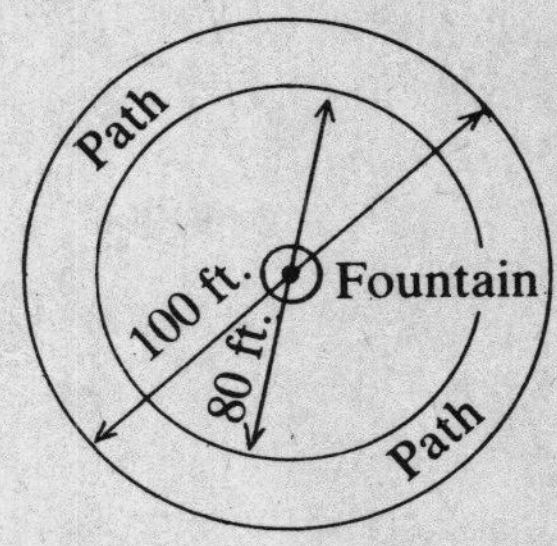

18. The fountain in the above illustration is located exactly at the center of the circular path. How many cubic feet of gravel are required to cover the circular garden path six inches deep with gravel?
    (A) 5400 cu. ft.
    (B) 4500 cu. ft.
    (C) 1250 cu. ft.
    (D) 450 cu. ft.
    (E) 5 cu. ft.

19. A business firm reduces the number of hours its employees work from 40 hours per week to 36 hours per week while continuing to pay the same amount of money. If an employee earned x dollars per hour before the reduction in hours, how much does he earn per hour under the new system?
    (A) $\frac{1}{10}$
    (B) $\frac{x}{9}$
    (C) $\frac{9x}{10}$
    (D) $\frac{10x}{9}$
    (E) 9x

20. A painter has painted one-third of a rectangular wall which is ten feet high. When she has painted another 75 square feet of wall she will be three-quarters finished with the job. What is the length (the horizontal dimension) of the wall?
    (A) 18 feet
    (B) 12 feet
    (C) 10 feet
    (D) 9 feet
    (E) 6 feet

STOP

END OF SECTION. IF YOU HAVE ANY TIME LEFT, GO OVER YOUR WORK IN THIS SECTION ONLY. DO NOT WORK IN ANY OTHER SECTION OF THE TEST.

SECTION VIII

Time—30 Minutes
25 Questions

Directions: In each problem below, either part or all of the sentence is underlined. The sentence is followed by five ways of writing the underlined part. Answer choice (A) repeats the original; the other answer choices vary. If you think that the original phrasing is the best, choose (A). If you think one of the other answer choices is the best, select that choice.

This section tests the ability to recognize correct and effective expression. Follow the requirements of Standard Written English: grammar, choice of words, and sentence construction. Choose the answer which results in the clearest, most exact sentence, but do not change the meaning of the original sentence.

1. It has been said that to be afraid of the dark is being afraid of all those things we cannot comprehend and, therefore, instinctively fear.
   (A) said that to be afraid of the dark is being afraid
   (B) said, that to be afraid of the dark, is being afraid
   (C) said being afraid of the dark is to be afraid
   (D) said that to be afraid of the dark is to be afraid
   (E) said that to be being afraid of the dark is to be being afraid

2. Hurtling through space, Anna saw a shooting star and was transfixed by the rare beauty of this sight.
   (A) Hurtling through space, Anna saw a shooting star and was transfixed by the rare beauty of this sight.
   (B) Anna saw a shooting star and was transfixed by the rare beauty of this sight hurtling through space.
   (C) Ann saw a shooting star hurtling through space and was transfixed by the rare beauty of this sight.
   (D) Anna saw, hurtling through space, a shooting star and was transfixed by the rare beauty of this sight.
   (E) Transfixed by the rare beauty of this sight, Anna saw a shooting star hurtling through space.

3. A study on the therapeutic value of pets as companions for the elderly has shown that cats are more superior than dogs as far as household companions are concerned.
   (A) are more superior than dogs as far as household companions are concerned.
   (B) are superior to dogs as household companions.
   (C) are superior to dogs as far as household companions are concerned.
   (D) are more superior to dogs as household companions.
   (E) are superior household companions than dogs.

4. Tibetan rugs are so expensive because the weaver still pursues his art as they have for centuries, by hand-dyeing all their wool and then knotting each thread individually to achieve a unique pattern for every piece.
   (A) the weaver still pursues his art as they have
   (B) the weaver still pursues his art as he has
   (C) weavers still pursue their art as they have
   (D) weavers still pursue their art as was done
   (E) the weaver still pursues his art as has been done

5. A number of prominent educators question whether the decreasing enrollment of students in colleges and universities is a reversible trend and fear that if the numbers do not go up, many institutions of higher learning will simply go out of business.
   (A) whether the decreasing
   (B) decreased
   (C) that the decreasing
   (D) if the decreasing
   (E) the decreased

6. If I was President, I would call an immediate halt to the development of all nuclear weapons.

(A) If I was President, I would call an immediate halt
(B) If President, I would call an immediate halt
(C) If I was President, I would immediately call a halt
(D) As President, I would call an immediate halt
(E) If I were President, I would call an immediate halt

7. A survey of American business schools concludes that female students are more concerned about job discrimination than male students.
(A) female students are more concerned about job discrimination than male students.
(B) female students are more concerned about job discrimination than male students are.
(C) female students, as opposed to male students, are more concerned about job discrimination.
(D) female students are more concerned about job discrimination than male students are concerned.
(E) female students are more concerned about job discrimination than their male counterparts.

8. The revelation that Shakespeare wrote certain of his plays expressly for Queen Elizabeth I lends credence to the theory that the dark lady of the sonnets was not Shakespeare's mistress nor any other woman the playwright had romanced but, in fact, the Queen herself.
(A) not Shakespeare's mistress nor any other woman the playwright had romanced
(B) neither Shakespeare's mistress or any other woman the playwright had romanced
(C) neither Shakespeare's mistress nor any other woman the playwright had romanced
(D) not Shakespeare's mistress or any other woman the playwright had romanced
(E) not Shakespeare's mistress neither any other woman he had romanced

9. The recent drop in the prime interest rate probably results from the Federal Reserve Bank's tight money policy and its effect on lending institutions rather than to the drop in the overall rate of inflation.
(A) its effect on lending institutions rather than to the drop in the overall
(B) its affect on lending institutions, as opposed to the drop in the overall
(C) it's effect on lending institutions, rather than from the drop in the overall
(D) its effect on lending institutions rather than from the drop in the overall
(E) the effect on lending institutions, rather than to the drop in the overall

10. Before they will sit down and resume bargaining, the strikers demand that management halt legal proceedings, including current court actions aimed at incarcerating demonstrators, and releases all strike leaders who have already been jailed.
(A) and releases all strike leaders who have already been jailed.
(B) and releasing all strike leaders who have already been placed in jailed.
(C) and release all strike leaders who have already been jailed.
(D) in addition to releasing all presently jailed strike leaders.
(E) but release all strike leaders who have already been jailed.

11. Since they shared so much when they were growing up, Elizabeth and Sarah have cultivated a very special friendship and even now confide their most intimate thoughts only to one another.
(A) to one another.
(B) one with the other.
(C) one with another.
(D) each to the other.
(E) to each other.

12. Henrik Ibsen's plays posed as great a challenge to middle-class Scandinavians' expectations of the drama that almost a century later Edward Albee will offer to theatergoers in America.
(A) that almost a century later Edward Albee will offer

(B) that, almost a century later, Edward Albee would offer
(C) as, almost a century later, Edward Albee did offer
(D) just as, almost a century later, Edward Albee offered
(E) as, almost a century later, Edward Albee would offer

13. Although Bill Tilden was perhaps the greatest tennis player of all time, his real accomplishments were overshadowed for many years by rumors about his personal life.
(A) Although Bill Tilden was perhaps the greatest tennis player of all time, his real accomplishments were overshadowed for many years by rumors about his personal life.
(B) Perhaps the greatest tennis player of all time, Bill Tilden's real accomplishments were nevertheless overshadowed for many years by rumors about his personal life.
(C) Perhaps the greatest tennis player of all time, rumors about his personal life overshadowed Bill Tilden's real accomplishments for many years.
(D) For many years Bill Tilden's real accomplishments were overshadowed by rumors about his personal life, despite being perhaps the greatest tennis player of all time.
(E) Although Bill Tilden's real accomplishments were overshadowed for many years by rumors about his personal life, perhaps he was the greatest tennis player of all time.

14. The commission studying mass transportation suggested that the Metropolitan Transit Authority hold off purchasing new subway cars and spend money instead on preventive maintenance of all cars, on repairs of substandard cars, on crime prevention in all stations and better lighting for the busiest stations.
(A) on crime prevention in all stations and better lighting for the busiest stations.
(B) on crime prevention in all stations, and better lighting for the busiest stations.
(C) on crime prevention in all stations and for better lighting in the busiest stations.
(D) on crime prevention in all stations, and on better lighting for the busiest stations.
(E) on the prevention of crime in all stations and for better lighting in the busiest stations.

15. Connoisseurs state unequivocally that the women in Paris are more beautiful than any other city.
(A) that the women in Paris are more beautiful than any other city.
(B) that the women in Paris are more beautiful than those in any other city.
(C) that Parisien women are more beautiful than in any other city.
(D) that, unlike any other city, Parisien women are more beautiful.
(E) that the women of Paris are more beautiful than the women in any other city.

16. The mayor's media advisor, together with his three top aides, are traveling with him on a tour of European capital cities.
(A) media advisor, together with his three top aides, are
(B) media advisor, also his three top aides, are
(C) media advisor, as well as his three top aides, is
(D) media advisor, along with his three top aides, are
(E) media advisor, all in the company of his three top aides, is

17. Lawyers and doctors alike both agree that something should be done about the rise in medical malpractice suits which are on the increase.
(A) alike both agree that something should be done about the rise in medical malpractice suits which are on the increase.
(B) alike agree that something should be done about the rise in medical malpractice suits.
(C) both agree that something should be done about the increasing rise in medical malpractice suits.

(D) agree that something should be done about the rise in medical malpractice suits, which are increasing.
(E) agree that something should be done about the rise in medical malpractice suits.

18. The obviously bitter actress stated that had the director known what he was doing, the play would have run for more than one night.
(A) had the director known what he was doing, the play would have run
(B) if the director would have known what he was doing, the play would have run
(C) if the director had known what he was doing, they would run
(D) had the director known what he was doing, they would run
(E) if the director knew what he was doing, they would have run

19. Dr. Smith's findings that emotions affect blood pressure are different from those published by his colleague, Dr. Loeb.
(A) affect blood pressure are different from those
(B) effect blood pressure are different from those
(C) effect blood pressure are different than those
(D) affect blood pressure are different than those
(E) affect blood pressure are different from that

20. Entering professional tennis as a talented but shy and awkward teenager, for the past eight years Chris Evert was the dominant force on the woman's circuit, a graceful and consistent player.
(A) Entering professional tennis as a talented but shy and awkward teenager, for the past eight years Chris Evert was
(B) A talented yet shy and awkward teenager when she entered professional tennis, for the last eight years Chris Evert has been
(C) Chris Evert entered professional tennis as a talented yet shy and awkward teenager, and was
(D) For the past eight years, having entered professional tennis as a talented yet shy and awkward teenager, Chris Evert has been
(E) Having entered professional tennis as a teenager who was talented yet shy and awkward, for the past eight years Chris Evert has been

21. The jurors agreed that of all the reasons the defense attorney gave for finding his client not guilty, the last two of them were the most absurd.
(A) the last two of them were the most absurd.
(B) the latter two were the most absurd.
(C) the last two of these were the most absurd.
(D) the last two of them were the absurdest.
(E) the last two were the most absurd.

22. The director of the Miss America pageant continues to maintain that the judges' ultimate choice is based less on the physical appearance of the contestant as on her intelligence, talent, and personality.
(A) as on
(B) and more on
(C) than on
(D) but more on
(E) than

23. The number of people jogging in New York City in the parks, in the playgrounds, and even in the streets, is at least ten times what they were a mere five years ago.
(A) is at least ten times what they were
(B) are at least ten times what they were
(C) is at least ten times what it was
(D) are at least ten times what it was
(E) is at least ten times what the numbers were

24. Insofar as poultry is still a good bargain and under a dollar a pound, the per-person consumption of chicken and turkey has increased in the last ten years, while that of the more expensive meats—beef, lamb, and pork—has declined.
(A) Insofar as poultry is still a good bargain and under a dollar a pound,

(B) Because poultry is still a good bargain and under a dollar a pound,
(C) For the reason that poultry is still a good bargain at under a dollar a pound,
(D) Because poultry is still a good bargain at under a dollar a pound,
(E) Insofar as poultry is still a good bargain, selling for under a dollar a pound,

25. Alicia de la Santina, <u>who danced with the famous Ballet de la France from 1942 to 1947, established</u> her own performance group, the renowned Ballet de Paris, in 1948.

(A) who danced with the famous Ballet de la France from 1942 to 1947, established
(B) who had danced with the famous Ballet de la France from 1942 to 1947, established
(C) who had been dancing with the famous Ballet de la France from 1942 to 1947, established
(D) who danced with the famous Ballet de la France from 1942 to 1947, had established
(E) dancing with the famous Ballet de la France from 1942 to 1947, established

STOP

END OF SECTION. IF YOU HAVE ANY TIME LEFT, GO OVER YOUR WORK IN THIS SECTION ONLY. DO NOT WORK IN ANY OTHER SECTION OF THE TEST.

ANSWER KEY—PRACTICE EXAMINATION II

SECTION I

1. B
2. D
3. D
4. B
5. A
6. D
7. D
8. C
9. A
10. A
11. B
12. D
13. A
14. B
15. B
16. C
17. E
18. C
19. C
20. D
21. C
22. E
23. C
24. A
25. D

SECTION II

1. D
2. E
3. C
4. C
5. E
6. A
7. B
8. A
9. E
10. A
11. C
12. C
13. D
14. C
15. E
16. C
17. C
18. D
19. A
20. D

SECTION III

1. D
2. E
3. C
4. B
5. C
6. C
7. B
8. C
9. D
10. E
11. B
12. C
13. B
14. B
15. D
16. D
17. E
18. D
19. E
20. B
21. B
22. C
23. A
24. E
25. A

SECTION IV

1. D
2. D
3. C
4. B
5. A
6. B
7. E
8. D
9. C
10. D
11. A
12. C
13. D
14. B
15. C
16. A
17. B
18. B
19. D
20. B
21. E
22. E
23. D
24. B
25. B

SECTION V

1. C
2. C
3. A
4. C
5. D
6. B
7. A
8. C
9. B
10. A
11. A
12. B
13. C
14. D
15. A
16. C
17. B
18. D
19. D
20. D

SECTION VI

1. C
2. B
3. C
4. D
5. C
6. B
7. A
8. C
9. E
10. D
11. B
12. A
13. D
14. B
15. E
16. A
17. E
18. C
19. A
20. B
21. E
22. B
23. E
24. C
25. E
26. B
27. D
28. D
29. B
30. A
31. A
32. D
33. E
34. D
35. B

SECTION VII

1. C
2. B
3. B
4. E
5. C
6. C
7. C
8. B
9. D
10. C
11. B
12. D
13. D
14. D
15. A
16. D
17. A
18. D
19. D
20. A

SECTION VIII

1. D
2. C
3. B
4. C
5. A
6. E
7. B
8. C
9. D
10. C
11. E
12. E
13. A
14. D
15. B
16. C
17. E
18. A
19. A
20. D
21. E
22. C
23. C
24. D
25. B

EXPLANATORY ANSWERS

Section I

1. **(B)** The author states that there are some good shows, but from the start to the end of the television day, the average is bad.

2. **(D)** He is telling the industry what it must do: "I intend. . . ." Hence (D). He is not defeated (A), nor hopeless (E). While he is righteous (C), the intention to prevail is dominant. There is no reconciliation, (B), at all.

3. **(D)** The whole thing is an extended shape-up-or-else statement, with justifications. (A) is not intended, and while there is an obligation to the listener or viewer, it is in seeking only to please the viewer that the author sees error; thus (A) is incorrect. (B) and (C) fail, since good children's shows are said to exist and it is only the steady diet of mystery, etc., which is objectionable. (E) fails because the teaching referred to is not classroom instruction.

4. **(B)** Literature and great traditions of freedom are urged as subjects for children's shows and these are certainly culture. None of the others are objected to, except cartoons, and there it is the massive doses only. The entire speech is a plea for moderation.

5. **(A)** (C) and (D) wrongly refer to air as the thing we breathe, while the author is referring to the broadcasting of television programs. (E) fails since the author nowhere opposes commercial television, but only insists that it should provide real service in return for using the common property that the airwaves represent. (B) has some merit since clearly the idea that the airwaves are owned by the people could be part—though only part—of an argument to say that the people should actually run everything to do with the airwaves through their government, but this is not part of the author's speech, and only if government oversight is to be equated with socialism can (B) ultimately be supported. We are, thus, left with (A), which is correct. While other rights may accrue to the people from their "ownership" of the airwaves, the right to have worthwhile use made of their property is certainly a permissible inference.

6. **(D)** The author states explicitly that the popularity of shows should not be the only criterion for selecting them. Since he has separated merit from popularity, he must believe that not all listeners or viewers know what is good for them. (A) and (C) have some appeal, but the author accuses the networks of catering to the nation's whims, which is hardly consonant with trying to do the right thing. He certainly does agree that they are failing, but that is not enough to justify choosing (A). The author's statements that there are some worthwhile shows is not enough to justify (C). (B) and (E) are flack.

7. **(D)** The citation of some good children's shows, even though they are overwhelmed by trash, is sufficient to choose (D). While (A) is not currently fashionable, the author is talking about meeting the needs of all of the population. (C) and (E) are directly stated, while (B) can be derived from the author's emphasis on opportunity of choice.

8. **(C)** There are two ways in which Minow refers to his own tastes in comparison to those of other people. First, he says that he finds little merit during the entire broadcasting day and says that the broadcasters to whom he is speaking would reach the same judgment if they sat and watched an entire

day's shows. So, he does not claim that he has better taste than the broadcasters, but rather that they, like he, would find the shows appalling. The second connection is between Minow's tastes and those of the general public. He says that most people would rather watch a Western than a symphony, and then he states that he likes Westerns and spy shows himself. What he objects to is the lack of choice, not the rank order or popularity as such. Thus he does not hold himself as having better taste than anyone, eliminating (A) and (B), and (D) since he does not speak of children's tastes at all. The appeal of (E), to the extent that it does appeal, is his first statement that television can be better than anything else, when it is good. But he means that in a simple and direct way and it is not some sort of complicated sneer. Don't exercise your imagination unnecessarily.

9. **(A)** Jargon is stated to be a technical term, though the passage notes that in farming and other old and widespread occupations, the words will often be generally familiar. (A), sun, is not a technical term in any field, while the other four are technical terms for, respectively, husbandry, farming, weaving, and carpentry.

10. **(A)** None of the answer choices has any statement of the topic of the passage, but only a general form. The passage is descriptive only; hence (A). (C) and (D) are not done, (E) seems unlikely in this rather dry passage. (B) has the slight merit of the fact that the description given is a sort of argument that the phenomenon described does exist, but that is not so well described as a belief. Hence (A), not (B).

11. **(B)** It is important not to let outside knowledge interfere with understanding how this author is using a term. Although guilds in the Middle Ages were hard to get into, (A), and often required apprenticeships, (E), this is not in the passage since it is modern times that are under discussion.

(D) is too strong and (C)'s references to secrets is a little strange since it is only the reports not the secrets that are broadcast; but the strength of (B) is that it is one of the two specific statements following the phrase at issue. (C), the second-best answer, is not precisely what is stated about popular science in the passage.

12. **(D)** Since the author chose vocabulary to write an article about, he most likely studied it since it reflects the best way to discuss things in the field, as the passage states. (A), (B), and (E) have little to do with the passage. (D) is preferable to (C) because (D) includes (C) and also refers to actually learning knowledge in the new field.

13. **(A)** Since the passage primarily concerns words and their use, meanings, and history, (A) is the best answer. There is no specific support for any of the other answers.

14. **(B)** The last two sentences give us our best evidence for time and place. Roentgen rays and wireless telegraphy are key terms. They are obsolete terms for X rays and radio, respectively, and certainly have an old-fashioned feel about them. The sentence with provincial in it tells us that the country of the author probably has knowledge of advanced science and many newspapers. The omission of radio and television from the list of media is also significant. (D) and (E) fail because of the date, since television and radio would surely be mentioned in those years. (A) fails since India was not a science center (nor a media center) in 1904. (B) is preferable to (C) since 1944 had radio and 1914 didn't.

15. **(B)** Since technical words come and go, (B) is very strong. (A) would only be true if words never left the language, which the passage does not say and common sense forbids. (C) fails since it refers to all words. (D) is shown to be false by the last sentence, if not the whole passage. (E) overlooks the author's position that such words as these are still technical words, even though common.

16. **(C)** These issues are discussed in the early part of the passage. The correct analysis of these four propositions depends largely on being sensitive to some restricted meanings of the words used in the passage. II is not

true even though the passage says that the use of jargon is "economical," because the commodity saved is time, not money. III fails for a similar reason. While the use of jargon permits "the precision of a mathematical formula," that does not mean that the jargon need be mathematical.

I is an advantage of jargon that is directly stated and is the real point of the comment on the economical nature of jargon. IV is also stated in the passage, deriving from the mathematically precise nature of jargon that that passage lauds. The qualifying phrase "for describing special topics" makes this proposition much easier to support since ordinary language can be perfectly precise for ordinary topics.

17. **(E)** I and III are clearly indicated by the phrase physical characteristics and cultures. II is a combination of the two. Food is a physical characteristic in terms of what is available, and the preparation is a cultural aspect. Hence, all three are referred to in the passage, (E).

18. **(C)** (B) is the result primarily of the Himalaya's sudden appearance, rather than glaciation, and (D) is of both. What we need is the idea of what would have been different if the existing plants had been entirely wiped out. (A) and (C) both speak to that, and (A) has some merit, though it is weakened by the word flourish, which seems extreme. Though the use of life without any adjective seems odd, this is done in both (A) and (C). In (A), however, there is no sense of development or implication. (C) tells us what would have been different to the concern of the passage at that point—the diversity and type of fauna and flora. Note that the word possibly in (C) protects it from the criticism that the Kunlun range cut off other life from coming in, as does the non-specific reference to nearby arid areas. (E) would only be chosen if all of the others were definitely bad.

19. **(C)** We know only two things about the Tibetan tea. First, it is in written quotes, which means it is not just regular tea. Second, it is a possible replacement for vegetables. These both fit (C) better than any of the other answer choices. If you were reluctant to choose (C) because it sounded unlikely, you are wrong for two reasons. First, and the most important, it is almost exclusively the relationship to the passage that matters. Second, that is what Tibetan tea really is.

20. **(D)** (A), (B), and (C) are all in the passage, but they serve the purpose stated in (D). (E) is not mentioned as mysterious.

21. **(C)** The passage is full of references to the findings of others, which supports (B) and (C). (A) is unsupported by the few statements made in the passage without references. None of the statements refer to any firsthand experience by the author, eliminating (A). There is no special emphasis on China to support (D), and there is much in the passage other than geology, (E). Between (B) and (C), one must choose between the strong items in each choice—"lifelong" and "only." While the passage displays some erudition, it is not clear that a lifelong study is indicated, but all of the information can come from books and almost all of it certainly does, hence, (C).

22. **(E)** Although Lattimore and Kawakita have different emphases as to the source of the polyandry, it is not stated nor required that polyandry must be either preserved from earlier forms or an efficient way of selecting the householder. The other answers reflect differences which are not required.

23. **(C)** Montesquieu is stated to believe that climate and soil are cultural determinants, that is, they determine what the culture of the inhabitants of an area will be. (D) is unrelated to this idea, and (E) focuses on the food, not the soil and climate as such. (A) and (B) mention only one of the two factors said to be important to Montesquieu. (C) clearly states the idea of soil and climate being determinative of culture.

24. **(A)** The term continental climate is used in the passage with only a partial explication of

what it might mean. However, the passage stresses the fact that the fauna and flora which were found in pre-glacial Tibet were typical of the entire region, though reduced in variety. Thus, the continental species are those found in a continental climate, the details of which you do not need to know.

(B) and (D) refer to events which are totally outside the scope of the passage and are therefore highly unlikely to be correct. (E) has the merit of referring to the location of the species and the idea that species are restricted to certain locations because of the environmental attributes of the locations. However, there is no mention of islands in the passage and, even more importantly, the fact that some species are not found on islands is not enough to classify it as continental in the way that term is used in the passage. Also, the idea of never being on any island of any sort is a little bizarre since doubtless there are islands in Tibet which have some of the species found in Tibet.

(C) has the merit of referring to the species' location in Asia, but it is not enough to just say "other parts" of Asia; Asia is very big. Also, the answer choice is not limited in any way and really means that these species are found all over Asia, which the passage makes clear is not the case.

25. **(D)** The only example of the spread of species that is mentioned in the passage is the *lack* of invasion from various outside areas into the Tibetan highlands. This is explained, as the geological emphasis of the entire passage would predict, by the geological fact that the Kunlun range is between Tibet and the nearest source of species already adapted to steppe conditions. (A) makes the claim that the situation in Tibet is the usual one—no spread—but the entire passage is predicated on the idea that the conditions in Tibet are highly unusual. (B)'s reference to human intervention is unrelated to the passage, except for the matter of tea coming from China, and that is a case of human intervention. (C) is logical insofar as it deals with densities of species, but it must be the competing species whose densities could possibly be an issue. In any case, the density of species is mentioned in the passage only with reference to Tibet itself, which would be the receiving area rather than the originating area. (E) is both unstated in the passage and illogical in the world and in the context of the passage. Weather conditions are precisely what does seem important to the survival of species.

Section II

1. **(D)** The minute hand will make one complete circle of the dial by 7:15. Then it will complete another half circle by 7:45. Since there are 360° in a circle, the arc travelled by the minute hand will be one full 360° plus half of another full 360°, yielding 360° + 180° = 540°.

2. **(E)** One way of solving this problem would be to convert each of the fractions to a decimal or find a common denominator so that a direct comparison can be made. This is too time-consuming. Instead, anytime the GMAT asks a question similar to this one, the student can be confident that there is very likely some shortcut available. Here the shortcut is to recognize that every answer choice, except for (E), is either equal to or greater than $\frac{1}{2}$, $\frac{7}{8}$ and $\frac{8}{9}$ are clearly much larger than $\frac{1}{2}$. $\frac{7}{12}$ must be greater than $\frac{1}{2}$ since $\frac{6}{12}$ is equal to $\frac{1}{2}$. But $\frac{6}{17}$ is less than $\frac{1}{2}$—$\frac{6}{12}$ would be $\frac{1}{2}$. So (E) is the smallest of the fractions. Even if the shortcut had eliminated only two or three answers, it would have been worthwhile.

3. **(C)** Even though it is not absolutely necessary to draw a figure to solve this problem, anyone finding the solution elusive will likely profit from a "return to basics:"

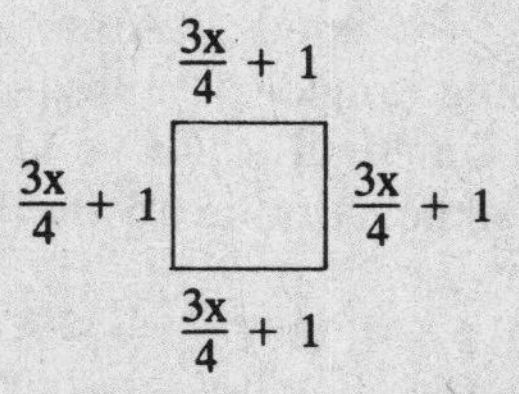

$$P = 4\left(\frac{3x}{4} + 1\right)$$

Quickly sketching the figure may help you avoid the mistake of multiplying the side of the square by another side, giving the area, answer (D), not the perimeter. The perimeter will be 4s, not s^2: $4(\frac{3x}{4} + 1) = \frac{12x}{4} + 4 = 3x + 4$.

4. **(C)** Average speed is nothing more than miles travelled over the time taken: rate speed $= \frac{\text{distance}}{\text{time}}$. The elapsed time here is 4 hours and 48 minutes. 48 minutes is $\frac{4}{5}$ hours. Our formula then will be: $\frac{240 \text{ miles}}{4\frac{4}{5} \text{ hours}}$. We attack the problem by converting the denominator to a fraction: $4\frac{4}{5} = \frac{24}{5}$, and then we invert and multiply:

$$\frac{240 \text{ miles}}{4\frac{4}{5} \text{ hrs.}} = \frac{240}{\frac{24}{5}} = \frac{5}{24} \times 240 = 50 \text{ miles/hr.}$$

Notice that setting up the problem in this way avoids a lot of needless arithmetic. This is characteristic of the GMAT. Most problems do not require a lengthy calculation. Usually the numbers used in constructing the questions are selected in a way that will allow for cancelling, factoring, or other shortcut devices. On the test, fractions are usually easier to work with than decimals.

5. **(E)** Multiplication is both associative and commutative. By associative, we mean that the grouping of the elements is not important—for example, $(5 \times 6) \times 7 = 5 \times (6 \times 7)$. By commutative we mean that the order of the elements is unimportant—for example, $5 \times 6 = 6 \times 5$. So (A), (B), (C), and (D) are all alternative forms for m(nop), but (E) is not: $(mn)(mo)(mp) = m^3nop$.

6. **(A)** There is an easy and a more complicated way to handle this question. The more complex method is to begin with the formula for the area of a triangle: Area $= \frac{1}{2}$ (altitude)(base). Since angle CBE is equal to angle E, BC must be equal to CE, and it is possible to reduce the altitude to the base (or vice versa). So Area $= \frac{1}{2}(\text{side})^2$. The area is 8, so $8 = \frac{1}{2}s^2$, and $s = 4$. Of course, s is also the side of the square, so the area of the square ABCD is s^2 or 16.

Now, an easier method of solving the problem is to recognize that BC and CE are equal to sides of the square ABCD, so the area of BCE is simply half that of the square. So the square must be double the triangle, or 16. A 45–45–90 right triangle is half of a square, and its hypotenuse is the diagonal of the square.

7. **(B)** Although some students will be able to solve this problem without the use of a diagram, for most drawing the floor plan of the closet is the logical starting point:

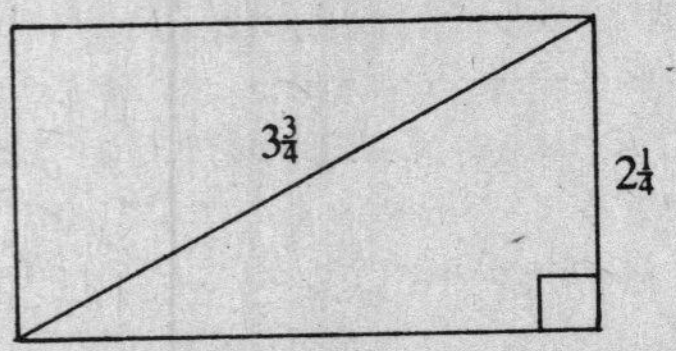

Now it becomes clear that the Pythagorean Theorem is the key to solving this problem. Once the dimensions are converted to fractions, the problem is simplified further: the triangle is a 3–4–5 right triangle ($\frac{9}{12}$, $\frac{12}{2}$, $\frac{15}{2}$). The two legs of the right triangle are simultaneously the width and length of the rectangle. So the area of the closet is: $\frac{9}{2} \times 6 = \frac{54}{2} = 27$.

8. **(A)** There are four times as many women as there are men, so if there are x men in the meeting, there are 4x women. This means that there is a total of 5x persons in the meeting (x + 4x). Since the men are x men out of a total of 5x, the men constitute one-fifth, or 20%. Choices (D) and (E) can be avoided by noting that there are more women then men in the room and men thus come to less than 50%.

9. **(E)** This is an unusual problem, one which requires careful reading rather than some clever mathematical insight. The question asks us to compare the fractions in the form $\frac{P}{Q}$ with the decimal .PQ. For example, we convert the fraction $\frac{1}{8}$ into the decimal .18 for purposes of comparison and ask how closely the second approximates the first. Since $\frac{1}{8}$ is .125, we see that the fit is not a very precise one. Similarly, with $\frac{2}{9}$, the corresponding decimal we are to compare is .29, but the actual decimal equivalent of $\frac{2}{9}$ is $.22\frac{2}{9}$. The equivalent for $\frac{3}{4}$ is .34, not even close to the actual decimal equivalent of .75.

Similarly, for $\frac{4}{5}$, the artificially derived .45 is not very close to the actual decimal equivalent of .80; but for $\frac{8}{9}$ we use the decimal .89, and this is fairly close—the closest of all the fractions listed—to the actual decimal equivalent of $\frac{8}{9}$, which is .888.

If you have difficulties in finding the decimals for fractions, try to relate the fractions to percentages, which are in hundredths, or to other, more common decimal-fraction equivalencies. For example, one-third is probably known to you as approximately .33 or 33%. A ninth is one-third of a third; hence a ninth is approximately 33%/3 = 11% or .11. Eight-ninths is thus 8(11%) = 88%.

10. **(A)** If a problem seems a bit too abstract to handle using algebraic notation, a sometimes useful technique is to try to find a similar, more familiar situation. For example, virtually everyone could answer the following question: Books cost \$5 each; how many books can be bought for \$100? The calculation goes: $\frac{1 \text{ book}}{\$5} \times \$100 = 20$ books. So, too, here the number of books which can be purchased per d dollars must be multiplied by the number of dollars to be spent, m: $\frac{b}{d} \times m$, or $\frac{bm}{d}$. Pursuing this line of attack, it might be worthwhile to point out that substitution of real numbers in problems like this is often an effective way of solving the problem. Since the variables and the formulas are general—that is, they do not depend upon any given number of books or dollars—the correct answer choice must work for all possible values. Suppose we assume, therefore, 2(b) books can be purchased for \$5(d), and that the amount to be spent is \$50(m). Most people can fall back onto common sense to calculate the number of books that can be purchased with \$50: 20 books. But of the five formulas offered as answer choices, only (A) gives the number 20 when the values are substituted: For b = 2, d = 5 and m = 50, (A) $= \frac{(2)(50)}{5} = 20$, (B) = (2)(5)(50) = 500, (C) $= \frac{5}{(2)(50)} = \frac{1}{20}$, (D) $= \frac{2 + 50}{5} = \frac{52}{5}$, (E) $= \frac{2 - 50}{5} = \frac{-48}{5}$ Substitution will take longer than a direct algebraic approach, but it is much better than simply guessing if you have the time and can't get the algebra to work right.

11. **(C)** The formula for the area of a square is *side times side*. Since the square has an area of 16, we know $s \times s = 16$, $s^2 = 16$, so side = 4. Then we compute the perimeter of the square as the sum of the lengths of its four sides: 4 + 4 + 4 + 4 = 16.

12. **(C)** Since John has more money than Mary, we note that x is greater than y. Then, John has less money than Bill has, so x is less than z. This gives us $x > y$ or $y < x$ and $x < z$. Thus (C), $y < x < z$.

13. **(D)** One way to attack this question is multiply the expression $(x - y)^2$ and then substitute the value 3 for x. $(x - y)^2 = 4$, so $x^2 - 2xy + y^2 = 4$. Then, if x = 3, we have $(3)^2 - 2(3)y + y^2 = 4$, or $9 - 6y + y^2 = 4$. Now we rewrite that in standard form (grouping like terms and arranging terms in descending order of exponents): $y^2 - 6y + 5 = 0$. At this juncture, the mathematicians will factor the expression on the left: $(y - 5)(y - 1) = 0$. Thus, the two roots of the equation are 5 and 1. So, 5 is a possible value.

Of course, a non-mathematical attack is also possible. We know that one of the five answers must be correct. So, we can simply try each one until we find one that will fit in the equation. For this we begin by putting 3 in for x: $(3 - y)^2 = 4$. We then test (A): $(3 - -5)^2 = (8)^2 = 64$ and $64 \neq 4$, so we know that −5 is not a possible value for y. On the othern hand, if we try (D): $(3 - 5)^2 = (-2)^2 = 4$, and 4 does equal 4. We have taken a shortcut here by not working each of the answer choices.

14. **(C)** There are several ways of running the calculation for this problem. One way is to reason: 10% of 360 is 36. Since 5% is one half of 10%, 5% of 360 is one half of 36, or 18. Since 10% of 360 is 36, and since 5% of 360 is 18, the difference between the two is 36 − 18 = 18.

15. **(E)** Again, perhaps the most natural starting point for a solution is working on the expression, rearranging by grouping like terms. $x^2 + 3x + 10 = 1 + x^2$. By transposing (subtracting from both sides) the x^2 term, we see that the x^2 is eliminated:

$$3x + 10 = 1, \text{ so } 3x = -9, \text{ and } x = -3$$

Although the x^2 term was eliminated from our initial expression, we know the value of x. It is now a simple matter to substitute -3 for x in the expression x^2, and we learn $x^2 = 9$.

16. **(C)** Proposition I is true. It is the geometry theorem that two lines parallel to a third must be parallel to each other.

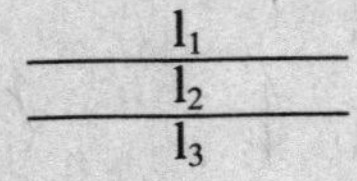

$l_1 \parallel l_2$
$l_3 \parallel l_2$
$\therefore l_1 \parallel l_3$

Proposition II is also necessarily true. Just as with lines, if two planes are parallel to a third plane, they must likewise be parallel to each other.

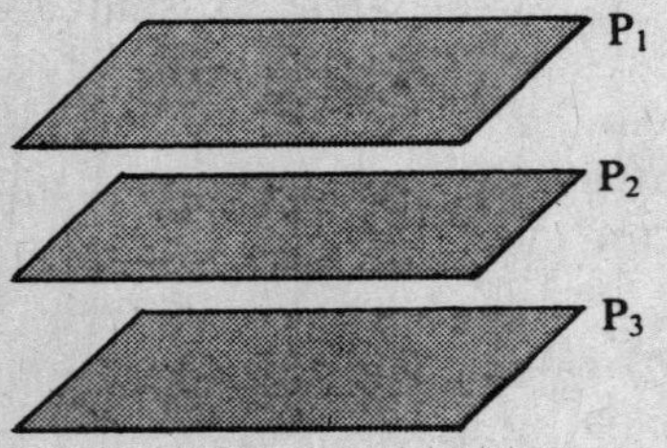

$P_1 \parallel P_3$
$P_2 \parallel P_3$
$P_1 \parallel P_3$

Proposition III, however, is not necessarily true. Two lines might be drawn in a plane parallel to another plane and yet intersect with one another:

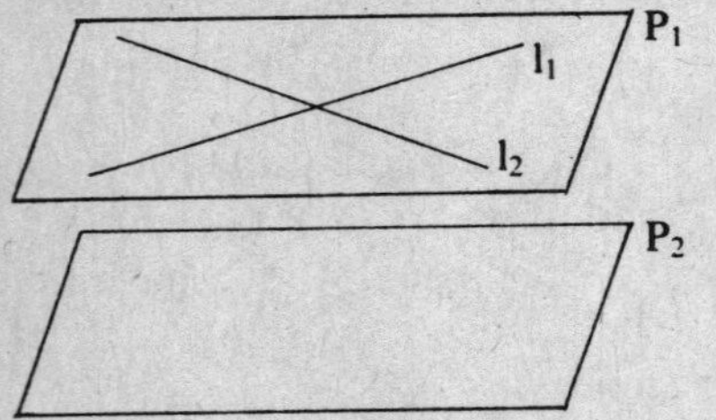

$l_1 \parallel P_2$
$l_2 \parallel P_2$
but $l_1 \nparallel l_2$

17. **(C)** We all know the simple formula that price minus discount equals discounted price—that much is just common-sense arithmetic. What we sometimes overlook, however, is the fact that the discounted price can be expressed either in monetary terms, e.g., \$5.00 or 37¢, or in percentage terms, e.g., 50% of the original price. In this case, the discount is given as a percentage of the original price. So we have, original price − 90¢ = 90% of original price; or, using x for the original price: $x - \$.90 = .9x$. This is an equation with only one variable, so we proceed to solve for x: $.1x = \$.90$, so $x = \$9.00$.

18. **(D)** We begin by computing the length of the side of the square ABCD. Since the x and y axes meet on the perpendicular, we have a right triangle formed by the origin (the point of intersection of x and y) and points A and B. Since point A has the coordinates (2,0), we know that OA is two units long—the x coordinate is 2. Similarly, point B is two units removed from 0, so OB is also two units long. Thus, the two legs of our right triangle are 2 and 2. Using the Pythagorean Theorem:

$$2^2 + 2^2 = s^2, \text{ so } s = \sqrt{8} = 2\sqrt{2}$$

Now that we have the length of the side, we compute the area of ABCD by side × side: $(2\sqrt{2})(2\sqrt{2}) = 8$.

19. **(A)** This problem is particularly elusive since there is no really clear starting point. One way of getting a handle on it is to manipulate the expression $\frac{x}{y} + \frac{n}{m}$. If we add the two terms together using the common denominator of my, we have $\frac{mx + ny}{my}$. We can see that this bears a striking similarity to the first equation given in the problem: $mx + ny = 12my$. If we manipulate that equation by dividing both sides by my, we have $\frac{mx + ny}{my} = 12$. But since $\frac{x}{y} + \frac{n}{m}$ is equivalent to $\frac{mx + ny}{my}$, we are entitled to conclude that $\frac{x}{y} + \frac{n}{m}$ is also equal to 12.

20. **(D)** This problem, too, is fairly difficult. The difficulty stems from the fact that its solution requires several different formulas. For example, we can conclude that (A) is necessarily true. MN is not a diameter. We know this since a diameter passes through the center of the circle. So whatever the length of MN, it is less than that of the diameter (the diameter is the longest chord which can be drawn in a circle). Since 2MO

would be equal to a diameter (twice the radius is the diameter), and since MN is less than a diameter, we can conclude that MN is less than 2MO. We also know that $z = y$. Since MO and NO are both radii of circle O, they must be equal. So we know that in triangle MNO, MO = NO; and since angles opposite equal sides are equal, we conclude that $z = y$. (B) requires still another line of reasoning. Since MN is greater than NO, the angle opposite MN, which is x, must be greater than the angle opposite NO, which is y. So x is greater than y. Finally, (E) requires yet another line of reasoning. If MN were equal to NO, it would also be equal to MO, since MO and NO are both radii. In that case, we would have an equilateral triangle and all angles would be 60°. Since MN is greater than MO and NO, the angle opposite MN, which is x, must be greater than 60°. So (D) must be the correct answer. A moment's reflection will show that it is not necessarily true that $x = y + z$. This would be true only in the event that MNO is a right triangle, but there is no information given in the problem from which we are entitled to conclude that $x° = 90°$.

Section III

1. **(D)** The area of a rectangle equals its length times its width, and the perimeter of a rectangle is the sum of its sides, or twice the sum of its length and its width. From (1) you can find the width of the rectangle:

   $5W = 20$
   $W = 4.$

   You can then find the perimeter of the rectangle:

   $2(L + W) = P$
   $2(5 + 4) = P = 18$
   From (2) you can also determine the length and width of the rectangle by setting up an equation with one unknown $x(x + 1) = 20$, where x equals the length and $(x - 1)$ equals the width. Then, solving for x:

   $x^2 - x - 20 = 0$
   $(x - 5)(x + 4) = 0$

   $x = 5$ or $x = -4$. Since a negative length is impossible, the length, x, is 5, and the width, $x - 1$, is 4. Thus the perimeter is $2(5 + 4) = 18$. To answer the question, it is not necessary to solve the equations and actually find the perimeter using (1) and (2) separately. It is sufficient (the name of the section is Data *Sufficiency*) to know that the length and width *can* be found by each of the two statements separately.

2. **(E)** From (1) or (2) separately, you know that the average can be either greater than 10 or less than 10; just think of groups of numbers that yield averages both less than 10 and greater than 10. For example, five 11's and five 1's yield an average of 6, but five 9's and five 15's yield an average of 12. Using (1) and (2) together will not produce an answer to the question either; the same two groups above can be used to answer the question either "yes" or "no."

3. **(C)** If $AX > BX$, $A > B$ if X is positive, but $A < B$ if X is negative because multiplying or dividing both sides of an inequality by the same negative number changes the direction of the inequality, but multiplying or dividing by a positive number does not change the direction. (2) by itself tells you nothing about A or B. (1) and (2) together, however, tell you that $A < B$. Thus the answer to the question is "no."

4. **(B)** In order for AB to be parallel to DE, you must be told either that $\angle BAC = \angle EDC$ or that $\angle ABC = \angle DEC$. Since (1) tells you only that DC = EC, and nothing about the relationship among the above angles, you do not know whether AB is parallel to DE. (2) tells you that AB is parallel to DE because $\angle EDC$ and $\angle BAC$ are equal corresponding angles.

5. **(C)** If the area of the rectangle is 16, the length and width are variable, e.g., 4 and 4, 8 and 2, 16 and 1, and thus the length of the diagonal is variable. If the perimeter is 16, the length and width are also variable, e.g., 1

and 7, 2 and 6, 3 and 5, and thus the length of the diagnoal is also variable. If (1) and (2) are both used, then the length must be 4 and the width must be 4, so that the diagonal, according to the Pythagorean Theorem, is $4\sqrt{2}$. Using (1) and (2) together gives two equations with two unknowns, an area equation and a perimeter equation, enabling you to determine the length and width of the rectangle and, therefore, the length of the diagonal by means of the Pythagorean Theorem.

6. **(C)** (1) tells you that $X + 6 < 186$ and $X < 180$ (subtracting 6 from both sides), which is not sufficient to answer the question. (2) tells you that $X + 8 > 186$ and $X > 178$ (subtracting 8 from both sides), which is not sufficient to answer the question. Both (1) and (2) together tell you that $178 < X < 180$ (X is greater than 178 *and* less than 180), which implies that X is 179 (since X must be a whole number).

7. **(B)** If (1) is true, then T may or may not be divisible by 15; for example, T could be 555, which is divisible by 15 (divisible means that the result of dividing is an integer with no remainder, or an integer rather than an integer plus a proper fraction), or T could be 348, which is not divisible by 15. (2) tells you that T is definitely not divisible by 15, because in order for an integer to be divisible by 15 it must also be divisible by 5 (since 5 is a factor of 15). An integer divisible by 5 must end in 5 or 0. Since in (2) the units digit is 3 (not 5 or 0), the integer is not divisible by 5 and hence not by 15. Thus, given (2) only, the answer to the question is "no."

8. **(C)** (1) gives you no idea of the size of the parallelogram and is therefore insufficient to answer the question. (2) by itself also is insufficient to answer the question because you don't know what shape the quadrilateral is. (1) and (2) together are sufficient to answer the question (the answer is 23) because the two unshaded triangles together have half of the area of the parallelogram: the area of the entire parallelogram is its base times its height. The area of the unshaded triangle on the left is *half* of its base times its height (which is the same as the height of the parallelogram), and the area of the unshaded triangle on the right is *half* of its base times its height (which is also the same as the height of the parallelogram). Since the bases of the two unshaded triangles together add up to the base of the parallelogram, the areas of the two triangles must be half of the area of the parallelogram, and the shaded region must be the other half.

9. **(D)** (1) by itself fixes the size of the cube completely and is therefore sufficient to answer the question (the answer is $\sqrt{3}$). Likewise, (2) by itself fixes the size of the cube completely, because from the length of the diagonals of the faces you can deduce that the sides are of length 1, and it is therefore sufficient to answer the question.

10. **(E)** (1) tells you nothing about the time the return journey took. Using (1) by itself, you can conclude only that the round trip took more than one hour. (2) by itself tells you nothing about how long the return journey or the round trip took. (1) and (2) together likewise tell you nothing about the length of time that any portion of the trip took.

11. **(B)** If (1) is true, you cannot answer the question without knowing the relative positions of points S and T. (Remember that geometric figures in the Data Sufficiency section are not necessarily drawn to scale, i.e., the lengths or sizes may not be what they appear to be.) If (2) is true, then the lengths of TU, ST, and RS are equal to each other, and therefore the answer to the question is "neither."

12. **(C)** If John has 5 more than Paul, there are two possible combinations: Paul could have 1 and John 6, or Paul could have 2 and John 7. Note that 3 and 8 are impossible since the total number of marbles is only 10. So (1) is not sufficient to answer the question. If Peter has half as many as John, there are three possible combinations: Peter could have 1 and John 2, Peter could have 2 and John 4, or Peter could have 3 and John 6. Again, (2) is not sufficient by itself. If both conditions are known, the only possibility is that Paul has 1, John has 6 and Peter has 3.

13. **(B)** (1) tells you nothing about the value of A. If A is positive, the answer to the question is "yes"; if A is not positive, the answer to the question is "no." Therefore, (1) by itself is insufficient to answer the question. In (2), since $A < 0$, $A + B < B$ (adding B to both sides of $A < 0$), so the answer to the question is "no."

14. **(B)** (1) tells you that x equals 1 or -1, so (1) is insufficient to answer the question. (2) tells you that x equals -1, so (2) by itself is sufficient to answer the question.

15. **(D)** In (1), if $\angle A = 55°$, then $\angle B = 180° - 55° = 125°$. Therefore, (1) is sufficient to answer the question. In (2), if $\angle D > 90°$, then $\angle B$ is also greater than 90° because $\angle B$ and $\angle D$ are corresponding angles with respect to parallel lines *l* and *m* and are therefore equal. So the answer to the question is "no" and (2) is sufficient.

16. **(D)** The area of a rectangle equals its length times its width. The length is given as 40. The perimeter (twice the sum of the length and the width) is given in (1), so the width can be found as follows:

$$2(L + W) = 140$$
$$2(40 + W) = 140$$
$$40 + W = 70$$
$$W = 30$$

Now you know the length and the width which are sufficient to find the area. In (2) you are given the length of the diagonal. By using the Pythagorean Theorem you can find the width as follows:

$$40^2 + W^2 = 50^2$$
$$W = 30$$

Now the area can also be found.

17. **(E)** If you divide both sides of the second equation by -2, the result is the equation in (1). Therefore, equation (2) is equivalent to equation (1). There are many solutions to equation (1)—and equation (2). For example, $A = 0$ and $B = \frac{-17}{3}$, and $A = 1$ and $B = -5$.

18. **(D)** In general, the relationship among the lengths of time that it takes for two persons or machines to perform a task is illustrated by the equation $\frac{1}{x} + \frac{1}{y} = \frac{1}{z}$, where x equals the number of units of time that it takes one person or machine to complete the task, y equals the number of units that it takes the other person or machine, and z equals the number of units that it takes both, working together, to complete the task. (1) tells you that the equation is $\frac{1}{x} + \frac{1}{2x} = \frac{1}{30}$, where x equals the number of minutes that it takes Joe to unload the bushels, y equals 2x equals the number of minutes that it takes Tom, and z equals 30 minutes, the time it takes Tom and Joe working together to unload the bushels. Since the equation can be solved for x, (1) is sufficient. Likewise, (2) is sufficient because it also yields one equation with one unknown, which may be solved for the unknown: $\frac{1}{45} + \frac{1}{x} = \frac{1}{30}$.

19. **(E)** (1) gives no information about B, so (1) is insufficient to answer the question. (2) tells you nothing about the relative values of A and B, but only that the square of (A + B) is positive, so (2) is also insufficient.

20. **(B)** If $\angle P < \angle Q$, it is possible for any one of the three angles to be a right angle, which would make the triangle a right triangle, or it is possible for none of the three angles to be a right angle, so (1) by itself is insufficient to answer the question. (2) tells you that $\angle R$ is a right angle ($\angle R = 90°$), since the sum of the three angles is 180°: $\angle P + \angle Q + \angle R = 180°$; $\angle P + \angle Q = \angle R$; $\angle R + \angle R = 180°$ (by substituting $\angle R$ for $\angle P + \angle Q$ in $\angle P + \angle Q + \angle R = 180°$); $2\angle R = 180°$; therefore $\angle R = 90°$ (by dividing both sides of the equation by 2). Thus (2) is sufficient to answer the question.

21. **(B)** In (1), if $K > 2L$, K could equal 3 and L could equal 0 ($K > L$); or K could equal -4 and L could equal -3 ($K < L$). In (2), if $K - L$ is positive, then $K - L > 0$ and $K > L$ (adding L to both sides in $K - L > 0$), so (2) is sufficient to answer the question.

22. **(C)** In this problem there are three unknown quantities. In order to determine

them, you need three equations. From the given conditions you can write $x + y + z = 7$, where x, y, and z represent the lengths of each of the three pieces. From (1) you can write $x = y + z$. These two equations are not sufficient to answer the question. From (2) you can write $y = 6$ or $z = 6$. Now, with both (1) and (2), there is sufficient information to arrive at an answer (3 equations and 3 unknowns). You need not solve the equations, but the longest piece is three feet six inches long, the shortest piece is six inches long, and the other piece is three feet long.

23. **(A)** Subtracting A from both sides in (1), $B > A$ or $A < B$. So the answer to the question is "no." From statement (2) you could get different results as follows: if $A^2 > B^2$, then A could equal 3 and B could equal 2 ($A > B$). Alternatively, A could equal -5 and B could equal 2 ($A < B$).

24. **(E)** In (1) N could be divisible by 6 and not by 12, e.g., $N = 18$. Alternatively, N could be divisible by 6 and by 12, e.g., $N = 24$. So (1) is not sufficient to answer the question. In (2) the same argument could be presented. A number divisible by 2 may or may not be divisible by 12. The two statements together are still not sufficient because any number divisible by 6 is automatically divisible by 2. So (2) gives no new information.

25. **(A)** An even number is always twice some whole number. So (1) yields the answer "yes." In (2) X could be, for example, $\frac{1}{3}$ (not a whole number) or 3 (a whole number). So (2) is not sufficient to answer the question.

Section IV

1. **(D)** (A) is incorrect because the "if" clause, expressing past condition contrary to fact, requires the past-perfect subjunctive ("had found"). (B) is wrong because the "possible conclusion" clause requires the perfect form of a modal auxiliary ("would have paid"). (C) fails because "fewer" refers to items that can be counted; tax, as a collective quantity, requires "less." (E) changes the meaning.

2. **(D)** (D) is not elegant but at least it is unambiguous and correct. Poor phrasing in (A) and (E) results in ambiguities: Do the columns contain volumes? Do the volumes have columns? (B) changes the tense and hence the overall meaning. (C) errs in agreement of subject and verb: the plural noun "libraries" must take the plural verb "contain."

3. **(C)** When seen from the context of the present, activities of ancient peoples should be described in the past (or past perfect) tenses. (A), (B), (D), and (E) put one or both of the ancient activities in the present or present perfect tenses. (D) also errs in adding three superfluous words. Only (C) is completely correct.

4. **(B)** (A), (C), and (D) require 14 words each to say what (B) says, more gracefully, in 12. (E) changes the meaning.

5. **(A)** (C) and E are incorrect because the clause expressing past condition contrary to fact requires past-perfect subjunctive ("had known"). (D) is incorrect because the clause stating a possible conclusion requires the perfect form of a modal auxiliary ("would have come"). (A) and (B) both use the correct verb forms in both clauses, but (B) adds "if"; this word is superfluous and alters the word order required by Standard Written English.

6. **(B)** (A) requires 15 words, and (C) 12, to say what B says in 11. (D) and (E) change the meaning.

7. **(E)** (A), (B), (C), and (D) are obviously confused: men whose landing and assault surprised the enemy could not have been prisoners at the time. (D) also confuses "affected" with "effected."

8. **(D)** Context indicates Jones is not afraid of bad weather; all that is required is a single negative. (A) uses a double negative ("Un-" and "neither . . . nor"). (C) incorrectly mixes the "either . . . or" and "neither . . . nor" constructions. (B) and (E) change the meaning.

9. **(C)** (A) requires 22 words to say what (C) says in 18. (B), (D), and (E) all change the meaning of the original; B also uses the singular verb "has" with the plural noun "recommendations."

10. **(D)** (A) is wordier than need be, fails to repeat "to" in the parallel structure ("to refine . . . to increase), and misplaces the modifier both. (B) and (C) needlessly substitute "utilized" for the short, simple "used." (E) uses a loose "also" instead of the tight "both" construction and incorrectly adds a comma.

11. **(A)** (B), (D), and (E) change the meaning. (C) omits the "do" needed to focus the contrast with married women who "do not."

12. **(C)** In its first two phrases, the original sentence establishes a pattern of parallelism ("Your . . . meddling, your . . . ridiculing). (A), (B), and (E) fail to continue the pattern. Both (C) and (D) do continue it ("your . . . departing"), but (D) adds three unnecessary words, leaving (C) as the best version.

13. **(D)** (A), (B), (C), and (E) each contain one or two errors in agreement of subject and verb. Plural subject "breeding and education" requires plural verb "establish," just as plural subject "occupation and income" requires "do."

14. **(B)** (A) and (C) are wrong because when a noun clause is used to pose this kind of indirect question, the conjunction required is "whether," not "if." (D) fails to link its "whether" clauses to the predicate with a verb. (C) and (E) err in using "is" instead of "are"; (E) also changes the meaning.

15. **(C)** (A) and (D) express simple result ("so impressed . . . that"), but (C) adds the sense of *to such an extent* ("so impressed . . . as to.") That this sense is the one intended is shown in the original by the second result "designate," which is in the infinitive form; the two results together then should be "so impressed . . . as to ignore . . . and designate. . . ." (B) takes more wordage than (C) to stress " to such an extent that," and "were to ignore" changes the time sense. (E) is not idiomatic.

16. **(A)** (A) is correct because the way to specify a "demand" that someone do something is in a "that" clause using the present subjunctive (*do,* "return"). (C) weakens the effect by confusing "demand that" with "demand for." (D) and (E) make incorrect use of the auxiliary verbs would and ought. With ought (E) even changes the meaning. (B) needlessly repeats "the members" instead of using the pronoun they.

17. **(B)** The original confuses two sources of punishment, the "referee's lack" and the referee himself, resulting in awkward use of "who" and needless use of both "punished" and "penalized." (C) better manages to link "referee" and "who," but it still requires both "punished" and "penalized." (D) and (E) change the meaning, (D) by implying that the referee is conscious of his "lack," (E) by adding "brutality."

18. **(B)** (A) and (E) suffer from faulty parallelism. When two or more phrases/clauses branch off from the same word, that word should come first and they should be in parallel structure ("responsible not only for . . . but also for . . ."). (C) and (D) have the right word order but a wrong word—the idiom is "not only . . . but also," and (C) changes the meaning. Futhermore, (A), (C), and (D) are wordy, using "the maintenance of order" when "maintaining order" will do.

19. **(D)** (A), (C), and (E) are marred by faulty parallelism: ancient Greek literature is compared with today's Greek people. (C) even leaves "literature" to be inferred, and (E) compares the ancient *Greek* with modern *Greeks.* (B) does achieve parallelism, but errs in using the plural (and here unidiomatic) verb "are containing" with the singular noun "literature." Only (D) lines up the ideas correctly.

20. **(B)** In (A), (C), and (D), the phrases about the "oldest brothers" are parentheti-

cal; they are not part of the subject. Steve, the true subject, is singular, requiring not "are" but "is," as in (B). In (E), "his oldest brothers" is linked with "Steve" by "and," thus creating a plural subject requiring not "is" but "are."

21. **(E)** In Standard Written English, "looked like" and "looked as if" are not synonyms for "appeared that," eliminating (A), (B), and (C). "Would have" (C) changes the meaning. "Appearances were that" and "would be crossing" make (D) wordier than the succinct, and correct, (E).

22. **(E)** (A), (B), and (D) incorrectly use "inferred" to mean "implied." (A) and (C) use the pronoun them instead of it (the antecedent is "plight").

23. **(D)** (A) and (C) each use two statements that can be condensed into one. (B) and (E) do condense them, but they fail in other ways: (B) uses faulty parallelism—a series of like items is awkwardly expressed in unlike forms, two nouns and a "how" clause—while (E) uses a dangling modifier—"rich and famous" here describes the traits instead of the men. (C) makes an error similar to (E). (D) achieves clarity and brevity by lining up like items in a series of like grammatical forms, and by placing modifiers next to the words they modify.

24. **(B)** (B) is correct because in likening two things, it puts the second into the same grammatical form as the first ("To insist . . . is to violate"). The others are incorrect because they put the second item in a different grammatical form: (A) and (E) use "violating" instead of "to violate"; (C) uses "to violate" instead of "violating"; and (D) has "violation" instead of "violating." (D) and (E) are also wordier than need be.

25. **(B)** (A) and (C) are redundant: "as well" means "also." The "which reduces" phrase in (C) and (E) may change the meaning, suggesting that only the damaged vision figures in the reduced survival potential. (D) and (E) need "also" after "but" to carry out the pattern of "not only . . . but also."

Section V

1. **(C)** This problem simply requires finding the value of the expression $2x + 3y$, when $x = 3$ and $y = 2$: $2(3) + 3(3) = 12$.

2. **(C)** You do not need a course in business arithmetic to solve this problem, only the common-sense notion that profit is equal to gross revenue less cost. Expressed algebraically, we have $P = GR - C$; then, transposing the C term, we have $C + P = GR$, which is read: cost plus profit (or mark-up) is equal to gross revenue (or selling price). In this case, $P = \$4$, $GR = \$20$: $C + 4 = 20$, so $C = 16$.

3. **(A)** The information given says that the 1970 student population is $2\frac{1}{2}$ times as great as the 1950 student population. So: '70SP = '50SP $\times 2\frac{1}{2}$, or '70SP = $500 \times 2\frac{1}{2} = 500 \times \frac{5}{2} = 1250$.

4. **(C)** We must test each of the answer choices. The question asks for the one choice in which the answer is not equal to $3n + 3$. In (A), for example does $300 = 3n + 3$? A quick manipulation will show that there is an integer, n, which solves the equation: $297 = 3n$, so $n = 99$. For (C), however, no integral n exists: $3n + 3 = 208$, $3n = 205$, $n = 68\frac{1}{3}$. So (C) is the answer we want. Another approach is to test each of the answer choices for being divisible by 3 since $3n + 3$ is divisible by 3 when n is an integer. If the sum of all the single digits in a number add to a number divisible by 3, the number is itself divisible by 3; if not, not (208, for example: $2 + 0 + 8 = 10$, is not divisible by 3). Being divisible by 3 does not mean an answer fits the conditions, but not being divisible by 3 means that it doesn't.

5. **(D)** The easiest approach to this problem is to draw the figures.

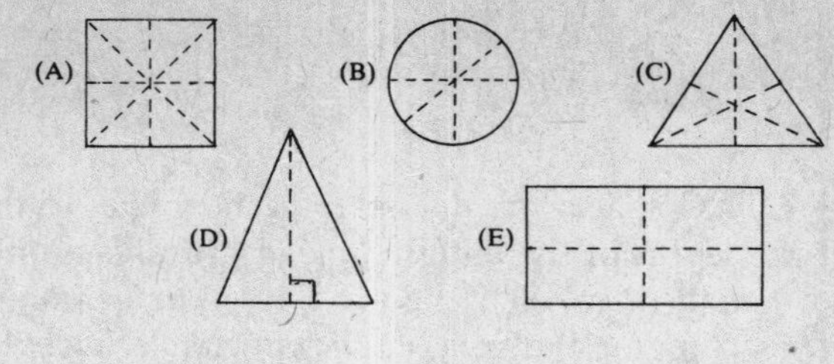

The dotted lines show possible lines of symmetry—that is, these are lines along which a paper cutout of the figure could be folded and the result will be that the two halves exactly match one another. (D) must be our answer, since it is the only figure with but one line of symmetry.

6. **(B)** This problem can, of course, be solved using an equation. We know that the laborer worked 8 hours @ \$8 per hour, but what we need to know is how much overtime he worked. We let x be the number of overtime hours: (8 hrs. × \$8/hr.) + (x hrs. × \$12/hr) = \$80. The \$12/hr. is the laborer's overtime rate—that is, \$8 × $1\frac{1}{2}$ = \$12. Now it is a fairly simple matter to manipulate the equation:

$$64 + 12x = 80$$
$$12x = 16$$
$$x = \frac{16}{12}$$
$$x = 1\frac{1}{3}$$

Since $\frac{1}{3}$ of an hour is 20 minutes, the laborer worked 1 hour and 20 minutes of overtime, which, when added to the standard 8 hours, gives a total work day of 9 hours and 20 minutes.

Now, it is not absolutely necessary to use an equation. The equation is just a way of formalizing common sense reasoning, which might have gone like this: Well, I know he made \$64 in a regular day. If he made \$80 on a given day, \$16 must have been overtime pay. His overtime rate is time-and-a-half, that is, $1\frac{1}{2}$ times \$8/hr, or \$12/hr. In the first hour of overtime he made \$12, that leaves \$4 more. Since \$4 is one-third of \$12, he has to work another one-third of an hour to make that, which is twenty minutes. So he works 8 hours at standard rates of \$64, one full hour of overtime for another \$12, and another $\frac{1}{3}$ of an overtime hour for \$4. So \$80 represents 9 hours and 20 minutes of work.

7. **(A)** Since MNOP is a square, we know that angle O must be a right angle, that is, 90°. From that we can conclude that arc NP is one-fourth of the entire circle. If arc NP is 4π units long, then the circumference of the circle must be 4 times that long, or 16π units. We are now in a position to find the length of the radius of circle O, and once we have the radius, we will also know the length of the sides of square MNOP, since MN and OP are both radii. The formula for the circumference of a circle is $C = 2\pi r$, so:

$$2\pi r = 16\pi$$
$$2\pi r = 16\pi$$
$$r = 8$$

So the side of the square MNOP must be 8, and its perimeter must be s + s + s + s or 4(8) = 32.

8. **(C)** The most direct way of solving this problem is first to compute the rate at which the water is filling the tank. Water is flowing into the tank at 800 cu. ft. per minute, but it is also draining out at the rate of 300 cu. ft. per minute. The net gain each minute, then, is 500 cu. ft. We then divide 3750 cu. ft. by 500 cu. ft./min., which equals 7.5 minutes. We convert the .5 minute to 30 seconds, so our answer is 7 min. 30 sec.

9. **(B)** A quick sketch of the information provided in the problem shows that we need to employ the Pythagorean Theorem;

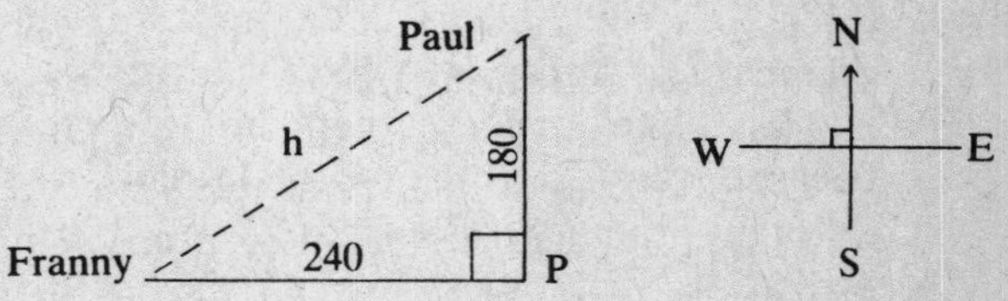

The shortest distance from Paul to Franny is the hypotenuse of this right triangle:

$$180^2 + 240^2 = h^2$$

It is extremely unlikely that the GMAT would present a problem requiring such a lengthy calculation. So there must be a shortcut available. The key is to recognize that 180 and 240 are multiples of 60—3 × 60 and 4 × 60, respectively. This must be a 3,4,5 right triangle, so our hypotenuse must be 5 × 60 = 300.

10. **(A)** This problem requires a very simple insight: Area of rectangle = width × length. What makes it difficult is that many students—while they are able to compute the area of any rectangle in which the dimensions are given—"freak out" when dimensions are expressed in terms of a variable rather than real numbers. Those who keep a cool head will say, "Oh, the area is the width times the length. The area here is $81x^2$, the length is 27x, therefore:

$$(W)(L) = \text{Area}$$
$$(W)(27x) = (81x^2)$$
Divide both sides by x:
$$(W)(27) = 81x$$
$$W = 3x$$

11. **(A)** To solve this problem, you must recognize that angle ABC is a right angle. This is because the triangle is *inscribed* in a semicircle (the vertex of the triangle is situated on the circumference of the circle), and an inscribed angle intercepts twice the arc. For example:

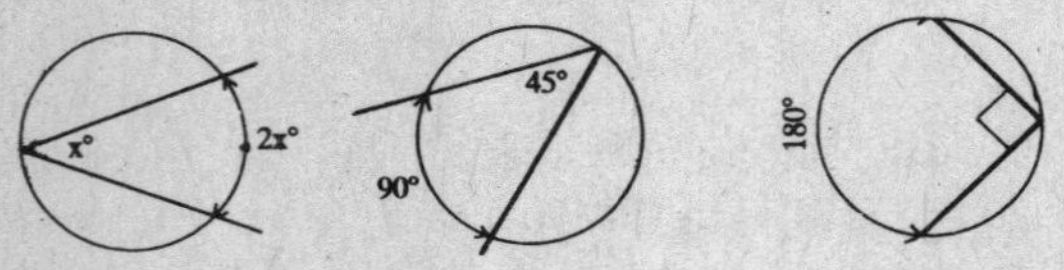

Once it is recognized that ABC is a right triangle, the shaded area can be computed by taking the area of the triangle from the area of the semicircle, or expressed in pictures:

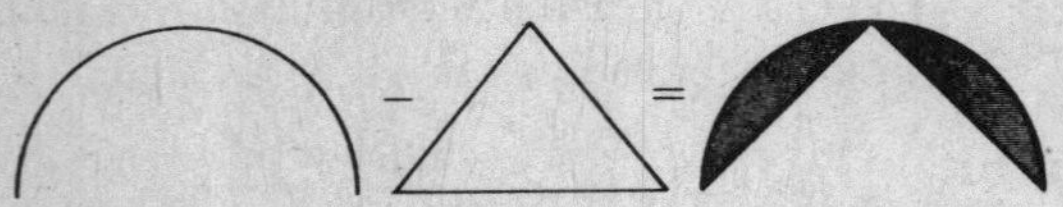

Line AC is the hypotenuse of ABC, so its length is:

$$AC^2 = (2\sqrt{2})^2 + (2\sqrt{2})^2$$
$$AC^2 = 8 + 8$$
$$AC = 16$$

AC is also the diameter of the circle, so the radius of the entire circle is 4 (radius is one-half diameter). We are now in a position to compute the area of the semicircle. Since the area of the entire circle would be πr^2, the area of the semicircle is $\frac{\pi r^2}{2} : \frac{\pi 8^2}{2} = 32\pi$.

Then we compute the area of the triangle. The area of a triangle is $\frac{1}{2}$ ab, and in any right triangle either of the two sides will serve as the altitude, the other serving as the base. For example:

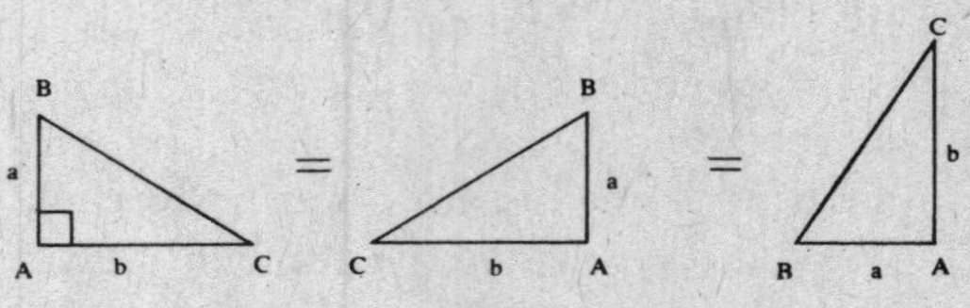

In this case, we have area $= \frac{1}{2}(2\sqrt{2})(2\sqrt{2}) = 4$. Referring to our pictorial representation of the problem:

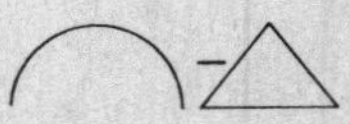 = 32π − 4.

12. **(B)** This problem does not actually need to be calculated. The symbol * is standing for a set of instructions. These instructions start with the square of the number and then add twice the number, which could be symbolized by * of $x = x^2 + 2x$. Since 12 squared is 144, the answer must be something in that general neighborhood, and the only answer that is close is (B) 168. The calculation would be $12^2 + 2 \cdot 12 = 144 + 24 = 168$.

13. **(C)** In the first trip, the motorist travels 120 miles at 60 m.p.h., which takes 2 hours. On the way back, he travels the same distance at 40 m.p.h., which takes 3 hours. His average rate is the total distance (240 miles) divided by the total time (5 hours), which yields 48 m.p.h.

14. **(D)** If angles BAD and BCD are right angles, they are equal. Angle BAC equals angle BCA, since they are base angles of an

isosceles triangle. Subtracting equals from equals, angle DAC equals angle DCA. Therefore, ACD is an isosceles triangle, and AD = CD.

15. **(A)** Let x = the cost.

$$\text{Then } x + \tfrac{1}{4}x = 80$$
$$4x + x = 320$$
$$5x = 320$$
$$= \$64 \text{ (cost)}$$
$$\frac{\text{Cost}}{\text{S.P.}} = \frac{64}{80}$$
$$= \frac{4}{5}$$

16. **(C)**

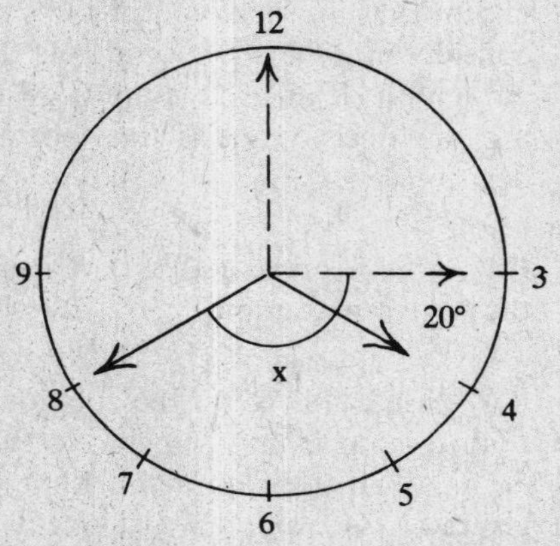

At 3:00, large hand is at 12 and small hand is at 3. During the next 40 minutes, large hand moves to 8 and small hand moves $\frac{40}{60} = \frac{2}{3}$ of the distance between 3 and 4; $\frac{2}{3} \times 30° = 20°$. Since there is 30° between two numbers on a clock $\angle x = 5(30°) - 20° = 150° - 20° = 130°$

17. **(B)** Area of sector $= \frac{120}{360} \cdot \pi \cdot 15^2$
$= \frac{1}{3} \cdot \pi \cdot 15 \cdot 15$
$= 75\pi$

18. **(D)** $\frac{17}{10}y = 0.51$
Multiplying both sides by 10, we get 17y = 5.1, or y = .3.

19. **(D)** $40\% = \frac{2}{5} \times 50 = 20$ girls attended
$50\% = \frac{1}{2} \times 70 = 35$ boys attended

$$\frac{55}{50 + 70} = \frac{55}{120} = \frac{11}{24} \qquad .458 = 45.8\%$$

```
       .458
24 )11.000
     96
     140
     120
      200
      192
```

Approx. 46%

20. **(D)** In order to find out the total production for the five days of round-the-clock production, you first need to know the rate of production for some time period and the number of that time period in the five days. To find the rate of production, we need to add the rate of production of the new machine ($\frac{x}{\text{hour}}$) to the rate of production of the old machine, which is $\frac{1}{8}$ as much ($\frac{x}{8}$ per hour). Adding these two together you get a total production rate of $x + \frac{x}{8} = (\frac{9}{8})x$ per hour. This must be multiplied by the number of hours in five days (5)(24) to give the total production: $\frac{(9)(x)(5)(24)}{8} = 135x$ transmissions.

Section VI

1. **(C)** The related major factor is reliability. Age is important only insofar as it makes for reliability.

2. **(B)** This is a major factor, as Barbara states in presenting the problem to her friends initially.

3. **(C)** This is an interesting sort of Minor Factor in that it is minor; first, because it relates to only one choice—Fastype—and, second, because its content is of subordinate rank anyway. By this is meant that "adjustments" are only of importance insofar as they promote "speed," an important need of Barbara's.

4. **(D)** Barbara assumes she can get the money when she needs it from a bank. It is not a difference between the options.

5. **(C)** Repair costs are part of total acquisition costs, a major factor. These are not operating repair costs.

6. **(B)** This is an independent line of discussion of each option. It is a difference between the options.

7. **(A)** It is made clear from the start that this is one of Barbara's aims.

8. **(C)** Remember that items concerning only one of the alternatives are normally Minor Factors. This contributes to #6.

9. **(E)** Nothing is mentioned or implied to this effect. Although common sense tells you that this would be anyone's goal, you are being examined on what the text says. Right now that is not what is on Barbara's mind, and does not help make her current decision.

10. **(D)** This is simply an unargued-for assumption Barbara makes right at the start.

11. **(B)** This is the same consideration as #6.

12. **(A)** This is the goal related to the (B) in #2.

13. **(D)** Provisions of a relevant contract are almost always (D)s. The existence of the penalty provisions allows Barbara to judge the significance of the differences in the reliability of the various options.

14. **(B)** This is the major factor associated with the goal of timely completion of her projects for the consortium.

15. **(E)** This consideration is never mentioned or implied.

16. **(A)** It is stated and/or implied several times that this is a goal.

17. **(E)** This is irrelevant any way you slice it.

18. **(C)** Transportation cost is a component of cost, a major factor.

19. **(A)** This is presented as a rationale for the entire expansion program in the initial paragraph.

20. **(B)** Some passages simply list major factors. The fourth paragraph serves this function here, and labor relations is cited as a principal consideration.

21. **(E)** The decision in focus is which of three publishing firms to acquire.

22. **(B)** The major factors are listed in the passage's fourth paragraph.

23. **(E)** Characteristics of Gilt Edge, Lovepages, and Enchanted Heart, not of Wells itself, must determine which selection is made. If you constructed an elaborate chain of reasoning to justify labelling this item as a (C), you read too much into the question.

24. **(C)** *Name recognition* is a major factor, but *a particular company's name recognition* is a minor factor. References to specific alternatives frequently signal minor factors.

25. **(E)** This idea would have been a factor, except that it was specifically excluded from consideration by the end of the fourth paragraph. If an idea is not used in discussing the decision, it is unimportant to the decision.

26. **(B)** This is presented as a major factor in the fourth paragraph.

27. **(D)** While this is a rather obvious assumption, it is far from irrelevant to the decision at hand. It is simply the kind of "background" assumption we naturally make but seldom think about. Nonetheless, it *is* an assumption, and one on which this decision is predicated.

28. **(D)** Wells has to assume this for their deliberations to make any sense. Certain propositions seem too obvious to count as major assumptions, but premises so basic that we cease to think about them are premises nonetheless.

29. **(B)** See the fourth paragraph of the passage.

30. **(A)** That this is a principal goal can be gathered from the first three paragraphs taken together.

31. **(A)** While only partly achievable by this particular decision, it is a goal.

32. **(D)** This is never mentioned as such, but the whole passage would be senseless were the board not making this assumption.

33. **(E)** In answering these questions, your first allegiance is to the text, and not to your outside knowledge. Nothing stated or implied in the passage leads us to believe that anything about Wells' advertising budget will help the board determine which of these three companies to buy.

34. **(D)** This is an easy question. The correctness of basic data cannot be irrelevant to the solution of a problem such as the board's, nor does it make sense as a decision *factor.* Accuracy is a basic background *assumption.*

35. **(B)** This is stated as a necessity at the passage's beginning only. It is not taken up again in the discussions of each company's appropriateness for acquisition. If the factor did not ring a bell, you ought to have scanned the passage for it.

Section VII

1. **(C)** First we must convert one and one-half yards into inches. There are 36 inches in a yard, so one and one-half yards must contain 36 + 18 or 54 inches. Now, to determine how many two-inch segments there are in 54 inches, we just divide 54 by 2, which equals 27. So there must be 27 two-inch segments in a segment which is one and one-half yards long.

2. **(B)** It is important to remember that the positive x values are to the right of the origin (the intersection between the x and y axes), and that the negative values on the x axis are to the left of the origin. Also, the positive y values are above the origin, while the negative y values are below the x axis.

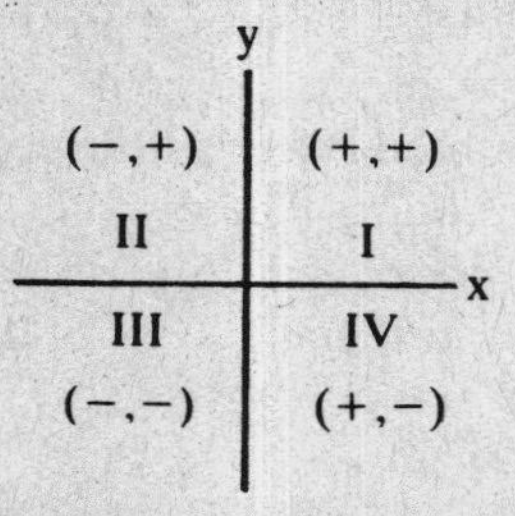

When reading an ordered pair such as (x,y) (called ordered because the first place is always the x-coordinate and the second place is always the y-coordinate), we know the first element is the movement on the horizontal or x axis (from left to right), while the second element of the pair gives us the vertical distance. In this case, we are five units to the left of the origin, so that gives us an x value of negative 5. We are 2 units above the horizontal axis, so that gives us the second value (y) of +2. Thus our ordered pair is (−5, 2), answer (B).

3. **(B)** The formula for computing the circumference of a circle is $2\pi r$. In this case our radius is 4, so the circumference of the circle is 8π. Now, P and Q will be as far apart as they can possibly be when they are directly opposite one another:

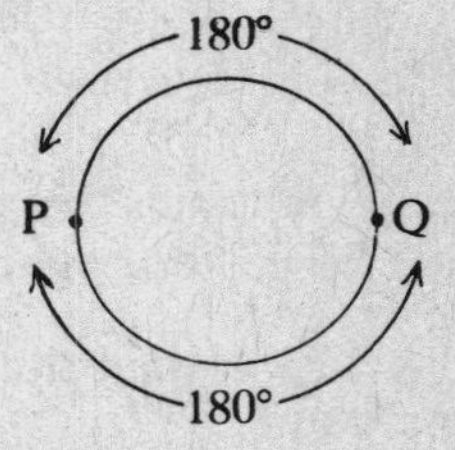

Or a half circle away from each other. So the maximum distance by which P and Q could be separated—measured by the circumference of the circle and not as the crow flies—is one-half the circumference, or 4π.

4. **(E)** Remember that a prime number is an integer which has only itself and 1 as integral factors. Thus, 13, 17, 41, and 79 are all prime numbers because their only factors are 13 and 1, 17 and 1, 41 and 1, and 79 and 1, respectively. 91, however, is not a prime number since it can be factored by 7 and 13 as well as by 1 and 91.

5. **(C)** The natural starting point here would be to draw the picture:

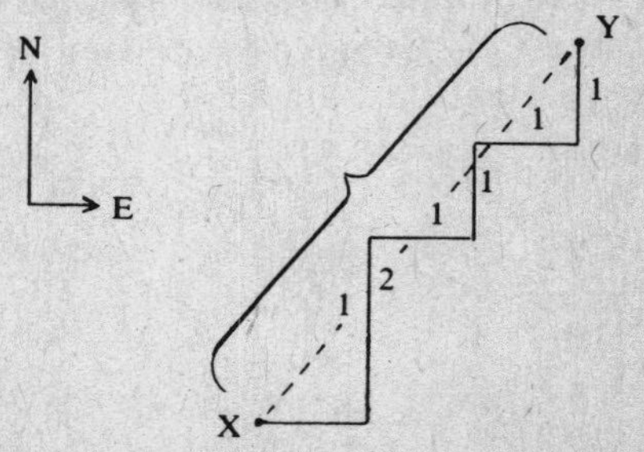

Since directions are perpendicular, we can perform the needed calculation with the Pythagorean Theorem. To simplify things, we can show that the picture on the previous page is equivalent to this:

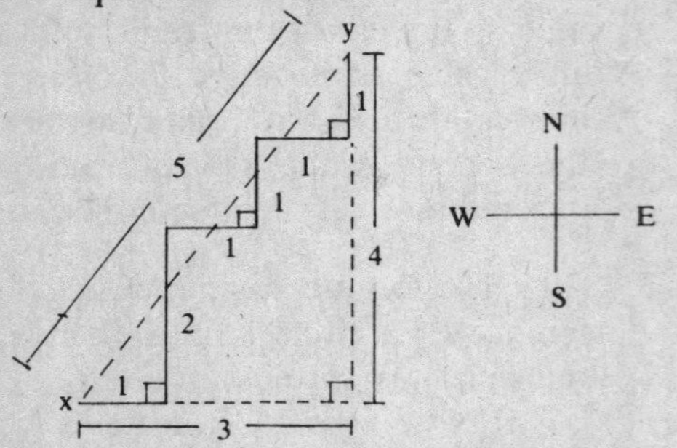

Now we can solve for the distance between X and Y with one use of the Pythagorean Theorem. Since the two legs of the right triangle are 3 and 4, we know that the hypotenuse must be 5. (Remember that 3, 4, and 5, or any multiples thereof, such as 6, 8, and 10, always make a right triangle.)

6. **(C)** Let us begin by substituting x, y, and z for ∠QPS and ∠TPR. Since ∠QPS and ∠TPR are equal, we know $x + y = z + y$, and since $y = y$, we know that $x = z$. As for (A) and (B), we do not know whether y is equal to x and z; it could be larger or smaller or equal:

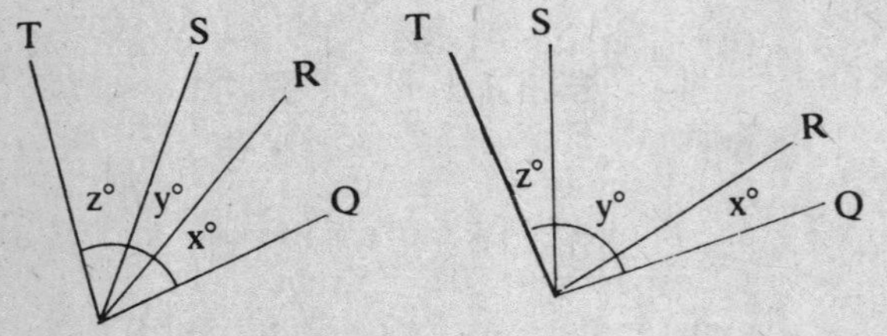

We can also eliminate (D), since we have no information that would lead us to conclude that all three are of equal measure.

7. **(C)** By this juncture the drill should be well known. We must begin by drawing a picture:

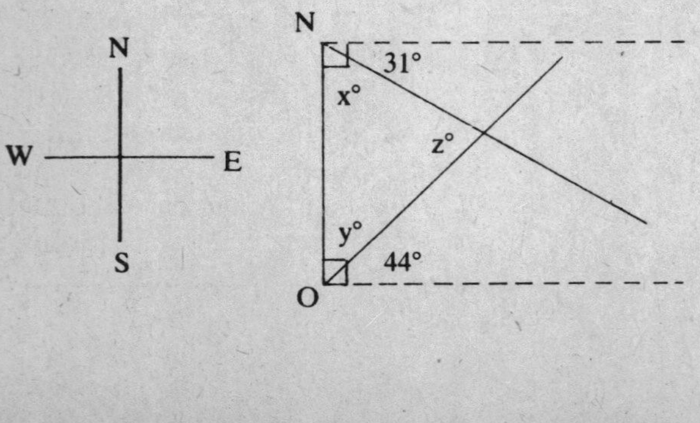

Now, since the angles at N and O are 90°, we can compute the magnitude of x and y − x = 90° − 31° = 59°, and y = 90° − 44° = 46°. Then, since x, y, and z are the interior angles of a triangle, we know $x + y + z = 180°$. Substituting for x and y, we have $59° + 46° + z = 180°$, and we solve for z: $z = 75°$. Since z is the angle of intersection between the two highways, our answer must be (C).

8. **(B)** Let us use x to represent the sum of money. Then we know that when x is divided equally by n, the result is \$60; or, expressed in formal notation: $\frac{x}{n} = 60$. We then know that when x is divided by n + 1 (that is the original number plus another child), the result is \$50, or $\frac{9}{n+1} = 50$. Now, let us manipulate these equations so that we isolate n:

$$\frac{x}{n} = 60 \qquad \frac{x}{n+1} = 50$$

$$\frac{x}{60} = n \qquad \frac{x}{50} = n + 1$$

$$\frac{x}{60} = n \qquad \frac{x}{50} - 1 = n$$

Since n = n, we know that $x/60 = x/50 - 1$, and we have an equation with only one variable: $x/60 - x/50 = -1$, so:

$$\frac{5x - 6x}{300} = -1$$

AND: $-x = -300$

SO: $x = 300$

The sum of money is \$300 and our answer is (B). (Note that you could also solve for n; in this case n = 5.)

9. **(D)** While it is possible to set up a formula for this problem, Original Price − Discount = Discounted Price, a little common sense is a better attack. The discount is 25% of the original price, and 25% of \$90 is \$22.50. If the item originally cost \$90, and we are getting a discount of \$22.50, the new price will be \$67.50.

10. **(C)** Let us begin our solution by dropping a perpendicular from the upper vertex of the triangle:

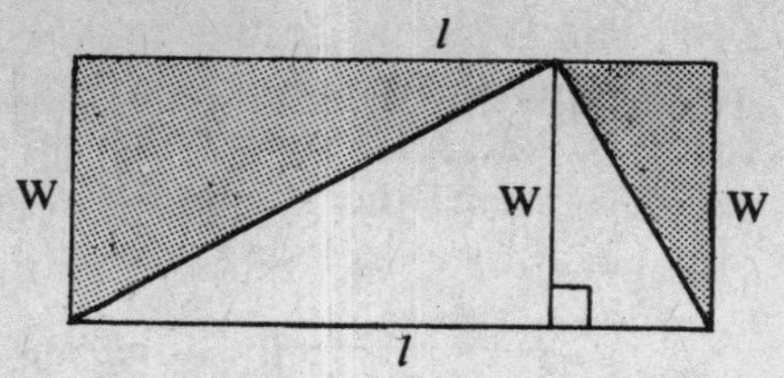

This divides the rectangle into two other rectangles, each with a diagonal running across it:

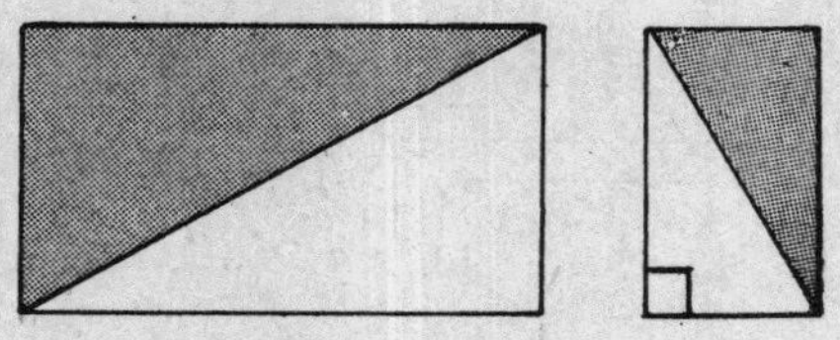

It should be intuitively clear that the diagonal of a rectangle divides the rectangle in half since all sides and angles are equal. Therefore, the left shaded area is equal to the left unshaded area and the right shaded area is equal to the right unshaded area, which means the total shaded area is equal to the total unshaded area. Thus, the triangle has half the area of the rectangle. This is actually the proof of the formula you use to find the area of a triangle—A = (height)(base)$\frac{1}{2}$. Remember this situation since it could easily come up in one problem or another.

11. **(B)** Since Earl and Ellen will be working together, we add their work rates:

$$\frac{\text{Number of tasks}}{\text{Time}} + \frac{\text{Number of tasks}}{\text{Time}} = \frac{\text{Number of tasks together}}{\text{Time}}$$

In this case:

$$\frac{45 \text{ envelopes}}{60 \text{ seconds}} + \frac{45 \text{ envelopes}}{90 \text{ seconds}} = \frac{300 \text{ envelopes}}{x \text{ seconds}}$$

Or: $\frac{45}{60} + \frac{45}{90} = \frac{300}{x}$

To make the arithmetic simpler, we reduce fractions:

$$\frac{3}{4} + \frac{1}{2} = \frac{300}{x}.$$

Then we add: $\frac{10}{8} = \frac{300}{x}$.

And solve for x: $x = 300(\frac{8}{10}) = 240$ seconds.

Since 240 seconds is equal to 4 minutes, our answer is (B). If you are not comfortable with fractions, you could have kept to minutes.

Another way to approach this problem would be to try to get the rate of each worker in envelopes per minute. Earl is already known to work at 45 envelopes per minute. Ellen takes $1\frac{1}{2}$ minutes for the same work. Thus, 45 envelopes are done in three half-minutes. 45 divides by 3 nicely, as we often find on the GMAT, so Ellen does 15 envelopes in $\frac{1}{2}$ minute or 30 envelopes per minute, 45 per minute + 30 per minute = 75 per minute, which means $\frac{300}{75}$ = 4 minutes.

12. **(D)** First, let us count the number of subjects having characteristic X. The first two categories are those subjects having X (25 which also have Y, 10 which do not have Y but do have X), which is a total of 35. Then those subjects having Y are entered in the first and third categories (25 also have X, 25 have Y but lack X), for a total of 50. Our ratio is $\frac{35}{50}$, which, when reduced by a factor of 5, is equal to $\frac{7}{10}$.

13. **(D)** This problem is a bit tricky, but not really difficult. When dealing with a ratio, say 4 to 1, it is important to remember that the number of parts is the sum of these two numbers. So we might say we have five parts—four parts are passenger vehicles, one part is all other vehicles— and that is how we get a ratio of 4 to 1. But this means that 4 parts out of the total of 5 parts are passenger vehicles, and 4 out of 5 is $\frac{4}{5}$, or 80%. Answer (E) makes the mistake of forgetting that although there are four times as many passenger cars as all other vehicles, the passenger vehicles constitute only $\frac{4}{5}$ of the total number.

14. **(D)** Let us logically approach this problem before even trying to calculate it. Although we have a 10% increase and then a 10% decrease, we must always ask ourselves "10% of what?" The increase was 10% of the original price, but the decrease was 10% of the higher price and consequently the decrease is bigger than the increase and the result at the end is less than the starting

price, which eliminates answer choices (A), (B), and (C). Similarly, on logical grounds, it is hard to see how a 10% decrease from a 10% higher price could be equal to an 11% decrease from the starting price; that seems too much, which leaves (D) as the answer.

If we wish to compute the answer, let us start by saying that the original price of the item is x. A 10% increase in that price will be one-tenth of x, or .1x. When we add the increase to the original price, we find our increased price is 1.1x. We must then take away 10% of that. Ten percent of 1.1x is .11x, and subtracting .11x from 1.1x, we get .99x. We started with x; we ended with .99x, so we lost .01x, which is 1%.

15. **(A)** Proposition I is necessarily true. Since lines l_m and l_n are prependicular to one another, a line that intersects l_m on the perpendicular must be parallel to line l_n.

Proposition II is not necessarily true. Line segment MN may fail to intersect l_m simply because it is too short—that is, if extended, for all we know MN will intersect l_n.

Proposition III is not necessarily true. Line l_o may intersect l_m at point P without plane y being perpendicular to plane x.

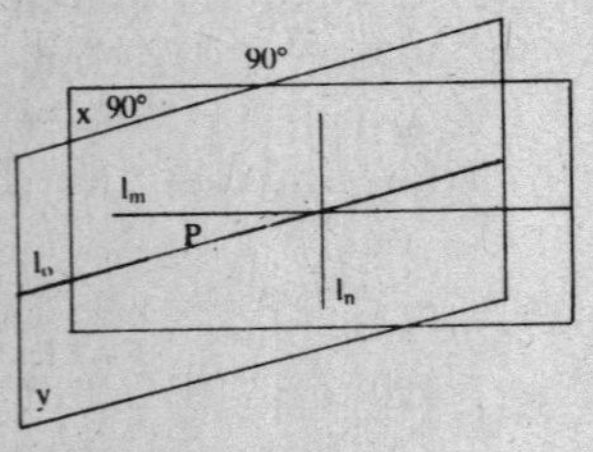

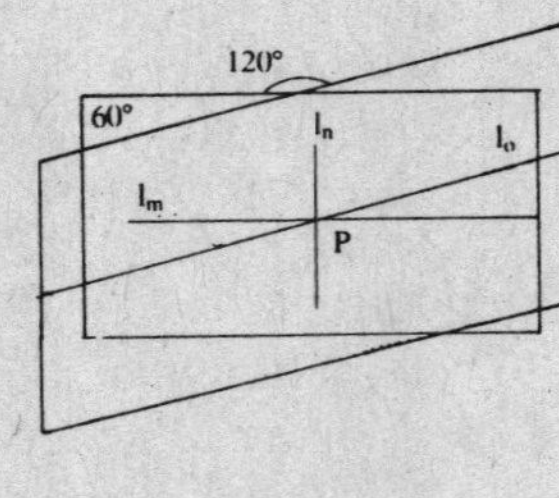

16. **(D)** Since the ratio of insects with X to those without X is 5:3, we know that $\frac{5}{8}$ of the population has X. (There are 8 equal units—5 + 3—5 of which are insects with X.) Then, of those $\frac{5}{8}$, $\frac{3}{8}$ are male. So we take $\frac{3}{8}$ of the $\frac{5}{8}$($\frac{3}{8}$ × $\frac{5}{8}$), and that tells us that $\frac{15}{64}$ of the total population are male insects with X.

17. **(A)** This is an interesting problem in that no formula is going to solve it. Instead, it requires the use of some good old common sense. Perhaps the solution is more easily visualized if we explode the cube.

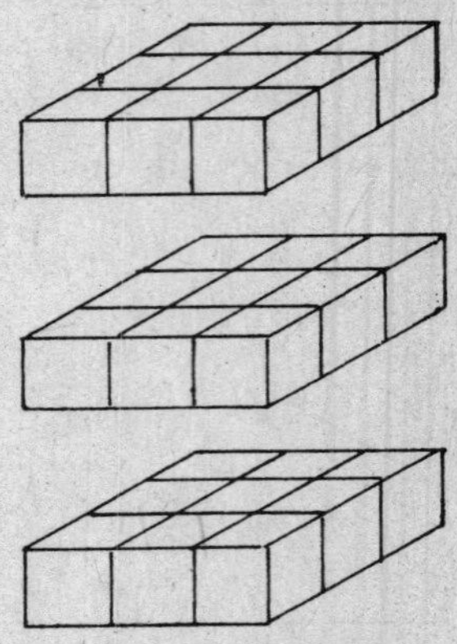

All of the small cubes on the top and the bottom layers will have at least one side painted. In the middle layer, the outer eight smaller cubes encircle the center cube, which is protected on top by the top layer, on the bottom by the bottom layer, and on the remaining four sides by the outside of the sandwich layer:

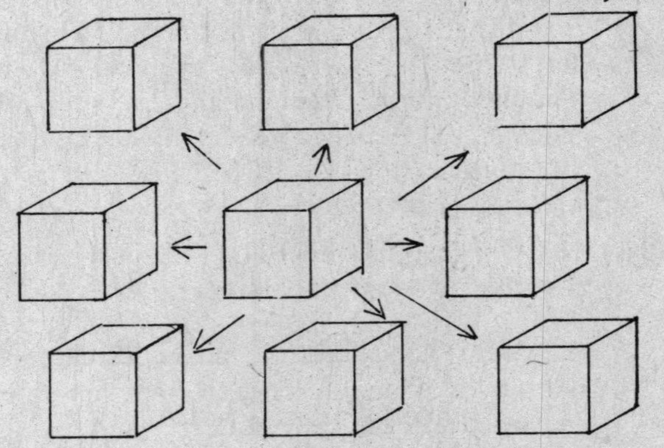

18. **(D)** The proper way to "visualize" this problem is to imagine that the gravel-covered walk will be a very squat-shaped cylinder with a donut hole removed (the circular region inside the walk). Expressed more abstractly, we need to compute the volume of a cylinder with a radius of 50 feet

($\frac{1}{2}$ of 100 = 50) and a height of 6 inches, or $\frac{1}{2}$ foot. Then we compute the volume of a cylinder with a radius of 40 feet ($\frac{1}{2}$ of 80 = 40) and a height of 6 inches, or $\frac{1}{2}$ foot. Then we subtract the second from the first and what is left is the volume we seek. Now, since both cylinders have the same height, it will be easier to compute the areas of the bases first and subtract before multiplying by $\frac{1}{2}$ foot.

Area of larger circle: Area = $\pi r^2 = \pi(50)^2 = 2500\,\pi$.

Area of smaller circle: Area = $\pi r^2 = \pi(40)^2 = 1600\pi$.

By subtracting 1600π from 2500π, we determine that the area of the garden path is 900π square feet. To determine the volume of gravel we need, we then multiply the figure by $\frac{1}{2}$ foot (the depth of the gravel), and arrive at our answer 450π cu. ft.

19. **(D)** Let d stand for the hourly rate under the new system. Since the employee is to make the same amount per week under both systems, it must be the case that:

$$\frac{\$x}{\text{hr.}} \text{ times } 40 \text{ hrs.} = \frac{\$d}{\text{hr.}} \text{ times } 36 \text{ hrs.}$$

Now we must solve for d:

$$40x = 36d, \quad d = \frac{10x}{9}$$

The problem can also be solved in an intuitive way. Since the employee is working less time yet making the same weekly total, he must be earning slightly more per hour under the new system than under the old. Answer (A) is just the naked fraction $\frac{1}{10}$, without making reference to monetary units. Answer (B) implies that the employee is making $\frac{1}{9}$ as much per hour under the new system as under the old—that would be a decrease in the hourly rate. Similarly, (C) says that the employee is making only 90% of his old hourly rate and that, too, is a decrease. Finally, (E) says that the employee is making *9 times* the hourly rate he made under the old system, a figure which is obviously out of line. The only reasonable choice is (D). The moral is: Even if you cannot set up the math in a technically correct way, use a little common sense.

20. **(A)** This problem must be solved in two stages. First, we need to calculate the total area of the wall. The information given in the problem states that $\frac{1}{3}$ of the job plus another 75 square feet equals $\frac{3}{4}$ of the job. In algebraic notation, this is:

$$\frac{1}{3x} + 75 = \frac{3}{4x}$$

$$75 = \frac{3}{4x} - \frac{1}{3x}$$

$$75 = \frac{5}{12x}$$

$$x = 180$$

So the entire wall is 180 square feet—that is, W × L = 180. We know that the height of the wall is 10 feet; so 10 × L = 180, and L = 18.

Section VIII

1. **(D)** (D) is correct because in likening two things it expresses them in like grammatical forms: "to be afraid of . . . is to be afraid of" (infinitives). (A), (B), and (C) fail because they compare unlike forms: "to be afraid" (infinitive) with "being afraid" (participle). (E) uses the same form for both parts, but it is an unnecessary combination of the two possibilities. (B) also uses commas incorrectly. Using the participle form in both parts would also be correct.

2. **(C)** The problem is raised by placement of the modifier "hurtling through." Who or what is hurtling, Anna [(A), (D)] , the sight (B), or the shooting star [(C), (E)]? Of the two clearest statements—(C) and (E)—(C) presents the facts in a better order.

3. **(B)** (A) errs in three ways: "superior" is already a comparative adjective and does not need the comparative form "more"; the idiom is "superior to," not "superior than"; and the "far as . . . concerned" phrase embodies an unneeded repetition. (C), (D), and (E) each make one of these errors; (E) also is awkward in its word order.

4. **(C)** A is incorrect because it switches from the singular ("weaver," "his") to the plural ("they"). Changing this segment to all singular, as in (B), would not tie in with "their wool" later in the sentence. So it is better to change all references to the plural, as in (C). (D) and (E) unpleasantly switch from the personal active to the impersonal passive.

5. **(A)** (C), (B), and (E) change the meaning; in (B) and (E) the result is gibberish. (D) would make sense but would not be Standard Written English: the required conjunction in such an indirect question is "whether."

6. **(E)** Since the writer talks of a condition contrary to fact (he is not President), he should use the subjunctive form "I were," as in (E). "I was," as in (A) and (C), would be acceptable in informal speech but not in Standard Written English. (B) is too elliptical. (C) and (D) slightly change the meaning: (C) makes the "halt" the President's very first action; (D) implies he has a realistic chance of being President.

7. **(B)** (A) and (E) err in being ambiguous: they could mean that females are more concerned about discrimination than about males. (D) goes further than it has to by repeating the full phrase "are concerned." All that is necessary is the key word "are," as in (B). (C) is not incorrect, but it is less graceful and too wordy.

8. **(C)** In Standard Written English, the negative correlative conjunctions "neither . . . nor" function together, as in (C). If one of them appears in a negating construction like (A), (B), or (E), the other should also appear, but in the appropriate order of "neither . . . nor." In (D), "or" is wrong because when it is used as a correlative conjunction, it appears only with "either," which would be contrary to the meaning here.

9. **(D)** (D) is correct because it extends the structure begun with "results from" by repeating the "from" at the crucial point. The others are incorrect. (A) uses "to" where "from" is needed; (B) confuses "affect" with "effect" and fails to extend the "results from" structure; (C) makes two errors in punctuation—neither the apostrophe nor the comma is used correctly; (E) repeats (A)'s error with an unnecessary comma.

10. **(C)** (C) is correct because after a verb like "demand" the action called for must be expressed in the subjunctive mood, e.g., "that management halt . . . and release. . . ." (B) uses the correct verb form but the wrong conjunction: "but" violates the meaning. (A), (B), and (D) all violate the parallelism required. (D) also creates an awkward final phrase.

11. **(E)** In Standard Written English, "each other" is the reciprocal pronoun for two persons, "one another" for more than two. Hence (E) is the only correct answer. In informal speech, (A) would be acceptable.

12. **(E)** (A) errs in three ways: it uses "as . . . that" instead of "as . . . as," which is required in comparing things to an equal degree; it fails to put "almost a century later" in commas, required since the phrase is non-essential; and it uses "will offer" where, in the sequence of tenses after the past verb "posed," the past form of "will" ("would offer") is required. (B) and (C) each correct only two of the three errors; (D), only one; (E) is entirely correct.

13. **(A)** The original is best because it relates the circumstances in the most logical, most dramatic order, and without error. (B) and (C) leave their opening phrase dangling: (B) links "the greatest player" not to Tilden, but to his "accomplishments"; and (C), to the "rumors"! (C), (D), and (E) fail to arrange the facts as effectively as (A) does; (D) is especially awkward.

14. **(D)** (A) errs in parallelism and in punctuation. A series of items branches off from the idea "spend money . . . on". Effective parallelism requires repetition of "on" before each item; effective punctuation requires a comma after each item standing before

"and." (B) supplies the comma but not the "on"; (C) and (E) supply "for" instead of "on" and no comma; (E) is wordier than need be.

15. **(B)** (A) creates ambiguity through faulty parallelism: are women being compared with women or with cities? (E) eliminates confusion by using strict parallel structure: "the women in Paris" is balanced by "the women in any other city." But (B) is better because it saves a word by using "those" instead of repeating "the women." (C) and (D) not only worsen the parallelism, they misspell "Parisian," ironically hitting on the French masculine form for the English adjective.

16. **(C)** The phrase about the "aides" simply supplies extra, parenthetical information. It is not part of the subject, which remains the singular "media advisor." (A), (B), and (D) therefore err in using the plural verb "are." (E) uses the correct singular "is" but reverses the facts—it's the "aides" who "are all in the company" of the "advisor."

17. **(E)** The original is repetitious: if "Lawyers and doctors . . . agree," then "alike" and "both" are superfluous; if there's a "rise in . . . suits," the clause "which are on the increase" is redundant. Only (E) avoids all these errors.

18. **(A)** (B) is wrong because the "if" clause, stating a past condition contrary to fact, requires a past-perfect subjunctive ("had known"). (C) and (D) are wrong because the "possible conclusion" clause requires the perfect form of a model auxiliary ("would have run"). (E) uses the wrong tense of the subjunctive. (B), (C), and (E) all needlessly add the "if" already implicit in the "had . . . known" construction, which is required in Standard Written English.

19. **(A)** (B) and (C) confuse "effect" with "affect." (C) and (D) use "than" instead of "from": things differ "from" one another. (E) uses the singular "that" instead of the plural "those" to refer back to the plural antecedent "findings." Only (A) avoids all these traps.

20. **(D)** (A) is poor on two counts: (1) "the past eight years," or past action continuing into the present, requires the present perfect ("has been") rather than the past tense ("was"); and (2) the two parts of the sentence that should be close for comparative purposes—"shy and awkward" and "graceful and consistent"—are separated. (C) echoes (1) and corrects (2) at the expense of vital information. (B) and (E) echo (2).

21. **(E)** In (A), (C), and (D), "of them" or "of these" is superfluous. In (B), "the latter" is incorrect. Since there are more than two items to refer back to, the correct term is "the last." (If four items were specified, the writer could refer to "the latter two," as distinct from "the former two," but "of all the reasons" implies many more than four.)

22. **(C)** In Standard Written English, the pattern is "less . . . than" and of course the two parts thus introduced should be in parallel structure. (A)'s use of "as" is totally unacceptable. (B)'s use of "and more on" might be acceptable in informal speech. (C) is illiterate. (E) uses the correct adverb, "than," but omits the "on" that cinches the parallelism.

23. **(C)** The subject of the sentence is singular ("the number"). Therefore verbs related to the "the number" should be singular (is, was) and a pronoun referring back to "the number" should be singular (it). (A), (B), and (D) each violate one or both of these requirements. (E) only appears to correct the error by substituting "the numbers" for "they" still makes an incorrect reference back to "the number."

24. **(D)** The original has two faults: "Insofar as" is used incorrectly—it means "to such an extent," not "because"—and "a good bargain" and "under a dollar a pound" are only loosely related by the conjunction "and." Only (D) corrects both faults. (E)'s solution for the second fault is good, but the sentence requires 15 words compared to (D)'s 13.

25. **(B)** Context indicates that of two past actions, "danced" and "established," one

occurred before the other. Therefore, the earlier action must be set in the past perfect tense ("had danced") as in (B). (C) is not incorrect, but there seems to be no reason for using the longer form, the past perfect progressive ("had been dancing"). (E), by using the participle "dancing" for the 1942 to 1947 action, blurs the distinction to be made from the 1948 action. (D) reverses the tenses required and so violates the time sense.

PART FOUR

GMAT GRADUATE SCHOOL LIST

GMAT GRADUATE SCHOOL LIST

The following schools require GMAT scores for admission to their graduate business programs.

Adelphi University
School of Business Administration
Garden City, NY 11530

Air Force Institute of Technology
Wright Patterson Air Force Base, OH 45433

Alabama Agricultural and Mechanical University
Normal, AL 35762

American Graduate School of International Management
Glendale, AZ 85306

American International College
Springfield, MA 01109

The American University
The Kogod College of Business Administration
Washington, DC 20016

Angelo State University
Business Administration Department
San Angelo, TX 76901

Appalachian State University
John A. Walker College of Business
Boone, NC 28608

Aquinas College
Department of Business Administration
Grand Rapids, MI 49506

Arizona State University
College of Business Administration
Tempe, AZ 85281

Arkansas State University
State University, AR 72467

Armstrong College
Berkeley, CA 94704

Armstrong State College
Savannah, GA 30314

Ashland College
Ashland, OH 44805

Assumption College
Worcester, MA 01609

Atlanta University
School of Business Administration
Atlanta, GA 30314

Auburn University
School of Business
Auburn, AL 36830

Augusta College
School of Business Administration
Augusta, GA 30904

Austin Peay State University
Clarksville, TN 37040

Avila College
11901 Wornall Road
Kansas City, MO 64145

Azusa Pacific University
Azusa, CA 91702

Babson College
Babson Park, MA 02157

Baldwin-Wallace College
Berea, OH 44017

Ball State University
College of Business
Muncie, IN 47306

Barry College
Miami, FL 33161

Baylor University
Hankamer School of Business
Waco, TX 76706

Bellarmine College
Louisville, KY 40205

Belmont College
Nashville, TN 37203

Bentley College
Waltham, MA 02154

Berry College
Graduate Studies in Business
Mount Berry, GA 30149

Bethany Nazarene College
Bethany, OK 73008

Bloomsburg State College
Bloomsburg, PA 17815

Boise State University
School of Business
1910 Campus Drive
Boise, ID 83725

Boston College
Graduate School of Management
Chestnut Hill, MA 02167

Boston University
School of Management
685 Commonwealth Avenue
Boston, MA 02215

Bowling Green State University
College of Business Administration
Bowling Green, OH 43403

Bradley University
College of Business Administration
Peoria, IL 61606

Brandeis University
Waltham, MA 02154

Brigham Young University
Graduate School of Management
Provo, UT 84601

Bryant College
Smithfield, RI 02917

Bucknell University
College of Business Administration
Lewisburg, PA 17837

Butler University
College of Business Administration
Indianapolis, IN 46208

California Lutheran College
Graduate Program in Business Administration
Thousand Oaks, CA 91360

California Polytechnic State University
School of Business
San Luis Obispo, CA 93401

California State College
California, PA 15419

California State College, Bakersfield
School of Business and Public Administration
9001 Stockdale Highway
Bakersfield, CA 93309

California State College, San Bernardino
School of Administration
550 State College Parkway
San Bernardino, CA 92407

California State College, Stanislaus
School of Business Administration
Turlock, CA 95380

California State Polytechnic University, Pomona
School of Business Administration
Pomona, CA 91768

California State University, Chico
School of Business
Chico, CA 95926

California State University, Dominquez Hills
School of Management
Carson, CA 90747

California State University, Fresno
School of Business
Fresno, CA 93710

California State University, Fullerton
School of Business Administration and Economics
Fullerton, CA 92634

California State University, Hayward
School of Business and Economics
Hayward, CA 94542

California State University, Humboldt
School of Business and Economics
Arcata, CA 95521

California State University, Long Beach
School of Business Administration
Long Beach, CA 90840

California State University, Los Angeles
School of Business and Economics
Los Angeles, CA 90032

California State University, Northridge
School of Business Administration and Economics
Northridge, CA 91324

California State University, Sacramento
School of Business and Public Administration
6000 Jay Street
Sacramento, CA 95819

California State University, San Diego
School of Business Administration
San Diego, CA 92115

California State University, San Francisco
School of Business
1600 Holloway Avenue
San Francisco, CA 94132

California State University, San Jose
School of Business
San Jose, CA 95192

California State University, San Luis Obline
Department of Business Administration
San Luis Obline, CA 93407

California State University, Sonoma
Department of Business Administration
Sonoma, CA 94928

Campbell University
Box 546
Buies Creek, NC 27506

Canisius College
School of Business Administration
Buffalo, NY 14208

Capital University
Department of Business Administration and Economics
Columbus, OH 43209

Carnegie-Mellon University Graduate School of Industrial Administration
Pittsburgh, PA 15213

Case Western Reserve University
School of Management
Cleveland, OH 41106

Centenary College
Shreveport, LA 71104

Central Michigan University
School of Business Administration
Mount Pleasant, MI 48858

Central Missouri State University
School of Business and Economics
Warrensburg, MO 64096

Central State University
School of Business
Edmond, OK 73034

Chaminade-University of Honolulu
Honolulu, HI 96816

Chapman College
School of Business and Management
Orange, CA 92666

The Citadel
Charleston, SC 29409

City University of New York
The Bernard M. Baruch College
School of Business and Public Administration
17 Lexington Avenue
New York, NY 10010

City University of New York
Graduate Center
33W. 42nd Street
New York, NY 10036

Claremont Graduate School
Department of Business Administration
Claremont, CA 91711

Clarion State College
School of Business Administration
Clarion, PA 16214

Clark University
Division of Business Administration
Worcester, MA 01610

Clarkson College of Technology
School of Management
Potsdam, NY 13676

Clemson University
College of Industrial Management and Textile Science
Clemson, SC 29631

Clemson University–Furman University
Furman University Campus
Greenville, SC 29613

Cleveland State University
The James J. Nance College of Business Administration
Cleveland, OH 44115

College of Insurance
New York, NY 10038

College of Notre Dame
Belmont, CA 94002

College of Saint Rose
Albany, NY 12203

College of Saint Thomas
St. Paul, MN 55105

College of William and Mary
School of Business Administration
Williamsburg, VA 23185

Colorado State University
College of Business
Fort Collins, CO 80521

Columbia University
Graduate School of Business
New York, NY 10027

Columbus College
School of Business
Columbus, GA 31993

Cornell University
Graduate School of Business and Public Administration
Ithaca, NY 14853

Creighton University
College of Business Administration
Omaha, NE 68178

Dartmouth College
The Amos Tuck School of Business Administration
Hanover, NH 03755

Delta State University
School of Business Administration
Cleveland, MS 38733

DePaul University
Graduate School of Business
Chicago, IL 60604

Dowling College
Oakdale, NY 11769

Drake University
College of Business Administration
25th and University
Des Moines, IA 50311

Drexel University
College of Business and Administration
Philadelphia, PA 19104

Drury College
Breech School of Business Administration
Springfield, MO 65802

Duke University
Fuqua School of Business
Durham, NC 27706

Duquesne University
Graduate School of Business and Administration
Pittsburgh, PA 15219

East Carolina University
School of Business
Greenville, NC 27834

East Tennessee State University
College of Business
Johnson City, TN 37614

East Texas State University
College of Business Administration
Commerce, TX 75428

East Texas State University at Texarkana
P.O. Box 5518
Texarkana, TX 75501

Eastern Illinois University
School of Business
Charleston, IL 61920

Eastern Kentucky University
College of Business
Richmond, KY 40475

Eastern Michigan University
Graduate Business Programs
Ypsilanti, MI 48197

Eastern New Mexico University
Portales, NM 88130

Eastern Washington State University
School of Business and Administration
Cheney, WA 99004

Eastern Washington University
Cheney, WA 99004

Emerson College
148 Beacon Street
Boston, MA 02116

Emory University
Graduate School of Business Administration
Atlanta, GA 30322

Emporia State University
Emporia, KA 66801

Fairfield University
Fairfield, CT 06430

Fairleigh Dickinson University
College of Business Administration
Teaneck, NJ 07666

Fairleigh Dickinson University
285 Madison Avenue
Madison, NJ 07940

Fairleigh Dickinson University
270 Montross Avenue
Rutherford, NJ 07070

Florida Agricultural and Mechanical University
Tallahassee, FL 32307

Florida Atlantic University
College of Business Administration
Boca Raton, FL 33431

Florida International University
School of Business and Organizational Sciences
Miami, FL 33199

Florida State University
School of Business
Tallahassee, FL 32306

Florida Technological University
College of Business Administration
Orlando, FL 32916

Fordham University
College of Business Administration
Bronx, NY 10458

Fordham University at Lincoln Center
Graduate School of Business Administration
New York, NY 10023

Framingham State College
Framingham, MA 01701

Furman University
Department of Economics and Business Administration
Greenville, SC 29613

Gannon University
Division of Business Administration
Erie, PA 16541

George Mason University
School of Business Administration
Fairfax, VA 22030

George Washington University
School of Government and Business Administration
Washington, DC 20052

George Williams College
555 Thirty-first Street
Downers Grove, IL 60515

Georgetown University
College of Business Administration
Washington, DC 20057

Georgia College
School of Business
Milledgeville, GA 31061

Georgia Institute of Technology
College of Management
Atlanta, GA 30332

Georgia Southern College
School of Business
Statesboro, GA 30460

Georgia State University
College of Business Adminstration
33 Gilmer Street, SE
Atlanta, GA 30303

Golden Gate University
536 Mission Street
San Francisco, CA 94105

Gonzaga University
School of Business Administration
Spokane, WA 99258

Governors State University
College of Business and Public Administration
Park Forest South, IL 60466

Grand Valley State College
College of Business and Administration
Allendale, MI 49401

Hartford Graduate Center
Department of Management
Hartford, CT 06120

Harvard University
Graduate School of Business Administration
Boston, MA 02163

Hofstra University
Graduate School of Business
Hempstead, NY 11550

Houston Baptist University
Department of Business Administration
Houston, TX 77036

Howard University
School of Business and Public Administration
Washington, DC 20001

Husson College
Bangor, ME 04401

Idaho State University
College of Business
Pocatello, ID 83209

Illinois Benedictine College
Lisle, IL 60532

Illinois Institute of Technology
Stuart School of Business Administration
Chicago, IL 60616

Illinois State University
College of Business
Normal, IL 61761

Indiana Central University
Department of Business Adminstration
Indianapolis, IN 46227

Indiana State University
Evansville Campus
Evansville, IN 47712

Indiana University
Graduate School of Business
Bloomington, IN 47405

Indiana University
School of Business
Fort Wayne, IN 46805

Indiana University
School of Business
Gary, IN 46408

Indiana University
School of Business
South Bend, IN 46634

Indiana University of Pennsylvania
School of Business
Indiana, PA 15705

Indiana University-Purdue
School of Business Administration
Fort Wayne, IN 46805

Iona College
School of Business Administration
New Rochelle, NY 10801

Jackson State University
Jackson, MS 39217

Jacksonville State University
Jacksonville, AL 36265

James Madison University
Harrisonburg, VA 22807

John Carroll University
The Graduate School
Cleveland, OH 44118

Kansas State University
College of Business Administration
Manhattan, KS 66506

Keller Graduate Schhol of Management
10 South Riverside Plaza
Chicago, IL 60606

Kent State University
Graduate School of Business Administration
Kent, OH 44242

LaGrange College
LaGrange, GA 30240

Lake Forest School of Management
Lake Forest College
Lake Forest, IL 60045

Lake Superior State College
Sault Sainte Marie, MI 49783

La Roche College
9000 Babcock Boulevard
Pittsburgh, PA 15237

LaSalle College
School of Business
Philadelphia, PA 19141

Lehigh University
College of Business and Economics
Bethlehem, PA 18015

Lewis University
Romeoville, IL 60441

Lincoln University
School of Business
San Francisco, CA 94118

Lincoln University
Jefferson City, MO 65101

Lindenwood College
St. Charles, MO 63301

Loma Linda University
Loma Linda, CA 92354

Loma Linda University
Riverside, CA 92515

Long Island University
Brooklyn Center
School of Business Administration
Brooklyn, NY 11201

Long Island University
C.W. Post Center
School of Business Administration
Greenvale, NY 11548

Long Island University
Manhattan College
Riverdale, NY 10471

Louisiana State University
College of Business Administration
Baton Rouge, LA 70803

Louisiana State University
Shreveport, LA 71105

Lousiana Tech University
College of Administration and Business
Box 5796, Tech Station
Ruston, LA 71272

Loyola College
Department of Accounting and Business Administration
Baltimore, MD 21210

Loyola University
School of Business Administration
Lewis Towers
820 North Michigan Avenue
Chicago, IL 60611

Loyola University
College of Business Administration
New Orleans, LA 70118

Loyola Marymount University
Los Angeles, CA 90045

Lynchburg University
School of Business
Lynchburg, VA 24505

Manhattan College
Riverdale, NY 10471

Mankato State College
School of Business
Mankato, MN 56001

Marist College
Poughkeepsie, NY 12601

Marquette University
The Robert A. Johnston College of Business Administration
Milwaukee, WI 53233

Marshall University
School of Business
Huntington, WV 25701

Mary Washington College
Box 1098 College Station
Fredricksburg, VA 22401

Marymount College of Virginia
Old Dominion and North Glebe Road
Arlington, VA 22207

Marywood College
Department of Business
Scranton, PA 18509

Massachusetts Institute of Technology
Alfred P. Sloan School of Management
Cambridge, MA 02139

McNeese State University
School of Business
Lake Charles, LA 70601

Memphis State University
College of Business Administration
Memphis, TN 38152

Mercer University in Atlanta
3000 Flowers Road
Atlanta, GA 30341

Mercer University
Macon, GA 31207

Miami University
School of Business Administration
Oxford, OH 45056

Michigan State University
Graduate School of Business Administration
East Lansing, MI 48824

Michigan Technological University
School of Business and Engineering Administration
Houghton, MI 49931

Middle Tennessee State University
School of Business and Economcis
Murfreesboro, TN 37132

Millsaps College
Jackson, MS 39210

Mississippi College
Division of Business and Economics
Clinton, MS 39058

Mississippi State University
College of Business and Industry
Mississippi State, MS 39762

Monmouth College
Department of Business Administration
West Long Branch, NJ 07764

Montclair State College
Upper Montclair, NJ 07043

Monterey Institute of International Studies
P.O. Box 1978
Monterey, CA 93940

Moorhead State College
Division of Business
Moorhead, MN 56560

Morehead State University
Morehead, KY 40351

Morgan State College
Department of Economics and Business
Baltimore, MD 21239

Mount Saint Mary's College
Emmitsburg, MD 21727

Mount Saint Mary's College
Hooksett, NH 03106

Murray State University
School of Business
Murray, KY 42071

New Hampshire College
Department of Business Administration
Manchester, NH 03104

New Mexico Highlands University
Las Vegas, NM 87701

New Mexico State University
College of Business Administration and Economics
Las Cruces, NM 88003

New York Institute of Technology
Division of Business and Management
888 Seventh Avenue
New York, NY 10019

New York University
Graduate Programs at Manhattanville
Purchase, NY

New York University
Graduate School of Business Administration
100 Trinity Place
New York, NY 10006

Niagara University
Niagara University, NY 14109

Nichols College
Dudley, MA 01570

Nicholls State University
College of Business Administration
Thibodaux, LA 70310

Norfolk State University
2401 Corprew Avenue
Norfolk VA 23504

North Carolina Central University
Durham, NC 27707

North Texas State University
College of Business Administration
Denton, TX 76203

Northeast Louisiana University
College of Business Administration
Monroe, LA 71209

Northeast Missouri State University
School of Business
Kirksville, MO 63501

Northeastern University
College of Business Administration
Boston, MA 02115

Northern Arizona University
College of Business Administration
Flagstaff, AZ 86011

Northern Illinois University
College of Business
De Kalb, IL 60115

Northern Kentucky University
Highland Heights, KY 41076

Northern Michigan University
Department of Business Administration
Marquette, MI 49855

Northrop University
School of Business
Inglewood, CA 90306

Northwest Missouri State University
School of Business Administration
Maryville, MO 64468

Northwestern State University of Louisiana
College of Business
Natchitoches, LA 71457

Northwestern University
Chicago Campus
301 East Chicago Avenue
Chicago, IL 60611

Northwestern University
Graduate School of Management
Evanston, IL 60201

Nova University
Fort Lauderdale, FL 33314

Oakland University
School of Economics and Management
Rochester, MI 48063

Ohio State University
College of Administrative Science
Columbus, OH 43210

Ohio University
College of Business Administration
Athens, OH 45701

Oklahoma City University
School of Business
Oklahoma City, OK 73106

Oklahoma State University
College of Business Administration
Stillwater, OK 74074

Old Dominion University
School of Business Administration
Norfolk, VA 23508

Oral Roberts University
School of Business
Tulsa, OK 74171

Oregon State University
School of Business
Corvallis, OR 97331

Pace University
Lubin Graduate School of Business
New York, NY 10038

Pace University
School of Business
Pleasantville, NY 10570

Pace University
White Plains Campus
55 Church Street
White Plains, NY 10601

Pacific Christian College
2500 East Nutwood Avenue
Fullerton, CA 92631

Pacific Lutheran University
School of Business Administration
Tacoma, WA 98447

Pacific States University
1516 South Western Avenue
Los Angeles, CA 90006

Pan American University
80 Fort Brown
Brownsville, TX 78520

Pan American University
Edinburg, TX 78539

The Pennsylvania State University
College of Business Administration
120 Boucke Building
University Park, PA 16802

Pennsylvania State University, Capitol Campus
Administration and Business Graduate and Undergraduate Programs
Middletown, PA 17057

Pepperdine University
School of Business and Management
Los Angeles, CA 90044

Philadelphia College of Textiles and Sciences
Marketing and Management
Philadelphia, PA 19144

Pittsburg State University
1701 South Broadway
Pittsburg, KS 66762

Plymouth State College
Plymouth, NH 03264

Polytechnic Institute of New York
Department of Business Management
Brooklyn, NY 11201

Portland State University
School of Business Administration
P.O. Box 751
Portland, OR 97207

Prairie View Agricultural and Mechanical University
Prairie View, TX 77445

Providence College
Providence, RI 02918

Purdue University—Calumet
Hammond, IN 46323

Purdue University
Krannert Graduate School of Management
West Lafayette, IN 47907

Queens College
1900 Selwyn Avenue
Charlotte, NC 28274

Quinnipiac College
Hamden, CT 06518

Regis College
West Fiftieth and Lowell Boulevard
Denver, CO 80221

Rensselaer Polytechnic Institute
Troy, NY 12181

Rice University
School of Business Administration
Houston, TX 77251

Rider College
School of Business Administration
Trenton, NJ 08648

Rivier College
Nashua, NH 03060

Robert Morris College
Coraopolis, PA 15108

Rochester Institute of Technology
College of Business
Rochester, NY 14623

Rockhurst College
Kansas City, MO 64110

Rollins College
Roy E. Crummer School of Business
Winter Park, FL 32789

Roosevelt University
Walter E. Heller College of Business Administration
Chicago, IL 60605

Rosary College
River Forest, IL 60305

Rutgers University
Graduate School of Management
Newark, NJ 07102

Rutgers University, Camden
Camden, NJ 08102

Sacred Heart University
Bridgeport, CT 06606

Saginaw Valley State College
School of Business and Management
University Center, MI 48710

St. Ambrose College
Davenport, IA 52803

St. Bonaventure University
School of Business Administration
St. Bonaventure, NY 14778

St. Cloud State University
College of Business
Saint Cloud, MN 56301

St. John's University
College of Business Administration
Utopia and Grand Central Parkways
Jamaica, NY 11439

St. John's University
College of Business Administration
Staten Island, NY 10301

Saint Joseph's College
Philadelphia, PA 19131

Saint Louis University
School of Business and Administration
St. Louis, MO 63104

Saint Mary's College of California
Moraga, CA 94575

St. Mary's University
School of Business and Administration
San Antonio, TX 78284

Salisbury State College
Salisbury, MD 21801

Samford University
School of Business
Birmingham, AL 35209

Sangamon State University
Springfield, IL 62708

Savannah State College
Department of Business Administration
Savannah, GA 31404

Seattle University
School of Business
Seattle, WA 98122

Seton Hall University
School of Business Administration
South Orange, NJ 07079

Shenandoah College and Conservatory of Music
Winchester, VA 22601

Shippensburg State College
Department of Business Administration
Shippensburg, PA 17257

Simmons College
Department of Business Administration
Boston, MA 02215

Southeast Missouri State University
Cape Girardeau, MO 63701

Southeastern Louisiana University
Hammond, LA 70401

Southeastern Massachusetts University
School of Business Administration
North Dartmouth, MA 02747

Southeastern University
Department of Business Administration
Washington, DC 20024

Southern Illinois University at Carbondale
School of Business
Carbondale, IL 62901

Southern Illinois University of Edwardsville
Division of Business
Edwardsville, IL 62026

Southern Methodist University
School of Business Administration
Dallas, TX 75275

Southern Oregon State College
Ashland, OR 97520

Southwest Missouri State University
Springfield, MO 65802

Stanford University
Graduate School of Business
Stanford, CA 94305

State University of New York at Albany
School of Business
Albany, NY 12222

State University of New York at Binghamton
School of Management
Binghamton, NY 13901

State University of New York
Center at Buffalo
Buffalo, NY 14214

State University of New York
Maritime College
Fort Schuyler
Bronx, NY 10465

Stephen F. Austin State University
School of Business
Nacogdoches, TX 75962

Stetson University
De Land, FL 32720

Stevens Institute of Technology
Department of Management Sciences
Hoboken, NJ 07030

Suffolk University
School of Management
Boston, MA 02108

Sul Ross State University
Department of Business Administration
Alpine, TX 79830

Syracuse University
Corning Center
Corning, NY 14830

Syracuse University
School of Management
116 College Place
Syracuse, NY 13210

Temple University
School of Business Administration
Philadelphia, PA 19122

Tennessee State University
Nashville, TN 37203

Tennessee Technological University
School of Business Administration
Cookeville, TN 38501

Texas A & M University
College Station, TX 77843

Texas Christian University
M.J. Neeley School of Business
Fort Worth, TX 76129

Texas Tech University
Lubbock, TX 79409

Texas Woman's University
Denton, TX 76204

Thomas College
Graduate School of Management
Waterville, ME 04901

Trenton State College
Trenton, NJ 08625

Trinity College
Washington, DC 20017

Trinity University
715 Stadium Drive
San Antonio, TX 78284

Troy State University of Ft. Rucker
Fort Rucker, AL 36360

Troy State University at Montgomery
Maxwell Air Force Base, AL 36112

Troy State University
Department of Business Administration
Troy, AL 36801

Tulane University
Graduate School of Business Administration
New Orleans, LA 70118

Union College and University
Schenectady, NY 12308

United States International University
School of Business Administration
San Diego, CA 92131

University of Akron
College of Business Administration
Akron, OH 44325

University of Alabama
Huntsville Campus
Huntsville, AL 35807

University of Alabama in Birmingham
School of Business
Birminham, AL 35294

University of Alabama
Graduate School of Business
University, AL 35486

University of Alaska
School of Business
Anchorage, AK 99504

University of Alaska
School of Business
Fairbanks, AK 99701

University of Alaska
Juneau Senior College
Juneau, AK 99801

University of Arizona
College of Business and Public Administration
Tucson, AZ 85721

University of Arkansas
College of Business Administration
Fayetteville, AR 72701

University of Arkansas
College of Business Administration
Little Rock, AR 72204

University of Baltimore
School of Business
Baltimore, MD 21201

University of Bridgeport
College of Business Administration
Bridgeport, CT 06602

University of California
Graduate School of Business Administration
Berkeley, CA 94720

University of California, Davis
Davis, CA 95616

University of California, Irvine
Irvine, CA 92664

University of California, Los Angeles
Graduate School of Management
Los Angeles, CA 90024

University of Central Florida
P.O. Box 25000
Orlando, FL 32816

University of Chicago
The Graduate School of Business
Chicago, IL 60637

University of Cincinnati
College of Business Administration
Cincinnati, OH 45221

University of Colorado
Graduate School of Business Administration
Boulder, CO 80302

University of Connecticut at Danbury
School of Business Administration
University of Connecticut
Storrs, CT 06268

University of Connecticut at Hartford
West Hartford, CT 06117

University of Connecticut at Stamford
Stamford, CT 06903

University of Connecticut
Department of Business Administration
Storrs, CT 06268

University of Dallas
Dallas, TX 75061

University of Dayton
School of Business Administration
Dayton, OH 45469

University of Delaware
Department of Business Administration
Newark, DE 19711

University of Denver
College of Business Administration
University Park
Denver, CO 80208

University of Detroit
College of Business and Administration
Detroit, MI 48221

University of the District of Columbia
1529 16th Street N.W.
Washington, DC 20036

University of Evansville
School of Business Administration
Evansville, IN 47702

University of Florida
Gainesville, FL 32604

University of Georgia
College of Business Administration
Athens, GA 30602

University of Hartford
200 Bloomfield Avenue
West Hartford, CT 06117

University of Hawaii
College of Business Administration
Honolulu, HI 96822

University of Houston: Clear Lake City
Houston, TX 77058

University of Houston
College of Business Administration
Houston, TX 77004

University of Idaho
College of Business and Economics
Moscow, ID 83843

University of Illinois
Department of Business Administration
Champaign, IL 61820

University of Illinois at Chicago
College of Business Administration
Box 4348
Chicago, IL 60680

University of Iowa
College of Business Administration
Iowa City, IA 52242

University of Judaism
6525 Sunset Boulevard
Los Angeles, CA 90028

University of Kansas
School of Business
Lawrence, KS 66045

University of Kentucky
College of Business and Economics
Lexington, KY 40506

University of Louisville
School of Business
Louisville, KY 40292

University of Lowell
Lowell, MA 01854

University of Maine
College of Business Administration
Orono, ME 04469

University of Maryland
College of Business and Management
College Park, MD 20742

University of Massachusetts
School of Business Administration
Amherst, MA 01003

University of Miami
School of Business Administration
Coral Gables, FL 33124

The University of Michigan
Graduate School of Business Administration
Ann Arbor, MI 48109

University of Michigan at Dearborn
4901 Evergreen Road
Dearborn, MI 48128

University of Michigan at Flint
1321 East Court Street
Flint, MI 48503

University of Minnesota
School of Business Administration
Duluth, MN 55812

University of Minnesota
School of Business
Minneapolis, MN 55455

University of Mississippi
School of Business Administration
University, MS 38677

University of Missouri, Columbia
College of Administration and Public Affairs
Columbia, MO 65211

University of Missouri, Kansas City
School of Administration
Kansas City, MO 64110

University of Missouri, St. Louis
School of Business Administration
St. Louis, MO 63121

University of Montana
School of Business Administration
Missoula, MT 59812

University of Nebraska, Lincoln
College of Business Administration
Lincoln, NE 68508

University of Nebraska, Omaha
College of Business Administration
Omaha, NE 68182

University of Nevada, Las Vegas
College of Business and Economics
Las Vegas, NV 89154

University of Nevada, Reno
College of Business Administration
Reno, NV 89557

University of New Hampshire
Whittemore School of Business and Economics
Durham, NH 03824

The University of New Mexico
School of Business and Administrative Sciences
Albuquerque, NM 87131

University of New Orleans
College of Business Administration
New Orleans, LA 70148

University of North Alabama
Florence, AL 35630

University of North Carolina, Chapel Hill
Graduate School of Business Administration
Chapel Hill, NC 27514

University of North Carolina, Charlotte
College of Business Administration
Charlotte, NC 28223

University of North Carolina, Greensboro
School of Business and Economics
Greensboro, NC 27412

University of North Carolina at Wilmington
Wilmington, NC 28401

University of North Dakota
College of Business and Public Administration
Grand Forks, ND 58202

University of North Dakota
Minot, ND 58701

University of Northern Iowa
School of Business
Cedar Falls, IA 50614

University of Notre Dame
College of Business Administration
Notre Dame, IN 46556

University of Oklahoma
College of Business Administration
Norman, OK 73019

University of Oregon
Graduate School of Management
Eugene, OR 97403

University of Pennsylvania
The Wharton School
Philadelphia, PA 19104

University of Pittsburgh
Graduate School of Business
Pittsburgh, PA 15260

University of Portland
School of Business Administration
Portland, OR 97203

University of Puerto Rico
San Juan, PR 00931

University of Puget Sound
School of Business and Public Administration
Tacoma, WA 98416

University of Rhode Island
College of Business Administration
Kingston, RI 02881

University of Richmond
School of Business
Richmond, VA 23173

University of Rochester
The Graduate School of Management
Rochester, NY 14627

University of St. Thomas
3812 Montrose Boulevard
Houston, TX 77006

University of San Diego
Department of Business Administration
San Diego, CA 92110

University of San Francisco
College of Business Administration
San Francisco, CA 94117

University of Santa Clara
Graduate School of Business and Administration
Santa Clara, CA 95053

University of Scranton
Scranton, PA 18510

University of South Alabama
Mobile, AL 36688

University of South Carolina
Graduate School of Business
Columbia, SC 29208

University of South Dakota
School of Business
Vermillion, SD 57069

University of South Florida
College of Business Administration
Tampa, FL 33620

University of Southern California
Graduate School of Business Administration
Los Angeles, CA 90007

University of Southern Mississippi
School of Business Administration
Hattiesburg, MS 39401

University of Southern Mississippi
Gulf Coast
Long Beach, MS 39560

University of Steubenville
Steubenville, OH 43952

University of Tennessee
College of Business Administration
Knoxville, TN 37996

University of Tennessee, Chattanooga
Department of Economics and Business Administration
Chattanooga, TN 37402

University of Tennessee, Martin
School of Business Administration
Martin, TN 38238

University of Tennessee
College of Business Administration
Nashville, TN 37388

The University of Texas, Arlilngton
College of Business Administration
Arlington, TX 76019

University of Texas, Dallas
Graduate Program in Management and Administrative Science
Richardson, TX 75080

University of Texas, San Antonio
College of Business
San Antonio, TX 78285

University of Texas at Tyler
3900 University Boulevard
Tyler, TX 75701

University of Toledo
College of Business Administration
Toledo, OH 43606

University of Tulsa
College of Business Administration
Tulsa, OK 74104

University of Utah
College of Business
Salt Lake City, UT 84112

University of Vermont
Burlington, VT 05405

University of Virginia
The Colgate Darden Graduate School of Business Administration
Charlottesville, VA 22906

University of Washington
Graduate School of Business Administration
Seattle, WA 98195

University of West Los Angeles
Culver City, CA 90230

University of Wisconsin at Eau Clair
Eau Clair, WI 54701

University of Wisconsin, La Crosse
School of Business Administration
La Crosse, WI 54601

University of Wisconsin, Madison
Graduate School of Business
Madison, WI 53706

University of Wisconsin, Milwaukee
School of Business Administration
Milwaukee, WI 53201

University of Wisconsin, Oshkosh
School of Business Administration
Oshkosh, WI 54901

University of Wisconsin at Parkside
Wood Road
Kenosha, WI 53140

University of Wisconsin, Whitewater
College of Business and Economics
Whitewater, WI 53190

University of Wyoming
College of Commerce and Industry
Laramie, WY 82071

Utah State University
College of Business
Logan, UT 84322

Valdosta State College
Department of Business Administration
Valdosta, GA 31698

Vanderbilt University
Graduate School of Management
Nashville, TN 37203

Villanova University: MBA Program
Villanova, PA 19085

Virginia Commonwealth University
School of Business
Richmond, VA 23284

Virginia Polytechnic Institute and State University
College of Business
Blacksburg, VA 24061

Wake Forest University
Babcock Graduate School of Management
Winston-Salem, NC 27109

Washington State University
College of Economics and Business
Pullman, WA 99164

Washington University
Graduate School of Business Administration
St. Louis, MO 63130

Wayne State University
School of Business Administration
Detroit, MI 48202

Webber College
Babson Park, FL 33827

West Georgia College
School of Business
Carrollton, GA 30118

West Texas State university
School of Business
Canyon, TX 79016

West Virginia College of Graduate Studies
Institute, WV 25112

West Virginia University
College of Business and Economics
Morgantown, WV 26506

Western Carolina University
School of Business
Cullowhee, NC 28723

Western Connecticut State College
Danbury, CT 06810

Western Illinois University
Macomb, IL 61455

Western Kentucky University
College of Business and Public Affairs
Bowling Green, KY 42101

Western Michigan University
College of Business
Kalamazoo, MI 49008

Western New England College
1215 Wilbraham Road
Springfield, MA 01119

Western New Mexico University
Silver City, NM 88061

Western Washington University
Bellingham, WA 98225

Wheeling College
Wheeling, WV 26003

Whittier College
Whittier, CA 90608

Wichita State University
College of Business Administration
Wichita, KS 67208

Widener College
Department of Business Administration
Chester, PA 19013

William Paterson College of New Jersey
300 Pompton Road
Wayne, NJ 07470

Williamette University
College of Business Administration
Salem, OR 97301

Wilmington College
New Castle, DE 19720

Winona State University
Winona, MN 55987

Winthrop College
Rock Hill, SC 29730

Worcester Polytechnic Institute
Worcester, MA 01609

Wright State University
College of Business and Administration
Dayton, OH 45435

Xavier University
College of Business Administration
Cincinnati, OH 45207

Yale University
School of Organization and Management
New Haven, CT 06520

York College of Pennsylvania
Department of Business Administration
York, PA 17405

Youngstown State University
School of Business Administration
Youngstown, OH 44555